INDIA'S SILENT REVOLUTION

CHRISTOPHE JAFFRELOT

India's Silent Revolution

The Rise of the Lower Castes in North India

Columbia University Press
New York

Columbia University Press
Publishers since 1893
New York

Library of Congress Cataloging-in-Publication Data

Jaffrelot, Christophe.
India's silent revolution : the rise of the lower castes in North India / by Christophe Jaffrelot.
p. cm. — (CERI series in comparative politics and international studies)
Includes bibliographical references and index.
ISBN 0-231-12786-3 (cloth : alk. paper)
1. Dalits—India—Political activity. 2. India—Politics and government—1947- I. Title. II. Series.
DS422.C3 J325 2002
323.3'224—dc21
2002073707

Columbia University Press books are printed on permanent and durable acid-free paper.

c 10 9 8 7 6 5 4 3 2 1

Printed in India

For Tara

ACKNOWLEDGEMENTS

It was in the early 1990s, when the 'Mandal affair' was at its peak, that I began working on the 'revolution' that North India is experiencing. It seemed to me that the kind of social change which was unfolding was a proper revolution because there was a transfer of power in the making from the upper castes to the lower castes in the bureaucracy and the political sphere in North India. One may argue that this revolution was not silent at all, given the vigorous anti-Mandal mobilisation and the lower castes' counter-mobilisation of 1990. But the phase of violent confrontation was short and circumscribed. The upper castes quickly adjusted themselves to the new balance of power and looked for other avenues of social mobility, out of the state, while the lower castes relied on the constitutional process – the reservations and the democratic *modus operandum*, in which their massive numbers were bound to benefit them. Since then, while the overall process remains largely unaccomplished, they are gradually, and more or less surreptitiously, taking over in North India. In that respect, North India is going the way South India – and, to a lesser extent, West India – have already gone.

This book took longer to write than I thought, for two reasons. First, it is largely based on data concerning the caste background of North Indian political personnel, the collection and verification of which have been time-consuming. It has been especially hard to identify the caste of the Members of Parliament or Legislative Assemblies who were elected in the 1950s, 1960s or 1970s, some of whom are no longer with us. But I needed this data to establish long-term trends and I made a point of cross-checking the information I was given. In Madhya Pradesh I had a head start, given the work involved in preparing my first book on the Hindu nationalist movement in Central India. For the other states I started from scratch. I spent hours with old-timers from every political party, in dusty offices in Bhopal, Jaipur, Agra, Lucknow . . . painstakingly combing through lists of hundreds of names. My thanks go first to these political veterans who often became as excited as I was by the delineation of their party's social profile – they were often surprised by the results!

India's Silent Revolution has also taken longer than the 'five-year plan' I had in mind originally, because I decided to write it directly in English. For French scholars working on India (or other countries), the choice of the most relevant language for scientific communication has become difficult. Their books, especially when they are based on hard and/or detailed fieldwork data, are mainly for their colleagues and advanced students. Now, this public could read them in English, and to write such books in English enables other colleagues and students abroad to have access to their content – something no book in French can really achieve, given the decline of our language in the international scientific community and the small number of books 'English-speaking' publishers translate. However, I would not have embarked on such an enterprise had not Michael Dwyer assured me that C. Hurst & Co. would take care of the edit-ing. My text, like *The Hindu Nationalist Movement* published by the same firm in 1996, has immensely benefited from the painstaking rewriting orchestrated by Michael Dwyer.

I am also grateful to the many colleagues and students who, over the years have commented upon the views expressed in this book, most of the time in a very encouraging and constructive manner. Among them, I would like to thank those who have either invited me to present these views or discussed them in one respect or another: Arjun Appadurai, Amrita Basu, Rajeev Bhargava, Kanchan Chandra, Gyan and Jayati Chaturvedi, Ian Duncan, Barbara Harris, Mushir and Zoya Hasan, Rob Jenkins, Anand Kumar, David Ludden, Owen Lynch, Gurpreet Mahajan, James Manor, Sujata Patel, V.B. Singh, Anne Vaugier-Chatterjee, Yogendra Yadav, Ashutosh Varshney, Steven Wilkinson, Andrew Wyatt, Eleanor Zelliot, Jasmine Zérinini-Brotel, and, of course, Bruce Graham, who read an early version of the manuscript with his inimitable care. Yet, this book owes more to Tara, through whom I discovered the happiness of being two for fieldwork.

In spite of all this support, the book has shortcomings, and they are entirely mine.

Paris, March 2002 CHRISTOPHE JAFFRELOT

CONTENTS

TABLES

INTRODUCTION

'We must make our political democracy a social democracy as well. Political democracy cannot last unless there lies at the base of it social democracy. What does social democracy mean? It means a way of life which recognises liberty, equality and fraternity as the principles of life. [. . .] On the 26th of January 1950, we are going to enter into a life of contradictions. In politics we will have equality and in social and economic life we will have inequality. [. . .] We must remove this contradiction at the earliest moment, or else those who suffer from inequality will blow up the structure of political democracy which this Assembly has so laboriously built up.' (Speech by B.R. Ambedkar on 25th November 1949, in *Constituent Assembly Debates*, New Delhi, Lok Sabha Secretariat, 1989, vol. IX, p. 979)

India claims the status of a democracy – 'the world's largest democracy' – and it holds serious arguments to defend this pretension. It is one of the few countries of the South with a stable parliamentary system and which has regularly held free elections on the basis of universal suffrage over the last five decades (these have been thirteen elections between 1952 and 1999). Turnout at these elections has risen gradually, peaking at 64.1% in 1984 and remained around the 60% mark throughout the 1990s. This achievement was partly due to the early and successful introduction of voting symbols associated with the various parties, a system that attenuated the effect of high illiteracy rates.[1]

In some parts of India the rule of law has been compromised by an increasing criminalisation of politics. Gangs associated with candidates (if not with parties) during elections, intimidate voters and/or capture ballot-boxes in the polling stations of constituencies deemed hostile to the candidate commissioning the operation called 'booth capturing'. Such practices are only prominent in a few states (mainly Bihar and Uttar Pradesh) and the Election Commission – an independent institution supervising the election process – tends

[1] See Bruce Graham, 'Electoral symbols and party identification in Indian politics' in P. Lyon and J. Manor (eds), *Transfer and Transformation: Political Institutions in the New Commonwealth*, Leicester University Press, 1982.

to order re-polls in polling stations where incidents have occurred. Thus, election results generally reflect the voters' inclination, their desire for change or continuity.

The Indian political system has undergone six political alternations emerging from general elections. In 1977 the Congress (R), led by Indira Gandhi, was routed by the Janata Party, a coalition of the main opposition parties. In 1980 Mrs Gandhi staged a comeback. In 1989 the Congress (I), with Rajiv Gandhi at the helm, was overthrown by an alliance of opposition parties, albeit less formalised than in 1977. In 1991 the Congress regained power but five years later it again lost the elections. In 1998, the Bharatiya Janata Party formed a parliamentary coalition, enabling a Prime Minister with a Hindu nationalist orientation to take power for the first time. Roughly the same coalition won again in 1999. Thus India has unique record among the non-western democracies in terms of the alternation of power, which has swung side to another in an almost banal fashion. True, the electoral process was suspended for twenty months, in 1975–7, due to the Emergency declared by President F.A. Ahmed at the request of Indira Gandhi; but this episode ended with the defeat of a ruling party whose authoritarianism had thoroughly displeased and alienated the electorate.

In addition to free election and the alternation of power, India fulfils another criterion of democracy, namely its capacity to maintain a relative separation of powers, most notably the independence of the judiciary. The latter is subject to continuous political pressure, but the Supreme Court as well as the High Courts – which operate at the State level – do pronounce verdicts that thwart the interests of the dominant political élite. In fact Indira Gandhi's infamous declaration of the Emergency was in response to a judicial decision, invalidating her election to the Parliament because of illegal practices during her 1971 election campaign.

The press is another pillar of Indian democracy because of its role in the political balance of power. Titles are multiplying, in English as well as in vernacular languages and newspapers rarely spare those who govern, a prime example being the media campaign that accused Rajiv Gandhi of having accepted bribes from the Swedish armaments firm, Bofors, and which was largely responsible for his electoral downfall in 1989. The illiteracy that still blights half of India's population is not an insuperable obstacle to the influence of the press because newspapers are frequently read and commented upon in public. In this way, the fifth estate helps in shaping public opinion and precipitating political debate in the villages.

However, one may object that democracy in India lacks any real substance, given the fact that – officially – 38% of the population were still living below the poverty line in the 1990s and that the institutional mechanisms of the Republic of India are superimposed on a social system that is dominated by the hierarchical logic of castes, and therefore seems *a priori* largely incompatible with the individualist and egalitarian values of democracy.[2] India, at least in its earlier incarnations, may therefore be an extreme case of political democracy without social democracy. This opposition that the Marxists expressed in terms of 'formal (or bourgeois) democracy' versus 'popular democracy', constitutes one of the *classicus loci* of political analysis. All the western democracies went through an elitist stage where democracy was purely political: parties competed electorally, but

[2] In Sanskrit classical literature Hindu society is divided into four *varnas*: the Brahmins (priests and literati), the Kshatriyas (the warriors), the Vaishyas (crafts- and tradesmen) and the *dvijas* (twice-born) category, while the Shudras appear as the servants of the categories mentioned above. In 1931 –Brahmins represented 6.4% of the population, the Rajputs, the principal caste of warriors, 3.7%, and the Banyas (mainly merchants composing the third order), 2.7%. The *varna* system encompasses a system of *jatis* which are the real castes. The word *jati* derives from '*jan*', 'to be born' and indeed the *jatis* are endogamous: one is born in the caste one's parents belong to; they are organised in a hierarchical way due to their status, given in terms of ritual purity, according to a continuum ranging from the Brahmins to the Untouchables. However qualitative leaps exist in this gradation since the *varna* system gives a structure to the profusion of *jatis*. Each *jati* belongs to a specific *varna*. The *jatis* of the 'twice-born' *varnas* naturally enjoy a higher status than those which are placed at the level of the Shudras and even more among the Untouchables. This hierarchy of inherited statuses is concomitant with one's economic function, sometimes to an extremely specialised degree. Originally every *jati* was defined by a professional specialisation: so Brahmins fulfil functions reserved to *literati* and priests avoiding manual work, especially if it implies forms of violence (like agriculture, which destroys micro-organisms) because non-violence is a brahminical ideal, which manifests itself also in a vegetarian diet. On the contrary, the main Untouchable *jati* of north India, the Chamars, are leather workers who are particularly impure not only because they treat organic matter, but also because they work with hides, the cow being the sacred animal *par excellence* of Hinduism.

elections, even by universal franchise, opposed candidates from the upper classes who, once in office, seldom advocated measures favouring the poor. Such an elitist view was first articulated by Edmund Burke, for whom – inequality being unavoidable in any society – the political representative should be men of superior ability who would not need to be accountable even to their electors. Others regarded democracy as residing primarily in the representativeness of the elected bodies: 'what seems important is less what the legislature does than how it is composed'.[3] Even if representative democracy does not imply that assemblies perfectly reflect the composition of society absolutely, the long-term exclusion of entire, large groups would be an insuperable impediment simply because the interests of these people would be neglected.

This scenario unfolded itself in India after independence. Democracy was immediately captured by the dominant classes. Bhim Rao Ambedkar, the main architect of the Indian Constitution, in his capacity of chairman of the Drafting Committee, highlighted this contradiction in a famous speech he made to the Constituent Assembly in 1949 – of which the most relevant portion has been cited as an epigraph to this introduction. In spite of Ambedkar's warnings, for decades politicians from India's social elite and representing their interests competed via different parties but alternated in power in a kind of closed circle. The many political parties masked a great social homogeneity because representatives of the social elite have always dominated the mainstream parties. The Congress, the dominant party till the 1970s, never gave political responsibilities to the lower classes at least not in North India.

Myron Weiner maintained that the Congress party instituted very early an 'open elite system' permitting 'aspiring social groups to gain a share of power within the party'.[4] According to Weiner, Congress leaders accommodated the demand for power by aspiring groups because of the party's endemic factionalism: the groups which were locked in such struggles willingly included emergent leaders from rising social groups in order to reinforce their own position. Interestingly, Weiner's book is based on case-studies from beyond the

[3] H.F. Pitkin, *The Concept of Representation*, Berkeley: University of California Press, 1967, p. 61. Pitkin's classic remains the best source on this debate.

[4] M. Weiner, *Party Building in a New Nation – The Indian National Congress*, University of Chicago Press, 1967, p. 470.

Hindi belt and my contention is that his model does not apply to this meta-region of North India.

The North-South opposition

Weiner's thesis is substantiated by the observations of many scholars working on South India. In Karnataka James Manor underlines that as early as the 1930s, intermediate cultivating castes like the Vokkaligas and the Lingayats collaborated with Brahmins in the Congress.[5] This arrangement partly resulted from the fact that these dominant castes[6] benefited early from the emergence of a local economy based on small farmer-proprietors. In the former princely state of Mysore – the heart of modern Karnataka – in the 1950s, 65.2% of the farmers made one third of their income from the land they owned. This socio-economic profile contributed to the formation of a larger social coalition behind the Congress Party.

In Andhra Pradesh too, the dominant castes gained momentum at the expense of the Brahmins. The Kapu and the Kamma, respectively 15.2 and 4.8% of the population in 1921, profited from the modernisation of agriculture, especially in the areas where the *raiyatwari* system (see intro) prevailed, hence the emergence of middle class peasant in their midst.[7] Gradually these groups joined Congress and captured its second line of leadership. As a result, in 1937–9, the Congress government of Madras was prepared to abolish the *zamindari* system where it prevailed in the province.

In Maharashtra, the bridge state between the North and the South, by the late nineteenth century the Brahmins almost monopolised administrative functions open to Indians as well as the professions.[8]

[5] J. Manor, 'Karnataka: caste, class, dominance and politics in a cohesive society' in F. Frankel and M.S.A. Rao (eds), *Dominance and State Power in Modern India. Decline of a social order*, vol. 1, Delhi: Oxford University Press, 1989, p. 340.

[6] The concept of dominant caste, introduced by the Indian anthropologist M.N. Srinivas, designates and upper – or an intermediate – caste which controls a large area of land and is numerous locally (M.N. Srinivas, *Social Change in Modern India*, New Delhi: Orient Longman, 1995 [1966], p. 10).

[7] G. Ram Reddy, 'The politics of accommodation – Caste, Class and Dominance in Andhra Pradesh' in Frankel and Rao (eds), op. cit., p. 274. The situation was naturally very different in the princely state of Hyderabad where the *jagirdars* and the *zamindars* reigned supreme over land.

However, the Marathas – a very large dominant caste which had participated in the modernisation of agriculture within the *raiyatwari* system – rapidly asserted themselves[9] and joined the Congress which had become a serious contender for power. The upper castes who then ran the party refused to allow them a large berth within the Congress governments of 1937 and 1946, but from 1950 onwards, the Congress was gradually dominated by Marathas.

Similar developments were notable by their absence in Northern India. To give only one example, in 1937, of the members of the Congress government of the United Provinces (today's Uttar Pradesh), two-thirds were from the upper castes. I suggest, therefore, that the Weiner thesis cannot elucidate the political trajectory of the Hindi belt and that the Congress' exclusion of the new, aspiring peasant elites was largely responsible for the conservative character of the party and, by extension, of Indian democracy as a whole. This meta-region – principally composed of Uttar Pradesh, Bihar, Madhya Pradesh and Rajasthan – indeed accounts for 40% of India's total population. In 1991 the four states were inhabited by 335 out of 844 millions people and sent 204 out of a total of 543 MPs to the Lok Sabha (the Lower House – Assembly of the People).

The two ages of democracy in India

The primary aim of this book is to demonstrate that North India lagged behind in terms of including new groups in the political system and to explain why the Congress cared very little about representing lower classes. The deviant attitude of the Congress *vis-à-vis* Weiner's model in the Hindi belt cannot be explained by differences in its factional configuration since the party was also faction-ridden in the North.[10] Other differences may provide us with clues. First, these two mega-regions always had a different caste profile. In the Hindi-belt, the caste system is traditionally the closest to the *varna* model

[8] G. Johnson, 'Chitpavan Brahmins and Politics in Western India in the Late Nineteenth and Early Twentieth centuries' in E. Leach and S.N. Mukherjee (eds), *Elites in South Asia*, Cambridge University Press, 1970, p. 105.

[9] J. Lele, 'Caste, Class and Dominance: Political Mobilization in Maharashtra' in Frankel and Rao (eds), op. cit., p. 153.

[10] For Uttar Pradesh see P. Brass, 'Factionalism and the Congress party in Uttar Pradesh', *Asian Survey*, Sept. 1964, pp. 1037–47.

with its four orders (Brahmins, Kshatriyas, Vaishyas and Shudras) and the Untouchables. In the South, the twice-born are seldom 'complete' since the warrior and merchant castes are often absent or poorly represented, as in Maharashtra and Bengal. By the same token the upper *varnas* are more numerous in the North: according to the 1931 census, the last one which interrogated caste, they represent from 13.6% (Bihar) up to 24.2% (Rajasthan) of the population whereas in the South, the proportion of the Brahmins and even of the twice-born is often low. In Andhra Pradesh, for instance, the Brahmins and the Kshatriyas represent respectively 3 and 1.2% of the population. In Maharashtra the twice-born are only marginally superior in numbers with 3.9% Brahmins, 1% Kshatriyas and 1.69% Vaishyas.

The North-South contrast derives also from the kind of land settlement that the British introduced in these two areas. While the *zamindari* system prevailed in North India, the *raiyatwari* system was more systematically implemented in the South. The former ossified the hierarchy of peasant society whereas the latter was more conducive to forms of social equality.[11] Both phenomena – the formula applied for the policy of land settlement and the caste structure – had a cumulative effect in the North since the *zamindars* often came from the largest caste of Kshatriyas, the Rajputs. This agrarian elite's dominant role was also reinforced because the British thought of its members as forming 'natural leaders', considered them to be their most reliable supporters and hence treated them well.[12] In addition, the Rajputs and other land-owning groups exerted power

[11] In the North, when the coloniser levied estate taxes, they often used intermediaries – mainly *zamindars* – who had been established under the Mughal Empire or the successor states. These intermediaries of the central authority, who were often Rajputs or Muslims of aristocratic descent, were allowed to levy taxes owed by the peasants against payment of tribute. They were recognised as land-owners by the British in exchange for the right to collect taxes in the rural areas. In the South, where the Mughal administration had been weak, the British found fewer *zamindars* (or the equivalent) and tended to select individual farmers as land-proprietors and direct taxpayers: hence the 'raiyatwari' system from 'raiyat' 'cultivator'. This was more conducive to the formation of a relatively egalitarian peasantry than the *zamindari* system.

[12] S. Freitag, ' "Natural leaders", Administrators and Social control: Communal Riots in the United Provinces, 1870–1925', *South Asia*, 1 (2) pp. 27-41.

in most of the princely states of North India. The princely states covered two-fifths of the sub-continent and accounted for one-fifth of the population but the highest concentration was in the Hindi belt. In Rajputana – the present-day Rajasthan – they numbered 22, and in the present-day Madhya Pradesh where there were 67 (35 in Vindhya Pradesh, 25 in Madhya Bharat and about a dozen in Chhattisgarh). The princely states were often conservatories of social order, as the Maharajas tried to preserve their territories from modern influences. They generally administered their state through a network of *zamindari* and *jagirdari* (who unlike the former had a police and even a judicial function in their domain).

My hypothesis is that the demographic weight of the upper castes and their role in the local power structure prepared the ground for the development of conservative ideologies and the establishment of the Congress's clientelistic politics. The role of ideology will be examined in the first chapter, through the impact of Gandhi's thought. Even though the Mahatma presented himself as a reformer, he was, in many respects, conservative, as evident from the manner in which he resisted the alternative, egalitarian agenda that Ambedkar was proposing in the 1930s. In northern India more than anywhere else his doctrine strengthened the conservatives within Congress. Ideology, however, often merely served as a justification for the pursuit of social domination. The Congress neglected the poor largely because the party apparatus was in the hands of upper caste notables who relied on 'vote banks politics' to win elections, an issue we shall study in chapter 2. The affirmative action policies which the Congress initiated or inherited from the British did not correct these defects since the quotas were not fulfilled in the administration and the Congress used the reservation of lower caste seats in the assemblies to its own advantage by co-opting docile Untouchable leaders. It also became adept at co-opting less pliable leaders simply to weaken lower castes parties, as we shall show in chapter 3. After the split in Congress in 1969 Indira Gandhi attempted to reform her faction of the party to transform it into an allegedly socialist cadre-based party. But her efforts came to nought and in fact she was less interested in socialist measures than in purely populist strategies which culminated in the imposition of a state of emergency (chapter 4). During this twenty-month period Indira Gandhi suspended a legally constituted state on the pretext of accelerating socio-economic development. It was as if political democracy was incompatible with social democracy because the ruling party depended too much on upper caste notables. Thus in the mid-1970s the Congress had reached a kind of stalemate since it was congenitally unable to reconcile political and social democracy in North India, the meta-region commanding the fate of the whole country. This development was to occur outside the party – and even against it.

The second age of Indian democracy began around the same period, in the late-1960s and – early 1970s. This new development did not follow the same pattern as in the South and in the West where the politicisation of the lower castes had prepared the ground for their political emancipation during the British Raj. South India evolved a pattern of low caste mobilisation based on an ethnic identity and the use of reservation policies introduced by the British (chapter 5), whereas North India remained the prisoner of Sanskritisation (see chapter 6). In fact, the lower castes became politicised at a later date when they realised that they needed to organise themselves in order to gain reservations in the framework of the affirmative action policies that India conceived – or envisaged – after independence (chapter 7). The socialists were the first to mobilise them around these issues. Unlike the communists, they regarded caste as a vehicle for exploitation as harmful as the class system and considered that they could rally lower caste voters around this issue. In the 1960s and 1970s, the mobilisation of the cultivating castes resulted from the conjunction of this 'quota politics' and the 'kisan (peasant) politics' of Charan Singh. A peasant leader, and Congress dissident, Charan Singh developed another kind of plebeian mobilisation based not on caste but on peasant identity. This move coincided with the growing affluence and assertiveness of small peasants in North Indian due to the Green Revolution. His political party, the Bharatiya Kranti Dal (Indian Revolutionary Party), founded in 1969, made inroads in the Congress strongholds of Uttar Pradesh (chapter 8). However, 'quota politics' and 'kisan politics' had many affinities and the socialists and Charan Singh realised that they needed to unite if they were to win power. Charan Singh was the main architect of the union of the opposition which culminated in 1977 with the formation of the Janata Party (chapter 9). Both strategies, the socialist one appealing to caste sentiment and Charan Singh's manipulation of peasant identity in order to mobilise the rural masses, were then implemented simultaneously. The former eventually prevailed in the 1980s–1990s. This process culminated with the announcement by V.P. Singh of the introduction of quotas for the lower castes in the central administration in 1990. The upper castes were so violently against this decision, that the lower castes organised a counter-mobilisation. They now formed interest groups and discovered the importance of co-operation in pressurising the political parties and indeed they rose to power in several North Indian states (chapter 10). Paradoxically, caste – certainly the politicized version of caste – was responsible for the democratisation of Indian democracy. This new age of democracy implicated the Scheduled Castes too since the Bahujan Samaj Party, a party led by Untouchables, jumped to one-fifth of the valid votes in Uttar Pradesh in the 1990s (chapter 11). No party could any longer ignore the lower castes but the issue remains unresolved, as I shall try to show in the last part of this book. How far can the lower castes sustain the political unity which may enable the plebeian parties to gain power and remain in office? Can the mainstream, upper-caste dominated parties like the Congress and the BJP adjust to this new challenge and circumvent this silent revolution?

Part I

CONGRESS IN POWER OR INDIA AS A CONSERVATIVE DEMOCRACY

The Indian National Congress, the main architect of the independence movement and the dominant political force after 1947, has been largely responsible for the social deficit of Indian democracy. Founded in 1885, it had already begun the conquest of power during the colonial period. In 1909 the British had established provincial assemblies, the legislative councils where Indian representatives were elected. Ten years later, a more ambitious reform had liberalised the electoral franchise and had handed over entire administrative sectors to Indian ministers who were responsible to these legislative councils, while British governors remained in charge of important domains. Finally, in 1935, this 'diarchy' was replaced by a proto-parliamentary regime at the regional level where the provinces of British India were largely ran by governments resulting from the elections. The 1937 elections allowed the Congress to gain power in seven provinces. After 1947, the party almost monopolised power in the states of the Indian Union until 1967 and at the centre until 1977.

The 'Congress system'[1] turned out to be conservative in its socio-economic orientation, contrary to the socialist programme advocated by its leaders. This trend stemmed from its strong emphasis on consensus which, in Gandhi's view, almost amounted to social organicism. However, it was primarily due to the social composition of the party since the intelligentsia at its helm, often from an upper caste elite, recruited notables who enjoyed a personal base in order to win elections. This vote bank politics was supplemented by the co-option of

[1] This expression was coined by Rajni Kothari and refers to the identification of the Congress with the state and the party's capacity to remain in power by adjusting to the movements of society ('The Congress system in India', *Asian Survey*, 4 (12) Dec. 1964).

Dalit leaders which weakened the political parties representing the lower castes. As a result, in North India at least, in the 1950–1960s the Congress partly owed its supremacy to the regrouping of the two extremes of the social system i.e. the upper castes and the Dalits.

1
THE GANDHIAN SOURCES OF CONGRESS CONSERVATISM

The origins of the Congress's ideology, as far as its social aspects are concerned, are to be found in the socio-religious movements which developed during the nineteenth century within the Hindu community. These movements often came about as a reaction to the proselytisation of Christian missionaries and the criticism of Indian society by the British. Be they missionaries or Utilitarians, the British denounced the indignity of the caste system and other social evils as early as the turn of the nineteenth century. Although they advocated ambitious reform programmes (against child marriage, and for the emancipation of women, etc.) the Hindu socio-religious reform movements often tried to legitimise as far as possible the hierarchical principles on which their society was based.[2] This effort undoubtedly reflected their social origins (all came from the upper castes[3]) as much as an incapacity to perceive the world through other categories. These socio-religious reform movements prepared the ground for the National Social Conference which developed parallel to the Congress. The NSC was indeed founded to deal with social issues and therefore to spare the Congress these difficult questions. However, the Congress

[2] K. Jones, *The new Cambridge History of India – III.1 Socio-religious Movements in British India*, Cambridge University Press, 1989. On the Sarvajanik Sabha, one of the movements which prepared the ground for the Congress in the Bombay Presidency, and especially on the social conception of its leader, M.G. Ranade, see R. Kumar, 'The new Brahmans of Maharashtra' in D.A. Low (ed.), *Soundings in Modern South Asian History*, Berkeley, CA: University of California Press, 1968, p. 115; on the Arya Samaj, which played a similar role in Punjab, and especially on the thought of its founder, see J.T.F Jordens, *Dayananda Saraswati: His Life and Ideas*, Delhi: Oxford University Press, 1978.

[3] R. Thapar, 'Imagined religious communities? Ancient history and the modern-search for a Hindu identity'., *Modern Asian Studies* (hereafter *MAS*), 23 (2), 1989, p. 229.

developed its own social doctrine, which became a key element of its ideology under Gandhi.

Reformism and social organicism in Gandhi's thought

Before Gandhi, Congress had laboriously started thinking about social reform. In the first decade of the twentieth century, in some of its regional branches debates were held about the conditions of the lower castes. In 1917 the Congressmen of Bombay Presidency passed a motion calling the party to discuss, during its next plenary session, a resolution on 'the necessity, justice and righteousness of removing all the disabilities imposed by religion and custom upon the Depressed Classes [an administrative euphemism introduced by the British which in fact refers to the Untouchables]. Those disabilities being of a most vexatious and oppressive character, subjecting those classes to considerable hardship and inconvenience by prohibiting them from admission into public schools, hospitals, courts of justice and public offices, and the use of public wells, etc.'.[4] These recommendations remained unheeded.

Gandhi had already shown some interest in the problem of Untouchability within the ashrams he had founded.[5] In the 1920 session of the Congress held at Nagpur – which consummated his rise to power – the first resolution voted was to condemn what he called the 'sin of untouchability'.[6] This text called upon Indians 'to rid Hinduism of the reproach of untouchability, and respectfully urge[d] the religious heads to help the growing desire to reform Hinduism in the matter of its treatment of the suppressed classes'.[7] In contrast to the motion proposed by the Congressmen of Bombay, Gandhi

[4] Cited in E. Zelliot, 'Congress and the untouchables, 1917–1950' in R. Sisson and S. Wolpert (eds), *Congress and Indian Nationalism, The Pre-Independence Phase*, Delhi: Oxford University Press, 1988, p. 183.

[5] Soon after the founding of the Sabarmati ashram, Gandhi told the other residents that he 'should take the first opportunity of admitting an untouchable candidate . . .', M.K. Gandhi, *An Autobiography or the Story of my Experiments With Truth*, Ahmedabad: Navajivan, 1995 (first edn 1927), p. 330.

[6] 'The sin of untouchability, *Young India*, 19.01.1921, in *The Collected Works of Mahatma Gandhi*, vol. XIX, Ahmedabad, Navajivan Trust, 1966, pp. 242-3.

[7] Cited in E. Zelliot, 'Congress and the untouchables, 1917–1950', op. cit., p. 185.

considered Untouchability to be more a religious than a social problem.

In 1920–1 he made more and more statements in favour of the Untouchables, as is evident from the many articles on this theme he published in his newspaper, *Young India.*[8] In 1922, The Congress Working Committee (CWC) set up a committee that was commissioned to prepare a plan to fight untouchability. But it never got off the ground, mainly due to a shortage of funds. Its president, Swami Shraddhananda, an Arya Samajist, who was very active on behalf of the Untouchables, resigned from this committee soon after. Following the old Congress strategy which until the beginning of the century had delegated thinking on social issues to other bodies such as the National Social Conference, the CWC in 1923 decided to handover the problem to the Hindu Mahasabha, a Congress offshoot whose interest in untouchability derived from the fact that it was perceived to be a vulnerable aspect of Hinduism *vis-à-vis* the Muslims.[9] Swami Shraddhananda, a member of the Hindu Mahasabha proposed in its extraordinary session of August 1923, a very ambitious four-point resolution:

(1) 'that the lowest among the depressed classes be allowed to draw water from common public wells;

(2) that water be served to them at drinking posts freely as is done to the highest among other Hindus;

(3) that all members of the [depressed] classes be allowed to sit on the same carpet in public meetings and other ceremonies with the higher classes; and

(4) that their children (male and female) be allowed to enter freely and, at teaching time, to sit in the same form with other Hindu and non-Hindu children in government national and denominational institutions.'[10]

These proposals were too radical for the Hindu Mahasabha which

[8] See, for example, Gandhi's 'Speech at Suppressed Classes Conference, Ahmedabad, 13.04.1921, in *Collected Works*, vol. XIX, op. cit., p. 569; 'Disappearing Untouchability', *Young India*, 27 Apr. 2001, in ibid., vol. XX, p. 41; and 'The Panchamas' *Young India*, 29 Sept. 1921, in ibid., vol. XXI, p. 213.

[9] C. Jaffrelot, *The Hindu Nationalist Movement and Indian Politics, 1925 to the 1990s*, London: Hurst, 1996, Chapter 1.

[10] J.T.F. Jordens, *Swami Shraddhananda – His Life and Causes*, Delhi: Oxford University Press, 1981, p. 137.

at the time was led by orthodox Hindus such as Madan Mohan Malaviya, one of the pillars of the Congress in the United Provinces since the 1890s. The question of untouchability was handed over to a subcommittee of Pandits, and a watered-down version of the Shraddhananda resolution was passed in the 1924 session: the Hindu Mahasabha recommended that Untouchables be given free access to schools, to wells and to temples but added that 'it was against the scriptures and the tradition to give the untouchables "*yajyopavit*" [the sacred thread worn by the "twice born"], to teach them Vedas and to interdine with them, and the Mahasabha hoped that the workers in the interests of unity would give up these items of social reform.'[11] Shraddhananda had already turned away from the Hindu Mahasabha, he found too little bold in its fight against Untouchability.

In 1929, the Congress made Madan Mohan Malaviya responsible for preparing its policies towards Untouchability. In doing so the party was responding to contradictory motives: for the Congress leadership only a staunch traditionalist like Malaviya could win over orthodox Hindus to the need for reform, but by choosing Malaviya the movement ran the risk of achieving nothing. In fact, Malaviya – who during the 1927 session of the Hindu Mahasabha had declared that Untouchability did not figure in the Shastras – contented himself with a tour of South India to advocate free access for Untouchables to wells, temples and public thoroughfares.[12]

This lost opportunity occurred with the tacit consent of Gandhi who led his first anti-Untouchability campaign in a very peculiar context. In 1924, the Dalits of Vaikham, in the state of Travancore, launched a *satyagraha* to gain access to a local temple, or at least to use the road adjacent to the temple. Gandhi supported this mobilisation and went to Vaikham, but his dialogue with the local priests did not bear fruit. The latter rejected all his compromise proposals and their arguments prompted him to re-examine his position about Untouchability, as indicated by Parekh:

> He had almost for the first time in his life come face to face with orthodox Brahmins and experienced the intensity of their prejudices. He saw that though they were wrong and confused, they felt strongly about their beliefs

[11] Cited in ibid., p. 142.

[12] Parmanand, *Mahamana Madan Mohan Malviya*, Benares Hindu University, 1985, vol. 2, p. 732.

and sincerely held that these had a scriptural basis. Gandhi seems to have thought that if he was to win them over, he had to earn their confidence and reassure that he was as much concerned to preserve Hinduism as the most orthodox among them.[13]

He lost interest in the Vaikham movement, and in various public meetings later declared himself to be a *sanatanist*, that is a follower of the *Sanatan Dharma*, the 'eternal religion' according to the orthodox Hindus. Gandhi continued to support the Untouchables' demands for access to temples but did so in a manner so as not to offend the high castes. Above all, he refrained from intervening in other causes which were more social than spiritual and hence more sensitive. For him equality before God mattered more than equality between men. This selective approach to Untouchability reflected Gandhi's attachment to a social structure which he considered to be potentially harmonious.

Asked by numerous 'progressive' readers of *Young India* to justify his position, in December 1920 Gandhi defended certain aspects of the caste system in a long article:

> Like every other institution it has suffered from excrescences. I consider the four divisions [the *varnas*] alone to be fundamental, natural and essential. The innumerable sub-castes are sometimes a convenience, often an hindrance. The sooner there is fusion, the better [. . .]. But I am certainly against any attempt at destroying the fundamental divisions [. . .].
>
> One of my correspondents suggests that we should abolish the caste [system] but adopt the class system of Europe – meaning thereby I suppose that the idea of heredity in caste should be rejected. I am inclined to think that the law of heredity is an eternal law and any attempt to alter that law must lead us, as it has before led to utter confusion. I can see very great use in considering a Brahmin to be always a Brahmin throughout his life. If he does not behave himself like a Brahmin, he will naturally cease to command the respect that is due to the real Brahmin. It is easy to imagine the innumerable difficulties if one were to set up a court of punishments and rewards, degradation and promotion. If Hindus believe, as they must believe, in reincarnation, transmigration, they must know that nature will, without any possible mistake, adjust the balance by degrading a Brahmin, if he misbehaves himself by reincarnating him in a lower division, and translating one who lives the life of a Brahmin in his present incarnation to a Brahminhood in his next.

[13] B. Parekh, *Colonialism, Tradition and Reform – An Analysis of Gandhi's Political Discourse*, New Delhi: Sage, 1989, p. 223.

Interdrinking, interdining, intermarrying, I hold, are not essential for the promotion of the spirit of democracy. [. . .] We shall ever have to seek unity in diversity, and I decline to consider it a sin for a man not to drink or eat with anybody and everybody.[14]

Such a discourse is revealing of Gandhi's adherence to certain mechanisms and even to the spirit of the caste system. He voices his belief in reincarnation, he highlights the necessity of maintaining one's rank (especially for the higher castes) as an element of natural regulation, and if he rejects the idea of a rigid hierarchy he appreciates the distribution of men in different castes as a factor of socio-economic complementarity and social harmony. He drew his inspiration from the view of the *varna* system as expressed in the founding myth of the Rig Veda, describing the birth of the Hindu society from the sacrifice of the primordial man: 'His mouth became the Brahmin / the Kshatriya rose from his arms / his hands became the Vaishya / from his feet was born the Shudra'.[15] This fourfold origin of society responds to an organicist *and* hierarchical logic. Referring occasionally to this myth, Gandhi defines the *varna vyavastha* as a model of social organisation which attributes to everyone a socio-professional vocation ensuring a harmonious functioning of the whole. His emphasis on socio-economic cohesion goes hand in hand with a denial of the hierarchical principle, which nevertheless is at the heart of the *varna* system:

The four *varna* have been compared in the Vedas to the four members of one body, and no simile could be happier. If they are members of one body, how could one be superior or inferior to another? If the members of the body had the power of expression and each of them were to say that it was higher and better than the rest, the body would go to pieces [. . .] It is this canker that is at the root of the various ills of our time, especially class and civil strife. It should not be difficult for even the meanest understanding to see that these wars and strifes could not be ended except by the observance of the law of *varna*. For it ordains that every one shall fulfil the law of one's being by doing in a spirit of duty and service that which one is born.[16]

[14] 'The caste system', *Young India*, 8 Dec., 1920, in *The Collected Works of Mahatma Gandhi*, vol. IX, op. cit., pp. 83-5.

[15] *Hymnes spéculatifs du Veda*, notes and translation by Louis Renou, Paris: Gallimard-UNESCO, 1956, p. 99 (Rig-Veda X-90).

[16] Cited in D. Dalton, 'The Gandhian View of Caste, and Caste after Gandhi' in P. Mason (ed.), *India and Ceylon: Unity and Diversity*, London: Oxford University Press, 1967, p. 175.

Gandhi echoes the metaphor of the body that was inherent in the aesthetic of the *varna* system. Now, as Schlanger has shown, metaphors of the body often aim to convince man of the unity of society.[17] If Gandhi tries to eliminate the hierarchical dimension of the caste system, he describes its organic rationale with arguments which leave little place for social mobility. For Gandhi, such mobility implies forms of competition which produce social tensions, as evident in the individualistic societies of the West. In *Hind Swaraj*, his vehement indictment of Western civilisation, that Gandhi wrote in 1908, he congratulated himself that, in contrast to Europe, India 'has had no system of life-corroding competition. Each followed his own occupation or trade, and charged a regulation wage.'[18] In the early 1920s this idea is still dominant in his mind when he writes in *Young India*:

> Historically speaking, caste may be regarded as man's experiment or social adjustment in the laboratory of Indian society. If we can prove it to be a success, it can be offered to the world as a leaven and as the best remedy against heartless competition and social disintegration born of avarice and greed.[19]

Gandhi justifies the hereditary character of the caste system by stressing the social harmony it procures and the economy of energy it allows. Each individual can then devote himself to his quest for salvation.[20] As the struggle to allow Untouchables to enter temples has previously shown, he values religious equality more than anything else: his notion of equality is confined to this domain and hardly admitted in the social world. Thus Gandhi's social reform operates only to the point where egalitarianism runs the risk of challenging social unity – which in practice is hierarchical.

The conflict between Gandhi and Ambedkar

Gandhi's hostility towards radical social reform is evident from his conflict with Ambedkar, one of the first Indian leaders who articulated an alternative, egalitarian view of society in the political arena. Ambedkar was a thinker as much as a political leader, as one might

[17] J. Schlanger, *Les métaphores de l'organisme*, Paris: Vrin, 1971, p.31. I am grateful to Olivier Herrenschmidt for drawing my attention to this book.

[18] M.K. Gandhi, *Indian Home Rule*, Madras, Ganesh, 1922, p. 64.

[19] *Young India* (5 Jan. 1921, p.2), cited in N.K. Bose (ed.), *Selections from Gandhi*, Ahmedabad: Navajivan Publishing House, 1948, p. 233.

[20] *Young India*, 29 Sept. 1927, p.327 cited in ibid., p. 232.

expect from his education, since he was awarded degrees –including a Ph.D. – in different subjects, ranging from economics to law. He was also interested in anthropology, a subject he studied at Columbia University, where he was enrolled from 1913–16. In 1916 he gave a paper entitled 'Castes in India. Their Mechanism, Genesis and Development' in which he intended to 'advance a Theory of Caste',[21] different from that of the western students of Indian society who, according to him, tended to over emphasise the criterion of race. For Ambedkar, caste was not a racial but a social phenomenon that emerged from the Brahmins' strategy of adopting a strictly endogamous matrimonial regime, prompting other groups to do the same in order to emulate this self-proclaimed elite. In fact, Ambedkar, as early as 1916, had gained an insight into practices that M.N. Srinivas was to analyse forty years later in terms of 'Sanskritisation' – a notion to which we return below.

As a corollary, he perceives that caste is not 'a unit by itself' but 'one within a System of Caste'[22]: '*caste in the singular number is an unreality. Castes exist only in the plural member*. There is no such thing as a caste: there are always castes. To illustrate my meaning: while making themselves into a caste, the Brahmins, by virtue of this, created non-Brahmin caste; or, to express it in my own way, while closing themselves in, they closed others out'.[23] The lower castes emulated the Brahmins because they adhered to the same value system. In doing so they admitted that the Brahmins were their superiors: one can certainly exert one's own domination by having the others believing in one's own superiority.[24]

For Ambedkar the *varna* system establishes a unique social structure since no other society has such 'an official gradation laid down, fixed and permanent, *with an ascending scale of reverence and a descending scale of contempt*'.[25] The specificity of the system lays in this 'graded inequality' which is a cause for obsessive anger for Ambedkar.[26]

[21] B.R. Ambedkar, 'Castes in India. Their Mechanism, Genesis and Development', *Indian Antiquary*, May 1917, vol. XLI, reproduced in *Dr Babasaheb Ambedkar Writings and Speeches*, vol. 1, Bombay: Government of Maharashtra, 1979, p. 22.

[22] Ibid., p. 20

[23] Ibid.

[24] Ibid., pp.17 et 19

[25] Ibid., p. 26 (emphasis added).

[26] For a remarkable analysis of these notions, see O. Herrenschmidt,

For Ambedkar, 'inequality is not half so dangerous as graded inequality'.[27] In a state of inequality, groups of a similar size oppose each other. In industrial societies, the labour class can revolt against the bourgeoisie; in the aristocratic regimes, the bourgeois can fight the aristocrats. But in a caste system, the dominated are too deeply divided to join hands against their oppressors:

> In a system of graded inequality, the aggrieved parties are not on a common level [. . .]. In a system of graded inequality there are the highest (the Brahmins). Below the highest are the higher (the Kshatriyas). Below the higher are those who are high (Vaishya). Below the high are the low (Shudra) and below the low are those who are lower (the Untouchables). All have a grievance against the highest and would like to bring about their downfall. But they will not combine. The higher is anxious to get rid of the highest but does not wish to combine with the high, the low and the lower, lest they should reach his level and be his equal. The high wants to over-throw the higher who is above him but does not want to join hands with the low and the lower, lest they should rise to his status and become equal to him in rank. The low is anxious to pull down the highest, the higher and the high but he would not make a common cause with the lower for fear of the lower gaining a higher status and becoming his equal. In the system of graded inequality there is no such class as completely unprivileged class except the one which is at the base of the social pyramid. The privileges of the rest are graded. Even the low is a privileged class as compared with the lower. Each class being privileged, every class is interested in maintaining the system.[28]

The mechanisms described by Ambedkar go even further since they are also at work *within* each *varna*, where they oppose different *jatis*. Otherwise, the Shudras would form a bloc which would be in a majority in the Hindu community. This analytical weakness notwithstanding, Ambedkar was the first low caste politician to offer such a sophisticated view of the caste system and to deplore the division of the lower strata of society, 'a disunited body [. . .], infested with the caste system in which they believe as much as does the caste

' "L'inégalité graduée" ou la pire des inégalités. L'analyse de la société hindoue par Ambedkar', *Archives Européennes de Sociologie*, 37 (1996), pp. 16–17.

[27] B.R. Ambedkar, ' Revolution', in *Dr Babasaheb Ambedkar Writings and Speeches*, vol. 3, Bombay: Government of Maharashtra, 1987, p. 320.

[28] B.R. Ambedkar, 'Untouchables or the Children of India's Ghetto', in *Dr Babasaheb Ambedkar Writings and Speeches*, vol. 5, Bombay: Government of Maharashtra, 1989, pp. 101–2.

Hindu. This caste system among the untouchables has given rise to mutual rivalry and jealousy and it has made common action impossible'.[29]

Using his sociological insights, Ambedkar endeavoured to reshape the Untouchable identity in order to enable them to assert themselves. The ultimate outcome of this undertaking is found in *The untouchables. Who were they and why they became untouchables*? Here, he once again rejects the racial theory of western scholars for whom the Untouchables descended from indigenous peoples subjugated by the Aryan invaders.[30] His interpretation is much more complex, and subtle. He explains that each and every society is subjected to invasions by external forces, each of which appears to be more powerful than its local counterparts. Suffering from dislocation, the latter give birth to new groups that Ambedkar calls the 'Broken Men' (or *Dalit* in Marathi).[31] After the conquering tribes become sedentary, they mobilise the Broken Men to protect villages from further incursions, thus establishing them on the periphery of clusters of habitations, not least because the villagers shun them.

These Broken Men became the first and most fervent followers of Buddha and remained so when most other converts returned to mainstream Hinduism. For Ambedkar, 'It explains why the Untouchables regard the Brahmins as inauspicious, do not employ them as their priest and do not even allow them to enter into their quarters. It also explains why the Broken Men came to be regarded as Untouchables. The Broken Men hated the Brahmins because the Brahmins were the enemies of Buddhism and the Brahmins imposed untouchability upon the Broken Men because they would not leave Buddhism'.[32] Yet Ambedkar did not consider that the Buddhist affiliation of the Broken Men was sufficient to explain why the Brahmins treated them so harshly. Another reason lay in the fact that the Untouchables refused to become vegetarians and continued to eat beef whereas the 'Brahmins made the cow a sacred animal'.[33]

[29] B.R. Ambedkar, 'Held at Bay' in *Dr Babasaheb Ambedkar Writings and Speeches*, vol. 5, Bombay: Government of Maharashtra, 1989, p. 266.

[30] B.R.Ambedkar, 'The untouchables. Who were they and why they became untouchables ?' in *Dr Babasaheb Ambedkar Writings and speeches*, vol. 7, Bombay: Government of Maharashtra, 1990, pp. 290–303.

[31] Ibid., p. 275.

[32] Ibid., p. 317.

[33] Ibid., p.350.

Thus, Ambedkar not only elaborated a profound theory of caste which culminates in the notion of graded inequality, but he also shaped new identities to promote the emancipation of the Untouchables. He endowed them with a separate, prestigious identity deriving from the special status of Buddhism in India. This creed provided the Untouchables with a strong ideological basis for questioning their subordinate rank in the caste system, all the more so given its egalitarian doctrine. Once they regard themselves as former Buddhists, they can overcome their divisions and mobilise against the caste hierarchies. However, Ambedkar found it hard to advance his cause because of the opposition of Congress leaders and, above all, of Gandhi.

During the second Round Table Conference, in which Ambedkar participated as a representative of the Depressed Classes, he demanded for them a separate electorate. Ambedkar believed that such electoral reform would transform his caste fellows into a solid interest group.[34] Gandhi objected, saying that it would mean the division of Hindu society, adding that he would oppose this move if necessary at the expense of his life.[35] When the British government, through the 1932 Communal Award, gave a separate electorate to the Depressed Classes he threatened to fast unto death in order to force the British authorities back down. The letter he sent on September 15, 1932, to the Bombay Government is highly revealing:

> . . . my intimate acquaintance with every shade of untouchability convinces me that their lives, such as they are, are so intimately mixed with those of the Caste Hindus in whose midst and for whom they live that it is impossible to separate them. They are part of an indivisible family. Their revolt against the Hindus with whom they live and their apostasy from Hinduism I should understand. But this, so far as I can see, they will not do. There is a subtle something quite indefinable in Hinduism which keeps them in it *even in spite of themselves.* And this fact makes it imperative for a man like me with a living experience of it to resist the contemplated separation even though the effort should cost life itself.[36]

'This subtle something' – which Gandhi had qualified as 'marvellous' a few lines above – is nothing less than the integration in a caste

[34] For Ambedkar's argument, see B.R. Ambedkar, *What Congress and Gandhi Have Done to the Untouchables*, Bombay: Thacker, 1946.

[35] Pyarelal, *The Epic Fast*, Ahmedabad: Mohanlal Maganlal Bhatt, 1932, p. 98.

[36] Cited in ibid., p. 115. Emphasis added.

system with its social and economic interdependence and its ritual complementarity but also, the integration being hierarchical, its marks of submission (the Untouchables work for the upper castes and Gandhi even candidly says that they live for them), its deference and simply its physical or symbolic violence, which explain that the Untouchables remain within the system 'in spite of themselves'! Gandhi of course is not blind to these defects but he sees in them the perversions of an older and more perfect order which needs to be restored, not through laws like the one giving a separate electorate to the Untouchables, but through social reforms. In the Round Table Conference he had eulogised the work undertaken by the upper castes reformers to reject the measures demanded by Ambedkar and he still expected from them a gradual transformation of the system which would preserve its unity. Two days after beginning his fast, in a conversation with Vallabhbhai Patel, one of his conservative lieutenants, he betrayed his concern for the upper castes:

> [The Untouchables] do not realise that the separate electorate will create division among Hindus so much that it will lead to blood-shed. 'Untouchable' hooligans will make common cause with Muslim hooligans and kill caste-Hindus. Has the British Government no idea of all this? I do not think so.[37]

Gandhi's fast naturally precipitated an upheaval throughout India. Madan Mohan Malaviya, who represented the upper caste interests in the Congress, organised a conference to which Ambedkar was invited to renegotiate the terms of the Communal Award. Successive drafts of the compromise were placed before Gandhi whose condition was fast deteriorating. Finally the 'Poona Pact' was ratified by the leaders of the Congress, who were considered as the *de facto* representatives of the upper castes, and Dalit leadership, including Ambedkar.[38] Gandhi, who professed to be above the fray and above caste, did not sign the text. It established a system of reserved seats and primary elections which granted 148 seats (instead of the 71 provided

[37] Cited in E. Zelliot, 'Gandhi and Ambedkar – A study in leadership' in J.M. Mahar (ed.), *The Untouchables in Contemporary India*, Tuscon: University of Arizona Press, 1972, p. 85.

[38] R. Kumar, 'Gandhi, Ambedkar and the Poona Pact, 1932' in J. Masselos (ed.), *Struggling and Ruling – The Indian National Congress, 1885–1985*, London: Oriental University Press, 1985, pp. 87–101.

for in the Communal Award) to the Depressed Classes in the provincial assemblies but which removed the principle of separate electorates: in 148 constituencies – where the Untouchables were numerous – the members of the Depressed Classes would elect four persons among them and these would be candidates for which the electorate as a whole would be called upon to vote.

In the wake of the Poona Pact, Gandhi threw himself wholeheartedly in the struggle against Untouchability: he established an 'Untouchability Abolition Week' in September–October 1932, launched a weekly journal, *Harijan*,[39] in February 1933 and campaigned on behalf of the Untouchables from November 1933 to July 1934. He also helped set up an All-India Anti-Untouchability League which was headed by a committee of 9 members, 3 of which were untouchables, of whom Ambedkar was one. Being in favour of abolishing the caste system, Ambedkar proposed that the League campaign for inter-caste marriages and meals. This suggestion was rejected by the high command of the league. The untouchables members resigned immediately. The League which was renamed Harijan Sevak Sangh (The Association of the servants of the Harijans) – with the help of funds provided by the capitalist G.D. Birla, the Mahatma's principal sponsor – was intended to help the Depressed Classes to come up, particularly in terms of education, and at the same time to favour some change in the mentality of the upper castes.[40] It concentrated on assisting the Dalits in a perspective which was strongly tinted with paternalism.[41] Its aim was not to abolish the caste system.

The conservative influence of Gandhi on the Congress in North India

Gandhi's view of Untouchability is a good indicator of his philosophy in regard to social reform. He had no wish to bring down the social structure but rather to reorganise it while avoiding (even preventing) its break-up. This approach manifested itself in an exacerbated concern for consensus: Gandhi always tried to resolve social conflicts

[39] 'Harijan' literally means 'children of Hari', i.e. God. See B. Ray (ed.), *Gandhi's campaign against Untouchability, 1933-1934*, New Delhi: Gandhi Peace Foundation, 1996.

[40] G.D. Birla, *In the Shadow of the Mahatma*, Bombay: Orient Longman, 1953, ch. 7.

[41] B. Parekh, *Colonialism, Tradition and Reform*, op. cit., pp. 238–9.

through conciliation. This is evident from the first farmers'agitation which he organised in Bihar in 1918, in Champaran district against the indigo planters. He treated the peasantry 'as a homogenous entity' in order to avoid seeing the slightest division: 'the domination of the planters is openly denounced as oppressive, but not that of the big Indian *zamindars* which nevertheless was basically of the same nature.'[42]

The Gandhian approach was (or gradually became) that of most Congressmen. In 1923 those of the Swaraj Party declared in their electoral manifesto:

> True it is that the Party stands for justice to the tenant but poor indeed would be the quality of that justice if it involves any injustice to the landlord. The Party believes that it is only by serving the true interests of both that it can find a solid base of Swarajya and is pledged to stand by the one as firmly as the other in its hour of need.[43]

By the late 1920s the Congress adopted a more radical position under the auspices of its new young, socialist wing, of which Jawaharlal Nehru was regarded as one of the leaders. In October 1930, within the framework of the Civil Disobedience movement, the Congress of the United Provinces launched a campaign to boycott agricultural taxes. These taxes were collected by Indian intermediaries, the *zamindars* and the *taluqdars*, who were upper caste Hindus (often Rajputs) or Muslims aristocrats. The tax strike was supported all the more by tenants and subtenants as the 1929 Great Depression had hit the Indian economy hard. Gandhi became worried that such a strike could provoke social tensions. In May 1931, he simultaneously published an 'Appeal to the *zamindars*' and a 'Manifesto to the *kisans* [peasants]' in which he indicated:

> The Congress expects every tenant to pay as early as possible all the rent he can, and in no case as a general rule less than 8 annas [subdivision of the rupee] or 12 annas as the case may be. But just as even in the same district there may be cases in which a larger payment is possible, it is equally possible that there may be cases in which less than 8 annas or 12 annas can only be

[42] J. Pouchepadass, *Planteurs et paysans dans l'Inde coloniale*, Paris: L'Harmattan, 1986, p. 264.

[43] Cited in P. Reeves, *Landlords and Governments in Uttar Pradesh*, Delhi: Oxford University Press, 1991, p. 220.

paid. In such cases I hope the tenants will be treated liberally by the Zamindars. In every case you will see that you get against payment a full discharge from your obligation for the current year's rent.[44]

After the Congress suspended its Civil Disobedience movement in March 1931 following the Gandhi-Irwin pact, party workers in the United Provinces immediately took the necessary measures to enable the tax to be collected.[45] The farmers' leaders, on the other hand, intensified their agitation, which occasionally turned violent and prompted local Congress leaders immediately to disavow them. For G. Pandey, 'these leaders laboured under ideological restrictions derived primarily from Gandhi's doctrine'.[46]

To counter the idea of class struggle Gandhi proposed the notion of 'trusteeship', a theory that rejected private property in favour of public ownership of goods: owners were called upon to consider themselves to be trustees of public property which they had to manage in the common interest.[47] The philosophy of 'trusteeship' rested partly on the reinterpretation of the *jajmani* system which dominated the rural economy in pre-colonial times and under British rule. This system eschewed private ownership of land; instead, agricultural produce was deemed to be the result of co-operation between different castes, and their remuneration – generally paid in kind – was a function of the work done.[48] Blacksmiths, for instance, received a part of the harvest in exchange for their work fashioning tools and ploughs; the Untouchables and other castes earned their share by threshing grain and other tasks. This system enabled the upper or/ and dominant castes to compel the castes dependent upon them for generations (particularly service rendering castes) to carry out difficult or menial tasks. Certain British observers ignored the relationship of dominance inherent in the *jajmani* system and thought of it only as

[44] Cited in G. Pandey, *The Ascendancy of the Congress in Uttar Pradesh 1926–1934*, Delhi: Oxford University Press, p. 105.

[45] Ibid., p. 183.

[46] Ibid., p. 101

[47] See M.K.Gandhi, *Socialism of My Conception*, Bombay: 1957, pp. 198–306 and J.D. Sethi (ed.), *Trusteeship. The Gandhian Alternative*, New Delhi: Gandhi Peace Foundation, 1986.

[48] M.L. Reiniche, 'La notion de jajmani: qualification abusive ou principe d'intégration?', *Purushartha*, vol.3, 1977, pp. 71–107.

a model of socio-economic cooperation. This explains how Blunt, in his famous 1931 report on the caste system in Northern India, defined the *jajmani* system as 'a circle of clients from whom the village artisan or menial receive fixed dues in return for regular services.' He added that 'The *jajmani* is undoubtedly a valuable asset, and many a villager derives at least as much of his income from this source as from his fields'.[49] Gandhi undoubtedly shared this interpretation and used it in order to present the *jajmani* system as based on conflict-free social relations. In 1931, he invited the *zamindars* to consider themselves as trustees – and not as owners – of their land, after which Congress would see to it that the farmers paid their taxes.[50]

Gandhi's views had a strong inhibitory influence on the emerging socialist-minded leaders of the Congress, including Jawaharlal Nehru. In 1929, while he was presiding over the Congress session in Lahore, Nehru declared himself to be a socialist and made a strong plea for a land reform policy that favoured the rise of 'owner-peasants'.[51] In 1930 he campaigned for a boycott of the taxes to which farmers were subjected in the United Provinces, and three years later he adopted a revolutionary tone in a pamphlet with an evocative title, 'Whither India?'. In this paper he regretted that the Congress had yet to question 'the social status quo'.

> Nothing is more absurd than to imagine that all the interests in the nation can be fitted in without injury to any. At every step some have to be sacrified for others [. . .] It is therefore essential that we keep this in mind and fashion our idea of freedom accordingly. We cannot escape having to answer the question, now or later, for the freedom of which class or classes in India are we especially striving?[. . .] To say that we shall not answer that question now is itself an answer and a taking of sides, for it means that we stand by the existing order, the status quo [. . .] India's immediate goal can therefore only be considered in terms of the ending of the exploitation of her people. Politically it must mean independence [. . .]; economically and socially it must mean the ending of all special class privileges and vested interests [. . .]

[49] E.A.H Blunt, *The Caste System of Northern India*, Delhi: S. Chand, 1969 [1931], p. 259.

[50] P.D. Reeves, 'The landlords' response to political change in the United Provinces of Agra and Oudh, India, 1921–1937', PhD thesis, Australian National University, Canberra, 1963, p. 268.

[51] Ibid., p. 260.

In a revolutionary period such as exists in the world today, it is a foolish waste of energy to think and act in terms of carrying on the existing regime and trying to reform it and to improve it. To do so is to waste the opportunity which history offers us once in a long while [. . .] Whither India? Surely to the great human goal of social and economic equality, to the ending of all exploitation of nation by nation and class by class, to national freedom within the framework of an international co-operation [and a] socialist world federation.[52]

In 1934, the left wing of the Congress – which regarded Nehru as one of its leaders – became a party within the party by creating the Congress Socialist Party. The CSP emerged largely to restrain Gandhi where the socialists 'felt he was not right and to strengthen him [. . .] where there was a danger of his being let down by the Right-wing [of the Congress].[53] But Gandhi rejected socialism as an ideology 'based on coercion' and class antagonism.[54] Nehru soon abandoned the radical overtones of his discourse, as suggested by his evaluation of the UP landlords in 1936:

Both these poor landowners and the middle landlords, though often intellectually backward, are as a whole a fine body of men and women, and, with proper education and training, can be made into excellent citizens. They have taken a considerable part in the nationalist movement. Not so the *taluqdars* and the big *zamindars*, barring a few notable exceptions. They have not even the virtues of an aristocracy. As a class they are physically and intellectually degenerate and have outlived their day; they will continue only so long as an external power like the British Government props them up.[55]

After Congress's electoral success in 1937, the UP government enacted a very modest boat of land reform which affected the big absentee-landlords.[56] The Tenancy Act, XVII of 1939 was anything but

[52] J. Nehru, *India's Freedom*, London: Union books, 1962, pp. 20–34.

[53] K.C. Mahendru, *Gandhi and the Congress Socialist Party*, Jalandhar, ABS, 1986, p. 21.

[54] Cited in ibid., pp. 29 and 31.

[55] J. Nehru, *An Autobiography*, New Delhi: Oxford University Press, 1987 (1936), p. 58.

[56] Z. Hasan 'Power and Mobilization: Patterns of Resilience and Change in Uttar Pradesh Politics', in Frankel and Rao (eds), op. cit., p. 151. In 1936, The United Provinces Congress had appointed an Agrarian Reforms Enquiry Committee whose conclusions had reflected the socialists' influence but remained ambivalent : 'The abolition of the zamindari system will have to take place in

bold. Smaller land holdings were not exempted from rent, contrary to what the Congressmen had promised during the election campaign, nor were rental arrears cancelled – non-payment of rent also remained a cause for expulsion from the land. The tenants had acquired a hereditary right to till the land on which they had been settled but they could still be expelled for non-payment of rent.[57] Only the larger landlords who employed a number of tenants were affected. The smaller *zamindars* – those paying less than Rs 250 in land tax per annum – remained largely untouched by this land reform.

To sum up, in the 1920–1930s the Congress, while emerging as a mass party as well as a party of government, manifested a rather conservative approach to politics which was in tune with Gandhi's views. The Mahatma's emphasis on social harmony was no doubt explained by his concern to safeguard the unity of the nation. On the occasion of the Second Round Table Conference, at which Congress and the British government resumed their negotiations after the conclusion of the Gandhi-Irwin pact six months earlier, he declared:

> 'The Congress claimed to represent over 85 per cent of the population of India, that is to say the dumb, toiling, semi-starved millions [. . .] the Congress claimed also by right of service to represent even the Princes [. . .] the landed gentry, the educated class [. . .] The Congress [. . .] claims to represent all minorities.'[58]

Gandhi's comments reflected his desire to constitute Congress as the emanation and the embodiment of the whole nation. It is consistent with the way he denied the existence of conflicts within the nation. This is a commonplace feature among freedom movements. In the case of Gandhi's Congress, however, this irenism assumes a special form. Gandhi's concern to avoid conflicts within

---

India, as in other countries, sooner or later. How it will take place will depend on the circumstances then existing and it is a little difficult to lay down hard and fast rules as to what should happen when such a contingency arises. We should like this changeover to take place with as little injury as possible to various groups. Conflict is inevitably an expensive process and it is always desirable to lessen conflict. Some of us are clearly of opinion that compensation be given to the expropriated zamindars, some other members of our committee are opposed to this idea of giving compensation [. . .] Some of us are in favour of peasant proprietorship of land, while others stand for the principle of State ownership.' (Cited P. Reeves, *Landlords and Governments*, op. cit., pp. 221–2)

[57] Ibid., pp. 232–3.

[58] Cited in Pandey, *The Ascendancy of the Congress*, op. cit., p. 101.

Indian society basically reflects his organic vision of the caste system. This social model, idealised in reference to the *varna* system, underlies his constant search for (re)conciliation. His concern for the unity of society and of the nation finds its expression in his opposition to separate electorates for the untouchables, as Ambedkar had demanded. Ambedkar, probably the first politician who proposed an alternative, egalitarian programme of social reforms, was also the only Indian leader Gandhi confronted by undertaking a fast unto death. His ideas were bound to re-emerge in the course of time, but in the 1930s–1940s he had lost one battle against Congress conservatism.

Gandhian doctrine inhibited the socialist-like tendencies of leftist-leaning Congressmen like Nehru and found an echo within the conservative Congress elite. In January 1948 the Mahatma disappears from the scene but Nehru, as Prime Minister, had now to deal with conservative Congressmen who used Gandhism to justify their views. As a result, there was little chance of putting into practice the progressive discourse of post-independence India that was enshrined in the 1950 Constitution.

Congress and social transformation: an empty discourse?

In his pioneering work on the Indian Constitution, G. Austin underlines that it 'is first and foremost a social document. The majority of its provisions are either directly aimed at furthering the goals of the social revolution or attempt to foster this revolution by establishing the conditions necessary for its achievement'.[59] In many respects, indeed, the Indian Constitution, proclaimed three years after Independence in 1950, reflects the progressive views of the westernised intelligentsia. Within the Constituent Assembly this group was represented by Nehru but also by Ambedkar, the chairman of the Drafting Committee. Wider notions of human rights were a source of inspiration in drafting the 'Fundamental Rights', a kind of preamble to the Constitution where equal rights – outlawed was discrimination on grounds of religion, of race, of caste (untouchability therein is abolished), of sex or of geographical origins – as well as respect for the liberty of speech and religion, are advocated strongly. Then follow in the Constitution the 'Directive principles of state policy'

[59] G. Austin, *The Indian Constitution – Cornerstone of a Nation*, Bombay: Oxford University Press, 1972, p. 50.

where it is anticipated that 'the state shall strive to promote the welfare of the people by securing and protecting as effectively as it may a social order in which justice, social, economic and political, shall inform all the institutions of the national life'.[60] Yet again, however, this framework was to be frustrated by the opposition of conservative Congressmen.

The social reform approach displayed by the Fundamental Rights and the Directive Principles could only be laid down with great difficulty in the Constitution itself, as evident from the debate around property rights, which mainly concerned compensation that had (or had not) followed on from the nationalisation of private property. The redistribution of land was the root cause of the controversy at a time when several states had already launched (sometimes as early as 1947) land reform. Nehru argued that state assemblies alone should decide the level of compensation, whereas, Patel, the Deputy Prime Minister, considered that those whose property had been nationalised should have the right to legal appeal.[61] The compromise formula finally evolved in 1949 provided that no one could be dispossessed of their property except by legal sanction and that the law had to indicate the level of compensation or the manner in which it would be calculated. Moreover the Acts in question had to receive the consent of the President of Republic and therefore of the government where Patel could virtually exert a veto.[62]

The debate around property rights is revealing of the opposition which Nehru confronted immediately after Independence: his socialism was no longer inhibited by Gandhi but hindered by the conservatism of many Congress members. These tensions were also exemplified by the debates on agrarian reform, the role of planning in the Indian economy and agricultural co-operatives.

The thwarting of land reform: the case of Uttar Pradesh

The Nehru government reactivated land reform after Independence but the framing of concrete measures was the responsibility of the states. The case of the United Provinces, renamed Uttar Pradesh after

[60] *The Constitution of India*, New Delhi: Government of India, 1983, art. 38, p. 20.

[61] See Austin, *The Indian Constitution*, op. cit., p. 97.

[62] Ibid., p. 98.

Independence, is certainly the most interesting one in North India. Here, the abolition of the zamindari system had been one of the main planks of the 1945–6 election campaign. Congressmen were encouraged to promote this theme since the 1935 Government of India Act – so far as the state assemblies were concerned – had lowered the electoral eligibility tax to an annual farm rent of ten rupees, which increased the rural electorate from 1.5 million to 4.6 million people. Within this electorate there were five tenants to each landlord.[63]

However, once the elections had been won and Independence gained, two antagonistic trends emerged within the UP Congress. The left wing and the Congress Socialist Party agitated for a co-operative system where family-based land-holdings would disappear and no compensation would be paid to the victims of land reform; whereas Charan Singh wanted to see Indian agriculture dominated by small peasant proprietors and did not rule out compensation payments.

Even though he said that his 'childhood was spent among peasants who bared bodied labour in the fields',[64] Charan Singh (1902–87), was born in a relatively well off family of Jat tenants from western Uttar Pradesh (Meerut district). After gaining a law degree and beginning an independent legal practice in 1928 he later joined Gandhi's Civil Disobedience movement and rose within the ranks of Congress as a peasant leader. In fact he had led peasant movements in western UP since 1929[65] and he began to reflect upon the need for land reform in the 1930s. In 1939 he wrote two pamphlets, *Peasant Proprietorship or Land to the Workers* and *Prevention of Division of Holdings Below a Certain Minimum.* The same year he proposed a 'Land Utilisation Bill' in the Legislative Assembly, where he had been elected in 1937, which sought to transfer proprietory rights over agricultural holdings in the United Provinces to tenants who would deposit ten times the annual rental in Government treasury to the account of the landlord.[66] This proposal was to be implemented in

[63] P. Reeves, B.D. Graham and J.M. Goodman, *A Handbook to Elections in Uttar Pradesh, 1920–1951*, Delhi: Manohar, 1975, pp. xxxix–xl.

[64] Cited in Gyanendra Rawat (ed.), *Chaudhury Charan Singh: sukti aur vichar*, New Delhi: Kisan Trust, 1995, chapter 8 (no page number).

[65] C. Singh, *Land Reforms in UP and the Kulaks*, Delhi: Vikas, 1986, p. 1.

[66] Sukhbir Singh Goyal, *Profile of Chaudhary Charan Singh*, New Delhi: Ompal Singh, 1978, p. 6.

the framework of the coming land reform. In 1947, he published a manifesto, *Abolition of Zamindari: Two alternatives*, where he opposed the co-operative system and advocated a family-based economy on the following grounds: first, that a society of peasant proprietors would strengthen democracy, and secondly, that private property would be the most effective inducement to productivity.[67] His ideas were later taken up in the report of the Zamindari Abolition Committee that was responsible for designing the land reform scheme in Uttar Pradesh.

This committee had been appointed by the Legislative Assembly of the United Provinces on August 8, 1946, under the chairmanship of Govind Ballabh Pant, the Chief Minister. One of its most influential members was Charan Singh, who was then Parliamentary Secretary to the former.[68] The report reflects the Gandhian view of an idealised, conflict-free rural society that was upheld by many Congress leaders[69] and Charan Singh's views on the peasantry.

The Gandhian overtone of the report primarily finds its expression in a recurrent concern for 'the revival of [. . .][the] village republics'[70] and the eulogy of the 'theory of trusteeship' which, according to the committee, 'has been widely misrepresented as defending the continuance of vested interests'.[71] In fact, it is 'a revolutionary doctrine' since 'The tiller of the soil would become its owner neither by organised violence nor by legislation but by a moral revolution; a re-

[67] C. Singh, *Abolition of Zamindari – Two Alternatives*, Allahabad: Kitabistan, 1947.

[68] Excerpts of his recent memorandum 'How to Abolish Zamindari' were occasionally reproduced *in extenso* in the report of the committee. See *Report of the United Provinces Zamindari Abolition Committee*, vol. 1, Allahabad: Government of the United Provinces, 1948, pp 495–6.

[69] A staunch socialist – Z.H. Lari, who wrote a minute of dissent to the report – excepted, the 15 members of the committee were all followers of Gandhi. Among those whose caste and community could be identified, five of them were Brahmins, two Banyas, one Rajput, one Jat and four Muslims.

[70] *Report of the United Provinces Zamindari Abolition Committee*, vol. 1, op. cit., p. 519.

[71] Ibid., p. 397. Hence a strong emphasis on the autonomy of the so-called 'village community' which is supposed, for instance, to 'adjust the revenue on individual holdings on the basis of valuation', with the sanction of the Government (ibid., p. 520).

volt not of the peasants, but of the conscience of the landlords themselves'.[72] Such sentences reflected a typically Gandhian view of the Indian village as virtually free from social conflicts, not only because of the potentially harmonious relations between those who cultivate and those who own land but also between the artisans and the other groups:

> [In contrast to the factory worker generated by the capitalist economy], the village craftsman is not exposed to the temptations or perils of a competitive economy. His work is, in a sense, a private enterprise carried on with the motive of private profit, but it is also a service to the village, in the performance of which he is assured a modest competence and a definite social status [. . .] The craftsman is, therefore, on the whole safe and content; he has neither the opportunity nor the desire to acquire vast wealth, his purely acquisitive and selfish instincts are not over-developed, nor does he run the risks that go with the opportunity of acquiring wealth [. . .].
>
> It is only when one considers all these aspects of our traditional way of life that one can realise the significance of the concept of '*dharma*' as attached to a man's calling and the duties of his station.
>
> [. . .] The village as a self-governing institution, the caste system and the joint family, were, all of them, institutions designed to bring individual purposes and economic motives into harmony with the well-being of the community as a whole, and to co-ordinate the interests of the individual with the interests of a larger group. [. . .] The organisation of our social life and our habits of mind are not individualistic, at any rate not to the same degree as those of an ordinary European. It is the realisation of this basic fact that constitutes the point of departure for the new scheme of land tenure that we propose.[73]

The Committee reproduces Gandhi's vindication of the caste system as a model of harmonious socio-economic co-operation. In this excerpt, the *jajmani* system is presented as tension-free, as if this type of social relations was not at all based on domination. The committee's concern for social harmony in the Indian village explains the timidity of its proposals. Its report stresses the fact that land redistribution 'would arouse a spirit of opposition among the substantial cultivators – landlords and tenants – and would inflict great hardship upon the landlords, whose income will, in any case, be

[72] Ibid., p. 398.
[73] Ibid., pp. 479–80, emphasis added.

reduced by our scheme for the abolition of zamindari'.[74] Obviously, the committee was not only afraid of generating social tensions in the villages, but also of 'pauperising' – the word is used elsewhere in the report[75] – the former landlords. Besides, according to its calculations, the cutting down of the largest holdings – those above 25 acres – would not appreciably reduce the number of uneconomic holdings and might cut the quantity of grain available on the market since small (or middle size) farmers tend to consume most of the grain they produce. The committee therefore concludes that 'the results achieved by the redistribution of land would [not] be commensurate with the discontent and hardship resulting from it' and therefore abstain from recommending that some 'limit be placed on the maximum area held in cultivation either by a landlord or a tenant'.[76]

The main thrusts of its reports lay in the abolition of intermediaries and the promotion of peasant-proprietors, as envisioned by Charan Singh, who subscribed to the mainstays of Gandhi's philosophy. In an article published a year after the submission of its report by the Zamindari Abolition Committee, he emphasised that any imitation of the techniques adopted following the Russian revolution would be contrary to the Mahatma's teachings, his own source of inspiration.[77] But he also valued the ethos of the entrepreneur although he remained committed to the Gandhian model of cottage industries. Although he remained committed to the Gandhian model of cottage industries, in this respect he is more an individualist than his fellow Congressmen. In 1949 he replied to Socialist and Communist criticisms that 'to call the *bhumidhar*, a peasant proprietor, that he will be, a capitalist, is a perversion of facts. He will not be performing a capitalist's real job of accumulating capital. And, although occasionally employing others, he will necessarily be performing an important and larger part of the manual labour himself'.[78] Charan Singh drew his inspiration from the Gandhian model of a decentralised economy, right up to the village level where the family would remain the basic unit of all production. Moreover he saw in the *bhumidhar*

[74] Ibid., p. 386.

[75] Ibid., p. 399.

[76] Ibid., p. 389.

[77] Charan Singh published an article along that lines in the *National Herald* (Lucknow) on Aug. 16, 1949 (reprinted in *Land reforms in UP and the Kulaks*, op. cit., pp. 28–9).

[78] Ibid., p. 33.

a guarantor of a centrist form of politics which, he hoped, would save India from the excesses of class struggle because by 'strengthening the principle of private property where it was the weakest, that is, at the base of the social pyramid, the reforms created a huge class of strong opponents of the class-war ideology'.[79] To his influence can be attributed the strong rejection of any form of collective farming on behalf of free enterprise, as set out in the Zamindari Abolition Committee report:

> If the production of an abundance of worldly goods cannot be organised except with the loss of individual freedom and happiness, many would prefer an economic system that produced less, provided it gave scope for the full development of human personality and did not lead either to war and imperialism, or to a totalitarian regime. Social values must not be sacrificed to economic efficiency. Reorganisation of agriculture should therefore be consistent with the economic freedom of the individual and the decentralisation of power, social, economic and political, which are necessary for the democratic way of life.[80]

At the maximum, the committee contemplated the development of co-operative farms which 'would be organised on the basis of voluntary association' and where the 'private property of the individual in his land would be recognised. . .'.[81] The promotion of peasant-proprietors was the main objective of the reforms and landless agricultural labourers, for instance, were largely ignored: they would be settled 'if excess [land] is available', to use Charan Singh's words in the report.[82]

Eventually, the Uttar Pradesh Zamindari Abolition and Land Reform Act recognised four categories of agricultural producers:

(1) the *bhumidhars* (meaning holders of land) were comprised mostly of former landlords, *zamindars* or *taluqdars*. Till then they had raised land revenue on behalf of the state, keeping a portion for themselves. This intermediariy status was abolished, as well as the possibility of their becoming tenants without guaranteed tenure. But they retained the ownership of the land which they cultivated, or whose cultivation they supervised and that they rented out for life

[79] Ibid., p. 40.

[80] *Report of the United Provinces Zamindari Abolition Committee*, vol. 1, op. cit., p. 477.

[81] Ibid., p. 505.

[82] Ibid., p. 496.

to tenants (this type of land tenure was called *sir* and *khudkasht*). Lastly, the *bhumidhars* continued to pay the same tax as before the reform, when they were authorised to keep approximately half of the taxes that they raised.

(2) The *sirdars* (meaning wielders of the plough) were liberated from the *zamindars* since they now paid their taxes directly to the government at the same fixed rate as before. Nor could they be expelled, hence their children inherited their land, but as it did not belong to them or their heirs, they could not sell or mortgage it. They could become *bhumidhars* by paying to the state ten times their former yearly land revenue, and then, in a second phase, ten times what they paid to the treasury annually.

(3) The *asamis* were the sub-tenants – till then known as 'tenants at will' – whose rights to the land they cultivated became hereditary though not transferable. This was a substantial improvement in their situation, but it remained a marginal category since the *asamis* cultivated no more than 5–10% of the available land.

(4) The *adhivasi* were peasants who worked without the benefit of a fixed contract. While their status remained precarious, after five years they could become *bhumidhars* or *sirdars* against payment of 'compensation'. The *adhivasis*' form of land tenure was transitional and was therefore abolished in 1954 by an amendment which transformed them into *sirdars* paying land revenue directly to the government.

The former *zamindars* were not victimised further. The aim of the reform was not to create on egalitarian peasantry, but to abolish the system of tax-collecting intermediaries to promote the development of peasant proprietors and to transform the old-fashioned landlords into entrepreneurs. This also explains why the committee was inclined to pay compensation to the ex-*zamindars*. The payment of the market value of their land was shelved not only because it was beyond the financial means of the state, but also because it would have perpetuated an 'inequitable distribution of wealth' and encouraged the ex-*zamindars* to continue 'to live as parasites, performing no service in return for their share of the wealth produced by others'.[83] But some compensation was seen by the UP Zamindar Abolition Committee

[83] *Report of the United Provinces Zamindar Abolition Committee*, vol. 1, op. cit., p. 395.

as necessary to give the victims of the reform 'an opportunity to find new and useful avocations [sic] by engaging in production activities'.[84] The compensation was obviously aimed at endowing the ex-*zamindars* with enough capital to invest in the modernisation of Indian agriculture: they were intended to become the spearhead of the new category of *bhumidhars.* Eventually, the committee recommended graded rates of compensation, the biggest zamindars getting less than the small ones.

Reflecting, as it did, the influence of Gandhian views and Charan Singh's sense of individual enterprise, the UP land reform was targetted not on small peasant proprietors but on the *bhumidhars* whose numbers grew steadily because of the entry of tenants whom the legislation had encouraged to purchase *bhumidhari* rights. Charan Singh considered that 'the abolition of the *zamindari* rights over land has given a great uplift to the self-respect of peasants and a great encouragement to peasants to work hard. This has greatly contributed to increase in production'.[85] Neale also considers that its impact was primarily psychological and therefore had an indirect economic effect: the former tenants, the *sirdars*, paid as much tax to the state as they did in the past to the *zamindars* but – except in case of *sir* and *khudkasht* land, – they now found themselves masters of their land and hence were all the more likely to invest in land improvement.[86] However, the ambivalent status of the *sirdars* had contradictory consequences. The fact that they could neither sell nor mortgage their land protected them against land transfers to money-lenders in reimbursement of their debts. More generally they were secured against the formation of large scale land holdings as had been accomplished by *kulaks* in Russia, although it also restricted the *sirdars*', access to credit on this basis, since they could not guarantee their borrowings.

Moreover the sums the tenants had to pay to become *bhumidars* was beyond the reach of most of them. Charan Singh had laid down the idea of a compensation fund, drawn from the contributions of

[84] Ibid., p. 399.

[85] Cited in Gyanendra Rawat (ed.), *Chaudhury Charan Singh: sukti aur vichar*, op. cit., ch. 8 (no page number).

[86] W.C. Neale, *Economic Change in Rural India : Land Tenure and Reform in Uttar Pradesh, 1800–1955*, New Haven: Yale University Press, 1962 and Daniel and Alice Thorner, *Land and Labour in India*, Bombay: Asia Publishing House, 1962.

tenants who wished to become *bhumidhars.* This would yield a small percentage of the 14 million rupees needed to compensate the *zamindars.* The indemnities anticipated for the smaller *zamindars* were particularly increased, 'as a means of reassuring those from whom Congress hoped to gain support after abolition was carried through'.[87] Only a few tenants were then able to subscribe to the fund for acquiring *bhumidhari* rights and in 1953 the government was obliged to suspend it when the amounts collected amounted to less than a quarter of the target.[88] Charan Singh had obviously over estimated the pull that land proprietorship – even at the cost of great financial sacrifices – exerts on the peasantry.[89]

Generally speaking, land reform in Uttar Pradesh left much to be desired. In 1963, following the mid-term appraisal of the third plan, the National Development Council (NDC) reviewed land reform implementation in several states, including Uttar Pradesh. It highlighted the main achievement as being the accession of 15 lakh (1.5 million) tenants and sub-tenants (holding about 20 lakhs of 2 million acres of land) to the status of *bhumidhars* but expressed its concern at the development of a form of land leasing called *batai.*[90] The general custom was for the tenure holder to pay the land revenue while the cost of cultivation was borne by the *bataidar* – or share-cropper – who paid half of the crop and half of the straw as rent. Usually the *bataidars* were forbidden from tilling the same land for any length of time lest they claim tenancy rights and such arrangements were usually not recorded in the land records: the *bataidars,* therefore, were like 'rack-rented tenants-at-will'.[91]

Land ceiling was another cause for concern. It had been eventually voted for in 1961 U.P. by the legislative assembly. But the ceiling was imposed at 40 acres of fair quality land, which was very high and its implementation was very slow: three and an half years after the law was enacted half of the cases had been dealt with (4,170 out of 8,052).[92]

[87] Reeves, *Landlords and Governments,* op. cit., p. 292.
[88] Ibid., p. 294.
[89] Singh, *Land Reform in UP,* op. cit., pp. 30–2.
[90] *Implementation of land reforms: A review by the Land Reforms Implementation Committee of the National Development Council,* New Delhi: Planning Commission, 1966, p. 12.
[91] Ibid., p. 129.
[92] Ibid., p. 133.

The lessons drawn from the agrarian reform carried out in Uttar Pradesh can be extended to other parts of India, as seen in the mixed assessment of the Land Reforms Implementation Committee of the NDC. In most states tenants were compelled to pay for the land they wished to acquire in ways designed to help the state compensate the landlords. Such rules naturally hindered the land redistribution process. In addition, landlords were often allowed to retain some of the land they cultivated or of which they were supervising the cultivation. The category of 'personal cultivation' which appeared in most of the agrarian reform laws was indeed ambiguous. Given the reluctance of most land owners to work the land, the simple fact of supervising work in the fields, that is to say, of residing on the farm, and not in town, was considered to be 'personal cultivation' in some states. Besides, under the pretext of restarting cultivation themselves, landlords could retain, within the quota limit reserved for it, large areas of land in their name under the designation 'personal cultivation'. They could also employ there tenants with few rights or even expel the older tenants.[93]

These arrangements were justified in the eyes of the legislature because, rather than aiming at an equal redistribution of land, the primary objective of the agrarian reform was to eliminate the big absentee landlords and promote a new category of peasant proprietors. The abolition of all kinds of intermediaries enabled 20 million tenants to establish direct contact with the state through the payment (or non-payment) of tax. Three million tenants and share-croppers acquired more than 7 million acres of land and 2 million acres of surplus land in excess of ceiling limits were taken possession of by the states. But on the other hand, 'substantial areas in some regions of the country were still cultivated through informal crop-sharing arrangements; ejectments [sic] of tenants still go on through the device of voluntary surrenders; the fair rent provisions were not enforced effectively in several cases; ceiling had been defeated through the well

[93] This clause enabled landlords to evict tenants who thus remained in a very precarious position: 'If a tenant, even though protected by law from eviction, "voluntarily" gave up his lease, the landowner could add this holding to others within the ceiling limit. Ignorant tenants, long used to regarding the local landlords as their social, economic and religious superior, were frequently cajoled or browbeaten into surrendering rights that they scarcely knew they had.' (H.C.L. Merillat, *Land and the Constitution in India*, New York: Columbia University Press, 1970, p. 113)

known device of transfers and partitions and not much land was made available for distribution to the landless and the small farmers'.[94]

This assessment of land reform considerably overlaps with that of Merillat, one of the most balanced and competent experts on this question:

> It undoubtedly diminished the wealth and power of some of India's very biggest landlords, and strengthened the hold on the land of larger numbers of cultivators who were somewhat less secure – in legal right, social position, and economic strength – before the reforms were effected. There was some shifting in the relative strength of those most privileged in all these respects to those somewhat further down the ladder of caste and of economic and political power. But the revolution benefited essentially the middle class. In terms of social justice and political pressures, the practicable changes could do little to satisfy the demands and hopes of the least privileged group who helped to work the land and depended upon it – landless labourers, share-croppers, and tenants without protected occupancy rights.[95]

Merillat's analysis is certainly apposite for rural North India: the big landlords lost their influence but remained a dominant category; the middle peasantry found itself strengthened, while the disadvantaged derived practically no benefit from the reform. As the *baitar* issue in Uttar Pradesh has already shown us above, the problem of tenancy could recur. In Rajasthan and Bihar the situation was even worse. In Rajasthan, while 130,000 tenants and sub-tenants gained ownership of 670,000 acres, the propriety rights conferred by law accrued only to tenants who held land at the commencement of the 1955 Act – new tenants did not enjoy any security of tenure.[96] In Bihar, too, there was no complete security of tenure since 'quite a sizeable area was cultivated by share-croppers called under-raiyats' who had at one time been ejected from their land and about whom no records existed anywhere.[97] Important aspects of the reforms were not even implemented. This was an especially pervasive problem in the case of land ceilings.

Each state limited the size of land holdings in order to avoid the

[94] *Implementation of Land Reforms,* op. cit., p. 16.

[95] H.C.L. Merillat, *Land and the Constitution in India,* op. cit., p. 79.

[96] *Implementation of Land Reforms,* op. cit., p. 12.

[97] Ibid., p. 48.

concentration of land and to redistribute some of the surplus. These land ceilings reflected the quality of the land: in Punjab, it was fixed at 30 acres of land yielding 410 kilos of wheat per acre; in Uttar Pradesh, at 40 acres of 'land of good quality' per family or 80 acres of poor quality land; in Bihar, at 20 acres of very good land and at 60 acres of hilly and sandy land; in the Bombay region at 24 acres of intermittently irrigated land or that planted with rice and at 12 acres of land of permanent irrigation, and in Rajasthan at 30 standard acres, which varied from 22 to 336 ordinary acres.[98] These ceilings were rather high, given the large number of marginal and landless peasants in these states. Moreover while the multiplicity of parameters at work complicated the calculation of the averages and the regulation of land-ceilings, there is no doubt that the state governments were very slow to implement them, especially in Rajasthan and Bihar where 100,000 to 150,000 acres would have become available as surplus land above the ceilings.[99]

Besides, fraud in land-ceilings continued well into the 1960s. The Planning Commission itself admitted that land reform had been affected by 'large scale evasions' and the Land Reforms Implementation Committee deplored the fact that in Madhya Pradesh the Ceiling Law provided for no penalty for non-submission of returns of surplus land by landholders, who were expected to inform the competent authority of the surplus land within three months of the appointed day.[100] One of the most common strategies for bypassing land ceilings consisted of a former *zamindar*, giving away some of his land to figureheads (from where comes the expression – *benami* — literally meaning 'nameless') drawn from among his family, employees, or friends. The *zamindars* had plenty of time to split up their land because the cases they took to court just after the passage of the land reform acts remained pending for years and the most significant ceiling laws were voted in the early 1960s – and enforced only three to four years later. As a result, in the early 1950s, land reform had failed to generate a much more egalitarian agrarian structure and things changed little in the next two decades, as shown in the Table 1.1.

These figures, of course, need to be qualified because one acre of

[98] Ibid., p. 51, p. 11, and Merillat, op. cit., p. 115.
[99] *Implementation of Land Reforms*, op. cit., pp. 12, 47.
[100] Ibid., p. 197.

Table 1.1. DISTRIBUTION OF OPERATIONAL HOLDINGS IN INDIA BY SIZE GROUP, 1953–72

Size of holding (acres)	*1953–4*[1] *(%)*		*1960–1*[2] *(%)*		*1973–4*[3] *(%)*	
	No. of house-holds	*Area operated*	*No. of house-holds*	*Area operated*	*No. of house-holds*	*Area operated*
Less than 2.5	54.80	5.93	39.07	6.86	60.3	9.2
2.5–5	15.91	10.86	22.62	12.32	16.4	14.9
5–10	14.87	19.63	19.80	20.70	12.9	22.6
10-25	10.51	30.30	13.99	31.17	8.1	30.4
25 and above	3.01	33.28	4.52	28.95	2.2	22.8
Total	100	100	100	100	100	100

[1] Government of India, *National sample survey*, 8th round.
[2] Ibid., 17th round.
[3] Ibid., 26th round.

Source : A. Kohli, *The State and Poverty in India. The Politics of Reform*, Cambridge University Press, 1987, p. 81.

fertile land is worth much more than one acre situated in a dry zone; nevertheless, Table 1.1 testifies to the marked concentration of land that still prevailed after land reform: in 1954, 54.8% of rural households possessed only 5.93% of the cultivated area, whereas 3.01% of rural households owned no less than one-third of it and these statistics do not include '*benami*' land. The situation had not changed much in 1961, when tenants still represented 23.56% of households working the land and 62% of them were in a precarious situation (for instance susceptible to being expelled within the scope of an extension of 'personal cultivation').[101] In 1968, the imposition of the agricultural land ceiling had permitted the redistribution of only one million of acres (of the 300 million acres of India's cultivable land), of which 450,000 acres alone were in the state of Jammu and Kashmir.[102]

Nehru's socialist discourse was clearly thwarted in its implementation. It was hampered by the conservative dimension of Congress ideology deriving from Gandhi's view of society, and by the strong

[101] F. Frankel, *India's Political Economy, 1947–1977: The Gradual Revolution*, Princeton University Press, 1978, p. 122.

[102] Ibid., p. 116.

attachment of many Congressmen to individual freedom and property rights. While Charan Singh echoed this sentiment about the peasantry, Patel did the same on a larger stage.

The problem of planning and the agricultural cooperatives

Patel opposed the creation of the Planning Commission that Nehru had long sought and which he imposed in January 1950, in a clamorous session of the Congress Working Committee.[103] The death of Patel in December that year undoubtedly made things easier for him. The Planning Commission, which had at first been relegated to a consultative body, grew in influence under the impulse of the Prime Minister's, who presided over it since its inception. In January 1955, at the Awadi session of Congress, Nehru proposed a resolution according to which 'planning should take place with a view to the establishment of a socialistic pattern of society where the principle means of production are under social ownership or control'. From that year, two important objectives of the Planning Commission developed, in relation, first, to the development of rural cooperatives on the Chinese model, but adapted to Indian conditions, and secondly, to the state regulation of the grain trade as a way of avoiding shortages in the most under-developed areas of the country.

In January 1959, at the Nagpur Congress session, Nehru pushed through a resolution which aimed to introduce new cooperatives within one year:

> 'The future agrarian pattern should be that of co-operative joint farming, in which the land will be pooled for joint cultivation, the farmers continuing to retain their property rights, and getting a share from the net produce in proportion to their land. Further those who actually work the land, whether they own the land or not, will get a share in proportion to the work put in by them on the joint farm.'[104]

This resolution, and the state regulation of the trade in grains prompted criticism within Congress with some leaders, such as N.G. Ranga, even leaving it to help launch the Swatantra Party, which was created with the support of business leaders fighting what they

[103] Ibid., p. 85.
[104] Cited in ibid., p. 162.

considered to be a drift of state power towards Marxism or the left. But the Nagpur resolution was not welcomed by most Congressmen and it remained a dead-letter. Since its aim was to establish co-operatives in most villages within three years, its implementation implied the recruitment and training of 70,000 party activists every year, yet only 600 party members agreed to take the relevant study course and hence the project was definitely abandoned as early as June 1959.[105]

Where co-operatives were established they did not necessarily equalize peasants' living conditions. On the contrary, they functioned only for procuring credit, purchasing tractors or creating seed pools and thus only those who already had some capital to invest in such a project benefited from them. In fact, the dominant castes quickly took over the management of many cooperatives and so reinforced their power of patronage.

The regulation of the grain trade met the same fate. Nehru's Minister for Agriculture, S.K. Patil, preferred to buy grain from the United States rather than exercise control over the merchants who belonged very often to the local Congress networks and on whose financial support it sometimes depended.[106] Here Patil acted in league with the Minister of Finance, Morarji Desai, who similarly disapproved of state intervention in the economy. These elements were not only conservative in disposition, but also by interest, because they knew how much the Congress depended on a network of local notables.

Before and after independence, Congress's conservative approach to politics derived partly from Gandhi's worldview. But it was not a purely personal idiosyncrasy. The Mahatma's emphasis on social harmony directly echoed the organicist overtone of the *varna* system which continued to exert some influence over the upper castes. More importantly, Gandhi endowed the conservative elite of the Congress with a very powerful armoury and helped unintendedly counter Nehru's push for reform. Many conservative Congressmen drew their inspiration from the Mahatma and opposed any radical change by arguing that social cohesion needed to be preserved. But they were also keen to protect their interests and those of their supporters.

[105] Ibid., pp. 169 and 171.

[106] Ibid., p. 174. In 1962, for instance, Patil went to the United States where 'he could persuade Mr Kennedy to provide India more rice.' (S.K. Patil, *My Years with Congress*, Bombay: V.G. Parchure, 1991, p. 105)

In Uttar Pradesh, even the limited reforms of Charan Singh were thwarted simply because the party was controlled by conservative notables. This scenario reflected the influence such local leaders exerted over the Congress. But the intelligentsia at the helm of the party was not purely progressive either.

2
THE CONGRESS: PARTY OF THE INTELLIGENTSIA, OR PARTY OF THE NOTABLES?

'As the level attained by the Congress organisation is uneven in different provinces and as several committees are controlled by Zamindars elements, the resolutions of the Congress cannot be implemented and remain in practice a dead letter. In such places, peasants will not receive that assistance from the Congress Committee to which they are entitled and their grievances will go unredressed for want of advocacy [. . .]

'In certain places the Congress organisation is controlled by professional men, merchants and moneylenders of the city and as their interests collide with those of the rural population, they cannot be expected to safeguard the interests of the peasantry.' (Narendra Deva's presidential address to the annual conference of the All India Kisan Sabha, Gaya, 1939 reproduced in Acharya Narendra Deva, *Towards Socialist Society*, Lucknow, Apala Publishing Cooperative Society, 1990 [1st edn, 1979], pp. 300 and 306)

The Congress was founded by the intelligentsia, that is to say, by persons socialised in Indian traditions but educated in English and trained by the British in the new professions.[1] Of the 2,361 delegates in the first three annual sessions of the party from 1885 to 1888 (in concurrent figures), 37% were lawyers, mainly practising advocates, 2.8% were medical doctors and 7.2% journalists.[2] Of the nearly 14,000 delegates at the 1889 to 1909 sessions, 39.3% were lawyers, 21% were traders, 19% were from the landed gentry and 3%

[1] This view of the intelligentsia draws on Ernest Gellner's definition who underlines that it 'should be treated as a separate sociological category, and certainly not confused with intellectual classes in general' and that it forms 'a class which is alienated from its own society by the very fact of its education' – (E. Gellner, *Thought and Change*, London, Weidenfeld and Nicolson, 1964, pp. 169–70).

[2] See A. Seal, *The Emergence of Indian Nationalism. Competition and Collaboration in the later Nineteenth Century*, Cambridge University Press, 1968, p. 278.

respectively doctors, journalists and teachers.[3] The social milieu that dominated Congress was unfortunately enough described 'as middle class'.[4] In fact they were recruited mostly from among the upper castes: 40% of the delegates in the annual session of the Congress between 1892 and 1909 were Brahmins, 49.5% of them non-Brahmins (of which many were from the high castes), 6.6% were Muslims, 1.5% Parsis and 0.8% were Christians.[5] The over-representation of the higher castes declined only slightly in the early 1920s as Gopal Krishna showed in one of the few articles on the social profile of the Congress cadres (see Tables 2.1).

Interestingly, the reduction by 12 percentage points in the share of Brahmins and Rajputs all worked to the advantage of the Muslims. However, the growing proportion of 'other Hindus and non-identified' suggested a slightly better representation of the intermediary and lower castes, a trend that went in hand with a diminution of the

Table 2.1. CASTE AND RELIGION OF DELEGATES TO THE ANNUAL SESSIONS OF THE CONGRESS, 1919–23 (%)

Castes and communities	*1919*	*1920*	*1921*	*1922*	*1923*
Brahmin	33.13	32.09	31.9	24.8	25.14
Rajput	5.42	1.85	1.84	2.07	2.95
Kayasth	16.26	14.19	10.42	6.8	6.21
Banya	2.4	2.46	3.06	1.77	1.18
Other Hindus and non-identified	29.51	31.48	28.8	36.09	36.98
Muslim	10.84	12.96	20.24	24.85	24.55
Sikh	–	1.23	1.22	2.66	2.36
Parsi	1.8	2.46	1.22	–	–
Christian	0.6	1.23	1.22	0.88	0.59
Total	100 N= 166	100 N=162	100 N=163	100 N = 338	100 N=338

Source: Adapted from G. Krishna, 'The development of the Indian National Congress as a mass organization, 1918-1923', *Journal of Asian Studies*, 25 (3), May 1966, p. 422.

[3] See P.C. Ghosh, 'The development of the Indian National Congress 1892–1909', Calcutta, 1960, p. 24, cited in J. Brown, *Modern India*, Oxford University Press, 1985, p. 180.

[4] See, B.B. Misra, *The Indian Middle Classes*, Oxford University Press, 1961.

[5] P.C. Ghosh, 'The development of the Indian National Congress', op. cit., p. 178.

Table 2.2. PROFESSION OF DELEGATES TO THE ANNUAL SESSIONS OF CONGRESS, 1919–23 (%)

Occupation	*1919*	*1920*	*1921*	*1922*	*1923*
Lawyer	64.6	64.4	50.9	23	21.3
Journalist	7.4	7.4	11.6	6.21	8.57
Doctor	4.3	3.7	4.29	4.7	4.73
Teacher	3.7	3.1	4.29	2.9	2.95
Landlord	4.3	4.9	2.45	2.36	1.47
Businessman	6.8	7.4	8.58	5.6	4.43
Activist	–	–	0.6	4.43	7.98
Other	4.9	5.6	6.13	6.8	6.5
Unknown	3.1	3.1	11.04	43.78	42.01
Total	100	100	100	100	100

Source: G. Krishna, op.cit., p. 422.

representation of the lawyers and an increase of the professions categorised as 'not known' (see Table 2.2).

The trends in the social composition of Congress from 1919 to 1923 identified by Krishna reflected the circumstances of the first pan-Indian anti-colonial mass agitation, the Non-Cooperation Movement, which led to the rallying of a growing number of peasants (notably tenants) to the national movement. For a while this diluted the over-representation of the upper castes belonging to the professions but, in fact, their domination over the political class remained intact.

This over-representation was a striking feature of the assemblies set up by the British. For instance, within the Imperial Legislative Council the percentage of lawyers among the non-official elected members[6] was 37, 26 and 33 respectively, after the elections of 1909, 1912, and 1916. And if we disregard the non-official members returned by a separate electorate (landowners, merchants and Muslims), these proportions were even more pronounced: 40, 45 and 54%. In 1916, lawyers represented 70% of the non-official members who were not returned within separate electorates.[7] In the Legislative Council of the Bombay Presidency, for example, the share of the non European and non-Muslim legislators who were in the legal profes-

[6] The official members were those who were appointed by the British.

[7] E. Montagu and F.J. Chelmsford, *Report on Indian Constitutional Reforms*, Calcutta: Superintendent of Government Printing, 1918, p. 54.

Table 2.3. CASTE AND COMMUNITY OF NON-MUSLIM MEMBERS OF THE ASSEMBLY OF BOMBAY PRESIDENCY, 1920–37[9]

	1920	*1926*	*1930*	*1937*
Brahmin	19.3	26	25	37
Maharashtrian	*15.3*	*17*	*22*	*29*
Gujarati	*4*	*9*	*2*	*8*
Kayasth (Prabhu)	2	–	–	–
Banya	6	11	10	9
Dubashi	2	–	–	–
Cultivators	23	36	32	22
Maratha	*17*	*17*	*22*	*14*
Patidar	*4*	*13*	*4*	*4*
Other	*2*	*6*	*6*	*4*
Lingayat	6	6	6	9
Scheduled Castes	–	2	2	12
Parsi	15.3	9	14	4
Other	27	9	10	6
Total	*100*	*100*	*100*	*100*

sion was respectively 47, 48, 34 and 34% after the elections of 1926, 1930, 1937 and 1946.[8] The over-representation of Brahmins was even more marked, as shown in Table 2.3.

The Congress elite was hardly the product of the middle class given the over-representation of the upper castes within its ranks. Such a description is also misleading because many members of the intelligentsia were politically conservative. They maintained links with the traditional notables and were themselves sometimes from this social milieu, be they merchants or landlords. These sociological realities were well illustrated by certain key Congress figures. This chapter examines the political sociology of the Congress in North India by looking at the careers of archetypical personalities of Allahabad and Jabalpur and by analysing aggregated data on the social composition of the party after independence.

[8] R. Sisson and L. Shrader, 'Legislature formation in Pre-Independent India: The issue of perequisites for democratic regimes' in P. Wallace (ed.), *Region and Nation in India*, New Delhi: Oxford and IBH, 1985, p. 201.

[9] Adapted from ibid., p. 203 and, for 1920, from L/P&J/9/28, India Office Library and Records (London).

The Congress intelligentsia – unevenly progressive

The Nehrus and the Malaviyas. In the first half of the twentieth century the politics of Allahabad was dominated by two families, the Nehrus and the Malaviyas. Motilal Nehru and Madan Mohan Malaviya were respectively their most prominent figures. Outwardly they appeared to be part of the same Congress intelligentsia, yet in spite of their many similarities, they occupied two ends of the ideological spectrum.

The Nehrus exemplified the upper caste families who had offered their administrative services to the varied kingdoms and empires that succeeded one another in the subcontinent. As Kashmiri Brahmins they belonged to a community which, along with the Kayasths, were over-represented among the educated elite.

One of the Nehrus' ancestors, Raj Kaul, from the Srinagar valley, was spotted in 1716 by a Mughal envoy and requested to come to Delhi. In exchange for his services in the administration, he was given villages as a *jagir.* His great-grandson, Lakshmi Narayan, continued this bureaucratic tradition by becoming the first *vakil* (advocate) of the East India Company at the Mughal court at Delhi. His son Ganga Dhar, the father of Motilal, was a police officer in Delhi when the 1857 Revolt broke out, an event that persuaded the entire family to move from Delhi to Agra. The family lost everything but very soon recovered their fortunes. Ganga Dhar's sons both learnt English, one becoming 'subordinate judge', the other the *diwan* of Khetri in Rajasthan. Motilal, who was much younger, followed the former. As a sign of the family's cosmopolitan culture, he was educated by a Muslim tutor and therefore read Arabic and Persian until he was twelve.[10] He then pursued his studies in English at Kanpur High School and later at the prestigious Muir College in Allahabad. He became an advocate in the early 1890s and was admitted to the Allahabad Bar in 1896, the highest judicial authority of the province. Motilal's taste for British culture had taken him to England as early as 1899 but his choice of clothing was very English even before then.[11] On his return, he

[10] B.R. Nanda, *The Nehrus – Motilal and Jawaharlal,* London: Geo. Allen and Unwin, 1962, p. 18.

[11] In fact, before his sudden shift to khadi as a consequence of his conversion to Gandhism in the early 1920s, 'Motilal Nehru had been considered almost a parody of the English gentleman. Although he had always continued to wear Indian styles of dress inside his own home, the public knew him as the

refused to abide by the purification rituals that were supposed to mitigate all travel beyond the 'black waters'. He was subjected to a social boycott by orthodox members of his caste but overcame it given the power he already wielded in Allahabad. His response to the boycott also reflected his basic agnosticism.

Motilal took an early interest in the Congress, so much so that in 1888 he was among the 1,400 delegates at the Allahabad session. In the early 1900s–1910s he sided with the Moderates, with whom he shared an admiration of Britain, as seen from his address to the first conference of Congress in the United Provinces, whose chairmanship he occupied in 1906:

> '[England] has fed us with the best food that her language, her literature, her science, her art and above all, her free institutions could supply. We have lived and grown on that wholesome food for a century and are fast approaching the age of maturity [. . .]. I firmly believe that he [John Bull] means well – it is not in his nature to mean ill [. . .]. It takes him rather long to comprehend the situation, but when he does see things plainly, he does his plain duty, and there is no power on earth – no, not even his kith and kin in this country or elsewhere – that can successfully resist his mighty will.'[12]

Motilal Nehru therefore strove simply to convince the British that they should introduce the English parliamentary system to India. The limited nature of the reforms of 1909 and 1919 disappointed him greatly, without diverting him from his chosen couse of action. The radicalisation of his nationalism in the early 1920s was in fact the result of the influence of M.K.Gandhi and of his son Jawaharlal. In spite of serious political differences, father and son shared basically the same political outlook, as is evident from the 'Nehru report'.

In 1928, in response to the Simon Commission the Congress prepared an alternative constitutional document whose drafting was assigned to Motilal, and in which he was helped by Jawaharlal. The Nehru Report rejected all conceptions of the nation that acknowledged intermediate bodies such as religious communities or castes.[13]

---

extravagant man of European fashion. . .' (E. Tarlo, *Clothing Matters: Dress and Identity in India*, London: Hurst, 1996, p. 102)

[12] Cited in Nanda, *The Nehrus*, op. cit., p. 60.

[13] *All Parties Conferences – 1928. Report of the Committee appointed by the Conference to determine the principles of the Constitution for Indian*, Allahabad: General Secretary of the AICC, 1920, p. 30.

The authors were convinced that religious sentiment would be gradually eroded by modernisation: individuals, and not castes or religious communities, were to be the building blocks of the nation, and their political identity would be shaped by their socio-economic position.[14]

These materialist conceptions reflected Jawaharlal's views. He visited Soviet Russia in 1927 and had seen his socialist conceptions confirmed. But his father had inculcated such ideas in him through his agnostic rationalism, a stand which carried with it its own dangers. During the 1926 election campaign, for instance, he was confronted by a new party, the Independent Congress Party, which tried hard to discredit him in the eyes of the Hindu electorate by accusing him of eating beef.[15]

Madan Mohan Malaviya, the principal opponent of the Nehrus in the United Provinces, was behind this campaign. From the late nineteenth century till his death in 1946 he epitomised the other, conservative Hindu, face of the Congress intelligentsia that prominent figures such as the Nehrus have often obscured and that the statistics do not reveal, since Malaviya, like the Nehrus, was a Brahmin trained in law and in journalism. He illustrates well the general analysis of Bruce Graham who has sought to define the Hindu traditionalists in Congress by referring to their attachment to Hindu culture and hence their involvement with associations protecting the cow as

[14] 'We are certain that as soon as India is free and can face her problems unhampered by alien authority and intervention, the minds of her people will turn to the vital problems of the day. How many questions that are likely to be considered by our future legislatures can be of a communal nature? There may possibly be a few now and then, but there can be no doubt that the vast majority of the questions before us will not be communal in the narrow sense. The result will be that parties will be formed in the country and in the legislature on entirely other grounds, chiefly economic we presume. We shall then find Hindus and Muslims and Sikhs in one party acting together and opposing another party which also consists of Hindus and Muslims and Sikhs. This is bound to happen if we once get going' (ibid., p. 49).

[15] J. Nehru, *A Bunch of Qld Letters*, London: Asia Publishing House, 1960. For more details on the use of communal issues in the framework of the rivalry between the Nehrus and the Malaviyas, especially the Ram Lila processions, see C. Jaffrelot, 'Hindu processions and Hindu-Muslim riots' in A. Basu and A. Kohli (eds), *Communal Violence and the State*, Delhi: Oxford University Press, 1998.

well as sacred places (temples, pilgrimage routes . . .) and promoting Hindi (as well as Sanskrit) and Ayurvedic medicine.[16]

Malaviya was the scion of a prestigious, orthodox Brahmin family. His father, Pandit Brajnath, was renowned for his command of the *Bhagwad Gita* and was patronised by local notables.[17] It is by virtue of his loyalty towards this family tradition that Madan Mohan Malaviya received the support of these *rais* (literally, the powerful, affluent men). Socialised in the Hindu tradition, Malaviya was educated at Muir College. He was then appointed editor-in-chief of *Hindustan* by the newspaper's founder, Rampal Singh of Kalakankar, a rich *taluqdar*.[18] He joined the Allahabad Bar soon after in 1891.[19] A member of Congress since its inception, he was elected to the Municipal Council of Allahabad and then to the Provincial Legislative Council. At every turn he defended conservative political ideas. He was an archetypal orthodox Brahmin who did not accept food except from the hands of a member of his own *jati*[20] and shrank from contact with anything that might desecrate his body and his Hindu soul.[21]

During the colonial period, the relation between conservative members of the intelligentsia and notables still harked back to the old pattern of the special rapport between Brahmins and the *rais*, whom the British also regarded as 'the natural leaders' of Indian society. To be more specific, it was rooted in the duties associated with religious donations which the Kshatriyas – be they a Maharajah or an ordinary landowner – and the merchants were obliged to make: financing festivals, feeding Brahmins, building temples and so on were necessary expenditures for them to maintain their status.[22] Thus

[16] B.D. Graham, 'The Congress and Hindu Nationalism' in D.A. Low (ed.), *The Indian National Congress*, Delhi: Oxford University Press, 1988, p. 174.

[17] S. Chaturvedi, *Madan Mohan Malaviya*, Delhi: Government of India, 1972, pp. 1–3.

[18] S.P. Sen (ed.), *Dictionary of National Biography*, vol. 4, Calcutta: Institute of Historical Studies, 1975, p. 233.

[19] S.L. Gupta, *Pandit Madan Mohan Malaviya*, Allahabad: Chugh Publications, 1978, pp. 5–6.

[20] Nand Lal Singh (ed.), *Mahamana Malaviyaji Birth Centenary Volume*, Benares Hindu University, 1961, p. 26.

[21] N.C. Kelkar, 'Malaviyaji : his personality and work' in *Malaviya Commemoration Volume*, Benares Hindu University, 1932, p. 1031.

[22] C.A. Bayly, 'Patrons and Politics in Northern India', *MAS*, 7 (3), 1973, p. 363.

in Allahabad the local notables, known as *rais*, supported the Hindu Samaj (Hindu Society) which was started in 1880 by M.M. Malaviya to defend the Hindu festivals of the region and in particular the annual Magh Mela which, it was thought, was threatened by the missionaries. This organisation spread to other provinces of northern India and then, in 1884, gave birth to the Madhya Hindu Samaj,[23] of which Malaviya was also the moving spirit.

While these associations were all patronised by rich merchants or bankers, Bayly see an essential innovation in the fact that they relied on the collaboration of *rais* and members of the intelligentsia (lawyers, teachers) whose competence – their fluency in English – was a prerequisite for communicating with the colonisers – Bayly refers to then as 'publicists'.[24] He regards the collaboration between these two groups as being the main factor in the growth of the Congress in the late nineteenth and early twentieth century. Indeed, the Congress relied on a network of associations, such as the Hindu Samaj (which sent delegates to the party's annual sessions), which were based on the collaboration of the *rais* and the publicists. The alliance formed by Ram Saran Das and Madan Mohan Malaviya is a perfect illustration of this type of social linkage. The former, a Khatri banker, backed the public enterprises of the latter and was content to occupy honorary functions in the associations he patronised.

The Hindu intellectual renaissance and the protection of the Hindu heritage were the two principal objectives of Malaviya and the Hindu Samaj. During the session organised by the latter in 1906, Malaviya won approval for a project to establish a Hindu University – which was later to become the Benaras Hindu University (BHU). Its blueprint, prepared in 1904, opened with remarks on the decadence of Indian society that Malaviya attributed to the 'loss amongst the Hindus of power, which, according to the sacred Hindu writings, supports the society, the power of religion, that denotes the name, even, of "Dharma" '.[25] He aspired to restore a system founded on hereditary social functions:

[23] *Speeches and Writings of Pandit Madan Mohan Malaviya*, Madras: G.A. Natesan, 1919, p. 3.

[24] C.A. Bayly, *The Local Roots of Indian Politics – Allahabad 1880–1920*, Oxford: Clarendon Press, 1975, p. 104.

[25] V.A. Sundaram (ed.), *Benares Hindu University, 1916–1942*, Benares, 1942, p. viii.

'The interests of social prosperity were provided for by assigning different functions of human society to different classes, whose duty and interest it was to perform these functions efficiently and hand down their knowledge, talents, skill and aptitude to their descendants [. . .] The functions thus assigned to each class as its *jati-dharma* were specialised by different families as their *kuladharmas* and were faithfully and efficiently performed for the well-being of the whole society, which was thus served by the classes and families composing it, as an organism is served by its constituent organs.'[26]

True to his Brahminical orthodoxy, Malaviya tried to resuscitate the spirit of the *varna* system even more literally than had Gandhi, in an overtly organicist perspective. The Benaras Hindu University was first debated in 1904 at a meeting presided over by the Maharajah of Benaras.[27] It then took ten years for Malaviya to find a site and to raise the necessary funds. The Hindu University Society delegation charged with collecting donations in northern India was led by members of the intelligentsia like Sunder Lal, a lawyer from Allahabad, who in 1906 became Vice Chancellor of the University of Allahabad. But it included a large number of *rais*, such as Sukhbir Sinha who led the Zamindars' Association[28] and Raja Rampal Singh of Kurri Sidhauli (a *taluqdar* whose money-lending activities were very lucrative and who dominated the British India Association of Oudh, the organisation of *taluqdars* in this sub-region of the United Provinces).[29]

Soon after the opening of the Benaras Hindu University, Malaviya was instrumental in relaunching the Hindu Mahasabha within the Congress in 1922 and he presided over its annual session on several occasions in the 1920s. The Hindu Mahasabha also relied on the collaboration of *rais* – even Maharajahs – and representatives of the conservative intelligentsia. Malaviya later distanced himself from the Hindu Mahasabha in order to create his own political party (within the Congress) in 1926, as mentioned above, and then the Congress

[26] Ibid., pp. xix–xx.

[27] J. Lütt, 'The movement for the foundation of the Benares Hindu University' in *German Scholars in India*, New Delhi: Cultural Department, Embassy of the Federal Republic of Germany, vol. 2, and S.L. Dar and S. Somaskandan, *History of the Benares Hindu University*, Benares: BHU, 1966, p. 88.

[28] Reeves, *The Landlords' Response*, op. cit., p. 63.

[29] F. Robinson, 'Municipal government and Muslim separatism in the United Provinces, 1883 to 1916', *MAS*, 7 (3), 1973, p. 401.

Nationalist Party in 1934.[30] Until his death in 1946, he therefore remained one of the most active traditionalist Hindus in Congress.

Malaviya was not an isolated example, however. Among his contemporaries is North India Rajendra Prasad, who was as important a figure in the Bihar Congress as was Malaviya in Uttar Pradesh, held similar views. He started his political career as a lieutenant of Gandhi during the Champaran *satyagraha*. In his account of this event, he never mentions the tensions *within* the local society he knew so well. For him, the exploiters of the peasants could not be the Indian landlords.[31] Like Malaviya, he was a lawyer who actively supported the Hindu Mahasabha in the 1920s.[32] Rajendra Prasad did not however belong to the same category as Malaviya, namely the conservative Congress intelligentsia. In contrast to him, Prasad was born in a rich Kayasth family which possessed a large *zamindari*.[33] The point is that Congress counted among its ranks not only conservative professionals who were closely linked to traditional notables, but also leaders who were *themselves* such notables. While few of these were *zamindars* with a purely rural base, many had commercial interests. This social profile is well illustrated by the case of Seth Govind Das, the grandson of a Jabalpur magnate, who played a major role in building the party in Madhya Pradesh.

Seth Govind Das in the footsteps of the 'natural leaders'. The British relied greatly on those whom they regarded as the 'natural leaders'

[30] M.M. Malaviya and M.S. Aney, *The Congress Nationalist Party – What it Stands for, Why Every Indian Should Support it*, Benares, August 1934.

[31] The last sentence of his recollection of the *satyagraha* is very revealing: 'The seed of Indian Swaraj has been truly sown in Champaran and the freedom which the poor, helpless down-trodden tenants of Champaran have secured against the educated, ever-vigilant and wealthy planters, living under the protecting wings of the powerful Government, is but a precursor of that larger freedom which Indians, trampled under the heels for centuries, are going to achieve in their struggle for *Swaraj*.' (Babu Rajendra Prasad, *Satyagraha in Champaran*, Madras: S. Ganesan, 1928, p. 266). He continued to hold traditionalist views all his life, as evident from the way he praised the traditional education of the Gurukuls (see his letter dated 22 Sept. 1960 in *Portrait of a President. Letters of Dr Rajendra Prasad written to Mrs Gyanvati Darbar*, vol. II, Delhi: Vikas, 1976, p. 196).

[32] He was Chairman of the Reception Committee of the Gaya session in 1922 (Rajendra Prasad, *Autobiography*, Delhi: National Book Trust, 1994 [1st edn 1957], p. 182).

[33] Ibid., p. 18.

of India, usually notables who were landlords or businessmen. In the countryside, *zamindars* or *jagirdars* played a pivotal role in this form of indirect rule, while notable merchants fulfilled similar functions in the urban context. Raja Gokuldas, a merchant from Jabalpur in present-day Madhya Pradesh, exemplifies this phenomenon.

Gokuldas's grandfather was a Marwari[34] from Jaisalmer. He had settled in Jabalpur around 1800 and made a fortune. His family's collaboration with the British crystallised during the 1857 Revolt when Gokuldas' father lent them enough money to purchase horses for an entire battalion, since the local authorities, cut off from the rest of India, could not obtain help from the government.[35] In recognition of his services the British decorated him with a belt studded with five diamonds.[36]

Gokuldas expanded the family enterprise by opening branches in Bombay, Calcutta and Rangoon and by investing in industry. His fortune permitted him to buy entire villages and thus he became a big *malguzar* (in the Central Provinces, the *malguzari* system was a variant of the *zamindari* system).[37] His peers next elected him to the presidentship of the first caste association, the Maheshwari Sabha.[38] His influence locally and beyond was partly due to his moneylending activities.[39] Among his debtors numbered municipalities, including Jabalpur, to which he loaned money to develop the town's waterworks.[40] Gokuldas lived at a time when notables began to stop acting as philanthropists pure and simple and, instead, lent money and contested elections in the hope of being rewarded with a seat by the local

[34] This merchant community originated from the Marwar region, in Rajasthan but had spread all over northern India in the nineteenth century. Taking advantage of the boost to commerce offered by modern communications, the Marwaris enriched themselves to the point of dominating the mercantile, and later industrial, sector of northern India, notably through families such as the Birlas. For more details see T.A. Timberg, *The Marwaris – From Traders to Industrialists*, New Delhi: Vikas, 1974.

[35] J. Mukerji, *Biography of Raja Gokuldas*, Bombay (no publisher), 1929, p. 12.

[36] Ibid., p. 15.

[37] Ibid., pp. 41–2.

[38] Ibid., p. 57.

[39] His biographer cites some fifty persons who, in the Central Provinces and elsewhere, borrowed from him 25,000 rupees or more (ibid., pp. 63–5).

[40] Ibid., p. 75.

electorate. The funding of public utilities (such as hospitals) besides purely religious works (the construction of temples and *dharamshalas*) were among the social obligations of merchants who were concerned to maintain their high rank. But they increasingly tended to sell these services – not only in monetary terms but also in terms of political appointments.

Gokuldas became a member and then the president of the Municipal Council of Jabalpur in the 1880s, after which his nephew succeeded him, without interruption, for the next eighteen years. No one dared to stand against Gokuldas who was repeatedly elected unanimously.[41] In 1887 he was nominated to the Council of the Viceroy in recognition of the help he gave to the British: whether it was a question of lodging troops in transit or aiding those leaving for the 'Russian border' he always readily offered them his services.[42]

The grandson of Gokuldas, Seth Govind Das, was to become the family's best known politician. He was denied the possibility of studying abroad[43] but received a modern education in India and was therefore a *de facto* member of the intelligentsia. Like Malaviya, however, he represented its conservative face. In spite of learning English, Seth Govind Das showed an early interest in Hindi to the point of becoming secretary, in 1916, of the Hindi Sahitya Sammelan (Conference of Hindi Literature),[44] an association founded in 1910 by a lieutenant of Malaviya, Purushottamdas Tandon, known for his Hindu traditionalism. In 1919, he became the president of the HSS of the Central Provinces.

Fascinated by Gandhi, he joined the Non-Cooperation Movement in 1920, fasted in order to compel his father to boycott the courts (so that he would not contest the rights of his tenants) and gave up his Calcutta shop which sold foreign clothes.[45] But then he joined the Swaraj Party which, within the Congress, attracted those who wanted to suspend the Non-Cooperation Movement. The Swaraj Party was in favour of contesting elections and so he stood in 1923 for elections to the Legislative Assembly. Interestingly, he contested

[41] Ibid., p. 88.

[42] Ibid., p. 89.

[43] B. Hooja, *A Life Dedicated – Biography of Govind Das*, New Delhi: Seth Govind Das Diamond Jubilee Celebrations Committee, 1956, pp. 23 and 28.

[44] Ibid., p. 40.

[45] Ibid., p. 55.

the elections in a constituency reserved for *malguzars*, where he was elected unopposed. The fact that a *malguzar* was elected on a Congress ticket was exceptional since the agrarian elite generally remained aloof from the nationalist movement. It is only because of the influence of Seth Govind Das and above all of his uncle that 'the *malguzars* and the rich of the region supported the Congress'.[46] In 1925, he was elected to the Council of State (the upper house of U.P.), for he 'cashed on the prestige and the position of his family'.[47] He was elected again in 1926. Seth Govind Das was obviously at the juncture of two worlds, the conservative intelligentsia and the traditional notables.

He was however less and less a *rais* and more and more a publicist: short of time, he gave up his business and instead launched a Hindi daily, *Lok Mat.* Das also became the president of Congress in the Central Provinces and then followed Gandhi during the Civil Disobedience movement of 1930,[48] for which he was immediately imprisoned.[49] As his father remained loyal to the British – and even collected land revenues on their behalf – he broke away from his family.[50] In 1934, he fought the elections in a general constituency[51] and was once again elected, a success he repeated in 1946 when he was elected unopposed to the Constituent Assembly.

His contribution to the making of the Indian Constitution showed that his ideology remained that of a Hindu traditionalist. Seth Govind Das was one of the most ardent defenders of the cow and a strong advocate of the elevation of Hindi to the rank of the national language. His speeches in support of this objective expressed great contempt for Muslim culture:

> 'I do agree that many Hindu poets and scholars have also created outstanding literature in Urdu. Despite this, I cannot help saying that Urdu has mostly drawn inspiration from outside the country [. . .] It is true we have accepted our country to be a secular State but we never thought that that acceptance implied the acceptance of the continued existence of heterogeneous cultures.

[46] Seth Govin Das, *Atma – Nirikshan* [autobiography], vol. 2, Delhi: Bharatiya Vishva Prakashan, 1958, p. 105.

[47] Hooja, *A Life Dedicated – Biography of Govind Das*, op. cit., p. 67.

[48] Ibid., p. 74.

[49] Ibid., pp. 77–9.

[50] Ibid., p. 86.

[51] Ibid., p. 91.

India is an ancient country with an ancient history. For thousands of years one and the same culture has all along been obtaining here. This tradition is still unbroken. It is in order to maintain this tradition that we want one language and one script for the whole country. We do not want it to be said that there are two cultures here.'[52]

Seth Govind Das even wanted the Constitution to be written in Hindi.[53] His attitude provoked unease among members from South India where Hindi was hardly spoken and English was the preferred idiom at the national level.[54] In advocating the prohibition of cow slaughter he spelled out his case in a purely Hindu traditionalist way, claiming that 'The problem of cow protection is a matter which has been associated with our civilisation from the time of Lord Krishna. To us it is not only a religious or economic but also a cultural problem'.[55]

On the whole, even though Seth Govind Das manifested the specific characteristics of the intelligentsia – he was a publicist, indeed a man of the press – his ideology remained that of a traditionalist Hindu. This mindset was well in tune with his social milieu, that of a *rais.* The break with his family did not prove irreconcilable: his father chose not to disown him and thus he inherited a significant fortune and a status that largely contributed to his exceptional electoral success after independence: he was elected without interruption to the Lok Sabha till 1971, a world record, according to the *Guinness Book of Records.*

In Uttar Pradesh too the Congress had 'natural leaders' in its ranks. As early as the 1920s, small and middle-size landowners joined Congress in massive numbers. They did so because it was on its way to power and also because it would not use this power against them, given its rejection of class struggle under Gandhi's influence. In the late 1920s, young *taluqdars* of Uttar Pradesh rallied around the Congress, which earned them the encouragement of Gandhi.[56] While

[52] *Constituent Assembly Debates* (hereafter, *CAD*), New Delhi: Lok Sabha Secretariat, 1989, vol. IX, p. 1328.

[53] Austin, *The Indian Constitution*, op. cit., p. 297 and vol.III, p. 222.

[54] T.T. Krishnamachari from the state of Madras thus denounced the 'linguistic imperialism' of the Hindi-speaking North in November 1948 (*CAD*, p. 234). See also to B. Pocker Sahib Bahadur's speech (ibid., p. 362).

[55] *CAD*, vol. VII, p. 223.

[56] Reeves, *The Landlords' Response*, op. cit., p. 257.

the Executive Committee of the Congress in the United Provinces never counted more than 3 *zamindars* a year, out of 21 members, in 1925–35,[57] at the lower level the local networks were recruiting many members from among the small *zamindars* and well-off tenants.[58] This network of rural leaders was developed after 1920 when the Congress, then under the sway of Gandhi, was engaged in the politics of mass agitation. It was to prove indispensable to the party in penetrating the countryside and mobilising the peasants.[59] As Congress acquired a pivotal role in Indian politics more and more (and bigger and bigger) *zamindars* joined its ranks. A particularly significant wave of affiliations occurred in the United Provinces before and after the 1945–6 elections which established the Constituent Assembly – during which Congress was confirmed as the dominant party. Many landowners hoped that they could influence the party from the inside.[60] In Bihar, for example, Rajputs and Bhumihars moved respectively from 8 and 15% of the Provincial Congress Committee in 1934, to 27 and 20% in 1946, whereas the share of the Kayasths, who traditionally dominated the party in this region fell from 54 to 20%.[61]

Obviously, the Congress was not merely the party of a progressive middle class. The intelligentsia certainly exerted a strong influence over it but it was recruited from the elite of the upper castes, a social group which often went hand in hand with Hindu traditionalism. Furthermore, these conservative elements kept close links with the notables of the landed aristocracy and the merchant castes.

Nevertheless, one should not exaggerate the contrast between the conservatives (whether from the intelligentsia or the notables) and the progressive intelligentsia numbers, many of whom retained close

[57] Pandey, *The Ascendancy of the Congress*, op. cit., p. 50.

[58] Bayly, *The Local Roots of Indian Politics*, op. cit., and L. Brennan, 'Political Change in Rohilkhand, 1932–52', PhD thesis, University of Sussex, 1972, p. 174 and pp. 182–3.

[59] See the case studies presented by Pandey in *The Ascendancy of the Congress*, op. cit., pp. 52–4.

[60] P. Reeves, 'Adjusting to Congress dominance: the UP landlords, 1937–1947', in R. Sisson and S. Wolpert (eds), *Congress and Indian Nationalism*, Delhi: Oxford University Press, 1988, pp. 171–3.

[61] R. Roy, 'Caste and Political Recruitment in Bihar' in R. Kothari (ed.), *Caste in Indian Politics*, New Delhi: Orient Longman, 1986 (1970), p. 242.

links with the other group when they were not dependent on them. For instance, Motilal Nehru was the lawyer to the family of Seth Govind Das, whose father was a great friend of his and whom he regarded as his son.[62] It was because of him that Seth Govind Das joined the Swaraj Party, of which he became treasurer. Similarly, after Independence, Jawaharlal Nehru, while officially disapproving of the inflow of conservative notables into the Congress, himself co-opted notables as part of genuine vote bank politics.

Congress 'Vote Banks' politics

After Independence, in a context changed by the advent of universal suffrage, conservative Congressmen feared that the socialist discourse of their party whould alienate the notables on whom it had relied in large part so far. This fear was especially obvious in UP where the upper castes represented a large proportion of the state's population. According to the 1931 census, the last one to ask questions about caste, the upper castes represented 20% of the population. Brahmins constituted 9.2%, the highest percentage in India, and Rajputs, 7.2%, among whom one could find a large concentration of *zamindars*. However, during the nineteenth century the tribute claimed by the British was such that many of them were obliged to hand over all or part of their *zamindari* to Banyas, Brahmins, or even Kayasths to whom they were heavily in debt. As a result, there were many landowners among these castes.

The peasants mostly belonged to lower and intermediate castes – two categories among the Shudras which must be carefully differentiated. Among the intermediate castes, the Jats formed the most significant group. They represented only 1.6% of the state population but were concentrated in western UP where they competed with the Rajputs for the status of dominant caste. They were hard working farmers. The lower castes were either service castes (e.g. Nais/barbers or Telis/toddy-tappers) or cultivating castes (Kurmis, Lodhis, Koeris, Gujars) or pastoral castes like the Ahirs (cowherds), a large caste representing 8.7% of the population.

The Congress leaders of UP came mostly from the upper castes and relied largely on this social milieu to maintain their ascendancy.

[62] Interview with Seth Govind Das by H.D. Sharma dated 4 Dec. 1967 (Oral History Transcript, Nehru Memorial and Museum Library, New Delhi), p. 9.

They therefore blamed Charan Singh for his zealous reformism when he launched the Zamindari Abolition scheme. One of his most virulent detractors was Sarvasri Sampurnanand, who was an ally of Madan Mohan Malaviya – he had helped him to re-launch the Hindu Mahasabha in 1922.[63] In the early 1950s – even before he became Chief Minister in 1954 – he launched an offensive against Charan Singh. After the setbacks recorded by Congress when three by-elections were won by non-Congress Rajput landowners, Sampurnanand circulated a very revealing note:

In India the *zamindars* have lost financially and in prestige and influence. Those of them who have to live in the villages, have, in many cases, to suffer the worst humiliation, but we have given them the vote, that is, the power of driving us out of office. There is absolutely no reason why, as a class, they should get reconciled to our regime [. . .] Only recently Charan Singh is reported to have said [. . .] that one of the subjects he, in other words, the Government, has in view, is to liquidate money lenders. This means creating another class of opponents who also wield considerable influence. It comes to this that we have antagonised practically every class which has so far possessed education, wealth, social status and, consequently, influence.

[. . .] The measures which we have adopted, and apparently intend soon to adopt, have had the definite tendency of affecting adversely the interests of the higher castes who, it must be remembered, have, in general, been the people from whom the Congress has derived the greatest measure of support in the past [. . .]

The work of uplift of the backward classes cannot stop. They have to be helped to achieve cultural and intellectual equality with those who have so far enjoyed these advantages and, of course, ever legitimate opportunity

[63] S. Sampurnanand, *Memories and Reflections*, Bombay: Asia Publishing House, 1962, p. 28 and J. Lütt, 'Die regionalen Wurzeln der Hindu Mahasabha', in H. Kulke and D. Rothermund (eds), *Regionale Tradition in Südasien*, Wiesbaden: Franz Steiner, 1985, p. 224. His Hindu traditionalism was evident from his interest in the culture of ancient India. He studied Sanskrit in order to read the Vedas in the original, on the basis of which he claimed that India was the original home of the Aryans who migrated from there to the east and to the west (Dr Sampurnanand, *Introduction to Vedic Studies*, Belgaum, Academy of Comparative Philosophy and Religion, 1969, p. 6). As Chief Minister between 1954 and 1960, his linguistic policy harmed Urdu, a language that he did not consider suitable for any official status (see B.D. Graham, *Hindu Nationalism and Indian Politics: The Origins and Development of the Bharatiya Jana Sangh*, Cambridge University Press, 1990, p. 118).

should be allowed to them to improve their economic position. But, at the same time, the game of baiting the higher classes must be suspended. We must, somehow win back their confidence. If the Soviets under Lenin could adopt the NEP, there is no reason why our statesmanship cannot rise equal to the task.[64]

The views of influential figures such as Sampurnanand led the Congress to accommodate upper caste notables. The party, in doing so, sought to use their social influence, in terms of economic leverage or physical intimidation. These were the sources of the notables' political clout and hence the starting-point of Congress's 'vote bank politics', an arrangement where votes 'can be delivered by local potentates acting as political intermediaries between the parties and the electorate'.[65] This party-building strategy relied on co-option of influential notables, in stark contrast to the cadre-based parties such as those developed by the communists or the Hindu nationalists.[66]

In Uttar Pradesh, the capacity of the Congress to co-opt local notables after independence was reflected in the social profile of the electoral candidates fielded by the Congress. Far from accommodating the low castes, the party continued to nominate upper caste politicians, as evident from the social background of its MLAs in the 1950s and early 1960s, when it dominated North Indian politics.

The over-representation of the higher castes among Congress MLAs is very high and continued to rise from 1952–62, from 58 to 61%, whereas the lower castes remained very under-represented with less than one-tenth of the MLAs. The Scheduled Castes accounted for one fifth to a quarter of the Congress group at the Assembly in Lucknow. Thus the two extreme poles of the caste system were the most represented here[67] although one should bear in mind that the large number of Scheduled Caste MLAs was due to the reservation

[64] Cited in Charan Singh, *Land Reforms in U.P. and the Kulaks*, op. cit., pp. 61–3.

[65] 'Voting behaviour in a developing society – A working paper', in CSDS, *Party System and Election Studies*, Bombay: Allied Publishers, 1967, p. 280.

[66] For a comparative study of the Congress and the Jana Sangh party-building patterns, see Jaffrelot, *The Hindu Nationalist Movement*, op. cit., ch. 3.

[67] These results are corroborated by other studies, such as that of Saraswati Srivastava (S. Srivastava, 'Uttar Pradesh, politics of neglected development' in I. Narain (ed.), *State Politics in India*, New Delhi: Meenakshi Prakashan, 1976, p. 352).

Table 2.4. CASTE AND COMMUNITY OF UTTAR PRADESH CONGRESS MLAs, 1952–62 (%)

	*% in UP**	*1952*	*1957*	*1962*
Upper castes	*20.4*	*58*	*56*	*61*
Brahmin	9.2	28	22	27
Rajput	7.2	13	15	19
Banya	2.4	8	8	8
Kayasth	1	5	6	3
Bhumihar	0.4	1	1	1
Tyagi	0.1	1	1	0
Other	0.1	2	3	3
Intermediate castes	*1.5*	*3*	*2*	*2*
Jat	1.5	3	2	2
Low castes	*41.9*	*7*	*6*	*6*
Yadav	8.7	3	2	2
Kurmi	3.5	2	2	2
Other	27.5	2	2	2
Scheduled Castes	*20.9*	*21*	*24*	*22*
Chamar	11.8	14	16	16
Pasi	3	3	2	1
Other	6.1	4	6	5
Muslim	*14.6*	*11*	*10*	*8*
Total	*100*	*100* *N =390*	*100* *N =286*	*100* *N =249*

* According to the 1931 census.

Source: Adapted from R.C. Meyer, 'The Political elite in an Underdeveloped Society: the case of Uttar Pradesh in India', PhD thesis, University of Pennsylvania, 1969 (Political Science), pp. 175-8.

system. In fact, Congress hardly bothered to promote this category of the population, as the composition of the UP Congress Committee in the1960s makes plain.

In 1968, three-fourths of the members of the UP Congress Committee were from the higher castes; there was not even one representative of the lower castes and one Scheduled Caste member among the presidents of its branches at the district or town level. The social profile of the Congress governments in the 1950s–1960s reproduces the same pattern.

The stability of the upper castes' over-representation in the UP government over three decades is astonishing. From the late 1930s

Table 2.5. CASTE AND COMMUNITY OF CONGRESS CADRES IN UTTAR PRADESH, 1964–8

	PCC members (1964)	*PCC members (1968)*	*District and city presidents (1964-8)*
Upper castes	*80*	*80.96*	*76.81*
Brahmin	35	33.34	36.23
Bhumihar	–	4.76	1.45
Kshatriya	10	9.52	18.84
Vaishya	25	23.82	13.04
Kayasth	10	9.52	5.80
Other	–	–	1.45
Low castes	*5*	–	*10.14*
Scheduled Castes	*5*	*4.76*	–
Sikh	-	*4.76*	*1.45*
Muslim	*5*	*4.76*	*5.80*
Unidentified	*4.76*	*4.76*	*5.80*
Total	*100*	*100*	*100*

Source: S. Srivastava, 'Uttar Pradesh', op. cit., pp. 352-3.

till the late 1960s the upper castes accounted for two-thirds (or even three quarters) of ministers and never less than 59% (Table 2.6). Unsurprisingly, Brahmins predominated till the late 1950s, but they tended to lose ground and by the 1960s the Banyas were the most numerous group in three governments out of four. Muslim representation steadily declined over the entire period. The Scheduled Castes always had a handful of ministers, which maintained their representation at a low rather than a marginal level. The most striking statistics concern the lower castes, which could manage only a couple of representatives. The Congress therefore appeared to be dominated by a tripolar elite of Brahmins/professionals (18% of the Congress MLAs were lawyers in 1952),[68] Banyas/businessmen and Rajputs/landlords. A similar pattern emerged in Bihar.

In Bihar, the upper castes represented only 12.7% of the population – according to the 1931 census. The Rajputs (4.1%) and Brahmins (4.6%) were relatively small in numbers. However, the Bhumihars (2.8%) – a dominant caste owning a lot of land – claim that they are Brahmins.[69] In Bihar most *zamindars* were Rajputs,

[68] R.C. Meyer, *The Political Elite*, op. cit., p. 171.

[69] Yet the Rajputs refuse to recognise them as Brahmins and consequently claim the second rank in the *varna* hierarchy, as elsewhere.

Bhumihars and Brahmins during the British Raj. While the province was mainly subjected to direct administration, the British allowed the *zamindars* wide-ranging prerogatives, especially after 1857, when they helped them to suppress the Revolt. Subsequently, the *zamindars* could go as far as seizing a tenant's personal possessions or harvest in repayment of debts.[70] As in Uttar Pradesh, most peasants belonged to low cultivating castes (Yadav, Kurmi, and Koeri etc.). Among them the cowherd caste of the Yadavs was most numerous – 11% of the population.

Just as in Uttar Pradesh, the Congress was dominated by the upper castes after Independence, but not to the same extent, as evident from the social profile of the party's MLAs. In the late 1950s and early 1960s the upper castes were not in a majority among the Congress MLAs and the lower castes represented 10 to 20% of them – a very high proportion in comparison to UP.

The over-representation of the upper castes was even more pronounced in the party apparatus, as evident from the composition of the Pradesh Congress Committee (PCC) of Bihar from 1947 to 1960. Table 2.8 does not indicate any trend. The share of the upper castes tended to decline but it remained at the same level in 1960 as in 1948. Within this apparent stability, Rajputs declined steadily whereas the Bhumihars were on the rise. In Bihar as in Uttar Pradesh, party cadres were more likely to come from the elite than the MLAs but in contrast to the situation of the UP Congress, the lower castes, who already represented about one-fifth of the Congress MLAs, remained between 10 to 20% of the PCC, a very high proportion.

The sociology of the Rajasthan Congress is closer to that of Uttar Pradesh. This has probably something to do with the demographic weight of the upper castes in both states. Rajasthan is the North Indian state where the upper castes are highest in number, just ahead of Uttar Pradesh (24.2% against 20%): Brahmins account for 8%, Rajputs 9.2% and Banyas 7%. The strength of the Rajputs was reinforced by the fact that most of the 22 princely states of Rajputana during the British Raj had Rajputs at the helm. However, a specific feature of Rajasthan is the high proportion of Jats, 9%, who could have balanced the Rajput domination. The fact that two of the princely states of Rajputana, Bharatpur and Dholpur, were governed by

[70] F. Frankel 'Caste, land and dominance in Bihar' in F. Frankel and M.S.A. Rao (eds), *Dominance and State Power in Modern India*, vol. 1, Delhi: Oxford University Press, 1989, pp. 58–9.

Table 2.6. CASTE AND COMMUNITY OF MEMBERS OF THE UTTAR PRADESH GOVERNMENT, 1937–67 (%)

Castes and communities	*1937*	*1947*	*1952*	*1954*	*1957*	*1960*	*1962*	*1963*	*1967*
Upper castes	*66.6*	*57.7*	*64*	*59*	*60*	*66.6*	*67.7*	*66.7*	*84.7*
Brahmin	33.3	21.1	28	22.7	30	14.8	16.1	28.6	23.1
Rajput	6.7	5.3	12	4.5	10	7.4	9.7	9.5	7.7
Banya/Jain	13.3	15.8	12	18.2	10	22.2	22.6	19	46.2
Bhumihar	–	–	–	–	–	3.7	3.2	–	7.7
Kayasth	13.3	15.5	12	13.6	6.7	3.7	3.2	–	–
Khatri	–	–	–	–	3.3	3.7	6.5	4.8	–
Amil	–	–	–	–	–	3.7	3.2	4.8	–
Other	–	–	–	–	–	7.4	3.2	–	–
Intermediate castes	–	*5.3*	*4*	–	*6.7*	*3.7*	*3.2*	*4.8*	–
Jat	–	5.3	4	–	6.7	3.7	3.2	4.8	–
Low castes	–	–	*4*	*4.5*	*6.6*	*3.7*	*6.4*	*4.8*	–
Kurmi	–	–	–	–	3.3	–	3.2	4.8	–
Murao	–	–	4	–	–	–	–	–	–
Yadav	–	–	–	4.5	3.3	3.7	3.2	–	–

Scheduled Castes	*13.3*	*5.3*	*12*	*18.2*	*10*	*11.1*	*16.1*	*14.3*	*7.7*
Muslim	*20*	*26.3*	*16*	*18.2*	*13.3*	*11.1*	*6.5*	*9.5*	*7.7*
Unidentified	–	*5.3*	–	–	*3.3*	*3.7*	–		
Total	*100*	*100*	*100*	*100*	*100*	*100*	*100*	*100*	*100*
	N=15	*N=19*	*N=25*	*N=22*	*N=30*	*N=27*	*N=31*	*N=21*	*N=13*

Source: *Sarvadhik Pichhra Varg Ayog Report*, Lucknow: Uttar Pradesh ki Sarkar, 1977 (Hindi), pp. 91-5.

Table 2.7. CASTE AND COMMUNITY OF CONGRESS MLAs IN BIHAR, 1957–62 (%)

	*% in Bihar**	*1957*	*1962*	
Upper castes	*12.7*	*44.29*	*43.16*	*(47.8)*
Brahmin	4.6	9.54	12. 75	(14.1)
Bhumihar	2.8	16.19	11.78	(13.6)
Rajput	4.1	14.28	13.24	(14.1)
Kayasth	1.2	4.28	5.39	(6)
Lower castes	*50*	*22.86*	*22.07*	*(24.4)*
Banya	0.6			(2.7)
Yadav	10.7			(8.2)
Kurmi	3.5			(6.5)
Koeri	4			(6.5)
Other	31.2			(0.5)
Scheduled Castes	*13.8*			*(17.4)*
Scheduled Tribes	*8.9*	*17.62*	*27.46*	*(1.1)*
Muslim	*12.2*	*11.43*	*7.35*	*(8.2)*
Bengali	*2.4*	*3.8*	–	*(1.1)*
Unidentified and others		*N=210*	*N=204*	*N=184*
Total		*100*	*100*	*(100)*

* According to the 1931 census.

Sources: C. Jha, 'Caste in Bihar Congress politics' in I. Narain (ed.), *State Politics in India*, Meerut: Meenakshi Prakashan, 1967, p. 583. The figures in brackets for 1962 come from H.W. Blair, 'Rising Kulaks and Backward Classes in Bihar', *Economic and Political Weekly* (hereafter *EPW*), 15 (2), Jan. 12, 1980, p. 68.

Jat dynasties, is noteworthy. The Rajputs controlled most princely states and at a lower level exercised the function of *jagirdar* or *zamindar*. In fact, their influence was as much political as cultural:

> . . .for over a thousand years the people of Rajasthan did not look up to the Brahmins as cultural models, nor did they adopt brahminical customs and life-styles to advance their ritual status. The people of Rajasthan did try to emulate the cultural norms and ritual forms adopted by their respective princes and *jagirdar* [who were Rajputs].[71]

Moreover the Congress was keen to co-opt Rajputs instead of offering the Jats or other groups political leverage which might be

[71] I. Narain and P. C. Mathur, 'The thousand year Raj: regional isolation and Rajput Hinduism in Rajasthan before and after 1947' in Frankel and Rao (eds), op. cit., p. 17.

Table 2.8. CASTE AND COMMUNITY OF MEMBERS OF THE PRADESH CONGRESS COMMITTEE OF BIHAR, 1947–60 (%)

	1947	*1948*	*1950*	*1952*	*1954*	*1955*	*1958*	*1960*
Upper castes	*78.57*	*61.92*	*75*	*73.69*	*57.89*	*60*	*66.77*	*61.9*
Brahmins	7.15	9.52	12.5	21.05	10.53	15	14.28	14.29
Bhumihar	14.28	14.29	12.5	21.05	21.05	20	23.81	28.56
Rajput	35.71	23.82	37.5	26.33	21.05	20	19.15	14.29
Kayasth	21.43	14.29	12.5	5.26	5.26	5	9.53	4.76
Low castes	–	*19.04*	*12.5*	*10.53*	*21.05*	*20*	*14.28*	*14.29*
Scheduled Castes	–	*4.76*	*6.25*	*5.26*	*5.26*	*5*	*4.76*	*4.76*
Scheduled Tribes	*7.15*	*4.76*	–	*5.26*	*5.26*	–	–	–
Muslim	*14.28*	*9.52*	*6.25*	*5.26*	*5.26*	*5*	*9.53*	*14.29*
Unidentified	–	–	–	–	*5.26*	*10*	*4.76*	*4.76*
Total	*100*	*100*	*100*	*100*	*100*	*100*	*100*	*100*

Source: R. Roy, 'Caste and political recruitment in Bihar', op. cit., p. 243.

used for power-sharing. Before Independence the 22 princely rulers of Rajputana were generally successful in curbing the penetration of modern ideas. The Congress was not even authorised to function in these states, where it went by the name of Praja Mandal (Association of the subjects or of the ruled). In Rajasthan, the office-bearers of the Praja Mandal, from 1919 to 1946, were recruited almost exclusively among the Brahmins (whose average proportion over the period stood at 47%), the Banyas (32%) and the Kayasths (6%). Rajputs represented only 4% of the total and the peasant castes (mostly Jats, probably), 10%.[72] The few Rajputs who had joined the Praja Mandal were hardly welcomed.[73] This situation was to change after Independence.

During the 1952 election, the Congress Chief Minister, Jainarain Vyas, a Brahmin, was defeated by the Maharajah of Jodhpur who had federated the opposition forces. Nehru then invited Rajput leaders to join the Congress, and to woo them more efficiently he offered them concessions regarding the envisioned land reform.[74] As a result, in 1954, Vyas – who had retrieved his post after being successful in a by-election – won the support of 22 Rajput MLAs who had been returned as Independents or under the banner of an opposition party. The proportion of Rajputs among the Congress candidates for the state elections shot up: their percentage increased from 2% in 1952 to 15% in 1957, at the expense, mostly, of the Brahmins who declined from 41 to 31%.[75] This trend stabilised in the following years, as is evident from the data collected by Sisson.

Table 2.9 reveals that even though the Congress remained dominated by Brahmins, it relied almost as much on Rajputs as on Banyas and Jats. Sisson's data, however, needs to be qualified. First, reserved seats are not taken into account; second, there is no precise information about the 'peasant castes', except for the Jats; third, we need to know the caste composition of the legislative party in order to evaluate the relative weight of the different groups in this arena.

The caste-wise distribution of the Congress MLAs confirms the over representation of the upper castes but this domination is not as

[72] R. Sisson, *The Congress Party in Rajasthan*, Delhi: Oxford University Press, 1972, p. 63.

[73] Ibid., p. 64.

[74] Ibid., pp. 139–40.

[75] Ibid., p. 135.

Table 2.9. CASTE OF CONGRESS CANDIDATES TO THE RAJASTHAN ASSEMBLY, 1952–67 (%)

	1952	*1957*	*1962*	*1967*
Upper castes	*66*	*70*	*68*	*70*
Brahmin	41	31	30	30
Rajput	2	15	13	12
Banya/Jain	17	14	18	16
Other	6	10	7	12
Peasant castes	*28*	*23*	*24*	*23*
Jat	20	18	18	16
Other	8	5	6	7
Muslim	*5*	*6*	*6*	*7*
Total	*100* *N=127*	*100* *N=125*	*100* *N=127*	*100* *N=122*

Source: Adapted from R. Sisson, *The Congress Party in Rajasthan*, op. cit., p. 135.

pronounced as in Uttar Pradesh. However, the lower castes are not so well represented as in UP – and certainly not as in Bihar. Disaggregating the category used by Sisson, the 'peasant castes', therefore enables us to show that the low castes were less represented in the Rajasthan assembly than in those of UP and Bihar. The Jats can hardly be regarded as a low caste like the Yadavs of Bihar simply because many of them have undergone rapid social mobility. Sisson and Shrader have shown than only 31% of the MLAs of the Vidhan Sabha elected in 1962 were still engaged in farming: 41% were lawyers, 14% civil servants and 11% social workers/professional politicians.[76]

The domination of the upper castes and the Jats over the Rajasthan Congress was even more prevalent in the party apparatus. From 1948 to 1965, the proportion of Brahmins in the Pradesh Congress Committee decreased from 46 to 39%, that of the Banyas fell from 33 to 19%, whereas that of the Rajputs rose from 1 to 7% and that of the intermediary peasant castes – mainly Jats – doubled from 9 to 18%.[77] The co-option of a growing number of Rajput notables in the early 1950s alarmed the Jats, who eventually provoked the fall

[76] R. Sisson and L.L. Shrader, *Legislative Recruitment and Political Integration: Patterns of Political Linkage in an Indian State*, Berkeley, CA: Center for South and Southeast Asia Studies, Research Monograph 6, 1972, p. 12.

[77] Sisson, *The Congress Party in Rajasthan*, op. cit., p. 133.

Table 2.10. CASTE AND COMMUNITY OF CONGRESS MLAs AND IN PARENTHESES OF ALL MLAs IN THE RAJASTHAN ASSEMBLY, 1952–67 (%)

	*% in Rajasthan**	*1952*	*1957*	*1962*	*1967*
Upper castes		*51.2 (61.6)*	*47 (47)*	*45.5 (47.2)*	*42 (46)*
Brahmin	8	22.1 (17.4)	24.4 (18.3)	20 (14.2)	18.7 (15.2)
Rajput	6	5.8 (30.5)	12.6 (17.1)	14.4 (19.3)	9.3 (15.8)
Banya/Jain	7	19.8 (11.1)	9.2 (8.6)	7.8 (11.4)	12.1 (13.6)
Kayasth	*n.a.*	3.5 (1.1)	0.8 (1.1)	2.2 (1.7)	1.9 (1.6)
Other			1.2 (0.5)	1.1 (0.6)	
Intermediate castes		*16.3 (15.8)*	*17.6 (16.6)*	*23.4 (16.4)*	*15.9 (13.6)*
Jat	9	16.3 (15.8)	17.6 (16.6)	22.2 (15.9)	15.9 (13.6)
Other (incl. Bishnoi)	*n.a.*		1.2 (0.5)		
Low castes	*n.a.*	*2.3 (3.2)*	*2.5 (4)*	*4.4 (6.3)*	*1.9 (3.3)*
Charan	*n.a.*		0 (0.6)		
Gujar	5	0 (1.6)	0 (1.1)	0 (3.4)	0.9 (2.2)
Kumhar	*n.a.*				0.9 (0.5)
Mali	3		0.8 (0.6)	1.1 (0.6)	
Yadav	*n.a.*	2.3 (1.6)	0.8 (1.1)	1.1 (1.1)	0 (0.5)
Others	*n.a.*		0.8 (0.6)	2.2 (1.1)	
Scheduled Castes	*17.3*	*20.9 (11.1)*	*21 (20)*	*14.4 (17)*	*15.9 (16.8)*
Scheduled Tribes	*12.4*	*4.7 (3.2)*	*7.6 (9)*	*10 (9.7)*	*14 (11.4)*
Muslim	*8*	*3.5 (3.2)*	*3.4 (2)*	*2.2 (1.7)*	*4.7 (3.3)*
Sikh	*1.5*	*1.2 (1.1)*	*0.8 (1)*		*1.9 (1.1)*
Unidentified		*0 (1.1)*	*0 (1)*	*0 (1.7)*	*3.7 (4.3)*
Total	*100*	*100* *N=86 (190)*	*100* *N=119 (175)*	*100* *N=90 (176)*	*100* *N=107 (184)*

* According to *Census of India, The Rajputana Agency*, vol. 27, except for SCs, STs, Muslims and Sikhs for whom the 1991 census had been used.

Source: Fieldwork, based on the list of MLAs of *Vidhan Bodhni – Traimasik Patrika* (Jaipur), Oct. 1997 (Hindi).

of Vyas in 1954. His successor, Sukhadia accommodated them.[78] In the mid-1960s, the upper castes represented still about two-thirds of the Rajasthan PCC and Jats almost one-fifth. The composition of the Congress governments shows the same domination of the upper castes and the Jats in the 1950s and1960s. They were relatively less elitist than the PCC but the upper castes were still in a majority in the 1960s and the Jats remained between one fifth and one fourth of the total.

The situation of Madhya Pradesh was close to that of Rajasthan in the sense that the state was also born, in 1956, by regrouping dozens of princely states – 25 in Madhya Bharat, the western part of

[78] K.L. Kamal, 'Rajasthan – Politics of declining feudal order' in I. Narain (ed.), *State Politics in India*, Meerut: Meenakshi Prakashan, 1976, p. 307.

Table 2.11. CASTE AND COMMUNITY IN THE CONGRESS GOVERNMENT OF RAJASTHAN, 1952–67

	1952	%	*1953*	%	*1954*	%	*1955*	%	*1957*	%	*1962*	%	*1967*	%
Upper castes	*9*	*81.9*	*6*	*75*	*6*	*75*	*4*	*44.4*	*7*	*49.9*	*13*	*56.4*	*21*	*53.9*
Brahmin	4	36.4	4	50	4	50	3	33.3	3	21.4	8	34.8	8	20.5
Rajput	1	9.1							1	7.1	1	4.3	4	10.3
Banya/Jain	3	27.3	2	25	2	25	1	11.1	3	21.4	3	13	6	15.4
Kayasth	1	9.1									1	4.3	3	7.7
Intermediate castes	*1*	*9.1*	*1*	*12.5*	*1*	*12.5*	*3*	*33.3*	*4*	*28.5*	*6*	*26.1*	*7*	*17.9*
Bishnoi									1	7.1				
Jat	1	9.1	1	12.5	1	12.5	3	33.3	3	21.4	6	26.1	7	17.9
Lower castes	*1*	*9.1*	*1*	*12.5*	*1*	*12.5*	*1*	*11.1*	–	–	*1*	*4.3*	*2*	*5.2*
Yadav	1	9.1	1	12.5	1	12.5	1	11.1	–	–	1	4.3	1	2.6
Kumhar													1	2.6
Scheduled Castes	–	–	–	–	–	–	*1*	*11.1*	*1*	*7.1*	*1*	*4.3*	*3*	*7.7*
Scheduled Tribes	–	–	–	–	–	–	–	–	*1*	*7.1*	*1*	*4.3*	*2*	*5.1*
Muslim	–	–	–	–	–	–	–	–	*1*	*7.1*	*1*	*4.3*	*2*	*5.1*
Sikh	–	–	–	–	–	–	–	–	–	–	–	–	*1*	*2.6*
Unidentified	–	–	–	–	–	–	–	–	–	–	–	–	*1*	*2.6*
Total	*11*	*100*	*8*	*100*	*8*	*100*	*9*	*100*	*14*	*100*	*23*	*100*	*39*	*100*

Source: As for Table 2.10.

the state, 35 in Vindhya Pradesh and a dozen in Chhattisgarh. In the 1950s, 170 out of 296 assembly constituencies and 20 out of 37 parliamentary constituencies were located in part or in whole on the territory of former princely states.[79] But the caste composition of Madhya Pradesh was specific. The upper castes represented 12.9% of the state population (5.7% Brahmins, 5.3% Rajputs and 2% Banyas), the lower castes, 42%, the Scheduled Castes 14% and the Scheduled Tribes an exceptionally high 22%.[80] In Madhya Pradesh, the Congress contented itself with co-opting former princes without paying too much attention to intermediary castes since there was no group within the peasantry as influential as the Jats in Rajasthan.

This process is well illustrated by the case of the Scindias. This dynasty was, in 1947, at the helm of one the largest princely states of northern India and it controlled – thanks to its own power and prestige and network of former *jagirdar* – nearly a one fifth of the assembly constituencies. In 1952, 'the Palace', the name under which the Scindias are known in Gwalior, discreetly supported the Hindu Mahasabha which emerged as the main rival to the Congress in Madhya Bharat. Nehru realised that it would pose a threat to his party. He therefore requested the Maharajah, Jivaji Rao, to side with Congress just before the elections of 1957. The Maharajah declined the invitation but the Maharani, Vijaya Raje Scindia, was persuaded to contest the elections under the Congress banner[81] and won with a large margin against the Hindu Mahasabha candidate. The Mahasabha lost ground throughout Madhya Bharat whereas Congress established a dominance which remained unchallenged till 1967 when 'the Palace' left the ruling party and once again sided with the Hindu nationalist opposition.

The Scindias owed their influence to several factors. First, they headed a network of ex-*jagirdar* and ex-*zamindar* who remained

[79] For more details, see Jaffrelot, *The Hindu Nationalist Movement and Indian Politics*, op. cit., p. 215.

[80] For more details, see C. Jaffrelot, 'The Sangh Parivar Between Sanskritisation and Social Engineering' in T.B. Hansen and C. Jaffrelot (eds), *The BJP and the Compulsions of Politics in India*, Delhi: Oxford University Press, 2001, pp. 22–71.

[81] V. Scindia with M. Malgonkar, *Princess – The Autobiography of the Dowager Maharani of Gwalior*, New Delhi: Times Books International, 1988, pp. 172–3.

very powerful at the grassroots level. Second, they could mobilise support among their agricultural and industrial enterprises, which employed thousands of people and represented considerable pools of capital. Third, they patronised several social and educational institutions (Jivaji Rao founded the Vikram University of Ujjain in 1956 with a donation of five million rupees).[82] Besides these material resources, the ruling family also benefited from being the object of social deference and devotion, at least in Madhya Bharat[83] where their patronage of the great religious festivals and temples added to their prestige.[84]

Until 1967, the princely families of Madhya Pradesh sided with Congress, either because they were anxious to remain in step with those in government or because they dared not oppose the entreaties to which they were subjected. In Madhya Bharat, in addition to Vijaya Raje Scindia, the Congress benefited from the support of Bhanu Prakash Singh (ex-Maharaja of Narsingarh) who was appointed a minister by Indira Gandhi in the late 1960s.

In Vindhya Pradesh, it received the backing of the former Raj Pramukh (governor of the province immediately after Independence), the Maharajah of Rewa, a state equal in size to all others in this region. As in many other states, here the Congress had been established as the Praja Mandal. A local Rajput *jagirdar*, Capt. Avadhesh Pratap Singh, who had been drawn to Gandhi in the early 1920s, played a significant role in developing the organisation – an indication of the role that upper caste landlords played in the making of the Congress in the region. After Independence Capt. Singh was nominated a member of the Constituent Assembly and became Chief Minister of Vindhya Pradesh. His son, G.N. Singh, who launched his political career as a student leader, was elected an MLA for the first time in 1952 and subsequently till 1967 when he became Chief Minister of Madhya Pradesh.[85] Another 'dynasty' of Congress Rajput

[82] *Hitavada*, 16 Oct. 1956, p. 1.

[83] For a description of how the Scindias were perceived in a village of the Gwalior region, see J.L. Chambard, *Atlas d'un village indien*, Paris: EHESS, 1980, p. 37.

[84] Till her death in 2001, Vijaya Raje Scindia patronised the Gopal Mandir of Ujjain, a holy city which is far away from Gwalior but which used to be part of Gwalior state.

[85] Interview with G.N. Singh, New Delhi, 16 Nov. 1997.

landowners was initiated by Siva Bahadur Singh, a big *zamindar* who was a minister in the first cabinet of Vindhya Pradesh. His son, Arjun Singh, – who also started his public career as a student leader – was first elected MLA in 1957 as an independent but then joined Congress in March 1960. Interestingly, he had asked to meet Nehru before joining his party and Nehru had given him 'his blessing'.[86]

In Chhattisgarh, from 1952 onwards the Congress won the support of the Maharajahs of Sarangarh (district of Raigarh) and Surguja, who contested elections under its banner, and the support of the Rani of Khairagarh (Padmavati Devi) and of the Maharajah of Kanker.[87] Thus, the Congress established its domination over Madhya Pradesh by aggregating 'vote banks' controlled by former princes or *jagirdars.*

From 1957 to 1967, the proportion of upper caste MLAs remained around 40-50%, which was less than in Uttar Pradesh but more than in Bihar. The intermediate castes and low caste Congress representatives in the Madhya Pradesh assembly were more numerous than in Uttar Pradesh but in fewer number than in Rajasthan (in respect of the intermediate castes) and Bihar (in respect of the low castes). In fact the most important non upper caste groups comprised Scheduled Castes and Tribals. But these MLAs, who were often uneducated, did not form powerful lobbies. In fact, they had been coopted because of the reservation system (see Chapter 3, below). They were, indeed, very few in the state government, where there was no reservation system.

Between the early 1950s and the late 1960s, the Congress governments of Madhya Pradesh comprised between two-thirds and three fourths of upper caste ministers, the second largest group being made up of Scheduled Castes leaders while Scheduled Tribes were even fewer in number. Most interestingly, the low castes were conspicuous by their absence, except in the 1964 government.

A comparison of the caste background of Congress MLAs in the four largest states of the Hindi belt in the 1950s and 1960s shows that Uttar Pradesh was certainly the most 'elitist': there upper caste MLAs represented between 56 and 61% of the total in 1952–62 whereas the lower castes comprised 6 to 7% of the total. The gap is

[86] Interview with Arjun Singh, New Delhi, 18 Nov. 1997.

[87] *Hitavada*, 5 Jan. 1952, 10 Nov. 1956, p. 3, and *Madhya Pradesh Chronicle*, 1 May 1963, p. 3 and 19 Jan. 1962, p. 6.

Table 2.12. CASTE AND COMMUNITY OF CONGRESS MLAs AND (IN PARENTHESES) OF ALL MLAs IN MADHYA PRADESH, 1952–67 (%)

	*% in MP**	*1957*	*1962*	*1967*
Upper castes	*12.9*	*40.1 (41.2)*	*51.2 (48.4)*	*44.5 (44.9)*
Brahmin	5.66	20.5 (20.4)	27.7 (21.5)	23.7 (21.8)
Rajput	5.29	7.4 (8.1)	12.1 (14.2)	10.7 (10.9)
Banya/Jain	2.1	10 (10.6)	6.4 (8.3)	7.1 (8.2)
Kayasth	0.49	2.2 (2.1)	4.3 (3.8)	2.4 (3.4)
Other	–	–	0.7 (0.6)	0.6 (0.6)
Intermediate castes	*1.11*	*0.4 (1.1)*	*0.7 (0.6)*	*0.6 (0.6)*
Maratha	1.11	0 (0.7)	0 (0.3)	0.6 (0.3)
Raghuvanshi	*n.a.*	0.4 (0.4)	0.7 (0.3)	0 (0.3)
Low castes	*41.44*	*5.1 (5.1)*	*9.2 (9.4)*	*10.5 (9.7)*
Lodhi	2.25	0.4 (0.4)		
Dangi	0.21		0 (0.3)	
Gujar	1.23	–	0 (0.3)	0.6 (1)
Jaiswal	0.7	–	0.7 (0.7)	1.2 (0.7)
Kirar	0.51	–		0 (0.7)
Kurmi	2.64	0 (0.7)	1.4 (1)	2.4 (2.4)
Pawar	*n.a.*	2.6 (2.1)	2.1 (1.7)	2.4 (1.4)
Teli	4.02	–	0 (0.3)	0.6 (1)
Yadav	5.29	–	0 (0.3)	
Sondhia Rajput	0.36	–	0 (0.3)	0.3 (0.3)
Soni	0.67	0.4 (0.4)	–	
Baghel	*n.a.*			0.6 (0.3)
Other	23.56	1.3 (1.1)	4.3 (4.2)	2.4 (1.6)
Scheduled Castes	*14.05*	*18.2 (15.9)*	*17 (14.4)*	*11.9 (12.8)*
Scheduled Tribes	*21.62*	*20.5 (18.3)*	*17 (20.1)*	*22.5 (20.4)*
Muslim	*3.85*	*1.7 (1.8)*	*4.3 (2.4)*	*0.6 (1)*
Other minorities	*0.29*	*0 (0.8)*	–	
Unidentified	*4.1*	*14 (16.5)*	*1.4 (4.2)*	*10.1 (10.6)*
Total	*100*	*100* *N=229 (284)*	*100* *N=141 (289)*	*100* *N=169 (293)*

* According to the 1931 census.

Sources: Fieldwork based on the bio data of the *Madhya Pradesh Vidhan Sabha sadasyon ka sankshipt parichay – 1957*, Bhopal, Madhya Pradesh sabha Sachivalay, 1961, *Madhya Pradesh Vidhan Sabha sadasyon ka sankshipt parichay – 1962*, Bhopal, Madhya Pradesh sabha Sachivalay, 1964 and *Madhya Pradesh Vidhan Sabha sadasyon ka sankshipt parichay – 1967*, Bhopal, Madhya Pradesh sabha Sachivalay, 1970.

Table 2.13. CASTE AND COMMUNITY OF MEMBERS OF THE CONGRESS GOVERNMENT IN MADHYA PRADESH, 1953–67

	1953 (%)	*1953*	*1957 (%)*	*1957*	*1962 (%)*	*1962*	*1964 (%)*	*1964*	*1967 (%)*	*1967*
Upper castes	*66.7*	*4*	*73.8*	*17*	*86.6*	*13*	*66.7*	*14*	*66.7*	*8*
Brahmin	50	3	34.8	8	40	6	38.1	8	33.3	4
Rajput	16.7	1	13	3	13.3	2	19	4	16.7	2
Banya/Jain	–	–	21.7	5	20	3	4.8	1		
Kayasth	–	–	4.3	1	13.3	2	4.8	1	16.7	2
Khatri	–	–	–	–	–	–	–	–	–	–
Low castes	–	–	–	–	–	–	*9.5*	*2*	–	–
Panwar	–	–	–	–	–	–	9.5	2	–	–
Scheduled Castes	*16.7*	*1*	*8.7*	*2*	*6.7*	*1*	*14.3*	*3*	*25*	*3*
Scheduled Tribes	–	–	*8.7*	*2*	*6.7*	*1*	*4.8*	*1*	*8.3*	*1*
Muslim	*16.7*	*1*	*8.7*	*2*	–	–	*4.8*	*1*	–	–
Total	*100*	*6*	*100*	*23*	*100*	*15*	*100*	*21*	*100*	*12*

Sources: As for Table 2.12.

not as striking in any of the other states: Bihar, in contrast, was the most 'democratic' with about 45% of upper caste MLAs in 1957–62 but 22–24% low caste MLAs. In between, Rajasthan and Madhya Pradesh have neat dissimilarities: while the upper caste Congress MLAs are as numerous in MP as in Rajasthan (40 to 51% as against, 42 to 48% in Rajasthan over the years 1957–67), low caste MLAs represent 5 to 10% of the total in MP, as against 2 to 4.4% in Rajasthan. This difference is due to the large share of the intermediate castes, mostly Jats, in Rajasthan (16 to 23%). In spite of these variations, the Congress party was clearly over-dominated by the upper castes in the Hindi belt.

This is reconfirmed by the caste background of the party MPs in this region. Table 2.14 erases the specificity of the different states since it concerns the MPs of Uttar Pradesh, Bihar, Rajasthan, Madhya Pradesh (or the regions which were to constitute this state before 1956), Delhi, Chandigarh and the Hindi-speaking districts of Punjab

Table 2.14. CASTE AND COMMUNITY OF CONGRESS MPs AND (IN PARENTHESES) OF ALL MPs ELECTED IN THE HINDI BELT, 1952–67 (%)

	1952	*1957*	*1962*	*1967*
Upper castes	*64.96 (65.02)*	*59.67 (59.35)*	*57.33 (56.14)*	*51.97 (56.2)*
Brahmin	30.46 (28.6)	21.02 (21.05)	21.33 (19.34)	22.05 (21.2)
Rajput	8.05 (10.7)	11.36 (13.98)	10 (15.09)	10.24 (13.82)
Bhumihar	4.02 (3.9)	4.55 (3.83)	5.33 (4.25)	2.36 (4.15)
Banya/Jain	9.8 (9.7)	10.23 (9.09)	8.67 (7.55)	6.3 (8.29)
Kayasth	9.2 (8.7)	9.09 (7.66)	6 (4.25)	4.72 (2.76)
Other	3.43 (3.42)	3.42 (3.84)	6 (5.66)	6.3 (5.98)
Intermediate castes	*0.57 (0.97)*	*1.71 (2.39)*	*1.34 (2.83)*	*3.15 (3.22)*
Jat	0.57 (0.97)	1.14 (1.91)	0.67 (2.36)	2.36 (2.76)
Low castes	*4.58 (4.39)*	*5.11 (6.22)*	*10.01 (9.43)*	*11.02 (9.67)*
Yadav	1.72 (1.46)	2.27 (2.39)	5.33 (4.72)	4.72 (4.61)
Kurmi	1.15 (1.46)	1.7 (2.87)	2 (2.36)	2.36 (1.84)
Panwar	0.57 (0.49)	0.57 (0.48)		0.79 (0.46)
Other	1.14 (0.98)	0.57 (0.48)	2.68 (2.35)	3.15 (2.76)
Scheduled Castes	*17.21 (15.57)*	*20.47 (18.67)*	*20.01 (18.85)*	*21.27 (17.97)*
Scheduled Tribes	*4.01 (5.84)*	*5.11 (6.22)*	*6 (6.6)*	*9.45 (7.83)*
Muslim	*5.75 (5.34)*	*5.68 (4.78)*	*4.67 (3.77)*	*2.36 (4.57)*
Other minorities	*1.14 (0.98)*	*1.14 (0.96)*	*0.67 (0.47)*	*0.79 (0.46)*
Sadhu			*0 (0.47)*	*0 (0.46)*
Unidentified	*1.72 (1.94)*	*1.14 (0.96)*	*0 (0.47)*	*0 (0.46)*
Total	*100*	*100*	*100*	*100*
	N=174 (206)	*N=176 (209)*	*N=150 (213)*	*N=127 (218)*

Source: Fieldwork.

(which were hived off to form Himachal Pradesh and Haryana in 1966). The strength of the Jats – which was especially prevalent in Rajasthan – is for instance diluted. It offers a more global picture of the caste background of Congress MPs in the wider Hindi belt between 1952 and 1967. Two significant trends emerge: first, the steady erosion of the proportion of upper caste MPs, and second, the increase in the share of low caste MPs. Yet, the upper caste MPs remained in a majority whereas the lower castes represent only one tenth of the deputies in 1967. The Congress tends to be slightly less 'elitist' than the other parties but it naturally contributes significantly to the upper caste domination of the assembly. The Lok Sabha of the 1950s and 1960s, at least for Hindi belt MPs, was clearly a case of elitist democracy. The elected bodies self-evidently did not reflect the composition of society, which largely explains the conservative nature of the Congress-dominated regime.

The conservative character of Congress in North India was largely the product of its Gandhian political culture and of its social profile. On the one hand conservative notables joined Congress because its ideology was compatible with their interests and their ethos, while on the other hand, the massive presence of conservative upper caste notables and the intelligentsia among the party's leaders reinforced its opposition to the social reform programmes of progressive elements in the leadership.

From the time of Motilal Nehru to the reign of Jawaharlal, the party had a remarkable over-representation of the upper castes in its ranks. This did not necessarily imply a conservative bias since the intelligentsia, even though it was largely Brahmin, had many social reform-oriented leaders in its midst. But for one Nehru, there were many Malaviyas. Even among the modern professionals, one finds many proponents of social conservatism. Moreover because Congress reached out to the notables of the merchant and agrarian milieus, it therefore co-opted many conservative, even traditionalist, Hindus like Seth Govind Das.

After Independence, the party leaders, including Nehru, recruited even more influential local personalities to serve its electoral interests, developing an interlocking network of 'vote banks' whose incumbents joined the nationalist intelligentsia in the party machine. Thus it was that in the two decades after Independence Congress established the supremacy of the upper castes in the political system of

North India. While it was almost a dominant party, the over-representation of the upper castes among its MLAs and MPs was striking.

The main upper castes – Brahmins, Rajputs and Banyas – which, together, control the Congress in North India largely coincide with the coalition of interests described by Bardhan as regrouping the 'dominant propertied classes'.[88] For him, the monopoly of power exerted by this coalition was not incompatible with a system of representative democracy. On the contrary, 'In a country where the elements in the dominant (though tacit) coalition are diverse, each sufficiently strong to exert pressures and pulls in different directions, political democracy may have a slightly better chance than elsewhere, particularly in view of the procedural usefulness of democracy as an impersonal (or least arbitrary) rule of negotiation, demand articulation, and bargaining within the coalition, and as a device for one partner to keep the other partner at the bargaining table within some moderate bounds.[89] This interpretation is in tune with one of the most stimulating theories of democracy initiated by D.A. Rustow and further elaborated by M. Olson. For the former, political democracy emerged as an almost unintended consequence of the conflict in which sectional elite groups are locked. In the context of 'a prolonged and inconclusive political struggle', one can expect 'a deliberate decision on the part of political leaders to accept the existence of diversity in unity and, to that end, to institutionalise some crucial aspects of democratic procedure'.[90] Olson uses the same premises when he suggests that democracy is 'permitted by the accidents of history that leave a balance of power or stalemate – a dispersion of force and resources that makes it impossible for any one leader or group to over-power all the other'.[91]

In India, rivalry between elite groups had not taken a very acute

[88] P. Bardhan, *The Political Economy of Development in India*, Oxford: Blackwell, 1984.

[89] P. Bardhan, 'Dominant Proprietary Classes and India's Democracy' in A. Kohli (ed.), *India's Democracy. An Analysis of Changing State – Society Relations*, Princeton University Press, 1990, p. 215.

[90] D. A. Rustow, 'Transitions to Democracy – Toward a Dynamic Model', *Comparative Politics*, 2 (3), April 1070, p. 355.

[91] Further elaborating this point, Olson hypothesizes that 'If no one leader can subdue the others or segregate his followers into a separate domain, then the alternative is either to engage in fruitless fighting or to work out a truce with mutual toleration.' (M. Olson, 'Dictatorship, Democracy, and Development', *American Political Science Review*, 87 (3), Sept. 1993, p. 573)

form but the dominant classes mentioned by Bardhan were definitely locked in a conflict. The groups in control of agriculture and those who commercialise their production and lend them money – the Banyas – were traditionally antagonistic. Both of them were targeted by the urban, educated intelligentsia who ran the government (through the Congress party) and the administration – partly because they entertained social-reform oriented ideals, partly because they wanted to assert their authority. These conflicts were bound to last – except if the state resorted to coercive, violent means – and the realisation that this deadlock might endure prompted the three groups to spell out a compromise that fits neatly with the democratic agenda as advanced by Bardhan. Instead of fighting each other, these elite groups thought of collaborate and pool their resources. Businessmen would fund the Congress party against the promise of a moderating of state intervention in the economy and *ad hoc* departures from the 'licence Raj' (which was a major source of corruption). Landowners would rally around the ruling party and allow it to mobilise their local influence at election time in return for a 'soft' implementation of land reform and state-control of the grain trade. The Congress professional politicians and the bureaucracy could assert their own power with the help of these two support bases. Democracy offered them all a flexible set of bargaining procedures which allowed for the division of the spoils, while resisting popular pressure. This interpretation provides a pragmatic explanation of the continuity of the democratic polity in India.[92] It also offers an explanation for its social defects. The bargaining form of collaboration between élite groups was congenial to political democracy but drastically limited the chances of success of a genuine policy of social distribution. India was bound to have political democracy without social democracy.

Certainly, in Delhi progressive elements tended to dominate the power structure with Nehru at the helm. But it became helpless in face of the inertia of the Congress apparatus in the states. As Atul Kohli has already emphasised, this is a clear case of loss of state autonomy, since, in the states, the Congress was dependent on local notables delivering 'vote banks'.[93] The way in which the land reform,

[92] For more details, see C. Jaffrelot, *La démocratie en Inde Religion. Caste et politique*, Paris: Fayard, 1998.

[93] A. Kohli, *The State and Poverty in India – The Politics of Reform*, Cambridge University Press, 1987, p. 57.

after the initial impetus given by Nehru, was diverted from its objectives can be explained in this perspective because its implementation was delegated to the state governments. However, the Centre itself reduced the autonomy of the state by admitting that the Congress needed the support of local notables. Congress was also adept at co-opting the emerging low caste leaders – thus often depriving Dalit parties of their political nascent elite.

APPENDIXES TO CHAPTER 2

Table 2.15. CASTE AND COMMUNITY OF CONGRESS MPs IN UTTAR PRADESH, 1952–62 (%)

	1952	*1957*	*1962*
Upper castes	*58.5*	*55.1*	*54.7*
Brahmin	33.3	27.7	21
Rajput	6.6	12.3	12.9
Banya/Jain	12	7.6	4.8
Kayasth	4	3	4.8
Bhumihar	1.3	1.5	3.2
Tyagi	1.3	1.5	1.6
Nayar	–	1.5	1.6
Khatri	–	–	4.8
Intermediate castes	*2.6*	–	*1.6*
Jat	2.6	–	1.6
Low castes	*0*	*1.5*	*3.2*
Yadav	–	1.5	1.6
Kurmi	–	–	1.6
Scheduled Castes	*22.6*	*21.5*	*24.2*
Muslim	*8*	*9.2*	*6.5*
Christian	*1.3*	*1.5*	–
Sadhu	*1.3*	–	–
Unidentified	*5.3*	*10.8*	*9.7*
Total	*100* *N=75*	*100* *N=65*	*100* *N=62*

Table 2.16. CASTE AND COMMUNITY OF CONGRESS MPs IN RAJASTHAN, 1952–62 (%)

	1952	*1957*	*1962*
Upper castes	*74.8*	*68.3*	*69.2*
Brahmin	41.6	15.8	15.4
Rajput	–	–	7.7
Banya/Jain	24.9	31.5	23.1
Kayasth	8.3	21	23
Scheduled Castes	*8.3*	*21*	*7.7*
Scheduled Tribes	*8.3*	*5.2*	*15.4*
Unidentified	*8.3*	*5.2*	*7.7*
Total	*100*	*100*	*100*
	N=12	*N=18*	*N=11*

Table 2.17. CASTE AND COMMUNITY OF CONGRESS MPs IN MADHYA PRADESH, 1952–62 (%)

	1952	*1957*	*1962*
Upper castes	*58.6*	*51.4*	*58.3*
Brahmin	44.8	25.7	37.5
Rajput	–	5.7	8.3
Banya/Jain	10.3	17.1	12.5
Kayasth	–	2.8	–
Other	3.4	–	–
Low castes	*6.9*	*5.6*	–
Panwar	3.4	2.8	–
Kurmi	–	2.8	–
Other	3.4	–	–
Scheduled Castes	*10.3*	*17.1*	*12.5*
Scheduled Tribes	*10.3*	*20*	*20.8*
Muslim	*3.4*	*2.8*	*4.17*
Sikh	*3.4*	*2.8*	*4.17*
Unidentified	*6.9*	–	–
Total	*100*	*100*	*100*
	N=29	*N=35*	*N=24*

3

THE CONGRESS PARTY AND THE SCHEDULED CASTES

RESERVATIONS AND CO-OPTION

Even though there is no reliable survey data on political allegiance in India before the late 1960s, most village studies and monographs suggest that a majority of Scheduled Castes voters supported the Congress party after Independence. Several factors were responsible for this voting pattern.

The Congress traditionally paid more attention to the Untouchables than to the other lower castes, who were sometimes treated almost as badly. This attitude derived from its well established tradition of socio-religious reform. First, some of the nineteenth-century socio-religious reform movements had a strongly egalitarian agenda and aspired to abolish the caste system. They naturally focused on the Untouchables who were the most obvious victims of the social system. Even when they had no such motivation, the socio-religious reform movements often focussed on the needs of the Scheduled Castes in order to dissuade them from rejecting Hinduism. The Arya Samaj, for instance, opened schools and orphanages and tried to upgrade the lower castes through the Shuddhi ritual in order to dissuade them from attending Christian schools and converting to Christianity. Arya Samajist Congress leaders such as Lajpat Rai were keen to reorient the Shuddhi movement towards the Untouchables so as to improve their condition.[1] A pro-poor discourse focussing on the Untouchability issue took shape in this context and, as we saw in

[1] In 1909 Lajpat Rai called out the upper castes in the following terms: 'The Hindus are going down in numbers. Your insolence towards the lower classes of Hindus is paid back by the latter turning their back on you. Mohammedanism and Christianity are extending their arms to embrace them and indications are not wanting of the readiness of the lower classes of Hindus to accept the hospitality of non-Hindu religions and social systems. Why? The reason is obvious.

Chapter One, Gandhi embraced it and further elaborated on it. The popularity of the Mahatma Gandhi among the Scheduled Castes was another obvious reason why they granted their electoral support to the Congress.

After Independence, this discourse became part of the official idiom of the new Republic. Nehru had already endorsed it in a more egalitarian vein, like most of the leftist leaders, and aspired to give it some substance. Article 17 of the 1950 Constitution abolished Untouchability and stated that 'its practice in any form is forbidden'. The Nehru Government also brought forward bills such as the one allowing Untouchables to enter temples and, in 1955, *The Untouchability (Offences) Act*, which aimed at protecting the Untouchables from any kind of discrimination.[2] These laws also enabled the Congress to woo the Scheduled Castes voters.

The Congress party was also able to attract the support of the Scheduled Castes because of the introduction of the reservation system and the concomitant access to education, the bureaucracy and the elected assemblies it was meant to usher in. This policy of affirmative action was partly a smokescreen since the quotas were often unfulfilled. But it enabled the ruling party to bargain and extend its patronage in exchange for electoral support. More importantly, Congress succeeded in projecting itself as the natural representative of the Scheduled Castes because of its skill in promoting or co-opting Untouchable leaders – including cadres of the parties established by Ambedkar – and getting them elected in the framework of the reservation system. Even if they had propagated revolutionary views in their early career, they often forgot them, once integrated to the political elite.

As a Hindu you won't touch him; you would not let him sit on the same carpet with you. You would not offer him water in your cups, you would not accept water or food touched by him; you would not let him enter your temples, in fact you would not treat him like a human being.' (Lala Lajpat Rai, 'The Depressed Classes', *The Modern Review*, July 1909, reprinted in D. Swaroop (ed.), *Politics of Conversion*, New Delhi: Deendayal Research Institute, 1986, p. 302)

[2] Among other things, the Act declares illegal any attempt to prevent members of the Scheduled Castes, on the ground of Untouchability, from entering temples, shops and restaurants, to practise some occupations, to use public wells or other sources of water, public accommodation, transport, hospitals, educational institutions and to wear jewellery.

The reservation policy: the smokescreen of the egalitarian discourse

During the British Raj quotas were first granted to the Scheduled Castes in educational institutions and the government services. As early as 1892, a network of schools reserved for the Untouchables was established. It enabled the state to boost the community's literacy rate to 6.7 and 4.8% respectively for boys and girls by 1921. The British pursued such programmes of affirmative action till 1947.[3] Their policy was even more ambitious where the state bureaucracy was concerned. In 1934 the Government reserved 25% of vacancies in the administration to Muslims and 8.3% to other minorities, including the Scheduled Castes, who then represented 12.5% of the population according to the Census. The latter quota was increased to this level – 12.5% – in June 1946 in order to observe a notion of proportionality.[4] This measure was extended by the first Indian government and, as the proportionality principle continued to apply, the Scheduled Castes quota was increased to 15% when the 1951 census indicated this to be their share of the population. The same quota was implemented in educational institutions.

However, most of these quotas remained unfulfilled, allegedly because of a lack of good candidates, but also because of a lack of goodwill among those in charge of recruitment.[5] In 1961, the Scheduled Castes represented 1% to 2% of the graduates of one age class[6] and, according to Galanter, only 6% of them really benefited from the redistributive effect of quotas.[7] As evident from Table 3.1, the quotas were only fulfilled in the two lower categories of the administration in the 1950s and 1960s, which meant that the lot of the Scheduled Castes changed very little. For instance, sweepers employed by the administration in the class 4 category come mostly from the Untouchable Bhangi caste.

[3] In 1944, for instance, a sum of Rs 300,000 for five years were disbursed for financing scholarships for low caste and Scheduled Castes students. (B.A.V. Sharma, 'Development of reservation policy' in B.A.V. Sharma and K.M. Reddy (eds), *Reservation Policy in India*, New Delhi: Light and Light Publishers, 1982, pp. 18–19)

[4] Ibid., pp. 2–3.

[5] M. Galanter, *Competing Equalities – Law and the Backward Classes in India*, Delhi: Oxford University Press, (1984) 1991, p. 94.

[6] Ibid., p. 61.

[7] Ibid., p. 108.

Table 3.1. DISTRIBUTION OF SCHEDULED CASTES IN CENTRAL GOVERNMENT SERVICES, 1953–87 (%)

	1953	*1961*	*1963*	*1967*	*1974*	*1980*	*1987*
Class 1	0.53	1.2	1.78	2.08	3.2	4.95	8.23
Class 2	1.29	2.5	2.98	3.1	4.6	8.54	10.47
Class 3	4.52	7.2	9.24	9.33	10.3	13.44	14.46
Class 4	20.52	17.2	17.15	18.18	18.6	19.46	20.09

Sources: The Commissioner for Scheduled Castes and Scheduled Tribes, *Report – volume 1*, New Delhi: Udyogshala, 1969 cited in S.N. Dubey and Usha Mathur, 'Welfare Programmes for Scheduled Castes. Content and Administration', *EPW*, 22 Jan. 1972, p. 167 (for 1961 and 1967) and cited in O. Mendelsohn and M. Vicziany, *The Untouchables: Subordination, Poverty and the State in Modern India*, Cambridge University Press, 1998, p. 135 (for all the other years).

Twenty years after independence, in 1967, the Indian state had far from satisfactorily implemented positive discrimination programmes. The quota for the Scheduled Castes was fulfilled in the fourth class only. In the higher echelons of the central administration they were very poorly represented. The same gap was obvious in the Public Sector Undertakings which were also covered by the reservation system.[8] By contrast, quotas in the assemblies were strictly implemented but they only contributed to the dependence of Scheduled Castes on upper-caste-dominated Congress.

Reservations and Politics. The fact that the reservation policies did not help the Scheduled Castes as much as it should have done must be considered in a wider context. It reflects the fundamental bias that hampered the entire reservation policy from the outset. Even in the colonial period the Congress party tried to down play the impact of reservations on Indian society, a reason that was mirrored in the conflict between Gandhi and Ambedkar. This dispute was eventually settled by the Poona Pact in terms which favoured the former's preferred option: in contrast to separate electorates, the new reservation

[8] In 1969, only 0.16% of class 1 employees were from the Scheduled Castes, 0.5% in class 2, 4.2% in class 3 and 12.8% in class 4. The Commissioner for Scheduled Castes and Scheduled Tribes, *Report*, vol. 1, New Delhi: Udyogshala, 1969 cited in S.N. Dubey and Usha Mathur, 'Welfare Programmes for Scheduled Castes. Content and Administration', *EPW*, 22 Jan. 1972, p. 167.

system did not allow the Scheduled Castes to designate their representatives. The Poona Pact did establish a Scheduled Castes electoral college charged with nominating in each constituency the four Scheduled Caste candidates who were then allowed to contest the elections. Thus the Scheduled Castes exerted a veto during the primary elections, but thereafter the successful Scheduled Castes candidate was inevitably elected in large part by the other castes since they were not a majority in any constituency. The Poona Pact also prevented the Scheduled Castes from winning representation that was proportional to their number. The 1935 Government of India Act gave them only 7 seats out of 156 in the Council of State, 19 out of 250 in the Central Assembly and 151 out of 1,585 in the different Provincial Legislative Assemblies.[9]

Naturally, the Constituent Assembly examined the matter closely – specially after Ambedkar, Nehru's Law Minister, was appointed Chairman of the Drafting Committee. Influential Hindu traditionalist leaders such as K.M. Munshi, who was also a member of the Drafting Committee, Seth Govind Das, Rajendra Prasad (the Assembly President) and Vallabhbhai Patel rejected any kind of separate electorate because, to use Munshi's words, which recalled Gandhi's arguments in 1932, they were 'part and parcel of Hindu community'.[10] Another Assembly Member even mentioned the fact that people had to consider 'the Scheduled Castes as belonging to Hindus [sic]'.[11] They all wanted to preserve the reservation system. However one of Ambedkar's disciples, S. Nagappa,[12] proposed an alternative, according to which in constituencies reserved to Scheduled Castes, these candidates winning not only a majority but also more than 35%

[9] For the provincial breakdown, see B.A.V. Sharma, 'Development of reservation policy', op. cit., pp. 15–16.

[10] Speech by K.M. Munshi, on 27 Aug. 1947, *CAD*, vol. V, op. cit., p. 227.

[11] Speech by S.L. Saksena, ibid., p. 235.

[12] Sardar Nagappa, a Mala from Andhra Pradesh, had joined Congress in 1930 and had been elected in Madras Assembly in 1937 and 1946. Within the Constituent Assembly he was the convenor of the Scheduled Castes members. In Delhi, he lived close to Ambedkar's house and saw him quite often: it is because of Ambedkar that he presented his project of 'qualified joint electorate'. Nagappa unsuccessfully contested the 1952 elections as a candidate of the Kisan Mazdoor Praja Party and then rejoined Congress. (R.K. Kshirsagar, *Dalit Movement in India and its Leaders*, New Delhi: MD Publications, 1994, pp. 282–3).

of the Untouchables' votes could be declared the victors. For Nagappa, such a system would have given more legitimacy to the Scheduled Caste MPs and MLAs:

> . . .today, if we are elected to reserved seats, when there is agrarian trouble, when the Harijans and the agriculturists are at loggerheads and when we go and appeal to these people, these Harijans, they say 'Get out man, you are the henchmen and show-boys of the Caste Hindus. You have sold our community and you have come here on their behalf in order to cut our throats. We don't accept you as our representative'. Sir, in order to avoid that, what I suggested is that a certain percentage of the Harijans must elect the candidate so that he may be able to tell them that he has the backing of some Harijans and he will have the prestige and voice as their representative.[13]

Upper caste assembly members reacted angrily to the proposal, all the more so as Ambedkar was absent. His name topped the list of the four assembly members who had supported Nagappa's amendment, but he had not come in person to defend it. Ambedkar had probably no hope of having it passed since a very similar proposal he had tabled in the sub-committee on minorities had been defeated. It held that non Scheduled Castes Hindu candidates should, before being declared elected, poll a minimum number of votes from among the minority communities, including the Scheduled Castes. Ambedkar alone voted for this resolution. Congressmen objected that it amounted to a reintroduction of the separate electorates through the back door, whereas Independent India ought to rid itself of such divisive influences. The sub-committee decided by a majority of 28 to 3 that there should be no separate electorates.[14] Nagappa's amendment caused the same kind of reactions in the Constituent Assembly[15] and Patel was swift to seal its fate:

[13] Speech on 28 Aug. 1947, *CAD*, vol. V, op. cit., p. 259.

[14] On the sub-committee's debates, see, B. Shiva Rao (ed.), *The Framing of India's Constitution. Select Documents*, vol. 2, Bombay: The Indian Institute of Public Administration, 1967, pp. 398–8 ff. H.J. Khandekar, another Mahar member of the Constituent Assembly who had opposed Ambedkar since the 1930s when he had supported Gandhi against the demand for separate electorates, congratulated himself in the assembly that Ambedkar had 'given up the idea of separate electorates and [that] he voted for the joint electorates in the meeting of the Advisory Sub-Committee' (*CAD*, vol. XI, op. cit., p. 741).

[15] See the much acclaimed speech by D. Velayudan, ibid., vol. V, p. 263.

So far as the Scheduled Castes are concerned, I do not think very much has to be said on this amendment, because I got a representation from a large majority of the Scheduled Castes representatives in this house, except one or two or three, that they are all against this amendment [Hear, Hear], and Mr Nagappa knew about it. But Mr Nagappa wanted to move his amendment to fulfil a promise or undertaking or at least to show his community that he was not purchased by the majority community! Well, he has done his job, but other people took him seriously and took a lot of time.[16]

Such an ironical speech substantiated Nagappa's plea: the Congress party expected nothing but docility from the Scheduled Castes. Patel even accused the Scheduled Castes of fomenting fissiparous tendencies:

To the Scheduled Castes friends, I also appeal: 'Let us forget what Dr Ambedkar or his group have done'. Let us forget what you did. You have very nearly escaped partition of the country again on your lines. You have seen the result of separate electorates in Bombay, that when the greatest benefactor of your community [Gandhi] came to Bombay to stay in Bhangi quarters it was your people who tried to stone his quarters. What was it? It was again the result of this poison, and therefore I resist this only because I feel that the vast majority of the Hindu population wish you well. Without them where will you be? Therefore secure their confidence and forget that you are a Scheduled Caste [. . .] those representatives of the Scheduled Castes must know that the Scheduled Castes must be effaced altogether from our society, and if it is to be effaced, those who have ceased to be untouchables and sit amongst us have to forget that they are untouchables or else if they carry this inferiority complex, they will not be able to serve their community.[17]

In other words, Patel is telling the Scheduled Castes that they should be ashamed of their demands, amounting to separatism, while their real hero, Gandhi, strove to keep the nation united. For Patel, it is up to the Scheduled Castes to regain the trust of the upper castes. The problem is psychological: the Scheduled Castes must erase their inferiority complex.

Eventually, the Constitution established a system of reserved seats for ten years, which has been extended every ten years ever since. The primary elections system was abolished, a decision which deprived the Scheduled Castes of a crucial political leverage. Article 330 (2)

[16] Speech on 28 Aug. 1947, in *CAD*, vol. V, op. cit., p. 270.
[17] Ibid., p. 272.

simply established quotas for the Scheduled Castes and the Scheduled Tribes in proportion to population, but their implementation took many different forms. In the reserved constituencies where the Scheduled Castes and Scheduled Tribes were in a majority, the seat would be automatically reserved for them. So far as the former were concerned, in 1952, it was the case for only 3 seats (all in West Bengal) and only one in 1957.[18] Most of the quota was filled with 'double' constituencies where SC/STs were not in a majority. However, these double constituencies were located in areas where the Scheduled Castes and Scheduled Tribes were comparatively numerous. There, two MLAs (or two MPs) were returned: one from the non-SC/non-ST candidates, the other one from the SC/ST candidates. So far as the Scheduled Castes were concerned, the system worked as follows: in 15% of the constituencies, where the Scheduled Castes were numerous, two seats were contested (in a very few constituencies a third seat was reserved to a Tribal) and each voter had two ballots (exceptionally three). Even if none of the Scheduled Castes candidates received the largest or the second largest number of votes, the one who had most votes among them won the reserved seat. However, if two Scheduled Castes (or Scheduled Tribes) candidates came first, they won both seats, as happened in 1957 in a constituency in Andhra Pradesh where one of the two seats was reserved for the Scheduled Tribes. Two tribal candidates came first and were elected whereas the third was V.V. Giri, an influential – Brahmin – Congress leader who became President of India in 1969. He brought the case before the Supreme Court, which upheld the election results as pronounced by the Election Commission.[19] The system was modified before the 1962 elections, ostensibly because the double consituencies were huge, but obviously because Giri's defeat had shown that both seats could be won by SC or ST candidates.

Since 1961 there have been only single constituencies. In 15% of them, where the Scheduled Castes are numerically predominant, candidates can only come from that community. Under the 1961 delimitation of parliamentary constituencies, 75 seats were reserved for representation by the Scheduled Castes. The proportion of the

[18] Election Commission, *Report on the second general elections in India, 1957*, vol. 1, New Delhi, 1959, p. 59 and Election Commission, *Report on the third general elections in India, 1962*, vol. 1, New Delhi, 1965, p. 7.

[19] Ibid., p. 8.

population made up of these castes in these constituencies varied considerably, but they never formed a majority, as is evident from the following table:

Table 3.2. DISTRIBUTION OF CONSTITUENCIES RESERVED FOR SCHEDULED CASTES IN 1961

% of Scheduled Castes	*No. of constituencies*
0-10	4
10-20	25
20-30	33
30-40	10
40-50	3

Moreover, 75% of the Scheduled Castes were in non-reserved constituencies.[20] A coalition of high and intermediate castes could thus return a Scheduled Caste candidate even if the Scheduled Castes chose not to vote for him. Congress had clearly become adept at co-opting Scheduled Caste leaders and getting them elected by mobilising non-Scheduled Castes voters. Galanter emphasises:

> The design of the legislative reservations – the dependence on outside parties for funds and organisations and the need to appeal to constituencies made up overwhelmingly of others – tends to produce compliant and accommodating leaders rather than forceful articulators of the interests of these groups.[21]

One of the Scheduled Caste leaders co-opted by the Congress, Jagjivan Ram, admitted that 'since one had to depend on the non-Scheduled Caste vote, one went along with the fortunes of the party'.[22]

Jagjivan Ram, Stooge of the Congress? Jagjivan Ram (1908–86) was a Chamar from Bihar whose family, as did Ambedkar's, benefited from the British policy of recruiting Scheduled Castes in the army – his father worked in a military hospital. Mendlsohn and Vicziany, who investigated the social background of successful Dalit leaders,

[20] M. Galanter, 'Compensatory discrimination in political representation', *EPW*, 14 (7–8), Feb. 1979, pp. 438–9.

[21] Galanter, *Competing Equalities*, op. cit., p. 549.

[22] Interview cited in F. Frankel, 'Caste, land and dominance in Bihar', op. cit., p. 83.

underlined that 'his and an employed brother's steady income was the basis for the growing prosperity for the family'.[23] He established the Ravidas Mahasabha in 1928 while studying in Calcutta. His objective was to unite the Untouchables – even though Ravidas was a tutelary figure for the Chamars only – and to engender social reform via sanskritization, rather than through the radicalism Ambedkar was advocating at that time: he exhorted the Depressed Classes 'to give up drinking and uncleanliness'.[24]

Jagjivan Ram joined Congress in 1930. He was inspired by Gandhi and was initiated into the party by Rajendra Prasad.[25] In September 1932, while Gandhi and Ambedkar were locked in conflict in Poona, Congressmen from Bihar – as Jagjivan Ram later recollected – 'sent telegrams to Mahatmaji intimating that I should represent *nationalist* Depressed Classes in the Poona parleys'.[26] He took part in the launch of the Bihar Anti-Untouchability League (Harijan Sevak Sangh) and Rajendra Prasad appointed him as secretary of the organisation. In this capacity he accompanied Gandhi on his Bihar tour in 1934.[27] Jagjivan Ram was promoted by Congress as a counterweight to the growing influence of Ambedkar. In 1934 the Depressed Classes League was established during the annual meeting of the Ravidas Mahasabha, clearly with the aim of balancing Ambedkar's movement. In 1935, the organisation was officially established in a meeting in Kanpur where Jagjivan Ram was appointed one of its secretaries. The objectives of the All India Depressed Classes League then reflected the Gandhian social programme and a sense of sanskritisation. For instance, it aimed (1) 'to promote good understanding and the spirit of genuine co-operation between the Scheduled Castes and other sections', (2) 'to act in union with the rest in order to develop healthy nationalism and evolve a well knit and compact body of Hindus' and (3) 'to take steps for improving their [the Depressed Classes'] religious, moral, educational, social

[23] Mendelsohn and Vicziany, *The Untouchables*, op. cit., p. 252.

[24] R.K. Kshirsagar, *Dalit Movement in India and its Leaders (1857–1956)*, New Delhi: MD Publications, 1994, p. 311.

[25] His biographer writes that 'when he came into contact with Dr Rajendra Prasad, he became a Gandhian' (ibid., p. 311).

[26] J. Ram, *Caste Challenge in India*, New Delhi: Vision Books, 1980, p. 44, emphasis added.

[27] Ibid., p. 45.

and political rights'.[28] In 1936, Ram became president of the Depressed Classes League. The Congress was so badly in need of a Scheduled Caste leader that his rise through the ranks was very rapid. A member of the Bihar Legislative Assembly in 1937, he was immediately appointed Parliamentary secretary.[29] He then became secretary of the Bihar Congress in 1940 and joined the All India Congress Committee. The fact that he was used by Congress to counteract Ambedkar was made explicit in 1946 when he led a delegation to the British Cabinet Mission, to present 'the view point of Nationalist Harijans and repudiate [. . .] the claim of Dr. Ambedkar and his organisation [. . .] to be the representative organisation of Harijans in India'.[30] Ram systematically contrasted the 'National Harijans' to the separatists who followed Ambedkar. In September 1946 he joined the Government – which Ambedkar would join only in August 1947. Ram kept one portfolio or another till the 1970s, remaining a key figure of the Congress Working Committee from 1948 till the mid-1970s; he even became President of Mrs Gandhi's Congress (R) in 1969.

Jagjivan Ram was co-opted by Congress because of his personal qualities – his intelligence and his energy – but also because his views on society were in tune with those of the upper caste leadership. He naturally projected himself – and was projected by the Congress – as a Scheduled Caste leader and the protector of the lower castes. And this is of course one of the reasons why he became an all India leader capable of attracting mass support. But his ideas were much less radical than those of Ambedkar and some of them even echoed Gandhi's organicist view of society. This is evident from the memorandum he

[28] Munshilal Gautam, *Bapusaheb Rajbhoj – In Search of Buddhist Identity*, Aligarh: Siddhartha Gautam Sikshan and Sanskriti Samiti, 1995, p. 16. Rajbhoj was the other secretary of the movement. Another indication of Jagjivan Ram's willingness to be associated with upper-caste dominated programmes was his participation in the meeting of the Hindu Mahasabha held under the presidentship of Madan Mohan Malaviya at Pune in December 1935 where he moved a resolution demanding that the Scheduled Castes should have access to the temples, schools, wells etc. (R.K. Kshirsagar, *Dalit Movement in India and its Leaders*, op. cit., p. 312)

[29] Rajendra Prasad, *Autobiography*, New Delhi: National Book Trust, 1994 (1957), p. 443.

[30] *The India and Pakistan Year's Book and Who's Who*, Bombay: Times of India, 1949, p. 800.

prepared for the sub-committee on Fundamental Rights of the Constituent Assembly. He opposed Ambedkar's demand for separate electorates and asked instead for 'joint electorates with the caste Hindus'. Indeed, he wanted 'to accelerate the assimilation of the other [other than racial and religious] minorities (such as the Scheduled Castes) in the parent body by bringing them to an equal level with others in that community'.[31] Ram's desire for social integration in the majority community and the metaphor of the body he alludes to suggest that he was imbued with the sanskritisation framework. He demanded reserved seats proportionate to the Scheduled Castes population in the assemblies, the administration and the executive. But he emphasised that these safeguards 'may be eliminated as soon as untouchability totally disappears'. For him, it would be the case '(i) when all Hindu temples are open to all castes [. . .], (ii) when water or eatables of any caste shall not be polluted by the touch of any other caste of the Hindu society, (iii) when in all religious and social functions of the Hindus, persons of all castes of Hindus may participate without any discrimination'.[32] The three criteria he uses to define Untouchability recall Gandhi's views since they centre on the religious dimension of the problem. The promotion of inter-caste marriages, that many social reformers advocated as a means of fighting Untouchability and the caste system, are not even mentioned. The endogamous character of caste in fact was not a problem for Jagjivan Ram because he was not against the caste system as such.

In Ram's *Caste challenge in India* (1980) he writes that 'The division of society into classes or guilds, though to some extent hereditary in character, was unavoidable in the early stages of the evolution of society.'[33] He tends to assume that the caste system established a division of labour which did not imply a strict hierarchy. Ram emphasised that Gandhi 'wanted to forge a greater unity and integration [. . .] through the abolition of untouchability and the revival of the "Chaturvarnic" concept [the system based on the four *varnas*] in all its pristine purity. Men are born equal but they are also born with varying inclinations, temperaments, attitudes and aptitudes. Their spiritual growth differs. Instead of letting struggle and competition

[31] 'Reply to the questionnaire received from Jagjivan Ram, April 3, 1947' in B. Shiva Rao (ed.), *The Framing of the Indian Constitution*, vol. 2, op. cit., p. 331.

[32] Ibid., p. 335.

[33] Ram, *Caste Challenge in India*, op. cit., p. 8.

determine and categorise these differences, would it not be infinitely better, he argued, if the Chaturvarnya and heredity were accepted as the law of nature and as the supreme regulatory principle of social life.'[34] Ram approved of this approach. According to him it was effective: because Gandhi 'did not start by challenging the basic assumptions behind the four-fold division of Indian society, and yet succeeded to a considerable extent, in shaking the very foundations of the system. The work begun by him has to be carried on'.[35] In contrast to Ambedkar, who converted to Buddhism, Ram praises Hinduism where 'There is the humanist and democratic assertion that man is the measure of everything, that all men are born free and equal, that the human personality is divine and unique'.[36] Such ideological stands suited the Congress leadership.

Most Scheduled Castes leaders co-opted by the Congress party shared the views of Jagjivan Ram but none of them benefited from the same upward mobility in the party apparatus. Ram was a useful exception who gave his caste brothers the illusion that such a rise to power was possible. In Uttar Pradesh, for instance, Brass underlines that 'The Scheduled Castes leaders who have been given Congress tickets in the reserved constituencies are non-militant and have no power in the local or state Congress organisations.[37] This analysis is substantiated by the caste composition of the Congress cadres and governments in Uttar Pradesh – and also in Madhya Pradesh, Rajasthan and Bihar – that was analysed in the preceding chapter.

Most Congress MPs elected in seats reserved to the Scheduled Castes can be qualified the same way as Brass did for local leaders. A survey conducted in 1962–4 showed that almost half of them did not utter a word in the Lok Sabha during this period, whereas only one fourth of those returned in general constituencies remained so tight-lipped.[38] When they spoke, they rarely dealt with

[34] Ibid., p. 42.

[35] Ibid., p. 20.

[36] Ibid., p. 16.

[37] P. Brass, *Factional Politics in an Indian State: the Congress Party in Uttar Pradesh*, Berkeley: University of California Press, 1966, p. 105. Brass adds that 'The numerous organisations in Uttar Pradesh for the advancement of the Scheduled Castes and "depressed classes" have been content to serve as agencies for the distribution of Congress patronage (ibid.).'

[38] M. Galanter, 'Compensatory discrimination in political representation', op. cit., p. 445. However, Galanter points out that Scheduled Caste MPs defend

crucial matters. For instance, there was no pressure exerted in the assembly to speed up the vote of the *Prevention of Atrocities against Scs/STs Act* which took place only in 1989! In fact, the two main consequences of the reservation system were the formation of a small elite which would otherwise have remained much more embryonic (the Rajya Sabha – in which there was no reservation – had only 13 Scheduled Caste members out of 228 in the 1960s) and the defence of collective interests. For instance Scheduled Caste MPs prevented the state from removing certain castes from the list of the Scheduled Castes, as some upper caste politicians demanded, by claiming that they were benefiting from upward mobility. On the other hand, they managed to include Dalit converts to Buddhism and even Christians among the Scheduled Castes eligible for scholarships (which were once reserved for Hindus or Sikhs).[39] But it took till 1990 for Dalits who converted to Buddhism to become eligible for reserved seats in the assemblies and quotas in the administration.

All in all, the Scheduled Caste MPs achieved little on behalf of their community. Nor did they pressure the government as they ought to have done had they been accountable to a separate electorate of Scheduled Caste voters. Finally the reservation system provided hardly any incentive for Scheduled Castes MPs or MLAs to foster the political consciousness of their caste fellows since they depended upon other voters to sustain their careers, especially after the abolition of the primary elections.

What party for the Scheduled Castes?

Ambedkar launched his first political party, the Independent Labour Party, in 1936. As its name suggests it did not confine its appeal to the Scheduled Castes. Ambedkar explained that 'The word "Labour" is used instead of the words "Depressed Classes" because labour includes the Depressed Classes as well'.[40] Indeed, the Scheduled Castes

---

material interests – such as university grants and subsidies – of their fellow caste members when they are in jeopardy.

[39] G. Narayana, 'Rule making for Scheduled Castes: Analysis of Lok Sabha Debates, 1962–1971', *EPW*, 15 (8), 23 Feb. 1980, pp. 433–40, and Galanter, 'Compensatory discrimination', op. cit., p. 444.

[40] *Independent Labour Party – Its Formation and its Aims,* Reprinted from the

only appeared under the guise of labourers in the party's 'aims and objectives', of which large sections were devoted to economic issues. State-sponsored industrialisation was presented as the top priority. The ILP also demanded labour laws to protect factory workers and improved educational facilities in technical institutions. The party even tried to project itself almost as a spokesman for the 'lower middle class',[41] of whom very few were Dalits. The word 'caste' appeared only in the last item of the ILP's programme: 'The party will also endeavour to prevent the administration from becoming the monopoly of any single caste or community. Consistently with efficiency of administration, the party will endeavour to bring about a fair admixture of all caste [sic] and communities in the administration of the Presidency'.[42]

This emphasis on socio-economic issues did not reflect socialist influences. Ambedkar always regarded Marxist-inspired ideologies as irrelevant to India. In *Annihilation of Caste*, he pointed out that 'Caste system is not merely a division of labour. *It is also a division of labourers*',[43] a formula directly derived from his notion of 'graded inequality'. Whereas socialism regards the class position *vis-à-vis* the means of production as the main criterion for analysis, for Ambedkar the root-cause of social domination lies in the caste hierarchy.[44] His main priority, therefore, was to unite the castes belonging to the same class but which regarded each other as ordered according to their respective status.

There was an evident contradiction between the ILP's programme and the caste-centred discourse of Ambedkar: on the one hand he pretended that his party represented the workers at large, on the other hand he did not recognise any substantive reality to this class and emphasised that caste was the basic unit of society. This contradiction emerged clearly in the 1937 elections. In Bombay Presidency, the ILP nominated 17 candidates – 13 in reserved constituencies (where 11 of them won) and 4 in general seats (where he gave tickets

---

Times of India (15th Aug. 1936), Bombay, Independent Labour Publications, no. 1, 1937, p. 3 in Ambedkar Papers (NMML), Reel no. 2, File no. 9.

[41] Ibid., p. 5.

[42] Ibid., p. 8.

[43] B.R. Ambedkar, *Annihilation of Caste*, New Delhi: Arnold Publishers, 1990, p. 47.

[44] Ibid., p. 42.

to high caste people, out of which 3 were successful).[45] Most ILP candidates were from the Scheduled Castes, and more especially from the Mahars. There was only one Mang (rope maker) and one Scheduled Caste candidate from Gujarat. The Chambhars (leather workers), whose socio-economic level was higher, were not represented on this list. For them, as for the Mangs, Ambedkar was a leader of the Mahars and the ILP represented this caste.

With 10 members in the Legislative Assembly of Bombay Presidency, the ILP became the second largest opposition party, behind the Muslim League. But it remained a marginal force, confined largely to Bombay. Ambedkar paid little heed to organisation, so much so, as suggested by his biographer, that the party relied mainly on his charisma:

> Ambedkar did not try to organise his political party on modern lines. He had no taste for individual organisation. There were no regular annual conferences, or general meetings of the organisations with which he was connected. Where and when he sat was the venue of conference and the time for decision. The President or the Secretary or the Working Committee had to fall in line with his arrangement. His followers were attracted to him by his integrity, ability, sacrifice and learning.[46]

In addition to these weaknesses, the party could scarcely claim to represent the working class when its cadres all came from the Scheduled Castes, and many Kunbis gradually distanced themselves from the party for this reason.[47] All these factors contributed to the demise of the ILP and its replacement by the Scheduled Castes Federation.

The Scheduled Castes Federation (Dalit Federation in Marathi) was founded in July 1942. As evident from the party's name, Ambedkar had given up the idea of broadening his political base to encompass the working class and instead stressed the need to unify the

[45] E. Zelliot, 'Dr Ambedkar and the Mahar Movement', Ph.D. thesis, University of Pennsylvania, 1969, p. 249, and R.I. Duncan, 'Levels, the communication of programmes, and sectional strategies in Indian politics, with reference to the Bharatiya Kranti Dal and the Republican Party of India in Uttar Pradesh State and Aligarh district (UP)', Ph.D. thesis, University of Sussex, 1979, p. 214.

[46] D. Keer, *Dr Ambedkar Life and Mission*, Bombay: Popular Prakashan, 1992 [first edn 1954], p. 480.

[47] G. Omvedt, *Dalits and the Democratic Revolution: Dr Ambedkar and the Dalit Movement in Colonial India*, New Delhi: Sage, 1994, p. 207.

Scheduled Castes across India. Scheduled Castes were presented as a minority, like the Muslims. One of the resolutions of the SCF Working Committee in September 1944 at Madras even emphasised that 'the Scheduled Castes are a distinct and separate element in the national life of India and that they are a religious minority in a sense far more real than the Sikhs and Muslims can be. . .'.[48] Thus the SCF not only demanded separate electorates but also a separate home land.[49] Another resolution pledged that the SCF would not accept Constitution that did not enshrine the following demands: a separate electorate for the Scheduled Castes, statutory representation within the executive system and villages reserved for them alone.[50] Ambedkar told his followers: 'You should realise what our object is [. . .] It is not fighting for a few jobs and for a few conveniences. It is the biggest cause that we have ever cherished in our hearts. That is to see that we are recognised as the Governing community'.[51] At a meeting organised by a railworkers union in Madras he said in the same vein that 'The capture of political power is far more important than organising trade unions'.[52] The SCF was established to achieve this end but the 1945–6 elections revealed how unrealistic this aim was. The SCF lost heavily in both the Legislative Assembly and Constituent Assembly elections gaining only two seats in the Legislative

[48] 'Political demands of Scheduled Castes – Resolutions passed by the Working Committee of the All-India Scheduled Caste Federation', App. XI to B.R. Ambedkar, *What Congress and Gandhi have done to the untouchables* in *Dr Babasaheb Ambedkar: Writings and Speeches*, vol. 9, Bombay: Government of Maharashtra, 1990, pp. 346–7.

[49] As early as 1926, Ambedkar had pointed out that the Untouchables should seek a separate homeland. In 1929 he had even expressed his readiness to visit Sind and the state of Indore – whose Maharajah he knew well – in order to find suitable sites for resettlement. (D. Keer, *Dr Ambedkar*, op. cit., pp. 63, 128)

[50] The SCF demanded that the government should include representatives 'from [the] general community and from [the] minority communities in a proportion to be specified in the Constitution' and that the Constitution provided 'for the transplantation of the Scheduled Castes from their present habitations and form separate Scheduled Caste villages away from and independent of Hindu villages'. ('Political demands of Scheduled Castes – Resolutions passed by the Working Committee of the All-India Scheduled Caste Federation', App. XI to B.R. Ambedkar, *What Congress and Gandhi have done to the Untouchables*, op. cit., p. 353)

[51] *The Liberator* (Madras) 26 Sept. 1944.

[52] Ibid., 24 Sept. 1944.

Assemblies, one in Bengal, the other in the Central Provinces and Berar. This setback largely reflected the party's weak organisation but also the voting system. The SCF had won more votes than the Congress in Bombay Presidency, the Central Provinces and Berar and Madras Presidency during the primary elections when the Scheduled Castes were the only voters, but the Congress succeeded in winning more seats thanks to non-Scheduled Castes voters.[53] In North India too some SCF candidates won the primary elections. In the United Provinces they achieved successes in Agra, Allahabad, Kanpur and, as far as the rural constituencies were concerned, Rae Bareli and Sitapur. But the party did not win a single seat, even if their results were encouraging in Agra where it received 21.9% of the valid votes and Kanpur where it got 11.1%.[54]

The first general elections after Independence, in 1951–2 brought no improvement in the SCF's fortunes. It won only two Lok Sabha seats, one in Hyderabad and the other in the Province of Bombay, where Ambedkar failed to gain a seat. He now realised that the Scheduled Castes would never be able to win power alone. The SCF had certainly sharpened their political consciousness, but it had also cut them off from other social groups and possible allies. In one of his last meetings, in Nagpur in October 1956 – he was to die two months later – Ambedkar suggested that the Scheduled Castes Federation should be dissolved and a new party formed instead. He invited party workers to forge links with leaders from non-Dalit communities. In fact he had already made overtures to socialist leaders, in 1954, and contested the Bhandera by-election on the same ticket as Ashok Mehta, the former General Secretary of the Praja Socialist Party. Ambedkar clearly wanted the SCF's successor to forge alliances with the socialists against Congress and the Communist Party.[55]

Even though it was officially founded in October 1957, ten

[53] *Jai Bhim* (Madras), 5 March 1946; Ambedkar papers, Reel 1/2; and E. Zelliot, 'Learning the use of political means: the Mahars of Maharashtra' in R. Kothari (ed.), *Caste in Indian Politics*, Hyderabad: Orient Longman, 1970, p. 53.

[54] P.D. Reeves, B.D. Graham and J.M. Goodman, *A Handbook to Elections in Uttar Pradesh 1920–50*, Delhi: Manohar, 1975, pp. 315-38.

[55] He was very worried that the CPI was attracting Scheduled Caste voters (J. Gokhale, *From Concessions to Confrontation: The Politics of an Indian Untouchable Community*, Bombay: Popular Pradesham, 1993, p. 216).

months after Ambedkar's death, the Republican Party of India nevertheless bore his stamp, and it returned to the grand design of the ILP, namely to represent all the poor not just the Scheduled Castes. Its constitution assigned it the mission to 'engage itself in organizing the down trodden masses of India particularly the Buddhists [mainly Mahar converts], Scheduled Castes, Scheduled Tribes and other Backward Classes'.[56]

According to Ambedkar, diluting the Dalit identity of the party would enable the RPI to make alliances, a project that started to materialise during the 'linguistic states' controversy. Initially Ambedkar had been hostile to the redrawing of the administrative map of the Bombay Presidency because the establishment of states speaking Gujarati, Marathi, Kannada and Telugu would have strengthened the dominant castes. In Maharashtra, for instance, the Marathas would have become the largest caste, by far, and reasserted their influence over the Scheduled Castes. However, regional feelings were such in Maharashtra that Ambedkar joined the communists and the socialists within the Samyukta Maharashtra Samiti (Committee for a United Maharashtra) which was intended to pressure the Government into creating a new Marathi-speaking province from the old Bombay Presidency. Ambedkar made this pragmatic alliance with the SMS in November 1956.

This agreement and the popularity of the linguistic state partly explained that the RPI was relatively successful during the 1957 elections. It won 4 Lok Sabha seats in the Province of Bombay (of which 2 were reserved for the Scheduled Castes) and 15 assembly seats. During the municipal elections, it won in 12 wards of Bombay and one of Ambedkar's lieutenants, P.T. Borale, became mayor. In the 1962 elections, the RPI expanded beyond Maharashtra, the state which was eventually created in 1960.

Even though Maharashtra remained the RPI's stronghold in terms of valid votes, it was in Uttar Pradesh that the party won most of seats. The main architect of the RPI in UP was Chhedi Lal Sathi, who was born in a poor, Kewat (fishing caste) family but educated and taken care of by Congress leaders: he was first a typist in the UP Congress office, secretary to Lal Bahadur Shastri, and then secretary to G.V. Pant when he was Chief Minister. Ambedkar attracted him into the

[56] Cited in Duncan, *Levels*, op. cit., p. 236.

Table 3.3. RPI ELECTION RESULTS, 1962 AND 1967
(*no. of seats and % of valid votes*)

	1962		*1967*	
	Lok Sabha	*Vidhan Sabha*	*Lok Sabha*	*Vidhan Sabha*
Andhra Pradesh	0 (0.96)	0 (0.40)	0 (0.50)	1 (0.27)
Bihar	–	–	–	1 (0.18)
Gujarat	0 (0.89)	0 (0.41)	0 (2.02)	0 (0.08)
Haryana	–	–	0 (2.32)	2 (2.9)
Himachal Pradesh	0 (6.56)	–	0 (2.33)	–
Karnataka	0 (3.86)	0 (0.82)	0 (3.1)	1 (0.77)
Punjab	0 (6.25)	0 (2.15)	0 (2.63)	3 (1.79)
Madhya Pradesh	0 (1.84)	0 (1.26)	0 (1.70)	0 (0.84)
Maharashtra	0 (11.66)	3 (5.38)	0 (12.71)	5 (6.66)
Rajasthan	–	–	0 (0.18)	0 (0.13)
Tamil Nadu	0 (1.54)	0 (0.45)	0 (0.20)	0 (0.20)
Uttar Pradesh	3 (4.27)	8 (3.74)	1 (4.07)	10 (4.14)
West Bengal	–	–	0 (0.66)	0 (0.01)

SCF in 1952 and he become the first president of the RPI in UP, a post he was to occupy till 1964.[57] In Uttar Pradesh the RPI polled well among Muslims who were distrustful of the Congress in the wake of the 1961 Aligarh riot, when the government had been lenient towards the Hindu assailants. The Muslims' response was to ally themselves with the Scheduled Castes against the upper castes who traditionally supported the Congress and the Jana Sangh.

In Aligarh district, the RPI won the Lok Sabha seat and two Vidhan Sabha seats in 1962. The new MP was B.P. Maurya, the son of an agricultural labourer from Khair, a *tehsil* of Aligarh district, who had learnt to read and write with a Catholic priest when he was still a child.[58] He joined Congress in 1941, after Gandhi and other leaders had visited Khair, but he met Ambedkar soon after in Delhi, and he realised that he was 'the real leader' because 'he knew our problems'.[59] In 1948 Maurya left Aligarh to pursue his studies in Agra, where he was associated with the Jatav movement (see below). He resigned from Congress and joined the SCF in 1948. He returned to Aligarh soon after and completed his L. Sc, LLB and LLM in Aligarh Muslim University where he became Assistant Professor of

[57] Interview with Chhedi Lal Sathi, Lucknow, 20 August 2000.

[58] H.R. Isaac, *India's ex-Untouchables*, New York: Harper Torchbooks, 1964, pp. 70–1.

[59] Interview with B.P. Maurya, New Delhi, 15 Nov. 1997.

Constitutional Law in 1960. In the meantime he had become the most popular leader of the RPI in Uttar Pradesh. He contested the Aligarh Lok Sabha seat in 1957, and lost, but won in 1962. Aligarh was a non-reserved seat and Maurya had been selected precisely because he had made a point of never contesting elections in reserved constituencies. He explains his success by the fact that he had been 'working day and night for 15 years among the landless labourers'. He also launched agitations, such as that to install a statue of Ambedkar in Parliament – he claims 300,000 people courted arrest throughout India. In April 1957, he had orchestrated a huge conversion meeting in which 100,000 Jatavs became Buddhists.[60] Such a mass conversion and the transformation of Hindu temples into Buddhist temples infuriated the upper castes. Riots followed and the police had to intervene. Maurya played a major part in the Jatav demonstration and he too was jailed. For Duncan 'By the beginning of the 1960s, Maurya had become the idol of the Jatavs of Aligarh district, his fame and reputation had spread to surrounding areas and he has well on the way to becoming a Scheduled Caste political leader of national status'.[61] It was no fluke that Maurya achieved such electoral success in Aligarh district, for it had the heaviest concentration of Chamars in Uttar Pradesh, accounting for 22% of the population. However, Maurya was able to broaden his base beyond his caste. True to the RPI's principles, he was persuaded that the Scheduled Castes had to ally with other groups, which is why he joined hands with Muslims who were disgruntled by Congress as exemplified in his 1962 election slogan: 'Jatav Muslim bhai bhai, Hindu kaum kahan se aye?', 'Jatavs and Muslims are brothers, where do the Hindus [community, nation] come from?'.[62] The coalition was the cornerstone of the RPI's success.

To consolidate its social base, the RPI emphasised socio-economic issues. In 1959 the party campaigned for land redistribution in Maharashtra.[63] In 1964, the fourth annual session of the party met

[60] He had become a Bhuddist in February 1957 in Aligarh and had therefore changed his name from Bhagwati Prasad Maurya to Buddha Priya Maurya.

[61] Duncan, *Levels*, op. cit., p. 274.

[62] Cited in ibid., p. 286. Another slogan was more aggressively directed against the upper castes: 'Thakur, Brahmans and Banyas, make their face black' (ibid.).

[63] On the Bhumiheen Satyagraha, see Gokhale, *From Concessions to Confrontation*, op. cit., pp. 225–6.

in Ahmedabad and again stressed this issue. Its Charter of Demands, published one year later, was also replete with economic issues: the implementation of the 1948 Minimum Wage Act, strict control of the distribution and prices of foodgrains, enlarging the recruitment of the Scheduled Castes and Scheduled Tribes in the government services etc.[64] The RPI's 1962 election manifesto also included demands for land nationalisation and the introduction of collectivised farming.[65]

This re-orientation of the party towards socio-economic issues dismayed the old Ambedkarites who still believed in the programme of the SCF, considered that the problems of the Scheduled Castes were absolutely specific and regretted that the RPI had diluted them in its programme.[66] This trend was especially disapproved of by B.K. Gaekwad (1902–71), a Mahar from Nasik district who had been asked by Ambedkar to organise the party in rural Maharashtra and who was regarded as its chief architect in the state. He was typical of the Mahar old guard, from a rural background and with little formal education, which insisted that the party should above all represent the Scheduled Castes. In the late 1950s they opposed the new generation of Dalit leaders who came from educated, urban background. B.C. Kamble – an advocate from Bombay – being the most notable of these.

Tensions were also due to factionalism: after the death of Ambedkar, the party underwent a leadership crisis which was all the more acute because he had not designated any successor. The conflict between Gaekwad and Kamble quickly transformed itself into a personal fight and led to the 1959 schism, Kamble forming the RPI (Durushta) which eventually merged with Congress.

Many other schisms followed. Ten years later, in 1969, Khobragade founded his own party after he was overlooked in favour of R.S. Gawai as the RPI (Gaekwad) candidate for the Maharashtra Legislative Assembly. Soon afterwards Gawai took over from Gaekwad at the helm of the party. Finally, Ambedkar's son, Bhaiyyasaheb, whose organisational skills were not his strongpoint, created his own party. By the early 1970s there were four RPIs – led by Gawai, Kamble, Khobragade and Ambedkar. Their rivalries had disastrous

[64] Duncan, *Levels*, op. cit., p. 245.

[65] Ibid., p. 251.

[66] Gokhale, *From Concessions to Confrontation*, op. cit., p. 220.

effects in electoral terms. In 1967, the two RPIs won 2.48% of the valid votes and only 5 assembly seats. In 1971–2, the three RPIs won one Lok Sabha seat but only 3 assembly seats. In both cases, these victories were confined to Maharashtra; the party had been routed everywhere else.

The RPI had also failed to expand because of caste politics. In Maharashtra it was still regarded as a Mahar party, and the other castes, especially the Chambhars stuck with the Congress. Their leaders opposed the Mahar Buddhist converts when they demanded reservations because they feared competition from a caste which was bigger than theirs and was already cornering most of the benefits from the reservation system.[67] In Uttar Pradesh the RPI was identified with the Chamars – more especially the Jatavs. Maurya himself prompted Muslim-Jatavs unity, without paying much attention to other Scheduled Castes.

All these handicaps were greatly aggravated by the Congress strategy of co-opting 'Untouchable notables' – to use Duncan's phrase. P.N. Rajbhoj was the first of Ambedkar's lieutenants to dissociate himself from his leader, in 1955. A Chamar by caste, Rajbhoj had been elected to the Municipal Council of Pune in 1928. He was first attracted by Gandhi and by 'Hindu' parties, such as the Hindu Mahasabha, which he joined in 1935 'with an avowed purpose of converting Chatur Varna society into Ekta Varna society'.[68] In 1935 he became Secretary – and co-founder with R.L. Biswas, M.C. Rajah and Jagjivan Ram – of the All India Depressed Classes League. He then took part in the Harijan Sevak Sangh but found considerable differences between its discourse and practice and consequently joined the ILP in 1940. Ambedkar then appointed him General Secretary of the SCF, in 1942, probably because he could balance the over-representation of Mahars among the office-bearers. He was elected MP from Sholapur in 1952 but left the SCF in 1955 to join the Congress party, which offered him a Rajya Sabha seat in 1957.

From the RPI, the first top leader who joined Congress was R.D.

[67] While they represented 35.11% of the Scheduled Caste population of Maharashtra, they received 82.83% of the total scholarships awarded to Scheduled Castes students in the state in 1967–8, while the Mangs – 33% of the Scheduled Castes population – received only 3.87% of the scholarships and the Chambhars – 22% of the SC population –, 10% of the scholarships. (Dubey and Mathur, 'Welfare Programmes for Scheduled Castes', op. cit., p. 170).

[68] Gautam, *Bapusaheb Rajbhoj*, op. cit., p. 11.

Bhandare (1916–88). A Mahar, Bhandare began his political career as a trade unionist and had been one of the first to join the SCF. He presided over the Bombay branch of the party. A co-founder of the RPI, he resisted Gaekwad's leadership and argued in favour of an RPI – Congress alliance. After joining Congress in 1966 he was appointed Governor of Bihar and then Andhra Pradesh.[69] In North India, B.P. Maurya shifted to the Congress in the early 1970s. He had been defeated as a RPI candidate in 1967. Then the party had lost heavily during the 1969 assembly elections. In the presidential elections that year, the RPI supported V.V. Giri, who eventually became Indira Gandhi's candidate. The Prime Minister called Maurya to finalise their collaboration and then asked him to join the Congress(R). As working president of the RPI he refused and instead proposed, an alliance, but Indira Gandhi told him that she wanted *him* in the party and hence he joined:

'I joined Congress because by that time there was no great opposition leader. No socialist. I joined Indira Gandhi against certain conditions which she fulfilled later: the preamble of the Constitution should refer to socialism; agricultural labourers should be guaranted minimal wages; land reform should be implemented. She agreed and I joined. She wanted me to become more civilised. I was very rough and tough so she sent me to the United States. When I came back she made me a Minister. I became close to her. And she has been very kind to me.'[70]

Maurya's justification of his shift from the RPI to Congress is revealing of the mechanisms of the co-option process: even though he claims that he had laid down his ideological pre-conditions for joining, these proved very shallow and he joined Indira Gandhi – rather than Congress – in order to obtain a ministerial post: he became Minister of State in the Ministry of Agriculture and Industry in 1974 – this was probably the real pre-condition. Before that, he had been given a Congress(R) ticket in 1971, in a non-reserved constituency, Hapur, where he had won with 62% of the valid votes. Interestingly, by the late 1960s he had already been subjected to 'the criticism now levelled at all the leaders that they are corrupt and open to bribes'.[71] Maurya – who was till then known 'for his fiery, witty,

[69] Kshirsagar, *Dalit Movement in India*, op. cit., p. 182.

[70] Interview with B.P. Maurya.

[71] O. Lynch, *The Politics of Untouchability: Social Mobility and Social Change in a City of India*, New York: Columbia University Press, 1969, p. 124.

and bitterly anti-Congress speeches'[72] – eventually adopted the Congress discourse on the Scheduled Castes: 'There is nothing like Dalit politics. This is a most confusing approach because Scheduled Castes and Scheduled Tribes are part and parcels of the entire society.' Such words echo Gandhi's analysis of the caste system and, indeed, Maurya remains respectful of the Mahatma.[73] Chhedi Lal Sathi followed the same route. He recounts how 'Mrs Gandhi came to (him) and said "We are in trouble; we are asking for socialism, so you join us, otherwise upper castes and the rich people will come" '. Sathi joined Congress in 1970 and became general secretary of the UP Congress in 1973.[74] The RPI was also affected by its attempts to ally itself with the Congress. In addition to Bhandare, in the late 1960s, Gaekwad and Maurya were favourably inclined towards such a policy. There was so much reluctance within the party that Gaekwad could only finalise a seat adjustment in 1971, when the RPI could only be a junior partner of the Congress. This relationship became even closer during the Emergency, when the RPI supported Indira Gandhi. In the 1977 elections, the main faction of the Ambedkarite movement, the RPI (Gawai), remained an ally of Congress, but it lost heavily, whereas the RPI (Khobragade) which had reached an agreement with the Janata Party and the Progressive Democratic Front –a regional party formed in Maharashtra by Congress dissidents – won alone Lok Sabha seat.

Far from emerging as a political force, the Scheduled Castes were marginalised politically during the first two decades of the Indian Republic, as the fate of Ambedkar's political parties testifies. They had a presence in the state apparatus thanks to compensatory discrimination programmes initiated by the British, but the quotas were not fulfilled – especially in the upper reaches of the administration. In the assemblies Scheduled Castes MPs and MLAs did not forcefully advocate the cause of their caste-mates since they were not accountable to them: there was not even one reserved constituency with a majority of Scheduled Castes voters.[75] In addition to these handicaps

[72] Ibid.

[73] Interview with B.P. Maurya.

[74] Interview with Chhedi Lal Sathi.

[75] Satish Saberwal draws the same conclusion from the situation prevailing in the Punjabi context: 'A constituency at the state level [. . .] would have a large

and most importantly, even before independence, the Congress had started co-opting Scheduled Caste leaders who were known for their Gandhian leanings, like Jagjivan Ram.

The Congress was thus successful in its attempts at containing the impact Ambedkar had started to make in the 1930s–1950s through political parties which oscillated between class-based mobilisations – like with the ILP and the RPI – and the defence of the Scheduled Castes alone. Ambedkar did not pay enough attention to the organisation of these parties and after his death nobody could succeed him with the same charisma and authority, so much so that the RPI also suffered from factional tensions. More importantly, the Congress became adept at co-opting RPI leaders and in negotiating seat adjustments with the party. This – initially – opposition force thus lost much credibility, and its leaders who defected to the Congress, like Maurya, toned down their militancy after they were accommodated in the power structure.

This Congress strategy was one of the reasons why it succeeded in attracting Scheduled Caste voters, who tended to cast their vote for individuals and follow their advice, irrespective of their party affiliation. The ruling party thus received support from groups which were poles apart in the social structure: besides a large number of upper castes (especially Brahmins), many Scheduled Castes people voted for it too. Brass described the Congress's support base as a 'coalition of extremes'.[76] Though very evocative, this phrase is misleading since it suggests that the two poles in question might command the same influence. In fact, the lower castes leaders within Congress depended on their upper caste patrons; the Congress system, in that sense, is a clientelistic arrangement.

---

majority of high caste voters, making the candidates less dependent upon – and therefore less responsive to – the Harijan vote. Support from high caste faction leaders is, therefore, crucial for success at this level [as well as at the level of the parliamentary constituency, one might argue].' (S. Saberwal, 'The Reserved Constituency. Candidates and consequences', *EPW*, 8 Jan. 1972, p. 79)

[76] P. Brass, 'The politicization of the peasantry in a North Indian state', *Journal of Peasant Studies* (hereafter *JPS*), 8 (1), Oct. 1980, pp. 3–36.

4

INDIRA GANDHI, THE POPULIST REPERTOIRE AND THE ABORTED REFORM OF CONGRESS

Nehru attempted to counter the conservative leanings of the Congress by launching the 'Kamaraj Plan' (named after the Tamil Nadu Chief Minister who monitored its operation), which was intended to revitalise the party by attracting new activists and restructuring its organisation. The plan enabled Nehru to ask for the resignation of 'rightist' ministers by arguing that they should be assigned new tasks in the process of reinvigorating the Congress party,[1] but its impact was limited because many senior party workers dragged their feet. Nehru died in 1964 and his successor, Lal Bahadur Shastri, 'was the creature of the party bosses who derived their power from the dominant landed groups that reorganisation would have displaced'.[2]

Indira Gandhi was swept to power in January 1966 largely because the Congress bosses saw her as inheriting the prestigious mantle of the Nehru family, a strong electoral asset, but also because they thought that she could be manipulated, given her relative lack of political experience. However tension between the 'Syndicate' – the press's name for the Congress bosses – and Indira Gandhi increased after the 1967 elections, which marked the party's first serious setback. Determined to emancipate herself from the Syndicate's tutelage, she legitimised herself with socialist slogans and solicited the support of the left wing of Congress, especially that of the Congress Forum for Socialist Action (FSA).

[1] Patil considered that he was displaced because he had 'removed all restrictions on food movements and [that] some of his colleagues who talked of socialism and tighter controls did not favor [his] policy. They were poisoning Jawaharlal's mind that controls could not be introduced as long as S.K. Patil remained in charge of Food and Agriculture Ministry.' (Patil, *My Years With Congress*, op. cit., p. 105)

[2] Frankel, *India's Political Economy*, op. cit., p. 246.

This conflict led, in 1969, to the first split in Congress, a development which might have precipitated a British-style two party system with Mrs Gandhi's Congress moving to the left, as its rapprochement with the CPI indicated. But her radical discourse notwithstanding, she did not refashion Congress along such lines. The party could not function without the established network of local notables to maintain its influence. Some radical measures were implemented in 1975–7, during the Emergency, but this period was in fact the culminating point of an authoritarian brand of populism that had been gaining momentum since the late 1960s.

Towards a new Congress?

In the 1967 elections the Congress won an all time low 283 out of 516 seats. The CFSA, to which Indira Gandhi turned for support derived from the Congress Socialist Forum which had been founded in 1957 in order to strengthen the party organisation and to endow it with a firm ideology. It had then immediately campaigned in favour of land reform and the cooperativisation of Indian agriculture.[3] The CSF, which had become dormant in the late 1950s, was relaunched in 1962 under a new name, the CFSA, by a group of congressmen made up of G. Nanda, Brahma Prakash Choudhury, K.D. Malaviya and Mrs Subhadra Joshi. After the 1967 elections, they received the support of ex-PSP cadres who had joined Congresss, men such as Chandra Shekhar, who seemed to be the leader of the 'young Turks' – as the press called this new generation of radicals.[4] The CFSA was able to act with increasing effectiveness as a pressure group within Congress as Mrs Gandhi was becoming well disposed towards its programme.

In May 1967 she persuaded the Congress Working Committee to adopt a 10-point programme which had been spelt out by the CFSA and contained the nationalisation of banks and insurance companies, the transfer of import and export monopolies to the state, the setting up of revenue and urban property ceilings, an employment programme for landless labourers and the abolition of the princes'

[3] Ram Singh Awana, *Pressure Politics in Congress Party. A Study of the Congress Forum for Socialist Action*, New Delhi: Northern Book Centre, 1988.

[4] J. C. Johari, 'Young Turks and the radicalisation of Congress leadership', *The Indian Journal of Political Science* (hereafter *IJPS*), April–June 1973, 24.

privileges and privy purses.[5] In July 1969, Mrs Gandhi published *Stray Thoughts*, which borrowed heavily from the ideas of the CFSA and the Young Turks.

The break-up with the Syndicate, which was increasingly critical of Mrs Gandhi, occurred during the presidential elections in August. Indira Gandhi campaigned for the trade-unionist V.V. Giri whereas the Congress bosses supported Sanjiva Reddy. The latter lost despite the support of most Congress MPs and the two rival groups then fought for control of the party. Indira Gandhi backed a petition by which the AICC members were required to elect a new Congress president to replace Nijalingappa, who was one of the Syndicate. In November 1969, the members who responded to Indira Gandhi's call elected a new party president and the split was consummated. Their party came to be known as Congress (R) – for 'requisition' and later for 'ruling' – whereas the Syndicate formed the Congress (O) – for 'organisation'.

Soon after, Indira Gandhi introduced bills in the Lok Sabha to nationalise the banks and abolish the privileges and privy purses of the princes. The Rajya Sabha, however, rejected the latter measure. The government then sought to obtain the same result by a presidential ordinance but the Supreme Court, on 15 August 1970, declared the move to be illegal as the Constitution guaranteed the rights of the princes. Indira Gandhi then dissolved the Lok Sabha on 27 December 1970.

She broke with the old Congress traditions during the mid-term election campaign. She tried to short-circuit the 'vote bank' system by presenting her programme directly to the people. In a broadcast to the nation, she declared in December 1970 that:

> The challenge posed by the present critical situation can be met only by the proper and effective implementation of our secular and socialist policies and programmes through democratic processes. Time will not wait for us.

[5] The CFSA strongly disapproved of the alliance between the Congress and 'feudal' as well as 'capitalist' elements. In 1969, it criticised the inclusion of Raja Kamakshya Narain Singh of Ramgarh in the Bihar Cabinet as a 'flagrant disregard of the previous decision and policy of the Congress' (Cited in R.S. Awana, *Pressure Politics*, op. cit., p. 249). Similarly, Chandra Shekhar accused M. Desai of having a pro-Birla bias in Parliament and Mohan Dharia criticised Bhanu Prakash Singh, Union Deputy Minister for Industrial Development for defending the privy purses and privileges of the princes.

Millions who demand food, shelter and jobs are pressing for action. Power in a democracy resides in the people. That is why we have decided to go to the people and seek a fresh mandate from them.[6]

The electoral campaign of 1971 exemplified her new style of politics. Before the split, the Congress combined a socialist-like discourse at the top and conservative practices at the local level where notables ensured the party's electoral success. After 1969 most of these notables sided with the Congress (O) because of affinities with the Syndicate bosses or because of the fears raised by Indira Gandhi's policies. Hence she would no longer rely on 'vote banks', which she had criticised as status quoist. She played a leading role in the election campaign, addressing 250 public rallies and hundreds of smaller meetings. Her slogan, very personal and demagogic was:

'Some say let us get rid of Indira Gandhi (*Indira Hatao*)
I say let us get rid of poverty (*Garibi Hatao*).'

The election manifesto of Congress(R), where most of the ten points spelled out by the CFSA had been reiterated,[7] projected the party as an agent of progress while the opposition parties (the Congress(O), the Jana Sangh and the Swatantra party) clubbed together in a Grand Alliance were described as conservative forces:

The alliance of reaction, composed of the Syndicate, the Jana Sangh and the Swatantra Party backed by vested interests, has been brought into being solely to fight against the progressive programmes of the Congress [. . .]

With the consolidation of the reactionary forces, we are confronted with the most crucial fight in our post-independence history. But we are determined to press forward with a programme of social change which is being challenged by disruptive and backward-looking elements who are clinging to ideas and methods which are obstructing growth and social advance. . . .[8]

To neutralise the influence of local leaders Indira Gandhi had the counting of votes moved from the local voting offices to the chief towns of the districts, where it was much more difficult for notables

[6] Cited in Awana, *Pressure Politics in Congress Party*, op. cit., p. 200.

[7] M.M. Sankhdher, 'The Election Manifestoes of Congress (R) and the Jana Sangh', *Journal of Political Science Review*, 6 (1), Oct. 1971–March 1972, pp. 40–55.

[8] 'Congress (R) Election Manifesto', in A. Moin Zaïdi, *Annual Register of Indian Political Parties* (hereafter *ARIPP*), vol. I, 1972–3, New Delhi: Orientalia, p. 117.

to check whether their 'clients' had voted correctly. The Election Commission reported that this measure 'eliminated to a large extent pre-election intimidation and post-election victimisation of voters belonging to the weaker, poorer and smaller sections of the community'.[9]

Not only did Indira Gandhi try to establish a bipolar political scene where forces of progress would be confronted by conservatives, she also attempted to change the social profile of her party. The Congress Parliamentary Board of the Congress (R) had recommended new rules for the selection of candidates : members of the Rajya Sabha and the state assemblies should, as far as possible, be discouraged from contesting the Lok Sabha elections in order to infuse fresh blood in the party. New faces did appear in some places. In Delhi, for instance, two women, Mukul Bannerji and Subhadra Joshi were newcomers, whereas A.N. Chawla – the head of the local Congress Seva Dal – H.K.L. Bhagat, the General Secretary of the Delhi Pradesh Congress Committee and Dalip Singh, the former President of Rural District Committee contested for the first time without being totally new to Delhi politics.[10] In Rajasthan, another area where there was some change, 'the agricultural castes were given some consideration in 1971', in comparison to 1967,[11] but the change was very limited:

> Jats were given some representation for the first time among the Congress nominees. But the upper castes were still in a majority and, among them the Banyas got the lion's share, even though 'monopoly businessmen' were not given tickets. Among the 23 Congress candidates, there were 8 lawyers, 6 businessmen and industrialists and 4 landlords.[12]

The renewal of the political elite induced by Indira Gandhi's politics was very limited indeed. The victory of the Congress (R), which secured 352 of the 451 seats in the Lok Sabha, induced some change in the ideological profile of the party's parliamentary group since

[9] Election Commission, *Report on the Fifth General Elections, India, 1971–72. Narrative and Reflective Part*, New Delhi: Election Commission, 1972, p. 203.

[10] P. Srivastava, 'Selection of Congress Party (R) candidates for Parliamentary seats in Delhi (1971)', *IJPS*, 6(1), Oct.1971–March 1972, pp. 29–38.

[11] I. Narain and M.L. Sharma, 'Election politics, secularization and political development : the fifth Lok Sabha elections in Rajasthan', *Asian Survey*, April 1972, 12 (4), p. 296.

[12] Ibid.

Table 4.1. CASTE AND COMMUNITY OF CONGRESS AND CONGRESS (R) CANDIDATES IN RAJASTHAN IN THE 1967 AND 1971 LOK SABHA ELECTIONS

Caste and community	*Congress 1967*	*Congress (R) 1971*
Brahmin	2	3
Rajput	1	3
Banya	10	7
Kayasth	2	1
Jat	–	3
Mali	–	1
SC/ST	7	7
Other	–	1
Total	22	23

Adapted from I. Narain and M.L Sharma, 'Election politics', op. cit., p. 296.

60 to 70 members of the CFSA were returned, but it did not involve any significant increase of the *social* representativity of the House.

The ruling Congress continued to rely on the coalition of extremes pattern. For example, Indira Gandhi promoted Jagjivan Ram in 1969 as President of the party organisation and the following year put him in charge of the ministry of defence, the most important portfolio he ever held. Above all she managed to co-opt Untouchable leaders who had a solid electoral base. That is how B.P. Maurya and Sathi became Congressmen as mentioned above. On the other hand, the upper castes still dominated the party.

While Congress MPs tended to be younger, better educated and more often involved in intellectual professions than in landowning, the majority were from the upper castes. The upper caste profile of the Congress MPs returned in the Hindi belt can be explained by the weakness of the CFSA in North India (except in Uttar Pradesh and Bihar), but the CFSA was in any case an elitist organisation. Among the 35 leaders associated with it from 1962 to 1973, 30 were from the upper castes and 28 were professionals.[13] The only non upper caste leaders of the CFSA were Ram Dhan, Mohan Dharia (two Scheduled Caste members), Brahma Prakash Choudhury, an Ahir based in Delhi (cf. infra) and Ram Lakhan Singh Yadav, from Uttar Pradesh (see below).

Yet, the CFSA was very particular about the social profile of the

[13] R.S. Awana, *Pressure Politics in Congress Party*, op. cit., p. 85.

Table 4.2. CASTE AND COMMUNITY OF THE MPs OF THE HINDI BELT AND OF CONGRESS(R) MPs OF THIS REGION, 1971

	All MPs	*Congress (R)*
Upper castes	*115 (52.4)*	*83 (49.6)*
Brahmin	61 (27.8)	50 (29.9)
Bhumihar	5 (2.3)	2 (1.2)
Rajput	29 (13.2)	16 (9.5)
Banya	12 (5.5)	9 (5.4)
Kayasth	4 (1.8)	3 (1.8)
Khatri	2 (0.9)	2 (1.2)
Nayar	1 (0.4)	–
Other	1 (0.4)	1 (0.6)
Intermediate castes	*10 (4.4)*	*7 (4.2)*
Jat	8 (3.6)	6 (3.6)
Bishnoi	1 (0.4)	1 (0.6)
Maratha	1 (0.4)	–
Low castes	*23 (10.4)*	*19 (11.4)*
Yadav	14 (6.4)	10 (6)
Kurmi	6 (2.7)	6 (3.6)
Panwar	1 (0.4)	1 (0.6)
Saini	1 (0.4)	1 (0.6)
Other	1 (0.4)	1 (0.6)
Scheduled Castes	*40 (18.3)*	*34 (20.4)*
Scheduled Tribes	*16 (7.3)*	*9 (5.4)*
Muslim	*10 (4.6)*	*9 (5.4)*
Sikh	*1 (0.4)*	*1 (0.6)*
Sadhu	*1 (0.4)*	*1 (0.6)*
Unidentified	*3 (1.4)*	*3 (1.8)*
Total	*219 (100)*	*167 (100)*

candidates for the 1972 state assemblies elections. In October 1971, its Central Steering Committee passed a resolution on 'Norms for issue of Party tickets' where it recommended that the selected candidates should be below thirty-five years of age, representative of 'Labour, Kisan, Women, Backward and Minority communities'. It insisted that party tickets should not be given to Congress (O) cadres who wished to join Congress (R) or to 'Those known to be associated with Big Business monopolies, Landlords, feudal orders, communal, caste, reactionary and vested interests'.[14]

[14] Ibid, p. 207.

It worked pretty well in Karnataka. In 1967, the two dominant castes, the Lingayats and the Vokkaligas (who represented respectively 15.5 and 12% of the state population) were accorded 85 and 63 seats (68.5% of the total and 80.5% of the non reserved seats). In 1972, each of the two communities were accorded only 45 seats (or 42% of the total number). Simultaneously, the lower castes got 52 nominees.[15] The Congress leader who led the party during these elections and became Chief Minister after its victory, Devraj Urs, was from these lower castes. Manor argues convincingly that Urs was the first Karnataka politician to prove that it was 'possible to break the control of dominant landed groups [or castes, that is the Lingayats and the Vokkaligas] over regional politics'.[16] Land reform was the main achievement of his government. It came into force in 1974, and under the new law share-cropping was abolished and almost the only persons 'eligible to hold land [were] those engaged in personal cultivation'.[17] This reform was implemented diligently thanks to a new network of 193 tribunals whose 'actions were not subject to prior approval by higher authority or to subsequent appeal'.[18] Almost 1,250,000 acres were thus distributed. As Manor pointed out, this reform was not primarily intended to help the landless peasants – largely Scheduled Caste labourers whose emancipation would have affected the interest of dominant landed castes such as the Lingayats –, but to end tenancies. Its principal aim, therefore, was to aid the cultivating – low – castes. Urs also implemented reservation schemes for these groups, which we shall examine in Chapter 6.

In Andhra Pradesh the Reddys also began to be sidelined by the Congress (R) whose strategy consisted in co-opting Dalit, Tribal and OBC leaders.[19] Party members from this caste rebelled and contested the elections as independents in 1972. The central leadership reacted by large scale expulsions, but half-way through it drew back and even

[15] I. Narain and M.L. Sharma, 'The Fifth State Assembly Elections in India', *Asian Survey*, March 1973, 13 (3), p. 325.

[16] J. Manor, 'Pragmatic Progressives in Regional Politics. The Case of Devraj Urs', *EPW*, annual number, Feb. 1980, p. 201.

[17] Ibid., p. 202.

[18] Ibid., p. 203.

[19] G. Ram Reddy, 'The politics of accommodation – Class, caste and dominance in Andhra Pradesh' in Frankel and Rao (eds), *Dominance and State Power in Modern India*, vol. I, op. cit., p. 284.

reinstated those who had been suspended. Apparently it realised that it was 'impossible to lead the party through direct contact with the base'.[20] Yet Indira Gandhi and the Chief Minister Narasimha Rao consistently initiated socio-economic programmes with the aim of 'weakening the hold of the rich peasantry over the "vote banks" provided by the poor peasants and landless'.[21] They succeeded to some extent, since the proportion of MLAs who were Reddys dropped from 25 to 22% between 1967 and 1972, whereas that of the low castes increased from 14.2% to 19.1%.[22]

Narasimha Rao, however, had to be removed in 1973 because he had alienated the dominant castes; his successor, Vengala Rao had to be more cautious.[23] However, the share of low caste members among the MLAs never declined below 18.7% in the following elections – an achievement that none of the Hindi-speaking states could emulate.

In North India the Congress (R) had not broken from its well entrenched collaboration between an upper-caste educated intelligentsia and notables from the merchant and landowning classes. The Congress headquarters resigned themselves to selecting only those who could win as party nominees.[24] Moreover the Congress leaders were often thwarted when they tried to diminish the power of the landed castes in favour of weaker sections within the party. Therefore, in most of the states where there was a 'drastic turnover of candidates and an infusion of new and younger faces', those recruited 'continued to be drawn from the same socio-economic base as in the past'.[25] The Central Steering Committee of the CFSA could only 'express its dismay and strong resentment at the manner in which Congress tickets

[20] D. Bernstoff, 'Eclipse of "Reddy Raj" ? The Attempted Restructuring of Congress Party Leadership in Andhra Pradesh', *Asian Survey* 8 (Oct. 1973), p. 973, and G. Ram Reddy, 'The 1972 Assembly Elections in Andhra Pradesh', *IJPS*,1 (June–Aug. 1972), pp. 87–93.

[21] R. Reddy, 'The politics of accommodation', op. cit., p. 284.

[22] Ibid., p. 305.

[23] Ibid., p. 284.

[24] See what happened in Haryana, for instance P. Singh, 'Haryana State Assembly Polls of 1968 and 1972', *IJPS*, 7 (April–Sept. 1973), pp. 143–64.

[25] S.A. Kochanek, ' Mrs Gandhi's pyramid : the New Congress' in H.C. Hart (ed.), *Indira Gandhi's India: A Political System Reappraised*, Boulder, CO: Westview Press, 1976, p. 107.

Table 4.3. CASTE AND COMMUNITY OF ANDHRA PRADESH MLAs, 1957–85 (%)

	1957	*1962*	*1967*	*1972*	*1978*	*1983*	*1985*
Brahmin	7.6	7.3	4.8	6.2	3.7	2	1.7
Reddy	25	27.6	25	21.9	24	25.8	22.7
Kamma	11.3	12.6	13.2	12.5	14.6	15.9	16.3
Muslim/Christian	3.6	2.3	3.1	5.2	3	3.7	3.7
OBC	12.6	13	14.2	19.1	18.7	20.7	20
Scheduled Castes/ Scheduled Tribes	17.3	22.3	19.1	19.5	19.7	18.3	18.3
Other	16.3	11.3	15.3	14.6	13.9	13.2	11.5
Unidentified	6	3.3	4.8	0.7	2	–	5.4
Total	*100*	*100*	*100*	*100*	*100*	*100*	*100*
	N=300	*N=300*	*N=287*	*N=287*	*N=294*	*N=294*	*N=294*

Source: G. Ram Reddy, 'The politics of accommodation', op. cit., p. 305.

were allotted'.[26] It especially regretted the nomination of former Congress (O) members who had applied for and been granted reintegration within the ruling party. The members who had crossed over from the Congress (O) were welcomed all the more warmly as the elections for the state assemblies were approaching. The Central Election Committee rejected or relaxed the rules which the CFSA had proposed for the selection of candidates and contented itself with recommending that a third of the outgoing members of the legislative assemblies should 'as far as possible' retire and declared being in favour of an 'adequate representation' of minorities, intellectuals, youths and weaker groups.[27]

The caste profile of the Assemblies remained almost unchanged in states where the Congress(R) won an overwhelming majority, like Madhya Pradesh (220 seats out of 296) and Rajasthan (145 out of 184). The upper caste MLAs represented more than 52% of the assembly in Madhya Pradesh and almost 42% in Rajasthan where the Jats rose to almost 16%. In both states the representation of the OBCs was below 10%. The situation remained by and large the same so far as the governments of these two states were concerned. (One must note, however, the rise of the subalterns in the MP government in the 1970s).

[26] Awana, *Pressure Politics in Congress Party*, op. cit., p. 210.

[27] 'Annual report presented by the General Secretaries in June 1972', in A. Moin Zaidi, *ARIPP*, vol. 1, op. cit., p. 89.

By contrast in Bihar non elite groups won a larger share of Congress tickets in 1972. Of the 258 constituencies where the Congress contested elections, Brahmins got 28, Rajputs 31, Bhumihars 25, Yadavs 31, other low caste people 44, Scheduled Castes 45, Scheduled Tribes 29 and Muslims 25.[28] But the low caste candidates were not as successful as the upper caste ones possibly because they were given the most difficult constituencies: the Congress(R)'s group in the Assembly comprised about 40% MLAs from the higher castes while hardly more than one fourth of them came from the lower and intermediary castes.[29] The sociology of the state political elite hardly underwent any change: 'the majority of Congress leaders both before and after the split, belonged to the class of big *zamindars* and contractors'.[30] Congress Chief Ministers tended to have the low and intermediate castes represented in their governments in the same proportion as the MLAs,[31] as was shown by the composition of the governments of Kedar Pandey, Abdul Ghafoor and Jagannath Mishra. The declining representation of the higher castes in Mishra's government did not benefit the lower and the intermediary castes but the Scheduled Castes and Scheduled Tribes and the Muslims.

In Uttar Pradesh, the rising stars of the Congress (R), Kamlapati Tripathi, who led the Uttar Pradesh government in 1971–3, and Hemwati Nandan Bahuguna, who later succeeded him in 1973–5, were both Brahmins who were not averse to politics conducted by vote banks. The former had inherited the ideological legacy of the Hindu traditionalists. He began his autobiography as follows:

> I belong to a Saryupareen Brahmin family. My family is a traditional one. We believe in idol worship and follow all those customs and traditions that are described in the Smritis and the Puranas.[32]

Tripathi immediately emphasised that he 'rebelled' and neither believed 'in untouchability nor in the fetters of caste and creed'.[33] But

[28] I. Narain and M.L. Sharma, 'The Fifth State Assembly Elections in India', *Asian Survey*, March 1973, 13 (3), p. 325.

[29] Mitra, *Caste Polarization and Politics*, op. cit., p. 124.

[30] S.C. Kashyap, *The Politics of Power – efections and State politics in India*, Delhi: National, 1974, p. 377.

[31] Frankel, 'Caste, land and dominance in Bihar', op. cit., p. 101.

[32] Pt Kamlapati Tripathi, *Freedom Movement and Afterwards*, Varanasi: Vishwavidyalaya Prakashan, 1989, p. 1.

[33] Ibid., p. 2.

Table 4.4. CASTE AND COMMUNITY OF MEMBERS OF CONGRESS GOVERNMENTS OF RAJASTHAN, 1967–74

	M.L. Sukhadia Govt. (1974)	*B. Khan Govt. (1971)*	*H. Joshi Govt. (1974)*
Upper castes	*53.9*	*40*	*53.4*
Brahmin	20.5	13.3	6.7
Rajput	10.3	13.3	20
Banya/Jain	15.4	6.7	20
Kayasth	7.7	6.7	6.7
Intermediate castes	*17.9*	*26.7*	*20*
Jat	17.9	20	20
Bishnoi	–	6.7	–
OBC	*5.2*	*6.7*	–
Yadav	2.6	–	–
Kumhar	2.6	6.7	–
Scheduled Castes	*7.7*	*6.7*	*13.3*
Scheduled Tribes	*5.1*	*13.3*	*6.7*
Muslim	*5.1*	*6.7*	*6.7*
Sikh	*2.6*	–	–
Unidentified	*2.6*	–	–
Total	*100*	*100*	*100*
	N=39	*N=15*	*N=15*

Source: As for Table 2.10, p. 76.

he admitted that he 'continued to observe those family traditions which were no impediment to social interest'.[34] While Gandhi inspired him most in overcoming caste taboos, for him 'Gandhian philosophy reflected the ancient Indian thought'.He was also a staunch supporter of Hindi. In 1947 he presided over the Hindi Sahitya Sammelan of the United Provinces and for 20 years he worked as the editor of two Hindi dailies *Aaj* and *Sansar*. Such a profile recalls that of Malaviya, whose family had a special equation with the *rais* of Allahabad and Benares because of its orthodoxy, the same way as Tripathi's family, which 'was treated with respect by the rajas and feudal lords because of [its] scholarship and pious living'. Those of

[34] Ibid., p. 29.

Table 4.5. CASTE AND COMMUNITY OF MEMBERS OF CONGRESS GOVERNMENTS OF MADHYA PRADESH, 1963–76 (%)

	S.C. Shukla Govt. (1969)	*P.C. Sethi Govt. (1972)*	*S.C. Shukla Govt. 1 (1975)*	*S.C. Shukla Govt. 2 (1976)*
Upper castes	*55.6*	*77.7*	*35.2*	*46.15*
Brahmin	33.3	33.3	17.6	38.46
Rajput	8.3	11.1	17.6	7.69
Banya/Jain	5.6	22.2	–	–
Kayasth	5.6	11.1	–	–
Khatri	2.8	–	–	–
OBC	*11.2*	–	*17.7*	*23.07*
Bairagi	2.8	–	–	–
Jaiswal	2.8	–	–	–
Kurmi	2.8	–	–	–
Pawar	–	–	11.8	15.38
Others	2.8	–	5.9	7.69
Scheduled Castes	*8.3*	*11.1*	*17.6*	*7.69*
Scheduled Tribes	*22.2*	*11.1*	*23.5*	*23.08*
Muslim	*2.8*	–	–	–
Unidentified	–	–	*5.9*	–
Total	*100* *N=36*	*100* *N=9*	*100* *N=17*	*100* *N=13*

Source: As for Table 2.12, p. 81.

them who had been 'initiated [in their sect] by members of the family 'had given a lot of land to them'.[35] However, Tripathi claimed that he supported the zamindari abolition schema after independence.[36] He was a member of the Zamindari Abolition Committee whose report has been studies in chapter one.

Bahuguna was of a different background and projected himself as a reformist as soon as he took over from Tripathi. He was immediately after one of his ministers, Lokpati Tripathi, who owned 4,532 acres registered in the name of fourteen – 'benami' – people.[37] In 1974, Bahuguna asked him and others who owned land in excess the amount permitted by the Ceilings Act to 'give up their excess lands

[35] Ibid., p. 27.

[36] Ibid., p. 95.

[37] Z. Hasan, *Quest for Power*, op. cit., p. 81.

Table 4.6. CASTE AND COMMUNITY OF MLAs IN THE ASSEMBLY OF UTTAR PRADESH, BIHAR, RAJASTHAN AND MADHYA PRADESH, 1972–5 (%)

	UP 1974	*Bihar* 1975*	*Rajasthan 1972*	*MP 1972*
Upper castes	*38.79*	*54.8*	*41.8*	*49.6*
Brahmin	16.25	18.3	13.6	24.7
Rajput	15.59	19.8	14.1	12.3
Banya/jain		–	12.5	9.6
Kayasth	6.95**	2	1.1	2.7
Khatri	–	–	6	0.3
Other	–	14.7	0.5	–
Intermediate castes	*6.95*	–	*15.8*	*0.3*
Maratha	–	–	–	0.3
Jat	–	–	15.8	–
OBC	*28.36*	*29.5*	*7.1*	*9.5*
Banya		4.6	–	–
Jat		–	–	0.3
Yadav		11.7	1.6	–
Kurmi		5.6	–	1.7
Koeri		5.6	–	
Kirar		–	–	0.3
Gujar		–	3.3	–
Mali		–	1.6	0.3
Teli		–	–	1.4
Panwar		–	–	2.1
Other		2	0.5	3.4
Scheduled Castes	*16.31*	*n.a.*	*16*	*13*
Scheduled Tribes		*n.a.*	*11.1*	*22.2*
Muslim	*9.6*	*13.2*	*3*	*2.1*
Sikh		*–*	*1*	*–*
Parsi		*–*	*–*	*0.3*
Undentified/Other		*2.5*	*3*	*2.7*
Total	*100*	*100*	*100*	*100*
	N=424	*N=197*	*N=184*	*N=292*

*Figures compiled on the basis of the unreserved seats only.

Sources: Fieldwork and, for Bihar, adapted from Blair, 'Rising Kulaks', op. cit., p. 67, and for UP, Z. Hasan, *Quest for Power*, op. cit., p. 251.

**This figure includes all the non-Brahmin and non-Rajput offer castes.

or resign from the government'.[38] Ten ministers warned that they would quit the government if Tripathi remained under such pressure, and several Congress MLAs threatened to withdraw their support

[38] Ibid., p. 82.

Table 4.7. CASTE AND COMMUNITY OF MEMBERS OF CONGRESS GOVERNMENTS OF BIHAR, 1972–7 (%)

	Kedar Pandey	*Abdul Gafoor*	*Jagannath Mishra*
Upper castes	41.20	45.57	31.55
Intermediate and low castes	29.45	19.57	18.95
Scheduled Castes	8.74	13.02	18.95
Scheduled Tribes	11.79	10.87	12.15
Muslim	5.85	10.97	12.15
Other	2.97	–	6.35
Total	*100* *N=13*	*100* *N=21*	*100* *N=15*

Source: Mitra, *Caste Polarization and Politics*, op. cit., p.133.

Table 4.8. CASTE AND COMMUNITY OF MEMBERS OF CONGRESS GOVERNMENTS OF UTTAR PRADESH

	K. Tripathi Govt. (1971–3)	*H.N. Bahuguna Govt. 1 (1973–4)*	*H.N. Bahuguna Govt. 2 (1974–5)*	*N.D. Tiari Govt. (1976–7)*
Upper castes	*59.1*	*42.4*	*42.9*	*40*
Brahmin	38.5	24.2	23.8	16
Rajput	15.4	15.2	14.3	12
Banya/Jain	2.6	–	4.8	4
Kayasth	–	3	–	4
Khatri	2.6	–	–	–
Others	–	–	–	4
Intermediate castes	–	*3*	*4.8*	*4*
Jat	–	3	4.8	4
OBC	*12.8*	*18.1*	*19.2*	*20*
Gujar	–	3	4.8	4
Kalwar	–	3	4.8	–
Kurmi	5.1	–	–	4
Lodhi	2.6	3	4.8	4
Yadav	5.1	9.1	4.8	8
Scheduled Castes	*15.4*	*12.1*	*9.5*	*8*
Muslim	*12.8*	*18.2*	*19*	*20*
Sikh	–	*3*	*4.8*	*8*
Unidentified	–	*3*	–	–
Total	*100* *N=39*	*100* *N=33*	*100* *N=21*	*100* *N=25*

Source: *Sarvadhik Pichhra Varg Ayog Report [Report of Most Backward Classes Commission]*, (Hindi), Lucknow: Uttar Pradesh ki Sarkar, 1977, pp. 98-101.

from Bahuguna. He had to accommodate them; but he was not such an ardent reformist anyway.

He remained keen to rely on local notables, including those from princely families. Despite the fact that he was from Garhwal district, he chose to contest the 1969 Assembly elections in the Allahabad region where he could find a safe seat. One of the former princely Rajput states of the United Provinces, Mandla, was located in this area. Sant Bux Singh, the local rajah, was already an MLA. He opted for the Congress (R). His younger brother Vishwanath Pratap Singh was inclined to enter politics. In this way 'V.P.Singh who had considerable influence in the Allahabad area because of his family connections, received ground signals that Bahuguna would like to promote him'.[39] It seemed that he preferred a Rajya Sabha seat but Bahuguna wanted him to contest the elections in order to profit from his influence during the election campaign.[40] Therefore in 1969 V.P.Singh and Bahuguna became MLAs in two adjoining constituencies.

The persistence of vote bank politics shows that the 1969 split did not bring about either a break from the 'old Congress' culture or the sociological renewal which could have matched the socialist discourse of Indira Gandhi. In fact, among the MPs and MLAs of the Congress (R) in the Hindi Belt, Brahmins and Rajputs (along with the Scheduled Castes) formed the largest groups. Some of these Brahmins did not even belong to the intelligentsia but were landlords. For instance Jitendra Prasad, who was first elected in 1971 was the son of a *zamindar* from Shahjahanpur who had joined the Congress during the freedom struggle. Prasad himself joined the Congress in 1969, just before the split.[41] Then he opted for the Congress (R) where his 'feudal' profile was no handicap. In fact, the Congress (R) even relied on princes, as evident from the situation prevailing in Madhya Pradesh.

In 1967, the princes of this state started to leave Congress because they were worried about the authoritarianism of the new Chief

[39] S. Mustafa, *The Lonely Prophet – V.P. Singh: a Political Biography*, New Delhi: New Age, 1995, pp. 20–1.

[40] J. Thakur, one of the most abrasive biographers of V.P. Singh, emphasised that Bahuguna simply needed 'some solid vote banks'. (J. Thakur, *V.P. Singh: The Quest for Power*, New Delhi: Warbler Books, 1989, p. 30). See also R. Bahuguna Joshi and R. Tripathi, *Hemvati Nandan Bahuguna*, Delhi, Rajkamal Prakashan, 1999, p. 202 (Hindi)

[41] Interview with Jitendra Prasad, 17 Nov. 1996, New Delhi.

Minister, D.P. Mishra. Most of these defectors joined the Jana Sangh in the wake of Vijaya Raje Scindia who returned to Hindu nationalism, the original fold of 'the Palace' of Gwalior. Nevertheless of the 36 'blue-blood' candidates who stood for election in 1967, 17 were still under the banner of Congress, which continued to enjoy the support of the Maharajah of Rewa.[42] Defections multiplied in the early 1970s when Indira Gandhi questioned the pensions and privileges that the princes had obtained after Independence in exchange for the merger of their states with the Indian Union. At the 1971 elections the Jana Sangh had six princely candidates in the Lok Sabha. However, once the abolition of their privileges and pensions was voted by parliament after Indira Gandhi's electoral success in 1971, most princes, who no longer had any interest in supporting the opposition, returned to the Congress fold. The Maharajah of Rewa was among them, and he was instrumental in having eight Congress MLAs returned in the 1972 assembly elections. In Rajasthan, the Maharajah of Kota similarly rejoined Congress after a brief sojourn in the ranks of the Jana Sangh, and he helped the ruling party to win all 16 assembly seats in his stronghold.[43] Of the 37 princes who contested the assembly elections, 24 stood on the Congress ticket among whom 17 of them in Madhya Pradesh.[44]

Thus Indira Gandhi followed the same vote bank politics as had her father's Congress. Nor did she manage to reform the party's organisation.

How to transform the Congress into a cadre-based party?

Mrs Gandhi repeatedly expressed her desire to transform the Congress (R) into a well structured party. She needed a strong political machine for obvious electoral reasons but also to push the administration to implement pro-poor policies, especially land reform.

In May 1972 a conference on the implementation of the electoral promises of the Congress (R), which gathered mainly the members of the Central government and the party's Chief Ministers, stressed

[42] B.R. Purohit, 'General elections in Madhya Pradesh' in S.P. Varma and I. Narain (eds), *Fourth Elections in India*, op. cit., p. 304.

[43] K. Bhargava, 'Rajasthan Politics and Princely Rulers', *IJPS*, 33 (4), Oct.–Dec. 1972, pp. 428–9.

[44] I. Narain and M.L. Sharma, 'The Fifth State Assembly Elections in India', op. cit., p. 325.

'the need for involving party workers in the socialist programme of the Congress. There is no doubt that the party has got to develop a cadre to act as watch-dog in the interest of the common man'.[45] A resolution of the AICC during its meeting of October 1972 reiterated this ambition:

> The party has to equip itself for a new role in the implementation of the broad, social, political and economic objectives of the nation. It has to be cast in a new mould to create and to energise a myriad of points of contact, at all levels of the party with the people on the one hand, and with the instruments of governance on the other. The party must not be content with a ritualistic endorsement of Government policy from time to time, it has to play a vital role in the forging of instruments which will concentrate people's will and energies on the task of social reconstruction.[46]

Since 1970, a plan to refashion the Congress (R) had been mooted in order to turn it into a 'suitable instrument for social transformation'. Jagjivan Ram, who had become the party president in 1969, thought that 'the Scheduled Castes, Scheduled Tribes, other backward classes and all the minorities should be drawn in larger numbers into the Congress and involved directly in its activities'.[47] It turned out to be wishful thinking. In Uttar Pradesh, the state Congress machinery had never been so dominated by the Brahmins: in 1973, 38 of the 75 presidents of the district and town committees came from this caste; there was not a single Jat and only two Kurmis and two Yadavs.[48]

Many congressmen who had opted for the Congress (O) in 1969 decided to join Mrs Gandhi's party after she won the 1971 elections. The Central Working Committee of the Congress (R) had ruled out such cross-over to comply with the line laid down earlier by the Congress Parliamentary Board. However, soon after the electoral success of the Congress (R), several Congress (O) politicians did join the party, to the chagrin of the Congress Forum for Socialist Action. Thus, compared to 1969 the party machinery underwent only a superficial transformation: the new entrants did not manifest any

[45] 'Annual Report presented by the General Secretaries in June 1972' in A. Moin Zaïdi, *ARIPP*, vol. 1 op. cit., p. 85.

[46] A. Moin Zaïdi, *ARIPP*, vol. 1 op. cit., pp. 194–5.

[47] Frankel, *India's Political Economy*, op. cit., p. 444.

[48] P. Brass, *Caste, Faction and Party in Indian Politics*, vol. 1, Delhi: Chanakya, 1984, p. 305.

higher doctrinal purity than their predecessors and often represented more or less the same social categories.

Leaders who had joined in or who were promoted in the party apparatus owed their 'election' to the all powerful will of Indira Gandhi, who over-centralised the party machine. The Working Committee dissolved the Pradesh Congress Committees and appointed new ones, including the PCC presidents. After 1971 the Congress presidents convened meetings of presidents and secretaries of district Congress committees. The Congress president was even given the power to nominate two representatives to each party committee.[49] This process was also fostered by the party's inability to elect its own leaders. In December 1972, the party elections gave rise to innumerable disputes (concerning, for example, corruption or intimidation of voters). The high command then imposed leaders – who had Mrs Gandhi's blessings – as heads of local party branches. These were the last party 'elections' (before the 1990s) – those of December 1975 were finally cancelled due to the fear of similar troubles.

These setbacks largely explain the difficulties of the Political Training and Cadre Building Department of the AICC. In July 1972, the Congress Working Committee had passed a resolution inviting the party to get more deeply involved into the social reform process, especially in the field of land redistribution.

> Committees may be formed at the central, state and district levels, of people committed to the idea of land ceiling to provide the main political impetus and direction to the process of reform by creating an awareness about what it stands for and why it is being undertaken. Special importance should be attached to the education of the poorer classes and their involvement in order to create a proper climate for reform. Political rallies and conventions may provide the platform and the instrument by which the redistribution programme is given the character of a mass movement. The need for disciplined

[49] S.A. Kochanek, 'Mrs Gandhi's pyramid : the New Congress', op. cit., p. 98. Congress Chief Ministers were similarly affected by the centralisation process : before the 1972 State elections, Indira Gandhi replaced those of Rajasthan, Andhra Pradesh, Assam and Madhya Pradesh. This centralisation process amounted to personalising power: in Kochanek's words, 'Mrs Gandhi's consolidation of power resulted in the creation of a pyramidal decision-making structure in party and government in which all key positions were staffed by loyal and trusted followers' (ibid., p. 105).

and devoted work by party cadres at various levels should be emphasised in this connection.[50]

K.D. Malaviya who was in charge of the Political Training and Cadre Building Department since 1971, later resigned, having failed to establish a network of activists. In fact he confided to Frankel that the party members 'were forever postponing the convening of these camps out of fear that they would be used to create a Marxist-style cadre that would not be bound by methods of democratic operation'.[51] This explanation reflects the traditional reservations of the Congress party – whether it be 'national', 'R' or 'O' – about the institutionalisation of a body of activists who would be likely to effectively reform society and therefore challenge their clientelistic networks and put their resources into question.

In May 1974 the CWC amended the party constitution with a view to set up a new category of members, the 'active members', who would have to receive specific training. The next meeting of the CWC in August assigned several priority tasks to the Congress elite among which was the implementation of land ceilings. In October it decided to organise training camps, spelling out that 'The camps should be austere and simple and the trainees would be required to live in the camp during the duration of the training'.[52]

The first camp took place at Narora (in Bulandshahr district in Uttar Pradesh) in November 1974. The Congress President D.K. Barooah inaugurated it and announced that the party intended to train 50–100,000 active members in such camps. This scheme eventually failed to materialise. Kochanek concludes that 'the Congress continued to remain a broadly aggregative electoral coalition, rather than a cohesive ideologically coherent party'.[53]

Indira Gandhi's incapacity to reform the Congress party partly explained her failure in carrying out her electoral pledges. During the 1971 election campaign, Congress (R) had promised in its manifesto that if voted to power, it would lower the land ceiling to 10 acres per family for irrigated land and 18 acres per family for land sustaining two crops.[54] These measures were passed but the government

[50] A. Moin Zaïdi, *ARIPP*, vol. 1 op. cit., p. 153.

[51] Cited in Frankel, *India's Political Economy*, op. cit., p. 483.

[52] Ibid., p. 177.

[53] S.A. Kochanek, 'Mrs Gandhi's pyramid : the New Congress', op. cit., p. 106.

[54] Zaïdi (ed.), *ARIPP*, vol. 1, op. cit., p. 134.

adopted flexible rules for other kinds of land: 27 acres for irrigated land providing one crop and 54 acres for dry land. In addition, the ceilings were applicable to families with five children; beyond that an additional area was provided for each additional child with the limit being fixed as twice the ceiling.[55] These rules were applied to a changing set of circumstances: over the last 25 to 30 years the landlords had learnt to divide their land among their relatives or to use their names to avoid exceeding the ceilings. Thus only 62,000 acres of land were redistributed. The obstructionist attitude of the state party leaders and the state governments was largely responsible for the minimal nature of this reform.[56] Only a reformed Congress (R), which would have become a party of social transformation, could have overcome these handicaps.[57]

In the mid-1970s Indira Gandhi came across roughly the same difficulties as her father in the implementation of her socialist programme since the Congress (R), like the undivided Congress before 1969 still relied on local elites who were hostile to reforms. The 1969, split had allowed Indira Gandhi to do away with the Syndicate bosses but some of them had rejoined the party after 1971 and, generally speaking, the Congress (R) continued to depend upon 'vote bank' leaders.

This state of affairs was not the direct cause of the Emergency which Indira Gandhi asked the President, F.A. Ahmed, to declare in June 1975, which was in fact the result of the increasing threat that the opposition posed to the government and the Allahabad High Court's verdict declaring Indira Gandhi's election void due to malpractices in the 1971 elections. However the declaration of the Emergency suspended the elective process and therefore conveniently freed Indira Gandhi from her dependence on the Congress notables. But would she be willing to use this new margin for manoeuvre for undertaking more radical reforms?

[55] This decision was made at the meeting of the CWC of 22 July 1972 (ibid., pp. 150–1).

[56] P.S. Appu, who had been appointed Land Reforms Commissioner in 1970 gives ample evidence of this 'lack of political will' (P.S. Appu, *Land Reforms in India*, New Delhi: Vikas, 1996, pp. 158–73).

[57] The attempt at regulating grain trade met the same difficulties. During the AICC meeting of October 1972 a resolution had been passed in order to stop the hike in grain prices which resulted from the merchants' speculative practices (A. Moin Zaïdi (ed.), *ARIPP, 1974–76*, op. cit., p. 424). However this determination did not materialise.

The Emergency: suspending democracy, a condition for social reforms?

Indira Gandhi immediately tried to justify the Emergency in the name of the socialist mission of the Congress. In her broadcast on July 1, 1975, in which she spelled out her tweenty-point programme, she declared that : 'There is only one magic which can remove poverty, and that is hard work sustained by clear vision, iron will and the strictest discipline'.[58]

Soon after she admitted that 'there is not much new in the programmes that were announced'. But she emphasised that 'what is new is that there is an atmosphere today when it is easier to implement what we want to do'.[59] What was wrong with the previous atmosphere ? The opposition demonstrated in the streets and the JP movement allegedly disrupted civil life. But the political context was also probably not conducive to social reforms because it was dominated by electoral contests in which Congress relied on notables with vested interests. Paradoxically, the democratic electoral system hampered socio-economic reforms. Indira Gandhi had tried to bypass these notables after the 1969 split but she had failed. The suspension of democracy gave the government the possibility of taking redistributive measures – and at least gave them the pretext of justification.

Indira Gandhi's 20-point programme for social progress *inter alia* promised the rapid enforcement of land ceilings, housing for landless labourers, the abolition of bonded labour and a moratorium on the debts of the weaker sections of society. In order to implement this programme, and especially land reforms, local committees were set up with full power to evaluate and correct inequalities. These '20 point programme committees' never functioned because they lacked the infrastructure to support themselves and the *panchayats* which were controlled by the local notables did not provide them with any help.

On the 18 and 19 August the AICC held a major conference on the question of land reform at which the leaders of the state govern-

[58] 'New Programme for Economic Progress – Shrimati Indira Gandhi's Broadcast' in D.V. Gandhi (ed.), *Era of Discipline – Documents on Contemporary Reality*, New Delhi: Samachar Bharati, 1976, p.18.

[59] 'From the Prime Minister's speech in Lok Sabha on July 22, 1975' in ibid., p. 28.

ments announced new land redistribution schemes. The government had the level of ceiling reduced in all the states and redistribution of land started immediately. By December 1975, about 540,000 acres had been declared surplus, out of which 250,000 had been taken possession of by the state government. Of these, about 90,000 acres were allegedly distributed to 52,000 persons.[60] North India was a particular target. In Uttar Pradesh, a survey of illegal encroachments on panchayat land showed that over 200,000 acres were illegally occupied. In Bihar, thousand of acres of *benami* land were similarly 'detected in Purnea, Saharsa and Champaran districts'.[61] According to Frankel, the government could do no better than implement the land ceilings established in 1972–3 but this was a step in the right direction since in 1976, 1.7 million acres were acquired by the government and 1.1 million acres redistributed. This achievement was 'attributable mainly to the disability placed on landowners in moving the courts for a stay against the committee's award, and the determination of the local authorities to reduce the time lag between scrutiny of landholdings, surrender to surplus area, government take over of the land, and distribution'.[62] Similarly the local administration pressed forward to implement the programme launched in 1972 and aimed to procure 4 million houses for landless rural labourers by 1979. According to Frankel, three-fourths of this target was achieved during the first year of the Emergency, mostly because of the efforts of two states, Gujarat and Uttar Pradesh.

Other authors maintain that the achievements of the Emergency government regarding land reform were most disappointing. Economists came to the conclusion that by July 1976 only 1.5% of the total area owned by rural households could be considered as surplus and of that 1.5%, about 16% was allegedly distributed.[63] As Das Gupta points out, 'this was probably the most effective way of revealing whether or not the real supporters of land-holders were in jail or in power'.[64]

[60] 'Land for the landless', op. cit., p. 268.

[61] Ibid., p.269.

[62] Frankel, *India's Political Economy*, op. cit., p. 552.

[63] Ranjit Sau, 'Indian Political Economy, 1967–77', *EPW*, 9 April 1977, p. 618, and P.S. Appu, *Land Reforms in India*, op. cit., p. 175.

[64] J. Das Gupta, 'A season of Caesars : emergency regimes and development-politics in Asia', *Asian Survey*, April 1978, 18 (4), p. 336.

According to the Rudolphs, the Emergency regime chose 'to talk left and act right'.[65] The corporatist dimension of the industrial political economy of the Emergency tends to substantiate this interpretation. State governments were asked to introduce 'bipartite councils at the shop floor and enterprise levels for all firms employing more than 500 persons, and bipartite apex bodies were brought into being by the centre in most major industries'.[66] A National Apex Body was also established to supervise the entire private industrial sector. It included representatives from three of the major trade unions (the All India Trade Union Congress, the Indian National Trade Union Congress and the Hindustan Mazdoor Sangh) as well as representatives of employers and manufacturers' organizations. The whole arrangement was justified by the need to restore harmonious social relations among workers and employers – a euphemism for industrial discipline. Indeed, many labour leaders were arrested and the Emergency regime made a point of reducing the number of man-days lost in industry by banning strikes. By contrast, the government were lenient towards those actions of the employers and management which contributed significantly to the loss of man-days.[67]

Business Standard candidly admitted that 'Within a month of the proclamation of Emergency and the decision not to have strikes and lock-outs, nearly 20,000 employees have been either retrenched or laid off by various multi-national business-houses'.[68] On 26 October 1976, the Union Labour Minister had to admit that lock-outs were responsible for most of the man-days lost (57% in January, 96% in July).[69] As a result of the new atmosphere, while the man-days lost through strikes roughly doubled in 1973–4, in 1975 'they remained high at 17 million during the first half but after the imposition of Emergency Rule declined drastically to only 2 to 4 million in the second half'.[70] Over the period January–April 1976, there were only 2.3 man-days lost through strikes, that is 83% less than over the same period in 1975.

[65] L.I. Rudolph and S. Hoeber Rudolph, 'To the brink and back : representation and the State in India', *Asian Survey*, April 1978, 18 (4), p. 390.

[66] Ibid., p. 388.

[67] Das Gupta, 'A season of Caesars', op.cit., p. 335.

[68] *Business Standard*, 29 Aug. 1975.

[69] *EPW*, 30 Oct. 1970, p. 1709.

[70] A.G. Frank, 'Emergence of permanent emergency in India', *EPW*, 12 March 1977, p. 465.

The Emergency regime also proved to be business-oriented because it declared a wage freeze – which certainly reinforced the deflationary trend, a cut from 8 to 4% of the minimum annual bonuses[71] and, more importantly, because it liberalised the 'Licence Raj'. Private enterprises were allowed to import more freely and to expand their share of the market. The Foreign Exchange Regulation Act of 1973 was amended in such a way as to reduce the tax on royalties earned by foreign companies and Indian firms also benefited from 'reductions in capital gains tax [and] reductions in the rates of taxation at the upper income and wealth brackets'.[72] In contrast to the mandate of socio-economic reform which the Emergency regime claimed it was pursuing, it, in fact, complied with liberal dogmas. It assumed 'that collective enrichment comes first, and that unequal enrichment of groups within the nation is a precondition of rapid development'.[73] Indira Gandhi's policy indeed led some analysts to regard the Emergency regime as reflecting the 'Indian bourgeoisie's bid for a "Brazilian model" capital intensive and export oriented subimperialist solution to its crisis of capital accumulation'.[74]

In spite of Indira Gandhi's claims, the Emergency regime was not 'pro-poor' but, in a way, perpetuated the previous arrangement where the 'dominant proprietary classes' monopolised power. For Blair, the national bourgeoisie, the landlords, the civil services, the military and the intelligentsia remained firmly entrenched in the state's political economy. He comments that 'The period of Emergency [. . .] can straightforwardly be explained as simply the continuation of the reality of the previous system with the pluralistic veneer of parliamentary democracy stripped away, leaving the underlying reality of elite class dominance'.[75]

In fact, Indira Gandhi's policy in the ten years of her first reign increasingly fulfilled the criteria of populism. This 'elusive and protean' notion[76] is often used loosely and therefore the sense in which

[71] *Far Eastern Quarterly Review*, 20 Feb. 1976.

[72] *EPW*, 4 Dec. 1976, p. 1884.

[73] Das Gupta, 'A season of Caesars', op. cit., pp. 340–1.

[74] Frank, 'Emergence of Permanent Emergency', op. cit., p. 470.

[75] Blair, 'Mrs Gandhi's Emergency, the Indian Elections of 1977, Pluralism and Marxism : Problems with Paradigms', *Modern Asian Studies* 2 (1980), p. 255.

[76] To use the words of Ionescu and Gellner in the 'Introduction' to G. Ionescu and E. Gellner (eds), *Populism – its Meanings and National Characteristics*,

we employ this concept needs to be clarified. In the words of Shils, populism 'proclaims that the will of the people as such is supreme over every standard, over the standards of traditional institutions, over the autonomy of institutions and over the will of other strata. Populism identifies the will of the people with justice and morality'.[77] In that sense Indira Gandhi resorted to a populist discourse when she claimed that she represented the will of the people, to such an extent that she could bypass institutions such as the judiciary. Immediately after her electoral success in 1971, Mrs Gandhi had the Constitution changed in order to implement other aspects of her programme. The 24th amendment voted on 4 August 1971 restricted the powers of the judiciary to control the procedure of constitutional amendments. The 25th amendment abolished compensation for the victims of nationalisation and declared the judiciary incompetent to challenge the decisions of the state in these matters.

Secondly, populism is also the discourse of these politicians who claim that they are above party politics and stand on the side of the workers against their exploiters.[78] It is therefore used by individual leaders who thereby try to establish a direct, personal relation between them and 'the people'. They profess to be one of the people and, at the same time, claim to be their defender and protector against enemies both domestic and foreign. Indeed the creation of a conspiracy theory is one of the devices resorted to by populist regimes. Indira Gandhi fulfilled this other criterion of populism when she claimed that she, alone, rose against the conservative Grand Alliance to protect the poor. And she dramatically personalised this relation between herself and The People during the 'Indira Hatao versus Garibi Hatao' campaign of 1971 when she deliberately short-circuited the Congress vote banks.

Thirdly, the populist discourse is a political device in the sense that the politicians who articulate it are not interested in promoting the interests of the poor. Populism is not an egalitarian ideology. Its aim

---

London: Weidenfeld and Nicolson, 1969, p. 1. Ernesto Laclau comes to the same conclusion in *Politics and Ideology in Marxist Theory, Capitalism – Fascism – Populism*, London: Verso, 1979, p. 143.

[77] E. Shils, *The Torment of Secrecy*, Melbourne: Heinemann, 1956, p. 98.

[78] This 'populism of the politicians' is one of the types of populism studied by Margaret Canovan in *Populism*, New York: Harcourt Brace Jovanovich, 1981, pp. 260 ff.

is to defuse demands rather than to implement social reforms. Therefore, personalities from the establishment as well as the rural elites may even support it (though from a distance given the rather unpredictable moves of its demagogic architects). Indira Gandhi, indeed, did not try very hard to implement the land reform she had promised and in the industrial domain she even resorted to conservative and authoritarian methods. When populist leaders do take social measures, it is generally in a rather authoritarian framework, such as the corporatist structures which also encompass trade unions.[79]

Yet, we must take a nuanced view of populism. A populist leader cannot stand entirely against the people. A discourse can only be repeated *ad nauseam* without any implementation up to a point. India's experiment with populism certainly culminated in an authoritarian regime, that is in the Emergency. But this anti-democratic rule permitted some social reforms and Indira Gandhi justified her authoritarian rule in the light of these achievements. This populism affected the previous balance of power in so far as the ruling party no longer relied as much on a network of state and local bosses but rather on the charisma of an all-India leader.

Thus in the mid-1970s, India was in the grip of a dilemma: in a democratic context the ruling party, in order to win elections, needed the support of local conservative notables; yet when electoral constraints disappeared, as during the Emergency, dependence on the network of notables was much less apparent and the party seemed to be in a better position to implement the social promises made by its high command. The Congress(R) was therefore facing a paradox – political democracy tended to exclude social democracy and vice-versa – and a dilemma since a decision in favour of one option or the other had to be made.

At the end of the 1970s of the Congress was confronted by a much greater challenge: the long-term social changes that saw – at least in North India – the rise to prominence of middle-ranking farmers from intermediate and lower castes. The mobilisation of this group

[79] Populism is basically anti-democratic since it relies on a strong personalisation of power justifying that counter powers (including the media and political parties) were sidelined: they are accused of dividing the nation and, more importantly, of interfering with the manner in which the leader interprets the will of the people. For more details see P.-A. Taguieff, 'Political Science confronts populism', *Telos*, no. 103, spring 1995.

seemed to offer a way out for Indian democracy because if it could be organised the influence of the notables would be eroded and the law of numbers more likely to prevail.

Weiner's thesis about the 'open elite system' of the Congress party in the 1960s does not fit with the situation prevailing in North India. His analysis was based on case studies from South and West India, but the Congress system was very different in the Hindi belt. In the four main states – Uttar Pradesh, Madhya Pradesh, Rajasthan and Bihar – the party remained dominated by elite groups from the upper castes, either professional politicians from the intelligentsia, businessmen or landlords.

The intermediate and lower castes – mostly cultivating castes – were conspicuous by their absence. They formed a marginal group among the Congress MLAs, the state party leaders and the state governments. Certainly, the Jats were well represented in the Congress of Rajasthan – even though the party tried to rather woo the Rajputs in the late 1950s –, but in Uttar Pradesh, where they started to form an emerging rural elite (in West UP at least), partly because of the land reforms initiated by Charan Singh, they were ignored.

In fact, the party had a more inclusive attitude *vis-à-vis* the Scheduled Castes, partly because they did not pose the same kind of threat to the elite groups as the rising 'middle castes', partly because the Indian establishment had a tradition of anti-Untouchability activism (be they moved by philanthropy or the fear of mass conversions by Dalits). However, the Scheduled Castes leaders who became influential figures in the Congress – like Jagjivan Ram – were often very moderate and even imbued with the ethos of Sanskritisation. Many of them had been initiated into the party by Gandhi or his lieutenants.

One of the reasons for the upper caste-dominated social profile of the Congress lay precisely in the impact of Gandhi's ideas. His emphasis on social cohesion – in a somewhat organicist manner – contributed to make the Congress systematically downplay class and caste conflicts: the British and their supporters among the richest landlords and businessmen were the only legitimate targets of the party. As a result, Ambedkar's movement was marginalised and proprietory classes, such as landowners and capitalists, did not hesitate to join a party they had little to fear from – and that they could influence from the inside.

The second reason for the large representation of such elite groups in Congress was that the party needed them. It needed the financial support of businessmen and it needed the landlords because they could deliver votes. Nehru himself institutionalised this vote bank politics by co-opting former Maharajahs and by nominating them in constituencies where they had a good chance of winning.

The social profile of Congress was not incompatible with democracy, as evident from Bardhan's analysis of the political attitude of the proprietory classes. But this democracy was bound to be largely formal and conservative. In order to win the support of the rural vote bank owners, for instance, the Congress had to dilute its policy of land reform.

Indira Gandhi tried to transform the Congress into a machine capable of sustaining the implementation of social reforms. She failed to refashion the Congress into a cadre-based party or to substantially change the social basis of her Congress (R) because she still depended on vote bank politics. The notables on which the party relied were still conservative and upper caste, but their importance diminished after Mrs Gandhi declared the Emergency. Though she then indulged in populist politics, some progressive schemes, such as land reform, began to be implemented.

The logical conclusion flowing from this survey of the Congress's trajectory till the 1970s suggests that it could only sustain political democracy at the expense of social democracy and promote social democracy when political democracy was not working, as in 1975–7. It is as if political democracy and social democracy were incompatible. This contradiction was especially evident in the North. In the South and in the West the situation was different because, as Weiner emphasised, the party had accommodated emerging cultivating castes. For us, the question now is why could these castes play such a role in the Congress there but not in the North?

Part II

THE UNEVEN EMANCIPATION OF THE LOWER CASTES

NON-BRAHMINS IN THE SOUTH, OBCS IN THE NORTH

The North/South contrast in terms of low caste mobilisation can be explained by several variables. We have noticed in the introduction that it derived from economic and social factors. First, the kind of land settlement that the British introduced in India differed from area to area. While the *zamindari* system prevailed in North India, the *raiyatwari* system was more systematically implemented in the South. Second, these two regions have a different caste composition. In the Hindi-belt, the caste system is the closest to the *varna* model with its four orders (Brahmins, Kshatriyas, Vaishyas and Shudras) and its Untouchables. In the South, the warrior and merchant castes are often missing or poorly represented, as in Maharashtra and Bengal. Correlatively, the upper *varnas* are larger in number than in the North

However, the caste factor does not explain the North/South divide only in arithmetic terms. In fact, the caste system underwent a more significant and early change *out of the Hindi belt.* This social system has been analysed by anthropologists as a 'sacralized social order' based on the notion of ritual purity.[1] In this view, its holistic character – to use the terminology of Louis Dumont[2] – implies that the dominant – brahminical – values are regarded by society as providing universal references, or role models. Hence the pervasiveness of Sanskritisation, a practice that Srinivas has defined as 'the process in which a "low" Hindu caste, or tribal or other group, changes its

[1] See Harold Gould, *The Hindu Caste System*, vol 1: *The Sacralization of a Social Order*, Delhi: Chanakya Publications, 1987.

[2] Louis Dumont, *Homo Hierarchicus*, Paris: Gallimard, 1966.

customs, ritual, ideology and way of life in the direction of a high, and frequently, "twice-born caste" that is the Brahmins, but also the Kshatriyas or even the Vaishyas'.[3] Low castes may for instance adopt the most prestigious features of the Brahmins' diet and therefore emulate vegetarianism. Such a process reflects a special coherence in society, all the groups admitting the values of the upper castes as *the* legitimate value system. Such coherence is not synonymous with cohesion. In fact, Sanskritisation itself bears witness to an aspiration for social mobility and therefore reflects social tensions: low castes constantly try to improve their social status by imitating the high castes and contest the position which has been assigned to them in the system. Moreover, the myths of origin of the low castes are always centered around the idea of an initial decline: even Untouchable castes claim to descend from Brahmin castes and argue that they have fallen because of the malicious intent of the upper castes.[4] Though Deliège points out that 'the untouchable myths are quite distinct from those of higher and even middle-range castes',[5] they do not reflect the existence of a separate, untouchable identity: 'they take caste for granted, and by stressing their brotherhood with Brahmans, they acknowledge the superiority of the latter'.[6] This is an excellent illustration of the Sanskritisation process. For Srinivas, 'the mobility associated with Sanskritization results only in *positional changes* in the system and does not lead to any *structural change*. That is, a caste moves up above its neighbours and another comes down, but all this takes place in an essentially stable hierarchical order. The system itself does not change'.[7] Indeed, the values sustaining the social system remain the same. While the Brahmins are the main objects of imitation,

[3] Srinivas, *Social Change in Modern India*, op. cit., p. 6.

[4] The myth of origin of the Chamars is very telling in this aspect: their original ancestor was the youngest of four Brahmin brothers who went to bathe in a river and found a cow struggling in quicksand. The youngest brother went to rescue the animal, but before he could do so it drowned, at which his brothers made him remove the carcass. They then turned him out of their caste and gave him the name of Chamar.(R.V. Russell, Rai Bahadur Hiralal, *The Tribes and Castes of the Central Provinces of India*, New Delhi: Asian Educational services, 1993 (1916) vol.2, p. 405)

[5] R. Deliège, 'The myth of origin of Indian Untouchables', *Man*, 28 (3), p. 534.

[6] Ibid., p. 546.

[7] Srinivas, *Social Change in Modern India*, op. cit., p. 6

Srinivas points out that the Sanskritisation process does not refer to them only. The Kshatriyas are often chosen as role models too. Pocock even suggests that there is a 'Kingly model of Hindu society'.[8] However this style of self-promotion does not simply rely on the imitation of the superior. In fact the second *varna* has been one of the main avenues for social mobility because the Shudras could take power and overthrow the Kshatriyas as rulers on the basis of mere numerical strength; Brahmins then legitimised their rise by evolving the required genealogies. Srinivas points out that 'the Kshatriya category was the most open one in the caste system'.[9] While this openness is a very important element in the promotion of the low castes, it does not question *the system* either since it has to be sanctioned by Brahmins who retain their paramount importance and whose values remain supreme.

Historically, low caste groups have also explored avenues for upward mobility through the *bhakti* movements and the sectarian model. Since the Buddha, gurus have continually questioned the caste system on behalf of the fundamental equality of men before god. Their disciples who were initiated into monastic orders abandoned caste as they formed new fraternities. Srinivas emphasised that the 'protest sects' in a way 'offered opportunities for mobility to members of the so-called low castes'.[10] However, this equality was otherworldly: it did not affect the social order. Ambedkar rightly pointed out that 'from the point of view of the annihilation of caste, the struggle of the saints did not have any effect on society'.[11] In the second part of this book I argue that the lower castes of North India tend to remain imbued with the ethos of Sanskritisation or with that of spiritual, otherworldly equality, whereas those of South and West India were able to emancipate themselves through collective mobilisation using primarily the idiom of ethnicity.

[8] D.F. Pocock, 'The Movement of castes', *Man*, May 1955, pp. 71–2. See also D.F. Pocock, *Kanbi and Patidar, A Study of the Patidar Community of Gujarat*, Oxford University Press, 1972.

[9] M.N. Srinivas, 'Future of Indian caste', *EPW*, 14 (7–8), Feb. 1978, p. 238.

[10] Ibid., p. 238.

[11] Cited in Keer, *Dr Ambedkar. Life and Mission*, op. cit., p. 109.

5

CASTE TRANSFORMATIONS IN THE SOUTH AND WEST

ETHNICISATION AND POSITIVE DISCRIMINATION

'It was too late in the day for me to defend what has been termed the Non-Brahmin movement. When its activities have spread from Bombay to Madras, from the Vindhya Mountains to Cape Comrin, its very extent and the lightning rapidity with which its principles have pervaded the country will be the best justification of the movement'. (Presidential address of the Raja of Panagal at the second session of the All-India Non-Brahmin Congress at Amraoti, 1925, cited in K. Kavlekar, *Non-Brahmin Movement in Southern India. 1873–1949*, Kolhapur: Shivaji University Press, 1979, p. 115)

While the caste system had never been a fixed institution, the socio-economic and political changes precipitated by the British Raj probably affected caste more directly than any previous change. Economic modernisation implied 'rapid industrialisation and physical mobility', and in 'these volatile environments it was not just the weak and deprived who sought to hedge themselves round with more tightly defined *jati* and *varna* identities'.[12] Till then, caste was confined to a reduced territory, delimited by matrimonial relations (in North India caste endogamy and village exogamy are compelling rules). The development of modern means of communication favored the territorial extension of the frontiers of caste and the emergence of horizontal solidarities. Transfers of bureaucrats out of their native place often generated feelings of anomie and made finding a suitable match for endogamous marriages more complicated; hence the need to create associations which could link members of the same caste.

However these associations were also by-products of the census, which was a key element in the formation of the colonial state. From 1871 onwards the British enumerated castes (like the religious groups)

[12] S. Bayly, *The New Cambridge History of India*, vol. IV. 3: *Caste, Society and Politics in India from the Eighteenth Century to the Modern Age*, Cambridge University Press, 1999, p. 263.

and therefore these 'human groups (castes) [we]re treated to a considerable extent as abstractable from the regional and territorial contexts in which they function[ed]'.[13] This process reinforced the construction of the state but the census also raised among several castes the sentiment of having interest in common since the colonial authorities did not content themselves with enumerating them – they also classified them. In 1901, the Census Commissioner, Risley, decided to rank *jatis* in their local context and according to their *varna*, which was a much more delicate enterprise. Caste associations were therefore created as pressure groups whose aim was to improve their rank in the census, a development that was especially prominent among the low castes. Each census provided castes with an opportunity to petition the government for a higher place in the order of precedence and for being recorded under new, Sanskritised, names. In northern India, sixteen castes did so in 1911 and twenty in 1921, including Kurmis, Gadariyas, Kacchi, Lodhs and Ahirs, who all wanted to be recognised as Kshatriyas.[14] This move was in keeping with the logic of Sanskritisation since the objective was not to opt out from the system but to rise within it according to its own rules and values.

However, caste associations paid more attention to non-ritual issues when the British started to use the Census classification, for example, in 'deciding which communities were "manly" enough to provide recruits for the colonial army':[15]

> It is no wonder that many Indians took these matters seriously, becoming skilled in manipulating the Census lists, and taking pains to communicate their views and claims about these processes both to other Indians and to the colonial authorities. Indeed, in the latter nineteenth century there were some Indians with appropriate scribal and statistical skills who launched their own caste enumeration projects, in some cases adapting colonial Census methods in order to supplement older forms of almanac data produced to popularise regional guru networks and holy places.[16]

[13] A. Appadurai, 'Number in the colonial imagination' in A. Appadurai (ed.), *Modernity at large – Cultural Dimensions of Globalization*, Minneapolis: University of Minnesota Press, 1996, p. 119.

[14] E.A.H. Blunt, *The Caste System of Northern India*, Delhi: S. Chand, 1969 (1931), p. 227.

[15] Bayly, *The New Cambridge History of India*, vol. IV. 3, op. cit., p. 125.

[16] Ibid., p. 126.

Caste associations were transforming themselves into interest groups and gradually acquired the features of mutual aid structures. They founded caste-specific schools and co-operative movements. The Rudolphs have underlined the modern character of the caste associations.[17] They behaved like collective enterprises with economic and political objectives which brings to mind the image of political 'lobbies'. They had their head office, their publications, their list of members, and their organisational chart. Generally, their leaders did not come from the most prestigious clans or families but from those of the castemen who were the most educated, able to negotiate with the state and often as ambitious as the political entrepreneurs of Joseph Schumpeter. In many cases, they came from the younger generation.[18]

However, the transformational potentialities of caste associations must not be exaggerated since they were not conducive to social change *per se*. This point needs to be made in the case of the lower castes associations especially. On the one hand, these associations were simply vehicles for Sanskritisation-oriented demands to be put to the state. On the other hand, they acted as pressure groups *vis-à-vis* the same state and as mutual aid structures. While the first dimension remained prominent in the North, it tended to vanish in the South where caste associations prepared the ground for an ethnicisation process.

The first important social change that caste associations achieved in the South probably concerns the unity of the caste groups. They successfully incited the sub-castes to adopt the same name in the Census and to break the barriers of endogamy, even if, within a caste, the members of the upper class still tended to inter-marry – but then it

[17] L. I. Rudolph and S. Hoeber Rudolph, 'The political role of India's caste associations' in I. Wallerstein (ed.), *Social Change: the Colonial Situation*, New York: J. Wiley, 1966, p. 448.

[18] Karen I. Leonard emphasises this dimension in her study of the Kayasths of Hyderabad (*Social History of an Indian caste. The Kayasths of Hyderabad*, Hyderabad: Orient Longman, 1994 [1978], p. 293.) She criticises the Rudolphs' reading of caste associations as 'tutorial experiences related to the modernisation of caste-based units and to their political mobilisation' because, for her, 'such associations are a defensive response to adverse administrative circumstances'. But both interpretations are not mutually exclusive. In fact, castes are more likely to form associations, which will play the role of interest groups in the political arena, when they feel threatened by changes in the state policies.

was more economic endogamy than purely caste-based endogamy. In her study of the Kayasths of Hyderabad, Leonard emphasises that 'the ease with which marriages across former boundaries are accommodated is striking'. For her, this change 'might confirm an ideological shift from caste to ethnicity and class'.[19] This process has been observed by Hardgrave in the case of the Nadars of Tamil Nadu whose caste association, the Nadar Mahajana Sangam was founded in 1910 and promoted what he calls 'caste fusion', as 'the unit of endogamy expanded'.[20] Barnett comes to a similar conclusion in his study of the Kontaikkatti Vellalars – again in Tamil Nadu – who are influential despite their small numbers since many of them are landlords. From 1920 onwards, the caste association has encouraged them to expand endogamy in new territories and to other Vellalars in order to make up for their numerical weakness. For Barnett these innovations confront the entire ideological field of caste hierarchy, since 'blood purity',[21] has lost its importance. The relevant unit is no longer the original *jati* but groups of castes, which represents 'the transition from caste to ethniclike regional caste blocs. "Ethniclike" because each such unit is potentially independent of other such units, defined and characterised by a heritable substance internal to the unit itself and not affected, in terms of membership in the unit, by transactions with others outside the unit. Rather than the conceptual holism of caste, we begin to see the antecedent autonomy of its component parts. In an ethniclike situation transactional ranking no longer orders the parts of the whole, and caste interdependence is replaced by regional-caste bloc independence'.[22]

However, one might argue that intermarriage only leads to caste fusion – to use Hargrave's words – which is only the first step of the ethnicisation of caste. Such a process also implies a collective history – at least a golden Age – and a separate, cultural identity. The subjective representation of the collective self is most important in this process. Caste is partly a mindset; it is based on beliefs in hierarchies relying on purity and impurity – what Ambedkar called 'graded

[19] Leonard, *Social History of an Indian Caste*, op. cit., p. 294.

[20] R. L. Hardgrave, Jr, 'Caste: Fission and Fusion', *EPW*, July 1968, pp. 1065–70.

[21] S. Barnett, 'Identity Choice and Caste Ideology in Contemporary South India' in K. David (ed.), *The New Wind – Changing Identities in South India*, The Hague: Mouton, 1977, p. 401.

[22] Ibid., 402.

inequality'. Alternative social *imaginaires* might be conducive to the emancipation of the lower castes. As M.S.A. Rao argues: 'The problem of identity is crucial in the formation of protest groups and for collective mobilisation':

> Deprived sections of society in different parts of the world have organised themselves into protest movements to fight against discriminations of various kinds based on colour, religion, caste and tribe. Their problem, however, has been one of establishing a new identity – the kind of image that they want to protect in order to gain self-respect, honour and status.[23]

Such a change in collective identity is precisely what is at stake in the process of ethnic identity – building by lower castes. This kind of caste ethnicisation is much more conducive to social change than caste associations or caste fusion pure and simple.

This process was partly shaped by European ideas, as propagated by the missionaries and the British schools. While castes have always been perceived in India as kin groups, the racial dimension that caste tended to acquire in the nineteenth century derived from European interpretations of Indian society. In 1792, William Jones had deduced from the discovery of the Indo-European linguistic family the notion of a common, original race whose branches had migrated towards Europe and India.[24] This theory was developed during the nineteenth century by German philologists such as Weber, Roth, Kuhn and Möhl (whose books were published in the 1840s–1850s). In their writings appear the notions of a 'Sanskritic race' or a 'Vedic people'. These speculations reached India from the late 1850s onwards through Max Müller, who tended to be somewhat more cautious, and Muir who published in 1860 a study on *The Trans-Himalayan Origin of the Hindus, and their affinity with the western branches of the Aryan race.*[25] Susan Bayly points out that 'many pre-independence ethnographers' from Britain 'portrayed India as a composite social landscape in which only certain peoples, those of superior "Aryan" blood, had evolved historically in ways which left them "shackled" by a hierarchical, Brahmanically – defined ideology

[23] M.S.A. Rao, 'Social Movements among the Backward Classes and the Blacks: Homology in the Sources of Identity' in M.S.A. Rao (ed.), *Social Movements in India*, Delhi: Manohar, 1984, pp. 191–2.

[24] P.J. Marshall, 'Introduction' in P.J. Marshall (ed.), *The British Discovery of Hinduism in the Eighteenth Century*, Cambridge University Press, 1970, p. 15.

of "caste". At the same time large numbers of other Indians – those identified in varying racial terms as Dravidians, as members of "servile" classes, aborigines, wild tribes, and those of so-called "mixed" racial origins – were portrayed as being ethnologically distinct from this so-called Aryan population, and were not all thought to belong to a ranked Brahmanical caste order.'[26] In addition to the ethnographers, the British administration imbibed these Orientalist categories and propagated them in society. In 1886, the Governor of Madras, Mountstuart Elphinstone, in his address to the graduates of the university of Madras emphatically declared: 'You are of pure Dravidian race. I should like to see the pre-Sanskrit element amongst you asserting itself rather more'.[27] Gradually, Non-Brahminism and Dravidianism coincided and the low castes looked at themselves as forming an ethnic category.

In order words, colonial ethnography was largely responsible for merging caste and race, and more precisely for equating the 'Aryans' with the upper castes and the Dravidians with the lowest orders of the Indian society. This perception prepared the ground for the interpretation of castes in ethnic terms outside the 'Aryavarta', the northern region where the Brahmanical pattern was supposed to have taken root. Indeed, this ethnicisation process was more prominent in western and southern India than in the North. So far, we have only mentioned examples from South India but in respect to caste ethnicisation, western and southern India followed a similar pattern. As M.N. Srinivas pointed out, 'Jotirao Phule's reforms, and his social thought anticipate the programme of the non-Brahmin Movement in Madras'.[28] In this chapter we shall investigate how far the lower castes of Maharashtra and Tamil Nadu followed parallel routes.

[25] I am most grateful to Bruce Graham for this information. See B. Graham, *Hindu Nationalism and Indian Politics – The Origins and Development of the Bharatiya Jana Sangh*, Cambridge University Press, 1990, p. 44.

[26] S. Bayly, 'Caste and "race" in the colonial ethnography of India' in P. Robb (ed.), *The Concept of Race in South Asia*, Delhi: Oxford University Press, 1995, p. 170.

[27] Cited in E. F. Irshick, *Politics and Social Conflict in South India. The Non-Brahman Movement, 1916–1929*, Bombay: Oxford University Press, 1969, p. 281.

[28] M.N. Srinivas, *Caste in Modern India and other essays*, Bombay: Asia Publishing House, 1962, p. 20.

The non-Brahmin movement in Maharashtra: an ideology of empowerment

Phule's bahujan samaj: the lower castes as autochthonous. Phule, as Srinivas suggested, certainly played a pioneering role in the formation of the non-Brahmin movement and more precisely in the ethnicisation of caste. This process is well illustrated by the Satyashodak Movement that he founded in Bombay Presidency in the late nineteenth century. It was not a caste movement since its aim was to represent the 'bahujan samaj', literally, the majority of the people, the masses. Jotirao Phule (1827-1890)[29] was a Mali (market gardener), a cultivating caste in close contact with towns where its members sold their products. In one such town, Poona, Phule attended a Scottish Mission school whose teaching played a catalysing role in shaping his anti-caste ideology. What he learnt about the Blacks in the United States suggested to him a comparison with the lower castes – hence his book, *Slavery* (1873) that he dedicated 'to the good people of the United States as a token of admiration for their sublime disinterested and self sacrificing devotion in the cause of Negro Slavery; and with an earnest desire, that my country men may take their noble example as their guide in the emancipation of their Shudra Brethren from the trammels of Brahmin thraldom'.[30] The writings of Thomas Paine exerted a special influence on Phule who discovered the notions of liberty and equality in *The Age of Reason* and *Human Rights.*

This source of inspiration developed in conjunction with that of Christianity. For Phule, Jesus Christ epitomises equality and fraternity. He also regards him as the spokesman for the poor. However, Phule did not convert to Christianity and even translated the Christian idiom into a new, indigenous discourse focusing on King Bali, the subterranean god who reigns in the underworld, according to Hindu mythology.[31] Through the vernacularisation of Christian values and symbols, Phule endowed his people with a new, positive identity.

More importantly he gave them a new history on the basis of some

[29] For biographical details, see D. Keer, *Mahatma Jotirao Phooley – Father of Indian Social Revolution*, Bombay: Popular Prakashan, 1974.

[30] J. Phule, *Slavery – Collected works of Mahatma Jotirao Phule*, vol. I, Bombay: Government of Maharashtra, 1991, p. xxvii.

[31] Phule, *Slavery*, op. cit., pp. 36–8.

of the findings of Orientalism. Phule used the Aryan theory to his own advantage: the fact that upper caste leaders traced their origin from Aryan conquerors[32] could be used to argue that they descended from foreigners and that their culture, including the caste system, was alien to India's original people. Phule, therefore, portrayed the Aryans as invaders who had settled in India at a later period to subjugate the autochthones and destroy their civilisation. For him, the low castes were their descendents. In this reinterpretation of the past, the invaders were identified as Brahmins whereas the indigenous groups were described as descending from the original ruling class, the Kshatriyas. In Phule's ideology, this category refers not to the second *varna* but includes all original Indians, from peasant castes to Untouchables.[33] For him, they formed a people, united by the bond of a common origin and of a warrior ethos:

> The Kshatriyas in India (the land of Baliraja) that is the original masters of the land here were known as Astiks, Pishachas, Rakshasas, Ahirs, Kakatas, Bhut, Kolis, Mangs, Mahars etc. They were extremely adept in fighting without the aid of arms and were famed as brave and valiant warriors. They were of an epicurean temperament and were given to the enjoyment of the goods things of life. The kingdoms of most of these rulers were in a prosperous condition, and it would be no exaggeration to say that the land of King Bali was literally flowing with milk and honey.[34]

This description not only presents the original rulers of India as brave warriors but also emphasises their martial manliness and sense of honour (they did not use weapons) as well as their good nature.

[32] The first Hindu nationalist ideologues of the late nineteenth and early twentieth century – from Dayananda to Tilak – borrowed heavily from the European orientalists. Among other themes, the one they used assiduously related to the common racial origin of the European and Indian peoples and its corollary, the southward migration which they interpreted as proving that the Hindus were the first race. This myth helped the first Hindu revivalists to regain their self-esteem but made the North-South divide more pronounced. For more details, see C. Jaffrelot, 'The Idea of the Hindu race in the writings of Hindu nationalist ideologues in the 1920s and 1930s: a concept between two cultures' in P. Robb (ed.) *The Concept of Race in South Asia*, op. cit., pp. 327–54.

[33] G. Omvedt, 'Jotirao Phule and the Ideology of Social Revolution in India', *EPW*, 11 Sept. 1971, p. 1971.

[34] *Collected Works of Mahatma Jotirao Phule*, vol. II, Bombay: Government of Maharashtra, 1991, p. 8.

Such a narrative prepared the ground for the stereotype of the 'good savage' that will be applied to the Indian aborigines but it stands in contrast to the ritually bound and fetishist brahmin. The king of these original Kshatriyas, Bali, is described by Phule as reigning over a rich country, this prosperity being the very reason for the Aryan invasions:

> The extreme fertility of the soil of India, its rich productions, the proverbial wealth of the people, and the other innumerable gifts which this favourable land enjoys, and which have more recently tempted the cupidity of the Western nations, attracted the Aryans. [. . .] The original inhabitants with whom these earth-born gods, the Brahmans, fought, were not inappropriately termed Rakshasas, that is the protectors of the land. [. . .] The cruelties which the European settlers practised on the American Indians on their first settlement in the new world had certainly their parallel in India in the advent of the Aryans and their subjugation of the aborigines. [. . .] They originally settled on the banks of the Ganges whence they spread gradually over the whole of India. In order, however, to keep a better hold on the people they devised that weird system of mythology, the ordination of caste, and the code of crude and inhuman laws to which we can find no parallel among the other nations.[35]

Phule was the first low caste leader who avoided the traps of Sanskritisation by endowing the low castes with an alternative value system. For the first time, they were presented as *ethnic groups* which had inherited the legacy of an antiquarian golden age and whose culture was therefore distinct from that of the wider Hindu society; second, his efforts on behalf of the low castes were not confined to his castemen only: he wanted to unite the *bahujan samaj*, and more especially the *Shudras* and the *Atishudras* (*dalits*). As Omvedt points out, Phule's 'non-Aryan' theory 'excluded Brahmans but did positively identify the peasant majority (that is the middle level castes of Kunbis, Malis, Dhangars etc) with untouchables and Tribals as one community, native inhabitants of Maharashtra'.[36] As early as 1853 he opened schools for Untouchables. He projected himself as the spokesman of the non-Brahmins at large and, indeed, kept targeting the Brahmins in vehement pamphlets where he presented them as

[35] Cited in G. Omvedt, *Dalit Visions*, New Delhi: Orient Longman, 1995, pp. 17–18.

[36] G. Omvedt, 'Jotirao Phule and the Ideology of Social Revolution in India', op. cit., p. 1974

rapacious moneylenders, corrupt priests eager to extort as much as they could from poor and ignorant villagers.[37]

Phule was also the first low caste organiser. In 1875 he was attracted to the Arya Samaj,[38] but kept his distance from the movement because he did not trust the upper caste reformers[39] who pretended to fight against the social system even though they observed its rules.[40] Phule also remained aloof from the Congress, which he regarded as a Brahmin movement.[41] Nationalism, according to him, was an illusion created by upper caste manipulation to conceal the inner divisions of Indian society.[42] He founded the Satyashodak Samaj in 1873 in order to strengthen the sentiment of unity among the low castes. He narrated pseudo-historical episodes bearing testimony to the traditional solidarity between the Mahars and Shudras[43] and protested against the Brahmins' stratagems for dividing the low castes.[44] In the late nineteenth century and early twentieth century, the Satyashodak idiom embraced rich peasants as well as agricultural tenants who belonged to very different castes and in some places 'the Satyashodak message seemed to have reached even the untouchable'.[45] A major spokesman of the non-Brahmin movement in Maharashtra in 1910–30, Mukundrao Patil, the son of Phule's colleague, Krishnarao Bhalekar, was a radical defender of the Untouchables even though he was a rich peasant. He advocated 'the general Satyashodak ideology, of opposition to Sanskritisation and assertion

[37] See, 'Priestcraft exposed' in J. Phule, *Collected Works of Mahatma Jotirao Phule*, vol. 2, op. cit., p. 67 and 'A poem about the crafty, cunning and spurious (religious) books of the Brahmins (A contrast between the comfortable lives of the Brahmins and the miserable lives of the Shudras)' in *Slavery – Collected Works of Mahatma Jotirao Phule*, vol. I, op. cit., p. 81.

[38] O'Hanlon, *Caste, Conflict and Ideology*, op. cit., p. 223.

[39] In 1885 Phule published a pamphlet implicitly directed against Ranade whom he criticised for his elitist conceptions and more especially for his condescending attitude *vis-à-vis* the peasants (J. Phule, 'A warning' in *Collected Works of Mahatma Jotirao Phule*, vol. II, op. cit. p. 48 ff.).

[40] Phule, *Slavery*, op. cit., pp. 58–9.

[41] Phule, *Collected Eorks*, vol. II, op. cit., p. 25.

[42] Ibid., p. 29.

[43] For instance he tells a story about how Mahars once had to attack 'Brahmins for liberating their Shudra brothers' (*Slavery*, op. cit., p. 25).

[44] Ibid., p. 49.

[45] M.S. Gore, *Non-Brahman Movement in Maharashtra*, New Delhi: Segment Books, 1989, p. 26.

of the "non-Aryan" unity of Maharashtrian natives'.[46] By that time, Phule's view of the non-Brahmins as non-Aryas had made an impact on the small Dalit intelligentsia. In 1909, Kisan Faguji Bansode (1870–1946), a Mahar from Nagpur, warned the upper castes in the following terms:

> The Aryans – your ancestors – conquered us and gave us unbearable harassment. At that time we were your conquest, you treated us even worse than slaves and subjected us to any torture you wanted. But now we are no longer your subjects, we have no service relationship with you, we are not your slaves or serfs. . . .[47]

The Satyashodak Samaj eventually attracted even Marathas such as the Jedhe family, from Poona, who realised 'the futility of a purely Maratha politics'.[48] Keshavrao Jedhe adopted 'the long-held Satyashodak view of history: Brahmans were outsiders to the country and to the ethnic community of true "Hindus"; they desired only their own caste superiority and consolidated their power through treachery, through falsification of historical records, and by weaving a web of religious slavery which set up a social hierarchy of superiority and inferiority and divided the masses'.[49]

Maratha princes such as the Maharajah of Baroda strongly approved of Phule's ideological commitments and donated large amounts of money to his movement.[50] A direct descendant of Shivaji, the Maharajah of Kolhapur, Shahu, who reigned between 1894 and 1922, was even more supportive.[51] While Shahu inherited the ideological legacy of Phule, he had a different perspective: as a prince, he was anxious to reassert his authority *vis-à-vis* the Brahmins who

[46] G. Omvedt, 'The Satyashodak Samaj and Peasant Agitation', *EPW*, 3 Nov. 1973, p. 1973.

[47] Cited in Omvedt, *Dalit Visions*, op. cit., p. 35.

[48] G. Omvedt, 'Non-Brahmans and Nationalists in Poona', *EPW*, annual number, Feb. 1974, p. 207.

[49] Ibid., p. 208.

[50] *Collected Works of Mahatma Jotirao Phule*, vol. II, op. cit. pp. 81 and 97. The Maharajah of Baroda also tried to uplift the Untouchables through education but he could not find teachers other than Muslims and Arya Samajists for his schools (*Presidential Speech of His Highness the Maharajah Gaekwar at the All-India Conference on the Abolition of Untouchability*, Bombay, 1918, p. 10).

[51] He had been educated by a former member of the ICS, S.M. Fraser who was also the tutor of Mysore and Bhavnagar, two other states where anti-

dominated the state's administration. For Shahu, the non-Brahmin repertoire fits in a strategy of empowerment of the lower castes.

Shahu Maharaj and non-Brahminism as an empowerment strategy for the lower castes. Maharashtra had a long history of Brahmins – Maratha conflict. From the seventeenth century, the Maharashtrians carved out a state for themselves at the expense of the Mughal empire. The dynasty then established by Shivaji Marathas claimed the status of Kshatriya. However, Maharashtrian Brahmins – and more especially the Chitpavans, a particular *jati* – never acknowledged the legitimacy of this development and usurped the throne in the eighteenth century. The Brahmins, moreover, took dramatic advantage of the British education system and of the new administration. By the late nineteenth century they almost monopolised the administrative functions open to Indians as well as the professions,[52] a situation that served as a backdrop to the anti-Brahmin feelings of Shahu Maharaj, the heir of Shivaji.

When he ascended the throne in 1895, Shahu 'found that there were no Marathas either in the administration, education or politics, and, on the other hand, there was a preponderance of Brahmins in these fields. Having observed this preponderance, Shahu Maharaj was determined to graft as many non-Brahmins in his administration as possible'.[53] This was the basis of his discourse against the Brahmins till the end of his life.[54] In 1918 he wrote a memorandum arraigning the Brahmins in revealing terms:

> The Brahmins, Bureaucracy here is not like the Priestly Bureaucracy. In priestly bureaucracy not only caste but learning is also necessary. A learned

Brahmin feelings developed early (Chandra Mudaliar, *The Kolhapur Movement*, Kolhapur: Shivaji Vidhyapith, n.d., p. 41).

[52] G. Johnson, 'Chitpavan Brahmins and politics in western India in the late nineteenth and early twentieth centuries' in E. Leach and S.N. Mukherjee (eds), *Elites in South Asia*, Cambridge University Press, 1970, p. 105.

[53] Mudaliar, *The Kolhapur Movement*, op. cit., p. 5.

[54] In 1919 he recalled: 'since my boyhood it has been my pride and a cherished object tô over-rule and beakdown Brahmin bureaucracy and the complaint is that non-Brahmin boys have been detained and not allowed to go for the University examination' (letter from Shri Shahu Maharaj to Col. Wodehouse, reprinted as Appendix 13 in Kavlekar, *Non-Brahmin Movement in India*, op. cit., p. 192.

Brahmin becomes a priest. In the Brahmin Bureaucracy it is the caste alone that is required. However low, wicked, unhealthy, immoral a man may be, being a Brahmin, he is supposed to be higher than a Prince or a General or an Admiral or any learned man of another caste. [. . .] If no step is taken [. . .] it will not be correct to say that the Princes rule India or I may even say that the British rule India but on the contrary it will be right to say that Brahmins rule India.'[55]

Power being the most important thing at stake, Shahu did as much as he could to empower the non-Brahmins in his state. He first realised that the low castes needed education to compete with the Brahmins. He first founded boarding houses and encouraged low caste leaders to do the same for the students of their castes[56] and then, in 1917, made primary education free and compulsory.[57] Simultaneously, he recruited Marathas in the administration of Kolhapur.[58] In 1902 he even reserved 50% of vacancies in the state administration for 'the members of the backward communities'.[59]

Even though he was 'intensely proud of his Maratha lineage',[60] Shahu cannot accurately be described as a Maratha leader because of its efforts to federate the low castes under larger categories such as 'backward communities' or 'non-Brahmins'. In the communal representation scheme that he introduced in 1920 in the Kolhapur municipality, 85 castes were grouped into 20 'unions of castes'. The Marathas, the Rajputs and the Kunbis formed a constituency in themselves.[61]

[55] 'Memorandum from Shri Shahu Maharaj to Lord Sydenham', reprinted as Appendix 41 in Kavlekar, *Non-Brahmin Movement in India*, op. cit., pp. 232–3.

[56] The caste composition of the Shahu Boarding House in 1944 shows that this institution was able to accommodate many low caste people: out of 388 students, 133 were Marathas, 65 from lower castes and 135 Dalits (Kavlekar, *Non-Brahmin Movement in India*, op. cit., pp. 67–8).

[57] Mudaliar, *The Kolhapur Movement*, op. cit., p. 8.

[58] Ibid., p. 6.

[59] Ibid., p. 21.

[60] I. Copland, 'The Maharaja of Kolhapur and the Non-Brahmin Movement 1902–10', *MAS*, 7, 2 (1973), p. 214. He was not only proud of his Maratha identity but also defended the interests of the Marathas. In 1919 he asked the British to revive the Maratha regiments (Kavlekar, *Non-Brahmin Movement in India*, op. cit., p. 204).

[61] Mudaliar, *The Kolhapur Movement*, op. cit., p. 27.

While Shahu was close to the Arya Samaj,[62] he embraced the ideology of Phule which had obvious affinities with his anti-Brahminism. He patronised the establishment of the Satyashodak Samaj in Kolhapur in 1911 and, following the *modus operandi* of the movement, he promoted inter-caste dining halls and had the *Inter-caste Marriage Act* passed in 1918 at Kolhapur.[63] In 1920 he appointed Maratha priests to circumvent the Brahmins and soon after established the Kshatriya Vedic School to train Maratha priests.[64]

Naturally, Shahu's actions were confined to his state. But his desire to empower the lower castes led him to expand his activities beyond Kolhapur, in British India. In Bombay Presidency Brahmins enjoyed a virtual monopoly in the administration of the British Raj[65] and this state of affairs partly explained the low caste mobilisation orchestrated by Jotirao Phule in the late nineteenth century. Shahu's strategy consisted in highlighting the poor condition of 'the Marathas and other backward communities'[66] to solicit the protection of the British. The colonial authorities, partly because they wanted to counter the Brahmin-dominated Congress, were prepared to implement some affirmative action policies in favour of the Marathas. Eventually, they reserved seven seats for 'the Marathas and allied castes' in the Legislative Council of Bombay Presidency in 1919. The Simon Commission report pointed out in 1930 that reservation was resorted to in this instance 'to safeguard *majority* communities, who were thought to be likely to be under the dominance of a strongly

[62] He asked Arya Samajists to come to Kolhapur and educate the lower castes (Kavlekar, *Non-Brahmin Movement in India*, op. cit., p. 198).

[63] Mudaliar, *The Kolhapur Movement*, op. cit., p. 26.

[64] The very name of this school suggests that Shahu was still acting in the framework of Sanskritisation. Indeed, he tried to secure for the Marathas the status of Kshatriyas and broke with the local Brahmins in 1900 when they denied his family's claim to this status and accordingly refused them the right perform certain rituals. He wanted to 'kshatriyaise' the Dalits too. He used to give them symbolic swords and Maratha names, calling them 'Suryavaunshi' and pretending that they could trace their lineage to the sun God, Surya.

[65] In 1886–7 of the 328 Hindus of the 'Executive and Judicial Service' 211 were Brahmins, 25 were Kshatriyas, 37 Prabhus (i.e. Kayasth), 38 Vaishyas and only one came from the 'Backward Classes' (Seal, *The Emergence of Indian Nationalism*, op. cit., p. 185).

[66] Shahu uses this phrase repeatedly, for instance in his 1918 memorandum to Lord Sydenham (op. cit., p. 226).

entrenched minority [e.g. the Brahmins]'.[67] One of the eleven seats returned by urban constituencies and six of the rural ones were reserved to 'Marathas and allied castes'. This decision strongly encouraged these castes to unite and mobilise for social advancement. During the preparation of the 1919 Montagu-Chelsmford reform, Shahu circulated a memorandum 'on the necessity of separate Communal electorates for the Marathas, etc., for electing members to the new Councils under the Reforms scheme', where he wrote:

> Being thus not a commercial or educated community, they [the Marathas] are poor, and without resources, influence and organisation. In this respect they are even worse of than Telis, Tilaris, Goldsmiths, Sutas, Lohars and even Mahars, Mangs and other Untouchables, to whom many a business line and handicraft are open [. . .] Five great monsters do a lot of mischief to the village agricultural community which mostly consists of the Marathas. The Kulkarni [Brahmin who often played the role of village accountant] is the biggest of them all [. . .] Next to the Kulkarni is the Brahmin Sawkar [moneylender] who has appropriated to himself a very large portion of the village lands. The third in this order is the school-master and his brother the college-professor in big cities [. . .] [The fourth] is the Brahmin bureaucracy watered and nourished by Government themselves. [. . .] The village priest, securely and permanently installed by Hindu religious puranas invented and developed to maintain the Brahmanic supremacy is the fifth monster.[68]

Shahu demanded separate electorates instead of reserved seats on which, he said, he was 'sure that weak, unprincipled undesirable Marathas will be elected who would be used by Brahmins as cat's paw for them to draw the apples out of the fire',[69] the same argument was to be articulated by Ambedkar.

Shahu not only emphasised the backwardness of the Marathas but also the fact that they represented more than themselves: they pretended to be the central element of a larger, backward group in order to pressurise the British more efficiently. The People's Union, whose patron was Shahu Maharaj, organised a Conference of the Hindu Backward Classes in June 1920. The conference did not only ask for

[67] Indian Statutory Commission, *Report of the Indian Statutory Commission*, vol. 1, Calcutta: Government of India, 1930, pp. 139.

[68] 'Note by H.H. the Maharajah of Kolhapur on the necessity of separate Communal electorates for the Marathas, etc., for electing members to the new Councils under the Reforms scheme', IOLR, L/P&J/9/14.

[69] Ibid.

the recognition by the state of a new administrative category that would be called 'the Hindu Backward Classes', but insisted also that the notion used by the British in their reservation policy, 'the Marathas and allied classes', should 'include all the Backward communities'.[70] Maratha leaders obviously aspired to play a pivotal role in the shaping of a caste federation. Therefore, the conference expressed 'an emphatic protest against the misleading statement made in public to the effect that the Marathas, Malis etc. do not belong to the Backward Classes when their percentage of education is very low'.[71] The main demand of the conference was that the eight seats reserved to the Marathas and allied castes in the Montagu-Chelmsford report should be extended to fifteen. Simultaneously, the Secretary of the Poona-based All India Maratha Mali Union made a similar representation to the British:

> The word 'Maratta' [*sic*] means all the backward classes. As a matter of fact not only the Marattas but all other allied communities have fought in the last world war for the Empire and all such communities are anxious to get the privilege of reserved seats in the council to be hereafter elected.[72]

Among the allied communities of Marathas, the Yadav Gavlis then opportunely discovered that they had strong affinities with the Marathas. The President of the Yadav Gavli Association, Raghunath Vithal Khedekar, was an exceptional personality whom we shall meet again while dealing with North India in the following chapter. Born in Bombay in 1873, his father had been private secretary of the Maharajah of Bhavnagar, one of the most progressive states as far as the upliftment of the lower castes were concerned. After studying medicine in Britain, he started practising in 1902 in Bhavnagar and Kolhapur, where he met Shahu Maharaj.[73] The first Yadav association had been founded in 1903 by a relative of his father.[74] In the

[70] 'Resolutions of the Conference of the Hindu Backward Classes', L/P&J/9/14, IOLR.

[71] Ibid.

[72] Letter without any date from the Secretary of the All India Maratha Mali Union to the President of the Joint Committee (L/P&J/9/14).

[73] For biographical details see, M.S.A. Rao, *Social Movements and Social Transformation – A Study of Two Backward Classes*, Delhi: Manohar, 1987, p. 139.

[74] Ibid., p. 176.

early 1920s, Khedekar protested that the Southborough Committee should consider the Yadav Gavlis as Marathas:

The Yadav Gavli community claims descent from the Great Yadav families to one which Shri Krishna the 8th incarnation of Vishnu belonged. The whole of the North India, Gujarat and Deccan were only ruled by the Kings of the Yadav families. [. . .] They have kept up their Kshatriya caste traditions, customs and occupations. [. . .] They have given considerable recruits to the government and have been regarded as Marathas and included in the Maratha regiments.[75]

In the end, the Yadav-Gavli association demanded the 'inclusion [of this caste] in the list of the Marathas and allied communities of the Deccan for franchise purpose'. Access to political power was of course the main reason for this social *rapprochement*. Eventually, Khedekar was deputed by the People's Union, the Deccan Ryots Association and the Yadav Gavli Association to make a representation to the Joint Select Committee. He explained:

If the term 'Maratha' be defined as meaning 'anti-Brahmin' in the regulation to be framed under the Indian Act, it will remove all misunderstandings and ill feelings in the Maratha castes and it will allow Jains and Lingayat castes to share the benefit of the reserved seats.[76]

Marathas, who had already forged a 'backward' front with the Malis and the Yadavs, were striving for an even larger coalition including the Lingayats and the Jains under the all-encompassing label of 'anti-Brahmins'. Certainly, the loose structure of the Marathas lent itself to this kind of aggregative strategy. They have no clear-cut subcastes and are so 'amorphous' that 'it is hard to tell in some cases, whether a group is Maratha or of another affiliation called Kunbi'.[77] This arrangement naturally 'facilitates incorporation into Maratha caste'[78] of other peasant castes.

[75] Letter from R.V. Khedekar, without any date, (L/P&J/9/14). Subsequently, Yadav leaders claimed that Shivaji's mother was a Yadav. (Rao, *Social Movements and Social Transformation*, op. cit., p. 148 and R.V. Khedekar, *The Divine Heritage of the Yadavas*, Allahabad: Parmanand, 1959)

[76] Letter from R.V. Khedekar, dated 18 May 1920, to the Joint Select Committee (L/P&J/9/14).

[77] H. Orenstein, 'Caste and the concept of "Maratha" in Maharashtra', *The Eastern Anthropologist*, 16(1), Jan.–Apr. 1963, p. 3.

[78] Ibid., p. 8.

But in spite of the Marathas' specificity, there is much to learn from this case study as to how state policies can indirectly refashion social groupings. The British policy of compensatory discrimination through quotas in the assemblies accelerated the transformation of castes into interest groups and fostered a process of amalgamation among the low castes. Leading castes such as the Marathas initiated federations whose aim was purely political. They had understood that the rules were those of the game of numbers, a strategy that proved rather successful in Maharashtra. Its architects could rely on the legacy of Jotirao Phule's Satyashodak Samaj,[79] which had established an idiom – the Bahujan idiom – encompassing all non-Brahmins. Another important factor was the pivotal situation of the Marathas who represented 20% of the population. While they were unable to federate all the non-Brahmins the mere fact that the British designated a category called 'Marathas and allied' showed that they had achieved partial success. Among these allies were the Kunbis, who were always regarded as more backward than the Marathas[80] but who now appeared in the same category. The Kunbis accounted for 10% of the population of Maharashtra and therefore contributed, to the irresistible rise to power of the Marathas from the late colonial period onwards.

For decades, the Maratha-dominated non-Brahmin movement remained hostile to a Brahmin-dominated Congress. Phule regarded its nationalist discourse as a fraud because a caste-ridden society could not be the basis for a proper nation and the anti-colonial discourse was anyway a device used by the Brahmins to maintain their domination. Shahu indicted the Congress from his usual viewpoint emphasising power relations. In his memorandum to Lord Sydenham, he arraigned the party because 'it has closed its eyes to the needs of, and done nothing for, the submerged classes and the aims of their leaders are to strive to keep down the masses to perpetuate the bureaucratic rule of their community'.[81] However, when the Marathas asserted themselves politically – whereby they won a substantial

[79] The Maharajah of Kolhapur claimed that he had inherited his views from the movement ('Note by H.H. the Maharajah of Kolhapur on the necessity of separate Communal electorates for the Marathas, etc., for electing members to the new Councils under the Reforms scheme', IOLR, L/P&J/9/14).

[80] The Kunbis have been classified as OBCs by the Mandal Commission.

[81] 'Memorandum from Shri Shahu Maharaj to Lord Sydenham', reprinted as Appendix 41 in Kavlekar, *Non-Brahmin Movement in India*, op. cit., p. 228.

number of reserved seats in the assemblies and realised that Congress was a strong contender for power – they tried to enter the party. The Brahmin Congress leaders knew that Maratha support represented a very valuable asset. Politicians such as N.V. Gadgil, a Chitpavan Brahmin who was fully aware that the nationalist movement could only acquire a mass-base if it attracted in low castes leaders, forged an alliance with K. Jedhe in the early 1930s.[82] A Maratha-dominated Satyashodak Samaj, which till then had remained aloof from the Congress decided to join the movement. Gradually, the Marathas rose to power within the party.

The Maharashtrian political trajectory is a good illustration of Weiner thesis about the inclusiveness of Congress. This regional pattern relied on two complementary factors, first the changing identity of the lower castes which emancipates themselves from Sanskritisation to embrace instead an ethnic repertoire, and, second, the shaping of new social categories by state reservation policies which correspond, more or less, to new, ethnicised identities.

However, one must take a nuanced view of this pattern. First, the two groupings did not fully coincide since Phule's *bahujan samaj* was larger than the administrative notion which, eventually became relevant one, i.e. 'Marathas and allied castes'. Second, this latter category did not become consolidated either because many Marathas refused to mix with lower castes and remained wedded to the Sanskritisation ethos. One of their numbers, Bhaskarrao Jadhav, typified such ambivalence: on the one hand he admitted 'the prevalence of Dravidian customs and racial intermixture among Marathas, and on the other assert[ed], without any qualification, [that] the Marathas are definitely "Aryan Kshatriyas" '.[83] Thus even those who had followed Phule's message for some while eventually joined hands with the Brahmin-dominated Congress, or were co-opted by it.

In spite of this ultimate failure to unite the non-Brahmins, the low caste movement of Maharashtra, from Phule to Shahu, had several very distinctive features with long-term implications: non-Brahmin castes were virtually endowed with a common ethnic background – as the original inhabitants of India – and this category was partly validated by the British policy of positive discrimination which had

[82] Omvedt, 'Non Brahmans and Nationalists in Poona', op. cit., p. 213.

[83] Omvedt, 'Jotirao Phule and the ideology of social revolution in India', op. cit., pp. 1974–5.

a profound impact because the low castes internalised the official categories as part of their quest for empowerment. The non-Brahmin movement is not only – or even primarily – based on ideas but also on social competition. Both dimensions – ethnicisation and empowerment – are complementary and form the core of the southern and western Indian pattern of low caste emancipation. Indeed, they are even more in evidence in the South.

From non-Brahminism to Dravidianism in Tamil Nadu

Caste associations against Sanskritisation. The associations that the lower castes developed in Tamil Nadu by the end of the nineteenth century emancipated themselves from the Sanskritisation ethos more quickly than possibly anywhere else in India.[84] This development was well exemplified by the case of the Nadars. This impure – but not Untouchable – caste of toddy-tappers met with some socio-economic success in the early nineteenth century when Nadar 'middlemen and money-lenders [. . .] began to acquire wealth'.[85] These Nadars started to claim high Kshatriya status – 24,000 of them returned themselves as Kshatriyas in the 1891 census – and they began to get Sanskritised, adopting, for instance, the sacred thread of the twice-born.[86] However, this emulation of their manner of life was very much resented by castes ranked above the Nadars, such as the Maravars (warriors). Indeed, the Nadars, by Sanskritising themselves did not display any compliance with the values of the caste system but tried to challenge it. Revisiting the notion of Sanskritisation, Srinivas emphasises that it may embody 'a strong element of protest against the high castes: "We dare you to stop us emulating you" seems to be the spirit underlying emulation'.[87] That was precisely the

[84] This development was largely due to the fact that the Sanskritic-categories had been super imposed on local society in a superficial way by the British administration. In pre-colonial Tamil Nadu, most of the avenues to social mobility 'did not involve the adoption of [. . .] Sanskritic practices . . .' (N. Subramanian, *Ethnicity and Populist Mobilisation*, Delhi: Oxford University Press, 1999, p. 17).

[85] R. Hardgrave, *The Nadars of Tamilnad: The Political Culture of a Community in Change*, Berkeley: University of California Press, 1969, p. 97.

[86] Ibid., pp. 108–9.

[87] M.N. Srinivas, 'Introduction' in M.N. Srinivas (ed.), *Caste – Its Twentieth Century Avatar*, New Delhi: Viking, 1996, p. xv.

attitude of the Nadars who even fight physically and killed Maravars and Brahmins in the context of growing hostility between them and upper castes in the late nineteenth century.[88] At the same time, the Nadars began to shun this aggressive variant of Sanskritisation to acquire a separate identity. Their caste association, the Kshatriya Mahajana Sangam, founded in 1895 and significantly renamed Nadar Mahajana Sangam in 1910, aimed to promote the general welfare of the Nadars, 'the interests and rights of the community', to start schools and to encourage the industriousness of the community.[89] These objectives were purely secular and showed that the association largely ignored Sanskritisation. In 1921 it called upon the Nadars to return their caste as Kshatriya in the census but it changed its mind soon after under the aegis of W.P.A. Soundrapandian, their main leader in the 1920s–1930s. He urged the Nadars to discard the sacred thread and to boycott the Brahmin priests, including for marriages. He advocated the adoption of the self-respect form of marriage (which was performed without the use of Brahmin priests) and inter-caste dinings.[90] In fact, Soundrapandian had become a disciple of E.V. Ramaswami Naicker, the chief ideologue of the non-Brahmin Dravidian movement in the 1920s–1940s. Naicker selected him as the president of the first Self-Respect Conference in 1929 and in his speech the Nadar leader showed that he had imbibed most of his mentor's doctrine. He declared, for instance, that 'From the time when the Aryans came to our land from the north and strengthened and consolidated their position in our land, a great calamity overtook the country. The foundations of our society were shaken'.[91]

This discourse reflects a process of ethnicisation along Dravidian lines. This was to be the next step, after the rejection of Sanskritisation, for the Nadars: first they emancipated themselves from the dominant, hierarchical value system, then they adopted an alternative, egalitarian and ethnic identity. Soon after, in 1935, the Nadar Mahajana Sangam requested the government of Madras Presidency to include the Nadars in the list of the backward classes 'so that fee concessions might be given to Nadars students'.[92] This caste thus epito-

[88] R. Hardgrave, *The Nadars of Tamilnad*, op. cit., pp. 110–11.
[89] Ibid., p. 132.
[90] Ibid., pp. 179–80.
[91] Ibid., p. 179.
[92] Ibid., p. 141.

mises the way low castes of Tamil Nadu simultaneously internalised the Orientalist discourse on Dravidian identity and British social categories of positive discrimination. In the following sections we shall look at the making of this non-Brahmin Dravidianism in a larger perspective.

The invention of the Dravidian. As mentioned above, British Orientalists emphasised the cultural specificity of southern Indians as Dravidians in the nineteenth century. The Revd Caldwell (1819–91) was especially successful in familiarising Tamil Nadu with the idea that Sanskrit had been brought to South India by Aryan, Brahmin, colonists and that the original inhabitants were Dravidians speaking Tamil, Telugu etc.[93] Tamil thinkers assimilated these views very promptly. In the 1890s, P. Sundaram Pillai considered that 'India south of the Vindhyas, the Peninsular India, still continues to be India proper',[94] because of its pre-Aryan culture. However, Dravidian identity was especially articulated by low caste leaders in their fight against Brahmins.

In the first decade of the twentieth century Iyothee Thass, a Pariah converted to Buddhism,[95] pointed out that ancient India had been prosperous and most humanely governed under Buddhist kings but that they had been dislodged from power by Brahmin invaders who imposed the caste system on them. The Buddhists were then marginalised and considered as unclean and base.[96] Their religion had endowed them with a specific culture that eschewed violence, forbade alcohol and so on.[97] Thass even maintained that in the past India was called Indirar Desam, the land of Indirar, Indirar being the name of the Buddha after he succeeded in controlling his five senses (*indiriyams*).[98] This original civilisation was none other than the Dravidian civilisation and Thass therefore chose to call its castemates, the Pariahs, 'Dravidas'.[99] Thus, as early as the late nineteenth

[93] N. Ram, 'Dravidian Movement in its Pre-Independence Phases', *EPW*, annual number, Feb. 1979, p. 381.

[94] Cited in Irshick, *Politics and Social Conflict in South India*, op. cit., p. 283.

[95] Cited in V. Geetha and S.V. Rajadurai, *Towards a Non-Brahmin Millenium: From Iyothee Thass to Periyar*, Calcutta: Samya, 1998, p. 43.

[96] Ibid., p. 72.

[97] Ibid., p. 92.

[98] Ibid., p. 96.

[99] Ibid., p. 108.

century, Non-Brahmin leaders claimed that the lower castes were the original inhabitants of India.[100]

Gradually, the non-Brahmin South Indian associations adopted the name 'Dravida' and the suffix 'Adi' – meaning initial, primordial – in their titles. The Pariah Mahajan Sabha, which had been founded in 1890, became the Adi-Dravida Mahajan Sabha, and in 1918 it appealed to the government to replace the pejorative word Pariah by Adi-Dravida, denoting the original inhabitants of Dravida land.[101] In 1917 an Adi-Andhra Mahajan Sabha had come into existence the same way. In fact, this association was initially called Andhra Panchama Conference but the chairman of its 1917 session, M.V. Bhagya Reddy (1888–1939), in his presidential address, declared that the so-called Panchamas (the fifth caste, the Untouchables) were the original sons of the soil and they were the rulers of the country'.[102] Hence the change of name of the Sabha. In the 1931 census about one-third of the Malas and Madhigas (Untouchables) gave their identity as Adi-Andhras.[103]

One of the most influential proponents of the Dravidian ideology was M.C. Rajah (1883–1947), a Pariah who became secretary of the Adi-Dravida Mahajan Sabha in 1916 and who had presided over the All India Depressed Classes Association since 1928. As a nominated member of the Madras Legislative Council since 1920, Rajah in 1922 moved a resolution recommending that the terms 'Panchama' and 'Parya' be deleted from the government records and the terms Adi-Dravida and Adi-Andhra substituted instead.[104]

The main architect of non-Brahmin Dravidianism, however, was E.V. Ramaswami Naicker, alias Periyar, a religious mendicant who had been completely disillusioned by the Congress and Gandhi while taking part in the Vaikham *satyagraha*.[105] He left Congress in 1925

[100] M. Ross Barnett, *The Politics of Cultural Nationalism*, Princeton University Press, 1976, pp. 315–16.

[101] Kshirsagar, *Dalit Movement in India*, op. cit., p. 72.

[102] Cited in Omvedt, *Dalit Visions*, op. cit., p ; 36.

[103] *Census of India*, 1931, vol. 23, Hyderabad State, part 1, Hyderabad: Government Central Press, 1933.

[104] S.K. Gupta, *The Scheduled Castes in Modern Indian Politics – Their Emergence as a Political Power*, Delhi: Munshiram Manoharlal, 1985, p. 5.

[105] Mohan Ram, 'Ramaswami Naicker and the Dravidian Movement', *EPW*, Annual Number, Feb. 1974, p. 219. Periyar organised *satyagrahas* before the Mahadevar temple in Vaikkom, 'which gained him two jail terms and the

after the Tamil Nadu Congress rejected two of his resolutions in favour of reservations for non-Brahmins. If Phule drew some of his egalitarian inspiration from Thomas Paine, Periyar was more impressed by Robert Ingersoll. Like Phule and Ambedkar, he was egalitarian in a western, individualist vein.[106] The notion of human dignity was so central to his thinking that after quitting Congress in the mid-1920s, he launched the Self-Respect Movement, whose key word was *Samadharma*, equality. But Periyar regarded it as much as a Buddhist as a Western notion.[107] Like Thass, he argued that the lower castes were descendants of the first Buddhists and endowed them with a Dravidian identity. Periyar argued that the Dravidian-Buddhists were ill-treated by the Aryan-Hindus because they opposed caste hierarchy.[108] He eschewed the Orientalist view that interpreted the conflict between the former and the latter in terms of race but emphasised this cleavage by refering to ethnic categories anyway:

> The Dravidians have a distinct origin in society, their languages are independent and belong to separate classes. The terms 'Aryan' and 'Dravidian' are not my inventions. They are historical realities. They can be found in any school boy's textbook that the *Ramayana* is an allegoric representation of the invading Aryans and the domiciled Dravidians has [sic] been accepted by all historians including Pandit Nehru and all reformers including Swami Vivekananda.[109]

Naicker established an equation between the Brahmins and the Aryan invaders. Himself the son of an affluent merchant from the Balija Naidu caste (an artisanal caste whose members had often turned to trade), he presented the lower castes as the Dravidians and used Dravidianism against the Brahminical elite. One of the resolutions of the first Provincial Self-Respect Conference in 1929 concerned the

---

honorific "Vaikkom Veerar" (Hero of Vaikkom)' title. (M.S.S. Pandian, ' "Denationalising" the Past. "Nation" in E.V. Ramaswamy's Political Discourse', *EPW*, 16 Oct. 1993, p. 2282).

[106] He said, for instance, 'A sense of self-respect and fraternity must arise within human society. Notions of high and low amongst men should disappear'. (Cited in Geetha and Rajadurai, *Towards a Non-Brahmin Millenium*, op. cit., p. 283.)

[107] Ibid., p. 421.

[108] Pandian, ' "Denationalising" the Past', op. cit., p. 2284.

[109] Cited in ibid., p. 2287.

boycott of Brahmin priests – especially for weddings: Naicker initiated 'Self-Respect weddings', celebrated without such priests; another resolution condemned the *varnashrama dharma*. Moreover, in the late 1920s, the movement had the Manu Smriti (the Laws of Manu) burnt on several occasions.[110] Naicker's hostility to the caste system was spelled out in terms of a return to the sources of the Dravidian culture: '*Samadharma* came to stand in for a cultural and civilizational alternative: a social order based on radically different principles from the present, which needed to rest on premises derived from a non-Aryan, non-Sanskritic ethos'.[111]

Periyar had an explicitly ethnic conception of the low caste identity, which he compared to the situation to the blacks in South Africa.[112] He 'conceived of the Dravidian community primarily in terms of a coalition of mega castes – the non-Brahmin Hindu castes of Tamil Nadu'.[113] The Non-Brahmins who all shared a Dravidian identity therefore had to unite. Such a *rapprochement* did indeed occur since the Nadar followers of W.P.D. Soundrapandian and Adi Dravidas (Untouchables) were the mainstays of the Self-Respect movement. But the Self-Respect movement attracted also Balaji Naidus (like Naicker himself), Vellalas (like S. Ramanathan, the second most important leader of the movement), Sengunthars (weavers – like C.N. Annadurai, Naicker's successor), Agamudaiyars (a cultivating caste), Minavars (fishermen), Mukkulathavar and even Chettis (merchants).[114]

The scope and strength of this social coalition must not be exaggerated since old lines of cleavage persisted. As in Maharashtra, the 'non-Aryans' did not form a solid block. All non-Brahmins did not back the Self-Respect Movement, nor were all the castes which were represented among its supporters fully behind it: there were many Nadars in the Congress ranks for instance. However, the ethnic basis of the Non-Brahmin discourse which, from Thass to Periyar combined Buddhist and Dravidian references, helped its leaders to unite

[110] Irshick, *Politics and Social Conflict in South India*, op. cit., p. 341.

[111] Cited in Geetha and Rajadurai, *Towards a Non-Brahmin Millenium*, op. cit., p. 352.

[112] Ibid., p. 297.

[113] N. Subramanian, *Ethnicity and Populist Mobilization*, op. cit., p. 103.

[114] Ibid., pp. 373–4 and E. F. Irshick, *Tamil Revivalism in the 1930s*, Madras: Cre-A, 1986, pp. 95–100.

the low castes and mobilise them. As in Maharashtra, this process could only materialise because of the simultaneous implementation of policies of positive discrimination by the British.

The Non-Brahmin as a bureaucratic creation: the quest for empowerment

According to Irshick, the British administrators of Madras Presidency were especially prompt in distinguishing Brahmins from Non-Brahmins in their rules and regulations.[115] Such distinctions had an important impact when they began to affect access to resources or power. Successive Madras governments were especially keen to use the state machinery as a device 'to reflect or represent the population they governed'.[116] In August 1919, for instance, the following order was issued:

> The time would appear to have now come when it is desirable to obtain in the administrative machinery of this country the services belonging to all various large sections of the community in India and it is impossible to do this unless special facilities are offered to Panchamas (Untouchables) and other backward classes.[117]

Previous Madras governments had realised since the late nineteenth century that the lower castes needed positive discrimination programmes in the realm of education because they were concerned by the over-representation of Brahmins in the administration.[118] The taxonomy they used was to have long-term effects. The Education Department divided first the Hindus into Brahmins and 'other Hindus' in 1870, then into Brahmans and 'Hindus not Brahmans' in

[115] E.F. Irshick, *Tamil Revivalism in the 1930s*, op. cit., p. 23.

[116] Ibid., p. 41.

[117] Ibid., p. 42.

[118] From 1892 to 1904, 15 out of 16 recruits to the State Civil Service were Brahmins, as were 77 out of 140 deputy collectors and 15 out of 18 deputy judges in 1912 (E. F. Irschick, *Politics and social conflict in South India*, op. cit., p. 223). This preponderance of Brahmins in the administration resulted from their over-representation in the University. In 1913, even though they represented only 3% of the population, Brahmins accounted for 72% of 'graduates' in Madras University. (P. Radhakrishnan, 'Backward Class Movements in Tamil Nadu' in M. N. Srinivas (ed.), *Caste – Its Twentieth Century Avatar*, op. cit., p. 368)

1874, into 'Brahmans, Vaishyas, Shudras and other Hindus' by the early 1880s, and, by the turn of the century, 'the classification had simply become Brahman and "non-Brahman" '.[119]

This dichotomous categorisation was internalised by the low castes which were included among the 'non-Brahmans'; they realised that by presenting themselves as 'non-Brahmans' they would form a large, influential group. Again, this new identity was over-determined by the quest for empowerment. This qualitative change was evident from 'The Non-Brahmin Manifesto', the text marking the formation of the Non-Brahmin movement in Madras.[120] The authors first contrasted their demographic weight as gleaned from the Census – 40.5 million people, as against 1.5 million Brahmins and their lack of influence: they gave the relevant figures regarding their position in the administration (in 1913, out of 128 District *Munsifs*, 93 were Brahmins), in the University, in the assembly and in the Congress. They mention, for instance, that out of fifteen representatives of the Madras Presidency Congress to the All India Congress Committee, there was only one non-Brahmin. They concluded that 'The social reactionary and the impatient political idealist, who seldom has his foot on solid earth, have now taken almost complete possession of the Congress.' Thus their basic argument is that the non-Brahmins' 'political interests [. . .] (as compared with those of the Brahmins who number only about a million and a half) have materially suffered' because 'they maintain no proper organisation for protecting or promoting their common interests . . .' Hence the formation of the Justice Party by the promoters of the Non-Brahmin manifesto.

The Justice Party used the British mapping of Indian society, based on the division into Brahmins and Non-Brahmins for affirmative action programmes. These positive discrimination policies fostered a common sense of purpose among low castes who had not previously collaborated: now they had to defend shared interests. The castes in question were not the lowest, however. Dominant castes like the Vellalas and the Kapus and merchant castes (mainly Chettiars) were at the helm, namely those groups ranking below the Brahmins who were eager to supplant them. This common aim became an even

[119] E.F. Irshick, *Tamil revivalism in the 1930s*, op. cit., p. 24.

[120] The complete text has been reproduced as an appendix to E. F. Irschick, *Politics and social conflict in South India*, op. cit., pp. 358-67.

stronger motivation when the British implemented a new reservation policy in the Legislative Councils.

The preparation of the Montagu-Chelsmford reforms in 1917–18 helped the Justice Party to consolidate its social base since it could make representations to British officials on behalf of Non-Brahmins. Interestingly, this category was not used systematically from the outset. In the memorandum that the Justice Party presented to Montagu in December 1917, there was a strong plea to grant Non-Brahmins a quota in the legislature and in all the branches of the administration. But the party did not rule out separate representations being given to the five Non-Brahmin groups, the Balija Naidus, the Pillais (a sub-caste of Vellalas), the Mudaliars (also a Vellala sub-caste), the Chettis and the Panchamas (Untouchables).[121] The Montagu-Chelmsford Report that was published in 1918 eventually denied a communal representation to all groups except Sikhs and Muslims but Non-Brahmins sought to influence the drafting of the Government of India Bill which was to implement the reforms. At this juncture the Justice Party considered only Non-Brahmins as a relevant category, thereby trying to subsume all sub-groups. K.V. Reddi Naidu, a Kapu, presented a memorandum before the Joint Select Committee in charge of finalising the Bill in London by endowing this administrative category with a strong separate identity: there was, he testified, 'a basic racial difference that separated Brahman from non-Brahman; the former were Aryans, the latter Dravidians'.[122] Both notions – Non-Brahminism and Dravidianism – were now coterminous in the discourse of the Justice Party.

The party's claim was accepted by the British and therefore Non-Brahmins were granted reserved seats in the Government of India Bill. However, in April 1920, Lord Chelmsford received a Memorandum protesting against the reservation of only 28 seats out of 65 for the Non-Brahmins in the Legislative Council of Madras. Again, the signatories emphasised their caste and ethnic differences in justifying their claim:

> The Brahmins differ from the non-Brahmins in caste, manners, customs and interests and even in personal law in some respects. The former are Aryans and the latter are Dravidians and thus they differ in race. In the past

[121] E.F. Irschick, *Politics and Social Conflict*, op. cit., p. 70
[122] Ibid., p. 150.

the Brahmins have practically monopolised all or almost all the seats in the Local and Imperial Legislative Councils. The disabilities under which the Non-Brahmins have been suffering were fully set out in the Memorandum which Rai Bahadur K.V. Reddi prepared and submitted to the joint Select Committee on Government of India Bill.[123]

During the 1920 election campaign, the leaders of the Justice Party requested 'all non-Brahmins in this presidency to immediately organise, combine and carry on an active propaganda so as to ensure the return to the reformed Council of as many non-Brahmin as possible'.[124] This tactic yielded dividends since the Justice Party came first in the elections and formed the government thanks to the sympathetic attitude of the British.

The First Communal Government Order, in 1921, asked the chiefs of all administrative services, the collectors and the district judges, to issue every six months a list of their recruits classified in six categories, Brahmins, Hindus non-Brahmin, Christian Indians, Muslims, Europeans and Anglo-Indians and others.[125] From the second semester of 1921 onwards, a readjustment started as the administration recruited 22% of Brahmins, 48% of non-Brahmin Hindus, 10% of Christian Indians, 15% of Muslims, 2% of Europeans and Anglo-Indians and 3% of others. In 1922, a Second Communal Government Order extended these quotas to all services and to all promotions[126] and in 1927, new quotas were established in the administration: 42% for non-Brahmins, 17% for Brahmins, 17% for Muslims, 17% for Anglo-Indians and Christians and 8% for the Depressed Classes whose leaders had claimed that they were left out by the previous quotas.[127]

[123] *The Humble memorial of the Non-Brahmins of Madras* (23 April 1920); IOLR, L/P&J/9/14.

[124] *Justice*, 29 March 1920 in IOR, L/P&J/9/14.

[125] For the complete text, cf. E.F. Irschick, *Politics and Social Conflict*, op. cit., p. 368.

[126] Ibid. p. 369 and followings.

[127] These quotas benefited mostly the non-Brahmin élite. Its first critics, therefore, were the Untouchables. In 1923, M. C. Rajah led a delegation before the Madras Government to protest against the neglect of the Depressed Classes by the Justice Party in the distribution of posts in the administration. He claimed a quota of 30%, and while he did not win the case the 'Depressed Classes' were added to the categories used so far. (P. Radhakrishnan, 'Backward Class Movement in Tamil Nadu', op. cit., p. 115)

The commitment of the Justice Party's governments confirms that the quest for empowerment was one of the driving forces sustaining the Non-Brahmin movement in Madras, one which exemplifies how positive discrimination helped forge a coalition among a wide array of castes. The scope of this coalition must not be exaggerated, however. The Panchamas, for instance, were left out by the Justice Party as soon as it gained power.[128] On the other hand, though limited, this coalition was more solid than that of the Marathas and their allied castes, because Dravidian identity acted as a cementing force. Irschick concludes that 'social change is based on pragmatism, utility and the degree to which it satisfies individual or perceived social needs in solving problems rather than the existence of ideology or the extent to which that ideology is believed in by members of society'.[129] Such distinctions between ideas and beliefs on the one hand and material interests on the other are not really relevant. In the case of Dravidianism and Non-Brahminism, both dimensions are intermingled and reinforced each other: the quest for empowerment might have been the most powerful driving force behind the mobilisation of Non-Brahmins but their movement was sustained by the emotional appeal of their ethnic Dravidian identity. Politicians certainly instrumentalised the Dravidian repertoire but identified with it at the same time. The fact that the quest for power was a basic motivation behind the demand for reservations was made explicit in 1917 by one of the founders of the Justice Party, T.M. Nair:

> We claim our social, moral and political rights, and our share of government appointments, not because we think that government appointments will transform the Non-Brahman communities into the most prosperous of mankind, but because government appointments carry with them political power, of which, as lord of the soil and inheritors of noble traditions, they must have their legitimate share.[130]

Such a discourse shows clearly that, while empowerment was a priority motive of the Justice Party, such a transfer of power was legitimate because Non-Brahmins were Dravidian sons of the soil.[131]

[128] E.F. Irschick, *Politics and Social Conflict*, op. cit., p. 188 and p. 192.
[129] E.F. Irschick, *Tamil Revivalism in the 1930s*, p. 260.
[130] Ibid., p. 43.
[131] Irschick himself, in the conclusion of his first 'classic' considers that the rise of the Justice Party can be explained by at least two factors: on the hand the resentment of non-Brahmins *vis-à-vis* the Brahmins' domination of the

The Tamil Congress and the accommodation of non-elite groups. The rise to power of the Dravidian/Non-Brahmin movement obliged the Congress to democratise itself more significantly than in most other regions of India, including Maharashtra. As everywhere else, the party was dominated by Brahmins until the 1930s.[132] This Brahminical domination was the main reason for the exit of low caste Congress activists like Naicker in the 1920s. In the 1930s Congress leaders began to realise that the Justice Party and the Self-Respect Movement were forces to be reckoned with, and they made 'attempts to incorporate even the lowliest groups under their leadership'.[133] In fact, they focused on the lowliest castes, the Untouchables, as usual. But the party was also able to attract low castes like the Maravars (who were considered as being almost a Criminal Caste by the British)[134] and Nadars. The rise to power of Kamaraj Nadar epitomises this new, accommodating attitude of the Congress party. Kamaraj, who had joined Congress when most of the Nadars regarded the party as Brahmin-dominated, was offered the chance of contesting – successfully – on a Congress ticket to the Legislative Council in 1937 and was elected President of the Tamil Nadu Congress Council in 1940. No other regional branch of the party had such a low caste leader at the helm at that time. These developments attracted Nadars to the Congress Party in large numbers.[135] However, C. Rajagopalachari, a Brahmin, remained the towering figure of the Congress of Tamil Nadu. He became Chief Minister in 1937 and again in 1947 but Kamaraj succeeded him in 1954. At that time, Brahmins represented only 5% of the MLAs, as against 17.2% in 1937,[136] which means that in the early 1950s, the representation of the Brahmins in the assembly was

---

administration and the emergence of a non-Brahmin elite suffering from acute frustration because of this state of affairs and, on the other hand, the fact that 'the work of Caldwell and Nallaswami Pillai on the origins and nature of "Dravidian civilisation" had met with a large, and growing, readership among first-generation college-educated non-Brahman caste Hindus' (*Politics and Social Conflict in South India*, p. 352).

[132] Ibid., p. 268 and 273.

[133] Irschick, *Tamil Revivalism*, op. cit., p. 145

[134] Ibid., p. 200.

[135] R. Hardgrave, *The Nadars of Tamilnad*, op. cit., p. 190.

[136] See S. Saraswati, *Minority politics in Madras state*, Delhi, Impex, 1974 and C. Baker, 'The Congress and the 1937 elections in Madras', *Modern Asian Studies*, Oct. 1976, p. 586.

almost proportionate to their share of the population. In contrast to what had happened in most of the rest of India, the Congress had accompanied a dynamic of democratisation in Tamil Nadu.

The socio-political trajectory of Tamil Nadu suggests a pattern of low caste mobilisation comprising at least four chronologically organised elements. First, the caste associations emancipate themselves of the Sanskritisation ethos or implement its *modus operandi* in such an aggressive way that it reflects egalitarian values, as in the case of the Nadars.[137] Second, the low castes find an alternative identity in Dravidianism, an ideology deriving from British Orientalism, which, in addition to giving them self-esteem and historical pride, creates an egalitarian, ethnic bond between a wide range of non-Brahmin castes (minus the lowest ones, the Untouchables). Third, the British policy of positive discrimination designs administratively social categories such as the Non-Brahmins for which posts are reserved in the state machinery – including the elected assemblies – and this reservation policy serves as a strong incentive for all the castes included in these umbrella category to associate in order to gain power. Fourth, the growing assertiveness of the lower castes leads a Brahmin-dominated Congress to accommodate these groups undergoing a process of upward mobility; the party thereby complies with Weiner's thesis and accompanies an overall democratisation of local politics.

Maharashtra did not fulfil all the criteria of this model but complied with its general spirit. While ethnicisation of caste was initiated by the Satyashodak Samaj, the Sanskritisation ethos, and caste practices more generally speaking, remained pervasive among Non-Brahmins, especially the Marathas. That was one of the reasons why caste ethnicisation in Maharashtra was not as powerful as Dravidianism in Tamil Nadu. Second, the quest for low caste empowerment – whose architect was Shahu Maharaj – did not generate the same sense of solidarity as among the Non-Brahmins of Madras Presidency precisely because there was no such category (the 'Non-Brahmins') in the administration of Kolhapur state or in the reservation policies of Bombay Presidency. As a result, Shahu and Khedekar had to argue – unsuccessfully – that the Marathas represented the 'backward classes' (a notion the British ignored) at large. Finally, the

[137] Hardgrave points out that 'the Nadars have a generally strong bias against the caste *system*' (R. Hardgrave, *The Nadars of Tamilnad*, op. cit., p. 258).

nucleus of castes which inherited the legacy of Shahu Maharaj merely gathered together Marathas and Kunbis. Their mobilisation led a Brahmin-dominated Congress to accommodate them and gradually, as in Tamil Nadu, the Brahmins lost power to these newcomers but most of them belonged to a dominant caste, the Marathas.

There are common features but also differences between the trajectories of Tamil Nadu and Maharashtra. In both cases, upwardly mobile groups made (more or less wide-ranging) alliances to dislodge Brahmins from their seats of power by articulating ethnic identities. They benefited from the British policy of compensatory discrimination based on the reservation of seats in the bureaucracy and in the assemblies. The very decision to grant such or such statutory representation to such and such group in these assemblies contributed to the crystallisation of new groups which resented their non- (or their under-) representation. The State was therefore indirectly reshaping society. Besides, the British officials helped the lower castes to get organised because they feared a Brahmanical conspiracy. In Maharashtra, the Chitpavan Brahmins were the first target of the British because of their implication in secret societies which were responsible for violent actions in the late nineteenth and early twentieth century. In Madras, the Brahmins were simply perceived as the most active Congress supporters.[138]

The differences between the Tamil trajectory and that of Maharashtra may be explained from several points of view. Upper castes were smaller in number in Tamil Nadu, a region where, correlatively the *varna* system is more 'incomplete' than in most Indian provinces. In contrast to the situation prevailing in Maharashtra where the Marathas, form a dominant caste *par excellence*, in Madras Presidency, 'it was rare for a "preponderant" caste type to represent more than a quarter of a district's population'.[139] The most important lesson emerging from this comparison can be spelled out in the following terms: Tamil Nadu and Maharashtra have evolved two variants of a pattern of low caste mobilisation of which ethnicisation and empowerment are the key terms. Western India developed a second

[138] Christopher Baker, *The Politics of South India 1920-1937*, Cambridge University Press, 1976.

[139] D. Washbrook, 'Caste, class and dominance in Modern Tamil Nadu: Non-Brahmanism, Dravidianism and Tamil Nationalism' in M.S.A. Rao and F. Frankel (eds), vol. 1, op. cit., p. 223.

variant since one of the neighbouring states of Maharashtra, Gujarat, was the crucible of a similar phenomenon that has been defined as 'caste federation'.

Caste federations: the case of Gujarat

Kothari and Maru have analysed caste federations as the strategy of individual caste associations which tried to shape such coalitions for political reasons:

> The concept of caste federation refers to a grouping together of a number of distinct endogamous groups into a single organisation for common objectives, the realisation of which calls for a pooling together of resources or numbers or both. By and large, the objectives pursued are secular and associational, although the employment of traditional symbols for evoking a sense of solidarity and loyalty towards the new form is not uncommon. The traditional distinctions between the federating groups are on the whole retained, but the search for a new organisational identity and the pursuit of political objectives gradually lead to a shift in group orientations.[140]

This definition was developed in the course of a study of the caste federation phenomenon in Gujarat where the 'Kshatriyas' exemplified this phenomenon. From the early 1900s the local Rajput leaders had constituted caste associations for promoting education.[141] In the late 1930s, the descendent of one of its leaders, Natvarsingh Solanki, wished to extend these associations to other castes which he considered as *Kshatriyas.*[142] He tried to refashion the social identity of those groups in order to allow others to join hands with the Rajputs and, in this way, to acquire more influence.

Gujarat's largest caste was the Kolis. They had been classified by

[140] R. Kothari and R. Maru, 'Federating of political interests : the Kshatriyas of Gujarat' in R. Kothari (ed.), *Caste in Indian Politics,* New Delhi: Orient Longman, 1986 [1970], p. 72.

[141] G. Shah, *Caste association and political process in Gujarat.* Bombay: Popular Prakashan, 1975, p. 33.

[142] '. . . I wondered why I had to work exclusively for the Rajputs. Why not work for all the members of the Kshatriya class? The Kshatriyas are a class, not a caste.' (Interview cited in M. Weiner, *Party building,* op. cit., p. 97). Solanki obviously plays on the relative ambiguity of the *varna* system since by contrast with *jatis* (of which the usual translation is 'castes'), *varnas* are generally presented as more flexible, being based on the criterion of socio-economic functions.

the British as a 'criminal caste' but claimed that they were Kshatriyas and resorted to genealogists to provide evidence of their aristocratic lineage. They sought recognition on a par with Rajputs. Some Koli clans had established matrimonial alliances with Rajputs, as those castes practised hypergamy.[143] Their ancestors had established small principalities before the British took over and they had retained some control over land under the Raj as landowners or big tenants. Many of them met the necessary conditions for being enfranchised when the British established provincial legislative councils. The democratisation of elective politics therefore enabled the Kolis to use their main asset, their numbers: in 1931 they represented about 20% of the population, almost the double of the Patidars (12.16%), the dominant caste, the main rival of the Rajputs, who represented only 4.85% of the population. Solanki opened his caste association to the Kolis for this very reason: to transform it into a mass organisation.

In 1947, the Kutch, Kathiawar, Gujarat Kshatriya Sabha was created after years of preparatory work. The word 'Kshatriya' was a useful umbrella label to bracket the Rajputs and the Kolis together. In fact, the Kshatriya Sabha is a good example of the way castes, with very different ritual status, join hands to defend their common interests. In this case, the Kolis and the Rajputs had the same enemies, viz., the Patidars. Certainly, this alliance has been legitimised in the idiom of 'tradition', by pretending that its components belonged to the same *varna*, but the use of the word Kshatriya was largely tactical and the original caste identity was seriously diluted. The Rajput leaders of the Kshatriya Sabha emphasised that a *Kshatriya* is not to be defined by descent but by military values. Political calculations had therefore social implications. Several taboos were abolished. Rajputs and Kolis of the Kshatriya Sabha shared meals[144] and the Koli elite married their daughters to lower Rajputs and this process fostered the Rajputisation of the upper Kolis. Kshatriyas tended to form a new caste. The use of terms like Koli Kshatriyas and Rajput Kshatriyas certainly show that the merger was far from complete.[145]

[143] L. Lobo, 'Koli Kshatriyas of North Gujarat: a shift from sanskritised mobility to politised mobility', *Eastern Anthropologist.* 42 (2). April-June 1989, pp. 176-7.

[144] R. Kothari and R. Maru, 'Federating for political interests: the Kshatriyas of Gujarat', op. cit., p. 73.

[145] L. Lobo, 'Koli Kshatriyas of North Gujarat', op. cit., p. 188.

But important dimensions of the caste system were eroded by the after-effects of what were basically socio-economic and political strategies. In fact, the main demands of the Kshatriya Sabha after Independence reflected a relative indifference to ritual issues in comparison to material objectives. For instance, the association claimed that the Kshatriyas were part of the 'Backward Classes' and therefore should benefit from reservations in the educational system and in the administration. This claim was the exact opposite of Sanskritisation.[146] The Kolis benefited more than the Rajputs from the Sabha, which created boarding schools, grants, loan systems etc. in favour of the poorest of their community. This development contributed to the emergence of a Koli intelligentsia which, even though it remained small gave the Koli masses a new confidence and self-esteem as a caste.[147] The members of this elite 'interact[ed] frequently and chart[ed] out common political strategies'.[148] From the 1950s, the Kshatriya Sabha traded off its electoral support for the Congress in exchange for tickets for its members as party candidates. The party was not very responsive, especially because the Patidars were influential in the Congress and disapproved of the Kshatriyas' land reform demands.[149] The Kshatriya Sabha therefore kept its distance from the Congress before the 1962 elections and have suffered a setback. Instead, the association gave its support, in exchange for large concessions, to the Swatantra Party, which became the leading opposition party in the state. This situation persuaded the Congress to change its strategy and to give tickets to Kshatriya candidates before the 1967 elections. The Kshatriya Sabha then supported the Congress, which regained a more comfortable majority than in 1962.[150]

While the 'Kshatriyas' of Gujarat represent the best example of caste federation, other instances occurred in South India. In the early 1960s, the Kallan, the Maravar and the Agamudiar, three lower castes who had already forged close ties with each other (especially ritual ones since they clamed that they descended from the same ancestors),

[146] G. Shah, *Caste Association*, op. cit., p. 78.

[147] L. Lobo, 'Koli Kshatriyas of North Gujarat', op. cit., p. 188.

[148] Ibid., p. 187.

[149] In addition, Congress leadership feared 'communalisation' of the party, and therefore declared that dual membership to a caste-association and to Congress were incompatible.

[150] G. Shah, *Caste Association*, op. cit., p. 127.

decided to adopt the same name, Mukkulator (lit. three castes), in order to merge and to influence local politics.[151] This development suggests that Dravidianism was not the only framework for caste mobilisation in Tamil Nadu but social phenomena like the making of the Mukkulator and the Non-Brahmin movement of the 1920–30s had obvious affinities: in both cases, low caste groups joined hands to improve their bargaining power. While the reservation policy of the British was at stake during the Madras Presidency, electoral competition set the agenda in the 1960s. But the same logic was at work.

The search for new forms of caste activity did not contribute to social change and to the rise of the low castes in the same way in Maharashtra, Tamil Nadu and Gujarat, but the above case studies suggest the emergence of a southern pattern – 'southern' meaning here 'south to the Vindhyas' or 'beyond the Aryavarta', to use the geographical categories of the non-Brahmin movement. In these areas, caste associations prepared the ground for two major developments, namely the ethnicisation of castes, of which the ideology of the 'bahujan samaj' evolved by Phule and the Dravidian movement were the best examples, and the grouping together of castes in a strategy of empowerment – the latter had several incarnations, ranging from Shahu's moves in Kolhapur, to the Tamil Non-Brahmin and the Gujarati federation of the 'Kshatriyas'. These strategies were to a large extent successful[152] and prompted the Congress to accommodate new groups in its ranks.

[151] L.I. Rudolph, 'The modernity of tradition: the democratic incarnation of caste in India', *American Political Science Review*, LIX, (4), Dec. 1965, p. 984.

[152] However, caste federations or caste alliances did not always achieve their objective, as is evident from the case of the Vaniyars, the largest caste of Tamil Nadu, with about 12% of the population in 1931. At the turn of nineteenth century, they were known as Pallis, tilled the land and occupied a rather low rank (though above the pollution line). In 1871, after the first census was published, Pallis who had already protested their low ranking, signed a petition in which they claimed the status of *Kshatriya.* The caste became Sanskritised by abandoning practices considered as unclean like widow remarriage, non-vegetarian diet, etc. From 1901 onwards this process was co-ordinated by a caste association, the Vanya Kula Kshatriya Sangham (VKKS – Association of the Kshatriya of the Fire Clan), which lobbied the British administration. In

In North India, none of these processes reached their logical conclusion even through the British Raj had generated the same context as in the South and in the West. Caste associations often followed the Sanskritisation path and neither prepared the group for an ethnic discourse no.

1921 the agricultural occupation – considered as degrading – of the Pallis was omitted from the census and in 1931 the name Pallis itself was replaced by Vanniya Kula Kshatriyas, which became Vanniyars in common parlance (L.I. Rudolph and S.H. Rudolph. 'The political role of India's caste associations', op. cit., pp. 454–61). After 1947, the VKKS tried to obtain posts in the administration and electoral tickets, in exchange for its support for Congress. As the party was not responsive, the Vanniyars decided to 'contest the elections in cooperation with the toiling masses' and therefore formed the Tamilnad Toilers' Party. Twenty-five of them were elected MLAs. The Congress, which could not secure a majority of seats in the Madras Assembly, sought the Vanniyars' support. The 'independent' Vanniyars and then the TTP MLAs agreed to support its government in return for ministerial seats. Finally, the TTP was later dissolved, its members joined the Congress and the VKKS became dormant. The Vanniyar movement gained momentum again in the 1980s but its decline, from the 1950s onwards, typified the way the Congress party could defuse caste mobilisations by coopting its leaders. (P. Radhakrishnan, 'Backward Class Movements in Tamil Nadu', in M.N. Srinivas (ed.), *Caste – Its Twentieth Century Avatar*, op. cit., p. 123)

6
WERE THERE LOW CASTE MOVEMENTS IN NORTH INDIA?

In North India also British policies had changed the social and political context in such a way that some castes felt the need to organise themselves. Indeed, the tendency of the Madras government to have all social groups represented in the state machinery was not peculiar to Tamil Nadu, even if it was more developed there. It reflected the British conception of political representation which strongly valorised the community.[1] Consequently, the Raj implemented reservation policies for the lower castes all over India. In the North, the Dalits were the first to benefit from this positive discrimination but it had much less of an impact on them. Generally speaking, the low castes did not profit by the reservation policy in the same way as they had in southern and western India.

This was largely due to the social context. While caste associations took shape at an early date, they operated within the logic of Sanskritisation and did not prepare the ground for caste federations. This is evident from the strategies of forward non-*dvija* castes like the Kayasths, as well as from that of low castes like the Yadavs and the Kurmis. Untouchable castes like the Chamars remained not only prisoners of Sanskritisation but also of the *bhakti*.

The Kayasths as Chandraguptas

Among the non-*dvijas*,[2] caste associations often served merely as vehicles for Sanskritisation in North India. The Kayasths of North

[1] See S.H. Beer, 'The representation of interests in British Government: historical background', *American Political Science Review*, vol. LI, 3, Sept. 1957, pp. 613–50.

[2] The associations representing twice born castes were often very conservative, as evident from the case of the Kanya-Kubja Brahmins, a *jati* widely found across Uttar Pradesh, Madhya Pradesh and Rajasthan. In 1884 a Kanya-Kubja caste association was created in Lucknow. An all India association grew out from

India were probably the first to show the way. In the late nineteenth century, Munshi Kali Prasad, a rich, Lucknow-based lawyer of this caste, wrote *Kayasthas Ethnology*, in which he showed 'to which of the four great divisions of the Aryans in India [the Kshatriyas] the Kayasthas belonged'.[3] Subsequently, the Kayasths claimed that they were the descendants of the Emperor Chandragupta. In 1873 Kali Prasad set up in Lucknow a fortnightly magazine *Kayastha Samachar* and a Kayasth Dharma Sabha whose main task was to educate the caste's children.[4] A primary school – Kayastha Pathshala – was opened in Allahabad for poor and orphan children of the caste which in 1877 became an Anglo-Vernacular middle school, then a high school, and, in 1895, an intermediate college. The Kayastha Conference was founded in 1886 on the basis of the Kayasth Dharma Sabha. The opening resolution it passed at its first annual meeting in 1887 stressed the need 'to improve the educational and moral status of the Community' by opening new schools for which money was raised by the association. It also tried 'to encourage the community to undertake commercial and other respectable pursuits and not to rely solely on clerical or literary avocations'.[5] The Conference aimed at uniting the Kayasths and therefore decided 'to prepare a National Directory of the Chandraguptavanshi Kayastha community', which was intended 'to promote union and co-operation by a knowledge

---

it in 1901 and established local branches all over the Hindi belt. It was founded to help the Kanya-Kubja Brahmins to compete with Kayasths, Banyas and other Brahmins of North India in terms of education and administrative jobs (R.S. Khare, *The Changing Brahmans. Associations and Elites Among the Kanya-Kubjas of North India*, University of Chicago Press, 1970, p. 32). It supported the development of educational institutions and boarding schools and sponsored grants and newspapers which were intended to foster solidarity within the caste. The number of local branches increased until the mid-1930s when it then declined, partly because of the Congress's opposition to caste movements. However, it started to rise again in the 1950s in order to protect the Kanya-Kubja Brahmins against the 'threat' posed by affirmative action measures in favour of the lower castes (ibid., p. 46).

[3] *A short account of the aims, objects, achievements and proceedings of the Kayastha Conference*, Allahabad: Conference Reception Committee Muttra, 1893, p. IV.

[4] L. Carroll, 'Caste, social change, and the social scientist: a note on the historical approach to Indian social history', *Journal of Asian Studies*, 35 (1), Nov. 1975, p. 67.

[5] *A short account*, op. cit., pp. 3–6.

of their distant and scattered brethren'.[6] It established mutual aid programmes for the neediest Kayasth families to finance their sons' education or their daughters' marriage. Parallel to this strong emphasis on socio-economic development, the conference did not neglect the initial Sanskritisation objectives of Kali Prasad. It had a temperance section and repeatedly – and allegedly successfully – requested the Kayasths to give up drinking.

The Kayastha Conference is revealing of the ambivalence of caste associations: on the one hand, it endeavoured to promote the status of the Kayasths in the logic of Sanskritisation; on the other, it was created to counter the restriction of job opportunities in the British administration.[7] The Kayastha Conference still endeavoured in the 1920s–1930s to Sanskritise caste rituals and invited its members to emulate the 'dvijas'. This policy stemmed from modern motives since its main objective was to standardise the Kayasth culture and create a homogenous social group.[8] But Sanskritisation remained the key idiom, with its emphasis on positional mobility instead of structural change, to use Srinivas' words. The situation of the Yadavs and Kurmis, suggests that this pattern applied also to lower castes.

Sanskritisation and Division among Yadavs and Kurmis

The term 'Yadav' covers many castes which initially had different names: Ahir in the Hindi belt, Punjab and Gujarat, Gavli in Maharashtra, Gola in Andhra Pradesh and Karnataka etc. Their traditional common function, all over India, was that of herdsmen, cowherds and milksellers.[9] In their 'Tribes and Castes of the Central Provinces of India', Russell and Hira Lal note that 'In former times the Ahirs had the exclusive right of milking the cow, so that on all occasions an Ahir must be hired for this purpose even by the lowest castes'.[10]

[6] Ibid., p. 8.

[7] W.L. Rowe, 'Mobility in the nineteenth century caste-system' in M. Singer and B.S. Cohn (eds), *Structure and Change in Indian Society*, New York, 1996 (1968), pp. 201–7.

[8] Carroll, 'Caste, social change and the social scientist', op. cit.

[9] M.S.A. Rao, *Social Movements and Social Transformation*, New Delhi: Manohar, 1987, p. 130.

[10] R.V. Russell and Rai Bahadur Hira Lal, *The Tribes and Castes of the Central Provinces of India*, vol. 2, New Delhi: Asian Education Services, 1993 (1916), pp. 35–6.

In practice, the Yadavs today spend most of their time tilling the land. At the turn of the century in the Central Provinces two-thirds of Ahirs were already cultivators and labourers while less than one third raised cattle and dealt with milk and milk products.

While the Yadavs are spread over several regions, they are concentrated in the Ganges plain where they account for 10% of the population. They form one of the largest castes in Bihar and Uttar Pradesh with respectively 11 and 8.7% of the population according to the 1931 Census. The 'caste regions' mapped by Schwartzberg show that they formed the largest caste in almost all the districts of northern Bihar and in much of eastern UP in 1931.[11] But the Yadavs are not a dominant caste, as pastoralism did not go hand in hand with land possession; furthermore, from the ritual point of view, Yadavs are traditionally regarded as low caste peasants:

> The very mention of the community invokes, in Bihar, the image of dull, miserly and loud-mouthed people lacking in grace and culture. Besides, the Yadavs are considered as to be unusually prone to casteism and violence.[12]

In the Central Provinces there is a local proverb: ' A Gaoli's quarrel: drunk at night and friends in the morning'. Russell and Hira Lal note that in this region, 'The Ahirs are also hot-tempered, and their propensity for drinking often results in affrays, when they break each other's head with their cattle-staffs'.[13] They are also associated with another image, that of placidity and peace because of their special relationship with cows. Another proverb cited by Schwartzberg says: 'The cow is in league with the milkman and lets him milk water into the pail'.[14] This association with the sacred cow explained that the Ahirs had 'a special relation to the Hindu religion',[15] notably because of their cult of Krishna. These links with the cow and Krishna were conducive to Sanskritisation, an attitude the Ahir caste associations developed assiduously.

[11] J. Schwartzberg, 'The distribution of selected castes in the Northern Indian plain', *Geographical Review*, Oct. 1965, p. 490.

[12] Tilak D. Gupta, 'Yadav ascendancy in Bihar politics', *EPW*, 27 June 1992, p. 1304.

[13] Russell and Hira Lal, *The Tribes and Castes of the Central Provinces of India*, vol. 2, op. cit., p. 37.

[14] Schwartzberg, 'The distribution of selected castes', op. cit., p. 490.

[15] Russell and Hira Lal, *The Tribes and the Castes of the Central Provinces of India*, vol. 2, op. cit., p. 29.

The Yadavs reportedly descend from immigrants from Central Asia, the Abhiras, who established kingdoms in North India, the most recent of which was built in Rewari, in Haryana in the seventeenth century.[16] The scion of the dynasty, Rao Bahadur Balbir Singh, established the Ahir Yadav Kshatriya Mahasabha in 1910. This association claimed that the Ahirs descended from the Yadu dynasty (hence the term Yadav) to which Krishna belonged, and that the Ahirs' real name was 'Yadavs' and that they were Kshatriyas.[17] To promote a warrior ethos and caste unity, association leaders could rely on the caste history since Ahirs had been deemed by British ethnography as coming from the same ethnic stock as the Abhira – and were known for their martial valour – the prince of Rewari took part in the 1857 Revolt, for instance. This is probably why M.S.A. Rao considers that the 'term Yadava refers to both an ethnic category and an ideology'.[18] Yadav leaders succeeded in their social fusion project since they persuaded their fellow caste members to downplay the endogamous units into which they were divided: there were even some inter-regional marriages. Fusion was made easier from the 1930s onwards when North Indian Yadavs migrated from their villages to urban areas and especially to Delhi. But this project did not incorporate a more ambitious ethnicisation process through which other Kshatriya castes would have been merged – as in a federation – because it remained imbued with the ideology of Sanskritisation.

The Ahirs willingly subjected themselves to Sanskritisation because of their special relation to the sacred cow but alas because the Arya Samaj exerted a significant Sanskritising influence over the Yadav movement. As early as 1895, the ruler of Rewari, Rao Yudhishter Singh (the father of Rao Bahadur Balbir Singh), invited Swami Dayananda to his state. Branches of the Arya Samaj flourished soon after and Rewari provided a base from which Arya Samaj *updeshaks* (itinerant preachers) operated in neighbouring areas.

The Sanskritisation impact of the Arya Samaj. The Arya Samaj has been too often regarded as purely Punjabi and confined to the urban

[16] M.S.A. Rao, *Social Movements*, op. cit., pp. 124–5.

[17] This claim was already made by one of the principal subcastes of the Ahirs in Northern India, the Jadwansi (Russell and Hira Lal, *The Tribes and the Castes of the central Provinces of India*, vol. 2, op. cit., p. 24).

[18] M.S.A. Rao, *Social Movements*, op. cit., p. 123.

middle class.[19] In fact, it made inroads in the adjacent states at a quite early date and attracted many low caste followers. Dayananda even started his 'campaign against heresy and orthodoxy' – to use the words of an Arya Samajist – in the Kumbha Mela held in Haridwar.[20] Subsequently, he toured in the United Provinces, in particular in the western part of this region. He visited Meerut eight times, for instance, between 1866 and 1880 – the Meerut City Arya Samaj was established as early as 1877 and others followed in Farrukabad (1879), Kanpur (1879), Benares (1880), Lucknow (1880). Eventually, the Srimati Arya Pratinidhi Sabha for the United Provinces of Agra and Awadh was founded in 1886.[21] These local branches gradually extended their influence in the countryside.

The Arya Samaj was well known for its anti-Brahmin stance. In *Sathyarth Prakash* (The Light of Truth), Dayananda has very strong words against 'the sectarian and selfish Brahmins',[22] 'these ignorant, sensual, hypocritical, irresponsible and vicious people'[23] who 'often dissuade persons from learning and ensnare them into their evil ways with the result that they lose health, peace of mind and wealth.[24] Dayananda reproached the Brahmins for exploiting the superstition of the Hindus by projecting themselves as the only intermediary between man and god, a monopoly he compared to that of the Catholic Pope and which, according to him, was evident from the Brahminical invention of idol worship: 'These Popes fill their pockets by playing fraud upon you. In the Vedas there is not even a word to sanction idol-worship or invoking invitation and dismissals'.[25]

Dayananda eulogised the Jats for forcefully resisting the Brahmins' 'Popish' attitudes. He narrates the story of a Jat whose father was dying and who was asked to give his only cow to the priest as a 'dying gift',[26] allegedly for helping the dying man to cross the river

[19] This is the main limitation of the otherwise path-breaking book by Kenneth Jones, *Arya Dharm – Hindu Consciousness in Nineteenth-Century Punjab*, Berkeley: University of California Press, 1976.

[20] *The Arya Samaj: A Renaissance – Svami Satya Prakash Sarasvati Speeches and Addresses*, vol. 2, Delhi: Vijay Kumar, 1987, p. 103.

[21] Ibid., pp. 105–6.

[22] Swami Dayananda, *The Light of Truth*, Allahabad: Dr Ratna Kumari Svadhyaya Sansthana, 1981, p.98.

[23] Ibid., p. 346.

[24] Ibid., p. 98.

[25] Ibid., p. 389.

[26] Ibid., p. 436.

Vaitarani 'in purgatory'. The Jat had to agree since the priest had already persuaded his relatives to put pressure on him. But he went to the priest's house soon after and accused him of being 'a great liar' since he had not taken the cow to the river bank but was milking it.[27] He then contested the authority of the *Garuda Purana*, the book the priest mentioned as dictating his conduct: 'This book has been written by your forefathers to secure livelihood for you. . .'[28] The Jat took the cow back to his home and Dayananda concludes, 'If other persons also behave like the Jat, then alone can the popish fraud be stopped'.[29]

However, Dayananda's indictment of the Brahmins did not amount to a rejection of the caste system. What he condemned was the hereditary nature of caste. He contended that in the initial *varna vyavastha* children were placed in each *varna* according to their individual 'merits, actions and temperaments'.[30] He specifically recommended that the 'fixture of the *varnas* according to merits and actions should take place at the sixteenth year of girls and twenty-fifth year of boys'.[31] Like Gandhi, Dayananda was not against caste as such since, according to him, provided it was not a hereditary system, caste endowed society with a virtually harmonious structure. Moreover, he considered that marriages should 'take place in the same *varna*s (classes) and the *varna* should be based on merits, profession and temperament'.[32] Thus endogamy, which is a pillar of the caste system, had to be enforced strictly. Nor did Dayananda fight caste taboos. For instance, he considered that a Brahmin needed only to eat food prepared by caste fellows because 'The nature of genital fluids made in a Brahman's body due to special kind of fooding is different from that made in Chandalas [Untouchables] body on account of bad diet. The body of the Chandalas is full of rotten particles due to rotten diet.'[33] Dayananda, therefore, maintained also the hierarchy in diets which is part of the caste system. He was obviously

[27] Ibid., p. 438.

[28] Ibid., p. 439.

[29] Ibid.

[30] Ibid., p. 114.

[31] Ibid., p. 115. He adds that this task should be handled by 'a syndicate of learned persons' who would 'decide after examination as to which is Brahman, which Kshatriya, which Vaishya and which Shudra'. (ibid., p. 483).

[32] Ibid., p. 110.

[33] Ibid., p. 334.

a clear proponent of Sanskritisation and for this reason the Arya Samaj exerted a strong influence in that sense over the lower castes of North India. The activities of the Arya Samajists among the Yadavs are a case in point.

The Arya Samaj *updeshaks* lobbied for the adoption of the sacred thread by the Yadavs and enrolled in the cow protection movement.[34] The Yadav ruler of Rewari, Rao Yudhishter Singh, true to his role as protector of the cows had already founded a Goraksha Sabha (cow protection association) in conjunction with the Arya Samaj – which was creating such *sabhas* all over North India. The cow protection movement which had been initiated in 1893 and relaunched on several occasions in the first two decades of the century, attracted many Yadavs who were anxious to emulate the upper castes by reaffirming their special commitment to the cow. In the Bhojpuri region, Pandey, who emphasised 'the special role of the Ahirs' in this movement points out that 'we have evidence here of a relatively independent force that added a good deal of power to cow-protection activities [. . .] – marginally "clean" castes who aspired to full "cleanliness" by emphasising the purity of their faith and the strictness of ritual adherence to it on the issue of cow-slaughter'.[35] Does this process represent 'a relatively independent force' or does it reflect the incapacity of the Ahirs to develop an alternative value system? Can such Sanskritisation amount to a strategy of emancipation?

Sanskritisation as a Strategy of Emancipation? Adopting a viewpoint similar to that of Pandey, Rao questions the opposition between Sanskritisation and egalitarianism in the case of the Yadavs. He argues 'the Yadavs were not imitating the "twice-born castes" when they were donning the sacred thread, but were challenging their monopoly over this privilege'.[36] Sanskritisation may amount to a form of social subversion, as Srinivas himself has pointed out. The practices of Nadars' associations have suggested that it may be part of a strategy of emancipation; but in that case Sanskritisation was a means of reconciling low ritual status with growing socio-economic

[34] Some of them did it ostensibly and Rajputs as well as Bhumihars retaliated violently in Bihar.

[35] G. Pandey, 'Rallying round the cow – Sectarian Strife in the Bhojpuri Region, *c.* 1888–1917' in R. Guha (ed.), *Subaltern Studies* II, Delhi: Oxford University Press, 1983, p. 104.

[36] Rao, *Social Movements and Social Transformation*, op. cit., p. 249.

assertiveness and of taking the first steps towards an alternative, Dravidian identity. Do we find the same combination in the case of the Yadavs?

One of the first Ahir caste associations, the Gop Jatiya Maha Sabha founded in 1912 in Bihar, is a case in point. It claimed that the Ahirs were Kshatriyas and asked its members to wear the sacred thread.[37] This attitude was fostered by purely secular motives, for as early as 1914, Ahirs had mobilised in Bihar against their *zamindar*. This movement, which gained momentum in the early 1920's targeted *zamindars* who bought the Ahirs' products 'at rates lower than those which prevailed in the bazaar'.[38] In Patna division, Ahir leaders organised meetings where they exhorted their caste fellows to unite and seek education, to use the sacred thread and to end the practice of *begari* (forced labour) for the upper castes.[39] The Kurmis and Koeris followed suit. The upper castes reacted by ostracising them and resorting to physical violence. Caste riots resulted in several casualties. This may be the same kind of aggressive Sanskritisation as in the case of the Nadars. According to Jha: 'The real motive behind the attempts of the Yadavas, Kurmis and Koeris at Sanskritising themselves was to get rid of this socio-economic oppression [of the *zamindar*]'.[40] In both cases, Sanskritisation was rooted in secular motives but there was a major difference between the two: the Ahirs did not challenge the value system on which caste was based on behalf of an alternative identity, in contrast to the Nadars' Dravidian ideology. The Yadavs tried to upgrade themselves while recognising the symbols of the Brahmins as superior,[41] whereas the Nadars – and

[37] P.C. Tallents, *Census of India, 1921*, vol. IV: *Bihar and Orissa, Part 1, Report*, Patna: Government Printing Press, 1923, p. 236.

[38] British report cited in H. Jha, 'Lower-Caste Peasants and Upper-Caste Zamindars in Bihar 1921–25: an analysis of sanskritization and contradiction between the two groups', *Indian Economic and Social History Review*, 14(4), 1977, p. 550.

[39] Ibid.

[40] Ibid., p. 556.

[41] The approach to the caste issue by historians belonging, like Gyan Pandey, to the school of Subaltern Studies has been criticised in the same way by Susan Bayly. She convincingly argues that: 'Historians of India's so-called "subalterns" have portrayed such initiatives as assertions of anti-authoritarian "resistance", especially when they took the form of collective action by low caste or "tribal" people against landlords, money-lenders, or agents of the colonial state.

the southern Non-Brahmins in general – disregard these values and shaped a new identity. In UP also, the Yadavs followed the Sanskritisation route, as is evident from the movements which they launched in the 1920s. N. Gooptu refers to a revealing pamphlet, 'Rules of the Ahir caste' (1927) which invited the Yadavs 'to return to/purer and original Hindu practices (Santana Dharma) in order to achieve higher ritual status'.[42]

The propensity of the Yadavs towards this basic kind of Sanskritisation in evident from their attempt at 'aryanising' their history. The first 'history' of the Yadavs was written by the father of R.V. Khedekar – whom we encountered in Maharashtra – Kithal Krishna Khedekar, in the late nineteenth century. This work was taken up by his son and published in 1959 under the title *The Divine Heritage of the Yadavs.* The book situates the origins of the Yadavs in the Abhiras and later in the ruling dynasties mentioned as Yadav in the Mahabharata and the Puranas. The descendants of Krishna naturally form the core group of this social heritage. But dynasties regarded as Jats and Marathas, like those of Kolhapur, Baroda and Bharatpur, are also included in this redrawing of history. This openness could have been part of an attempt at federating different castes but the Yadav 'historians' pretended that their caste was superior to the Jats and Marathas. The ethnic dimension of their 'narrative' is therefore much narrower than that of Phule or of Dravidian ideologues. In the wake of Khedekar, K.C. Yadav and then J.N.S. Yadav – two of the most prolific Yadav intellectuals – based their claim on inscriptions which may suggest that the Abhiras were the main ruling dynasty of North India as early as the second century BC.[43] Rewari was generally presented as the last representative of the Abhira kingdoms.

This largely mythical history enabled Yadav intellectuals to invent

---

In fact, few of these battles involving "tribal" and "low caste" campaigners were attempts to disavow caste as a system of perceived oppressions and discriminatory practices. In most cases, far from embracing anti-hierarchical "castlessness", these were attempts by people in comparatively advantaged – circumstances to take over the conventions of purity and hierarchy and then turn them to their advantage. (Bayly, *The New Cambridge History of India*, vol. IV.3, op. cit., pp. 231–2).

[42] N. Gooptu, *The Politics of the Urban Poor in Early Tweintieth-Century India*, Cambridge University Press, 2001, p. 207.

[43] See J.N. Singh Yadav, *Yadavas through the Ages*, Gurgaon, Yadav Publications, 1992.

a golden age. Khedekar pretends that 'Even in the vedic age the Yadavs were upholders of the Republican ideals of Government' under the aegis of Krishna himself'.[44] More importantly, he stresses the Aryan origins of his caste. For him, the Yadavs were those 'ancient Aryans who were the custodians of this Bharat Varsha and who possessed the highest virtues which attracted God to be incarnated amongst them, to play with them, to sing the sweet melody of the Bhagavad Gita in order to bring peace and prosperity in the world. Without the help of the Yadavs, Shri Krishna could not have done anything'.[45]

This narrative certainly aims at giving the Yadavs an ethnic identity, but this ethnicisation process is embedded in the Sanskritisation logic. In contrast to the lower caste leaders of Maharashtra and South India who tried to invent a Bahujan or a Dravidian identity which presented the Shudras and the Untouchables as the original inhabitants of the country *against* the Aryans, the Yadavs claim that they *are* Aryans in order to enhance their status *within* caste society. Pinch cites 'Yadav-Kshatriya historians who, in the 1930s, held that Yadavs were "the ancient citizens of the land of the Aryans" – they did not pre-date the Aryan invasions. On the contrary, they were described as having "their origins in the main Chandravamsh [lunar line] branch of kshatriyas" '.[46] Six decades later, the same sense of Sanskritisation continued to prevail among the official ethnography of India. In the late 1990s, the Anthropological Survey of India published several volumes on 'India's communities', where it was said that the clans of the Ahirs 'recognise the *varna* system, six of them identify themselves as Kshatriya and five as Vaishya'.[47] Similar comments were made *vis-à-vis* the Yadavs who 'trace their descent to lord Krishna of Yadu lineage which is mentioned as the second division of the Rigvedic Aryans'.[48]

Sanskritisation remained the doctrine of the All India Yadav

[44] Cited in ibid., p. 16.

[45] Cited in ibid., p. 15. K.C. Yadav also points out that Ahirs were 'the descendents of the Yaduvanshi Aryas' (K.C. Yadav, *Ahirwal. Itihas evan Sanskriti*, Gurgaon, Haryana Historical Society, 2000, p. 17).

[46] W.R. Pinch, *Peasants and Monks in British India*, Delhi: Oxford University Press, 1996, p. 90.

[47] K.S. Singh (ed.), *People of India: National Series: India's Communities*, vol. IV, Delhi: Oxford University Press, 1998, p. 56.

[48] Ibid., vol VI, p. 3693.

Mahasabha, through which Khedekar federated regional associations based in Punjab, the United Provinces and Bihar in 1924 but which was developed under the guidance of Rao Balbir Singh, the ruler of Rewari who was to be elected to the Punjab assembly in 1937 on a Hindu Mahasabha ticket.[49] The programme of the AIYM advocated vegetarianism and teetotalism. It militated in favour of the adoption of the name 'Yadav' all over India[50] and so far as material interests were concerned, it incited the Yadavs to embrace new professional careers and put pressure on the British to make the army recruit Yadavs as officers.[51] Thus, like most of the caste associations, the AIYM combined Sanskritisation and the defence of the Yadavs' interests. But such a craze for Sanskritisation as the only identity discourse had become rather uncommon among the associations of the lower castes in Maharashtra and South India in the 1920s–30s.

In addition to their inability to evolve an alternative, ethnic identity the Yadavs failed to develop caste federations or even looser caste combines, as their aborted alliance with the Kurmis and the Koeris testifies.

The Triveni Sangh, an aborted caste combine. Like the Yadavs, the Kurmis are concentrated in Bihar and UP where they represented respectively 3.6 and 3.5% of the population in 1931. They generally work as cultivators and are regarded as middle caste peasants but like the Yadavs, they claim to be Kshatriyas.[52] The ground for this claim was prepared by the Ramanandi *sampraday* which, as other sectarian movements, 'welcomed shudras as equal members of the monastic community'.[53] The Ramanandis exerted a strong ideological influence over the Kurmis. Monks codified caste myths, established for them 'genealogical ties to either Ram or Krishna' and inculcate them

[49] K.C. Yadav, *Elections in Punjab – 1920–1947*, Delhi: Manohar, 1987, p. 85.

[50] Rao, *Social Movements and Social Transformation*, op. cit., p. 141.

[51] Ibid., p. 142.

[52] William Pinch emphasises that the Kurmis 'thought of themselves not as cosmically created servants (shudra) devoid of any history, but as the descendants of divine warrior clans (kshatriya) firmly rooted in the Indian past' (W.R. Pinch, *Peasants and Monks in British India*, op. cit., 1996, p. 6).

[53] Ibid., p. 139.

'a pure lifestyle' based on vegetarianism, teetotalism etc.[54] By the late nineteenth century, Kurmi leaders were the first among the low castes to fashion caste stories emphasising 'an ancient past of kshatriya distinction that had long since deteriorated into present-day Shudra dishonour'.[55] These stories, which were gradually propagated by printed bulletins, relied on Vaishnava mythology as spelled out by the Ramanandi order. Kurmis were presented as descending from Ram's two sons, Kush and Lav – the Kushwahas (Koeris, Kachhis and Muraos) also claim that Kush was their ancestor but interestingly no attempt at merging these two groups ever occurred.[56]

The first Kurmi caste association was founded in 1894 in Lucknow to protest against the British decision to reduce the recruitment of Kurmis in the police. The Kurmis of Awadh then created a Kurmi Sabha and declared that other castes like the Patidars (from Gujarat), the Kapus (from Andhra Pradesh), the Vokkaligas (from Karnataka), the Reddys, the Naidus (from Madras Presidency) and the Marathas (from Maharashtra), were also Kurmis.[57] The association gained momentum during the 1901 census when it claimed that Kurmis were Kshatriyas. The All India Kurmi Kshatriya Mahasabha, which was officially registered in Patna in 1910, combined the defence of the caste's secular interests and Sanskritisation. While it canvassed for the use of the sacred thread,[58] it also petitioned for quotas in the administration as 'backward classes'[59] but met a lukewarm response.

Kurmis and Yadavs, even though they occupied similar social positions failed to unite. The first attempt was made in Bihar in the 1930s. It involved the Yadavs, the Kurmis and the Koeris, a caste of agriculturists representing 4.1% of the state population.[60] Members of these three castes joined hands in 1930 to contest the local district

[54] Ibid., p. 82.

[55] Ibid., p. 89.

[56] Ibid., pp. 90–1.

[57] K.K. Verma, *Changing Role of Caste Associations*, New Delhi: National, 1979, p. 14.

[58] Ibid., p. 30.

[59] Ibid., p. 35.

[60] According to a pre-independence official account, 'Amongst all the cultivating classes in Bihar, the most advanced are the Koeries or Kushwaha Kshatriyas. Simple in habits, thrifty to a degree and a master in the art of market-gardening, the Koeri is amongst the best of the tillers of the soil to be found

board elections. They lost badly but in 1934 formed the Triveni Sangh, a political party named after the confluence of three rivers, (the Ganges, the Yamuna and the Saraswati) in Allahabad. In 1936 about one million members had allegedly paid the four-anna (one-quarter of a rupee) fee.[61] However, at roughly the same time, in 1935, the Congress formed the Backward Class Federation 'to counter what they viewed as the dangerous class features of the Triveni Sangh and Kisan Sabha movements'.[62] Congressmen deprived the low caste movement of some of its leaders by co-opting Kurmi leaders (such as Birchand Patel) and Yadavs (such as Ram Lakhan Singh Yadav) and later refused to give tickets to Triveni Sangh candidates.[63] The party suffered a serious setback during the 1937 elections but in the few places where it won – like Arrah and Piro in Shahabad district – upper caste landlords retaliated violently.[64] The Triveni Sangh therefore failed because of the co-option of its leaders by congressmen who were to become adept at doing so, as we know; and also because of the strength of the caste system and its pervasive ethos of 'graded inequality': the upper castes were prompt to mobilise in order to preserve their domination, but the low castes of the Triveni Sangh were unable to unite effectively. The Yadavs, for instance, could not look at themselves as being on a par with the Kurmis, largely because of their superiority complex. Rao underlines that the Yadavas 'consider themselves to be natural leaders of backward classes'.[65] Their leaders used pseudo-historical grounds for lending weight to their claim: they argued that their caste fought against injustice during the Dwapara Yug under the leadership of Krishna and that they should now show the way in the battle against upper caste exploitation.

Years later the Kurmis tried to play a pivotal role in another kind of caste combine. During the thirtieth session of the All India Kurmi Kshatriya Sabha, some delegates suggested that the word 'Kshatriya' should be removed from the name of the association. In the same vein it was decided to constitute a caste federation with the Koeris. The

---

anywhere in India.' (D. R. Sethi, 'The Bihar cultivator' in W. Burns (ed.), *Sons of the soil*, Delhi: Government of India, 1944 [1941], pp. 72–3)

[61] Pinch, *Peasants and Monks in British India*, op. cit., p. 134.

[62] Ibid., p. 134.

[63] Ibid., p. 135.

[64] Ibid.

[65] Rao, *Social Movements and Social Transformation*, op. cit., p. 158.

Kurmis' leaders were planning to create a union they called 'Raghav Samaj' – after one of the names of the Lord Ram –, a choice they justified by presenting the Kurmis and the Koeris as descending respectively from Lav and Kush. This attempt, in which Biharis played a leading role[66] came to nought because of caste rivalries between the Kurmis and the Koeris.

The failure of the Yadavs, Kurmis and Koeris to form caste federations in North India reflects their inability to establish an encompassing category like the Dravidian Non-Brahmins or the Kshatriyas of Gujarat. Caste associations remained the basic unit of 'Shudra politics'; and their main achievement consisted in uniting individual castes. For instance, in 1928, the Simon Commission was petitioned by the All India Kushwaha Kshatriya Mahasabha, 'on behalf of the kori, kachchi and murao castes'.[67] The fact that the Kushwaha label stood for three sub-castes of market gardeners shows that this caste association promoted the fusion process, though not to a very large extent: this process cannot be compared with caste federations in Gujarat, for instance.

This example reconfirms that low castes unite more effectively when they attempt to pressurise the state. Precisely, there was not much at stake for the low castes of North India in this respect, since they were not given reserved seats or administrative jobs by the British. The situation was different in the case of the Scheduled Castes.

The North Indian Untouchables, Sanskritisation and bhakti

The Dalits of North India were also exposed to the influence of the Arya Samaj from the turn of the twentieth century. Briggs emphasises that 'During 1911, preceding the Census enumeration, both the Arya Samaj and the Mohammedan communities made special efforts to enrol Chamars [Untouchable leather workers], especially those who were Christians'.[68] This competition was part of the politics of numbers. In 1911 there were only 1,551 Arya Samajist Chamars in

[66] While the sessions of the Sabha were often presided over by Marathas, Patidars etc., in the 1970s about 30% of the executive bureau members were from Bihar (and 17%–18% from Uttar Pradesh).

[67] *Report on the working of the system of government – United Provinces,* op. cit., p. 160.

[68] Geo. W. Briggs, *The Chamars,* Calcutta: Association Press, 1920, p. 238.

the United Provinces, but most Jatav leaders who were to play a major role in Dalit politics, were exposed to the Arya Samaj. Their name, in itself, was very revealing. Jatavs were Chamars, who claimed descent from the Yadu race, which, allegedly, entitled them to be known as Kshatriyas. The Arya Samaj missions were responsible for propagating these views. They were especially successful in enrolling in their schools the sons of Agra Chamars who had become rich thanks to the leather trade.[69] Manikchand Jatavaveer (1897–1956), one of the founders of the Jatav Mahasabha in 1917, was a teacher in an Agra school run by the Arya Samaj.[70] Sunderlal Sagar (1886–1952), another co-founder of the Sabha in Agra, was even versed in Sanskrit – so much so that he was called Pandit.[71] They all preached moral reform, vegetarianism, teetotalism and temperance as means of achieving a purer status.[72] That was also the first inclination of Swami Achhutanand (1879–1933) who was to become the most important Scheduled Caste leader of the United Provinces in the 1920s and1930s.

Swami Achhutanand and the Adi-Hindu movement. Swami Achhutanand was also a Chamar. He was born in a village in Farukkabad district in the United Provinces. His father was a soldier and his uncle a *subedar* in the army of British India – like Ambedkar's, his family benefited from the government's policy of recruiting Untouchables into the military.[73] While he was still very young he was attracted by the itinerant life of Hindu ascetics. He followed his *guru* in Bengal and Gujarat till he was 24 and then joined the Arya Samaj, working as an *updeshak* under the name of Hariharnanda, from 1905 till 1912, mainly in Shuddhi Sabhas which were charged with 'purifying'

[69] O. Lynch, *The Politics of Untouchability – Social Mobility and Social Change in a city of India*, New York: Columbia University Press, 1969, pp. 68–9.

[70] R.K. Kshirsagar, *Dalit Movement in India and Its Leaders*, New Delhi: MD Publications, 1994, p. 230.

[71] Ibid., p. 321.

[72] Kshirsagar mentions many other Jatav leaders with Arya Samajist backgrounds such as Pandit Patramsingh (1900–72) in Delhi (ibid., p. 290), Puranchand (1900–70) in Agra (ibid., p. 301) and Ramnarayan Yadavendu (1909–51) also from Agra (ibid., p. 374).

[73] Chandrika Prasad Jigyansu, *Swami Achhutanand*, Lucknow: Bahujan Kalyan Prakashak, 1960, p. 7 (Hindi). A disciple of Bhaodanand (see below), Jigyansu (1885-1974) was a Buddhist preacher.

Untouchables.[74] But then he turned against the Arya Samaj and harshly criticised the organisation, under his new name, Swami Achhutanand (deriving from '*Achhut*', Untouchable). In a violent indictment of the Arya Samaj, he declared: 'This sect has been constructed in order to save the Brahmin religion from the attacks of the Christians and Muslims. [. . .] Its profession of purification are a fraud and a clever verbal gimmick of the *varna* system'.[75] He ridiculed the Arya Samaj's schemes of inter-caste marriage, asking its leaders why they had not also arranged such marriages among the twice-born if they were true reformers. In a conference he organised in Allahabad in 1930 he attacked the Arya Samajist reinterpretation of the *varna* system in the following terms:

> 'Earlier, caste and *varna* were based on birth. Now, they are being said to be derived from the talents and achievements of a person as preached by the Arya Samaj. If this is true then left the *dwij* [twice-born] marry their sons with our simple and homely daughters for the next generation as to vindicate this truth.'[76]

Swami Achhutanand enunciated the outlines of his Adi-Hindu philosophy for the first time in 1917 in a collection of poems and couplets. He argued that the Untouchables were the first inhabitants of India, the rightful owners of the land. The Aryans came from outside, 'as refugees' who, by resorting to tactics and strategies, captured power and subordinated the autochthonous people: 'They did not win over our own ruler by their good and noble deeds but by clever manoeuvres and later called them demons and Asuru and Satan. They destroyed our culture and civilisation and made us untouchables and outcastes in the heart of our own society.'[77]

Swami Achhutanand maintains that the Adi-Hindus had their roots in the Indus Valley civilisation of Harappa and Mohendjo Daro. He explained the difference between Shudras and Untouchables by arguing that, with the coming of the Aryans, those sections of the defeated who accepted the *varna* system became Shudras and those who did not became Untouchables. Those who ran away to live in

[74] Ibid., p. 100.
[75] Ibid., p. 12.
[76] Ibid., p. 100.
[77] Ibid., p. 8.

the forest or the mountains became tribals or Adivasis.[78] The Adi-Hindu philosophy was well crafted in order to promote the unity of the Shudras, the Untouchables and the Tribals since it endowed these three groups with a common cultural and ethnic background : once upon a time, they were part and parcel of the same people. Swami Achhutanand – like Ambedkar – paid little attention to the Adivasis but he did try to unite the two other groups politically: 'If these two categories were to come together and make an organisation then they would count for 20 crores and become the most important majority group – the Bahujan Samaj – in society and could make a government of their own. . .'.[79] Swami Achhutanand adopted the same expression – Bahujan Samaj – as Phule. However, the organisation he launched in 1919 was called the All India Achhut Caste Reform Sabha, a clear indication that the Dalits were his first target. According to his biographer, the first Adi-Hindu council was started in Andhra, then in Delhi in 1922, in Madras (the Adi-Dravid Sabha) and in Punjab (the Adi-Dharma Mandal). In Lucknow and in Poona a journal named *Adi-Hindu* was launched and, in Punjab, another newspaper, *Adidas,* was also published to publicise the ideas of Swami Achhutanand.[80]

The Adi-Hindu movement gained momentum in 1922 when Swami Achhutanand protested against Gandhi's Non Cooperation Movement and especially his boycott of the Prince of Wales's visit. Swami Achhutanand emphasised that the Congress was an organisation of 'twice born Brahmans who are as foreign to India as are the British'.[81] He argued that the Untouchables should not oppose the British; on the contrary, the colonial era was an opportune time for demanding their basic rights. He said he was in favour of the visit of the Prince of Wales, a stand the British appreciated : when the Lothian Committee organised its hearings in Lucknow, he was called upon to testify about the Untouchables' conditions.

[78] Ibid., p. 55.

[79] Ibid., p. 86.

[80] He also started a newspaper in Kanpur, called initially *Achhut* but whose name was later changed to *Adi-Hindu* (ibid., pp. 100–1). In addition to these periodicals, he published books propagating his ideas. But they came out after he died in 1933 under revealing titles, *The Creation and the Progress of Humanities* and *The Civilisation of the Aborigines in India.*

[81] Ibid., p. 12.

The Congress leaders took exception to his pro-British stand. He was accused of being a Christian in disguise and an agent of the British paid for to divide the Hindu community. But in fact, the congressmen's hostility came from the way he was mobilising the Untouchables against the caste system. His strong criticism of the Manusmriti was especially resented. A poem called 'Manusmriti is burning us' was read at the end of the UP Adi-Sabha Conference in 1927, the same year in which Ambedkar had the text burnt in Mahad. In response, the Arya Samaj started an All India Shraddhanand Dalitodwar Sabha whose objective was to break up the Adi-Hindu movement.[82] With the help of G.D. Birla, M.M. Malaviya also started an All India Achhutodwar Sabha, which organised meetings between 1924 and 1927. Later on it merged with the Congress-backed All India Dalit Varg Sabha.

However, Swami Achhutanand's attitude towards the caste system remained problematic because his egalitarian discourse was largely framed in a religious mould drawing its inspiration from the *bhakti* tradition. Indeed, he adopted the same style as many Dalit saints before him.[83] After severing his links with the Arya Samaj, Swami Achhutanand studied the writings of the Sikh Gurus, Kabir, Dadudayal, Namdev and Redam Sahib. He borrowed from them a very particular method of exposition[84] and discovered social equality in religion:

> Our religion is the way of the *saints* or the *sufi* way. This has been our religion for centuries or even longer. Our religion has produced hundreds of saints and their preachings constitute our religion. Our mothers and sisters since centuries have been praying to the mother earth because this land is the land of our forefathers and their forefathers. We do not need any other religion ; our religion is already with us. We do not need any purification. Ours is the oldest religion, even older than the sufis of Palestine. Gautam Buddha

[82] Ibid., p. 42.

[83] According to C.P. Jigyansu, 'His style of address was poetic and musical, similar to the Bhakti leaders of the sixteenth or seventeeth century, but his discourse was radical and biting' (ibid., p. 22).

[84] He 'relied a lot on the discourse of the Bhakti movement. Singing, chanting formed an essential part of his meetings'. Furthermore, Swami Achhutanand organised some of his meetings during religious functions. In 1931 he held a conference on the preachings of Kabir at the Allahabad Maherkumbha Mela (ibid., pp. 75–6).

propagated this religion. There is no discrimination or inequality or untouchability in it, as it is practised by the Brahmins. There is no high caste or low caste persons there is only the human race and all are equal before God.[85]

Swami Achhutanand emphasises that the Untouchables are India's original inhabitants and hence the torchbearers of its most ancient religion. This creed recalls the *bhakti* cults since it emphasises the worship of saints and equality before God. The *bhakti* cults, however, were not likely to promote the emancipation of the lower castes because they delinked equality before God from social equality.

Gooptu, who stressed the fact that the Adi Hindu movement arose in the wake of the resurgence of *bhakti* cults among the Untouchables in the late nineteenth and early twentieth century,[86] concludes that 'the criticism of the caste system by the Adi Hindu leaders was rather limited and had a narrow focus on the lack of rights or opportunities for the Untouchables':

The leaders did not jettison the notions of 'low' or 'impure', but concentrated on proving that such stigma and disabilities should not be attached to them due to caste status. Nor did they attempt to question the concept that work was inherited. Instead they claimed that 'low' work was not the true inheritance of the Untouchables. It was largely to buttress this claim that they asserted their pre-Aryan ancestry as the original rulers of India, for it enabled them to argue that they should re-inherit the ancient rights of which they had been deprived.[87]

Far from establishing a separate identity that would pull the Untouchables out of the caste system, the Adi Hindu movement used their so-called original identity as a means of promoting their status *within* the system. Thus the *bhakti* resurgence did not imply a radical

[85] Cited in ibid.

[86] N. Gooptu, 'Caste and labour: Untouchable social Movements in Urban Uttar Pradesh in the Early Twentieth Century' in P. Robb (ed.), *Dalit Movements and the Meaning of Labour in India*, Delhi: Oxford University Press, 1993.

[87] Ibid., p. 291. In her conclusion, Gooptu further argues that 'The Adi Hindu leaders thus did not pose a direct threat to the caste system, even though their conception of it as an instrument for imposing social inequalities implied a critique of ritual hierarchy' (ibid., p. 298).

questioning of their belonging to Hinduism. They questioned Brahminism by adhering to a popular tradition but their practise of this religious cult recalls the *modus operandi* of the Hindu sects – which directly derived from *bhakti* – whose egalitarian impact has always been otherworldly.[88] In his study of the Adi-Hindu movement, R.S. Khare points out that its *bhakti*-based 'spiritual equalitarianism' does not really provide an alternative ideology to the caste system, but has more a 'cathartic' effect: this 'ideology remains shy of radical political options'.[89]

The movement also suffered from organisational weaknesses. By 1924 local Adi Hindu Sabhas had been set up in only five cities in UP (Kanpur, Agra, Lucknow, Benares and Allahabad). In fact the Adi-Hindu movement remained chiefly confined to Agra and Kanpur. Besides, the movement's leaders gradually became more interested in getting a seat in the local power structure, as it developed after the 1919 reform than in collective mobilisation.[90]

In addition to these limitations, the movement did not manage to unite the Untouchables. In terms of commensalism its leaders failed to organise intercaste-dining ceremonies.[91] Nor could Untouchable leaders in North India agree about their strategy *vis-à-vis* the British and the Congress. In the early 1930s a break-away faction of the movement which was prepared to collaborate with the Congress formed the Depressed Classes League.

While the government evolved affirmative action policies which could have provided the basis for strategies of empowerment, the North Indian Dalits did not take full advantage of these opportunities, the Jatavs being a case in point.

The Jatavs, reservation policies and sanskritisation. In contrast to the North Indian Shudras, the Untouchable castes were granted special representation in the assemblies by the British. The 1919 Montagu-Chelmsford reform gave them nominated members (there were two

[88] See, D.N. Lorenzen (ed.), *Bhakti religion in North India*, Albany, NY: SUNY Press, 1995.

[89] R.S. Khare, *The Untouchable as himself*, Cambridge University Press, 1984, p. 2, p. 49 and p. 89.

[90] N. Gooptu, *The Politics of the Urban Poor in Early Twentieth Century India*, Cambridge University Press, 2001, p. 171.

[91] S.K. Gupta, *The Scheduled Castes in Modern Indian Politics: Their emergence as a political power*, Delhi: Munshiram Manoharlal, 1985, p. 290.

nominated representatives of the Depressed Classes – the official designation of the Untouchables – in the Legislative Council of Bihar and Orissa, one in the United Provinces, four in the Central Provinces – as opposed to ten in Madras Presidency where they attracted almost as much attention as the Non-Brahmins who got twenty eight seats).[92] The next bout of reform, the 1935 Government of India Act, had a significant impact since it reserved many more seats in the assemblies to the Untouchable castes – which were now known as 'Scheduled Castes': twenty in the United Provinces, fifteen in Bihar and twenty in the Central Provinces and Bihar (as against thirty in Madras Presidency).[93]

Understandably, the run-up to this reform process aroused great interest among the Untouchable castes. For instance, when the Indian Statutory Commission – better known as the Simon Commission, after its president – was appointed in 1928 to elicit the views of the different protagonists – including associations representing the major groups of Indian society, the All India Shri Jatav Mahasabha submitted a very telling memorandum:

> Our Mahasabha is fully alive to the fact that there can be no advancement so long as there is no real improvement in the political status of a community. It is idle to attribute the depression of the depressed classes to the religious and social system of the Hindus. If Government were to improve their political status by giving them honorary offices, adequate representation on local bodies and legislatures and in public services commensurate with their numerical strength, their social position would automatically improve and social injustice would become a thing of the past. For social position of the depressed classes would rise *pari passu* with the rise in their economic condition – a thing which is inconceivable in the case of any community without advancement of its political status.[94]

Such a discourse reflects the same strategic sense of empowerment as that displayed by the Non-Brahmins in Madras Presidency. However, these views were not appreciated by all the Scheduled Castes –

[92] Indian Statutory Commission, *Report of the Indian Statutory Commission*, vol. 1, op. cit., p. 144.

[93] J.P. Eddy and F.H. Lawton, *India's New Constitution*, London: Macmillan, 1935, p. 212.

[94] Cited in Gupta, *The Scheduled Castes in Modern Indian Politics*, op. cit., p. 243.

not even by all the Jatavs. In fact their mobilisation was impeded by the activism of the Harijan leaders who sided with the Congress. For instance, a special meeting of the United Provinces Depressed Classes Conference, held in Agra on 14–15 April 1928, protested against the participation of the Adi-Hindu movement in the deliberations of the Simon Commission.[95] The Jatav movement got especially divided after the Depressed Classes League was founded at Lucknow in 1935 by R.L. Biswas with Jagjivan Ram as General Secretary and P.N. Rajbhoj as Secretary. The moving spirit behind this association – at least one of its chief architects – Dharam Prakash, was a staunch Arya Samajist who opposed Ambedkar's strategy in favour of conversion and was elected to the Constituent Assembly, and then to the Rajya Sabha, on a Congress ticket.[96]

In the 1930s one of the main divisions among the Dalit leaders opposed the proponents of joint electorates with reserved seats, such as Bohre Khem Chand, the president of the All India Shri Jatava Mahasabha (and vice president of the All India Depressed Classes Association), and those who supported Ambedkar's demand for separate electorates, such as the United Provinces Adi-Hindu (Depressed Classes) Association.[97] This cleavage more or less coincided with that setting the proponents of Sankritisation against those who were more favourably inclined towards an egalitarian, Ambedkarite strategy. The former tended to dominate the Jatav movement in the 1930s. After the publication of the White Paper which was to be the basis of the 1935 Government of India Act, the Agra based Jatav Conference sent a memorandum to the Deputy Secretary to the Government of India where it was said:

> The Jatavs are the descendants of Yadu, the founder of Jadav [*sic*] tribe, from which the great Hero of Maha Bharat, Lord Krishna, came. But this position of superiority could not remain intact. Our community fell down from that great height to this degraded status in the Hindu fold [. . .] our present position is the outcome of the age-long inhumane oppression of Brahminism on the Kshatriyas. We, Kshatriyas of the past, are labouring under various sorts of disabilities, restrictions and religious injunctions imposed on us by the Orthodox Hindus. [. . .] But we are at loss to understand the exclusion

[95] Kshirsagar, *Dalit Movement in India*, op. cit., p. 144.

[96] Ibid., pp. 208–9.

[97] Gupta, *The Scheduled Castes in Modern Indian Politics*, op. cit., p. 280.

of our (Yadav) Jatav community from the list of the Scheduled Castes given in the White Paper. The result of this horrible negligence would, no doubt, be the sacrifice of the interests of our community.[98]

Such a discourse suggests that, while the Jatavs were eager to benefit from reservations for the Scheduled Castes, the organisation was still operating in the framework of Sanskritisation. Lynch points out that 'The Jatavs were not attempting to destroy the caste system; rather they were attempting to rise within it in a valid, though not licit, way'.[99]

Things began to change when Buddhism started to attract low caste leaders. Bahdant Bhaodhanand Mahasthvir (1874–1952), a Buddhist monk, played a pioneering role. He attended the first Depressed Classes Conference organised by Ambedkar in 1928 and, henceforth preached Buddhism among the Dalits – whom he regarded as India's aborigines – in Lucknow.[100] Subsequently, Ambedkar himself had a strong impact on the Jatav movement in the 1940s, so much so that local Dalit leaders could involve their separate Buddhist identity to neutralise the influence of Sanskritisation. Even those who did not convert to Buddhism regarded the Untouchables as descending from the original Buddhists and, therefore, prided themselves on being the original Indians: 'Buddhist identity [. . .] replaced Sanskritic Kshatriya identity'.[101] The Jatav movement could therefore rely on the same ethnic ground as the Bahujan movement in Maharashtra and the Dravidian movement in Tamil Nadu. Also, for the Jatavs, 'political participation' became a 'functional alternative' to Sanskritisation,[102] in the sense that they tried to achieve social mobility through access to power. This empowerment process was fostered by the colonial policies of positive discrimination and gradual democratisation, since both phenomena incited the caste to transform itself into a pressure group and assert itself as a collective body. However, such a change was confined to the Jatavs of Agra. Apart from the president of the Scheduled Caste Federation of the United Provinces, Piarelall Kureel (1916–84), who was a Kureel

[98] Memorandum of Jatav Conference of Agra, in IORL/P&J/9/108.

[99] Lynch, *The Politics of Untouchability*, op. cit., p. 75.

[100] Chhedi Lal Sathi, *Bharat ki aam janata shoshan mukt va adhikar yukt kaise ho?*, Lucknow: Bahujan Kalyan Printer, 1992, pp. 84-6 (Hindi).

[101] Lynch, *The Politics of Untouchability*, op. cit., p. 206. See also p. 93.

[102] Ibid., p. 7.

from Unnao district, most of Ambedkar's supporters were Jatavs from Agra.

A similar development occurred among the Mallahs (who claimed they should be called Nishads). These castes of fishermen and boatmen distanced themselves from the Arya Samaj in the 1920s. Babu Ramcharanji (1889–1935), who founded the All India Nishad Maha Sabha in 1920, joined the Adi-Hindu movement in 1925 and became president of the Adi-Hindu Sabha in 1927.[103] In 1933 the All India Nishada Sabha claimed that 'the Mallahs are the descendants of the ancient Nishadas and Chandalas of the Vedic age and they themselves and the Hindus in general regard them as such up to the present time'.[104]

Most other Scheduled Castes of North India remained imbued with the ethos of Sanskritisation, often fostered by Arya Samajist influences, as evident in the case of the Dhobis (washermen). In 1935, after the Government of India Act was made public, the All India Dhobi Association protested against the exclusion of their caste from the Scheduled Castes. This decision had been made under pressure from other associations such as the United Provinces Razak (Dhobi) Association which had links with the Arya Samaj. The president of the latter organisation, for whom Dhobis were Kshatriyas, considered that to bestow his caste fellows with the status of Untouchables would be 'a stigma on character and ability, an obstruction to self-advancement and improvement'.[105] Similar conflicts happened in the case of the Khatiks, an Untouchable caste of butchers,[106] the Dusadhs (pig herders)[107] and the Koris. The Bundelkhand Prantia Kori Sabha, which claimed 20,000 members, passed a resolution in 1936 to support the view that 'the Koris of India have always been classified amongst the touchable castes with the right to Samskaras' and that in the Manusmriti they were 'held to be born

[103] Kshirsagar, *Dalit Movement in India*, op. cit., p. 173.

[104] Letter from the President of the All India Nishada Sabha to the Home Member (Government of the United Provinces), dated 27 March 1933, in IORL/P&J/9/108.

[105] Letter from the President of the United Provinces Razak (Dhobi) Association, 22 June 1936, IORL/P&J/9/108.

[106] Letter from the Government the United Provinces, dated 3 July 1934, IORL/P&J/9/108.

[107] Kshirsagar, *Dalit Movement in India*, op. cit., p. 84.

of a Kshatriya in a Vaishya mother'. In its memorandum to the secretary of state for India the association referred to resolutions passed by caste panchayats in a dozen districts in between Lahore and Jhansi, its headquarters.[108] Other Koris were more interested in being registered as Scheduled Castes to benefit from reservations, but they were in a minority and belonged to the younger generation.

This point is also well illustrated by the salt manufacturers of North India, the Noniyas, who belong to the lower orders of the Shudras. In 1898 a rich notable of the caste established an association claiming for the Noniyas the status of Cauhan Rajputs. The 'New Cauhans' undertook ritually to don the sacred thread, something the upper castes strongly objected to. For Rowe, the 'Cauhan Movement' provided the Noniyas with 'a mechanism which allowed them to reduce the discrepancy between their contrasting positions in the ritual and economic hierarchies'; however the movement 'does not challenge but rather upholds the traditional stratification system'.[109] Interestingly, in the early 1960s, the 'new Cauhans' still considered the RPI 'as "the dirtiest party in India" (i.e. in its opposition to caste it encourages interdining of castes and intercaste marriage…)'.[110] However, the youngest generation was dissociating itself from this standpoint and becoming more politicised.

In his typology of the low caste movements, Rao distinguished five categories.[111] The first is characterised by 'withdrawal and self-organisation'. It is epitomised by the Ezhavas movement in Kerala which has many common features with the traditional *bhakti* way of contesting caste by resorting to sectarian arrangements (a Guru leads his group 'out of society' to promote its self-esteem).[112] The second one, illustrated by the Yadavs, is based on the claim of 'higher

[108] *Memorandum to the Secretary of State for India, through the Reforms Commissioner U.P., Naini Tal*, 10 Oct. 1936, IOR. L/P&J/9/108.

[109] W.L. Rowe, 'The New Cauhans: a caste mobility movement in North India' in J. Silverberg (ed.), *Social Mobility in the Caste System in India*, The Hague/Paris: Mouton, 1968, p. 74.

[110] Ibid. p. 75.

[111] Rao, *Social Movements and Social Transformation*, op. cit., pp. 211ff.

[112] The Ezhavas, were, till the nineteenth century, considered as Untouchables. They represented more than one fourth of the state's population and specialised in toddy (palm wine) distillation. They mobilised at the end of the nineteenth century at the instigation of Shri Dharma Paripalana Yogam.

varna status' and fits with the Sanskritisation pattern. The third one extols 'the virtues of the non-Aryan [Dravidian] culture'. It took shape in South India and in Maharashtra to a lesser extent. The fourth one negates Hinduism by embracing Buddhism – like the Ambedkar movement. The last one relies on Marxist ideology. For Rao, except in the latter, in all these movements 'the religious element forms an essential part of protest ideology'.[113] I would argue that religion is not an essential feature of the Dravidian movement, compared to ethnicity and that the same thing can be said about the Maharashtrian movements, not only the Satyashodak Samaj, that Rao ignores, but also, to a large extent, the Ambedkar movement, in which Buddhism is more perceived as providing a prestigious identity than as a religious creed.

Rather, the low caste movements can more pertinently be regrouped in two broader categories: first, the reform movements situating themselves within the Hindu way of life, be they relying on the mechanisms of Sanskritisation or on the *bhakti* tradition; and second those which are based on an ethnic or a western ideology with a strong egalitarian overtone. The Yadav movement – and to a lesser extent the Ezhavas – can be classified in the first group whereas all the other ones belong to the second category. Interestingly, none of the latter ones has a North Indian origin.

The egalitarian movements stemming from the ethnicisation of caste are typical of southern and western India. As mentioned above, they do not result only, or even primarily, from ideological motives. These movements are indeed sustained by strategies of empowerment stimulated by affirmative action programmes. Such developments did not take place in Northern India – the Adi-Hindu movement (partly) excepted.

To explain the difference between the Hindi belt movements and those which emerged beyond the Deccan, Rao emphasised that in North India Brahmins were 'generally backward with regard to modern education and government employment',[114] compared to the Kayasths and the Banyas and that, therefore, a non-Brahmin movement could not crystallise as it had in the South where the Brahmins attracted general resentment because they monopolised elite functions. This is not the only reason, however. The fact that the

[113] Ibid., op. cit., p. 217

[114] Ibid., op. cit., p. 11.

upper castes were numerous and benefited from land settlement procedures (the *zamindari* system) which were much less egalitarian than the Tamil *raiyatwari* system, for instance, reinforced their domination as already mentioned in the introduction to this book. In this chapter I focused on yet another factor, the resilience of Sanskritisation. This option did not reflect any downplaying of socio-economic issues. In fact, we have investigated the socio-economic ground of some Sanskritisation strategies among the low castes of Bihar. Sanskritisation was probably the key factor inhibiting low caste politics in North India not only because it tended to make the lower castes internalise the hierarchical framework of the caste system but also maintained their divisions according to the principle of 'graded inequality' that Ambedkar so pertinently emphasised.

The resilience of this mindset is well illustrated by the attitude of the North Indian princes. Whereas the rulers of Kolhapur, Baroda, Bhavnagar and Mysore lent determined support to the non-Brahmin movements, those of Rewari (Yadav), Bharatpur (Jat), Gwalior (Maratha) and Dholpur (Jat) – to cite only some of the non-upper caste Maharajahs tended to support the caste system. All of them entertained close links with the Hindu nationalist movement at one stage or another. As mentioned above, the ruler of Rewari joined the Hindu Mahasabha in the 1930s. The Maharajah of Dholpur presided over the Jat Mahasabha, whose Sanskritised Hinduism has been noted by N. Datta.[115] The Maharajah of Bharatpur supported the RSS.[116] In Gwalior, the Maharajah Jivaji Rao – who married a Rajput – supported the Hindu Sabha, and his main lieutenant the Sardar C.S. Angre – also a Maratha – became one of its 'zonal organisers' for the 1951–2 elections.[117]

As a result, the lower castes of northern India had to seek leaders from beyond North India. Maratha princes, for instance, were very much in demand. In the late 1910s, Kurmi leaders from the United Provinces asked the Maharajah of Baroda, and later Shahu Maharaj from Kolhapur, to preside over the annual session of their caste association. When the latter had second thoughts about his participation,

[115] Datta, 'Arya samaj and the Making of Jat Identity', op. cit., p. 115.

[116] S. Mayaram, *Resisting Regimes. Myth, Memory and the Shaping of a Muslim Identity*, Delhi: Oxford University Press, 1997, p. 171.

[117] For more details, see Jaffrelot, *The Hindu Nationalist Movement and Indian Politics*, op. cit., pp. 109–10.

the former urged him to 'kindly consider over the effects which [his] refusal would have *on the mind of the people of the North*'.[118] Similarly, the secretary of the Somvanshi Arya Kshatriya Dnyan Vardhak Samaj, a Yadav based in Gwalior, asked Shahu Maharaj to accept the leadership of his caste fellows who had 'been looking in since long for an able guide to lead them on to enlightenment'.[119]

The resilience of Sanskritisation had a major impact on the low caste movements of North India because it prevented them from establishing their claim on ethnic grounds and from shaping large coalitions like the non-Brahmin groupings or at least from forging caste federations. In contrast with what prevailed in southern and western India, their organisation went no further than caste associations. However, the mobilisation of the low castes was also hindered by the limited scale of the reservation policy in North India. The Scheduled Castes benefited from such programmes but were unable to capitalise on this framework, as had the Non-Brahmins in Madras, for instance – partly because of their lack of education and means; partly because they remained imbued with the spirit of Sanskritisation and 'graded inequality'. The low castes, on the other hand, did not benefit from affirmative action programmes. They started to mobilise and form larger fronts precisely when the State extended its compensatory discrimination policy to what became known as the 'Other Backward Classes'.

[118] Letter from Sampatrao Gaekwar to Shri Shahu Maharaj dated 19 March 1919. Reprinted in Kavlekar, *Non-Brahmin Movement in Southern India*, op. cit., p. 191.

[119] Letter from K.N. Yadav to Shri Shahu Maharaj, dated 26 Feb. 1920. Reprinted in ibid., p. 177.

7

CASTE AS THE BUILDING BLOCK OF THE 'OTHER BACKWARD CLASSES'

THE IMPACT OF RESERVATIONS

While affirmative action programmes for the low castes were first implemented in South India, they were gradually applied all over India. The new administrative categories, such as the Other Backward Classes, that these policies created played a major role in the formation of low caste fronts in the Hindi belt.

As mentioned above, the term 'backward classes' was first used in the 1870s by the Madras administration in the framework of an affirmative action policy favouring the under-educated. While the list of 'backwards' increased and widened, growing from 39 to 131 communities by the 1920s, the Untouchables claimed the right of being treated as a distinct class. Hence the sharing out of the 'backwards' between 'Depressed Classes' (Untouchables and Tribals) and 'Castes other than Depressed Classes' which was decided in 1925.[1] If Tamil Nadu appears to be a precursor, the central administration gradually moved in the same direction and eventually tried to harmonise the local classifications.

The time-honoured expression of the government to designate the lower and intermediate castes was first 'Depressed Classes', a group for which seats in local and national assemblies were reserved from 1919 onwards. However, after the 1935 Government of India Act, the Untouchables were designated as 'Scheduled *Castes*' and the denomination spread throughout the provinces of British India. Untouchables continued to be designated by the term 'Scheduled Castes' even after Independence, when the lower castes were referred to as 'Other Backward *classes*'. Nehru used the term during his first speech,

[1] P. Radhakrishnan, 'Backward Classes in Tamil Nadu, 1872–1988', *EPW*, 10 March 1990, pp. 509–17.

on December 13, 1946, before the Constituent Assembly, in his Objectives Resolution. He announced that special measures were to be taken in favour of 'minorities, backward and tribal areas and depressed and other backward classes,'[2] but did not elaborate further. The Constituent Assembly did not clarify this notion but raised the stakes since the OBCs, as they came to be called, were eligible for affirmative action programmes. The state thus created an administrative category which it then had to fill. What were the relevant criteria for identifying the OBCs: lack of education, poverty, occupation or caste? The debate went on for several decades and contributed to the crystallisation of a fragile OBC coalition in North India in the 1950s and '60s.

How to discriminate positively? The constitutional debate

Within the Constituent Assembly the notion of the 'other backward classes' that Nehru had used in his speech was taken up by the 'Advisory Committee on rights of citizens, minorities and tribal and excluded area' which was set up on January 24, 1947 to prepare the articles dealing with these matters. The committee chairman, Vallabhbhai Patel, created several sub-committees, and the one in charge of fundamental rights was the first to reflect upon the reservation issue. It recommended that 'The State shall not discriminate against any citizen on grounds only of religion, race, caste, sex, place of birth' and that there should be 'equality of opportunity for all citizens in matters of public employment'.[3] Ambedkar, who sat on the sub-committee, suggested an amendment whereby the proposal would not 'prevent the Government from prescribing a certain proportion of posts of public service for the minorities – whoever they may be'.[4] The sub-committee's discussions then led its members to define these minorities as 'any backward class of citizens which, in the opinion of the state, is not adequately represented in the services under the State.' This clause was eventually voted by the Constituent Assembly

[2] *Constituent Assembly Debates* (hereafter *CAD*), vol. 1, New Delhi: Lok Sabha Secretariat, 1989, p. 59.

[3] Draft of the report of the sub-committee on fundamental rights to the Advisory Committee (3 April 1947) in B. Shiva Rao (ed.), *The Framing of India's Constitution – Select Documents*, op. cit., p. 171.

[4] Ibid., pp. 204–5.

and became Article 16(4) of the Indian Constitution. In the very first constitutional debates a key element of the reservation policy has thus been representation in the state apparatus. The reason why this was emphasised, rather than education for instance, was not clearly spelled out but Ambedkar probably bore some responsibility for it. For him job quotas in the administration were the best means of empowering the lower castes.

The framing of the reservation policy by the Advisory Committee implied that its beneficiaries could be identified. This was easy in the case of the Scheduled Castes and Scheduled Tribes since they would continue to be enumerated in the census, but they were not the only 'backwards'. In the report that Vallabhbhai Patel, as Chairman of the Committee, submitted on 8 August 1947, the last clause, which dealt with financial alleviation for the 'backwards' set out the criteria which could be used to define the OBCs:

> Provision shall also be made for the setting up of a statutory Commission to investigate into the conditions of socially and educationally backward classes, to study the difficulties under which they labour and to recommend to the Union or the Government, as the case may be, the steps that should be taken to eliminate the difficulties and the financial grants that should be given and the conditions that should be prescribed for such grants.[5]

Even when qualified in this way, the notion of 'Backward Classes' remained vague. This worried some of the Constituent Assembly members, especially those from the North who were much less familiar with it than those from the South.[6] But the Committee in charge of drafting the Constitution refused to be more specific. One of its senior members, K.M. Munshi, retorted that 'it is perfectly clear that the word "backward" signifies that class of people – does not matter whether you call them untouchables or touchables, belonging to this community or that – a class of people who are so backward that a special protection is required in the services and I see no reason why any member should be apprehensive of regard to the word "backward" '.[7] By mentioning the Untouchables Munshi made the situation even more confused since the case was settled in so far as the

[5] *CAD*, vol. V, op. cit., p. 249.

[6] For instance, Dharam Prakash, from Uttar Pradesh, suggested that Depressed Classes or Scheduled Castes should be used instead of the nebulous notion of 'backward classes' (ibid., vol. VII, p. 687).

[7] Ibid., vol. VII, debate of 30 Nov. 1948, p. 697.

Scheduled Castes were concerned. He was obviously reluctant to delineate the limits of a clear cut category of 'backward classes', different from the Untouchables, which he was more than willing to help, as were most congressmen. Moreover, Munshi brought to the attention of the Scheduled Castes Assembly members that the quotas in favour of their caste-fellows had never posed any problem and that 'we, members who do not belong to the Scheduled Castes, have in order to wipe out this blot on our society, been in the forefront in this matter'.[8] Munshi's discourse prepared the ground for the Congress strategy of co-option of the Scheduled Castes, thereby circumventing the intermediate castes which, eventually, could challenge the upper castes' domination.

Ambedkar also felt no need to spell out more precisely the meaning of the epithet 'backward', but for different reasons. He seemed to be apprehensive that a clear-cut definition of the OBCs would transform them into an all powerful social coalition involving the bulk of society:

> 'A backward community is a community which is backward in the opinion of the state Government [. . .]. If the local government included in this category of reservations such a large number of seats [*sic*], I think one could very well go to the Federal Court and the Supreme Court and say that the reservation is of such a magnitude that the rule regarding equality of opportunity has been destroyed. . . .'[9]

In addition to the vagueness that shrouded the Other Backward Classes' category, some Constituent Assembly members regretted that less was done for them than for the Scheduled Castes[10] who already benefitted from quotas. But the low castes did not have a spokesman of Ambedkar's calibre. In fact, it seems that within the Constituent Assembly they were hardly represented at all. According to Austin, among the twenty most influential people who were drafting the Constitution, not one was from the low castes 11 were Brahmins, 2 Amil, 1 Kayasth, 1 Banya, 1 Rajput, 1 Scheduled Caste, Ambedkar, 2 Muslim and 1 Christian).[11]

[8] Ibid.

[9] Ibid., p. 702.

[10] Chandrika Ram, returned from Bihar, put it thus: 'We have provided so many privileges to Harijans on the ground that they are backward and I fail to understand why the same argument should not be applied for providing reservations for the backward classes' (ibid., p. 688).

[11] Austin, *The Indian Constitution*, op. cit., Appendix III.

The only advocate of the low castes was Punjabrao Deshmukh, who did not belong to this category but was a Maratha from Amraoti (Maharashtra). In August 1949 he introduced an amendment according to which all the 'classes and communities' of India would be represented within the administration according to their numeric strength. A passionate plea accompanied his proposal:

'It appears to me that the development in India has been lop-sided, one-sided. About 80 per cent of the people take no part as far as your cultural affairs are concerned, so far as the civilised things of life are concerned. There is a blackout so far as they are concerned; an iron curtain between them and the rest; unless every community, especially the larger and more popular communities advance equally and the advanced communities afford them opportunities for development, the advancement of India will be impossible [an argument Lohia made a few years later]. All that I demand is fairness and justice for the millions of people who are not in a position to come forward and compete with you. . .'[12]

Regarding the delineation of the 'Backward Classes', Deshmukh regretted that they were 'likely to be defined in a very limited and restricted manner' because, he said, 'it is not the claim of only the Scheduled Castes that they are backward, it is not the tribal people alone who should be considered backward; there are millions of others who are more backward than these and there is no rule nor any room so far as these classes are concerned'.[13]

Deshmukh again spoke out in favour of reservations for the lower castes in November 1949 when article 335 came up for discussion. This article indicated that 'The claims of the members of the Scheduled Castes and the Scheduled Tribes shall be taken into consideration, consistently with the maintenance of efficiency of administration, in the making of appointments to services and posts in connection with the affairs of the Union or of a state'. Deshmukh wanted the Other Backward Classes to be mentioned along with the Scheduled Castes and Scheduled Tribes. Thakur Das Bhargava, from the Congress, objected that the Scheduled Castes and Scheduled Tribes should be 'given more rights than the "backward classes" since they were 'more backward'.[14] Deshmukh replied that the Assembly was 'going to exclude the backward classes simply because they have not formed

[12] Ibid., vol. IX, p. 603.
[13] Ibid., p. 604.
[14] *CAD*, vol. X, p. 548.

themselves into one group or agitated'.[15] That might well have been true but Deshmukh was in a minority.

Deshmukh's proposal of reserving jobs to all the 'backwards' (especially, as he proposed, on a population basis) prompted two objections which, since then, have been deployed time and time again. First, several members of the high castes insisted that the need for administrative efficiency precluded the recruit of unskilled applicants, and second that the multiplication of quotas would erode incentives for meritorious candidates as fewer and fewer posts would be filled through competitive examinations. Pool Singh, a deputy from the United Provinces, rejected those arguments, replying first that 'equal merit presupposes equal opportunity and I think it goes without saying that the toiling masses are denied all those opportunities which a few literate people living in big cities enjoy' and, second, that 'if the administration is to be efficient as my friends want it to be, then you must have people in the job who know something about the job an who come from the masses. Otherwise the administration will lose touch with the masses'.[16] These arguments in favour of affirmative action in the government services had few takers in the Constituent Assembly, since even the Scheduled Caste deputies had little interest in the discussion and put their own problems forward. Ambedkar concluded the discussion by repeating that it was not useful to define the Backward Classes in detail as some deputies urged him to:

> 'Everybody in the province knows who are the backward classes, and I think it is, therefore, better to leave the matter, as has been done in this Constitution to the Commission which is to be appointed, which will investigate into the conditions of the state of society, and to ascertain which are to be regarded as backward classes in this country.'[17]

Ambedkar here referred to one of the above mentioned proposals spelled out by the Advisory Committee's chairman, Patel, which eventually became Article 340 of the Indian Constitution, voted on 26 January 1950:

> The President [of the Republic] can by decree nominate a Commission formed by persons he considers to be competent to investigate, within the Indian territory, on the condition of classes suffering of backwardness as well

[15] Ibid.
[16] Ibid., p. 616.
[17] Ibid., p. 630.

in social as in educational terms, and on the problems they meet, the way of proposing measures which could be taken by the Central or a State Government in order to eliminate difficulties and improve their condition.[18]

In this article, as in article 16(4), the word 'class' has been preferred to 'caste',[19] phrasing that reflected the leftist inspiration of Nehru and others and a widespread idea that India had to move away from caste-like social organisations. However, because the OBCs had to be identified on the basis of backwardness in social and educational terms, the issue was left wide open and discussions continued through the early 1950s even through a Commission was supposed to decide the case. Ambedkar systematically emphasised that caste was responsible for social backwardness but Nehru's views were different. This contrast became strikingly apparent in the debate on the first amendment to the Constitution, which was voted in reaction to the 1951 decision of the Supreme Court in a case involving Madras State.[20] The judgement struck down state reservations in educational institutions on the ground that it violated Article 15(1) and Article 29(2) where the fundamental principle of non-discrimination was emphasised.[21] The amendment, which was inserted as Article 15(4), stipulated that the state should not be prevented from 'making any special provision for the advancement of any socially and educationally backward classes of citizens or for the Scheduled

[18] *The Constitution of India (As modified up to the 15th August 1983)*, Government of India (s.l., s.d.), p. 178.

[19] Article 340 refers to 'socially and educationally backward classes' while Article 16 (4) refers to 'backward classes of citizens'. It reads: 'Nothing in this article shall prevent the State from making any provision for the reservation of appointments or posts in favour of any backward class of citizens which, in the opinion of the State, is not adequately represented in the services under the State'.

[20] Another decision of the Supreme Court regarding the Madras State's reservation policy about government jobs and a 1951 Bombay High Court decision were also involved (See 'Analysis of the Judgements of Supreme Court and the High Courts leading to the First Amendment of the Constitution', in *Report of the Backward Classes Commission*, Second Part, vol. III, New Delhi: Government of India, 1980, p . 1 and Galanter, *Competing Equalities*, op. cit., pp. 164–5).

[21] Article 29(2) states that 'No citizen shall be denied admission into any educational institution maintained by the State or receiving aid out of State funds on grounds only of religion, race, caste, language or any of them'.

Castes and the Scheduled Tribes'. The debate in Parliament primarily focused on the definition of the 'backward classes'. Ambedkar made it clear that, for him, what were called backward classes were 'nothing else but a collection of certain castes'.[22] Nehru was much less specific:

> 'We have to deal with the situation where for a variety of causes for which the present generation is not to blame, the past has the responsibility, there are groups, classes, individuals, communities . . . who are backward. They are backward in many ways – economically, socially, educationally – sometimes they are not backward in one of these respects and yet backward in another. The fact is therefore that if we wish to encourage them in regard to these matters, we have to do something special for them.
>
> [. . .] We want to put an end to . . . all those infinite divisions that have grown up in our social life . . . we may call them by any name you like, the caste system or caste religious divisions etc.'[23]

Nehru certainly acknowledged the pernicious influence of the caste system but he did so almost reluctantly – caste does not appear in his primary list of factors of backwardness – and for reasons different from Ambedkar's. He regretted the divisive effect of the social structure, at a time when he wanted to build a strong, united India and did not regard the need to fight caste as a priority objective in achieving social change. For him, economic modernisation would eventually eradicate caste and communal feelings, all these legacies of the past that had to be blamed for 'backwardness'.

The first amendment episode was revealing of the conflicts arising from any attempt at defining social backwardness. What should be the relevant criterion: caste, class, education? The work of the first Backward Classes Commission and of the judiciary was to nourish this vibrant debate.

The first 'Backward Classes' Commission or the partial concealment of caste

The first Backward Classes Commission was appointed on 29 January 1953. It consisted of eleven members, mostly low caste representatives but its president, Kakasaheb Kalelkar, was a Brahmin. One of the most famous prose writers of Gujarat, he was a Gandhian who

[22] *Parliamentary Debates,* vol. XII – 13 (Part II), col. 9006.
[23] Ibid., col. 9616.

had taken part in the Freedom Movement.[24] Its main terms of reference were to determine the criteria for identifying the socially and educationally backward classes, to establish a list of these classes and to examine their difficulties in order to propose steps to improve their condition.

The first task assigned to the commission, identifying the backward classes, turned out to be the most delicate. Eventually, a majority of the Commission's members selected four criteria for defining the OBCs: (1) low social position in the traditional caste hierarchy of Hindu society;[25] (2) lack of general educational advancement among the major section of a caste or community; (3) inadequate or no representation in the Government service; and (4) inadequate representation in the field of trade, commerce and industry.[26] Caste was not the only criterion but it was a key element. The Commission drew up a list of 2,399 castes, representing about 32% of the Indian population, as forming the bulk of the 'socially and educationally backward classes'. It had to extrapolate from the British census data to do so and advised the Government of India to re-establish castes enumeration in the 1961 census to obtain more accurate statistics.[27]

In order to redress the backwardness of the OBCs the Commission formulated two main recommendations. First that they should benefit from a 70% quota in technical education institutions (including disciplines such as applied sciences, medicine, agriculture, veterinary studies and engineering).[28] Second quotas had to be reserved for them in central and state administrations: 40% of the vacancies in classes III and IV, 33.3% in class II and 25% in class I.[29] The Com-

[24] R. Vyas, *The Glory of Gujarat*, Ahmedabad, Akshara Prakashan, 1998, p. 158. Another Gandhian and veteran of the anti-British struggle, Narayan Sadoba Kajrolkar, took part in the Commission as a representative of the Scheduled Castes. He was a Rohidas (or Chamar) but ran a flourishing food-processing business (For biographical information, see *The Indian and Pakistan Year Book and Who's Who – 1949*, vol. 35, Bombay: The Times of India, 1949, p. 747).

[25] However, the existence of Muslim or Christian 'backward castes' was also recognised (*Report of the Backward Classes Commission*, vol. 1, Delhi, Government of India, 1955, p. VI).

[26] Ibid. p. 46.

[27] Ibid. vol. 3 (*Minutes of Dissent*), pp. 14–15, and vol. 2 (*Lists*).

[28] Ibid. p. 125.

[29] Ibid. p. 140.

mission had noticed that many of the low caste representatives they interviewed were very keen to find employment in the administration. They candidly admitted that they valued posts in the bureaucracy because of 'The scale of pay in Government service, security of employment, power and prestige and the scope to distribute patronage. . . '.[30]

The Commission's responses to the two main terms of reference, the identification of the 'backward classes' and the reservation scheme, did not meet with unanimous approval: five of the eleven members of the Commission dissociated themselves from the report. S.D. Singh Chaurasia's minute of dissent drew its inspiration from Ambedkar. Chaurasia, a lawyer from a well-off family, who was based in Lucknow, had attended Ambedkar's first Depressed Classes Conference organised by Ambedkar in 1928.[31] He had been associated with the United Provinces Hindu Backward Classes League since its inception in 1929. He had coined the term 'Hindu Backward' in the early 1930s to avoid that of 'Depressed Classes' which conveyed the notion 'of untouchability in the sense of causing pollution by touch'.[32] Chaurasia dwelled on the fact that the 'backward classes' were basically Shudras, i.e., those who descended from the original inhabitants of India.[33] He cited Ambedkar when giving evidence to the Commission to stress the point that according to the Untouchable leader education and access to power should be the key elements of any reservation policy. Ambedkar had even said that the lower castes would benefit most from the formation of a small elite comprising people like himself: 'I am one of those highly qualified and educated persons who are on *Marke Ki Jagah* (Key post). I can control any wrong being done'.[34] Accordingly, Chaurasia focused on the need for the backward classes to 'snatch away the power' from the upper castes[35] and thus demanded reserved seats in the Assemblies on a population basis for twenty years.[36] His minute of dissent was the only one advocating more concessions for the backward classes.

[30] Ibid. p. 139.

[31] C.L. Sathi, *Bharat,* op. cit., pp. 87-9.

[32] Cited in Galanter, *Competing Equalities,* op. cit., p. 158. Chaurasia became a Rajya Sabha Member in 1974 and then affiliated himself to the Janata Party.

[33] Ibid., vol. III (Minutes of Dissent), p. 29 and p. 33.

[34] 'Minute of dissent by Shri S.D.S. Chaurasia', in ibid., p. 75.

[35] Ibid., p. 21.

[36] Ibid., p . 67.

Table 7.1. THE OBC POPULATION ACCORDING TO THE FIRST BACKWARD CLASSES COMMISSION

	Total population (1951)	*Estimated population*	*% of OBC population*
Assam	9,043,707	2,865,934	31.6
Bihar	40,225,947	15,321,746	38.1
Bombay	35,956,150	11,009,745	30.6
Madhya Pradesh	21,247,533	7,902,586	37.2
Madras (including Andhra)	57,016,002	12,680,945	22.2
Orissa	14,645,946	1,356,373	9.3
Punjab	12,641,205	2,565,087	20.2
Uttar Pradesh	63,215,742	26,010,161	42.6
West Bengal	24,810,308		9.1
Andhra		added in Madras	
Hyderabad	18,655,108	13,766,090	73.8
Madhya Bharat	7,954,154	1,936,980	24.4
Mysore	9,074,972	5,963,902	65.7
PEPSU	3,493,685	442,397	12.7
Rajasthan	15,290,797	3,431,326	22.4
Saurashtra	4,137,359	1,216,475	29.4
Travancore-Cochin	9,280,425	912,272	9.8
Ajmer	693,372	297,699	42.9
Bhopal	836,474	294,534	35.2
Himachal Pradesh and Bilaspur	1,109,466	315,101	28.4
Coorg	229,405	63,727	27.8
Delhi	1,744,072	317,906	18.2
Kutch	567,606	201,170	35.4
Manipur	577,635	35,490	6.1
Tripura	639,029	69,432	10.6
Vindhya Pradesh	3,574,690	1,376,307	38.5
Andaman & Nicobar Islands	30,971	–	–
India	356,829,485	113,510,830	31.81

Source: *Report of the Backward Classes Commission,* vol. III, op. cit., pp. 14–15.

*These calculations of the population and percentage of OBCs are not based on all the 2,399 castes declared to be OBCs by the Commission but on 837 castes only. The total actual figures for OBCs would be much higher had all the statistics been available.

The other dissenters, on the contrary, were worried that the report gave too much importance to caste compared to other socio-economic indicators and feared that caste-based quotas would prolong and deepen casteism instead of releasing India from its social system.[37] Kalelkar himself, in a last minute *volte face*, undermined the report of his Commission by using similar arguments. In a 23-page covering letter he denigrated the report he had just signed. His main point of departure was that he had eventually come to disapprove of the methods used by the Commission: 'It is only when the report was being finalised that I started thinking anew and found that backwardness could be tackled on a basis or a number of basis other than that of caste'.[38] Why did he have this last minute change of mind? Was it due to 'the warning of well-wishers of the country' (including senior politicians) he mentioned in his letter?[39] Was it because, as a true Gandhian, he couldn't help but justify the 'traditional' caste system? For him 'It was perhaps the only way through which they [contemporary India's ancestors] could teach the nation to forget and rise above racial, clannish, tribal and similar biological groupings of society and to accept a workable arrangement of social existence based on cultural hierarchy and occupational self-government'.[40] More importantly, perhaps, Kalelkar recalls that 'the nation has decided to establish a classless and casteless society, which also demands that backwardness should be studied from the point of view of the individual and, at the most, that of the family'.[41] Besides like other dissenters he feared that caste-based quotas would foster 'Communalism and Casteism [which] are bound to destroy the unity of the nation and narrow down the aspirations of the people'.[42] Last but not least, Kalelkar made a plea in favour of reservation based on economic criteria which would enable the government 'to remove the

[37] See 'Minutes of dissents' by Anup Singh, who said 'My opposition to reservation springs from the fear that reservation on caste or class basis will accentuate caste feelings, thus jeopardising the chance of national cohesion and solidarity' (ibid., p. 3); Arunanghsu De, who had the same opinion (ibid., p. 5); and P.G. Shah, who would have preferred to measure backwardness on an economic and literacy basis at the family level (ibid., p. 13).

[38] *Report of the Backward Classes Commission*, vol. 1, op. cit., p. vi.

[39] Ibid., p. xiv.

[40] Ibid., vol. I, p. iv.

[41] Ibid.

[42] Ibid., p. xiii.

bitterness which the extremely poor and helpless amongst the upper class [*sic*] Hindus feel that they are victimised for no fault of their own'.[43] He suggested that the state should extend its help to all families with an income of less than Rs 800 a year. Kalelkar submitted his own criteria for identifying the OBCs without any reference to caste on the basis of these considerations.[44] He also dissented from some of the Commission's recommendations. While he supported those concerning educational institutions,[45] he said he 'was definitely against reservation in government services for any community for the simple reason that the services are not meant for the servants but they are meant for the service of the society as a whole.'[46] Interestingly Kalelkar objected to any reservations in classes 1 and 2 but was prepared to accept a 49% quota in classes 3 and 4 'where there is already an ample percentage of backward people' – this is a candid admission that since the lower castes did the most degrading tasks, it should continue.[47] As a result, Kalelkar, whose appointment as chairman of the Commission had, understandably enough, not been 'very much welcomed by the backward class people', according to Chaurasia,[48] on his own initiative, introduced in his report contradictions of which its detractors took advantage.

The Kalelkar Commission Report was primarily submitted to the Home Minister, Govind Ballabh Pant, a Brahmin known for his qualities as an administrator – he had been Chief Minister of UP in

[43] Ibid., p. vii.

[44] His list comprised women, residents of rural area, 'those who are driven to the necessity of working with their own hands', 'those labouring under the sun and in open air', unskilled workers, landless peasants, those who do not have enough or any capital, those who are 'working as mere clerks', those with poor and uneducated parents, those who lack ambition and have no opportunities, those who have no means of support, the inhabitants of backward regions, the illiterates, those incapable of understanding the modern world and using its avenues for social mobility and those who believe in magic, in superstition and in fatality. (*Report of the Backward Classes Commission*, vol. 1, Delhi: Government of India, 1955, pp. xiv–xv)

[45] Even though he considered that if the backward classes 'have neglected education, it is because they had no use of it. Now that they have discovered their mistake it is for them to make the necessary effort for making up the leeway' (ibid., p. viii).

[46] Ibid., vol. I, p. iv.

[47] Ibid., p. ix.

[48] 'Minute of dissent by Shri S.D.S. Chaurasia', op. cit., p. 17.

1937–9 and again in 1946–54 – but also for his conservative views – even though his biographer concedes that 'with the war on Untouchability, his orthodox living vanished'.[49] Pant quickly dismissed the report. First he opportunistically emulated a typically Nehruvian argument by considering that 'With the establishment of our society on the socialist pattern [. . .], social and other distinctions will disappear as we advance towards that goal'.[50] He also claimed that 'Large sums of money have been spent by Governments both at the Centre and in the States on the work of reconstruction and development during the period of the first Plan resulting in an expansion of employment opportunities in the public services and elsewhere, and in the raising of the per capita income. The benefits of this nation-wide endeavour have been shared by all citizens'.[51]

More importantly, Pant disapproved of the use of caste as the most prominent criterion for identifying the backward classes. He considered that 'the recognition of the specified castes as backward may serve to maintain and even perpetuate the existing distinctions on the basis of caste'.[52] The 'tone and temper' displayed in Chaurasia's minute of dissent, according to Pant, brought 'into prominence the dangers of separatism inherent in this kind of approach'.[53] Moreover, by establishing a list of 2,399 castes forming the backward classes, the Commission, according to him, counted 'the bulk of the country's millions' as coming within this category and therefore its report was useless and only reminded Indians that their country was backward.[54] Pant agreed 'that some positive and workable criteria should be devised for the specification of the socially and educationally backward classes' but he suggested that *ad hoc* surveys should be held and that the state governments should be asked to establish their own list.[55]

The report was tabled before Parliament accompanied by a memorandum by Pant on 3 September 1956, but was not even discussed. The Deputy Registrar General conducted a 'pilot survey to see if

[49] M.C. Rau, *Govind Ballabh Pant*, Bombay: Allied Publishers, 1981, p. 334.

[50] *Memorandum on the report of the Backward Classes Commission*, Delhi: Ministry of Home Affairs (n.d.) p. 2.

[51] Ibid.

[52] Ibid.

[53] Ibid.

[54] Ibid.

[55] Ibid., p. 3.

backwardness could be linked to occupational communities instead of caste', to no avail.[56] Nehru's government eventually decided in May 1961 that there was not even any need for an all India list of OBCs – and that, consequently there would be no reservation policy at the Centre. Pant informed the Chief Ministers of the decision in a very revealing circular:

> If we go in for reservations on communal and caste basis, we swamp the bright and able people and remain second-rate or third-rate. I am to learn how far this business of reservation has gone on communal consideration [. . .]. Let us help the backward groups by all means but never at the cost of efficiency.[57]

The Ministry of Home Affairs addressed all the State Governments again in August 1961 to declare that while they had 'the discretion to choose their own criteria for defining backwardness, in the view of the Government of India it would be better to apply economic tests than to go by caste'.[58]

However, the Kalelkar report did have some repercussions. A motion was moved to discuss it in the Lok Sabha in October 1964 but the debate effectively took place more than a year later, in November 1965 and only with great difficulty since the quorum was filled only intermittently.[59] B.P. Maurya challenged the official view that economic disparities were the root-cause of inequality because they arose from the caste hierarchy. Not surprisingly, R.M. Harjanavis, the Minister of State for Education, replied on behalf of the government that caste-based reservations would 'perpetuate the caste [system?] because a caste is going to get, on the basis of that caste, certain preferential treatment'.[60] He concluded therefore that he was not 'quite sure that the interest of the backward classes is preserved by reservations'.

The way the Kalelkar Report was dismissed in the Lok Sabha debate, by the central government and, even before that, by Pant and

[56] *Report of the Backward Classes Commission*, First Part, vols I and II, New Delhi: Government of India, 1980, p. 2.

[57] Letter of J. Nehru to the Chief Ministers of 27 June 1961, in J. Nehru, *Letters to the Chief Ministers, 1947–1964*, Delhi: Oxford University Press, 1989, vol. V, pp. 456–7.

[58] Cited in *Report of the Backward Classes Commission*, First Part, vols I and II, New Delhi: Government of India, 1980, p. 2.

[59] *Lok Sabha Debates*, vol. 48, Debates of 25 November 1965, cols 3915ff.

[60] Ibid., col. 3975.

most of its minutes of dissent as well as Kalelkar's covering letter bore testimony to Congress's reluctance to recognise caste as a legitimate criterion for affirmative action. Caste and caste-based reservations were disregarded in favour of economic criteria, socialist programmes or national unity, even though these claims contradicted article 16(4) of the Constitution in which economic criteria are not mentioned. Anyway, they were often pretexts masking the desire to maintain the status quo.

The AIBCF and the quotas: an ephemeral low-castes front

Although its report was shelved the first Backward Classes Commission was a milestone for the low caste movement in North India. In order to determine the needs of the OBCs, the Kalelkar Commission had sent a detailed questionnaire to various representative organisations, eliciting a strong response: the Commission received 3,344 memoranda, in addition to the 5,636 persons interviewed.[61] Kalelkar himself admitted:

> It is clear that the ferment has reached the masses. They have, for the first time in thousands of years, shed their traditional resignation to fate and started hoping that their condition can be improved, that they will be able to take their rightful place in the social structure of to-morrow and that they will have their due share in all schemes of national advancement.
>
> The immediate effect of this ferment was marked in the form of uneasiness and impatience, and some measures of bitterness also, in the minds of the people. These symptoms cannot be ignored because they are indicative of the birth of a new energy which must be canalised into creative effort and constructive activity. *There remains no longer any belief in the sanctity of the caste-hierarchy having been established by the will of God.*[62]

Such comments acknowledged the decline of a hierarchical social order and implicitly admit that the Commission had brought new hope to certain castes which quickly acquired a new assertiveness. The impact of the first Backward Classes Commission thus reconfirmed that the state was shaping new social categories, like the Non-Brahmins, not only by framing them officially but also by consulting representatives of the new categories in question which helped to refashion each group's particular identity. These people were after all

[61] Galanter, *Competing Equalities*, op. cit., p.170.

[62] *Report of the [First] Backward Classes Commission*, vol. 1, op. cit., pp. 6–7. Emphasis by the present author.

members of the growing number of associations representing the lower castes. In 1954 there were 88 organisations 'working for the Backward Classes in 15 states, of which 74 represented individual communities, and 14, Backward Classes in general on a local or state basis'.[63] Two of the largest of such institutions in North India were the UP Backward Classes Federation, which had been founded in 1929, and the Bihar State Backward Classes Federation, which had been created in 1947. The All India Backward Classes Federation emerged from these two state organisations. The name of the organisation is not unimportant since it reflects an attempt at amalgamating the lower castes in a new, encompassing category and at imbuing them with a new identity.

The AIBCF was created on the same day as the Constitution was proclaimed, on 26 January 1950 in order to protest against the scant attention paid in this document to the OBCs. Its architect, and president, was Punjabrao Deshmukh who had thoroughly supported the backward castes during the Constituent Assembly debates. His last speech in the Assembly ran parallel to that of Ambedkar who provided the epigraph to the present book's introduction:

> This parliamentary democracy is essentially meant for maintaining the *status quo.* It is not meant to bring about a radical change from the existing state of affairs. We are going to keep the various institutions intact. We want to keep the various layers of society where they were and from that point of view I would not be surprised if this Constitution does not last long, because it does not answer the aspirations of the man in the street at the present time [. . .]
>
> the people who are known as the backward communities of India, have not been treated as fairly as I would have liked them to be. [. . .] it would be very desirable that the sympathy which we show towards the Scheduled Castes and Scheduled Tribes should also, in a measure, be extended to these people who have yet to see any benefits accruing from the freedom that we have achieved. . . .[64]

A graduate from Oxford with an LLB from Lincoln's Inn, Deshmukh had practised as an advocate before entering politics as a standard Congress notable: from chairman of Amraoti district council he became a member of the legislative council and the Minister of education, public works and development and agriculture in the govern-

[63] Galanter, *Competing Equalities*, op. cit., p. 162 .
[64] *CAD*, vol. XI, p. 777.

ment of the Central Provinces and Berar in 1930.[65] In 1926 he had founded the Berar Shetkari Sangh (or Farmer's Association) and later the Bharat Krishak Samaj (Farmers' Forum). But he had also been the president of the Kurma [Kurmi] Kshatriya Mahasabha in 1944,[66] and set up in 1949 the Scheduled Castes, Scheduled Tribes and Other Backward Classes Scholarship Board, and then the AIBCF in 1950. Before that, it was largely due to him that in March 1948 scholarships for the OBCs were created by the government. He later pressured the government to appoint the first Backward Classes Commission by which time Deshmukh had joined Nehru's government as agriculture minister in 1952.[67]

Not only was Deshmukh not from among the OBCs, he was not even from North India. Like Khedekar – and to a lesser extent, Shahu Maharaj – he came from Maharashtra and attempted to organise the generally leaderless low castes of North India. More broadly, he projected himself as leader of the OBCs by establishing the AIBCF, as president of which he submitted a memorandum to the Kalelkar Commission in which he 'pleaded for a reservation of 60% of the vacancies [in the administration] for the Other Backward Classes'.[68] The way the Kalelkar Report was dismissed in 1956 offended many members of the AIBCF. However, Deshmukh, who remained Agriculture Minister till 1962, refused to break with Congress. In 1958 the AIBCF even thanked the government for extending various welfare schemes to the OBCs and requested the state governments to place OBC students in educational institutions reserved for Scheduled Castes and Scheduled Tribes where vacancies existed.[69] The Congress, once again, had successfully co-opted a non-upper caste leader and circumvented his erstwhile militancy. In fact, Deshmukh was hardly radical. His discourse even had Gandhian overtones when he emphasised the need to promote 'the homogeneity of the Indian

[65] *Who's Who in Lok Sabha*, 1962, pp. 117–19, and S.P. Singh Sud and A. Singh Sud, *Indian Elections and Legislators*, Ludhiana: All India Publications, 1953, p. 125.

[66] *The Indian and Pakistan Yearbook and Who's Who – 1949*, Bombay: The Times of India, 1949, p. 719.

[67] A.B. Kholi, *Directory of Union Ministers, 1947–1987*, New Delhi: Reliance Publishing House, 1988, p. 33.

[68] *Report of the [First] Backward Classes Commission*, vol. 1, op. cit., p. 139.

[69] Galanter, *Competing Equalities*, op. cit., p. 174.

society'[70] and 'the noblest religion on earth, namely, the Hindu religion'.[71]

Deshmukh's reluctance to emancipate himself from the Congress and its Gandhian discourse alienated the most radical members of the AIBCF. The movement split in 1957 and Deshmukh's opponents created the Indian National Backward Classes Federation[72] under the leadership of R.L. Chandapuri. This organisation formed a political party but merged a few months later (10 November 1957) with the Socialist Party. The AIBCF, weakened by the split of 1957 and by Deshmukh's ageing leadership, remobilised itself after his death in 1965.

His successor, Brahma Prakash Chaudhury, a Yadav from Delhi, was also a lifelong Congressman. He had been the secretary of the Delhi Pradesh Congress Committee in 1946–51, then its President in 1951–2 and again in 1959–60. He was elected MLA for the first time in 1952 and became Chief Minister, a post he occupied till 1955. He was first returned to the Lok Sabha from Delhi Sadar in 1957 but moved to Outer Delhi in 1962 because this rural constituency was dominated by cultivating castes, including his own, the Yadavs.[73] Within Congress, Chaudhury is really the exception that proves the rule given that he was the first OBC Chief Minister to emerge from the party's ranks. This privilege, however, can be explained by his relatively moderate character, in which Chaudhury resembled Deshmukh: the Congress promoted low caste leaders, provided they were pliable. However, Chaudhury was more dynamic than Deshmukh and, more importantly, he was a Yadav. Henceforth, the

[70] *CAD*, vol. XI, p. 778.

[71] Ibid., p. 776. The last speech of Deshmukh in the Constituent Assembly needs to be cited fully here: 'I would not have minded if we had given some place to the noblest religion on earth, namely the Hindu religion, and even if we wanted that the Constitution should remain secular, even if we had declared that this shall be a Hindu State, I have not the slightest doubt that the Constitution would have remained as secular as wanted it to be, because there is no religion on earth which is more secular in its character than Hinduism.' (Ibid., pp. 776–7)

[72] Letter of R. L. Chandapuri to R. M. Lohia, of 15 June 1957, in R.M. Lohia, *The Caste System*, Hyderabad: Rammanohar Lohia Samata Vidyalaya Nyas, 1978 [1964], p. 38.

[73] *Lok Sabha Who's Who – 1962*, New Delhi: Lok Sabha Secretariat, 1962, p. 63.

AIBCF would benefit from the political activism and organisational ability of the Yadav Mahasabha and other associations which supported caste-based quotas.[74] The mid-1960s offered a favourable context for the activities of the AIBCF in this regard.

The issue of caste-based reservations, in the wake of the Kalelkar Commission, had aroused a new kind of solidarity among the lower castes in order to promote their socio-economic interests. In Bihar, where the Yadavs dominated the OBC movement, Frankel regards it as a real turning point, at least for the younger generation, which was emancipating itself from the logic of Sanskritisation:

> Instead of the 'old fantasy' of emulating Brahmans and Kshatriyas to achieve 'Twice born' status, they turned their attention to secular goals, particularly the promised reservations in professional and technical institutions and the higher ranks of the government services. Very quickly, in an effort to push implementation of the reservation policy, they shifted their reference group from the upper castes to that of the 'Backward Classes'. They also changed their emphasis from social activities to political mobilisation, underlining the need to overcome sub-caste division in order to maximise the power of the 'backward' vote.[75]

During its March 1966 annual meeting in New Delhi the AIBCF mobilised one thousand activists, with many speakers exhorting them to overthrow the 'Brahmin-Banya Raj'. Resolutions were passed requesting the government to publish lists of OBCs, to increase grants for low caste students and to introduce educational and administrative quotas on a population basis.[76] One of the resolutions specified that the reservation policy had to rely on caste criteria:

> The Federation is of the firm opinion that even though ultimately a class of people are to be judged by the economic well-being, in the transition period when large sections suffer from social disabilities in addition to economic poverty it would not be in the national interest to determine backwardness in terms of economic criteria alone. Social backwardness – as laid down in the Constitution – can only be determined in terms of castes and communities to which the stigma applies as a whole. . . .[77]

[74] Rao, *Social Movements and Social Transformation*, op. cit., p. 156.

[75] Frankel, 'Caste, Land and Dominance', op. cit., p.86.

[76] K. C. Yadav, *India's Unequal Citizens – A Study of the Other Backward Classes*, Delhi: Manohar, 1994, pp. 65–6.

[77] See 'Resolutions of the Backward Classes Federation Conference, 12 March 1966', Appendix 2 to M.S.A. Rao, *Social Movements and Social Transformation*, op. cit., p. 262.

For the AIBCF, which asked for the implementation of the Kalelkar report, caste had to be considered as the basic unit for evaluating backwardness and distributing the benefits of compensatory policies, not least because the stigma affecting the lower castes was 'a serious handicap' and even 'the root-cause of economic backwardness'.[78]

The AIBCF developed under the aegis of Brahma Prakash Chaudhury in a political context that was marked by the debate on the Kalelkar report and the concurrent mobilisation of the lower castes, as epitomised by the role of the All India Yadav Mahasabha. The 1968 conference of the Yadav Mahasabha, for instance, had campaigned for the implementation of the Kalelkar Report and for caste-based reservations.[79] The AIBCF was almost relaunched by Chaudhury in this context. It began publishing a *Backward Classes Review* in 1968, for instance.[80]

Backward caste associations found in the notion of 'OBC quotas' a good reason to down play their narrow identity and merge it in a broader front which could pressure the state more effectively. In the early 1970s, the All India Kurmi Mahasabha allied with the Koeris and sought a merger of all the 'backward classes'. At its 1972 session, its slogan was 'Pichara Jagao Desh Bachao' ('"Backwards", wake-up and rescue the country'). One resolution sought to allow non-Kurmis to belong to the association while another asked for the appointment of a Public Service Commission for the Backward Classes.

The trend was short-lived. First, Yadav domination of the AIBCF was resented by other low castes. Jai Narayan Singh Yadav had become its general secretary in 1959 and when Brahma Prakash Chaudhury took over from Deshmukh, the Yadavs tightened their grip on the Federation.[81] They maintained their influence throughout the 1960s. During the 1962 Indo-China war, Yadav soldiers acquitted themselves well of their task in Ladakh and some were decorated for valour. This episode fostered the Yadavs' pride in their martial traditions and they immediately asked the government to establish a

[78] *Backward Classes Review* 1(4–5), p. 10, cited in Galanter, *Competing Equalities*, op. cit., p. 210.

[79] M.S.A. Rao, 'Political Elite and Caste Association: A Report of a Caste Conference', *EPW*, 3, 1968, pp. 779–82.

[80] Galanter, *Competing Equalities*, op. cit., p. 210.

[81] Rao, *Social Movements and Social Transformation*, op. cit., p. 156. In Uttar Pradesh also, in 1961, a Yadav, Bachan Ram Yadav (MLA) became the Vice President of the U.P. Backward Classes Association (ibid., p. 157).

Yadav regiment, along the same lines as the Rajput or Sikh regiments. The claim was rejected but the Yadavs, after they showed their bravery in the 1965 war, reiterated their demand. In 1966, the AIYM held its annual conference in Ettawa, with Mulayam Singh Yadav as chairman of the reception committee and Rao Birendra Singh – the scion of the Rewari dynasty – as president. One of the resolutions of the subjects committee asked for the implementation of the Kalelkar report. However, the Yadavs could not help but adopt a hegemonic attitude *vis-à-vis* the other OBC castes covered by the report. Ram Lakhan Singh Yadav – a Congress leader from Bihar[82] – declared that the Yadavs 'were leading the 90% of the [Indian] population which was backward'[83] and B.P. Mandal, who was then Chief Minister of Bihar (see below), declared that the Yadavs 'should lead the revolution'.[84] The last day of the conference being devoted to the backward classes as a whole, other low castes and landless Scheduled Castes spoke on the need for the backward classes to unite. But the Kurmis were reluctant to accept the Yadav leadership and within the Yadav fold itself some influential leaders disapproved of the broader notion of backward identity that 'radicals' such as Mulayam Singh Yadav and B.P. Mandal promoted.

The President himself, Rao Birendra Singh, true to his leanings towards Sanskritisation, stressed in his address that it was 'a sign of weakness on the part of the Yadavs to consider themselves a backward community and urged that they should become politically awakened and integrated',[85] as if asking for reservations was a sign of separatism. Instead, he emphasised the Yadav regiment issue. In a signed memorandum submitted in November 1968, Rao Birendra Singh pointed out that Yadavs, 'like the Rajputs, Jats, Sikhs and Marathas, are a martial race'. He even added out that the 'Yadav community [was] not a caste but a race'.[86]

[82] Like Brahma Prakash Chaudhury, Ram Lakhan Singh Yadav had held responsibilities in the Congress since the 1940s: he had been General Secretary and then President of the PCC of Bihar, a Congress MLA since 1952 and a minister (Parliament of India, *Tenth Lok Sabha Who's Who*, New Delhi: Lok Sabha Secretariat, 1992, p. 865).

[83] Rao, *Social Movements and Social Transformation*, op. cit., p. 156.

[84] Rao, 'Political Elite', op. cit., p. 781.

[85] Ibid.

[86] 'All India Yadava Mahasabha – Memorandum', Appendix 1 to Rao, *Social Movements and Social Transformation*, op. cit., pp. 258–9.

In Ettawa, Rao Birendra Singh also described the Yadavs as peasants (*kisans*). He advocated the formation of Vishal Haryana, a new province where Yadavs and Jats would be in the majority, 'so that *kisan* could seize political power'.[87] The Rewari family have always oscillated between Sanskritisation and *kisan* politics. Rao Balbir Singh, even though he had links with the Hindu Mahasabha, had joined the Zamindar party soon after it was established by Chhotu Ram (see below). The party then represented the interests of the four major cultivating castes of Punjab, the Jats (Chhotu Ram's caste), the Yadavs, the Gujars and the Rajputs. The affinities between the Yadav dynasty and a Jat-led party are not so difficult to fathom since in Punjab, Delhi and part of Uttar Pradesh the former 'occupied a rank equal to that of Jats and Gujars with commensal relations including smoking from the same *hukka*'.[88] After the demise of Chhotu Ram in 1945, Rao Birendra Singh, succeeded him at the helm of the Zamindar Party. He was elected to the Punjab Legislative Council in 1954 and then joined Congress to become deputy minister and then Minister. He was again elected an MLA on a Congress ticket in 1957, 1962 and 1967 but then defected. He was elected leader of the Samyukta Vidhayak Dal and became Chief Minister of Haryana for a few months and founded a new party, the Vishal Haryana Party, soon after. The political inclinations of the Rewari family, either Sanskritisation or *kisan* politics, could only weaken the 'backward front'. Rao Birendra Singh was perhaps an old fashioned Yadav but he was re-elected as President of the AIYS at the Ettawa conference. In a very perceptive rejoinder to M.S.A. Rao's analysis of the Ettawa conference, Dhanagare emphasised the division within the Yadavs between the advocates of reservations and the followers of Rao Birendra Singh – the former were 'the economically underprivileged Yadavs' whereas the latter represented 'the class consisting of well-off Yadavs'.[89] This cleavage opposed the proponents of compensatory discrimination in caste terms and those who remained wedded to Sanskritisation and 'integration'. The AIBCF was directly affected by these cleavages since the Yadavs were the most active of the lower castes. The federation also failed to sustain the mobilisation of the 1960s because the

[87] Ibid.

[88] Rao, *Social Movements and Social Transformation*, op. cit., p. 131.

[89] D.N. Dhanagare, 'Political Elite and Caste Association – A Comment', *EPW*, 30 Nov. 1968, p. 1852.

implementation of caste-based quotas gradually became a remote possibility. It therefore became less attractive, and the AIBCF was almost defunct by the early 1970s.

The mobilisation of the backward castes on the quota issue in the 1960s contributed more than any other movement had previously done to the crystallisation of a low caste front in North India. The state policy of affirmative action was largely responsible for this development. It had invented a new socio-administrative category – the OBCs – in which the low castes were bound to recognise their common interests, and, by subsuming their caste identity and joining hands as 'backward classes', could press the state into granting them reservations. This strategy of empowerment had already been implemented by the Non-Brahmin movement in the South during the colonial era; the Kalelkar Commission created a favourable context for its reproduction in the North. However, the mobilisation orchestrated by the AIBCF could not be sustained for long because of divisions among the lower castes (mainly between Yadavs and Kurmis) and because of differences *within* the individual low castes, such as the Yadavs, whose leaders of the AIYM supported quota politics whereas others remained imbued with the Sanskritisation ethos. As a result, the low castes were unable to exert enough pressure on the states of North India to grant substantial reservations. In contrast, the reservation policies of South Indian states consolidated the political identity of the low castes.

Reservation policies: the North-South contrast

In North India, the post-Kalelkar mobilisation was ephemeral and resulted in few significant concessions from the Congress state governments. In the South, by contrast, the 1960s were marked by an increase of quotas in favour of the OBCs. Table 7.2 clearly brings out the contrast between the North and the South: it shows that the North Indian Backward Classes Commissions were appointed – at the most – in the 1970s and 1980s whereas most southern states had designated theirs in the 1960s and sometimes even before. In fact, there was already a tradition of caste-oriented positive discrimination in South India (as discussed in chapter 5 above in the case of Tamil Nadu) before independence. This was challenged by the judiciary but revived in the 1960s and 1970s, whereas the North continued to lag behind.

Table 7.2. STATE BACKWARD CLASSES COMMISSIONS AND COMMITTEES IN 20TH CENTURY INDIA

	Chairman	*Date of appointment*	*Submission of report*
Mysore	L. Miller	1918	1921
Bombay	O.H.B. Starte	1929	1930
Jammu and Kashmir	–	1931	1932
Mysore (reorganised)	R. N. Gowda	1960	1961
Maharashtra	B. D. Deshmukh	1961	1964
Kerala	Vishvanathan	1961	1963
Kerala	G. K. Pillai	1965	1966
Kerala	N. P. Damodaran	1967	1970
Jammu and Kashmir	B. P. Gajendragadkar	1966	1969
Jammu and Kashmir	J N Wazir	1969	1969
Andhra Pradesh	Mahohar Prasad	1968	1970
Tamil Nadu	A. N. Sattanathan	1970	1971
Bihar	Mungeri Lal	1971	1976
Karnataka	L.G. Havanur	1972	1975
Gujarat	A. R. Baxi	1972	1976
Uttar Pradesh	Chhedi Lal Sathi	1975	1977
Jammu and Kashmir	A. S. Anand	1976	1977
Kerala	–	1976	1977
West Bengal	Chhedi Lal Sathi	1980	1980
Madhya Pradesh	Ramji Mahajan	1980	1983
Gujarat	V. V. Rana	1981	1985
Karnataka	T. Venktaswamy	1985	1987
Gujarat	R.C. Mankad	1987	1987
Karnataka	O. Chinnappa Reddy	1989	1990
Haryana	Gurnam Singh	1990	1991

Source: Adapted from K.C. Yadav, *India's Unequal Citizens*, op. cit., p. 7

Reservations in South India: Political Schemes Under Judicial Constraints. The Indian affirmative action programmes in the government services undoubtedly stemmed from Mysore state, where over-representation of Brahmins in the administration gave the lower castes a strong incentive to organise. The Praja Mithra Mandali, which came into being in 1917, made representations in this respect to the Maharajah, who was himself from a 'Shudra' community, the Urs.[90] The latter then asked the Chief Justice of the Chief Court, Leslie Miller, to prepare a report on the importance of non-Brahmins

[90] J. Manor, *Political Change in an Indian State: Mysore, 1917–1955*, Delhi: Manohar, 1977, p. 60.

in the administration. The Miller Commission resorted to the notion of 'Backward Classes' to designate groups other than Brahmins, Europeans and Anglo-Indians and recommended that they be granted, in the next seven years, half of the highest and a third of the lowest grades in the administration.[91] The Maharajah decided to implement these measures in 1921.

The other pioneer region was Madras Presidency. As mentioned in chapter 5, in this province the British had long been concerned about the over-representation of Brahmins and favoured the caste-based positive discrimination of the Justice Party in the early 1920s. This policy was continued by the Congress government in the late 1930s. After Independence, in November 1947, the category of Hindu non-Brahmins was again subdivided and won a larger share of posts: 43% of the administration jobs went to non-Brahmin Hindus, 14% to 'Backward Hindus', 14% to Brahmins, 14% to Scheduled Castes, 7% to Anglo-Indians and Christian Indians and 7% to Muslims.[92] After the promulgation of the Indian Constitution in 1950, quotas based on religious criteria were abolished and the Scheduled Castes quota was redesigned on a population basis. As a result, the Scheduled Castes enjoyed a 15% reservation and the Other Backward Classes 25% in the administration and then in technical schools. For the cumulative impact of these measures see Table 7.4.

In 1947 Brahmins occupied 40.5% of the 'gazetted posts' and 27.7% of the 'non-gazetted posts' and non-Brahmins respectively 34.9% and 48.1%.[93] Other southern states promoted the lower

[91] O. Chinnappa Reddy, *Report of the Karnataka third Backward Classes Commission*, vol. 1, Bangalore: Government of Karnataka, 1990, pp. 11–12.

[92] A. N. Sattanathan, *Report of the Backward Classes Commission Tamil Nadu*, vol. I, Madras: Government of Tamil Nadu, 1974, pp. 27–8.

[93] Ibid., p. 90. By the late 1960s, the OBCs had acquired a considerable influence in strategic posts of the administration, the Secretariat (which controls the bureaucracy of the state), and the 'Collectorate' whose services collect the taxes and take major decisions regarding the budget:

Table 7.3. OBC IN THE SECRETARIAT AND IN THE 'COLLECTORATES' IN TAMIL NADU, 1970 (%)

	Non-gazetted posts	*Gazetted posts*
Secretariat	39.8	20.8
'Collectorates'	47.5	24.8

Source: Adapted from Sattanathan, *Report of the Backward Classes Commission*, op. cit., pp. 140.

Table 7.4. COMPOSITION OF THE ADMINISTRATION OF THE PROVINCE OF MADRAS AND TAMIL NADU BY CASTES AND COMMUNITIES, 1927–70

Year	*1927*[a]	*1935*		*1947*		*1951*[b]		*1969–70*[c]	
		Gazetted posts	*Non-gazetted posts*	*Gazetted posts*	*Non-gazetted posts*	*Gazetted posts*	*Non-gazetted posts*	*Gazetted posts*	*Non-gazetted posts*
Brahmins	51.6	40.7	44.4	40.5	27.7	22.7	17.2	16	15.7
Non-Brahmins,	18.8	23.4	37.8	34.9	48.1	47.1	53.8	51.6	67.2
(incl. Backward Castes)						(6.6)	(12)	(12.9)	(44.8)
Scheduled Castes		0.6	0.6	1.3	2.8				
Muslims	5.9	6	7.4	6.9	11	10.9	13.7	6.4	3.8
Anglo-Indians and Christian Indians	23.7	29	9.7	16.2	10.1	15.2	9.1	19.3	7.7

[a] The 1927 figures concern the Deputy Collectors, the Deputy Superintendents of Police, the Executive Assistants, Executive Engineers and Assistant Engineers, the Civil Surgeons and Civil Assistant Surgeons
[b] The 1951 figures constitute the average of only two administrative departments, the Police and the fiscal services
[c] The 1969-70 figures concern only three districts of Tamil Nadu, Chingleput, Ramanathapuram and Tiruchirappalli.

Source: A.N. Sattanathan, *Report of the Backward Classes Commission*, op. cit., pp. 90-1.

castes in the administration to a similar degree. In the princely states of Travancore and Cochin, which formed Kerala in 1956, Ezhavas together with – substantial – Christian and Muslim minorities, obtained in 1936 representation in the state administration on a population basis and, in 1937, a quota of eight seats in the state assembly.[94] In South India, either in princely states – such as Mysore or Travancore-Cochin – or in regions ruled by the British – like Madras Presidency –, reservation policies had enabled the lower castes to win a large share of the bureaucracy before 1947. These policies proved more difficult to implement after Independence.

In 1950 the promulgation of the Indian Constitution proved a major challenge for the reservation policies of the southern states. Their affirmative action programmes were first contested before the courts because they contradicted the fundamental rights regarding equality and the notion of equal opportunities. As noticed above, the first amendment was passed in 1951 as a reaction to this new trend. But the southern states continued to face adverse judicial reviews from judges who questioned that their quotas really benefited 'socially and educationally backward classes' and not castes. This conflict crystallised in the early 1960s when the central government and the Supreme Court turned out to be equally hostile to caste-based quotas. Soon after the cabinet rejected the Kalelkar Report on the ground, *inter alia*, that its definition of the backward classes relied to a too large extent on caste criteria, the Supreme Court gave a landmark judgement based on the same premises in the 1963 *Balaji v. State of Mysore* case.

In 1959, three years after the merger of Mysore state in a new entity of the same name – it was renamed Karnataka in 1973 –, the government established a list of 165 castes designated as 'Backward Classes' and gave them a quota of 57% of the posts in the administration. The High Court contested the validity of the whole exercise as it relied on caste criteria which were not recognised by the Constitution.[95] The government then appointed a 'Backward Classes Commission' which concluded that it was difficult to dissociate social 'backwardness' from caste but added to this criterion the level

[94] Yadav, *India's Unequal Citizens*, op. cit., pp. 148–50.

[95] O. Chinnappa Reddy, *Report of the Karnataka Third Backward Classes Commission*, vol. 1, Bangalore: Government of Karnataka, 1990, p. 13.

of education and the under-representation of castes in the administration. The Commission recommended the attribution of a quota of 50% for the 'Backward Classes' in the administration – 22% for the 'backward' and 28% for the 'most backward'. However, the Lingayats – the dominant caste of the state – protested their exclusion from this quota. In 1962, it was increased by the state government in order to include them. Eventually 15% of the places in engineering and medical colleges were reserved for the Scheduled Castes, 3% for the Scheduled Tribes and 50% for the Backward Classes.

The Supreme Court struck down this measure in 1963 in the 'Balaji Case' – for two reasons: because it disapproved of quotas whose total exceeded 50% of the posts in the administration or places in educational institutions[96] and because it considered that caste should not remain a predominant criterion of affirmative action. The place of residence, occupation or literacy rate should be equally important in the identification of the backward classes. Marc Galanter convincingly argues that the Supreme Court's judgement was especially hostile to taking caste *ranks* into account as a measure of backwardness. On the other hand, it was prepared to regard caste as a relevant *unit* for assessing low literacy rates and any other form of social backwardness. But the Court failed to make this distinction clear and therefore 'encouraged the notion that "caste" was in all respects eliminated from the selection of Backward Classes'.[97] As a result of the *Balaji* case, the government of Mysore abandoned the basis of caste and decided upon an interim measure to classify backwardness on the basis of economic conditions and occupation. However, this arrangement 'did not benefit the truly Backward Classes or Castes, which required to be helped but mostly benefited certain dominant communities such as Brahmins, Lingayats and Vokkaligas'.[98]

All the Southern states' affirmative action policies were affected by the Balaji-based jurisprudence. In Kerala, the government had granted in 1957 a quota of 35% to the OBCs in professional schools and of 40% in the administration (against 10% to the Scheduled

[96] Cited in Galanter, *Competing Equalities*, op. cit., p. 401

[97] Ibid., p. 192.

[98] Chinnappa Reddy, *Report of the Karnataka Third Backward Classes Commission*, op. cit., p. 15.

Castes and Scheduled Tribes). This procedure was contested before the Kerala High Court which in 1964 struck down the government's order classifying Ezhavas and Muslims as Backward Classes on the ground that the only test that had been applied was that of caste and community.[99] That yeat the state government appointed a Backward Classes Commission under the chairmanship of G.K Pillai. It emphasised economic criteria and eventually recommended in its report that OBC members earning more than 6,000 rupees a year should be deleted from the list. The government took this recommendation into account for the education quotas, but retained the old list for the administration. These dispositions were contested before the Court and a new Backward Classes Reservation Commission was appointed by the government in 1968. The Commission excluded from the OBCs list those earning more than 8,000 rupees a year and restricted the quotas in the administration to 38%. The Chief Minister Achuta Menon accepted these recommendations in 1973, to the great displeasure of the OBCs, but his successor, Vasudevan Nair, re-established a quota of 40% for the OBCs, in addition to the 10% reservation for the Scheduled Castes and Scheduled Tribes.

A similar development occurred in Andhra Pradesh which inherited its affirmative action policy from the British since it had been part of Madras Province till 1953. In 1960, when Andhra Pradesh was awarded its current state boundaries, quotas reserved for the OBCs in the administration represented 38% of the posts (against 17% for the Scheduled Castes and Scheduled Tribes).[100] In 1963, the Congress state government established quotas for OBC candidates to 'Medical Colleges'. A complaint was lodged against this decision before the High Court of Andhra Pradesh and the judges, following the Balaji judgement, quashed the government's decision because the quotas relied on caste criteria.[101] The same pattern repeated itself in 1968. The government appealed to the Supreme Court, which upheld the judgement. The first Backward Classes Commission was appointed two weeks later in April 1968: it recommended a quota of 30% for the OBCs, not only in every sector of the administration,

[99] Galanter, *Competing Equalities*, op. cit., p. 195.

[100] *Report of the Backward Classes Commission*, Hyderabad: Government of Andhra Pradesh, 1970, p. 108.

[101] Ibid., p. 7.

but also in the local authorities (Panchayats, District Boards, and Town Councils).[102] The government reduced this figure to 25% but the matter was again referred to the High Court which, in 1972, declared the report as unconstitutional, for the same reason as in 1963 and 1968. The government referred to the Supreme Court which then reverted the High Court's decision, arguing that even if the caste criterion had been used for establishing the list of OBCs, the castes included in the final list definitely suffered from social and educational backwardness.[103] The backward castes thus eventually won the case after years of litigation. As mentioned in chapter 4, one of the reasons for this achievement was the political will of the state Congress. After the 1969 split, the Congress(R) considered that the social basis of the party had to be enlarged not only through populism but also by co-opting Dalit, Tribal and OBC leaders. The case of Andhra Pradesh suggests that, in the 1970s, the Supreme Court questioned the maximalist interpretation of Balaji and recognised caste as an important criterion of backwardness. It was especially evident in Tamil Nadu where the political impetus was sanctioned with sympathy by the judges.

In Tamil Nadu, the Congress strategy of accommodating low caste politicians such as Kamaraj – who was Chief Minister in 1954–63 – could not contain the rise of the Non-Brahmin-based Dravidian movement, which had undergone major changes before Independence because of the *rapprochement* between the Justice Party and the Self-Respect movement of Naicker, who joined the Justice Party in 1935. In 1944 Naicker transformed this party into the Dravida Kazhagam. In 1949 one of his lieutenants, C.N. Annadurai, who had grown more radical in his demand for a separate Dravidistan, split up and created the Dravida Munnetra Kazhagam (DMK). This party projected itself as not only militantly Dravidian, but also as the spokesman for the lower castes. It became a strong rival to Congress, especially after Kamaraj went to Delhi to become President of the Congress party, and even won the 1967 elections. Soon after, the DMK government of Karunanidhi set up a commission in 1969, mainly to assess the effectiveness of the measures so far taken in favour of the backward classes. The A.N. Sattanathan Commission

[102] Ibid., p. 116.

[103] Yadav, *India's Unequal Citizens*, op. cit., p. 152.

looked at the actual number of OBCs by using the 1921 census, the most complete one so far as castes were concerned, and concluded that they represented 52% of the state's population of whom 23% were classified as 'Most Backward Classes'.[104] This report *inter alia* recommended the increase of the OBCs quotas in the administration from 25% to 33%,[105] 16% out of the 33% being reserved for the 'Most Backward Classes'.[106] On the basis of the report, in 1971 the government established a quota of 31% (instead of 33% recommended by the Backward Classes Commission)[107] so that these 31%, added to the 18% reserved for the Scheduled Castes, left more than 50% of posts open for competitive entrance. This decision could have been invalidated by the courts anyway because the Sattanathan report had adopted a caste-based definition of the backward classes,[108] but the judges accepted the new reservation policy established on this basis.[109]

A similar scenario unfolded in Karnataka in the 1970s. In 1972, the new Congress Chief Minister, Devraj Urs, whose career was referred to in chapter 4, restarted the reservation process which had been frozen with *Balaji*. He appointed another 'Backward Classes Commission' under the chairmanship of L.G. Havanur who undertook a very systematic investigation into the conditions of OBCs in the state. Half of its eight criteria selected for identifying backwardness directly referred to caste: the prejudice entertained by the upper castes, the 'low status or inferiority associated with their castes', 'social taboos against inter-dining and inter-marriage' and 'age-old

[104] A. N. Sattanathan, *Report of the Backward Classes Commission Tamil Nadu*, vol. I, op. cit., p. 40.

[105] Ibid., p. 94.

[106] This quota within the quota was justified by the fact that 9 OBC castes representing 11.3% of OBCs occupied 48.2% of the 'gazetted posts' reserved for the OBCs (ibid., p. 143).

[107] Ibid., p. 148.

[108] To cite the report: 'Social backwardness is a matter of local or regional opinion based on taboos and other concepts in a hierarchical society' (ibid., p. 36).

[109] When the government, shortly after, raised the quota reserved for OBCs and Scheduled Castes in medical schools up to 41%, opponents from the upper castes referred the matter to the Supreme Court, denouncing in particular the unconstitutionality of quotas based on caste criteria; but the court upheld the decision (Yadav, *India's Unequal Citizens*, op. cit., p. 133).

social customs'.[110] For the first time, the majority of the Lingayat subcaste were not considered as OBCs, which prompted demonstrations on their part. The Commission recommended a 26% reservation for the backward castes and communities in its 1975 report. The Devraj Urs government implemented it in an amended form since more quotas were created not only for the backward classes. The total reservations in the government services of the state therefore now covered 66% of the posts. The Government Order was questioned before the High Court by way of some Writ Petitions but it was upheld in 1985, except for some minor parts, which meant that caste had become a much more acceptable criterion for identifying backwardness, even for the judiciary.[111]

South India's experiment with reservations confirms that a specific pattern of low caste politics has crystallised in this meta-region. The many low caste people who considered themselves to be from a different ethnic – Dravidian – origin than the upper castes had early fostered a non-Brahmin movement, so much so that Non-Brahminism and Dravidianism largely coincided and mutually reinforced each other. The political parties arising from this milieu, with the support of the British and Shudra princes, established affirmative action programmes which started to dislodge Brahmins from the establishment even before 1947. After independence, the political agenda of the main parties still emphasised reservation policies for the benefits of the OBCs. The judiciary then compelled them to revise the criteria under which these classes were defined since in the 1950s and 1960s the courts interpreted the Constitution in such a way that 'backwardness' could not be equated with a low caste ranking. Most governments pursued a determined reservation policy under this tight constraint, which loosened in the 1970s when more and more judges admitted caste as an important criterion.

[110] Cited in Galanter, *Competing Equalities*, op. cit., pp. 239–40.

[111] The case was brought before the Supreme Court which asked the government to appoint another 'Backward Classes Commission'. But the report was indicted for other reasons than its reliance on caste as a major criterion. One of the judges, O. Chinnapa Reddy even said: 'Social status and economic power are so woven and fused into the caste system in Indian rural society that one may without hesitation, say that if poverty be the cause, caste is the primary index of social backwardness, so that social backwardness is often readily identifiable with reference to a person's caste.' (Cited in A. Prasad, *Reservational Justice*, op. cit., p. 83)

Western India: an Intermediate Pattern. While Galanter considers that South India and West India – Maharashtra and Gujarat – followed the same pattern of affirmative action,[112] to my mind, these two states – which were carved out from Bombay Presidency in 1960 – represent a different way of dealing with reservations.

In Maharashtra the Marathas, who had been steadily gaining control of the Congress party since the 1930s, had already established their presence in the administration when India became independent. In Bombay Presidency, they were well represented among the gazetted officers and dominant among the non-gazetted officers as is evident from Table 7.5.

Given the share of the administration they had already cornered, the Marathas were unlikely to support any large-scale policy of positive discrimination in favour of lower castes, especially after the 1950 Constitution granted quotas proportionate to their population to the Scheduled Castes. In 1961, the Maharashtra government appointed a Backward Classes Commission under the chairmanship of B.D. Deshmukh who submitted his report in 1964. He recommended new quotas in the administration and in the education system: 13% for the Scheduled Castes (including the Buddhist Mahars), 7% for the Scheduled Tribes, 4% for other tribes (nomads etc.) and 10% for the 'other backward communities'.[113] The government accepted these recommendations. In 1974, the OBCs benefited from a new measure, a 10% quota in the teaching profession.[114] This reservation policy was much more timid than in South India where, by that time, most of the states tried to implement at least 25% quotas for the OBCs. Even so, these concessions were partly reversed in 1979 when Chief Minister Sharad Pawar, a Maratha, decided to reserve 46% of the posts for the poor including the forward castes (those who earned less than 400 rupees a month). The matter was referred to the High Court, which declared it ill founded because economic criteria were not a sufficient basis for positive discrimination. The mere fact that the state government proposed such a measure bore testimony of the limited influence of the OBCs compared to the Marathas.

In Gujarat the lower castes had asserted themselves through the Kshatriya movement in the 1960s. This caste federation turned out

[112] Galanter, *Competing Equalities*, op. cit., p. 181.

[113] *Report of the [second] Backward Classes Commission – First Part*, op. cit., p. 9.

[114] Yadav, *India's Unequal Citizens*, op. cit., p. 161.

Table 7.5. CASTES AND COMMUNITIES IN THE ADMINISTRATION OF BOMBAY PRESIDENCY, 1949 (%)

	Gazetted officers	*Non-gazetted officers*
Marathas and allied castes	19.7	41.1
Brahmins	44.5	20.3
Depressed classes	0.5	7.8
Muslims	6.5	13
Others	28.8	17.7
Total	100	100
	N=3,077	N=105,464

Source: Reply of Chief Minister B.G. Kher to a question in the Bombay Legislative Assembly, cited in *CAD*, vol. XI, op. cit., p. 916.

to be a political interest group with greater leverage than caste associations, simply because it represented more people. Many Kshatriyas joined the Congress (R) after the Congress split in 1969, whereas most of the party bosses remained with the Congress (O). Kshatriyas gradually gained control over the state Congress. Madhavsingh Solanki, a Kshatriya of low birth, became Chief Minister in 1976 and appointed a majority of ministers from the same background.[115] During the electoral campaign of 1977 he initiated a new caste alliance regrouping the Kshatriyas, the Harijans (Scheduled Castes), the Adivasis (tribals) and the Muslims (hence the acronym 'KHAM'). This KHAM alliance was largely responsible for the Congress success in the 1980 elections. Between 1957 and 1990 the number of upper caste Congress MLAs decreased from 33 to 6% and those with a Patidar background remained stable at about one fourth of the total, whereas the Kshatriyas increased from 12% to 25% and the KHAM MLAs at large from 39 to 55%.[116] The Congress of Gujarat was therefore pursuing the democratisation process it had initiated under the pressure of the Kshatriyas.

[115] One third were Kshatriyas, one was tribal and two were Scheduled Castes. (G. Shah, 'Gujarat Politics in the Post-Emergency Period', *IJPS*, 55(3), July–Sept. 1994, p. 237)

[116] Ibid., p. 237. See also S. Mitra, 'The perils of promoting equality: the latent significance of the anti-reservation movement in India', *Journal of Commonwealth and Comparative Politics* (hereafter *JCCP*), 25 (3), Nov. 1987, pp. 298–301, and J. R. Wood, 'Reservations in doubt: the backlash against affirmative action in Gujarat, India', *Pacific Affairs*, 60 (3), autumn 1987, pp. 418–19.

This change in the social profile of the ruling party had repercussions on the state's reservation policies.[117] The Solanki government, in order to strengthen its electoral basis among 'KHAM', appointed a 'Socially and Educationally Backward Classes Commission' in 1972. In its 1976 report it recommended reserving 10% of posts in technical 'colleges' (medicine, engineering, agriculture, etc.) for the OBCs and that the same quota should be applied in class III and IV of the administration (only 5% were to be reserved for the OBCs in class I and II).[118] These dispositions were implemented in 1978 by the Janata government. They were hardly more progressive than those of the government of Bombay. While western India has obvious affinities with the reservation pattern of South India, Maharashtra and Gujarat have been less generous with the OBCs.

The Hindi Belt's conservative approach to affirmative action. In his typology, Galanter groups together the states of 'the eastern-middle band, stretching across India from Assam in the northeast through West Bengal and Orissa, across Madhya Pradesh to Rajasthan'[119] because they never even established a list of OBCs before the 1980s. In contrast, he brackets together Uttar Pradesh, Punjab, Bihar and Jammu and Kashmir as an intermediate group, claiming that the last two states 'approximate[d] the peninsular pattern [of South and West India]'.[120] This classification is questionable because the Hindi belt states share many more common features between themselves than with other regions of India. Even though they adopted early lists of OBCs, the states of Uttar Pradesh and Bihar had a very conservative approach towards reservations.

In Bihar, the Congress government drew up a list of the backward classes comprising two categories as early as 1951: the 79 castes of Annexe 1 were considered to be more backward than the 30 others of Annexe 2. However these two categories were only used for awarding educational benefits such as post-matriculation scholarships. They did not serve as a basis for quotas in the administration.

[117] The state of Saurashtra, that had merged with Gujarat when it was created, had appointed a Backward Classes Commission in 1953 but the Kutch area did not possess a list of OBCs. (*Report of the Socially and Educationally Backward Classes Commission*, Government of Gujarat, 1976)

[118] Ibid., pp. 126–7.

[119] Galanter, *Competing Equalities*, op. cit., p. 181.

[120] Ibid., p. 184.

In 1953 a Congress MLA, Bajnath Singh, proposed that 25% of the posts should be reserved in the administration for the OBCs, but due to pressure from his own party he had to withdraw it.[121]

After the judgement of the Supreme Court in the Balaji Case (1963), Patna High Court declared these lists invalid in 1964. The political context turned out to be more favourable to the OBCs in the late 1960s and early 1970s when the decline of the Congress in the state allowed left-wing parties to come to power, on their own or within a coalition, and low caste MLAs to put pressure on the Congress. In 1971, Daroga Prasad Rai, the first Yadav Congress Chief Minister, thus appointed the first Bihar Backward Classes Commission under the chairmanship of Mungeri Lal. The Commission also identified two categories of OBCs, the 'Most Backward Classes' (93 castes) and the 'Backward Castes', and recommended that 26% of the posts in the administration and 24% of the seats in the educational system, should be reserved for these two categories.[122] The subsequent Congress governments never implemented these recommendations. The Janata Party tried to do so in 1978 for the first time amid loud protests from the upper castes. The government largely fell because of this issue, a development we shall scrutinise in the following chapter.

A similar scenario unfolded itself in Uttar Pradesh where the Congress party refused quotas for many years. As early as 1945, the government of the United Provinces had established a list of 37 Hindu 'Backward Castes' and 21 Muslim 'Backward Castes' in order to help them gain educational benefits. Two lists of 'Other Backward Classes' were subsequently drawn up in 1955: the first – comprising 15 castes – for the establishment of a quota in the administration, the second – 59 castes – for the reservation policy in the education system. In 1958, these lists were revised and 37 Hindu Castes and 21 Muslim castes were identified but no quota was implemented. While in Bihar in the late 1960s and early 1970s, OBC Chief Ministers supported affirmative actions (one of them even appointing a Backward Classes Commission), nothing of the kind happened in Uttar Pradesh. The first Backward Classes Commission was only appointed in October 1975 by the government of H.N. Bahuguna. It was

[121] Hebsur, 'Reactions to the reservations for Other Backward Classes', op. cit., p. 157.

[122] Ibid.

the by-product of a deal between the state Congress leader and former members of the RPI who had defected to the ruling party, the Congress (R), in 1969 'on the assurance that the Uttar Pradesh Government would appoint a Backward Classes Commission'.[123] One of them, Cheddi Lal Sathi, was therefore appointed chairman of the Uttar Pradesh Most Backward Classes Commission in 1975.[124] The fact that the Congress government had specified that the Commission had to deal with the *Most* Backward Classes reflected its desire to restrict the scope of reservations to the less assertive of the low castes – those which could pose no threat to the upper castes. But it reflected also Sathi's concern that 'at least something should be given to the MBCs'.[125]

The members of the Commission took their job seriously since they toured to Tamil Nadu, Kerala, Karnataka and Andhra Pradesh where Backward Classes Commissions had already been appointed and where 'considerable progress had been made in the uplift of these classes'.[126] Once again, North India was trying to learn from South India and to emulate its achievements regarding the elevation of the low castes. More importantly, they collected data about the representation of 41 castes (Hindu and Muslim) classified among the Most Backward Classes in the four grades of the bureaucracy in 45 districts. This survey showed that the MBCs were poorly represented in the state administration (see Table 7.6). Not surprisingly, the MBCs were more numerous in the lower classes of the UP administration. Even there, however, they were certainly less represented than the Scheduled Castes which benefited from quotas.

The report of the Sathi Commission, submitted in June 1977, established three lists: the first, the Most Backward Classes, included 36 castes, whose common denominator was the insignificance of their landed property; the second, the Backward Classes, regrouped 18 castes whose members generally owned some land (Yadav, Kurmi,

[123] Hasan, *Quest for Power*, op. cit., p. 143.

[124] The two other members of the commission were Malkhan Singh Saini, a Saini (a caste of market gardeners) and Sitaram Nishad, a Nishad (a caste of boatmen and fishermen). (*Sarvadhik Pichhra Varg Ayog Report* [Report of the Most Backward Classes Commission], Hindi), Lucknow: Uttar Pradesh ki Sarkar, 1977, p. 12)

[125] Interview with Chetti Lal Sethi.

[126] *Sarvadhik Pichhra Varg Ayog Report*, op. cit., p. 14.

Table 7.6. REPRESENTATION OF 41 MBCs IN ADMINISTRATION OF 45 DISTRICTS OF UTTAR PRADESH, 1977 (%)

Classes of the administration	*No. of members of the MBCs*	*% of members of the MBCs*
Class 1	1	0.29
Class 2	11	1.54
Class 3	492	3.55
Class 4	1,308	10.96

Source: *Sarvadhik Pichhra Varg Ayog* (Report of the Most Backward Classes Commission), Hindi, Lucknow: Uttar Pradesh ki Sarkar, 1977, p. 74.

Gujar), the third list consisted of 23 Muslim castes. The MBCs accounted for 21.36% of the state population, the BCs, for 20.22% and the Muslim BCs, for 5.82%. Therefore, the OBCs represented 51.4% of the population of Uttar Pradesh but the Commission, knowing that the Scheduled Castes and Scheduled Tribes benefited from quotas of 20%, recommended 29.5% reservations for the OBCs 'in accordance with the Superme Court's opinion that reservation should not exceed 50%'.[127] In a disaggregated form, it meant that the MBCs, the BCs and the Muslim BCs were respectively granted 17%, 10% and 2.5% of the posts in the administration. The Commission submitted its report in 1977 soon after the Janata Party's success in the state elections. As in Bihar, the implementation of the backward classes report by the Janata government evoked strong protests from the upper castes and was the root-cause of its demise – as we shall see below.

The late appointment of the backward classes commissions in Bihar and Uttar Pradesh, and then the difficulties met by the state governments in implementing them, suggest that there is more a difference of degree than in kind between these states and those of Galanter's 'eastern-middle band' category. In Madhya Pradesh, for instance, the Congress government appointed the Mahajan Commission in 1980, only five years after Uttar Pradesh. The bulk of states displaying the strongest reluctance to reservation policy are in the Hindi belt.

[127] Ibid., p. 75.

The notion of the 'Other Backward Classes' and the reservation policies relying on it met with differing responses. In the South and in the West, this category eventually substituted itself into that of 'Non-Brahminism', a long established phenomenon. The implementation of caste-based policies of positive discrimination was hindered by the judiciary while there was a certain consensus in their favour among the political parties. In stark contrast, in the Hindi belt, an upper-caste dominated Congress resisted the institutionalisation of this notion and its correlative affirmative action programmes. However, the reports which were commissioned by the state in relation to these policies helped foster the mobilisation of the low castes. At an all-India level, the Kalelkar Commission initiated the crystallisation of the low castes by recommending caste-based positive discrimination. In the North it even helped the low castes to move towards a form of group consciousness. It was a new step in the process of reshaping caste identity.

The next step was to be accomplished by political actors. From the late 1960s onwards, the OBCs were to advance through the socialist movements and Charan Singh's political parties. The former – especially the parties of Ram Manohar Lohia – were quick to use reservations as a means of politicising the lower castes. While the southern pattern of low caste mobilisation linked ethnicisation and strategies of empowerment, what one can call 'quota politics', in the North the latter was the key factor.

Part III

QUOTA POLITICS AND KISAN POLITICS

COMPLEMENTARITY AND COMPETITION

8

THE SOCIALISTS AS DEFENDERS OF THE LOWER CASTES, JAT POLITICIANS AS ADVOCATES OF THE PEASANTS

The North Indian politicians who promoted the cause of the low castes were few in number till the late 1960s. The Congress party was dominated at the centre by progressive leaders who did not regard caste as a relevant category for state-sponsored social change and relied on conservative notables at the local level. The communists were in no position to give much hope to the low castes of the Hindi belt either; their influence remained confined to Kerala and West Bengal, where they certainly introduced substantial land reforms and education programmes.[1] In the North, their support peaked at 4.5% of the valid votes in UP in 1967 and 10.7% in Bihar in 1971. But the growing marginalisation of the two communist parties in North India was largely determined anyway by the scant attention they paid to the lower castes *qua* castes. True to their analysis of social struggle in terms of class conflict, they concentrated on organising the working class and economic change, namely the nationalisation of the means of production. Caste was ignored on the grounds that it was bound to be submerged by class. Dealing with 'this resistance to

[1] On West Bengal, see A. Kohli, *The State and Poverty in India: The politics of reform*, Cambridge University Press, 1987, chap. 3.

dealing with caste', Omvedt underlines that 'the communists universally adopted the Gandhian term "harijan" without much concern for whether it would appeal to the people concerned.'[2]

For Menon, Kerala Brahmins such as E.M.S Namboodiripad found in Marxism an ideology that allowed them to rehabilitate the Brahmins against the Dravidian anti-Brahmin ideology. Indeed, Namboodiripad referred to the caste system, monitored by the Brahmins, as a scientific division of labour and a necessary stage in the transition towards a modern mode of production.[3]

West Bengal, the other communist stronghold, where the Communist Party of India (Marxist) first came to power in 1967 and which they have been governed since 1977 was one of the few states which had neither established lists of Other Backward Classes nor introduced quotas for them in the administration till the 1990s. The West Bengal government appointed a committee to investigate the matter in 1980 but its report recommended that 'Poverty and low levels of living standards rather than caste should [. . .] be the most important criteria for identifying backwardness' and therefore that programmes should be designed 'for the economic development and educational advancement of the groups who are below the poverty line. . .'.[4] Jyoti Basu, the then West Bengal Chief Minister, while appearing before the Mandal Commission, pointed out that 'caste was a legacy of the feudal system and viewing the social scene from the casteist angle was no longer relevant for West Bengal'.[5]

The implementation of the Mandal Commission Report in 1990 was received sceptically by CPI(M) top leaders, Bhogendra Jha and Somnath Chatterjee. But these two Brahmins were criticised by the party's eleven OBC MPs.[6] As far as the CPI was concerned, it became

[2] Omvedt, *Dalit Visions*, op. cit., pp. 40–1. The CPI included its opposition to discrimination based on caste in its 'Programme of the Democratic Revolution' only in 1948.

[3] D.M. Menon, 'Being a Brahmin the Marxist Way: E.M.S. Namboodiripad and the Past of Kerala' in Daud Ali (ed.), *Invoking the Past: The Uses of History in South Asia*, Delhi: Oxford University Press, 1999, pp. 55–87.

[4] *Report of the [Second] Backward Classes Commission*, op. cit., p. 11.

[5] Ibid., p. 46.

[6] K.C. Yadav, *India's Unequal Citizens*, op. cit., p. 92. Yadav suggests that this stand was due to the over-representation of the upper castes among the communist office bearers. He substantiates his claim by showing that in Bihar a large number of the CPI and CPI(M) leaders were Bhumihars (ibid., pp. 120–1).

aware of the necessity to take caste seriously in to account in 1992, in the post-Mandal context partly under the impetus of Inderjit Gupta. This belated realisation may well have come too late to help the communists to recover in North India.[7] The Socialists, in fact, were the first to consider the lower castes as a pertinent social and political entity.

The Socialists and the Low Castes

The Socialists began to focus on the peasants' condition at a time when the Congress leadership was still rather urban-oriented. The programme that circulated before the founding conference of the Congress Socialist Party (CSP), held in Patna in May 1934, advocated the 'organisation of the peasants in Kisan Sanghs [peasant associations]'. It promised to work for 'the elimination of landlordism and the redistribution of land to the peasants'.[8] Socialists like Narendra Deva dared actively to depart from the Gandhian doctrine of 'trusteeship' by pitching tenant against landlord and thus preaching class struggle at the village level.[9] Narendra Deva, who was born in Sitapur (United Provinces) in a Khatri family, who had 'some Zamindari interests',[10] was probably the first Socialist ideologue of India. He presided over the inaugural Congress Socialist Conference in 1934 when he justified the creation of the CSP in sociological terms: the Congressmen's 'social basis being very narrow they really feel stronger by entertaining the belief that they are acting in interests of society as a whole'[11] but the Congress, according to Deva, badly needed to promote 'an alliance between the lower middle class and

[7] The appointment of Raja, a Dalit, as Secretary of the National Council of the CPI, however, suggests that the party has realised the need for promoting low caste people in the party apparatus (interview with D. Raja in Paris, 28 March 2000).

[8] 'Draft Proposals for the Formation of a Congress Socialist Party', in S. Mohan, H.D. Sharma, V.P. Singh and Sunilam (eds), *Evolution of Socialist Policy in India*, New Delhi: Janata Dal, 1997, p. 56 and p. 59.

[9] Acharya Narendra Dev, 'The Peasant in Indian Revolution', in ibid., pp. 96–112.

[10] H.D. Sharma (ed.), *Selected Works of Acharya Narendra Deva*, vol. 1, 1928–40, New Delhi: Radiant, 1998, p. xxxvi.

[11] A. Narendra Deva, 'Presidential Address at Patna Congress Socialist Conference', in ibid., p. 11.

the masses'.[12] This was the objective he assigned to the CSP.[13] For its leaders, the masses in question were primarily to be found in the village. They played an active part in the establishment of the All India Kisan Sabha, founded in 1936 in Lucknow. Narendra Deva was its president in 1939 and in his presidential address he justified its establishment as he had done with that of the CSP: as many Congress local committees 'are controlled by Zamindar elements [. . .], it is exactly in such places that the existence of the Kisan Sabhas will be mostly needed to carry on their day-to-day struggle':[14] 'The Kisan organisation is therefore necessary to exert revolutionary pressure on the Congress to adopt more and more the demands of the peasants'.[15]

The use of the word 'peasant' in Narendra Deva's speeches and writings is rather ambiguous for he was aware that the 'peasantry is not a homogenous class'.[16] In 1939 he said that 'the interests of the village poor can best be served in the present stage by mobilising the peasantry as a whole and not by splitting in into its various sections . . .'.[17] But this was a tactical device stemming from the weakness of the rural masses *vis-à-vis* urban society: to divide the peasants would have still made things worse. Narendra Deva did not want to indulge in what he called 'peasantism', a synonym for what I term 'kisan politics' (see below). This 'ism' looks at all questions 'from the narrow and sectional viewpoint of the peasant class [. . .]. It believes in rural democracy, which means a democracy of peasant proprietors [. . .]. It has the outlook of the middle peasant who has been influenced by modern ideas and is based on petty

[12] Ibid., p. 12.

[13] Narendra Deva was very lucid about the social profile of the Congress. In 1939, he wrote: 'In certain places the Congress organisation is controlled by professional men, merchants and moneylenders of the city and as their interest collide with those of the rural population, they cannot be expected to safeguard the interests of the peasantry. The result is that there are acute antagonisms between the town and the country and the Congress has very little hold on rural areas.' ('Presidential address at All India Kisan Conference', in ibid., pp. 168–9)

[14] Ibid., p. 162.

[15] Ibid.

[16] Ibid., p. 165.

[17] Ibid., p. 165.

bourgeois economy. In its crude form it would mean a kind of narrow agrarianism and an insatiable desire to boost the peasants in all possible places'.[18]

Narendra Deva's programme was very different since it drew on Marxist theories and the Soviet experiment: 'Our objective will be to re-educate the main mass of the peasantry in the spirit of socialism and to bring the bulk of the peasantry into line with socialist reconstruction through the medium of co-operative societies [. . .]. And this co-operative commonwealth must have a democratic base, in the shape of free peasants'.[19]

This programme – very similar to the measures Nehru would try to implement twenty years later through the Nagpur resolution – also implied land distribution and the abolition of all middlemen, such as the *zamindars*, between the tiller and the state. While Narendra Deva, true to his Marxist leanings, thought in terms of class interests,[20] he did not totally ignore caste. In his Presidential Address at the All India Kisan Conference of 1939 he emphasised that the 'agricultural labourer suffers from double bondage. The peculiar caste system of India has degraded him in the social scale. The social reform movement, which seeks to abolish untouchability, is therefore to be welcomed. It will raise his social status and will serve to make him conscious of human dignity. But unless the material and moral condition of his life is immediately improved social reform movement, however beneficent it may be, will not go a long way to make him a valuable self-respecting member of society'.[21]

This reference to caste – the only one, almost, in Deva's selected works covering the years till 1948 – suggests first, that untouchability is the only issue at stake – there's no mention of the need to abolish caste as such; secondly, it assumes that social reform should dispense of this curse; and thirdly, that the pre-condition for the annihilation of Untouchability is material and moral progress – the Marxist,

[18] Ibid., p. 169.

[19] Ibid., pp. 178–9.

[20] For Surendra Mohan, a veteran socialist who joined the CSP in 1946 in Uttar Pradesh, 'They were guided totally by the concept of class. They were marxist and even those who were not did not take caste questions into consideration' (interview with S. Mohan, New Delhi, 4 Nov. 1995).

[21] A. Narendra Deva, 'Presidential Address at All India Kisan Conference', op. cit., p. 167.

materialist analysis continues to prevail, at least to a certain extent.[22] The first official indictment of caste by the CSP came in 1947 in its policy statement at the annual party conference:

In India, apart from economic inequalities, there are social inequalities, particularly among one of the communities, namely the Hindus. The system of castes is anti-social, undemocratic and tyrannous, inasmuch as it divides men into high and low, touchable and untouchable, curtails human liberties and interfere with economic activities.[23]

After Independence the Socialists gradually highlighted the importance of caste when it appeared that land reform might not solve all the problems of rural India and that 'in the framework of a democratic system certain sections of the society had to be mobilised'.[24] The CSP, which became a party on its own, the Socialist Party, after severing its links with Congress in 1948, made an election pact with Ambedkar's Scheduled Castes Federation in 1952. It was even prepared to enter into a political federation with this party. The proposal

[22] It does not mean that Narendra Deva was not a strong proponent of equality. In fact, he was a militant egalitarian and this inclination probably accounts for his interest in Buddhism – he was an avid reader of studies on the Buddha and planned to write a book 'on Buddhist philosophy' in 1943 while in jail (H.D. Sharma (ed.), *Selected Works of Acharya Narendra Deva*, vol. 2, 1941–8, New Delhi: Radiant, 1998, p. 35). But this sense of equality tended to bypass caste. The need to abolish caste is mentioned for the first time in Narendra Deva's *Selected Works* in 1945, in an address to students (ibid., p. 80). In the Presidential address he delivered at the seventh Annual Conference of the Socialist Party that was held in Patna in 1949, he did not mention the word caste even though the address was entitled 'The Caste System and Democracy'. He emphasised that India 'should make every effort towards the social, economic and cultural advancement of the backward classes'. (Narendra Deva, *Towards Socialist Society. Collection of Writings and Speeches*, Delhi: Apala Publishing Cooperative Society, 1990 (1997), p. 117)

However, he stuck to an economicist perspective ('it is necessary to lay special stress on the equality of opportunities with a view to achieving economic progress') (ibid., p. 116). In fact, Narendra Deva remained imbued with a Marxist-like class analysis and was fascinated by 'the example of Soviet Russia'. He said, for instance: '. . . if we want to unite the people and invoke their cooperation in preparing the foundations of a new life, we shall have to follow the Russian example' (ibid., p. 116).

[23] 'Policy Statement of Socialist Party' in Sharma (ed.), *Selected Works of Acharya Narendra Deva*, vol. 2, op. cit., p. 287.

[24] Interview with Surender Mohan, New Delhi, 4 Nov. 1995.

came to nought because Ambedkar regarded the Kisan Mazdoor Praja Party (KMPP) of Kripalani, with which the SP was simultaneously preparing a merger, as reactionary.[25]

The 'rising star'[26] of the Indian socialist movement, Rammanohar Lohia, a Banya by caste was probably the first, to really incorporate caste in the movement's ideology.[27] He had been one of the founders of the CSP and in 1954 became general secretary of the Praja Socialist Party, which resulted from the merger of the SP and the KMPP of Acharya Kripalani. Disagreeing with most PSP leaders, who were inclined to collaborate with Congress, Lohia launched his own Socialist Party in 1956. A laborious reunification process led to the foundation of the Samyukta Socialist Party in 1964, before a new split took place in 1965, giving birth to a new PSP. Lohia remained at the helm of the SSP till his death in 1967, by which time it had become the largest socialist force in India.[28]

The PSP – old or new – displayed little interest compared to the Lohiaites in uplifting the lower castes. A survey conducted in 1967–8 showed that its leaders and MPs belonged to the upper caste urban intelligentsia: 75% of its forty top leaders were from the upper castes (including 50% of Brahmins) whereas the low castes accounted for only 12.5%. Half of them were professionals – as against 12.5% who were engaged in agriculture,[29] a fact reflected in the party's opposi-

[25] Ibid.

[26] The expression is from Nehru, whose relations with Lohia soured quickly after independence (G. Mishra and B.K. Pandey, *Rammanohar Lohia – The Man and His Ism*, New Delhi: Eastern Books, 1992, p. 12).

[27] K.R. Jadhav, 'Dr. Lohia on reservation policy' in B.A.V. Sharma and K.M. Reddy (eds), *Reservation policy in India*, New Delhi: Life and Life Publishers, 1982, pp. 38–9. He was not the only socialist leader to pay great attention to caste issues, of course. S.M. Joshi, for instance, considered that 'In this country, social inequality born out of the Varnashram and the caste system with its ghastly appendage of untouchability was a greater challenge than economic inequality and exploitations.' (S.M. Joshi, 'The Way to Socialist Alternative' in Mohan, Sharma, Singh and Sunilam (eds), *Evolution of Socialist Policy in India*, op. cit., p. 265)

[28] P.R. Brass, 'Leadership Conflict and the Disintegration of the Indian Socialist Movement: Personal Ambition, Power and Policy' in P.R. Brass, *Caste, Faction and Party in Indian Politics*, vol. 1, New Delhi: Chanakya, 1984, pp. 155–88.

[29] L.P. Fickett, 'The Praja Socialist Party of India – 1952–1972 : A final assessment', *Asian Survey*, Sept. 1973, 13(9), p. 831.

tion to Lohia's proposal of reserving 60% of administrative jobs for the low castes.[30]

In contrast, Lohia, who first championed the peasant's cause, gradually emphasised the abolition of caste. In his early career, he focussed, like Narendra Deva, on the economic issues of rural India. He was elected President of the Hind Kisan Panchayat in 1950 and prepared a 13-point programme which included 'parity between agricultural and industrial prices, a ceiling on personal income to be fixed at Rs 1,000 and no agriculturist household to have less than 12.5 acres and more than 30 acres of cultivable land'.[31] He took part in several demonstrations against the shortcomings of the land reform – including the high compensation given to former *zamindars* – and the eviction of tenants. Yet he began taking an interest in caste issues in 1952 in a series of lectures to a socialist study circle.[32]

For Lohia the caste system was responsible for the recurrent invasions India endured in its long history because it 'renders nine-tenths of the population into onlookers, in fact listless and nearly completely disinterested spectators of grim national tragedies'.[33] Fighting caste was therefore not only necessary for the emancipation of the subaltern groups but also and foremost because it weakened India in such a way as the 'dvija [twice born] have also suffered grievously from this atrophy of the people'.[34] However, social justice was his primary motivations: to those who favoured an analysis in terms of class he objected that 'caste is the most overwhelming factor in Indian life'.[35]

> Many socialists honestly but wrongly think that it is sufficient to strive for economic equality and caste inequality will vanish of itself as a consequence. They fail to comprehend economic inequality and caste inequality as twin demons, which have both to be killed.[36]

Lohia considered that political action needed to be supplemented

[30] Ibid., pp. 828–9.

[31] Mishra and Pandey, *Rammanohar Lohia*, op. cit., p. 41.

[32] Ibid., p. 151.

[33] R. Lohia, 'Towards the destruction of castes and classes' (1958), in R. Lohia, *The Caste System*, Hyderabad: Rammanohar Lohia Samata Vidyalaya, 1979 (1964), p. 81.

[34] Ibid., p. 102.

[35] Ibid., p. 79.

[36] R. Lohia, 'Class organisations: instruments to abolish caste' (1953), in ibid., p. 20.

by the reform of caste, and he fought one of its cornerstones, endogamy, advocating not only marriage between *jatis* but also between *varnas*, between the 'twice borns' and the Shudras.[37] He even went so far to advocate marriage to someone from another caste as a precondition for entry into the administration. Such measures were suggested by one of the resolutions of the All India End Caste Conference organised under his auspices at Patna in 1961[38] and became an article of faith of the Samyukta Socialist Party.[39]

Lohia partly drew his inspiration from Ambedkar. While Jagjivan Ram's duplicity left him cold – 'although he is known to flatter and kow-tow to the caste Hindus when he deals with them, he is reported to sing to the bitter tunes of hatred in exclusively Harijan meetings'[40] –, he was fascinated by Ambedkar. After the latter's death, in 1956, he wrote to Madhu Limaye, one of his lieutenants, as follows:

> It had always been my ambition to draw him [Ambedkar] into our fold, not only organisationally but also in full ideological sense, and that moment seemed to be approaching [. . .] Dr. Ambekar was to me, a great man in Indian politics, and apart from Gandhiji, as great as the greatest of caste Hindus. This fact had always given me solace and confidence that the caste system of Hinduism could one day be destroyed.[41]

But Lohia was no 'Ambedkarite'. What militated against him lending the former his support were his Marxist leanings, his admiration for Gandhi and the fact that he was less interested in the conditions of the Untouchables than in the backward classes – which he often called 'the shudras' –, perhaps because the former already had their political party, unlike the latter. In 1957, after the division of the All India Backward Classes Federation, one of the fractions trans-

[37] R. Lohia, 'The two segregations of caste and sex' (1953) in ibid., p. 4.

[38] R. Lohia, 'End caste conference resolutions' in ibid., p. 139. This conference also pleaded for the Indian people to abandon caste taboos regarding eating practices and other communal activities.

[39] One of the items of the programme adopted at the first conference of the SSP in 1966 read: 'Inter-Varna marriage should be deemed a qualification for Government employment. Inter-dining among Government servants twice a year should be made compulsory.' ('The Socialist Programme' in Mohan, Sharma, Singh and Sunilam (eds), *Evolution of Socialist Policy in India*, op. cit., pp. 260–1)

[40] Letter to Madhu Limaye, 1 July 1957, in ibid., p. 37.

[41] Ibid., p. 36.

formed itself into a political party but later merged with the Socialist Party, as mentioned in chapter 7. This fusion was based on ideological affinities as evident from the letters between R.L. Chandapuri, the leader of the secessionists, and Lohia. In one of these Lohia explained his support for the system of grants for low caste students and that a quota should be set aside for them in the administration – from where the higher castes had to be dislodged.[42] Lohia had, by then, become one of the staunchest supporters of positive discrimination – what he called 'unequal opportunities' –, not only in favour of the Scheduled Castes but also of the backward castes:

> When everybody has an equal opportunity, castes with the five thousand years old traditions of liberal education would be on top. Only the exceptionally gifted from the lower castes would be able to break through this tradition.[. . .] To make this battle a somewhat equal encounter, unequal opportunities would have to be extended, to those who have so far been suppressed.[43]

For Lohia such policies touched upon the core issue of India, whereas the Marxists' views about revolution or Nehru's policy of nationalisation amounted to 'vested interest socialism' because none of these things would change India:

> Workers with the brain are a fixed caste in Indian society; together with the soldier caste, they are the high-caste. Even after the completed economic and political revolution, they would continue to supply the managers of the state and industry. The mass of the people would be kept in a state of perpetual physical and mental lowliness, at least comparatively. But the position of the high-caste would then be justified on grounds of ability and in economic terms as it is now on grounds of birth or talent. That is why the intelligentsia of India which is overwhelmingly the high-caste, abhors all talk of a mental and social revolution of a radical change in respect of language or caste or the bases of thought. It talks generally and in principle against caste. In fact, it can be most vociferous in its theoretical condemnation of caste, so long as it can be allowed to be equally vociferous in raising the banner of merit and equal opportunity. What it loses in respect of caste by birth, it gains in respect of caste by merit. Its merit concerning speech, grammar, manners, capacity

[42] 'I think that the *dvijas*, in special conditions, should not get government services.' (Letter from Lohia to R.L. Chandapuri, dated 4 Sept. 1957, in ibid., p. 43)

[43] R. Lohia, 'Towards the Destruction of Castes and Classes' (1958) in ibid., p. 96.

to adjust, routine efficiency is undisputed. Five thousands years have gone into the building of this undisputed merit.[44]

Lohia did not entertain any romantic idea of the Indian lower orders – 'the Shudra too has his shortcomings. He has an even narrower sectarian outlook'[45] – but he thought they definitely deserved special treatment and should be 'pushed to positions of power and leadership'.[46] He was against affirmative action in the education system[47] but emphasised the need for administrative and electoral quotas. Once again he was following Ambedkar's strategy of empowerment that the non-Brahmin movement had already implemented in the South. In 1959, the third national conference of the Socialist Party expressed the wish that at least 60% of administrative posts be reserved for Other Backward Classes.[48] This recommendation was reiterated at the fifth annual session of the party, in April 1961, a few months before the third general elections.[49] Subsequently, the programmes or election manifestos of Lohia's successive parties promoted the notion of 'preferential opportunities', as in the programme adopted by the first Conference of the SSP held in April 1966:

> It should be remembered that equality and equal opportunity are not synonymous. In a society characterised by a hierarchical structure based on birth, the principle of equal opportunity cannot produce an equal society. The established, conventional notions about merit and ability must result in denial of opportunities in actual practice for backward castes, harijans, adibasis [tribals] etc. The principle of preferential opportunities alone will ensure that the backward sections will catch up with the advanced ones in a reasonable period of time.[50]

[44] Ibid., pp. 96–7.

[45] R. Lohia, 'Class organisations: Instruments to abolish caste' (1953), in ibid., p. 13.

[46] Ibid., p. 13.

[47] He tried to justify this stand in 1958 by saying: 'Let the backward castes ask for two or three shifts in schools and colleges, if necessary, but let them never ask for the exclusion of any child of India from the portals of an educational institution.' ('Towards the Destruction of Castes and Classes', 1958, p. 104)

[48] Ibid., p. 135.

[49] Ibid., p. 142.

[50] 'The Socialist Programme', in Mohan, Sharma, Singh and Sunilam (eds), *Evolution of Socialist Policy in India*, op. cit., pp. 258–9.

This document again recommended a quota of 60% for the backward sections of society – comprising then the Scheduled Castes, Scheduled Tribes, the OBCs and women – but extended it to 'all spheres', not only the administration, but also, apparently, the education system and the elected assemblies. These reservations were intended to give a share of power to the low castes; it was an empowerment scheme. Indeed, the SSP programme diagnosed that the weakness of the 'people's movement' resulted from its divisions but also from 'the preponderance of upper caste leadership in [the] major political parties'.[51] To show the way, the SSP nominated a large number of candidates from non-elite groups and the socialists had more OBC MLAs elected than any other political party in the states where they achieved their best results, namely Uttar Pradesh and Bihar.

Bihar as a Socialist Laboratory for 'Quota Politics'. Bihar had been the cradle and the birthplace of socialism in India since the foundation of the CSP in Patna, the state capital. In the 1950s and 1960s the socialist parties together polled between 20 and 25% of the valid votes, except in 1962 (see Table 8.1).

The 1967 election was a milestone not only because Congress lost power for the first time but also because this event was largely due to the growing assertiveness of low caste leaders, a process to which the ruling party had inadvertently contributed. Before the elections, the outgoing Chief Minister, K.B. Sahay, a Kayasth, depended on Bhumihar and Rajput factions who demanded much in return. To free him from their tutelage, Sahay had to rely more and more on OBC leaders. He organised a cabinet reshuffle which reduced the share of upper caste ministers from 50 to 40% and increased that of the backwards from 10 to 20%.[52] The latter were mainly upper backward. For instance, Sahay appointed a Yadav, Ram Lakhan Singh Yadav, and a Kurmi, Deo Saran Singh, as ministers. However, before the 1967 elections, Ram Lakhan Singh Yadav asked Sahay that 60% of Congress nominations be given to the OBCs, the figure recommended by Lohia. The higher caste leadership of the party rejected his demand but the episode tended to crystallise a lower caste front against the higher castes.

[51] Ibid., p. 260.

[52] S.N. Chaudhary, *Power-Dependence Relations: Struggle for Hegemony in Rural Bihar*, Delhi: Har-Anand, 1999, p. 218

Table 8.1. ELECTION RESULTS OF SOCIALIST PARTIES DURING THE FIRST FOUR GENERAL ELECTIONS
(*% of valid votes*)

	1952 SP	*1952 KMPP*	*1957 PSP*	*1962 PSP*	*1962 SP*	*1967 PSP*	*1967 SSP*
All India	10.6	5.8	10.4	6.8	2.7	3.1	4.9
Bihar	21.3	3.4	21.6	12.7	6.1	7.4	17.8
Uttar Pradesh	12.9	4.9	15.3	10.4	8.6	3.7	10.3

Source: D. Butler, A. Lahiri and P. Roy, *India decides*, New Delhi: Living Media, 1989, pp. 84-85.

Table 8.2. CASTES AND COMMUNITIES OF THE MLAs OF THE THREE MAIN PARTIES OF BIHAR, 1967
(*absolute values and %*)

	Congress	*SSP*	*Jana Sangh*
Upper castes	55 (42.97)	31 (46.26)	6 (25)
Intermediate and lower caste	28 (21.87)	27 (40.29)	8 (33.3)
Scheduled Castes	23 (17.97)	7 (10.44)	5 (20.8)
Scheduled Tribes	14 (10.93)	1 (1.49)	5 (20.8)
Muslims	8 (6.25)	1 (1.49)	
Total	*128 (100)*	*67 (100)*	*24 (100)*

Source: R. Mitra, *Caste Polarisation and Politics*, Patna: Syndicate Publications, 1992, p. 120.

On the socialist side, Karpoori Thakur played a leading part in the assertion of the OBCs and his activities explained the rise of the SSP at the expense of the Congress. A long-time socialist who had taken part in the Quit India Movement as a CSP member, Thakur belonged to a low caste classified among the 'Most Backward Classes' of Bihar, the Nais (barbers). He had been joint secretary of the Bihar Kisan Committee in 1948–52 and of the Bihar Socialist Party. He had been returned without any interruption as an MLA since 1952 and was one of Lohia's lieutenant in the SSP. In 1967 he popularised the following slogan: 'Socialists ne bandhi gangh/ Pichara pave saumee sath' (now Socialists are determined to get 60% reservations for the backwards).[53]

The decline of Congress during the 1967 assembly elections, from

[53] Ibid., p. 221.

41.35% to 33% of the valid votes, partly due to the fact that it could no longer retain the OBC support, prevented it from winning a majority of seats in Bihar,[54] whereas the SSP jumped from 6% to 18% of the valid votes and from 7 to 68 seats. The opposition parties, the communists, the Jana Sangh and the socialists formed a coalition called Samyukta Vidhayak Dal (SVD – the united parliamentary group), of which the SSP was the largest component. A former high caste (Kayasth) congressman, Mahamaya Prasad Sinha,[55] became Chief Minister, but the deputy Chief Minister was no other than Karpoori Thakur. In five months the SVD government, took some significant measures such as abolishing land revenue and prohibiting the use of Hindi in public.[56] The Socialist strategy of promoting and mobilising of the low castes largely explains the success of the SSP and the election of a large number of low castes MLAs in the late 1960s (see Table 8.3).

While the rise of the OBCs at the expense of the upper castes is not that dramatic, it is not insignificant either, especially if one looks at the declining share of Brahmins (from 17% to 12% of the MLAs returned in non-reserved constituencies) and the growing proportion of Yadavs, whose rise put them just behind the Rajputs (18.05% as against 23.15% in 1969).[57] Backward caste leaders could now exert much more leverage in obtaining new concessions, as evident from the growing share of ministerial portfolios they obtained in the late 1960s and early 1970s (see table 4.7).

Chandapuri, the President of the All India Backward Classes Federation, was approached by the Congress and agreed to back the party provided one of the backward castes was named at the head of the government,[58] and it was B.P. Mandal who agreed to take up the post.

[54] The mid-term elections of 1969 produced very similar results to those of 1967, including in terms of the MLAs' caste-wise distribution (among the SSP MLAs, the share of the intermediary and low castes members remained unchanged but that of the higher castes rose to 33.9%).

[55] Sinha had defected from the Congress in December 1966 to form the Jan Kranti Dal because he was sure that the Congress would be defeated.

[56] Among the Socialists, Lohia had been especially hostile to the use of English because it gave the élite groups a monopoly of the language of politics and administration and added one more hurdle for low caste upward mobility.

[57] Blair, 'Rising kulaks and backward classes in Bihar', op. cit., p. 68.

[58] Frankel, 'Caste, land and dominance in Bihar', op. cit., p. 90.

Table 8.3. CASTE AND COMMUNITY OF THE MLAs RETURNED IN NON-RESERVED CONSTITUENCIES IN BIHAR ASSEMBLY, 1962–9 (%)

	1962	*1967*	*1969*
Upper castes	*59*	*55.1*	*53.9*
Brahmin	17.2	13.2	12.3
Rajput	23.8	22.2	23.5
Bhumihar	12.6	14.8	14.8
Kayasth	5.4	4.9	3.3
OBC	*28.8*	*31.6*	*32.1*
Banya	3.3	5.3	6.2
Yadav	11.7	15.2	18.5
Kurmi	7.1	5.3	3.3
Koeri	6.7	5.8	4.1
MBC	*1.7*	*2.9*	*2.5*
Muslim	*8.8*	*7.4*	*7.8*
Bengali	*1.7*	*2.9*	*3.7*
Total	100	100	100
	N=242	N=243	N=242

Source: Blair, 'Rising Kulaks and Backward Classes in Bihar', op. cit., p. 67.

Bindeshwari Prasad Mandal, a Yadav who presided over the second Backward Classes Commission in 1978, had been elected an MLA on a Congress ticket in 1952 and 1962. He defected from the Congress in 1965 because the SSP offered him better opportunities; indeed, he obtained the ministerial portfolio of health in the SVD government in 1967 in spite of the fact that he had been elected in the Lok Sabha and not to the state assembly.[59] Lohia asked Madhu Limaye to persuade him to relinquish the post of minister but he refused and left the SSP to form the Shoshit Dal, or 'party of the oppressed', with 40 low caste dissident MLAs, including a number from the SSP. Madhu Limaye lamented that 'as soon as power came, SSP men broke up into caste groups. They equated the [Lohia's] policy with casteism! [. . .] Castemen belonging to other parties were felt to be closer than one's own Party comrades belonging to other castes'.[60] While one may indeed regret that once again Congress had managed

[59] Parliament of India, *Sixth Lok Sabha Who's Who*, op. cit., p. 341.

[60] M. Limaye, *Birth of Non-Congressism*, Delhi: B.R. Publishing Corporation, 1988, p. 155.

to divide in order to rule by co-opting opponents from the lower castes, such developments, which were the logical outcome of the Socialist policy, had some positive aspects: castes were transforming themselves into interest groups and forming socio-political coalitions like the non-Brahmins of South India. It meant that the low castes could not be integrated in vertical linkages as easily as during the heyday of the Congress system. Thus transformed, the low castes certainly lent themselves to manipulation by political entrepreneurs like B.P. Mandal, but the Mandal government episode brought out a positive development: the politicisation of caste and the growing solidarity between lower caste MLAs from different parties had become so pronounced that to topple the SVD government the Congress had no choice but to support one of the Shoshit Dal leaders – this is how B.P. Mandal became the first OBC Chief Minister of Bihar, in February 1968. He remained in office only a few months because the ruling coalition was very heterogeneous but he was to be followed by other non-elite leaders: of the nine Chief Ministers who governed the state from March 1967 to December 1971, only two were from the high castes.

However, Scheduled Castes leaders soon became interested in playing the game of the upper castes. When the Bihar Congress decided to support Mandal, sixteen upper caste congressmen led by the ex-Chief Minister Binodanand Jha (a Brahmin), left the party to form the Loktantrik Congress Dal. He toppled the Mandal ministry by allying with Scheduled Castes MLAs such as Bhola Paswan Shastri whom he promoted as the future Chief Minister. A counter-strategy to the rise of the low castes was taking shape through the activation of the traditional clientelistic links that the Congress upper-caste politicians maintained with their Scheduled Caste allies. The Scheduled Castes bore grievances towards the SVD regime since not one of them had been appointed to M.P. Sinha's cabinet. Shastri was Chief Minister for less than 100 days and then President's rule was imposed. The February 1969 elections left no party with a clear-cut majority and President's rule was imposed again in July.

After the February 1970 election, when the Congress(R) was still in a minority but in a better position to regain power, it appointed, as mentioned above, a Yadav, Daroga Prasad Rai, as Chief Minister. Rai reduced the share of the upper castes in his cabinet to an all-time low 33%, as much as that of the Scheduled Castes and Scheduled

Tribes, whereas the OBCs remained at 20%. Rai took the socialist discourse of Indira Gandhi literally. Denouncing the domination of the higher castes, he appointed an OBC as Chief Secretary and set up a Backward Classes Commission, the Mungeri Lal commission which was entrusted with reporting on the lag which the OBCs had incurred in socio-economic terms and education. The Brahmins within the ruling party, under L.N. Mishra's leadership, immediately expressed their objections. Mrs Gandhi shared their concern and Rai was obliged to resign. He had governed for barely ten months but his successor was Karpoori Thakur, who was supported by a large coalition of parties opposed to Congress. Thakur however could not hold on to power for more than six months.

The rise of the low castes came to a halt after the 1972 elections with the Congress(R)'s return to power, as noted above. Congress once again resorted to its strategy of co-opting the leaders of weaker groups that the higher castes had no reason to fear. This unequal coalition brought to the fore the vertical, clientelistic arrangement of the 'Congress system'. But it was not a restoration, and the socialist strategy of low caste mobilisation had now crystallised in such a way that it was bound to be reactivated more effectively one day.

The growing assertiveness of the lower castes in Bihar in the 1960s was largely a by-product of the socialist strategy. I have analysed it in terms of quota politics because a major feature of the programme of Lohia and his followers was spelled out in terms of reservations: the SSP not only reserved a large share of its electoral tickets to the lower castes, but the party also demanded quotas for these castes in the administration. Both developments fostered the low castes' mobilisation and sense of solidarity. This strategy thus contributed directly and indirectly to the democratisation of the social background of Bihar's politicians.

Quota politics was thus over-determined by the state's positive discrimination policies. The socialists had not invented anything: the procedure of what Lohia called 'unequal opportunities' was already there. The socialists simply mobilised the lower castes in order to have these policies implemented and extended. The Socialist quota politics benefited from the groundwork of the AIBCF, especially after Chandapuri's faction joined hands with Lohia. As in the South at the time of the Justice party, quota politics and the state's reservation policy had become two sides of the same coin, which contributed to the empowerment of the lower castes through the administrative and educational reservation policies and through the introduction of quota politics into party politics. However, another path to empowerment, parallel to quota politics, developped in the 1960s, namely *kisan* politics, an ideology of social transformation which mobilised the rural poor by emphasising their common interests and separate identity as peasants.

Kisan politics and the mobilisation of the Jat farmers

Kisan politics made its impact in Uttar Pradesh under the aegis of a Jat leader, Charan Singh, at the same time as the Socialists were – albeit briefly – rising to power in Bihar in the late 1960s. Jat farmers had long been the crucible of *kisan* politics because they embodied the independent-minded peasant proprietor, not only in UP but also in neighbouring Punjab, its real birthplace.

Changes in Jat identity in the nineteenth century. The Jats are especially numerous in the Punjab plain where they 'commonly are several times as numerous as the second most popular castes'.[61] But they are also the dominant caste in West Uttar Pradesh and in some parts of Rajasthan. This is probably one of the reasons why they have always found the Brahmins' superiority difficult to accept, which partly explains why many of them followed the reformist movement of the Sadhs.[62] This creed, which showed no respect for the Brahmins (and even did without them for all ritual matters), was the sectarian remedy for caste oppression open to the Jats.[63]

In the late nineteenth century, the Arya Samaj's success among the Jats was probably accounted for by its affinities with the Sadh's credo. They especially appreciated Dayananda's hostility to Brahmins. The first Jats to join the Arya Samaj were those of Hissar district where Lala Lajpat Rai practised law and also those of Rohtak in the 1880s and 1890s. One of the first-Jat 'converts' to the Arya Samaj was a medical practitioner, Ramji Lal Hooda who was attracted to the movement in 1883 by Lajpat Rai's father, Radha Krishan, who was

[61] J. Schwartzberg, 'The Distribution of selected castes', *Geographical Review*, 15 (1965), p. 488.

[62] N. Datta, *Forming an Identity: A Social History of the Jats*, Delhi: Oxford University Press, 1999, p. 7.

[63] Ibid., pp. 38–9.

his Persian teacher.[64] Lajpat Rai describes him as the first spokesman of the Arya Samaj among the Jats: 'Ramji Lal's house was a centre for the Jats of the entire division [. . .] By his ability and his skill as a physician and surgeon and his hospitality, Dr. Ramji Lal spread his religion amongst thousands of Jats. . .'[65] Indeed, Hooda played a major role in organising Jat Sabhas (and the Jat Mahasabha) and in spreading, via this channel, the Arya Samajist ideology among his caste fellows. In 1921 he became President of the Arya Samaj in Hissar and then contributed to the development of Shuddhi Sabhas. These associations were intended – to use his own terms – to 'bring back those persons who were converted long ago, to the Vedic fold'.[66] In 1923 he became President of the Shuddhi Sabha covering the districts of Hissar and Rohtak which reconverted a Jat who had embraced Islam. But, in fact, these Shuddhi Sabhas 'purified' many Jats – and lower castes – even when they were Hindus in order to transform them into 'twice borns'.[67]

Even though the Arya Samaj claimed that Shuddhi promoted equality, this ritual drew its inspiration and its procedure from the Brahminical tradition and adhered to the logic of Sanskritisation.[68] The 'Jats were told not to consume alcohol or meat, minimise their

[64] In his diary he says 'I owe every good things in my life since 1881 to him' (M.M. Juneja and K. Singh Mor (eds), *The Diaries of Dr Ramji Lal Hooda*, Hissar: Modern Book Co., 1989, p. 47).

[65] Cited in M.M. Juneja and K. Singh Mor, 'Introduction', in ibid., p. 14.

[66] Ibid., p. 244.

[67] These activities had developed by the turn of the century under the aegis of Ram Bhaj Datt, the president of the Shuddhi Sabha who described the ritual of shuddhi in the following terms: 'The ceremony is everywhere the same. In all cases the person to be reclaimed has to keep Brat (fast) before the ceremony [which culminates with the passing of the sacred thread in the case of low caste converts] [. . .] The very act of their being raised in social status makes them feel a curious sense of responsibility. They feel that they should live and behave better and that they should act as Dvijas [twice borns]. It has thus, in the majority of cases, a very wholesome effect on their moral, social, religious and spiritual being. As to treatment, the Arya Samaj treat the elevated on terms of equality.' (Cited in *Punjab Census Report, 1911*, p. 150)

[68] For more details, see C. Jaffrelot, 'Militant Hinduism and the Conversion Issue (1885–1990): From Shuddhi to Dharm Parivartan. The Politicization of an "Invention of Tradition" ' in J. Assayag (ed.), *The Resources of History. Tradition and Narration in South Asia*, Paris: Ecole Française d'Extrême Orient, 1999, pp. 127–52.

expenditure on wedding and ceremonial displays, and refrain from singing cheap songs and watching lewd pictures during the fairs'.[69] The Arya Samaj exerted over the Jats such a strong Sanskritisation effect that men like Hooja opted for a vegetarian diet.[70] Its preachers argued during long ritual debates that they were twice born Kshatriyas opposing them to orthodox Hindus (*shastarth*).[72] The All India Jat Mahasabha, 'an offshoot of the Arya Samaj, formed in Muzaffarnagar in 1905',[73] developed the same discourse under the auspices of Jat princes. Like the ruling family of Rewari, the Maharajahs of Bharatpur and Dholpur – both of them Jats – stressed the Kshatriya identity of their caste.[74] The Maharajah of Dholpur, while he was president of the Jat Mahasabha in 1917–18, supported the development of the Arya Samaj in his state.[75] The brother of the Maharajah of Bharatpur, Ragunath Singh, who relaunched the Jat Mahasabha in 1925, was known as a 'protestant reformer' because of his strong arya samajist leanings.[76]

Besides its opposition to the Brahmins and its sense of Sanskritisation, the Arya Samaj had affinities with the most specific characteristic of the Jats, their sense of industry. From its early days the Arya Samaj, with its strong emphasis on the notion of self help, displayed a spirit of enterprise – partly because many Arya Samajists came from the merchant castes, partly because of their nationalist concern for self sufficiency. They were the first, in the 1880s, to set up indigenous enterprises, the precursors of the Swadeshi movement. Exasperated by the imposition in 1893 of an 'excise tax' on Indian cotton, Mul Raj, the founder-president of the Lahore Arya Samaj, set up associations selling only *deshi* (made in India) clothes.[77] The following year

[69] Datta, *Forming an Identity*, op. cit., p. 71.

[70] Juneja and Singh Mor (eds), *The Diaries of Dr Ramji Lal Hooda*, op. cit., p. 159.

[71] Datta, *Forming an identity*, op. cit., p. 74.

[72] Ibid., p. 79.

[73] Ibid., p. 76. See also N. Datta, 'Arya Samaj and the Making of Jat Identity', *Studies in History*, 13(1), 1997, p. 107.

[74] Datta, *Forming an Identity*, op. cit., p. 161 and p. 165.

[75] Juneja and Singh Mor (eds), *The Diaries of Dr Ramji Lal Hooda*, op. cit., p. 198.

[76] Interview with his grandson, Raghuraj Singh, Bharatpur, 16 August 2000.

[77] Lajpat Rai, *Autobiographical Writings*, Joshi (ed.), Delhi: Jullundur University, 1965, p. 96.

he initiated the first bank with purely Indian capital, the Punjab National Bank[78] and then the Bharat Insurance Company.

This sense of enterprise was well in tune with the industrious ethos of the Jats. In his *Tribes and Castes of the North West Provinces and Oudh*, Crooke writes:

> The Jat takes a high rank amongst the cultivating races of the provinces. He is simply a slave to his farm [. . .]. He never dreams of taking any service except in the army, he is thrifty to the verge of meanness and industrious beyond comparison.[79]

Such orientalist stereotypes were in accordance with local proverbs. Blunt cites one in Hindi: '*Jat mara tab janiye jab terahwin guzar jae*' (Never be sure that a Jat is dead till the days of mourning for him are over);[80] whereas Schwartzberg mentions another in English: 'The Jat's baby has a plough-handle to play with'.[81] As Byres emphasises, 'the Jats are the archetypal working peasantry of northern India',[82] women even work in the fields, which is the exception in this type of intermediate caste. The ideal Jat owns his land and cultivates it with the nuclear family.[83]

The agrarian system of the Jats predisposed them to such a production-oriented lifestyle. This system was known as '*bhaichara*' because, customs (*chara*) were observed by a community (*bhaia*) for the management and distribution of land'.[84] But far from implying

[78] P. Tandon, *Banking Century: A Short History of Banking in India and the pioneer: Punjab National Bank*, New Delhi: Penguin, 1989, p. 152.

[79] Cited in Blunt, *The Caste System in Northern India*, op. cit., pp. 265–6.

[80] Ibid., p. 266.

[81] Cited in J. Schwartzberg, 'The Distribution of selected castes', *Geographical Review*, 15 (1965), p. 488.

[82] Byres, 'Charan Singh (1902–87): An Assessment', *JPS*, 15 (2), Jan. 1988, p. 142.

[83] A British handbook of the 1940s presenting the peasant castes described the Jats as follows: 'With traditions deeply rooted in agriculture they are a sturdy and independent race, loyal alike to their land and to its service in arms. Wherever a Jat community is found, there one can look with certainty for a high standard of cultivation, a long-standing tradition of hospitality, an independent outlook, directness of speech and loyalty to one's salt'. (Khan Sahabzada, 'The Jat Cultivator' in W. Burns (ed.), *Sons of the Soil*, Delhi: Government of India, 1944 [1941], p. 43)

[84] Jagpal Singh, *Capitalism and Dependence. Agrarian Politics in Western Uttar Pradesh, 1951–1991*, Delhi: Manohar, 1992, p. 10.

any collectivist *modus operandi*, or any hierarchical arrangement, this system had truly individualist connotations. As M.C. Pradhan points out:

> In the *bhaichara* system, land was equally divided among the lineages (*thoks*) of the founding ancestors or original conquerors. This system of land tenure was a Jat idea because Jats did not acknowledge the rights of their chiefs to the sole proprietorship of land conquered and colonised by them.[85]

In fact, *bhaichara* communities, after occupying a certain area, divided it between villages (from a minimum of 8 to 84) and all village affairs were managed by *khaps* (clan councils). Clan headship was hereditary and the chief was called the Chaudhari.[86] Jagpal Singh pertinently emphasises that 'land was not owned communally in the *bhaichara* villages. Under this system the peasant-proprietors had individual and hereditary rights on the land'.[87] And he adds: 'Production was carried out by the family members of peasant-proprietors, though sometimes Jats cultivated land as tenants in one plot and proprietors in another. They are called peasant-proprietors by virtue of their proprietorship over land and the family's participation in the production process.'[88] This system stood in stark contrast with the other agrarian arrangements of North India – *zamindari*, *taluqdari*, *jagirdari* or *malguzari* – where tillers did not own the land, which was controlled by landlords who also acted as intermediaries between the peasants and the state and therefore levied taxes. Obviously, the *bhaichara* system offered a suitable context for the development of the Jats' individualist industriousness. Thus the Jat Arya Samajists shaped their own emancipatory identity from their relatively subordinate status by combining the Sanskritised teaching of the *updeshaks* and this strong working ethic. Chhotu Ram is one such case in point.

Chhotu Ram, the Architect of Kisan Politics. Chhotu Ram was born in 1881, the son of an illiterate small Jat peasant proprietor in a village in Rohtak district, where he was to enter public life under the patronage of Ramji Lal Hooda. Remarkably intelligent, he studied

[85] M.C. Pradhan, *The Political System of Jats in North India*, Oxford University Press, 1966, p. 34.
[86] Ibid., pp. 1–6.
[87] Singh, *Capitalism and Dependence*, op. cit., p. 11.
[88] Ibid., pp. 11–12.

in Delhi at St Stephen's High School and then at St Stephen's College. After gaining his BA in 1905 he became assistant private secretary of Raja Rampal Singh of Kalakankar in Pratapgarh district (United Provinces), who had already supported Madan Mohan Malaviya's newspaper, *Hindustan*, in which Chhotu Ram was given an opportunity to write. But he resumed his studies, passed his LLB and set up his practice in Agra and then in his home district, Rohtak, in 1912.

Chhotu Ram was therefore one of the first Jat peasants to become part of the intelligentsia. In fact, he became an organic intellectual in the Gramscian sense since he constantly lobbied on behalf of those from his own background.[89] As early as 1907, he wrote in *The Imperial Fortnightly* an article entitled 'The improvement of India village life' which established the mainstays of the ideology of the *kisan*. He deplored that Indian villages were so backward and considered that 'no progressive society can afford to allow such a large and important section to remain stationary'.[90] Chhotu Ram wanted the individual to deploy his sense of entrepreneurship. This was to be one of the basic principles of the *kisan* ideology, that is of the peasant proprietor. Such an entrepreneurial individualism was supported by his Arya Samajist allegiance.[91]

[89] In fact Chhotu Ram was the first politician to articulate in analytical terms the opposition between rural and urban India. This attitude initially resulted from the cultural shock of his studies in Delhi: 'My seven years of study at Delhi brought me into close contact with students from the highly cultured sections of Delhi society. My relations with them were always entirely cordial, but, in friendly banter, these urban comrades always styled their school and college fellows from the countryside as rustics, clowns and pumpkins. Jats came in for particularly heavy share of these epithets.' (Cited in M. Gopal, *Sir Chhotu Ram – A Political Biography*, Delhi: B.R. Publishing Corporation, 1977, p. 16)

As he was to later reveal, in 1942, Chhotu Ram then felt 'that inchoate desire which in later years grew into a powerful passion for uplifting my class, educationally, socially, economically and politically' (ibid.)

[90] Chhotu Ram 'The improvement of Indian Village Life' in K.C. Yadav (ed.), *The Crisis in India*, Kurukshetra, Haryana Historical Society, 1996, p. 72. Among the factors which hindered the modernisation process, Chhotu Ram mentioned the joint-family and the 'old patriarchal system' whose main consequences was that 'the individual does not put forth his best efforts. Also, the advanced members of the family cannot introduce reforms without disturbing the peace of the house. This is a great hindrance in the way of social reform'.

[91] Chhotu Ram entered 'Vedic' in the column against religion specified in

However, Chhotu Ram emphasised the threats the merchant castes and urban-dwellers – groups that held dominant positions within the Arya Samaj – at large posed to the *kisans*. Ramji Lal Hooda had already distanced himself from the upper caste milieu from which most leaders of the Arya Samaj came. He wrote, for instance, in his diary that Banyas 'are always the friends of gain and have no appreciation of friendship or past obligations'.[92] Chhotu Ram joined Congress in 1917 but left it soon after because it was controlled by urban Arya Samajists and more especially Banyas. With Mian Fazl-i-Husain, a Muslim leader who was equally eager to organise the peasants in Punjab, he formed the National Unionist Party in the early 1920s. In 1923, the party's election manifesto focussed on the needs of 'the backward classes' –, which did not benefit from a 'just and fair' representation in the public services of the province and were exploited by 'the economically dominant classes'.[93] This term – the backward classes – was used as a synonym for the peasants as indicated by the party's promise to 'preserve intact the Punjab Land Alienation Act as a measure of protection to backward classes'.[94]

After the 1923 electoral success of the NUP, Fazl-i-Husain became Chief Minister of Punjab and Chhotu Ram Minister of Agriculture in 1924. He was thus largely responsible for amending the Land Revenue Act so as to fix the term of a normal settlement at a minimum of forty years and the state's share at a maximum of 25% of net assets in passing the Regulation of Accounts Bill. This pro-

---

the admission form of the intermediate examination to show that he fully adhered to Dayananda's doctrine (ibid., p. 14).

[92] Juneja and Singh Mor (eds), *The Diaries of Dr Ramji Lal Hooda*, op. cit., pp. 226–7. Hooda was also positively inclined towards the uplift of the lower castes. One entry of his diary reads: 'A meeting of the lower caste [*sic*] was held at Devi Bhawan, and all the Municipal wells were opened for all Hindus including "Achhoots". There is some opposition in certain quarters, but the opponents will realise their mistake after some days' (ibid., p. 282).

[93] Cited in M. Gopal, *Sir Chhotu Ram*, op. cit., p. 59.

[94] Cited in ibid. Chhotu Ram wanted to protect peasants from traders who brought agricultural products at low prices and acted as greedy moneylenders. As a result, the peasant's indebtedness reached unbearable levels and they eventually had to sell their land. This phenomenon was such a cause of concern for the British that they passed in 1900 the *Land Alienation Act*, which made very difficult the transfer of land from agricultural to 'non–agricultural tribes'. However, the Act had many loopholes and Chhotu Ram felt moved to organise the peasants.

tected debtors against the malpractices of moneylenders and made the Punjab Land Alienation Act work in favour of the "agricultural tribes". The NUP government also reduced water rates so that cultivators got better conditions for irrigation. Last but not least, the Punjab Agricultural Produce Marketing Act reformed the marketing committees of the *mandis* (agricultural market places), with peasants representing two-thirds of their members and traders one-third. Gokul Chand Narang, an Arya Samajist leader who owned several sugar mills protested that 'Through this legislation, penny worth peasants would sit alongside millionaire *mahajans* [banyas] in the committee'. Chhotu Ram replied: 'The Jat deserves no less respect than the Arora mahajan [Aroras are *Banyas* from Punjab]. [. . .] The time is not far off when the hard working peasant would leave the worshippers of money far behind'.[95]

This reply reveals how Chhotu Ram's thinking moved from the notion of 'Jats' to that of 'Peasants', suggesting that an equation could be established between both in his mind. The Jat was intended to be the rallying point of all the castes tilling the land. Chhotu Ram propagated the idea of *biradari* (peasant brotherhood) among the Ahirs, Jats, Gujars and Rajputs – hence the acronym AJGAR (cobra).[96] As Datta points out, Chhotu Ram 'used two entwined languages: one was of Jat cultural assertion and the other was that of a homogeneous rural community embodying elements of peasant culture'.[97]

Chhotu Ram is especially remarkable because he introduced in Indian politics a clear distinction between rural and urban India, what was to be known at a later stage as the famous 'Bharat versus India' slogan. In the mid-1930s he wrote in the *Jat Gazette*:

> O you rich people reside in towns, whilst the poor *zamindar* owns only a plough.[. . .] You (townsmen) enjoy rich food, the *bechara zamindar* [the hapless zamindar][98] gains his share of cheap brown sugar and coarse rice, and that too by mortgaging some of his utensils with the shopkeeper.[99]

[95] Cited in ibid., p. 108.

[96] Datta, *Forming an Identity*, op. cit., p. 108.

[97] Ibid., p. 112.

[98] He pointed out that 'In some provinces *zamindars* are different from peasants. But in the Punjab the two are synonymous. Here the agriculturist who has proprietary rights in land is the one who actually ploughs it.' (Cited in Datta, *Forming an Identity*, op. cit., p. 97)

[99] Cited in ibid., p. 104.

On the other hand, Chhotu Ram exhorted the peasants to 'shed their fatalistic outlook, acquire a vision and gain self-confidence and self-respect':[100] 'I want to see the Punjab peasant prosperous and united [. . .] awakened and standing on his feet, in action and organisation'.[101]

With Chhotu Ram, the Jats thus invented a new idiom of politics, *kisan politics*, which emphasised socio-economic cleavages. Such an agenda was bound to offer this caste – and other peasant castes – an alternative identity on the way to social emancipation. Logically enough, another Jat, Charan Singh, articulated this ideology after independence.

Charan Singh and Kisan Politics. Charan Singh's discourse was replete with references to his lowly origins[102] and spelled out an egalitarian agenda: 'For creating an egalitarian society the rains of power of the country should lie in the hands of the 80% of the population, uneducated and poor, which lives in the villages'.[103] Yet he represented more than anything else the class of peasant proprietors which he had begun to shape with the land reform he had initiated in Uttar Pradesh after Independence.

Our assessment of Charan Singh's land reform in chapter 2 suggested that he identified himself with the interests of peasants-proprietors from an early date. As far back as 1939 he successively introduced in the Legislative Assembly of the United Provinces a Debt Redemption Bill, which brought great relief to indebted cultivators, an Agriculture Produce Market Bill that was intended to protect cultivators against the rapacity of traders and a Land Utilisation Bill which should have transferred the proprietary interest in agricultural holdings to the tenants who deposited ten times the annual rent to the government as compensation to the landlord.[104] Like Chhotu Ram, Charan Singh was eager to protect the peasants from merchants, moneylenders and the urban population as a whole. In

[100] Ibid., p. 106.

[101] Cited in ibid.

[102] Sometimes with autobiographical references such as 'My own childhood has been spent amongst the peasants who bare bodied toiled and laboured in the fields.' (Cited in G. Ravat (ed.), *Chaudhary Charan Singh: Sukti aur Vichar*, New Delhi, Kisan Trust, 1985, chap. 6 [n.p.])

[103] Ibid.

[104] Goyal (ed.), *Profile of Chaudhary Charan Singh*, op. cit., pp. 6–7.

1939 he manifested a sharp awareness of the latent conflicts between rural and urban India:

In our country the classes whose scions dominate the public services are either those which have been raised to unexampled prominence and importance by the Britisher, e.g. the money-lender, the big *zamindar* or *taluqdar*, the *arhatia* or the trader, or those which have been, so to say, actually called into being him – the *vakil* [advocate], the doctor, the contractor. These classes have, in subordinate cooperation with the foreigner, exploited the masses in all kinds of manner during these last two hundred years. The views and interests of these classes, on the whole, are, therefore, manifestly opposed to those of the masses. The social philosophy of a member of the non-agricultural, urban classes is entirely different from that of a person belonging to the agricultural rural classes.[105]

For Charan Singh, Nehru epitomised this elitist, urban-oriented attitude in Indian society:

This supreme city dweller administrator had no knowledge whatsoever about life conditions of the millions of helpless Indians who live in the villages of India. He, who had only knowledge of the western principles of economy learnt in the Oxbridge university education system, was given the charge of administering the growth of the country. He got carried away towards these ready-made theories and concepts, which promised comparatively higher national production. He had imagined that by a public ownership of the industries the country could get a high level of production.[106]

According to Charan Singh priority had to be given not to industry but to agriculture. To implement a rural-oriented economic policy, the administration had to be staffed by the sons of farmers because only an official who understood and thought like a peasant could effectively solve his problems.[107] Charan Singh's view of affirmative action is therefore very different from that of Lohia or Ambedkar: for him it is a way of making an agriculture based on peasant-proprietors more efficient; for them it was a way of empowering the lower

[105] C. Singh, 'Why 50 per cent of government jobs should be reserved for sons of agriculturists' in Charan Singh, *Land Reforms*, op. cit., p. 203.

[106] G. Ravat (ed.), *Chaudhary Charan Singh: sukti aur vichar*, op. cit., chap. 8 [n.p].

[107] Ibid. He even said: 'If in the public services the number of those coming from peasant and rural sectors can be increased, not only the entire state administration will function as per desired expectations but its efficiency will considerably increase.' (Ibid.)

castes. In 1939, Charan Singh even proposed a 50% quota in public administration in favour of the sons of the farmers. The All India Jat Mahasabha supported Charan Singh's proposal although he was less wedded to caste affiliations as such.

Instead he wanted to subsume caste into a new peasant identity. This approach was undoubtedly dictated by his own social background since his caste, the Jats, occupied an intermediary position and were not numerically dominant. Though, technically, they have to be classified as Shudras, the Jats form a dominant caste and are therefore locked in conflicts with lower castes working for them as labourers or acting as their tenants. Second, in Uttar Pradesh the Jats represent only 1.2% of the population: so Charan Singh obviously, had good reasons to forge a '*kisan*' identity emphasising the opposition between peasants and town-dwellers in order to transcend caste divisions and promote peasant solidarity. In Charan Singh's discourse, '*kisan*' tended to be synonymous with 'villager', whereas, in reality, as Thorner points out in one of his studies published in the 1950s, precisely when Charan Singh was implementing his reform, *kisans* were situated between the 'maliks' – landlords and rich landowners – and the 'mazdoors' – poor tenants, sharecroppers and landless labourers. They are small landowners and substantial tenants who work the fields and have property interests but not on the same footing as the '*maliks*'.[108]

As revenue minister in charge of land reform in Uttar Pradesh after Independence, Charan Singh's strategy had been to promote the interests of the middle class peasantry by abolishing the *zamindari* system. His approach largely explains the moderate and selective character of the Uttar Pradesh land reform and later his conflict with Nehru. In 1959, in the Nagpur session of the Congress, he vigorously opposed the projected introduction of agricultural co-operatives announced by the Prime Minister. He even published a book, *Joint farming x-rayed: The problem and its solution*, where he proposed a strategy of global development radically opposed to that of Nehru.[109]

[108] D. Thorner, *The Agrarian Prospect in India*, Delhi University Press, 1956.

[109] Charan Singh wrote this book while he was out of office. He had resigned in April 1959 because of several disagreements with Sampurnanand, the Chief Minister, and was replaced as Revenue Minister by Hukum Singh. (M. Johnson, 'Relation Between Land Settlement and Party Politics in Uttar Pradesh', Ph.D. thesis, University of Sussex, 1975, p. 145)

In some ways *Joint farming x-rayed* is the first manifesto of *kisan* politics in post-independence India. Questioning the need for a rapid, state-sponsored industrialisation as advocated by Nehru, Charan Singh proposed to give priority to agriculture and to promote it by developing small farmer holdings, the only way according to him to generate the surpluses that were needed for industrial investment.[110] For him, agricultural co-operatives would have annihilated the productivity gains resulting from the elimination of the *zamindar* – like intermediaries because this would have jeopardised the independence of the farmers:

> The thought that land has become his [the peasant's] and his children's in perpetuity, lightens and cheer his labours and expands his horizon. The feeling that he is his own master, subject to no outside control, and has free, exclusive and untrammelled use of his land drives him to greater and greater effort. [. . .] Likewise any system of large-scale farming in which his holdings are pooled must affect the farmer, but in the reverse direction. No longer will he be his own master; he will become one of the many; his interest will be subordinated to the group interest.[111]

Obviously, economic rationality is not the only reason for rejecting agricultural co-operatives. Charan Singh admits that 'Ultimately it is not a question of economic efficiency or of form of organisation, but whether individualism or collectivism should prevail'.[112] Indeed he defends then *kisans*' way of life, not only their material vested interests. According to him 'The peasant is an incorrigible individualist; for his avocation, season in and season out, can be carried on with a pair of bullocks in the solitude of Nature without the necessity of having to give orders to, or, take orders from anybody'.[113] Charan Singh spells out a very romantic view, even a mystique of the *kisan*,

[110] Charan Singh spells out this argument rather late in the book but it is his starting point : 'Industrialisation cannot precede but will follow agricultural prosperity. Surpluses of food production above farmers' consumption must be available before non-agricultural resources can be developed.' (Charan Singh, *Joint Farming X-rayed – The problem and its solution*, Bombay: Bharatiya Vidya Bhavan, 1959, p. 251)

[111] Ibid., pp. v–vi.

[112] Ibid., p. 107. He subsequently emphasised that 'Collective farming is against human character'. (Cited in Ravat (ed.), *Chaudhury Charan Singh: sukti aur vichar*, op. cit., n.p.

[113] Singh, *Joint Farming X-rayed*, op. cit., p. 104.

as the man in communion with Nature (a word that he writes with a capital n) and the only one able to sustain its harmony.

There is a nutritional cycle in Nature, without maintenance of whereof Mother Earth will refuse to yield any crops at all. Nature has so ordained that whatever the earth produces is the nutrition of all living things including man, but whatever part of this nutrition is left unutilised and, therefore, rejected by the body of man, beast, bird, or insect, is the nutrition of Mother Earth which had, in the process of producing nutrition for the animal world, got exhausted and become hungry. If this night-soil and farm-yard waste are composted (along with dead vegetation) that is, properly treated, and returned to the earth, the nutritional cycle becomes complete, and our fields will never disappoint us and will continue giving us an ever-enduring supply of food.[114]

Naturally, 'a small farmer can best help complete' the cycle in nature.[115] First because being a *kisan* implies the use of draught animals which will produce the manure earth needs. Charan Singh argues, rather dramatically, that 'with tractors taking the place of bullocks [. . .], India will soon end up with a desert' because the peasants 'will have to apply chemical fertilisers instead of dung or compost, which is the best form of organic matter for fertilising the soil and best means of soil conservation'.[116] In addition to his living in harmony with nature, the *kisan* displays virtues which Charan Singh does not hesitate to present grandiloquently:

[114] Ibid., p. 266.

[115] Ibid., p. 50.

[116] Ibid., p. 268. The first argument presented against the use of machine was of course basically economic since it concerned the fight against unemployment: 'India has a huge population and a limited cultivable land surface, and mechanisation would throw out of work thousands of men' (ibid., p. 79). This argument is also offered in favour of non-capital intensive small-scale industry. Here Charan Singh claims to be in the footsteps of Gandhi (ibid., p. 213). Indeed, his eulogy of decentralised, village-based economy reminds us of the Mahatma. However, his developmental project differs from Gandhi's on one fundamental issue. Whereas the Mahatma recommended the pooling of all goods and highlighting their collective value, Charan Singh champions the right to property because he belongs to a class of farmers which he helped to promote and which he himself rightly calls 'peasant-proprietors'. In a latter edition of *Joint Farming X-rayed*, where the subtitle has become part of the title, Charan Singh elaborates on this point. He attributes the economic lag of India to the dominant mentality, the Brahmanical value system, which depreciates work and

Agriculture is a profession where the peasant has to fight nature and thus has to learn daily the lessons of perseverance. As a consequence there grows in him solidity and a capacity to bear hardships. In this way, such a personality is born which cannot grow in any other profession.[117]

Charan Singh defends the way of life and the interests of the peasant-proprietors but not those of other social groups, especially the landless peasants. He regards the Jat household as his model and considers, therefore, that 'The existence of landless agricultural labour [. . .] is not essential to peasant farming'.[118] Referring, *en passant*, to the labourers' condition, he notes that 'If wages have at all to be paid, in view of the fact that a large supply of idle labour is almost always available, the wages paid need only be subsistence wages'.[119] Charan Singh was against any land reform that applied too low a ceiling and gave land to everybody because it would multiply holdings that would be 'uneconomic' and hence weaken the peasant-proprietor pattern. For him '[t]here should be a provision in law that the allocated land is not further subdivided but the allocated position will be given to a single heir'.[120] He thought that the average ceiling should be fixed at about 30 acres because, in his view, this is the optimum area of land that one man can manage.[121] By setting the level at which a holding was deemed to be non-viable at 30 acres Charan Singh betrayed his preference for one group of peasants over another. This was tantamount to shelter from land redistribution a whole

---

turns man into a fatalist. Only those people who have followed the teaching of reform movements such as the Arya Samaj have developed their enterprising spirit. He is one of them and claims to follow the founder of this movement. (C. Singh, *India's Poverty and its Solution*, New York: Asia Publishing House, 1964, p. 319, n.7)

[117] Ravat (ed.), *Chaudhury Charan Singh: sukti aur vichar*, op. cit., chap. 8 [n.p].

[118] Singh, *Joint Farming X-rayed*, op. cit., p. 88.

[119] Ibid., p. 168.

[120] Ravat (ed.), *Chaudhury Charan Singh: sukti aur vichar*, op. cit., chap. 8.

[121] Singh, *Joint Farming X-rayed*, op. cit., p. 90. In 1955, Charan Singh had sent a long letter to the chief editor of *The National Herald* explaining that there were no more than 35,000 farms whose holding represented more than 30 acres and that the surpluses which could be obtained from this source would not exceed 750,000 acres, a very small proportion of the 40 million cultivable acres in the state. (Singh, *Land Reforms*, op. cit., p. 162)

class of middle class farmers who had sometimes grown rich. Not only that, but according to Charan Singh any surplus land obtained by putting a ceiling on large holdings should be redistributed 'to sub-basic holders rather than landless people'. For Charan Singh, the latter 'have to be drawn to industries, trade, transport and other non-agricultural avocations'.[122] In fact '[i]f the landless labourers do not go to other industries then the country will not progress. . .'.[123] Twenty years after the publication of *Joint Farming X-rayed*, Charan Singh was asked what was his programme for the landless peasants, he admitted that he did not regard them as peasants and that there was no land left for them.[124] Concerned about the implications of Charan Singh's politics, Partha Chatterjee warned that if his 'appeal succeeds in finding a stable home in peasant consciousness, it will be impossible at any future time to politically unite owner-peasants, large or small, with the landless'.[125]

In spite of this selective defence of the rural masses, Charan Singh systematically attempted to project himself as the spokesman for village India, against the city-based, parasitic elite, presenting the village community as a harmonious whole. He claimed that a village 'was always a stronger moral unit than a factory. The sense of the community was a vital thing among the peasantry, providing a natural foundation for collaboration or co-operative action'.[126] Like Gandhi – from whom he explicitly drew inspiration[127] – he completely ignored the deep social contradictions and class antagonisms between landowners, tenants, sharecroppers and labourers and dwelt instead on consensual processes of conflict resolution. He thus claimed that 'Differences or disputes amongst the villagers were settled

[122] Ibid., p. 137.

[123] Ravat (ed.), *Chaudhury Charan Singh: sukti aur vichar*, op. cit., ch. 8 [n.p].

[124] Ho Kwon Ping, 'The rise of the aging sun', *Far Eastern Economic Review*, 103 (2), 12 Jan. 1979, p. 81.

[125] Chatterjee, 'Charan Singh's Politics', *A Possible India – Essays in Political Criticism*, Delhi: Oxford University Press, 72.

[126] Singh, *Joint Farming X-Rayed*, op. cit., p. 270.

[127] For instance he shared Gandhi's reluctance towards the machine: '. . . we must follow the path advocated by Mahatma Gandhi [. . .] According to this path, we must stop the production of consumer goods by machines and in its place the existing cottage industries be made operational.' (Ravat (ed.), *Chaudhury Charan Singh: sukti aur vichar*, op. cit., ch. 8 [n.p])

mostly by discussion on a basis of equity guided by the village elders, the priest or the teachers, again, as a tradition and out of the self-same sense of being one community'.[128]

Charan Singh paid little heed to caste.[129] When he did, he drew his inspiration from Dayananda. He once said: 'Arya Samaj is my mother and Maharishi Dayanand is my Guru'.[130] He took up the Arya Samajist theory that belonging to a caste was originally not hereditary but determined by merit and individual competence.[131] From that he deduced an ironic view of society which has strong Gandhian overtones:

> The method of combining functional skill with new castes was an ingenious way of establishing social harmony by giving the newcomer an assured economic position within Hinduism, and this continued to hold the field as long as the economic basis of the Hindu social order remained stable. The system served as a social insurance for the weak and the unsuccessful. Instead of being thrown in a maelstrom, every member of the society knew his place and has a source of living, which was secure from encroachments or grasping proclivities of his neighbour.[132]

While such a discourse echoes Gandhi's view as much as it does those of the Arya Samaj, in contrast with the Mahatma he was less inclined to rehabilitate the traditional social system, preferring instead, simply to abolish the caste system. As early as 1939, he proposed a resolution to the Congress Legislature Party according to which 'no enquiries should be made into the caste of a Hindu candidate who seeks admission into an educational institution or any of the public services'.[133] Ten years later he submitted a note to the Chief Minister of Uttar Pradesh, G.B. Pant asking the government not to help finan-

[128] Singh, *Joint Farming X-Rayed*, op. cit., p. 272.

[129] In *Joint Farming X-Rayed* he referred to it only once to deplore that 'dignity of labour, without which no wealth can be produced, is foreign to the conception of caste founded on birth' (ibid., p. 259).

[130] Cited in Ravat, *Chaudhury Charan Singh*, op. cit., ch. 6.

[131] 'Swami [Dayananda] set the criteria for excellence and knowledge at the place of birth' (ibid.).

[132] Singh, *India's Poverty*, op. cit., p. 329.

[133] An observer, *Who is a Casteist?*, New Delhi: Kisan Trust, 1984, p. 21. Similarly, he proposed in 1951 that 'no Congressman shall either be a member or participate in the proceedings of an organisation whose membership is

cially the educational institutions named after a particular caste.[134] He did so again, in 1953, in a note where he suggested that 'only those persons shall be allowed to enter the legislature and gazetted services of the State or the Union who, if they marry or have married after a certain date, have done so outside their caste, or, if they are bachelors, propose to do so.'[135] Charan Singh was prepared to amend the Constitution to see this reform implemented. In 1954 he wrote to Nehru along these lines, justifying his fight against caste by evoking its divisive impact and his own personal story: 'Men like me know from experience what it means to be born in castes other than those which are regarded or regard themselves as privileged.'[136] But he never projected himself as a spokesman for the low castes.

Charan Singh was torn between two considerations so far as positive discrimination in favour of the lower castes was concerned. This ambivalence was especially evident from his conflict with C.B. Gupta in the early 1960s. Soon after he took over as Chief Minister, Gupta questioned the relaxation in the age criteria for the reccruitment of backward caste candidates for the police, a measure that G.B. Pant's government had granted. He wanted Charan Singh – who was Home Minister – to rescind the concession. Singh replied that the backward classes represented 53% of the population of Uttar Pradesh, whereas there were only 35 gazetted officers from those out of 3,250 in 1946–7, and 25 out of 5,250 in 1954–5. He also emphasised that there were only twenty-two OBC MLAs among the Congress Legislature Party, as against thirty-three among the opposition MLAs.[137] Finally he reminded Gupta that the southern states had reserved posts for the backward classes in their bureaucracy and that the Kalelkar Commission had recommended likewise. But he concluded his note by saying that while he was not inclined to question the

---

confined to a particular caste or castes or indulge in spreading hatred against other castes.' (Cited in An Observer, *Who is a Casteist?*, op. cit., p. 27)

[134] Ibid., p. 22.

[135] Ibid., p. 24. He reiterated this proposal in the 1964 edition of *Joint-Farming X-rayed* (Singh, *India's Poverty*, op. cit., pp. 353–4).

[136] Cited in An Observer, *Who is a Casteist?*, op. cit., p. 31. Nehru replied that such a low or constitutional amendment would 'offend the basic principle of individual freedom' (ibid. p. 32).

[137] Indeed, the low castes were comparatively more numerous in the social-

relaxation in the entry conditions for OBC candidates, he in no way favoured reservation of posts for them in the services or seats in the legislatures.[138] Charan Singh did not want to develop positive discrimination but rather to see caste abolished. He did not highlight caste cleavages but championed the interests of the peasants against those of the town.

To sum up: Charan Singh represented peasant-proprietors and his entire strategy consisted in forging a *kisan* identity in which all agricultural workers would recognise their common interests and mobilise behind him. So in building as broad a coalition as possible, he emphasised the dichotomy between urban and rural India.

> There has always been lack of equilibrium, rather a sort of antagonism between cities and the countryside. This is particularly so in our land where the gulf of inequality between the capitalist class and the working class pales into insignificance before that which exists between the peasant farmer in our village and the middle-class town dweller. India is really two worlds – rural and urban.[139]

This discourse excludes any kind of solidarity between workers and peasants and ignores the internal divisions of rural society, either in terms of economic disparities or social conflicts, which govern village life. Nor did he seek to mobilise followers on a caste basis.[140]

Charan Singh's *kisan* politics enabled him gradually to build a coalition encompassing the cultivating castes ranging from OBCs to intermediate castes. This coalition, in fact, was the old AJGAR grouping that Chhotu Ram had already developed in Punjab, minus the Rajputs.[141] While, unsurprisingly, there was no representative of

---

ist groups of the Uttar Pradesh legislative assembly in 1962: 31% for the SSP as against 23% for the PSP (against 14% for the Jana Sangh and 8% for the Congress). (A. Burger, *Opposition in a Dominant Party System*, Berkeley, University of California Press, 1969, p. 55)

[138] An Observer, *Who is a Casteist?*, op. cit., p. 59.

[139] Singh, *India's Poverty and its Solution*, op. cit., p. 212.

[140] He did not hide his antipathy for Brahmins and the parasitic, anti-work culture they embody but nor did he try to cash in on anti-Brahmin feelings or caste cleavages.(Byres, 'Charan Singh', op. cit., pp. 143–4).

[141] For Kalelkar, the AJGAR coalition included the Rajputs, the final 'R' standing for them, but it was no longer true with Charan Singh's *kisan* politics (*Report of the [first] backward classes commission*, op. cit., p. XXII).

the (often landless) Untouchable castes in this grouping, it included a wide range of castes, from the OBCs to intermediate and upper castes. Mulayam Singh Yadav was among the Yadav followers whom Charan Singh attracted in the 1960s – he was first elected as an MLA in 1967. Interestingly, he was introduced to the Chaudhuri by another OBC, Jairam Verma,[142] who was not even a Yadav but a Kurmi, a sign that Charan's Singh appeal to the cultivating castes extended beyond the AJGAR coalition.[143] *Kisan* politics had gradually found (and shaped) its constituency. But the Congress party ignored this emerging group and its principal spokesman.

Charan Singh's marginalisation within the Uttar Pradesh Congress

The case of the Jats shows clearly that contrary to what Weiner observed in areas other than the Northern Hindi-speaking states, in Uttar Pradesh the Congress hardly bothered to accommodate the interests of this emerging group of peasant proprietors or to co-opt some of its members. In fact the party harboured within its ranks one of its main leaders, in the person of Charan Singh, but again and again he was prevented from implementing the measures which would have benefited the rising peasantry.

One of his rivals within Congress, the Rajput leader, Thakur Hukam Singh, opposed the large scale land consolidation policies which Charan Singh enacted as Revenue Minister, a policy that served above all the interests of middle farmers whose productivity was

[142] Lal and Nair, *Caste vs Caste – Turbulence in Indian Politics*, Delhi, Ajanta, 1998, p. 32.

[143] Jai Ram Verma was one of the first OBC leaders of the Congress. He was a member of the Uttar Pradesh Government in 1957–60, and in 1962–7. Then he followed Charan Singh out of Congress and became one of his ministers in his 1970 government. He was the first Kurmi to be given such responsibilities within Congress. In fact, he drew the dividends from his early involvement in the freedom movement – which was then an avenue for upward socio-political mobility: he took part in anti-British activities in 1936 when he was 30, and then in the individual *satyagraha* (1941) and the Quit India Movement (1942). He was jailed repeatedly till 1945 for his militancy – and rewarded by a Congress ticket in 1946 (when he was elected to the UP Assembly) and by a seat at the AICC in 1950. (*Who's Who in Legislative Assembly 1962–67*, Lucknow: U.P. Legislative Secretariat, 1963, p. 82)

hampered by the scattered nature of their holdings.[144] The party's leaders in the state eventually acceded to Thakur Hukam Singh's wishes and replaced him as Revenue Minister in 1959 and held the post until 1967.

Another bone of contention between Charan Singh and the other Congress leaders concerned relations between the farmers and the urban merchants who bought their produce. As early as 1938, Charan Singh had proposed a bill to protect farmers from illegal trading practices. However, the Act was passed only in 1964 because of the stubborn resistance of several congressmen, including C.B. Gupta, a Banya close to the merchants' lobby who was Chief Minister of UP in 1960–3.

Another conflict that set Charan Singh against the UP Congress leadership concerned the taxation of villagers. Farmers were taxed very lightly. In addition the *bhumidhars* and *sirdars* had obtained an assurance in 1947 that there would be no increase in their taxes for forty years. In 1962 C.B. Gupta drafted a bill implying a 50% tax increase, which the farmers had to pay. Charan Singh reacted with a long note where he listed all the taxes which were already levied on the farmers. He also underlined the differential between the price of agricultural products and that of manufactured goods, which generated an imbalance in the terms of exchange between urban and rural dwellers.[145] The bill was abandoned but this controversy reflected a deep division.

In the 1964 edition of *Joint Farming X-Rayed* Charan Singh expressed his bitterness in a sad ironical tone:

> It cannot be seriously disputed that, had those in whose hands lies the power to make policies in India, their roots laid in the soil of their own country and their fingers on the pulse of their peasantry, we would have progressed much faster, at least, in the sphere of agriculture. But views and sentiments of the peasants are seldom shared by those at the top today. Political leadership of the country vests almost entirely in the hands of those who come from the town and, therefore, have an urban outlook. They may have an intellectual sympathy for the rural folk, but have no personal knowledge and psychological appreciation of their needs, problems and handicaps. Not only this: our leaders and the intelligentsia are nurtured on text-books written in conditions entirely different from our country or which are mostly inspired by the

[144] Johnson, *Relation between land settlement and party politics*, op. cit., pp. 57 and 103.

[145] Ibid., pp. 151–88.

ideology of Marx who had made no special study of the rural problems. That is mainly why Mahatma Gandhi's powerful advocacy in favour of a truly Indian approach to India's problems notwithstanding, we are under the spell of economic, political and social ideas and doctrines that we may have received ready-made from foreign oracles – western oracles till yesterday and eastern today.[146]

More importantly, Charan Singh had political ambitions, and he resented the way upper caste Congressmen threatened his attempt to become Chief Minister of UP. C.B. Gupta was preferred to him even though he had twice lost an election the Assembly during the current term, 1957–62, and was not even a MLA. Thereafter, in 1963, the post was offered to Sucheta Kripalani, who was not even from Uttar Pradesh.

The Congress displayed shortsightedness in marginalising Charan Singh because in the 1960s the social basis of his *kisan* politics had mushroomed. First, the land reform, even though it had been limited, had enabled some tenants to become peasant-proprietors. In India at large, from 1953–4 to 1971–2, the share of landowners possessing more than 10 acres decreased from 13.5% to 10.3% of rural households and finally represented 53.2% of the cultivated area in 1972, as against 66.5% in 1953–4. At the same time the share of those owning 2.5 to 10 acres increased in proportion to rural households (85.5% in 1954–5 and 89.6% en 1970–2) and finally represented 46.7% of the total cultivated area, as against 36.4% in 1954–5 (for more details, see table 1.1, p. 44).

In Uttar Pradesh, the share of landowners owning more than ten acres decreased from 7.6% to 5.3% of rural households between 1953–4 and 1971–2. This upper category owned 'only' 29% of the cultivated areas in 1971–2, as against 38% in 1953–4. In the same period, the smallest households increased in number since those possessing less than 2.5 acres represented 15.6% of the total in 1971–2, as against 12.1% in 1953–4. The intermediary group of those operating between 2.5 and 10 acres met a different fate. Their share of the total of rural households fell from 35.8% to 33.1%, but the ground area they represented rose from 49.9% to 55.3% of the total. This development would not have been significant had these middle peasants not benefited from the second, most important event of the 1960s, the Green Revolution.

[146] Singh, *India's Poverty and its Solution*, op. cit., p. 411.

Table 8.4. DISTRIBUTION AND SIZE OF OPERATIONAL HOLDINGS LAND IN UTTAR PRADESH , 1953–72

Size of class operational holdings (acres)	*1953-4 Households* %	*Area operated* %	*1960-1 Households* %	*Area operated* %	*1971-2 Households* %	*Area operated* %
0–1	35.6	2.2	37.2	2.4	39.5	2.8
1–2.5	21	9.9	21.2	10.4	22.2	12.8
2.5–5	20.4	20.4	20.1	20.6	20.5	25.4
5–10	15.4	29.5	14.4	28.1	12.6	29.9
10–25	6.5	26.5	6.1	25	4.8	23.4
25 +	1.1	11.5	1.2	13.5	0.5	5.6

Source: A. Kohli, *The State and Poverty in India*, op. cit., p. 213.

The Green Revolution enabled the small and middle peasants who had some investment capacity to commercialise their surpluses. This 'revolution' stemmed from the introduction of high yielding seeds in 1965–6, but also from the development of irrigation and the use of chemical fertilisers, especially in Punjab and West Uttar Pradesh. In Uttar Pradesh at large between 1960–1 and 1982–3, wheat production increased fourfold and progressed from 27% to 58% of the food products. Using these figures Zoya Hasan points out that the peasants who benefited most from this growth were those who possessed at least ten acres and could, therefore invest in new seeds, fertilisers and irrigation. In the early 1970s, 27.65% of these farms of more than 10 acres, were managed by middle caste farmers and 52.07% by upper castes. The former represented 31.33% of rural households in the state and accounted for 23.58% of the cultivated land whereas the latter represented 15.63% of the rural households but 40.7% of cultivated land.[147] It is among the middle caste peasants that one finds a large number of those whom the Rudolphs have called the 'bullock cart capitalists'.[148]

The Jats of western Uttar Pradesh and Haryana grew wealthy, notably thanks to the increase in sugar cane production resulting from extensive irrigation programmes in the framework of the Green Revolution.[149] The assertion of these middle farmers, among whom the Jats were over-represented largely explains the growing success of Charan Singh's *kisan* politics in the 1960s.

After the 1967 elections, which the Congress won by a small margin, C.B. Gupta was again preferred to Charan Singh for Chief Minister. The latter refused to join the government allegedly because Gupta did not agree to sack two ministers who did not enjoy a good

[147] Hasan, 'Patterns of resilience and change', op. cit., p. 169. These figures must be referred to with care because big landlords can appear in the middle peasant category simply because they have divided their land among relatives, friends or subordinates (*benami*).

[148] Rudolph and Rudolph, *In Pursuit of Lakshmi*, op. cit., p. 336.

[149] D.N. Dhanagare, 'The green revolution and social inequalities in rural India', *Bulletin for Concerned Asian Scholars*, 2 (20), April 1988, pp. 2–13. For a more monographic assessment of the social impact of rural modernisation in west Uttar Pradesh, see K. Siddiqui, 'New Technology and Process of Differentiation: Two Sugarcane Cultivating Villages in Uttar Pradesh', *EPW*, 25 Dec. 1999, pp. A139–A152.

reputation.[150] According to another interpretation it was because Gupta refused to appoint thirteen of Charan Singh's followers – that is one third of the government – as cabinet ministers and ministers of state.[151]

Charan Singh left the Congress with sixteen of his mostly non upper caste supporters: nine of these MLAs were Yadavs and Kurmis, four were Brahmins and Rajputs and two were from the Scheduled Castes. This muting enabled Charan Singh to topple C.B. Gupta's government and to replace him as Chief Minister with the help of opposition parties, with which he formed a coalition called the Samyukta Vidhayak Dal, as in Bihar. For the first time in Uttar Pradesh it was not a 'twice born' who occupied the highest post in the state. In addition 43% of ministers and state secretaries came from the intermediary, lower and Untouchables castes. Its composition was in stark contrast to C.B. Gupta's government (Table 8.5).

The coalition supporting Charan Singh included communists, socialists, RPI members and Jana Sanghis. Within this grouping the bones of contention were many.[152] The most important dispute concerned Charan Singh's opposition to the demand of the communists and the socialists concerning the abolition of land revenue on farms of less than 6 acres[153] because, according to him, it was desirable that the farmer pay it to feel fully committed to land ownership. This argument was in tune with his entrepreneurial logic, which had been used earlier in the land reform of Uttar Pradesh. The SSP and the CPI then withdrew their support from the government, which finally fell in February 1968.[154]

The failure of the SVD government showed that a major handicap

[150] Goyal (ed.), *Profile of Chaudhury Charan Singh*, op. cit., p. 41.

[151] Johnson, *Relation between land settlement and party politics*, op. cit., p. 188.

[152] For instance, Charan Singh was criticised by the Jana Sangh for cutting the margins of intermediaries and traders, who formed a major component of the right wing Hindu electorate. The Jana Sangh also protested against the requisitioning of the 500,000 tonnes of grain – finally reduced to 200,000 – in order to alleviate the victims of food shortage because it penalised the big landlords (ibid., p. 198).

[153] Anirudh Panda, *Dhartiputra Chaudhuri Charan Singh*, Ghaziabad: Ritu Prakashak, 1986, p. 104.

[154] For more details, see Paul Brass, 'Coalition politics in North India', *American Political Science Review*, 57 (4), Dec. 1968, pp. 1174–91.

Table 8.5. CASTE AND COMMUNITY GOVERNMENTS OF C.B. GUPTA AND CHARAN SINGH, 1967

	C.B. Gupta's government	*Charan Singh's government*
Upper castes	*9*	*12*
Brahmin	2	3
Rajput	1	5
Banya	5	1
Bhumihar	1	1
Other		2
Intermediate castes		*1*
Jat		1
Other backward classes		*7*
Yadav		3
Gujar		1
Kurmi		1
Lodhi		1
Jaiswal		1
Scheduled Castes	*1*	*4*
Muslim	*1*	*3*
Christian		*1*
Total	*11*	*28*

Source: *Sarvadhik Pichhra Varg Ayog Report* (Report of Most Backward Classes Commission), (Hindi), Lucknow: Uttar Pradesh ki Sarkar, 1977, p. 95.

of the lower caste leaders lay in their dependence on the other opposition parties which did not share the same interests. In this regard the SVD's short-lived experiences began a series of alternating governments which ended in failure. However, the change of government in Uttar Pradesh reflected the impact of the socio-economic rise of the middle-caste peasants on the political sphere, even though the effects of the Green Revolution were more pronounced in West Uttar Pradesh than in other areas.

The comparison of Charan Singh's *modus operandi* in UP and the situation in Bihar suggest that two means of mobilising and empowering the non-elite groups have been used more or less successfully in the 1960s. The strategy of the socialists – who were in the forefront in Bihar – relied more on caste identities and positive discrimination whereas Charan Singh resorted instead to a *kisan* politics that was intended to subsume caste divisions to engineer peasant solidarity against the urban elite. Both trends converged in the 1970s through the emergence of new political parties.

From the BKD to the BLD: the emergence of a new political force. In contrast to the many people who left the Congress and rejoined it after it came back to power, Charan Singh did nothing of the sort and even remained deaf to the calls of Indira Gandhi.[155] Two days before becoming Chief Minister in April 1967, he created his own party, the Jana Congress, which soon merged with the Bharatiya Kranti Dal (BKD – The Indian party of revolution). The BKD, founded on the initiative of Congress dissidents like Humayun Kabir, had initially been intended to be a national party.[156] Its inaugural convention took place in Indore (Madhya Pradesh) in autumn 1967, but the largest delegations came from Bihar, Uttar Pradesh and West Bengal. Some of the representatives coming from the latter state – beginning with Kabir – left the party when they failed to impose a conciliatory line towards the Congress, and the remaining Bengalis were expelled in 1969 because they were seeking alliance with the communists.[157] In April 1969, Charan Singh became president of the BKD, after which it appeared to develop as a regional party. This trend was confirmed during the 1968–9 elections when the BKD won 21.3% of votes in Uttar Pradesh as against 1.5% in Haryana, 2.1% in Bihar and 1.7% in Punjab. In Uttar Pradesh, the party's primary source of support were the Jats from the West, that is, from the same caste and region as Charan Singh. In the Aligarh district Duncan has established a clear correlation between Jat domination and the BKD vote, which was positive in almost all the constituencies.[158] Elsewhere Charan Singh attracted support from lower peasant castes. Satpal Malik, one of his supporters, points out:

> Charan Singh was popular amongst the farmers because he fought against Nehru, against cooperative farming and again, within Congress, he fought against vested interests [. . .]. Anywhere, the Congress committees were

[155] Brass, 'Chaudhuri Charan Singh – An Indian political life', *EPW*, 25 Sept. 1993, p. 2088.

[156] Fickett Jr., 'The politics of regionalism in India', *Pacific Affairs*, XLIV (2), summer 1971, pp. 201–3.

[157] Johnson, *Relation between land settlement and party politics*, op. cit., p. 250.

[158] Duncan, *Levels*, op. cit., pp. 156 and 175.

headed by Guptas [Banyas]. So the farmers knew that we were fighting for them. In eastern and central UP, the Kurmis and Yadavs get rights on the land because of the Zamindari abolition done by Charan Singh. He was their hero.[159]

Charan Singh however was concerned to make his party represent all the farmers. Once free from the responsibility of Chief Ministership he set about restructuring it by replacing members of the *ad hoc* local committees with representatives of the smaller peasantry from the lower castes.[160] These efforts made little impact since, in 1970, 56.7% of the presidents and general secretaries of the BKD district branches were still from the upper castes (18.9% Brahmins and 22.2% Rajputs) against 33.3% from the intermediary and the lower castes (8.9% Jats, 16.6% Yadavs, and 7.8% Kurmis).[161] It was clear that, in order to strengthen the party Charan Singh had to co-opt established leaders and notables, and he could only find them among the higher castes. However, he succeeded in giving party tickets to a large number of non-upper caste candidates in the mid-term elections of 1969 – caused by the absence of majority in the legislative assembly – the BKD fielded 115 candidates from backward and intermediary castes, as against only twenty-three on the Congress side.[162] This strategy certainly helped the BKD to become the second largest party in the state assembly, with 98 seats against 211 for the Congress. This electoral breakthrough of the BKD – and then of its successor, the BLD, which won 106 seats in 1974 – explains the rise of the OBCs among the UP MLAs in the late 1960s and early 1970s from 13% in 1962 to 29% in 1967, 27% in 1969 and 28% in 1974. In parallel with this trend the percentage of the upper castes declined and remained around 40% in 1967–74 – as against 53% in 1962.[163]

In 1969, the electoral success of the BKD was due not only to the fielding of OBC candidates but also to its capacity to rally a number of outgoing MLAs who had not been given a fresh ticket by Congress and who felt sufficiently bitter about it to cross over to the opposition. Of the 402 candidates of the BKD, 79 were former MLAs (of which 44 were outgoing). The party therefore benefited from

[159] Interview with Satpal Malik, New Delhi, 25 Oct. 1998.

[160] Duncan, *Levels*, op. cit., p. 258ff.

[161] Ibid., p. 262.

[162] Hasan, 'Patterns of resilience and change in Uttar Pradesh', op. cit., p. 182.

[163] Hasan, *Quest for Power*, op. cit., p. 251.

the influence of these political leaders and their own 'electoral machinery'.[164] In spite of this performance, Charan Singh was not in a position to form the government and C.B. Gupta became Chief Minister once again. But the Congress party split soon after. C.B. Gupta joined the Congress (O) and Charan Singh's BKD allied with Indira Gandhi's Congress (R), which enabled him to form a coalition government. The social composition of both governments showed that C.B. Gupta and Charan Singh were representing two contrasting constituencies (Table 8.6).

Interestingly, in Charan Singh's government, which lasted only eight months, out of ten Brahmin Ministers, nine were from the Congress (R), and out of eight OBCs five came from the BKD. The BKD/Congress alliance worked rather well in Uttar Pradesh but it

Table 8.6. CASTES AND COMMUNITY IN THE GOVERNMENTS OF C.B. GUPTA AND CHARAN SINGH, 1970

	C.B. Gupta's government	*Charan Singh's government*
Upper castes	*32*	*20*
Brahmin	15	10
Rajput	8	6
Banya	3	1
Kayasth	2	
Bhumihar	1	1
Khatri	1	1
Other	2	1
Intermediate castes		*2*
Jat		2
OBC	*3*	*8*
Yadav	2	5
Kurmi		1
Lodhi	1	1
Mallah		1
Scheduled Castes	*5*	*9*
Muslim	*4*	*6*
Sikh	*1*	
Total	*45*	*45*

Source: As for Table 8.6, pp. 96–7.

[164] Johnson, *Relation between land settlement and party politics*, op. cit., p. 299.

met difficulties at the Centre over the issue of the abolition of the princes' privy purses. Charan Singh opposed this measure on the pretext that it was a breach of a promise given by Sardar Patel to the Princes.[165] Though short-lived, this second experiment with power helped the BKD to establish its image as a *kisan* party. In 1974 it won more seats than in 1969 – 106 as against 98. The party was attracting more farmers, including well-off ones, notables who offered their vote banks to the BKD. Rashid Masood is a case in point. He joined the party in the mid-1970s to become General Secretary of the district branch of Saharanpur. He was the son of a *zamindar* who farmed 300 acres and who had been elected an MLA as an independent in Nakur (Saharanpur district) in 1967 and 1969. After contesting in 1974 as an independent, Masood joined the BKD because this party represented the farmers:

'Basically, I am a *khaksha*, a *kisan* and our interests lied with Chaudhary Charan Singh. Why should I have gone to Congress – a party of monopolists? Not *banyas*, who were with Jana Sangh, but industrialists [. . .]. When you pronounce the name of Chaudhury Charan Singh, immediately everyone would know it pertains to something rural. That was our basic ideology. In India, the *kisan* was the most neglected creature. He produced for others and was never properly paid. That movement started with the Unionist party in Punjab, with Chhotu Ram. He started the fight for big *zamindars* but basically they fought for *zamindars*. And for the first time in Indian history, someone raised his voice for the people who were *supposed to be* with land [. . .]. A *kisan* is who is tilling the land, but under the definition of the Lok Dal [Charan Singh's party after 1974], all those who either till the land or owe their livelihood to land *or tiller*, that is the artisans who are making tools for tillers and those who are living, even landless labour, from cultivation.'[166]

Rashid Masood, who was to be an MP four times and General Secretary of the Lok Dal in 1980, gave in this interview a significant definition of Charan Singh's *kisan* politics. Basically he was a *zamindar* himself, a notable whose family enjoyed enough influence to win elections but he found it useful to subsume the division of rural India under the label of '*kisan*'. The BKD offered landlords like him an ideological platform which enabled them to forge an anti-urban and

[165] Panda, *Dhartiputra Chaudhri Charan Singh*, op. cit., p. 113.
[166] Interview with Rashid Masood, New Delhi, 28 Oct. 1998 (emphasis added).

anti-businessmen coalition in which they could play a pivotal role: they projected themselves as *kisans* and even as rural people, and through this they could instrumentalise this encompassing category to promote their own, elitist interests. This case provides us with a good illustration of Paul Brass's findings.

Brass analysed the mechanism underlying the rise of the BKD on the basis of detailed calculations. He hypothesised that, since the 1950s middle caste peasants increasingly resented Congress rule. On the one hand the policies of the governments of Delhi and Lucknow annoyed them because they suffered from the structural weakness of agricultural prices; on the other hand 'control over agricultural patronage in the districts was maintained by Congress supporters among the local landed elites, who naturally favoured themselves and their closest allies in distributing inputs and credits'.[167] Till the late 1960s, the middle class peasantry expressed its hostility towards Congress largely by supporting independent candidates (like Masood's father) who received an average of 20% of the vote in election after election until 1967. They then shifted to the BKD. Indeed, the Congress vote fell by only 10% in 1969 and 1974.[168] Similarly, the Jana Sangh declined only marginally from 21.7% to 18% between 1967 and 1969. Thus the BKD did not grow at the expense of other parties. The smaller socialist parties comparatively suffered more (the PSP fell from 4% to 1.7% and the SSP from 10% to 8% between 1967 to 1969). Apart from independent candidates, the socialist parties had indeed been the only ones to receive a proportionately higher vote from the low castes.[169]

The election results in Meerut district for the UP legislative assembly provides a good illustration of this process. While Congress declined by 10% between 1967 and 1969 and the Jana Sangh by only 4%, the BKD succeeded in gaining 36% of the valid votes, largely because of the declining influence of the independents (who had already dropped from 24% to 5% in 1967) and the Socialists, who declined from 16% to 6% between 1967 and 1969.[170] Jagpal Singh

[167] Brass, 'The politicisation of the peasantry in a North Indian State – Part 2', *JPS*, 8 (1), Oct. 1980, p. 31.

[168] Brass, 'The politicisation of the peasantry in a North India State – Part 1', *JPS*, 7 (4), July 1980, p. 410.

[169] Brass, 'Uttar Pradesh' in Weiner (ed.), *State politics in India*, Princeton University Press, 1968, p. 86.

[170] Singh, *Capitalism and Dependence*, op. cit., p. 130.

also shows that in Meerut district, the Lok Dal – Charan Singh's party in the early 1980s – was supported by middle and rich peasants, most of them Jats.[171] However, 'just before 1969 elections he [had] accepted the need for ceiling on landholdings and redistribution of land and it was included in the election manifests of BKD'.[172] Such a move, which was certainly intended to broaden the base of the party, helped Charan Singh to mend fences with the Socialists – their social support bases partly overlap and were partly complementary.

In the late 1960s, the electoral success of the Socialists in Bihar and Charan Singh in Uttar Pradesh reflected the growing mobilisation of the middle peasantry from the intermediate and low castes, emerging groups that the Congress ignored at its own peril. The Socialists and Charan Singh represented two different political traditions. The former's strategy for social emancipation, which was first articulated by Lohia, put a strong emphasis on caste. Like Ambedkar, Lohia regarded caste as the basic unit of Indian society and amended his Marxist views accordingly. His aim was to encourage the coalescence of the lower castes in order to destroy the upper castes' domination. Paradoxically, he tried to promote equality by manipulating caste categories. Charan Singh, on the other hand, focused on *kisan* identity. He tried to promote a new rural solidarity in order to subsume caste and class divisions. This *modus operandi* reflected his own quest for power since the crystallisation of a cleavage between urban and rural India would enable him to mobilise a majority of Indian society behind him.

These two strategies gained momentum in the 1960s and 1970s in North India but they were not novel. In fact, Socialist quota politics used the reservation policy categories implemented by the state. Lohia was in the footsteps of the Justice Party, except that he did not imbue the lower castes with any ethnic identity and nor did he use the notion of Non-Brahmins that the British had introduced but rather that of 'Backward Classes' that had been institutionalised by the 1950 Constitution and popularised by the Kalelkar Commission. In fact, the Socialist success of the late 1960s in North India occurred in the wake of the mobilisation that the AIBCF had orchestrated to implement the Kalelkar Commission Report. Charan

[171] Ibid., pp. 132–5.
[172] Ibid., p. 127.

Singh's tactics were also rooted in Jat political culture. The industriousness of this caste prepared the ground for such developments as early as the 1920s when Chhotu Ram created *kisan* politics in Punjab. Either in Punjab or in Uttar Pradesh, this political culture had affinities with the Jat ethos of the peasant-proprietor.

In this chapter, I have identified quota politics with Bihar and *kisan* politics with Uttar Pradesh because these states and these strategies were closely associated with their respective locales but Lohia was active in UP, his birthplace, and *kisan* politics was also present in Bihar, especially among the Bhumihars, a caste whose characteristics are reminiscent of the Jats of UP. In fact, Swami Sahajanand implemented this very same strategy almost as early as Chhotu Ram in Bihar.[173]

The contrast between quota politics and *kisan* politics does not

[173] See Walter Hauser, *Sahajanand on Agricultural Labour and the Rural Poor*, Delhi, Manohar, 1994. Born in Ghazipur District (eastern UP) in 1889, Swami Sahajanand took the vow of renunciation in 1907 but remained involved in the promotion of his caste's interests through the Bhumihar Brahman Mahasabha with which he was associated till the 1920s. Like the Jats, the Bhumihars are a dominant caste in several parts of East UP and Bihar where they own much land and till it too. And like the Jats, they were first involved in a Sanskritisation process, claiming Brahmin descent, a status the British recognised in the 1911 census. (E.A.H. Blunt, *The Caste System of Northern India*, op. cit., p. 227) Swami Sahajanand first pursued this Sanskritisation path but in a slightly different way since he claimed that in the old time 'agriculture was the Chief occupation of the Vaishyas [the merchant caste]'. (W. Hauser (ed.), *Sahajamand*, op. cit., p.13) However, Sahajanand gradually distanced himself from caste associations and paid more attention to the peasant as a socio-economic category, so much so he played a key role in the establishment of the *kisan sabhas* of Bihar in the 1930s:

> We have seen an effort for some time, both directly and indirectly, to confuse the movement of agricultural labourers with the caste movement of the socially most depressed members of the society [. . .] The one unfortunate consequence of this development has been that the basic problems of the agricultural labourers have been ignored and in their place only some broad questions have been raised. This had limited to a few particular castes what is a large and complex range of issues involving all *khet mazdoors.* (Ibid., p. 73)

As Walter Hauser points out in his introduction to his translation of Sahajanand's 1941 book, *Khet Mazdoor*, this expression, *khet mazdoor* and *kisan*

need to be exaggerated either. These two routes had parallel objectives: they aimed at dislodging the upper caste urban elite from the

are used interchangeably by Sahajanand, and he employs 'the term *kisan* in a general sense in referring to both peasants and agricultural labourers'. (Ibid., p. 6) His definition of *kisan* is indeed encompassing:

> Generally, only those whose chief means of livelihood is agriculture should be called kisans, which means that those who are not primarily dependent on agriculture cannot make this claim [. . .]. But that person whose family's principal means of livelihood is labour, though generally not regarded as a *kisan*, should not be taken out of the category (*shreni*) of *kisan* so long as he subsists by working at least in the field of petty landholders (*chote mote khetihar*) and does not work on vast plantations or large farms. The sum and substance is that so long as there is any hope of acquiring even some small plot of land and subsisting by cultivating that land, he can be called *kisan*. (Ibid., pp. 54–5).

Even the agricultural labourers who have no land but hope to acquire some in the future are *kisans* according to this definition. Obviously, Sahajanand who represents the upper caste rural elite tries to design a social category that this elite could mobilise for promoting its own interests – under the garb of advocating the common interests of the *kisans*. He admitted that quite candidly when he wrote:

> The reason for considering them (the labourers) as *kisans* has to do with the issue of their 'organisation' and movement. We must think of them as *kisans* so that their movement rather than being organised as a labour movement be organised like that of the *kisans* and only to gather with the *kisans*. (Ibid., p. 62)

As a result, Sahajanand exhorts the farmers to 'treat the agricultural labourers on the basis of equality and brotherhood'. (Ibid., pp. 92–3) But this equality is spelled out in rather odd terms since he describes the labourers as 'literally the arms and legs of the *kisans*'. (Ibid., p. 93). Such a metaphor harks back to the organicist *imaginaire* sustaining the caste system. Indeed, Sahajanand's view of the peasantry is far from egalitarian and the solidarity between its components are bound to be limited. For instance, he is opposed to any land reform:

> When the *kisan* himself is dying and not only grasping every inch of his land, but also feverishly searching out for more land, then how can he lend his ears to the plea of conveying land to the *khet mazdoors*? (in ibid., p. 96)

For Sahajanand, the solution to the landlessness of the labourers lay in the increase of the land under cultivation and the modernisation of agriculture. This process will deprive half of the labourers from their job but they 'will find employment in new industries and workshops' because the 'full introduction

sites of power. Both were power-oriented. That was explicit in the case of quota politics since the empowerment of the lower castes was a recurring claim and in the case of *kisan* politics it was clear from Charan Singh's ambitions. This is the main reason why the Socialists and Charan Singh joined hands in the 1970s, preparing the ground for a larger coalition which culminated in the Janata Party.

---

of scientific methods in agriculture means that there will need to be a large number of new factories to produce the necessary tools and equipment for engaging agriculture. (Ibid., p. 101)

Therefore, Sahajanand tries to enrol the labourers in the *kisan* movement – the Kisan Sabha at least – but he is not interested in taking up their claims (regarding land redistribution for instance). He only aims at having them supporting the demand of the peasant proprietors, who according to him have distinctively common interests, such as the development of irrigation. (Ibid., p. 96)

The peasant proprietor is Sahajanand's role model, hence his rather romantic view of the *kisan*. Sahajanand established a mystique of the peasant almost at the same time as Chhotu Ram in Punjab. He wrote, for instance: 'The *kisan* of course carries on his cultivation with his bullocks and other animals. He loves them very much unless and until he has fed the cattle he will not eat himself. He may go without food but his cattle can never go hungry.' (Ibid., p. 93) Sahajanand candidly admitted once that he had set up the Kisan Sabha 'to get the grievances of the Kisans redressed by mere agitation and propaganda and thus to eliminate all chances of clashes between the *Kisans* and *zamindars* which seemed imminent [. . .] and thus threatened to destroy all the all round unity so necessary to achieve freedom. Thus I began the organised Kisan Sabha as a staunch [class?] collaborator.' (Cited in L. Singh, 'The Bihar Kisan Sabha Movement – 1933–1939', *Social Scientist*, 20 (5–6), May–June 1992, p. 29)

9

THE QUEST FOR POWER AND THE FIRST JANATA GOVERNMENT

Far from being mutually exclusive, quota politics and *kisan* politics have many ideological affinities and areas of overlap. They try to promote the interests of *roughly* the same groups, yet they regard them from two different viewpoints: as castes or as peasants. The adverb 'roughly' needs to be emphasised because quota politics is more concerned with the OBCs and – to a lesser extent – the Scheduled Castes, who are generally small peasants or labourers, whereas *kisan* politics focuses on intermediate castes (like the Jats) and OBCs who own land, as small or middle peasants but, sometimes, as well-off farmers too. The small and middle peasants from the OBCs represent the social intersection of these two constituencies. They formed an important and growing group in the 1970s and Charan Singh and the Socialists soon realised that it might well be the pivot of a larger coalition which could vote them to power.

The quest for power, here, refers to the personal ambition of leaders such as Charan Singh but also to the empowerment agenda of the lower castes. It was the root-cause of the merger of a section of the Socialists and the BKD and, to a lesser extent, of the formation of the Janata Party. By appointing the Mandal Commission, the Janata government showed that the proponents of *kisan* politics were also prepared to rally around quota politics.

The BLD: a joint venture

Several individual careers bear testimony of the porosity between *kisan* politics and quota politics. In addition to the case of Mulayam Singh Yadav, Satpal Malik exemplifies the first Socialists who became Charan Singh's supporters. Malik was the son of a Jat *zamindar* 'owning a big patch of land but cultivating it himself'.[1] He was

[1] Interview with Satpal Malik, 25 Oct. 1998, New Delhi. Malik's father was

inspired by Lohia while he was a student and later at Meerut College because 'Lohia was the centre for anti-establishment thinking in North India' and 'a bridge between Gandhi and Marx'.[2] Malik was president of the student union of Meerut College in 1965–9 and took part in many agitations, some of which landed him to jail. In 1969 he was offered a ticket for the Assembly elections by the district president of the BKD; he declined the offer because 'Charan Singh was not our ideal, as socialists. The socialists wanted land revenue to be abolished. Charan Singh opposed it.' In 1973 Charan Singh approached Malik directly because he thought they had much in common including an Arya Samajist background. Malik, who was to become a minister in V.P. Singh's government, turned out to be more responsive this time and joined the BKD.

In the late 1960s and early 1970s the socialists were in disarray. Lohia died in 1967 and his lieutenants fought each other. The faction of Madhu Limaye and George Fernandes – which was especially strong in Maharashtra – wanted to drop Lohia's policy of non-Congressism and merge with the PSP (which had already negotiated seat adjustments with Congress) whereas the faction led by Raj Narain was willing to pursue the 'non-congressism' line and opposed merger with the PSP. This faction was especially strong in Uttar Pradesh, Raj Narain's home state.[3] Raj Narain, a Bhumihar by caste, played a leading role in the *rapprochement* with Charan Singh. Associated with the CSP since its inception in 1934, he had left Congress in 1958 to join the PSP and became chairman of the Socialist Party in 1961. Having followed Lohia, he became general secretary of the SSP. The Indian *Who's Who* mentions that he was 'imprisoned 58 times for a period totalling about 15 years in connection with student's and socialist movements'[4] and that he 'invariably found himself at the centre of controversy and agitations'.[5] Raj Narain, indeed,

---

a freedom fighter from Meerut district. His anti-British activities were such that he was disowned by his family and had to leave his village.

[2] Ibid.

[3] Brass, 'Leadership conflict and the disintegration of the Indian socialist movement', op. cit., p. 162.

[4] *Sixth Lok Sabha Who's Who – 1977*, New Delhi: Lok Sabha Secretariat, 1977, p. 479.

[5] G. Singh (ed.), *India's Who's Who Year Book 1977–78*, New Delhi: Alfa Publications, (n.d.), p. 27.

epitomises the propensity of Indian socialists to agitate and debate – including among themselves, and not necessarily on substantial issues. (The proliferation of factions in socialist politics is largely the result of this tendency.)

Raj Narain had few if any ideological affinities with Charan Singh – except that the Bhumihars of East UP (he was from Varanasi district) were almost in the same position as the Jats of West UP. But he regarded the BKD as a good ally against Congress in order to win power. Charan Singh did not appreciate the socialists' mentality. According to Malik, 'he was afraid that he had to follow their ways. He was not for demonstrations every day and this and that'.[6] But Charan Singh knew that the social base of the Socialists and of his own party overlapped and in any case he needed allies against the Congress party.

Under Raj Narain's and Charan Singh's influence, in 1974 the SSP and BKD merged to form the Bharatiya Lok Dal (BLD – Indian People, Party) with Charan Singh as President. Soon after, the Swatantra Party also merged with the BLD, even though this liberal party did not share any social or peasant-oriented concerns since it had emerged in the late 1950s as the mouthpiece of business and landlord interests against Nehru's economic policy.[7] Obviously, Charan Singh was eager to make his party grow by any means, to build a political force which could dislodge Congress and serve his personal ambitions.[8]

Even before the formation of the BLD, the BKD had adopted some aspects of quota politics. For instance, it had proposed that 20% of unskilled jobs in all factories both in the public and private sector should be reserved for Scheduled Castes.[9] It had also 'agreed to reservations of jobs for Backward Castes in 1971 much against Charan Singh's own inner urge'.[10] In 1974 the party's manifesto for the Uttar Pradesh elections contained a revealing paragraph on this question:

> While the socially and educationally backward classes, other than Scheduled Tribes and castes, both Hindu and Muslim, constituted more than half of

[6] Interview with Satpal Malik.

[7] H.L. Erdman, *The Swatantra Party and India Conservatism*, Cambridge University Press, 1967.

[8] 'Charan Singh, for power, could do anything', according to Satpal Malik.

[9] An observer, *Who is a casteist?*, op. cit., p. 54.

[10] Ibid., p. 62.

our people, they have little or no place in the political and administrative map of the country. [. . .] While, therefore, *BKD regards any kind of reservation as a vicious principle*, it has, at long last, come to the conclusion that there is no way out but that a share in Government jobs, say 25 percent, be reserved for young men coming from these classes, as recommended by the Backward Classes Commission . . .[11]

The alliance between the socialist agenda based on caste politics and reservations and the proponents of *kisan* politics was fostered by the JP movement. While many other forces – including the Hindu nationalists – took part in it, the socialists were well represented in this movement partly because its epicentre was in Bihar, their own stronghold.

Charan Singh, in stark contrast, 'was not very enthused with it. He said that it would lead us to anarchy. He was not very happy with all this disorder'.[12] According to Satpal Malik, 'he had told that, had Indira Gandhi made him Home Minister he would have dealt with this JP movement'.[13] He was, indeed, prepared to join Congress in 1975, had the Prime Minister 'changed some of her colleagues and policies'.[14] But nothing of the kind happened and the socialists were exerting more and more influence over the BLD – so much so that 'Charan Singh was afraid that the Socialists eventually dominate his party'[15] and the JP Movement at large. These socialists were still promoting quota politics. Madhu Limaye, as convenor of the JP Movement Programme Committee in 1975, drafted a document where one could read:

Caste hierarchy based on birth is the biggest obstacle in the path of achieving social equality. In an unequal society, the doctrine of judicial equality and equal opportunity cannot by itself remove caste disabilities. The doctrine of preferential opportunity, therefore, had to be invoked in order to enable the backward sections to come up to the level of the upper castes. Reservation in the services that we have today have not enabled us to overcome the disabilities from which our suppressed communities suffer. [. . .] This must change, and these people and other backward classes should be enabled to

[11] Cited in ibid., p. 62.
[12] Interview with S. Malik.
[13] Ibid.
[14] Ibid.
[15] Ibid.

secure, through preferential opportunities and reservation, the substance of power.[16]

Limaye emphasised the empowerment dimension of affirmative action schemes the same way his mentor, Lohia, had done. There was little room left for *kisan* politics in this 'programme'. During the Emergency, however, Charan Singh re-established some of his influence. He cashed in on his own image as the main architect of unity among the Indian opposition which, since the formation of the BLD in 1974, he had striven hard to achieve by merging parties together – as much as he could under his chairmanship.

The creation on the Janata Party resulted from the merger of the BLD, the Jana Sangh, the Socialist Party, the Congress (O) and the Congress for Democracy – the product of a break-away faction of Congress led by Jagjivan Ram. Charan Singh could not dominate it – largely because other leaders like Morarji Desai, the Prime Minister, were wary of his personal ambitions – but the party further promoted the combination of quota politics and *kisan* politics already initiated by the BLD.

The Janata experiment

In 1977 the Janata Party election manifesto promised a 'policy of special treatment' and even a 'New Deal for weaker sections'. If voted to power it would 'reserve between 25% and 33% of all appointments to government service for the backward classes, as recommended by the Kalelkar Commission'.[17] However, most of the manifesto's promises were addressed to the *kisans.* One of the party's objectives was to narrow down the 'rural-urban disparities' by giving 'the farmer [. . .] remunerative prices'. The Janata Party did not speak about land reform but about 'agrarian reform', which should be covering 'tenurial relationships, ownerships and consolidation of holdings' and abolish landlordism.[18] Moreover, Charan Singh, as Union Home

[16] M. Limaye, 'Socio-economic Programme of JP Movement' in S. Mohan *et al.* (eds), *Evolution of Socialist Policy in India*, op. cit., p. 314.

[17] 'The 1977 Janata Party Election Manifesto', Appendix IV to J.A. Naik, *The Great Janata Revolution*, New Delhi: S. Chand, 1977, p. 157.

[18] Ibid., p. 149. On the top of this *kisan* discourse, the manifesto promised to launch a 'New village Movement' which was intended to 'bring new life, hope

Minister in Morarji Desai's government, regarded the 'three decades of Congress rule in post-Independence India as essentially elitist and urban oriented' and considered that the Janata Party had to maintain 'its live-links with the villages, with agriculture, with cottage and village industries, and generally with the uplift of our *kisans*'.[19]

Two major components of the Janata, the former Congress(O) of Prime Minister Morarji Desai and the Hindu nationalist Jana Sangh 'were unwilling to concede primacy' to Charan Singh.[20] He was expelled from the government because of the way he had criticised the Cabinet's weakness *vis-à-vis* Indira Gandhi (who, according to him, should have been tried for atrocities committed during the Emergency) and, more importantly, because of his attempt at destabilising Desai – whose post he coveted (he had accused his son, Kanti Desai, of corruption, for instance). Charan Singh organised a huge '*kisan* rally' attended by 5 million farmers in Delhi in December 1978 and he was re-inducted in the government as Deputy Prime Minister and Minister of Finance soon after.[21] His 'kulak budget', of 1979 to use the media's catch phrase, reduced indirect taxes on mechanical tillers, diesel for electric water pumps and chemical fertilisers by 50% in some cases; it lowered interest rates for rural loans; increased subsidies for small-scale irrigation; and earmarked funds for rural electrification and grain-storage facilities.[22] Charan Singh also succeeded in transferring indirect taxes on chemical fertilisers from producers to manufacturers and in raising sugarcane prices.[23] The Janata experiment was too short-lived to implement all these measures but Charan Singh had unquestionably become the rallying point of the *kisans.* During the Janata era, he raised the peasants' concerns in such a way that they became central to political debate – so much so that

---

and dignity to rural India seen as viable communities of functional rural clusters. . .' (ibid., p. 155)

[19] Charan Singh, 'The Emergence of Janata Party – A Watershed in Post-Independence Politics' in S. Mohan *et al.* (eds), *Evolution of Socialist Policy*, op. cit., p. 325 and p. 327.

[20] A. Varshney, *Democracy, Development, and the Countryside – Urban, Rural Struggles in India*, Cambridge University Press, 1995, p. 104. Most of this paragraph draws from this book.

[21] Ibid.

[22] Ibid., p. 105.

[23] P. Brass, 'Congress, the Lok Dal, and the Middle-Peasant Castes', op. cit., pp. 14–15.

they were taken up by farmers' movements in most states,[24] among which the Bharatiya Kisan Union of Tikait (a Jat who had been close to Charan Singh – the moving spirit behind the BKU) and the Shetkari Sangathana of Sharad Joshi in Maharashtra were noteworthy.

While Charan Singh tried to promote the *kisans*' interests, he was less active in so far as the reservation policy was concerned. As Deputy Prime Minister he suggested to the government that 25% of administrative posts should be reserved for OBCs[25] but he did not push the issue further, perhaps because it aroused too many objections within the Janata. Regarding reservations for the Scheduled Castes, he considered that they should be withdrawn so far as promotions were concerned because they had led 'to heart-burning and great inefficiency in services'.[26] And he added 'Nor should there be any reservation in education, particularly of Medicine and Engineering'.

However, 1977 was a milestone in the quest for power of the lower castes and the *kisan*, as evident from the social profile of MPs who had been returned in the Hindi belt, all of whom – except three – were from the Janata Party, stark evidence indeed that the Congress party had been routed.

The comparison between the 1977 figures and those of the previous elections – including 1971, when the Congress had been so successful – suggests interesting conclusions. Even though the change is not dramatic, one can observe obvious contrasts: for the first time, upper caste MPs represent fewer than 50% of Hindi belt MPs. Correspondingly, he share of intermediate castes and OBCs increased from 14.2% to 20%; however the Janata Party remained much more elitist than its parliamentary group, as evident from the caste background of the members of its National Executive (see Tables 9.1 and 9.2).

The overwhelming dominance of the upper castes – and, among them of the Brahmins – in the Janata Party National Executive was mainly due to the social profile of the ex-Congress (O) and ex-Jana Sangh. Besides the resilience of the upper castes in the party apparatus, the rise of the OBCs was unevenly distributed state-wise, as evident from the social composition of the assemblies of Madhya Pradesh,

[24] For details see T. Brass (ed.), *New Farmers' Movements in India*, London: Frank Cass, 1995.

[25] Brass, 'Chaudhuri Charan Singh', op. cit., p. 2089.

[26] Cited in Hasan, 'Patterns of Resilience', op. cit., p. 191.

Table 9.1. CASTE AND COMMUNITY OF HINDI BELT MPs, 1971 AND 1977

	1971	*1977*
Upper castes	*53.9*	*48.2*
Brahmin	28.31	16.37
Rajput	13.7	13.27
Bhumihar	2.28	3.1
Banya/Jain	5.48	8.4
Kayasth	2.28	3.1
Other	1.83	3.98
Intermediate castes	*4.11*	*6.64*
Jat	4.11	5.75
Maratha		0.89
OBC	*10.1*	*13.3*
Yadav	6.39	6.19
Kurmi	2.28	3.98
Panwar	0.46	
Other	0.92	3.09
Scheduled Castes	*18.26*	*17.7*
Scheduled Tribes	*7.31*	*7.08*
Muslim	*4.57*	*5.75*
Other minorities	*0.46*	*0.44*
Sadhu	*0.46*	
Unidentified		*0.89*
Total	*100* *N=219*	*100* *N=226*

Source: Fieldwork.

Rajasthan and Bihar. In Rajasthan and Madhya Pradesh, two states where the ex-Jana Sangh, an upper-caste-dominated party, was the largest component of the Janata, the OBCs represented respectively 15% and 7% of the MLAs, whereas the upper castes formed 44% to 49% of the assembly. Upper caste domination was even more evident in the state governments since the upper castes represented 62–69% of the ministers. In UP their percentage was even higher, but the share of the OBC reached 17.4%. By contrast, in Bihar, the percentage of upper caste MLAs fell to 35.3% and that of OBCs rose to 27.7%. More important, the low castes represented 38% of the government, 9 percentage points more than the upper castes.

Table 9.2. CASTE AND COMMUNITY
JANATA PARTY NATIONAL EXECUTIVE

	1978
Upper castes	*72.09*
Brahmin	39.53
Rajput	4.65
Banya/Jain	13.95
Kayasth	6.98
Sindhi	2.33
Other	4.65
Intermediate castes	*4.66*
Jat	2.33
Patidar	2.33
OBC	*9.32*
Ezhava	2.33
Kurmi	2.33
Nair	2.33
Yadav	2.33
Scheduled Castes	*4.65*
Muslim	*4.65*
Unidentified	*4.65*
Total	*100* *N=43*

Source: Fieldwork

These figures largely explain why the first attempts at re-launching the reservation policy took place in Bihar. The Janata Party had won the state elections throughout the Hindi belt in June 1977 and since the ex-BLD was stronger in Uttar Pradesh, Bihar and Haryana, whereas the ex-Jana Sangh was well entrenched in Madhya Pradesh, Rajasthan and Himachal Pradesh, the former obtained the Chief Ministership of the first three states and the latter that of the last three states.[27]

In Bihar, the Janata Party was dominated by S.N. Sinha, a Congress (O) Rajput leader, and Karpoori Thakur, who, after the SVD episode, had been Chairman of the SSP and Deputy Chief Minister in 1970–2. The former was supported by Rajput MLAs, who

[27] P. Brass, 'Congress, the Lok Dal, and the middle-peasant castes : An analysis of the 1977 and 1980 Parliamentary elections in Uttar Pradesh', *Pacific Affairs*, 54, 1 (spring 1981), p. 14.

Table 9.3. CASTE AND COMMUNITY OF THE MLAs RETURNED IN BIHAR, RAJASTHAN AND MADHYA PRADESH, 1977

	Bihar	*Rajasthan*	*MP*
Upper castes	*37.2*	*43.9*	*46.6*
Brahmin	5.8	12.5	21.3
Rajput	16.6	13	10.6
Bhumihar	11.4	–	–
Banya/Jain	–	15.8	10
Kayasth	3.4	1.1	3.1
Khattri	–	0.5	1.3
Other	–	1	0.3
Intermediate castes	–	*14.5*	*0.9*
Maratha	–	–	0.9
Jat	–	14.5	–
OBC	*29.6*	*7*	*14.3*
Banya	2.5	–	–
Jat	–	–	0.3
Yadav	15.7	1.5	1.6
Kurmi	3.7	–	3.1
Koeri	4.9	–	–
Lodhi	–	–	0.6
Teli	–	–	1.6
Panwar	–	–	2.2
Gujar	–	4	–
Other	2.8	1.5	4.9
Scheduled Castes	*13.8*	*17*	*13.4*
Scheduled Tribes	*8.6*	*7*	*20.4*
Muslim	*7.7*	*5*	*0.9*
Sikh	–	*2*	*0.3*
Unidentified/Other	*2.1*	*3*	*3.1*
Total	*100* *N=324*	*100* *N=200*	*100* *N=320*

Sources: For Bihar, adapted from H.W. Blair, 'Rising Kulaks and Backward Classes in Bihar', op. cit., p. 67; for Rajasthan and Madhya Pradesh, fieldwork.

represented about 21% of the MLAs, and the latter by the low castes, who had been elected in large numbers since their share in the Vidhan Sabha had jumped from 29.5 to 38.5% of the total between 1975

Table 9.4. CASTES AND COMMUNITIES IN THE GOVERNMENTS OF BIHAR, RAJASTHAN, UTTAR PRADESH AND MADHYA PRADESH, 1977

	Bihar	*Rajasthan*	*UP*	*MP*
Upper castes	*29*	*62.6*		*68.8*
Brahmin	*n.a.*	31.3		37.5
Rajput	*n.a.*	12.5		15.6
Banya/Jain	*n.a.*	18.8		9.4
Kayasth	*n.a.*			6.3
Intermediate castes	*n.a.*	*12.5*		
Jats	*n.a.*	12.5		
OBC	*38*		*17.4*	*6.2*
Yadav	*n.a.*		13.1	3.1
Teli	*n.a.*		–	3.1
Lodhi	*n.a.*		4.3	
Lower Backward	*4*			
SC (and ST for Bihar)	*17*	*18.8*	*8.7*	*9.4*
Scheduled Tribes	*n.a.*			*9.4*
Muslim (and Bengali for Bihar)	*13*	*6.3*	*4.3*	*6.25*
Total	*100*	*100*	*100*	*100*
	N=n.a.	*N=16*	*N=23*	*N=32*

Sources: As for Table 9.3. For UP, C.L. Sathi, *Pichhre vargon ka arakshan*, Lucknow: Bahujan Kalyan Publishers, 1982, p. 118.

and 1977. Among them, the Yadavs were the most successful with 20% of the MLAs (as against 11% in 1975).[28] Even though he belonged to the Most Backward Castes, Thakur was recognised as their representative by the Yadavs and even though he was a former socialist, Charan Singh chose him as his nominee. Thakur's government, for the first time in the state, had more OBC (42%) than upper caste (29%)[29] ministers but among the latter the Lower Backwards were very few compared to the Yadavs who got the lion's share. After laborious debates within the Janata Party, where the upper castes showed much reluctance towards any ambitious reservation scheme, in November 1978 Thakur announced the following quotas, which relied on the classification in OBCs and MBCs of the Mungeri Lal Commission, in the state administration:

[28] H. Blair, 'Rising Kulaks and Backward Classes in Bihar', op. cit., p. 69.
[29] Ibid.

	%
Other backward classes	8
Most backward classes	12
Scheduled Castes	14
Scheduled Tribes	10
Women	3
Economically backward	3

As noticed by R.K. Hebsur in the second Backward Classes Commission Report, 'Thakur was only pursuing the Lohia line of further mobilising the backward classes',[30] even if he amended this approach by following the Mungeri Lal Commission and distinguished MBCs from OBCs. According to Blair, the new reservation policy concerned only 1,800 jobs per annum (since the administration recruited 9,000 new employees each year) and was therefore a 'symbolic' measure.[31] However, Frankel underlines that the new quotas would have affected the Kayasths who represented 40% of the upper layer of the state administration.[32] And symbols are nonetheless important: even if it did not damage the upper castes' interests to a great extent, Thakur's scheme called the social order into question. This is probably the main reason why upper caste students demonstrated violently against the new reservation policy, burning buses and attacking trains – even to the extent of having one derailed. Government property and buildings were devastated. The agitation was supported, behind the scenes, by the former Jana Sangh which disapproved of the policy's impact on its upper caste electoral basis and of the fact that it divided along caste lines Hindu society, the constituency it was anxious to represent. The ex-Jana Sangh therefore withdrew its support to Thakur on 19 April 1979 and provoked the fall of the Bihar government with the help of a group of Scheduled Castes MLAs close to Jagjivan Ram, the then Deputy Prime Minister.

The *rapprochement* between the ex-Jana Sangh and Scheduled Castes MLAs was partly due to tactical calculations since the former

[30] R.K. Hebsur, 'Reactions to the Reservations for Other Backward Classes' in *Report of the Backward Classes Commission – Second Part*, New Delhi: Government of India, 1980, p. 157. However, the socialists themselves had become divided over the reservation issue with Ramanand Tiwari leading the upper castes' opposition to positive discrimination.

[31] Blair, 'Rising Kulaks and Backward Classes in Bihar', op. cit., p. 66.

[32] Frankel, 'Caste, Land and Dominance in Bihar', op. cit., p. 110.

was prepared to support Jagjivan Ram's claim to the Prime Ministership in order to replace Desai. But this alliance also reflected the persistence of the pattern defined by Brass as a 'coalition of extremes'. The rise of the OBCs, that was epitomised by Thakur's reservation policy, worried the upper castes as much as the Scheduled Castes. In the village, the latter were often landless agricultural labourers working for Yadav or Kurmi farmers and therefore they had antagonistic class interests. In 1982, 96.7% of the Scheduled Castes had either no land or a miniscule holding.[33] The distribution of housing plots to these people and the establishment of minimum wages during the Emergency had made relations between labourers and farmers – whether from the OBCs or from upper castes – more tense. Conflicts arose, for instance, about wages.

In 1979, the toppling of Karpoori Thakur enabled a Scheduled Caste leader, Ram Sunder Das, to take over as Chief Minister but the upper caste members were in a majority in his government, 50% as against 20% of OBCs (and no MBCs).[34] In July 1979, this government amended Thakur's reservation policy in such a way as any recruitment of SC/ST, OBC and MBC candidate on a 'merit' basis would be deducted from the quotas. For instance, if 2% of MBC people joined the Bihar administration by passing the competitive examination for posts, which were not covered by the quota, this quota would be reduced in the same proportions. The same rule was to be applied for the other quotas.

A similar scenario unfolded in Uttar Pradesh where the large Janata Party victory enabled Charan Singh to appoint one of his lieutenants, Ram Naresh Yadav, as Chief Minister. Like Takur, Yadav was also a socialist. In his own words, he 'came in contact with Acharya Narendra Deva, the eminent socialist leader and thinker of the country during University life and dedicated himself to the cause of socialism'.[35] Like many socialists he became close to Charan Singh in the 1960s and 1970s and as Chief Minister implemented *kisan*-friendly policies by increasing the procurement price of wheat to

[33] In Uttar Pradesh, in 1981, 56.52% of the landless holdings were Scheduled Castes (Hasan, 'Patterns of resilience and change in Uttar Pradesh', op. cit., p. 169).

[34] Blair, op. cit., p. 9.

[35] G. Singh (ed.), *India's Who's Who and Year Book, 1977–78*, New Delhi: Alfa Publication, 1978, p. 29.

Rs 115[36] and supporting high prices for sugar cane, which had been affected by poor rains.[37] On the other hand, he paid great attention to the reservation policy. He did not implement the recommendations of the UP Backward Commission whose report, submitted in June 1977, provided for a 29.5% total reservation for OBCs and MBCs, because such a large quota – in addition to the 20% for the Scheduled Castes – would have been rejected by the upper castes, even within the Janata Party. Upper caste ministers still represented on overwhelming majority of the UP government (see table 9.4). In his Government Order of 20 August, 1977, Yadav provided for the following scheme of reservations for state services and for industrial training institutes:

	%
Other backward classes	15 in Class I, II and III
	10 in Class IV
Scheduled Castes	18
Scheduled Tribes	2
Physically handicapped	2
Dependants of freedom fighters	5
Ex-military officers	8

The new reservation policy met with strong protests throughout Uttar Pradesh. In some areas civil servants themselves took part in the agitation, which was marred by violence in the eastern districts.[38] As in Bihar, 'the Jana Sangh group articulated the disapproval of upper castes over the potential challenge to their primacy'[39] and withdrew its support in favour of Banarsi Das, of the Congress(O). Banarsi Das froze all the reservation schemes announced by Ram Varesh Yadav, Quotas were not complemented at a national level either.[40]

[36] K. Lieten, 'The Janata as a Continuity of the System', *Social Scientist*, Dec. 1980–Jan. 1981.

[37] *EPW*, 2 Dec. 1979.

[38] R.K. Hebsur, 'Reactions to the Reservations for Other Backward Classes' in *Report of the Backward Classes Commission – Second Part*, New Delhi: Government of India, 1980, p. 161, and Hasan, *The Quest for Power*, op. cit., p. 146.

[39] Ibid

[40] After he became Prime Minister, Charan Singh proposed to reserve 25% of central government jobs for the OBCs, a measure that had to be dropped after the President objected that the caretaker government had committed itself

The alliance strategy of the Socialists and Charan Singh bore fruit since it culminated in the formation of the Janata government, in which both groups played a pivotal role. The bad news, however, was that they could not gain power alone – they needed allies – and that the Janata government was too heterogeneous to implement a consistent policy regarding positive discrimination or the promotion of rural interests. Its socialist and BLD components tried to push through a programme of quota politics and *kisan* politics but the Congress(O) of Morarji Desai and the Jana Sangh were not prepared to let an over-ambitious Charan Singh occupy centre stage or allow these new reservations to reduce the proportion of the upper castes in the bureaucracy. The Hindu nationalist party, which was strongly associated with the urban, upper caste middle class resisted any pro-peasant and pro-OBC policies and feared that such moves would strengthen the BLD in North India, its own stronghold.

The tensions between the BLD and the Socialists on the one hand and the Congress(O) and the Jana Sangh on the other led to the schism of June 1979 when Charan Singh founded the Janata Party (S)[41] receiving Indira Gandhi's support to become Prime Minister. It was the first time that a non-upper caste and a rural leader occupied the post and in his speech on Independence Day, on 15 August 1979, he accordingly focused on rural issues,[42] even if he tried to correct the anti-city portrait that the media were assiduously painting of him at that time. The appointment of Charan Singh generated a great deal of excitement among the *kisans* and the OBCs. The OBC leader Ram Lakhan Yadav, commenting upon this event, considered that 'a great enlightenment came to the Backward classes' and that it 'combined all Backward Classes together'.[43] This enthusiasm was short-lived

---

not to indulge in decisions 'which might amount to electoral initiatives'. (Galanter, *Competing Equalities*, op. cit., p. 187)

[41] 'S' for secular because he reproached the Janata regime for promoting Hindu communalism by accepting Jana Sangh leaders who pay allegiance to the RSS. On this 'dual membership' issue, see, Jaffrelot, *The Hindu nationalist movement and Indian politics*, op. cit., ch. 8.

[42] He said, for instance that he regarded it as a priority 'to establish cottage industries in the villages'. ('Charan's Singh's Speech on Independence Day', reproduced in R.K. Hooda, *Man of the Masses – Chaudhary Charan Singh, First Peasant Prime Minister of India*, New Delhi: Chaudhary Hari Ram and Sons, 1979, p. 77)

[43] Cited in Chaudhury, op. cit., p. 217.

since the Congress withdrew its support even before the vote of confidence and the Lok Sabha had to be dissolved, the 1980 elections bringing Indira Gandhi back to power. In states like Uttar Pradesh and Bihar the Congress largely owed its success to the reconstitution of the old coalition regrouping upper castes (mainly Brahmins), Scheduled Castes and Muslims. The OBCs were sidelined once again. In Uttar Pradesh, the Congress party nominated 120 Brahmins as against 26 OBCs for the elections to the Legislative Assembly.[44] Soon after returning to power in UP, the Congress removed in 1981 the age extension in favour of the OBCs applying for recruitment in the police. (The Janata Party government had increased by 5 years the age-limit for the OBCs). In Bihar, the Congress(I) highlighted its policy in favour of the landless labourers in 1975–7 to attract Scheduled Castes voters during its election campaign.[45] However, the return of the Congress did not mean that ideas instilled and the social dynamics of the Janata period would not one day re-emerge.

The Janata governments of Bihar and UP had failed to implement their reservation policies but their very attempt showed that quota politics was gaining momentum in North India. This trend was also well illustrated by the appointment (and then the report) of the second Backward Classes Commission. The North was becoming more conscious of the reservation issue. Charan Singh himself almost switched to this strategy, a move which represented one more step in the direction of the Socialists.

The Mandal Commission: the reservation issue revisited at the Centre

On 20 December 1978 the Prime Minister Morarji Desai announced the government's decision to appoint the second Backward Classes Commission, whose terms of references were close to those of the earlier one: it had to determine the criteria defining the OBCs and to recommend the measures, such as reservations in the administration, which could contribute to their social emancipation.[46] Twenty years after the appointment of the Kalelkar commission, the Centre re-launched quota politics. Desai might have done so reluctantly and

[44] An Observer, *Who is a casteist?*, op. cit., p. 42.

[45] Frankel, 'Castes, Land and Dominance in Bihar', op. cit., p. 115.

[46] *Report of the [second] Backward Classes Commission – First Part,* op. cit., p. vii.

with some after thoughts,[47] but the report of this Commission was to make a major impact. In contrast to the Kalelkar Commission, this body had no upper caste members but only OBCs,[48] of whom three out of five were MPs or ex-MPs. The Chairman of the Commission, Bin-dhyeshwari Prasad Mandal, as we know, was a Yadav who had been elected MP in Bihar in 1967 on a SSP ticket and who had been briefly its Chief Minister in 1968. He was an important figure in the Janata Party – in 1980 he had been a member of the party's Central Election Commission. Unsurprisingly, the 'Mandal Commission' advocated the Socialist policy of positive discrimination. Its report read:

> To treat unequals as equals is to perpetuate inequality. When we allow weak and strong to compete on an equal footing, we are loading the dice in favour of the strong and holding only a mock competition in which the weaker partner is destined to failure right from the start.[49]

In India, the Mandal report argued, the caste system was the root-cause of structural inequality and therefore notions of merit could not apply in the same way as they did in an individualistic society: it 'is an amalgam of native endowments and environmental privileges'.[50] The Mandal Commission had therefore no inhibition in recognising caste as the main factor in the backwardness of the OBCs: 'Caste is also a class of citizens and if the caste as a whole is socially and educationally backward, reservation can be made in favour of such a caste on the ground that it is a socially and educationally backward class of citizens within the meaning of Article 15(4)'.[51] Yet, the Commission did not regard caste as the sole criterion for the definition of the OBCs. In fact, it evolved an index based on eleven indicators subdivided into three categories – social, educational and economic. Three of the indicators were concerned with caste: whether the group was regarded as backward by others, whether it depended

[47] For Lal and Nair, Desai appointed the second Backward Classes Commission as 'the usual answer of most governments in India to silence strident demands without acceding to them' Lal and Nair, *Caste vs Caste*, op. cit., p. 90.

[48] One of them, Dina Bandhu Sahu had to resign on the ground of ill-health, but he was replaced by a Scheduled Castes former MP, L.R. Naik.

[49] Ibid., p. 21.

[50] Ibid., p. 23.

[51] Ibid., p. 62.

on manual labour and whether or not its members married at a young age. The three educational indicators tried to measure the proportion of children attending school and obtaining their matriculation. The four economic indicators concerned the family's assets, whether at least one quarter of the group had a *kuccha* (proper) house, whether they had easy access to water and whether they had taken out loans.[52] Ultimately social indicators were given heavier weighting than other criteria and thus the OBCs were defined as caste-groups. This is evident from Table 9.5 where the Commission ventured to present an overview of Indian society under the title 'Distribution of Indian Population by Caste and Religious Groups'.

The table was criticised by scholars because it drew on several sources (the 1931 census for the forward castes and the 1971 census for the SC/STs and the religious groups) and arrived at a figure of 52% for the OBCs through a roundabout route.[53] Yet it did for the first time provide a statistical straight-point which could be used for affirmative action and was not reliant only on caste criteria – economically disadvantaged Brahmin and Rajput sub-castes had been previously classified as OBCs for instance.[54]

After identifying the OBCs, the Mandal Commission recommended that 27% of posts in the administration and public sector should be reserved for them, a conclusion that reflected an Ambedkarite and Socialist-style approach to compensatory discrimination since the objective was to give the OBCs access to power, not jobs:

> It is not at all our contention that by offering a few thousands jobs to OBC candidates we shall be able to make 52% of the Indian population as forward.

[52] Ibid., p. 52.

[53] P. Radhakrishnan wrote for instance that the Mandal Commission's 'estimate of the OBC population is a hotpotch, arrived at by subtracting from 100 the population percentages for SCs, STs and non-Hindus (22.56 and 16.16 respectively) as per the 1971 Census, and the percentage for "forward Hindus" ' (17.58) as extrapolated from the incomplete 1931 Census, and adding to this derived sum (43.7) about half of the population percentage for non-Hindus (8.4)'. He also criticised the fact that for 'its "socio-educational survey", supposedly its most comprehensive inquiry, the Commission selected only two villages and one urban block from each district' (P. Radhakrishnan, 'Mandal Commission Report: A Sociological Critique' in Srinivas (ed.), *Caste – Its Twentieth Century Avatar*, op. cit., p. 207).

[54] For a list of these Brahmin and Rajput sub-castes see Prasad, *Reservational Justice*, op. cit., pp. 68–9.

Table 9.5. DISTRIBUTION OF INDIAN SOCIETY BY CASTE AND COMMUNITY ACCORDING TO MANDAL COMMISSION

	% of total population
Scheduled Castes and Scheduled Tribes	*22.56*
Scheduled Castes	15.05
Scheduled Tribes	7.51
Non-Hindu communities, religious groups	*16.16*
Muslims	11.19
Christians	2.16
Sikhs	1.67
Buddhists	0.67
Jains	0.47
Forward Hindu castes and communities	*17.58*
Brahmins (including Bhumihars)	5.52
Rajputs	3.9
Marathas	2.21
Jats	1
Vaishyas/Banyas	1.88
Kayasthas	1.07
Others	2
Remaining Hindu caste/groups to be treated as OBCs	*43.70**
(Religious groups which may also be treated as OBCs)	*(8.40)*
Total	*100*

*Derived figure.

Source: *Report of the Backward Classes Commission – First Part*, op. cit., p. 56.

But we must recognise that an essential part of the battle against social backwardness is to be fought in the minds of the backward people. In India Government service has always been looked upon as a symbol of prestige and power. By increasing the representation of OBCs in government services, we *give them an immediate feeling of participation in the governance of this country.* When a backward class candidate becomes a Collector or a Superintendent of Police, the material benefits accruing from his position are limited to the members of his family only. But the psychological spin off of this phenomenon is tremendous; the entire community of that backward class candidate feels socially elevated. Even when no tangible benefits flow to the community at large, the feeling that now it has its 'own man' *in the 'corridors of power'* acts as morale booster.[55]

[55] *Report of the [second] Backward Classes Commission – First Part*, op. cit., p. 57. Emphasis added.

The report modestly presents access to, and the exercise of, power from a psychological point of view but its ambitions were greater than that: it goes on to say that 'reservation will certainly erode the hold of the higher castes on the services',[56] and this was one of its objectives, albeit one balanced by the attention paid to education. In contrast to Lohia's reluctance to introduce reservation in schools and universities, the Mandal Commission Report recommended that 27% of 'seats should be reserved for OBC students in all scientific, technical and professional institutions run by the Central as well as State Governments'.[57] The Commission resigned itself to maximum quotas of 27% in order to remain within the limits of the 'law laid down in a number of Supreme Court judgements'[58] after the Balaji case.

When the North lags behind: reservation policies outside the Hindi Belt in the 1980s

The Mandal Commission prepared its report at a time when the states of South and West India were forging ahead with new reservations schemes. In the South, these developments were related to the rise to power of regional parties which often represented the lower castes, the DMK being a prime case in point. The All India Anna Dravida Munnetra Kazhagam (AIADMK) – a party born from a split of the DMK and which had gained influence over it – and the Telugu Desam Party emulated its strategy in the 1970s–1980s.

In 1978 the government of M.G. Ramachandran, the president of the AIADMK, decided to implement one of the recommendations of the Sattanathan Commission that had gone unheeded, namely to exclude from quotas OBCs whose income exceeded 9,000 rupees a year. This measure provoked vehement protests among the OBCs and it was apparently one of the reasons for the electoral setback of the AIADMK in 1980.[59] M.G. Ramachandran immediately revoked the decision and even raised the OBC quota from 31% to 50%. Upper castes members went to the Supreme Court which, in its judgement of 15, October 1982 asked the government to appoint a

[56] Ibid.

[57] Ibid., p. 59.

[58] Ibid., p. 58.

[59] Yadav, *India's Unequal Citizens*, op. cit., p. 134.

Commission. It recommended a quota of 32% for the OBCs so that total quotas whould not exceed 50% but M.G. Ramachandran preferred to bury the report.[60]

Andhra politics was even more clearly dominated by leaders advocating the cause of the low castes in the 1980s after the rise to power of the Telegu Desam Party, a regionalist organisation whose electoral basis largely consisted of OBCs. In 1983, shortly after its success in the state elections, Rama Rao, its founder-president and then Chief Minister, increased the OBC quota from 25% to 44% in the state administration. The High Court declared the decision invalid because the total quotas now exceeded 50%. Rama Rao withdrew his project, which triggered off violent street demonstrations from the OBCs,[61] evidence of their newly found self-assurance.

The OBCs had not only gained new assertiveness but had also been empowered to a certain extent. In 1982, they made up 28.6% of Andhra civil servants and were well represented in the entire administration, except among the IAS elite, the last stronghold of the Brahmins.[62] Ultimately they were to benefit substantially from reservations because of the political determination of the main parties but also because of a shift in attitude of the courts, an issue to which we return below.

In Gujarat, shortly after its return to power in 1980, the Congress appointed a second 'Backward Classes Commission' in order further to cultivate its low caste support. This Commission, in its report of 1983, recommended that caste be abandoned as a criterion for defining quotas and that the existing quota should be increased from 10% to 28%. Solanki kept the findings secret until January 1985 –

[60] Ibid., p. 135. The increase of the quotas granted to the OBCs in Tamil Nadu had already restricted the number of places available to Brahmins, who had either to opt for the private sector, or to migrate to the North or to go abroad (mostly to England or the United States) to forge a career in medicine or in engineering. After the introduction of quotas in the 1920s already, many Brahmins left for Bombay. (R.K. Hebsur, 'Reaction to the reservations for Other Backward Classes', Bombay, Tata Institute of Social Sciences 1980, in *Report of the Backward Classes Commission*, second part, vols III–VII, New Delhi: Government of India, 1980, pp. 147–50)

[61] P. Brass, *The New Cambridge History of India – The politics of India since independence*, Cambridge University Press, 1990, p. 212.

[62] G. Ram Reddy, 'The politics of accommodation – Class, caste and dominance in Andhra Pradesh', op. cit., pp. 300–2.

two months before the state elections – and then supported the increase in quotas up to 28% but without abandoning the caste criterion. He even appointed a new Commission in order to identify more 'backward castes'.[63] These decisions partly explain the excellent showing of the Congress (I) in the March 1985 state elections, after which Solanki formed a government in which fourteen ministers out of twenty were 'Kshatriyas'. This triggered off violent reactions from the upper castes. Their opposition to quotas had already been manifested in 1981 when riots had broken out – in particular in Ahmedabad – to protest against quotas granted since 1975 to Scheduled Castes in 'Medical Colleges'.[64] In fact, these quotas had remained unfulfilled: in 1979–80, Scheduled Castes and Scheduled Tribes students numbered only 507 out of 4,500 (instead of the nominated 945, according to the 10% quota) and in 1984, only 34% of seats reserved for the OBCs were effectively occupied.[65] The violent response of the upper caste seemed even less justified in 1985 when, once again, students were in the forefront of the protest. They formed the All Gujarat Education Reforms Committee and began attacking symbols of the state (bus stations, post-offices, schools . . .), forcing the cancellation of examinations. The High Court imposed a stay order on the implementation of the measures but violence continued unabated and on 5 July the deliberate derailment of a train, which injured more than 200 people, led Solanki to resign. His successor, Amarsingh Chaudhari cancelled the increase in the quotas and in June 1987 appointed a new Commission presided over by R.C. Mankad. Thus the 1985 riots (and their impact) revealed the limits of the reservation policy in Gujarat: in contrast with the South, positive discrimination measures were facing mounting opposition from the upper castes fearful of reduced opportunities and of a challenge to their pre-eminent status.

[63] U. Baxi, 'Reflections on the reservations crisis in Gujarat' in V. Das (ed.), *Mirrors of Violence: Communities, Riots and Survivors in South Asia*, Delhi: Oxford University Press, 1990, pp. 215–39.

[64] P. K. Bose, 'Social mobility and caste violence – A study of the Gujarat riots', *EPW*, (16) 18 April 1981, pp. 713–16

[65] I. P. Desai, 'Anti-reservation agitation and structure of Gujarat Society', *EPW*, May 1981, p. 821, and U. Baxi, 'Reflections on the reservations crisis', op. cit., p. 217.

The Lok Dal fighting for Mandal

It is in this context that the Mandal Commission Report was first discussed in the 1980s. Charan Singh had launched a new political party, the Lok Dal, soon before the 1980 elections, one of whose 'aims and objects' was to establish 'a socialist society, consistent with maintenance of individual freedom',[66] a good summary of the party's attempt to combine Lohia's legacy and *kisan* politics. Indeed, while Charan Singh was its president, its vice-president, Raj Narain, and its general secretary, Madhu Limaye, were both from socialist backgrounds, like many secretaries (such as Rabi Ray)[67] and members of the National Committee (such as Karpoori Thakur and George Fernandes).[68] Its National Executive Committee, in addition to Jat leaders (Satpal Malik and Devi Lal) comprised many OBC, mainly Yadavs, such as Hukum Deo Narain Yadav, Chandrajeet Yadav, Brahma Prakash Chaudhary and Sharad Yadav. Table 9.6 reveals that the Yadavs were the second largest group, after the Jats, in the Lok Dal National Executive in the 1980s. The Brahmins remained in large numbers, mainly because there were many Brahmins among the Socialists but they were no more numerous than the Yadavs in the mid- and late 1980s. In fact, the overall proportion of upper caste members of the Lok Dal National Executive declined from about one third to about 27% over the 1980s.

The 1980 election manifesto of the Lok Dal also combined the Socialist legacy and *kisan* politics. On the one hand it advocated farmer's interests: it pleaded for 'the replacement of farm tenancy by peasant-proprietorship' – which summarised what should be 'land reform' – and promised that, if the Lok Dal was voted to power, the state would 'intervene in the market to protect the farmer and ensure that he is not compelled to make distress sales' – not a word about landless labourers or those not engaged in commercial production.[69] On the other hand, the manifesto devoted a paragraph to the eradication of caste and went back to the old idea 'to give preference in

[66] See 'The Lok Dal' in A.M. Zaidi, *ARIPP-1979*, New Delhi: S.Chand, 1980, p. 385.

[67] Interview with Rabi Ray, New Delhi, 24 Oct. 1998.

[68] However, many Socialists had stayed in the Janata Party.

[69] Lok Dal, 'Election Manifesto – 1980 mid-term poll' in ibid., pp. 396–7.

Table 9.6. CASTE AND COMMUNITY IN THE NATIONAL EXECUTIVE OF LOK DAL

	1980	*1981*	*1984*	*1987*
Upper castes	*33.34*	*29.62*	*29.28*	*27.08*
Brahmin	11.11	14.81	12.20	10.42
Rajput	8.33	7.41	9.76	4.17
Banya/Jain	2.78	3.70	4.88	4.17
Bhumihar	2.78			
Kayasth	5.56	3.70	2.44	2.08
Khatri	2.78			2.08
Nayar				2.08
Tyagi				2.08
Intermediate castes	*16.67*	*22.21*	*17.08*	*18.75*
Jat	11.11	14.81	12.20	18.75
Reddy	2.78	3.70		
Vokkaliga	2.78	3.70	2.44	
Other			2.44	
OBC	*25*	*18.52*	*19.51*	*16.67*
Gujar				2.08
Kurmi	11.11	7.41	2.44	4.17
Nai	2.78	3.70		
Yadav	11.11	7.41	17.07	10.42
Scheduled Castes	*5.56*	*3.70*	*2.44*	*6.25*
Christian	*5.56*	*7.41*	*4.88*	*4.17*
Muslim	*11.11*	*11.11*	*12.20*	*16.67*
Unidentified	*2.78*	*7.41*	*14.63*	*10.42*
Total	*100*	*100*	*100*	*100*
	N=36	*N=27*	*N=41*	*N=48*

Source: Fieldwork.

recruitment to gazetted services to those young men who have married outside their own caste'.[70]

The same dual strategy was evident from the Lok Dal's attitude to reservations. The party was eager to expand positive discrimination not only to OBCs but also to 'kisan communities',[71] yet its MPs were at the forefront of the fight to implement the Mandal Commission Report.

[70] Ibid., p. 407.

[71] 'Lok Dal and Reservation, Statement, April 1981', cited in Hasan, 'Pattern of resilience and change', op. cit., p. 187, n.76.

The Report was submitted to Indira Gandhi's government in December 1980 but it was put before the Lok Sabha only on 30 April 1982, when there was barely a quorum in the House, a clear indication of the ruling party's priority. The most vehement speakers were Lok Dal MPs such as Chandrajit Yadav who emphasised what to him was its main finding: the fact that 'the other backward classes constituted 52% of our population'.[72] OBC leaders were obviously realising that their 'community' was a majority and could form an unbeatable constituency. Ram Vilas Paswan was also very combative in the debate even though he was not an OBC but a Dusadh (the member of a Scheduled Caste of pig herders). Paswan had a socialist background – he had been secretary of the Bihar SSP – and joined the Lok Dal in 1974, to become the secretary of the party Bihar unit.[73] When he appeared before the Mandal Commission he suggested that 'the existing percentage of reservation for OBCs should be increased and greater educational facilities provided to them' but he also added that 'in case the family income of a candidate exceeded Rs. 10,000 per year, [an OBC applicant] should not be given the benefit of reservations'.[74] In the 1982 Mandal debate he adopted an Ambedkar-like position in denouncing caste hierarchy as inherent in Hinduism, invoking the Law of Manu to this end.[75] The senior Congress representative then in the House, the Defence Minister, R. Venkataraman objected that the essence of Hinduism was found not in Manu but in the Gita whose hero, Krishna 'was a Yadava',[76] an attempt at flattering the Sanskritization tendencies of the Yadavs. Venkataraman went on to claim that the Mandal Commission Report, which had identified 3,743 castes, contradicted the findings of the Kalelkar Commission, which 'identified somewhere 2,000 and odds' such

[72] Lok Sabha Secretariat, *Lok Sabha Debates*, New Delhi, vol. 31, Aug. 11, 1982, col. 359. Chandrajit Yadav also used this opportunity to recall that the 'Yadav community has also made a great sacrifice for the country' in the 1962 war and that it was unfair to them not to create a Yadav regiment (ibid., cols 518–19).

[73] Paswan had been first elected in the Bihar Assembly at the young age of 23 in 1969 and to the Lok Sabha in 1977 in Hajipur (*Who's Who in Lok Sabha – 1977*, op. cit., p. 422).

[74] *Report of the [second] Backward Classes Commission*, op. cit., p. 45.

[75] Lok Sabha Secretariat, *Lok Sabha Debates*, New Delhi, vol. 31, 11 August 1982.

[76] Ibid., col. 562.

castes. According to him, neither could it be reconciled with the lists established by the states.[77] More importantly, he expressed the view that the reservation policy 'should be extended to include economically backward people'[78] and concluded that 'this is only a point of view; this is not the decision of the Government'. This decision was never implemented since the Congress was not interested in developing affirmative action. On 15 January 1982, Indira Gandhi had announced a new 20-point programme which emphasised health care, welfare programmes for women and greater provision of education.[79] A few days after the Lok Sabha debate, the Home Minister, Giani Zail Singh, gravely declared that 'the recommendations made by the Commission raise important and complex issues which have wide and deep implications for the country as a whole' but that 'the Central Government have forwarded the Report of the Commission to the various State Governments for obtaining their views'.[80] That was the only action taken by the Congress.

The tabling of the Mandal Commission Report before the Lok Sabha – which had been set for mid-February and then postponed – marked the partial conversion of Charan Singh to the notion of quota-politics:

> The founding fathers of our Constitution have clearly provided that the socially and educationally backward castes in our society be given reservation in services so that they would be able to come on a par with other forward castes. But the ruling Congress party during its thirty-one years rule instead of implementing the provisions of the constitution in relation to the backward castes has perpetuated the age-old domination of the so-called high castes over the backward castes. The recommendation of Kaka Kalelkar commission regarding the backward classes, which was submitted to the government in 1955 have not been implemented till date. It is as if here was a deep-seated conspiracy hatched by the upper castes and capitalists to thwart the rightful urges and aspirations of the backward castes, Harijans and Girijans [Tribals] to have their rightful place in the Indian society. It is

[77] Ibid., col. 558.

[78] Ibid., col. 560.

[79] 'AICC Circulars', in Zaidi, *Annual Register of Indian Political Parties – 1982*, op. cit., p. 570.

[80] *Memorandum explaining action taken on the report of the second backward classes commission*, New Delhi: Government of India, Ministry of Home Affairs, 1982, pp. 5–6.

heartening to note that these depressed sections of the Indian community have now risen from their age-long slumber and are now prepared to fight for their rights. They are bound to be victorious, as they constitute the majority of the Indian society.

It was for the first time during the post-independence period that a political party, viz. the Janata Party in its election manifesto for Lok Sabha elections in 1977 pledged itself to implement the recommendations of Kaka Kalelkar Commission Report and the Janata Party's pledge was actualised in Bihar under the stewardship of Karpoori Thakur who was the Chief Minister at the time. The Janata Party appointed the Mandal Commission as per the provisions of the Constitution to review the situation and make appropriate recommendations for the welfare of the backward castes. The Cong. (I) Government at the centre has been in possession of the said report for the last one year but has not yet published it despite its repeated assurances in the Parliament to put [it] on the table of the House. It seems the recommendations of the Mandal Commission would meet the same fate as the previous Kaka Kalelkar Commission Report unless the backward castes start a massive people's movement to compel the Government to implement them. Hence I make this fervent appeal to all the backward castes, Harijans and Girijans to join a massive rally on 18 February 1982 at Noon which is also the opening day of the Budget session of Parliament at the Boat Club near Parliament House in New Delhi. Let this rally be the precursor of a long-drawn-out battle of all the have-nots against the monopolists to assert their rightful place in the Indian society'.[81]

On 18 February 1982 Charan Singh held a meeting outside the Lok Sabha to exert pressure on the MPs to adopt the report's recommendations. However the Lok Dal was in no position to fight for the report's implementation. First, the staunchest candidates of reservations, the socialists, were not very strong in the party. But Charan Singh did not take all the Socialists with him when he left the Janata Party, which was still led by Chandra Shekhar. Surendra Mohan and Ramakrishna Hedge remained its general Secretaries and Ashok Mehta, N.G. Gore and Ramand Tiwari members of its National Executive. They acted as a lobby in favour of the OBCs and thus the party's 1980-election manifesto emphasised that it 'will see that the recommendations of the [Mandal] Commission are expeditiously processed and acted upon when they are received'.[82]

[81] Cited in R. Ray, Preface to 'An Observer', op. cit., pp. 5–6.

[82] Janata Party, 'Election Manifesto 1980 Mid-Term Poll' in Zaidi, *The Annual Register of Indian Political Parties* (hereafter *ARIPP*), New Delhi:

In addition to the division of the Socialists between the Janata Party and Charan Singh's party, the latter was also to split. In 1982, Devi Lal, a Jat leader from Haryana and Biju Patnaik – the strongman of Orissa – Karpoori Thakur, George Fernandes, Sharad Yadav, H.N. Bahuguna and Ram Vilas Paswan were expelled for 'anti-party activities'.[83] According to Rashid Masood, the chief whip of the Parliamentary group, they had to be expelled because 'they opposed Charan Singh. There was nothing ideological. It was purely personal, factional'.[84] The expellees formed the LD (K) (for Karpoori) and Charan Singh the LD (C) (for Charan). Devi Lal, Sharad Yadav and Bahuguna rejoined Charan Singh before the 1984 elections but his Lok Dal won only two seats, this fragile unity being shattered after his death on 29 March 1987. The acting president – who was supposed to help an ageing President, Charan Singh, was H.N. Bahuguna. Ajit Singh, his son, was one of the general secretaries, and the heir apparent. When Charan Singh died, they both claimed his legacy and a new split ensued, with Bahuguna founding the LD (B) and Ajit Singh the LD (A).

Thirdly, Lok Dal leaders were not uniformly interested in seeing the implementation of the Mandal Commission Report. According to Rashid Masood, during the Janata phase Charan Singh and his lieutenants supported the appointment of the Backward Classes commission because they 'thought then that all the *kisans* would benefit from it, including jats'.[85] However, Jats were not classified as OBCs by the Mandal Commission and therefore supporters of Charan Singh from this caste lost interest in the issue. Charan Singh himself later softened the party's lower caste image – he preferred to return to his former discourse that rejected caste *en bloc*:

> Our party is of poor people whether those poor may belong to village or to city or whether of high castes or backward castes or Scheduled Castes. Our party is of farmers and artisans, to whatever religion or sect they may belong

---

S. Chand, 1980, p. 301. In 1983, other Socialists joined the Janata Party and became its office-hearers in the JP, such as Madhu Dandavate and Yamuna Prasad Shastri. They were joined in 1986 by George Fernandes and Mrinal Gore.

[83] See the long argument by the Lok Dal National Executive, which met on 25 August 1982 in, Zaidi, *The Annual Register of Indian Political Parties – 1982*, New Delhi: S. Chand, 1982, pp. 673–9.

[84] Interview with Rashid Masood.

[85] Ibid.

to, whether they are proprietors of their land or are mere landless labourers [. . .] We are against caste system and regard casteism as the greatest enemy of our society, country and democracy. Casteism leads to all round degradation, that is for persons practising casteism, character, ability and capacity have no appeal.[86]

In fact, the 1987 split of the LD resulted also from the desire of Yadav leaders – such as Mulayam Singh Yadav – to emancipate themselves from Jat tutelage. Interestingly, only 5 of the 18 Uttar Pradesh Lok Dal MLAs continued to support, Ajit Singh but not one Jat left him.[87]

To sum up, while quota politics and *kisan* politics crystallised in the 1960s as two distinctive methods of promoting social transformation, they had many similarities and their social constituencies overlapped to such an extent that the proponents of the former, the Socialists, and of the latter, Charan Singh and his group, began to make common cause in the 1970s. This *rapprochement* was intended to catapult their coalition to power. It was partly successful since the Janata Party enabled the Socialists and Charan Singh's followers to sit in government at the Centre for the first time. But the other components of this party – the ex-Congress(O) and the ex-Jana Sangh – were associated with social groups – mainly the upper caste middle class –that the Socialists and Charan Singh were eager to dislodge from their privileged position. Thus reservations was one of the factors that precipitated the collapse of the Janata coalition.

An important outcome of the Janata government however was the appointment of the Mandal Commission, which had fewer inhibitions than previous, similar commissions regarding the use of caste as a relevant criterion for identifying the Other Backward Classes. Its approach was bound to relaunch quota politics. The Lok Dal – which gathered together proponents of quota politics and *kisan* politics once again under the aegis of Charan Singh – epitomised the growing synthesis of these two currents. Gradually, quota politics was taking over. Charan Singh himself supported this development for some

[86] 'Presidential address by Ch. Charan Singh. Lok Dal National council', in A.M. Zaidi (ed.), *ARIPP*, New Delhi: Indian Institute of Applied Political Research, 1985, p. 501.

[87] M. Jain, 'Backward Castes and Social Change in U.P. and Bihar', in Srinivas (ed.), *Caste – Its Twentieth Century Avatar*, op. cit., p. 147.

time in the 1980s, even though *kisan* politics was still his favourite option. Tension beween the two camps remained prevalent within the Janata Dal but the strategy of this party led ultimately to the rise of quota politics.

10

THE JANATA DAL AND THE RISE TO POWER OF THE LOW CASTES

Twenty-two years after the first Janata experiment, a second one started with the rise to power of the Janata Dal in 1989. Once again, its success was due to North Indian voters since 101 of the 143 seats won by the JD came from the four largest states of the Hindi belt. It was a significant achievement for a party that had been founded one year before on 11 October 1988. But the JD had not started from scratch.

While the Janata Party had been a very heterogeneous coalition-like party ranging from the Socialists to the Hindu nationalists, the Janata Dal primarily amalgamated only two currents of Indian politics, that of the Socialists and of Charan Singh. This state of affairs was evident from the identity of the parties it incorporated, mainly the Lok Dal (A) of Ajit Singh and the Lok Dal (B) of Devi Lal, and from the long list of Socialist leaders who became office-bearers of the Janata Dal – Madhu Dandavate, George Fernandes, Surendra Mohan, Sharad Yadav and Ram Vilas Paswan. Such heterodox origins brought with them their own problems, as the controversy over the name of the party showed. Till the last minute it was intended to be called the Samajwadi Janata Dal (Socialist People Party) but Devi Lal strongly objected to the epithet 'Socialist' and it had to be removed.[1] Eventually, in the competition between proponents of *kisan* politics and of a socialist strategy the latter prevailed and the rise to power of the JD went hand in hand with the new assertiveness of the lower castes.

Quota politics takes over

The Janata Dal's discourse on social justice was heavily loaded with socialist references. Its president, V.P. Singh, implicitly claimed that

[1] S. Mustafa, *The Lonely Prophet – V.P. Singh, a Political Biography*, New Delhi: New Age International, 1995, p. 110.

this brand of socialism underpinned his political beliefs. As mentioned above, he was the scion of a Rajput lineage which had been the ruling family of a small princely state near Allahabad and hence was ironically referred to as the 'Raja of Manda'. V.P. Singh was first involved in the Sarvodaya movement but had then been co-opted by the Congress Party to become MLA and then MP, though he resisted becoming just another notable in the vote bank pyramid. He rose to power as Chief Minister of Uttar Pradesh in 1980–2 and was then appointed Finance Minister by Rajiv Gandhi, a post where he launched an unprecedented campaign against business tax evasion. He then manifested his socialist credentials by claiming that he was 'to the Congress what JP was to the Janata'.[2] In early 1987 having antagonised big business he was transferred to the defence portfolio but went ahead with his anti-corruption drive in his new post and was later forced to resign. He showed the same zeal out of power by denouncing the corruption that allegedly surrounded the purchase by the army of field guns from Bofors, allegations that implicated top Congress leaders, including Rajiv Gandhi. He was therefore expelled from Congress in July 1987. The small party he then founded the Jan Morcha, gathered together a few Congress dissidents[3] but it played a pivotal role in the foundation of the Janata Dal and became the rallying point of other opposition parties with which it formed the National Front. V.P. Singh declared at that juncture that the Left was his 'natural ally' and indeed he kept referring to the founding fathers of Indian socialism.[4] The day after he was sworn in as Prime Minister, on 3 December 1989, in his First Address to the Nation, Ram Manohar Lohia and Jaya Prakash Narayan were the only names he mentioned as his mentors.[5]

[2] Cited in J. Thakur, *V.P. Singh – The Quest for Power*, New Delhi: Warbler Books, 1989, p. 6.

[3] Among them, however, were congressmen who had first been acolytes of Lohia and /or Charan Singh like Satpal Malik. (Interview with Satpal Malik, 25 Oct. 1998, New Delhi)

[4] In practice, however, V.P. Singh continued to benefit from the kind of vote bank politics he had initiated himself while supporting Bahuguna as 'the Rajah of Manda'. Another ex-ruler, Kanwar Rewati Raman Singh (from Baraon state), who had been elected MLA five times since 1974, helped him to be elected in 1989 in a constituency with which he had lost touch. (Interview with Raman Singh, Paris, 20 May 1998)

[5] V.P. Singh, 'Towards a Just Society' in Mohan, Sharma, Singh and Sunilam (eds), *Evolution of Socialist Policy in India*, op. cit., p. 357.

The Janata Dal focussed less on class than on caste and turned towards positive discrimination as its main social remedy. The programme it adopted during its inaugural session promised that 'Keeping in view special needs of the socially and educationally backward classes, the party [if voted to power] shall implement forth-with the recommendations of the Mandal Commission'.[6] The party was prepared to show the way and promised to allot 60% of tickets in the general election to 'the weaker sections of society'. Before that, V.P. Singh had promised to apply the 60% reservation to the party apparatus. This 60% quota was an old socialist idea that Lohia had propagated in the 1960s but it could not be implemented at the time of the nomination of the Janata Dal state party presidents because of the opposition of Devi Lal.[7] Once again, an aspect of the socialist approach was contradicted by a Jat trying to implement Charan Singh's strategy.

The JD, indeed, was also an instrument of *kisan* politics. Devi Lal, the then Chief Minister of Haryana, had won the 1987 state election largely because he had announced that if voted to power he would waive the cooperative loans up to Rs 20,000.[8] The 1989 election manifesto of the National Front promised to do the same with 'Loans upto Rs 10,000 of small, marginal and landless cultivators and artisans'.[9] Most of the items regrouped under the heading 'Rural Economy' favoured peasant-proprietors:

> Not less than 50 per cent of the investible ressources will be deployed for the development of rural economy. Farmers will be assured of guaranteed remunerative prices for their produce, a countrywide network of godowns and warehouses, remission of debts, provision of cheap credit, removal of unreasonable restrictions on movement of agricultural produce, crop insurance, security in land holding and strict implementation of land reforms and improved access to water resources.[10]

The only promise which directly concerned agricultural labourers was one about land reform, though once in power the JD barely tried to implement it. By contrast, Devi Lal – who became Deputy Prime Minister with the agriculture portfolio and had Sharad Joshi as one

[6] Ibid., p. 343.

[7] Mustafa, *The Lonely Prophet*, op. cit., p. 115.

[8] Varshney, *Democracy, Development, and the Countryside*, op. cit., p. 141.

[9] *Dignity to Nation, Commitment to People – National Front Manifesto, Lok Sabha Elections, 1989*, New Delhi: V.P. Singh, 1989, p. 18.

[10] Ibid., p. 6.

of his advisors, with a cabinet rank – waived all agricultural loans under central jurisdiction, up to Rs 10,000.[11] Yet, *kisan* politics was not pursued as resolutely by the V.P. Singh government as 'quota politics', for two reasons. From a pragmatic point of view, V.P. Singh was more eager to cater to the needs of the lower castes, especially the OBCs, than to those of the middle peasants (who were more numerous among intermediate castes such as the Jats) because this constituency had already been won over by Ajit Singh and Devi Lal. From an ideological point of view, like most socialist leaders of the JD, V.P. Singh believed less in economic and financial support than in the reform of society's power structure. Moreover, with 4 OBC ministers, his government had the highest representation so far (in terms of percentage) in the Union government.[12] And positive discrimination remained, for him a relevant technique of empowerment. The 1989 National Front election manifesto promised that 'Implementation of reservation policy will be made effective in government, public and private sector industrial undertakings, banking institutions, etc. . , by resorting to special recruitment drives so as to fulfill their quotas within the shortest possible time'[13] and that 'The recommendations of the Mandal Commission will be implemented expeditiously'.[14] While V.P. Singh did not dare to extend the reservation system to the private sector, he reasserted in the Presidential address that Venkataraman spelled out before both Houses of Parliament on 20 December 1989, that 'the government will take appropriate steps to implement the recommendations of the Mandal Commision'.

The Prime Minister announced this decision in a one and a half page *suo moto* statement in both Houses of Parliament on 7 August 1990, the related Office Memorandum being issued six days later. He justified it in his Independence Day Address on 15 August by the need to give 'a share to the poor in running the Government'.[15] He explained that he would have liked to reserve 40% of seats in Parlia-

[11] Varshney, *Democracy, Development, and the Countryside*, op. cit., p. 143.

[12] V.A. Pai Panandiker and A.K. Mehra, *The Indian Cabinet. A Study in Governance*, New Delhi: Konark Publishers, 1996, p. 74.

[13] *National Front – Lok Sabha Elections 1989 Manifesto*, New Delhi: V.P. Singh, Convenor, National Front, 1989, p. 26.

[14] Ibid., p. 27.

[15] V.P. Singh 'Justice for the Poor' in S. Mohan *et al.* (eds), *Evolution of Socialist Policy*, op. cit., p. 360.

ment and the State assemblies for the 40% poor of India, but quotas in the bureaucracy was already a major achievements, given the power wielded by the administration:

We believe that no section can be uplifted merely by money. They can develop only if they have a share in power and we are prepared to provide this share. In this year of justice, in memory of Dr. Bhimrao Ambedkar [whose birth centenary was then to be celebrated soon in 1991] the Government has recently taken a decision to give reservation to the backward classes in jobs in Government and public sector. It is being debated as to how many persons would get benefit out of it. In a sense, taking into account the population of this country, the Government jobs account for only one per cent and out of this one per cent if one fourth is given to anyone, it cannot be a course for his economic betterment though it may have some effect. But our outlook is clear. *Bureaucracy is an important organ of the power structure. It has a decisive role in decision-making. We want to give an effective* [*sic*] *here in the power structure and running of the country to the depressed, down-trodden and backward people.*[16]

As for most socialists before him, the caste system was V.P. Singh's main target and he analysed the institution in terms of power relations: without the prior transformation of the power structure, he suggested, social reform would only help the upper caste benefactors to keep a clean conscience and perpetuate the *status quo*. This approach did not please the proponents of *kisan* politics. Devi Lal had been appointed by V.P. Singh to chair a committee for the implementation of the Mandal report but, according to the latter, he 'did not take much interest [in it]'.[17] He had strong reservations *vis-à-vis* such schemes because of the exclusion of the Jats from among the OBCs.[18] It seems that he tried, and failed, to persuade the government to alter their view[19] and Devi Lal therefore convened no more than a couple of meetings to prepare for the implementation of the report. V.P. Singh then asked the Minister of Social Welfare, Ram

[16] Ibid., p. 361. Emphasis added. See also V.P. Singh's statement in Parliament on 27 August 1990 in *V.P. Singh Selected Speeches and Writings, 1989-90*, New Delhi: Government of India, 1993, p. 216.

[17] Cited in Mustafa, *The Lonely Prophet*, op. cit., p. 171.

[18] Interview with Ajay Singh – one of the Jat Ministers in V.P. Singh cabinet – New Delhi, 28 Oct. 1997.

[19] Interview with P.S. Krishnan, New Delhi, 4 April 1998. P.S. Krishnan was Secretary to the Ministry of Social Welfare who prepared the implementation of the Mandal report for R.V. Paswan.

Vilas Paswan, to do the job. All the Jat ministers objected strongly that their caste should be included in the list of OBCs.[20] A petition was organised among the MPs and 107 signatures were collected among Jat and Muslim leaders who also wanted some of their co-eligionists to be recognised as OBCs.[21] According to Satpal Malik, V.P. Singh was 'very clever and asked Surjeet Singh [the General Secretary of the CPI(M), a party of the ruling coalition] to write against it. He wrote a letter saying that the Jats could not be back-wards because they had been kings in Patiala and Bharatpur'.[22] V.P. Singh made a vague promise 'but nothing came' and he announced the implementation of the Mandal Commission Report only a few days after Devi Lal resigned from his government.

Devi Lal apparently had never reconciled himself with the fact that he could not become Prime Minister and resented the lack of support offered by the Janata Dal leaders to his son, Chauthala, the Haryana Chief Minister, whose opponents contested the legality of his election to the Haryana assembly. Fundamentally, V.P. Singh's policy did not accord with the wishes of Devi Lal. In fact, the social potential of V.P. Singh's reforms was perceived as posing a threat to the *kisans'* interests in so far as it might encourage the assertiveness of tenants and agricultural labourers from the lower castes. Devi Lal's resignation in fact consummated the collapse of Charan Singh's coalition. As a result, the OBCs reinforced their position in the JD, as evident from the caste background of the JD MPs of the Hindi belt in 1991 and that of the National Executive of the Janata Dal in 1994; in both cases Jat representation was noticeably low-compared to the OBCs.

While in 1989 Jats represented more than 13% of JD MPs in the Hindi belt, this percentage had fallen to 1.89% by 1991. The main beneficiaries of this development were the OBCs, whose share jumped from an already very high 27% to 39%, also at the expense of the upper castes whose representation almost halved. The JD was becoming an OBC party. Among its office-bearers also, the percentage of Jats became negligible in the early 1990s while OBC representation

[20] Satpal Malik claims that he was the first minister to ask for the inclusion of the Jats (interview with S. Malik).

[21] Interview with Rachid Masood.

[22] Interview with S. Malik.

Table 10.1. CASTE AND COMMUNITY OF THE JD, SP AND RJD MPs RETURNED IN THE HINDI BELT, 1989–98 (%)

	JD 1989	*JD 1991*	*JD+SP 1996*	*JD+SP+RJD 1998*
Upper castes	*31.78*	*16.98*	*14.29*	*16.67*
Brahmin	7.48	1.89	4.76	
Bhumihar	1.87	1.89		
Rajput	17.76	13.21	7.14	16.67
Banya/Jain	0.93			
Kayasth	2.80		2.38	
Khatri				
Tyagi	0.93			
Intermediate castes	*13.08*	*1.89*		
Jat	13.08	1.89		
OBC	*27.10*	*39.62*	*54.76*	*47.92*
Yadav	15.89	22.64	33.33	25
Kurmi	4.67	9.43	4.76	8.33
Lodhi	0.93			
Kachhi	0.93		2.38	
Gujar				
Koeri	2.80	5.66	4.76	6.25
Mali	0.93		2.38	
Panwar	0.93	1.89		
Other			7.14	8.32
Scheduled Castes	*18.7*	*24.53*	*14.29*	*18.75*
Scheduled Tribes	*1.87*			
Christian		*1.89*	*2.38*	*2.08*
Muslim	*7.48*	*13.21*	*14.29*	*14.58*
Unidentified		*1.89*		
Total	*100 N=107*	*100 N=53*	*100 N=42*	*100 N=48*

Source: Fieldwork.

reached 24% (see Table 10.2). Upper caste representation remained prominent, amounting to one third of the National Executive.

The most ardent supporters of 'quota politics' were probably not unhappy that Devi Lal left the Janata Dal because *kisan* politics was

Table 10.2. CASTE AND COMMUNITY OF THE MEMBERS OF THE JANATA DAL NATIONAL EXECUTIVE, 1994

	1994
Upper castes	*33.11*
Brahmin	11.51
Rajput	5.04
Bhumihar	1.44
Banya/Jain	3.60
Kayasth	1.44
Khandait	2.88
Khatri	1.44
Nayar	3.60
Other	2.16
Intermediate castes	*13.68*
Jat	0.72
Kamma	1.44
Lingayat	3.60
Maratha	2.88
Patidar	0.72
Reddy	2.88
Vokkaliga	1.44
OBC	*24.47*
Banya	0.72
Ezhava	0.72
Gujar	1.44
Koeri	0.72
Kurmi	2.16
Saini	1.44
Yadav	4.32
Other	12.95
Scheduled Castes	*4.32*
Scheduled Tribes	*3.60*
Christian	*2.16*
Muslim	*5.76*
Sikh	*2.16*
Unidentified	*10.79*
Total	*100*
	N=139

Source: Interviews in the Janata Dal office (New Delhi).

merely serving the interests of the peasant-proprietors and maintaining the social status quo in the countryside. The old Socialist and Ambedkarite approach based on an anti-caste discourse and affirmative action was apparently more promising.

Caste polarization around Mandal

For V.P. Singh Mandal was not a mass employment scheme and indeed the new quota of 27% represented relatively few jobs. Of the 204,288 appointments that were made in the bureaucracy in 1988, 55,158 jobs would have been given to OBCs according to the new reservation policy. In fact, the number of posts was declining (from 226,781 in 1985 to 204, 288 in 1988), whereas the number of candidates was increasing (from 2.4 millions in 1985 to 2.9 millions in 1988).[23] But the quota was even more strongly resented by the upper castes who regarded administration as their monopoly. In 1980, OBCs represented 12.55% of the Central Services and Scheduled Castes and Scheduled Tribes 18.72% (in Class I services, the OBCs represented less than 5%, as against 90% of high castes).[24] Moreover quotas for the Scheduled Castes and Scheduled Tribes very often remained unfulfilled.

Uttar Pradesh was a case in point. In 1984, 93.8% of the principal secretaries and secretaries to the government were from the upper castes[25] (including 56.3% Brahmins) and this was also the case for 86.6% of the heads of departments[26] and 93.2% of the section officers. At the local level, 78.6% of the District Magistrates were from

[23] *India Today*, 15 Sept. 1990, pp. 36–7.

[24] These figures were based on replies furnished by 30 Central Ministries and Departments and 31 attached and subordinate offices and public sector undertakings under the administrative control of 14 ministries (For the complete statistical figures, see *Report of the [second] Backward Classes Commission*, op. cit., p. 42).

[25] Interestingly, Verma *et al.* have classified the Jats as upper caste 'considering their asset base, occupational profile, educational and other attainments and representation in the services under the state'. (H.S. Verma, R. A. Singh and J. Singh, 'Power Sharing: Exclusivity and Exclusion in a Mega State', Monograph presented to the panel on 'Deprivations, Backwardness and Social Transformation of the Backward Classes' of the All India Sociological Conference, 29–31 Dec. 1993, Mangalore, p. 9)

[26] Ibid., p. 15. The figures cited by Verma *et al.* are based on the data from

the upper castes in 1985, including 41.1% of Brahmins and 25% of Kayasths.[27] In the public state units, 94.5% of the managing directors were from the upper castes in 1984.[28]

Verma *et al.* therefore conclude that 'the Secretariat set up, where the real state power rests, is still completely in the hands of the U[pper] C[astes]. Its exercise is controlled by the Brahmins and state power is being used in alliance with other 'twice born' castes. The representation of the OBCs is generally notional and in some of the key sub-structures like the police headquarters, judiciary and the direct employment recruiting agencies it is totally absent'.[29] In fact, the Scheduled Castes were better represented than the OBCs in the state administration because of reservations. However the same authors emphasise that one of the strategies of upper caste bureaucrats consisted in 'Keeping a large number of positions outside the scope of reservations' and that direct recruitment was limited generally to Class II positions and that higher positions were filled with promotions.[30] Besides, most quotas were not fulfilled. In 1992, according to the Ambedkar Mahasabha, an association of Scheduled Castes officers, quotas for the Scheduled Castes and Scheduled Tribes were not fulfilled in UP; the gap was still 14.72% in Class I, 12.75% in Class II, 7.74% in Class III and 2% in Class IV.

The upper caste middle class was very apprehensive that the quasi-monopoly it exerted over the administration would be dismantled. In addition to social scientists who contested the accuracy of the Mandal Commission Report,[31] many sections of the media opposed it for reasons which reflected the fears and anti-reservation prejudices of the upper castes and middle classes.[32] *India Today* exemplified this

---

the National Integration Department of the UP Government. According to the authors they still underestimate the over domination of the upper castes in the state apparatus.

[27] Ibid., p. 17.

[28] Ibid., p. 19.

[29] Ibid., p. 20.

[30] Ibid., pp. 27–8.

[31] See, for instance, M.N. Srinivas, 'The Mandal formula', *Times of India*, 17 Sept. 1990, Ramashray Roy, 'Fiction into fact', *Indian Express*, 30 Aug. 1990, S.C. Dube, 'A retrograde fetish', *Hindustan Times*, 3 Sept. 1990, and K.L. Sharma, 'A Backward Step', ibid., 19 Sept. 1990.

[32] See, for instance, the articles of Swapan Dasgupta ('Curse of Mandal', *Times of India*, 14 Aug. 1990) and Arun Shourie ('Sub-standard by definition',

trend on several occasions. According to the magazine, 'The OBCs, besides being powerful land-owners, already exercise considerable political clout'. *India Today* even dared to equate the new reservation policy and South African apartheid[33] and accused the lower castes of making no effort at upward mobility, knowing that they would continue to enjoy benefit of reservation schemes:

> Families that have benefited from job reservations have not raised their real standards of living because they have not practiced family-planning. In a vicious circle, they produce more children and ask for more reservations. Right now reservations reach only the individual who benefits from the collective backwardness of his caste.[34]

This kind of discourse, which was aimed at the Scheduled Castes, again is revealing of the upper castes' paranoia (at least in demographic terms) and anger. They resented the new quotas which questioned their dominanted of the bureaucracy and of the social hierarchy.

Soon after V.P. Singh announced the implementation of the Mandal Commission Report, upper caste students mobilised organisations such as the Anti-Mandal Commission Forum which was based in Delhi University. Of its 19 strong executive committee members, 17 were from landowning families from Bihar.[35] In Uttar Pradesh, the Arakshan Virodhi Sangharsh Samiti (Committee for the Struggle against Reservations) and the Mandal Ayog Virodhi Sangharsh Samiti (Committee for the struggle against the Mandal Commission) were founded by students who were often from the upper castes but

---

Indian Express, 23 Aug. 1990, 'The Stench of Casteism', ibid., 24 Aug. 1990 and 'Mandal Report : the Juggernaut', ibid., 25 Aug. 1990). These two columnists were to rally around the BJP in the early 1990s (Shourie became a BJP Rajya Sabha member in 1998 and a Minister in Vajpayee's government in 1999). Retrospectively, Dilip Padgaonkar, the then editor of the *Times of India* offered excuses to journalists: 'I think some among us got carried away. After all, the phenomenon was a novelty in North India. And also, I think, there was a sentiment that with this single announcement, the divisiveness relating to caste had been put on the front-burner of Indian politics and those who make and read newspapers, particularly the English language ones, are more embarrassed to discuss caste than sex and money.' (*Times of India*, 19 Nov. 1992)

33 P. Pachauri, 'New Reservation Policy – Apartheid, Indian Style', *India Today*, 15 Sept. 1990, p. 38.

34 *India Today*, 30 Sept. 1990, p. 31.

35 *India Today*, 31 Oct., 1990.

Table 10.3. CASES OF SELF-IMMOLATION, SUICIDES AND CASUALTIES OF POLICE FIRING DURING ANTI-MANDAL AGITATION

	Self-immolations (incl. unsuccessful attempts)	*Suicides (incl. unsuccessful attempts)*	*Persons killed in police firing*
Delhi	20	3	5
Haryana	22	32	6
Uttar Pradesh	25	28	16
Madhya Pradesh	27	5	–
Gujarat	10	3	–
Bihar	8	12	12
Chandigarh	7	8	1
Rajasthan	12	8	–
Punjab	6	30	1
Himachal Pradesh	9	13	9
Andhra Pradesh	3	6	–
Tamil Nadu	2	–	–
Jammu & Kashmir	1	1	1
Maharashtra	–	3	–
Orissa	–	–	7
Assam	–	1	–

Source: *National Mail*, 12 Jan. 1991.

also from the lower middle class. They wanted to 'abolish all reservations including reservations for the Scheduled Castes',[36] a demand which led the Dalit and OBC leaders to get closer. They 'feared that their hopes of government patronage would be thwarted by a coalition of lower castes'[37] which they were largely shaping themselves by provoking a new cleavage between forward castes (including Jats)[38] and lower castes. Teachers mobilized too. North Indian universities, like the administration were dominated by upper caste teachers.[39] As early as 17 August professors of Delhi University objected that the implementation of the Mandal report would divide society and unjustly penalize individual merit.[40] The student agitation started in

[36] Z. Hasan, *Quest for Power*, op. cit., p. 155.

[37] Ibid.

[38] The Jat-dominated BKU was explicitly against caste-based quotas and favored, like the BJP, an economic criterion for job reservations.

[39] For more details on the universities of Uttar Pradesh, see H.S. Verma *et al.*, 'Power sharing', op. cit., p. 23.

[40] *Hindustan Times*, 19 Aug., 1990, p. 1.

Delhi where it soon turned violent.[41] North India was the epicentre of this campaign on account of the upper caste students' mobilisation, and the behind the scene activities of the BJP, Congress and Devi Lal in Haryana.

The most famous case of self-immolation by students protesting against Mandal was that of Rajiv Goswami, a twenty-year-old student from a middle class Brahmin family – his father was employed in the postal service – who was a Delhi University Student Union (DUSU) activist. After a nine-day protest fast he set fire to himself on 19 September, 1990. He survived in spite of severe injuries and became a symbol of the student movement, the site of his suicide attempt becoming known as Yurbani Chowk (the Place of Sacrifice).[42] In the wake of his protest Goswami was elected President of DUSU in 1991. He was the first of 152 people – mostly students – who tried to immolate themselves, of whom 63 succeeded. *India Today* and other media added to the emotionally charged atmosphere by publishing front-page photographs of these often gruesome events.

Immediately after the first anti-Mandal demonstrations, leaders of the Janata Dal counter-attacked. On 26 August, the Delhi branch of the party organised a pro-Mandal rally at which Sharad Yadav claimed: 'We will show them within 15 days how many people are behind us if they don't come back to their sense. . . .'[43] V.P. Singh went to Patna for a rally where slogans such as 'Brahmin saala desh chhado'! (Bastard Brahmins, get out of the country!) were heard. Thus, 1990 was marked by an exacerbation of the cleavage between upper castes and lower castes, an atmosphere which explains at that time the emotional value of the OBC as a social category.

The main achievement of V.P. Singh was clearly to forge a broad coalition of castes under the OBC label and, consequently, to contest the elite-groups' domination more effectively than ever before. The 'OBCs' had become a relevant category for the lower castes because they had a vested interest in it, namely the quotas promised by the Mandal Commission report: many of those who were earlier known as 'Shudras' internalized this administrative definition of their identity in the early 1990s simply because they thought they could derive

[41] A. Prasad, *Reservational Justice*, op. cit., pp. 58–9.

[42] *India Today*, 15 Oct. 1990, p. 15, and *Hindustan Times*, 25 Sept. 1990, p. 1.

[43] Cited in ibid., 3 Sept. 1990.

benefits from it. However, this category also crystallized because of the attitude of the upper castes who had rejected such reservations in the administration. The cleavage between upper castes and lower castes had suddenly been reinforced by a collective, open hostility from the former and even by the unleashing of violence.

The judiciary was to enshrine officially this new role of caste. In September 1990, in the context of acute violence, the Supreme Court was approached by an upper caste plaintiff, Indra Sawhney, who contested the constitutionality of V.P. Singh's decision of implementing the Mandal report. It issued a stay order. When the Congress returned to power nine months later in June 1991, Prime Minister Narasimha Rao tried to defuse the frontal opposition between upper castes and lower castes by creating a new quota for the 'economically backward', irrespective of caste. However, in its final judgement in December 1992, the majority of the Supreme Court admitted that caste could be a major criterion in the identification of the Other Backward Classes: 'A caste can be and quite often is a social class in India. If it is backward socially, it would be a backward class for the purposes of Article 16(4).' And the judges went on: 'Since caste represents an existing, identifiable social group/class encompassing an overwhelming minority of the country's population, one can well begin with it and then go to other groups, sections and classes'.[44] On the other hand, the Supreme Court considered that 'A backward class of citizen cannot be identified only and exclusively with reference to economic criteria',[45] and therefore they held as invalid and struck down the Office Memorandum dated 25 September 1991 through which Narasimha Rao had tried to provide 10% additional reservations to the 'economically backward' upper castes. The Mandal case judgement also questioned the 50% rule established by 'Balaji'. A majority of the judges considered that, 'While 50% shall be the rule, it is necessary not to put out of consideration certain extraordinary situations inherent in the great diversity of this country and the people'.[46] (This sentence referred to the fact that in

[44] 'Summary of Issues, Judgement and Directions in Indra Sawhney v. Union of India', reproduced as Annexure 1 to Prasad, *Reservational Justice*, op. cit., p. 308.

[45] Ibid., p. 309.

[46] Ibid., p. 309.

some regions non-upper caste groups represented overwhelming majorities).

The reservation policy and the judicial review have come a long way from the first and the second backward classes commissions. Gradually caste has become the legitimate criterion for the definition of 'backwardness' and the 50% limit has lost some of its inviolability. These new developments made the crystallisation of an OBC political identity much easier. The low castes began to share a common political identity that was expressed in terms of the OBCs *vs* the upper castes: caste had become the building block of a larger social coalition. The process that had been aborted in the wake of the furore surrounding the Kalelkar Report was reaching its logical conclusion.

The electoral fallout of the Mandal affair

The OBC phenomenon helped the low castes to organise themselves as an interest group, outside the vertical, clientelistic Congress-like patterns. This coalesence enabled the low castes to benefit from their main asset, their massive numbers, during elections. Indeed, the share of OBC MPs increased in the late 1980s and early 1990s as low caste voters become more aware of their common interests and decided to vote for candidates from their own social milieu (with 52% of Indian society the OBCs represented in many constituencies an unbeatable majority).

As mentioned in the previous chapter, the proportion of upper caste MPs in the Hindi belt fell below 50% for the first time in 1977 while the share of the intermediate castes and the OBCs increased from 14.2% to 20%. But the return of the Congress in the 1980s saw the return of many upper caste MPs, especially in 1984. The percentage of OBC MPs increased again after the Congress lost power in 1989 – it even doubled from 11.1% in 1984 to 20.9% in 1989, largely because the Janata Dal, the winner of the ninth general election, had given tickets to many OBC candidates. The proportion of upper caste MPs thus fell for the first time below 40%. More interestingly, in contrast to what happened in the 1980s, the share of OBCs among MPs continued to grow in 1991, in spite of the Congress' comeback, and in 1996, when the BJP became the largest party in the Lok Sabha. This trend was evolving at the expense of the upper castes, because all the political parties were now giving a larger number of tickets to OBC candidates. This was precisely the goal V.P. Singh had envisaged.

For V.P. Singh, in India, political power used to follow 'the contours of the social power structure' since the ruling party usually drew its influence from local notables. It is not that the Congress 'did not do anything for the deprived sections' but the distribution of governmental benefits was made in the clientelistic framework of vote bank politics: 'the relationship was a transactional one, not transformational. That is we give you benefits, you give us power'. Hence he regarded the main achievement of the Mandal affair as being the transfer of power from elite groups to the subalterns:

> Now that every party is wooing the deprived classes, with every round of elections more and more representatives of the deprived sections will be elected. This will ultimately be reflected in the social composition of the local bodies, state governments, and the central government. A silent transfer of power is taking place in social terms.[47]

This silent revolution was achieved without recourse to violence. It was implemened gradually, since it was based on the quota strategy, an incremental approach to social change that eventually prevailed at the expense of *kisan* politics: Charan Singh and Devi Lal had tried to unite the peasants, in the process stressing the peasants' identity and common interests, rather than caste affiliation, whereas V.P. Singh emphasised caste identity by using the issue of reservation for the OBCs. As a result, the Jats deserted the Janata Dal, with many of them, in western Uttar Pradesh at least, associating themselves with the upper castes and hence the BJP. V.P. Singh was criticised by disciples of Charan Singh for the way he divided the *kisan*[48] but

[47] V.P. Singh, 'Power and Equality – Changing Grammar of Indian Politics', reproduced in Prasad, *Reservational Justice*, op. cit., pp. 316–17.

[48] Brass, 'Chaudhuri, Charan Singh', op. cit., p. 2090. V.P. Singh was also under pressure from other National Front leaders who did not approve of his socialist-like strategy. In late August 1990 Biju Patnaik, the Orissa Chief Minister, asked him to take economic criteria into account in identifying the OBCs (see his letter to the Prime Minister in *Indian Express*, 30 Aug. 1990). Jyoti Basu, the CPI(M) Chief Minister of West Bengal asked him for the same thing. It was decided, in a meeting of the Cabinet Committee on Political Affairs, that 5% to 10% of administrative jobs would be reserved for the poor from the upper and intermediate castes. (*India Today*, 15 Sept. 1990) But this concession was rather hypothetical since it would have increased the sum of the quotas to 54.5–59.5%.

Table 10.4. CASTE AND COMMUNITY OF MPs ELECTED IN THE HINDI BELT, 1980–99 (%)

	1980	*1984*	*1989*	*1991*	*1996*	*1998*	*1999*
Upper castes	*40.88*	*46.9*	*38.2*	*37.11*	*35.3*	*34.67*	*30.9*
Brahmin	18.22	19.91	12.44	16.29	15.49	12.44	11.3
Rajput	11.56	15.49	15.11	14.03	14.03	13.33	10
Bhumihar	3.11	2.65	2.22	1.81	1.77	1.78	3.2
Banya/Jain	4.89	5.31	3.11	1.81	1.77	3.56	2.7
Kayasth	0.89	1.33	2.22	1.81	1.33	1.78	0.9
Other	2.21	2.21	3.1	1.36	0.89	1.78	2.8
Intermediate castes	*5.33*	*5.31*	*8*	*5.43*	*7.53*	*8.89*	*6.4*
Jat	4.89	4.87	6.67	5.43	6.64	7.11	5.4
Maratha	0.44	0.44	0.89		0.89	0.89	0.5
Other			0.44			0.89	0.5
OBC	*13.74*	*11.1*	*20.87*	*22.6*	*24.8*	*23.56*	*22.2*
Yadav	5.33	6.19	9.33	7.69	8.41	6.67	7.2
Kurmi	4.44	1.77	7.11	9.95	7.08	7.56	5
Lodhi	0.44	0.44	1.78	1.36	1.77	1.78	0.9
Koeri	0.44		0.44	0.91	0.44	1.33	0.5
Gujar	0.44	0.89	0.44	0.91	0.44	0.89	0.5
Mali	0.89	0.44	0.44	0.45	0.89		0.5
Panwar			0.44	0.91	0.44		
Jaiswal					0.89		1.4
Other	1.76	1.32	0.89	0.45	4.41	5.32	6.2
Scheduled Castes	*17.78*	*17.26*	*17.78*	*18.1*	*18.14*	*18.22*	*17.8*
Scheduled Tribes	*7.56*	*7.52*	*7.56*	*8.14*	*7.52*	*7.56*	*7.3*
Muslim	*11.56*	*9.73*	*5.78*	*4.52*	*3.54*	*5.33*	*5*
Other minorities	*0.89*	*0.44*	*0.44*	*0.9*	*0.89*	*0.89*	*0.9*
Sadhu	*0.44*			*0.9*			*0.9*
Unidentified	*0.89*	*2.21*	*0.89*	*1.36*	*2.21*	*0.89*	*9*
Total	*100*	*100*	*100*	*100*	*100*	*100*	*100*
	N=225	*N=226*	*N=225*	*N=221*	*N=226*	*N=225*	*N=221*

Source: Database compiled on the basis of interviews.

his tactic enabled the OBCs to rise to power. This phenomenon, in conjunction with that of the rising electoral participation of the low castes, prompts one to consider, as Yogendra Yadav did recently, that India has experienced in the 1990s a 'second democratic upsurge'.[49] A transfer of power is certainly taking place as we have tried to show

[49] Y. Yadav, 'Reconfiguration in Indian politics. State Assembly Elections, 1993–95', *EPW*, 13 Jan. 1996, p. 96.

by studying the social profile of political personnel, but this analysis needs to be qualified from three points of view. First, this phenomenon has not spread evenly all over the Hindi belt ; second, the OBCs are still very much divided, with those benefiting from the ongoing democratisation of Indian democracy forming a new elite which is derived from only a few castes; and lastly, the main political parties', the Congress and the BJP, have decided to counter this 'silent revolution'.

Geographical unevenness

The rise of the OBCs is distributed unevenly throughout the Hindi belt. This is evident from the social profile of the MPs of the four largest states of this region, Uttar Pradesh, Bihar, Madhya Pradesh and Rajasthan. In Rajasthan, the OBCs remained as poorly represented in the late 1990s as in the early 1980s, with only 12% of MPs. The percentage of upper caste MPs has fallen from 40% in 1980 to 28% in 1999, but the main beneficiaries of this change have been the Jats who have now more MPs than the upper castes. Changes have been incomparably more dramatic in all the other three states where the turning point occurred systematically in the late 1980s and early 1990s. In Madhya Pradesh and Uttar Pradesh, the percentage of upper caste MPs has declined from about 50% in 1984 to about 40% in 1998 whereas the share of OBC MPs jumped from 7–10% in 1984 to 22–25% in 1998. While this increase occurred as early as 1989 in UP, MP had to wait two more years for the impact of Mandal to translate into change in the caste background of the deputies. However, the most dramatic change happened in Bihar where OBC MPs have been more numerous than the upper castes in 1991, 1996 and 1998. Again, 1989 and 1991 were real milestones because of the electoral success of the Janata Dal and then the after-effects of the Mandal affair.

The changes in the social profile of MPs need to be compared to those affecting these states's assemblies and governments. In Bihar, the trend that was evident from the Lok Sabha figures is even more pronounced when one looks at those of the Vidhan Sabha. While there were 36.33% upper castes and 33.33% OBCs among the Bihar MLAs in 1985, five years later, the former were reduced to 32.81%

Table 10.5. CASTE AND COMMUNITY OF MPs ELECTED IN RAJASTHAN, 1980–99

	1980	*1984*	*1989*	*1991*	*1996*	*1998*	*1999*
Upper castes	*40*	*40*	*36*	*32*	*36*	*20*	*28*
Brahmin	12	12	12	12	16	8	12
Rajput	4	12	20	12	12		8
Banya/Jain	20	16	4	4	8	12	4
Kayasth				4			
Sindhi	4						4
Intermediate castes	*20*	*16*	*28*	*28*	*28*	*36*	*32*
Bishnoi						8	8
Jat	20	16	24	24	24	24	24
Maratha			4	4	4	4	
OBC	*12*	*12*	*8*	*8*	*8*	*8*	*12*
Gujar	8	8	4	8	8	4	4
Yadav	4	4	4		4	4	
Others							4
Scheduled Castes	*16*	*16*	*16*	*16*	*16*	*16*	*16*
Scheduled Tribes	*12*	*12*	*12*	*12*	*12*	*16*	*12*
Muslim		*4*		*4*			
Unidentified						*4*	
Total	*100* *N=25*	*100* *N=25*	*100* *N=25*	*100* *N=25*	*100* *N=25*	*100* *N=25*	*100* *N=25*

Source: Fieldwork.

and the latter ranked first with 34.74%.[50] In 1995, the gap had widened with OBC MLAs representing 45.5% of the assembly and upper castes MLAs less than 19%. In 1995 not only was the number of OBC MLAs almost ten percentage points above the OBC MPs, but they also represented many more castes. No less than twelve castes classified among the 'Most Backward Classes' were represented in the Assembly, as against three only among the MPs.

The growing influence of the OBCs is even more evident from the social composition of the first government of Laloo Prasad Yadav, to whom we will turn below. While the upper castes represented 29% of the government of Karpoori Thakur and the OBCs 38%, in 1994,

[50] I am grateful to Anand Kumar, Centre for the Study of Social Systems, Jawaharlal Nehru University (New Delhi), for these figures

the latter was almost twice as numerous than the former with an all time high of 46.5% of ministerial posts.

In contrast to the situation in Bihar, the OBCs of Madhya Pradesh – a state about which we have said little so far – have no tradition of political organisation and mobilisation.[51] Undoubtedly, the fragmentation of the low castes stunted feelings of solidarity among them. With the exception of the Yadavs, none of the OBCs represents

Table 10.6. CASTE AND COMMUNITY OF MPs ELECTED IN MADHYA PRADESH, 1980–99

	1980	*1984*	*1989*	*1991*	*1996*	*1998*	*1999*
Upper castes	*50*	*47.5*	*40*	*33.3*	*32.5*	*35*	*37.5*
Brahmin	30	22.5	15	10.26	15	15	17.5
Rajput	7.5	12.5	10	15.38	10	10	12.5
Banya/Jain	10	10	12.5	2.56	5	5	7.5
Kayasth		2.5	2.5	5.13	2.5	5	
Khatri	2.5						
Intermediate castes	*2.5*	*2.5*	*2.5*	*2.56*	*2.5*	*2.5*	*2.5*
Maratha	2.5	2.5	2.5	2.56	2.5	2.5	2.5
OBC	*5*	*7.5*	*15*	*20.5*	*25*	*22.5*	*22.5*
Bairagi		2.5					
Kachhi					2.5		
Kirar					2.5	2.5	2.5
Kurmi	2.5	2.5	7.5	15.38	10	12.5	7.5
Lodhi			7.5	2.56	5	2.5	5
Pankha							2.5
Panwar				2.56	2.5		
Teli					2.5	5	2.5
Yadav	2.5	2.5					
Others							2.5
Scheduled Castes	*15*	*15*	*15*	*15.38*	*15*	*15*	*15*
Scheduled Tribes	*22.5*	*22.5*	*22.5*	*23.08*	*22.5*	*22.5*	*22.5*
Muslim	*5*	*5*	*2.5*	*2.56*			
Sikh			*2.5*	*2.56*	*2.5*	*2.5*	
Total	*100* *N=40*	*100* *N=40*	*100* *N=40*	*100* *N=39*	*100* *N=40*	*100* *N=40*	*100* *N=40*

Source: Fieldwork.

[51] *Report of the [second] Backward Classes Commission*, First Part, op. cit., p. 11.

Table 10.7. CASTE AND COMMUNITY OF MPs ELECTED IN UTTAR PRADESH, 1980–99

	1980	*1984*	*1989*	*1991*	*1996*	*1998*	*1999*
Upper castes	*36.47*	*51.78*	*36.48*	*44.05*	*42.36*	*40.48*	*24.7*
Brahmin	17.65	24.71	14.12	23.81	18.82	15.48	11.76
Rajput	12.94	20	18.82	19.05	17.65	21.43	9.41
Banya/Jain	1.18	1.18					
Bhumihar	2.35	1.18	1.18	1.19	3.53	2.38	1.18
Kayasth	2.35	2.35	1.18		1.18		
Khatri		1.18					2.35
Tyagi		1.18	1.18				
Other					1.18	1.19	
Intermediate castes	*4.71*	*3.53*	*5.88*	*2.38*	*4.71*	*5.95*	*1.18*
Jat	4.71	3.53	5.88	2.38	4.71	5.95	1.18
OBC	*16.48*	*10.59*	*25.88*	*23.8*	*24.72*	*22.61*	*24.71*
Bharbhunja							1.18
Gujar		1.18					
Jaiswal					1.18	1.19	3.53
Kachhi	2.35		2.35	1.19	2.35		
Koeri				1.19			
Kurmi	7.06	2.35	9.41	9.52	8.24	8.33	5.88
Lodhi	1.18	1.18	1.18	1.19	2.35	2.38	
Mali					1.18		
Nishad	1.18				1.18		
Panwar			1.18	1.19			
Shakya							1.18
Torak					1.18		
Yadav	4.71	5.88	11.76	8.33	4.71	7.14	7.06
Others				1.19	2.35	3.57	5.88
Scheduled Castes	*21.18*	*20*	*21.18*	*23.81*	*21.18*	*21.43*	*21.18*
Christian							*1.18*
Muslim	*21.18*	*14.12*	*10.59*	*2.38*	*4.71*	*7.14*	*9.41*
Sadhu				*2.38*			*2.35*
Unidentified				*1.19*	*2.35*	*2.38*	*15.29*
Total	*100 N=85*	*100 N=85*	*100 N=85*	*100 N=84*	*100 N=85*	*100 N=84*	*100 N=85*

Source: Fieldwork.

more than 5% of the state population.[52] Regional contrasts were also very significant, since none of these castes was evenly spread across

[52] For more detailed, see C. Jaffrelot, 'The Sangh Parivar Between Sanskritization and Social Engineering' in Hansen and Jaffrelot (eds), *The BJP and the Compulsions of Politics*, op, cit., pp. 40–61.

the whole state: while the Yadavs accounted for more than 5% of the population in Chhattisgarh and Vindhya Pradesh, they were weak in Madhya Bharat; while the Telis (oil-pressers) were the largest caste in Chhattisgarh, they accounted for fewer than 3% of the population of the other regions. A similar argument could be applied, although to a lesser extent, to the Kurmis in Vindhya Pradesh and to the Lodhis in Mahakoshal.

The weakness of the OBCs also stems naturally from the demographic weight of the upper castes: according to the 1931 census in Madhya Bharat and Vindhya Pradesh, the '*dvijas*' and the Kayasths represent about one-fifth of the population whereas in Mahakoshal and Chhattisgarh they account for, respectively, 12 and 3.5%. Their

Table 10.8. CASTE AND COMMUNITY OF MPs ELECTED IN BIHAR, 1980–99

	1980	*1984*	*1989*	*1991*	*1996*	*1998*	*1999*
Upper castes	*40.74*	*44.43*	*37.05*	*19.22*	*27.77*	*24.07*	*36.73*
Brahmin	11.11	14.81	7.41	1.92	7.41	5.56	6.12
Rajput	16.67	14.81	16.67	7.69	11.11	11.11	14.29
Bhumihar	11.11	11.11	5.56	7.69	3.70	3.70	12.24
Banya/Jain		1.85			1.85		
Kayasth	1.85		7.41	1.92	3.70	3.70	4.08
Other		1.85					
OBC	*24.07*	*18.51*	*29.63*	*36.54*	*37.04*	*38.89*	*28.57*
Banya	1.85	1.85			1.85	5.56	2.04
Bijoy						1.85	
Dhanuk						1.85	
Kewat					1.85	1.85	2.04
Koeri	7.41	1.85	7.41	5.77	5.56	5.56	2.04
Kurmi	1.85		5.56	13.46	5.56	9.26	6.12
Nonia		1.85	1.85				
Yadav	11.11	12.96	14.81	17.31	22.22	12.96	16.33
Others	1.85						
Scheduled Castes	*14.81*	*14.81*	*14.81*	*15.38*	*14.81*	*14.81*	*14.29*
Scheduled Tribes	*9.26*	*9.26*	*9.26*	*11.54*	*9.26*	*9.26*	*8.16*
Christian	*1.85*		*1.85*	*1.92*	*1.85*	*1.85*	*2.04*
Muslim	*9.26*	*11.11*	*5.56*	*11.54*	*7.41*	*11.11*	*6.12*
Unidentified		*1.85*	*1.85*	*3.85*	*1.85*		*4.08*
Total	*100 N=54*	*100 N=54*	*100 N=54*	*100 N=54*	*100 N=54*	*100 N=54*	*100 N=54*

Source: Fieldwork.

Table 10.9. CASTE AND COMMUNITY OF THE MLAs IN 1995 BIHAR LEGISLATIVE ASSEMBLY, 1980–99

	Numbers	*%*
Upper castes	*61*	*18.8*
Brahmin	12	3.7
Rajput	22	6.8
Banya/Jain	2	0.6
Bhumihar	16	4.9
Kayasth	6	1.8
Marwari	2	0.6
Khatri	1	0.3
Backward castes	*148*	*45.5*
Banya	9	2.7
Teli	4	1.2
Yadav	88	27.2
Kurmi	15	4.6
Koeri	25	7.7
Munda	5	1.5
Nishad	1	0.3
Sonar	1	0.3
Most backward castes	*17*	*5.1*
Bhuiyan	1	0.3
Gangota	2	0.6
Gaud	1	0.3
Kahar	1	0.3
Kharbar	1	0.3
Mehtar	1	0.3
Nai	1	0.3
Nonia	1	0.3
Dhanuk	1	0.3
Rajwanshi	1	0.3
Rajwar	1	0.3
Kewat	3	0.9
Mallah	2	0.6
Scheduled Castes	*43*	*13.3*
Chamar	11	3.4
Dhobi	3	0.9
Dome	2	0.6
Dusadh	21	6.5
Pasi	6	1.8
Scheduled Tribes	*21*	*6.3*
Adivasi	3	0.9
Ho	3	0.9
Oraon	6	1.8
Santhal	9	2.7
Sikh	*1*	*0.3*
Muslim	*23*	*7*
Unidentified	*9*	*2.7*
Total	*323*	*100*

Source: Adapted from *Muslim India*. N° 176, August 1997, p 345.

Table 10.10. CASTES AND COMMUNITIES IN BIHAR GOVERNMENT, 1980s AND 1990S (%)

	Chandra Shekhar Singh (1983)	*Bindeshwari Dube (1985)*	*Laloo Prasad Yadav (1st govt as in 1994)*
Upper castes	44	62	27
Backward castes	18	25	35.2
Most backward castes	6	12	11.3
Muslim and Bengali	19		11.3
Scheduled Castes and Scheduled Tribes	12		15.5
Total	*100*	*100*	*100*
	N=(N.A.)	*N=(N.A.)*	*N=71*

Source: Adapted from F. Frankel, 'Caste, land and dominance in Bihar', op. cit., p. 118, and S.N. Chaudhary, *Power-Dependence Relations*, op. cit., p. 219.

strength does not depend on this demographic advantage alone; in fact the domination of the Rajputs was especially marked in Madhya Pradesh because of the large number of former princely states. In Madhya Bharat and Vindhya Pradesh demographic weight and socio-political domination are concomitant (the Rajputs represent, for instance, the largest caste in Madhya Bharat with more than 9% of the regional population). Moreover, in contrast with Uttar Pradesh and Rajasthan where the Jats are locally recognised as the dominant caste in several places, in Madhya Pradesh the intermediate (or middle) castes who could have acted as the spearhead of anti-establishment movements are not numerous enough: the Marathas represent an almost negligible percentage, many of them belonging to the elite of the princely states whose ruling families were from the same social milieu. They tended, therefore, to emulate the Rajputs.[53]

This sociological context partly explains the comparatively small number of OBCs among the MLAs. But the trend that we have observed in the case of the MPs begun earlier here since the upper caste MLAs declined from about 40% in 1980 to almost one-third eighteen years later (as against 37.5% of MPs in 1999), whereas the OBCs rose from about 16% in 1980 to 22% eighteen years later (as against 22.5% of MPs in 1999). In contrast to most other states of the Hindi belt, the Mandal effect was less evident in Madhya Pradesh because

[53] This Kshatriyaisation process was well illustrated by several marital alliances such as the wedding of Jivaji Rao Scindia with Vijaya Raje Scindia.

the share of OBC MLAs had already begun to rise in the early 1980s. Yet it increased by 4 percentage points between 1990 and 1993.

The change in the social composition of the state government is very similar to that of the assembly in the sense that the share of the upper castes tended also to decline. However, this trend was not linear because it largely depended on which party was in office. After ups and downs, the Congress governments of Digvijay Singh maintained the share of the upper castes below 40% throughout most

Table 10.11. CASTE AND COMMUNITY OF MLAs IN MADHYA PRADESH ASSEMBLY, 1980–98 (%)

	1980	*1985*	*1990*	*1993*	*1998*
Upper castes	*40.3*	*40.7*	*40.9*	*37.1*	*35.6*
Brahmin	19.7	16.9	15.9	15.3	12.2
Rajput	11.3	15	12.5	12.8	15.3
Banya/Jain	5.9	7.2	10	7.5	6.9
Kayasth	2.5	1.3	1.3	0.9	0.6
Khatri	0.6	0.3	0.6	0.3	
Other	0.3		0.6	0.3	0.6
Intermediate castes	*0.9*	*0.3*	*0.3*	*0.6*	*0.9*
Maratha	0.3	0.3	0.3	0.6	0.9
Patidar	0.6				
OBC	*16.1*	*18.6*	*18.7*	*22.7*	*22*
Jat	0.3		0.3	0.3	
Yadav	0.9	1.9	2.5	2.5	2.8
Kurmi	4.4	4.1	3.1	5	6.3
Kirar	0.3	0.3	1.3	0.6	0.9
Lodhi	0.9	0.9	1.3	1.6	2.2
Mali	0.3	0.6	0.3	0.6	
Teli	0.9	1.6	1.9	2.2	1.6
Panwar	1.9	2.2	2.5	1.6	0.3
Other	6.2	7	5.5	8.3	7.8
Scheduled Castes	*14*	*13.3*	*13.7*	*14.3*	*14.7*
Scheduled Tribes	*24.4*	*24.4*	*23.7*	*23.4*	*23.4*
Muslim	*1.9*	*1.6*	*0.9*		*1.6*
Sikh	*0.3*	*0.3*	*0.6*	*0.9*	*0.9*
Christian	*0.3*			*0.3*	*0.3*
Unidentified/other	*1.6*	*0.6*	*0.3*	*0.3*	*0.6*
Total	*100 N=320*	*100 N=320*	*100 N=320*	*100 N=320*	*100 N=320*

Source: Fieldwork.

of the 1990s. This decline benefited not only the OBCs – who represented about one-fifth of the cabinets in the 1990s – but also the Scheduled Tribes. There were 25% of Tribals in his first government, approximately their share of the general population.

While the 1985 elections sent a smaller number of upper caste candidates and a larger number of OBCs to the assembly, the 1985 Congress government was massively dominated by upper caste politicians, a clear indication that the party was not, in fact, democratising itself. Things hardly changed in 1990 because the BJP won the elections and maintained a strong representation of the upper castes in the cabinet. But Digvijay Singh's governments in 1993 were

Table 10.12. CASTE AND COMMUNITY OF MEMBERS OF MADHYA PRADESH GOVERNMENTS, 1980–95

	1980–4	*1985–6*	*1990–2*	*1993–5*
Upper castes	*40.9*	*57.1*	*51.7*	*36.2*
Brahmin	18.2	38.1	19.4	13.9
Rajput	13.6	19.0	6.5	16.7
Banya/Jain	6.8		19.4	5.6
Khatri			3.2	
Kayasth	2.3		3.2	
OBC	*18.2*	*14.3*	*22.6*	*19.4*
Jat			3.2	
Yadav	2.3	4.8	3.2	8.3
Kurmi	4.5	4.8	6.5	2.8
Kirar			3.2	
Lodhi			3.2	
Mali				2.8
Teli			3.2	2.8
Panwar	4.5			
Other	6.8	4.8		2.8
Scheduled Castes	*13.6*	*9.5*	*6.5*	*8.3*
Scheduled Tribes	*15.9*	*4.8*	*9.7*	*25.0*
Muslim	*2.3*	*4.8*	*3.2*	*2.8*
Sikh	*2.3*	*4.8*		*2.8*
Christian				*2.8*
Unidentified	*6.8*	*4.8*	*6.5*	*2.8*
Total	*100* *N=32*	*100* *N=21*	*100* *N=31*	*100* *N=36*

Source: Fieldwork in Bhopal.

much less upper caste dominated. We shall return below to the Madhya Pradesh Congress's ability to integrate non-elite groups.

Like Madhya Pradesh, Uttar Pradesh occupies an intermediary position in so far as the changing social profile of its political personnel is concerned. Congress domination was for many years reflected in the over-representation of the upper castes in the government and in the assembly, but circumstances changed even more dramatically than in Madhya Pradesh in the 1990s.

The trend shown in Table 10.13 confirms the one that was evident from the changing profile of the UP MPs, but it is more pronounced. If one goes by the 1993 elections, the impact of Mandal is not as dramatic as in the case of Bihar, but more significant than in Madhya Pradesh. The erosion of the upper caste MLAs is marked, from almost 40% in 1980 and 1985 to about one third in the 1990s, with the same acceleration at the time of the Janata Dal's rise to power in 1989. However, as early as 1985 – as in Madhya Pradesh – the share of the OBCs rose to almost 20% and the Janata Dal victory of 1989 simply helped the lower castes to consolidate their gains. The impact of such electoral success on the social profile of the Uttar Pradesh government was more obvious, since in 1989 the cabinet of Mulayam Singh Yadav had fewer upper caste and more OBC ministers (but fewer from Scheduled Castes) than the previous Congress governments, as is evident from Table 10.14.

Rajasthan is the only state where the graph of MPs and that of MLAs is almost perfectly parallel. The state followed the general trend in so far as the decline of the upper castes is concerned as their percentage reached its lowest point in 1990, namely 31%. However, this development – as in the case of the MPs – did not benefit the OBCs (who remained very under-represented in 1993, with only 7% of MLAs) but rather the Jats, whose share rose to 20.5% in 1993.

The persisting under-representation of the OBCs is even more marked in the state governments. Though the figures regarding ministers must be treated with caution given the high percentage of 'unidentified caste and community' in the late 1980s and 1990s, it seems that the percentage of OBCs is declining. The proportion of Jats, by contrast, is increasing – as in the Assembly – and that of the upper castes oscillates between 30% and 40% without any linear trend.

Whether we look at the social profile of MPs, MLAs or state

Table 10.13. CASTE AND COMMUNITY OF MLAs IN UTTAR PRADESH ASSEMBLY, 1980–96

	1980	*1985*	*1989*	*1991*	*1993*	*1996*
Upper castes	*39.4*	*39.4*	*32.5*	*39*	*26.5*	*37.7*
Intermediate castes	*1.6*	*1.9*	*1.6*	*2.4*	*2.3*	*2.3*
OBC	*13.7*	*19.2*	*22.7*	*25.2*	*29.9*	*24*
Scheduled Castes	*21.7*	*21.8*	*22*	*22.1*	*22*	*21.2*
Scheduled Tribes	*0.2*	*0.2*	*0.2*	*0.2*	*0.2*	*0.2*
Muslim	*12.1*	*12.2*	*9.4*	*5.5*	*7.5*	*9*
Sikh	*0.9*	*0.7*	*0.2*	*0.2*	*0.2*	*0.4*
Anglo Indian	*0.2*	*0.2*	*0.2*	*0.2*	*0.2*	*0.2*
Unidentified	*9.9*	*4.2*	*10.7*	*5*	*10.8*	*4.7*
Total	*100*	*100*	*100*	*100*	*100*	*100*
	N=424	*N=426*	*N=427*	*N=420*	*N=427*	*N=424*

Source: Fieldwork by Jasmine Zerinini-Brotel as published in Christophe Jaffrelot and Jasmine Zérinini-Brotel, 'La montée des basses castes dans la politique nord-indienne', *Pouvoirs*, 90 (1999), p. 80 Zoya Hasan has published more detailed data for the 1980 assembly. At that time, the Brahmin MLAs represented 27% of the assembly, the Rajputs 14% the upper OBC 6%, the Scheduled Castes 20% and the Muslims 10% (see Z. Hasan, 'Power and Mobilization: Patterns of Resilience and Change in Uttar Pradesh Politics', in F. Frankel and M.S.A. Rao (eds), *Dominance and State Power*, vol. 1, op. cit., p. 176.)

governments, the rise of the OBCs has occurred unevenly throughout the Hindi belt. The most dramatic change has occured in Bihar where OBC MLAs are now in proportion to their population. If the representation of OBCs in Uttar Pradesh and Madhya Pradesh is not

Table 10.14. CASTE AND COMMUNITY OF MEMBERS OF THREE UTTAR PRADESH GOVERNMENTS, 1985–89

	N.D. Tiwari 1985	*V.B. Singh 1987*	*Mulayam Singh Yadav 1989*
Upper castes	*51.4*	*52.9*	*42.85*
Brahmin	21.6	*n.a.*	28.57
Rajput	24.3	*n.a.*	7.14
Bhumihar	–	*n.a.*	7.14
Kayasth	2.7	*n.a.*	
OBC	*13.5*	*11.8*	*21.42*
Yadav	2.7	*n.a.*	7.14
Kurmi	2.7	*n.a.*	7.14

Contd.

Gujar	–	*n.a.*	7.14
Other	8.1	*n.a.*	
Scheduled Castes	*18.9*	*20.6*	*14.28*
Muslim	*10.81*	*11.8*	*21.42*
Unidentified	*2.7*	*2.9*	–
Total	*100* *N=37*	*100* *N=34*	*100* *N=14*

Sources: C. Jaffrelot and J. Zérinini-Brotel, 'Accommodating the lower castes? UP and MP after Monital', in R. Jenkins (ed.) *Comparing Politics Across Indian States* (forthcoming) for the governments of N.D. Tiwari and V.B. Singh. R. Singh and A. Yadav, *Mulayam Singh*, New Delhi: Konark, 1998, p. 93 for the 1989 government of Mulayam Singh Yadav.

yet in proportion to their demographic weight, they have achieved a considerable increase over the last ten years, especially among MLAs. By contrast Rajasthan lags behind. Unsurprisingly, the rise of the OBCs is more significant at the state level than among the MPs who take part in national politics: India's silent revolution is a gradual one. In addition to this geographically eneven distribution, the OBCs also suffer from internal divisions in all these states.

Are the OBCs a social and political category?

In 1996, one member of the UP Backward Classes Commission observed that 'the OBC which was a constitutional category has now become a social category'.[54] Yadav's analysis follows a similar trajectory in his remarkable article about the 1993 elections where he wrote: 'The expression "OBC" has [. . .] travelled a long way from a rather careless bureaucratic nomenclature in the document of the Constitution to a vibrant and subjectively experienced political community'.[55] However, the notion that the OBCs form a new 'political community' or even a 'social category' needs to be qualified. While low caste solidarity increased during the Mandal affair, when caste polarisation was acute, it was much less prevalent from the mid-1990s onwards and the very notion of OBCs has lost some of its relevance in understanding political behaviour.

Grassroot mobilisation or Yadav manipulation? While Yadavs and Kurmis alone had representatives in the Lok Sabha till the 1970s, new

[54] Cited in Hasan, *Quest for Power*, op. cit., p. 164.
[55] Yadav, 'Reconfiguration in India politics', op. cit., p.102.

Table 10.15. CASTE AND COMMUNITY OF MLAs IN RAJASTHAN ASSEMBLY, 1980–98

	1980	*1985*	*1990*	*1993*	*1998*
Upper castes	*36*	*37.5*	*31*	*36*	*31*
Brahmin	13.5	16.5	10.5	11.5	9.1
Rajput	11.5	11.5	8	14	12.2
Banya/Jain	10	8	10	10	7.6
Kayasth	0.5	1	0.5	-	0.5
Khatri	0.5		1		0.5
Sindhi	–	0.5	1	0.5	1
Intermediate castes	*19*	*16.5*	*18.5*	*20.5*	*20.3*
Including: Jat	19	16	18.5	20.5	18.8
OBC	*6*	*8*	*10*	*6*	*8.6*
Yadav	1.5	1.5	2	1	2.6
Mali	1.5	2	3	1	0.5
Gujar	3	3	3	3	2
Kumhar	–	0.5	0.5	-	0.5
Other	–	1	1.5	1	3
Scheduled Castes	*17.5*	*17*	*18*	*18.5*	*17.8*
Scheduled Tribes	*13*	*14*	*14.5*	*13.5*	*14.1*
Muslim	*5*	*4*	*4*	*2.5*	*6.1*
Sikh	*0.5*	*1*	*2*	*1.5*	*1*
Unidentified	*3*	*1.5*	*1.5*	*1*	*1*
Total	*100* *N=200*	*100* *N=200*	*100* *N=200*	*100* *N=200*	*100* *N=197*

Source: Fieldwork.

castes have joined the political arena in the 1980s (Lodhis, Koeris, Gujars, Malis) and in the 1990s (such as the Jaiswals, the Telis and the Kacchis – two castes which I have classified among the 'others' in table 10.4). However, the rise of the OBCs is above all the rise of the Yadavs and the Kurmis, as their share of MPs testifies: together they represent some 15% of North Indian MPs, as many as the Brahmin or Rajput deputies, in the 1990s. The share of the Yadavs and the Kurmis has grown to such an extent that each of these castes represents about one-third of OBC MPs in North India since 1989.

Even though the Kurmis organised themselves as early as the Yadavs did by means of caste associations, the Yadavs have been at the forefront of the OBC mobilisation from the very beginning. The leader of the All India Backward Caste Federation in the 1960s and

Table 10.16. CASTE AND COMMUNITY OF MEMBERS OF RAJASTHAN GOVERNMENT, 1980–98

	1980	*1982*	*1985*	*1987*	*1990*	*1993*	*1998*
Upper castes	*43.2*	*52.4*	*33.4*	*35*	*29.8*	*40*	*33.3*
Brahmin	15.9	14.3	20	20	12.8	13.3	13.3
Rajput	6.8	14.3	6.7	10	8.5	16.7	10
Banya/Jain	20.5	19	6.7	5	8.5	10	10
Kayasth		4.8				–	
Intermediate castes	*9.1*	*14.3*	*6.7*	*15*	*17*	*13.3*	*16.6*
Including: Jat	9.1	14.3	6.7	10	14.9	13.3	13.3
OBC	*9.1*	*9.6*	*6.7*	*5*	*6.4*	*6.6*	*3.3*
Yadav	4.5	4.8	6.7		4.3	3.3	
Mali	2.3						
Gujar	2.3	4.8		5	2.1	3.3	3.3
Scheduled Castes	*22.7*	*14.3*	*20.1*	*25*	*14.9*	*16.7*	*16.7*
Scheduled Tribes	*9.1*	*4.8*	*20.1*	*5*	*8.6*	*3.3*	*10*
Muslim	*4.5*	*4.8*	*6.7*		*4.3*	*3.3*	*10*
Sikh	*2.3*				*2.1*	*3.3*	
Unidentified			*6.7*	*15*	*17*	*13.3*	*10*
Total	*100*	*100*	*100*	*100*	*100*	*100*	*100*
	N=44	*N=21*	*N=15*	*N=20*	*N=47*	*N=30*	*N=30*

Source: Fieldwork.

1970s, Brahma Prakash Chaudhury, was a Yadav. B.P.Mandal was himself a Yadav and after the Janata Dal took over in 1989 the Yadavs campaigned in favour of the report's implementation more actively than anybody else. Laloo Prasad Yadav, the then Chief Minister of Bihar, Mulayam Singh Yadav, the then Chief Minister of Uttar Pradesh and Sharad Yadav, the Minister for Textile and Food Processing in V.P. Singh's government were among the most determined Yadav leaders. The latter was already one of the few Yadav leaders with a national reputation. A native of Madhya Pradesh where he was elected MP in 1974 during the JP Movement, he moved to Budaun (Uttar Pradesh) where he was elected in 1989 and then to Mahdepura (Bihar), B.P. Mandal's home village, where he was returned to the Lok Sabha in 1991.[56] His influence was also felt in Haryana where he allied with Devi Lal in 1987 and attracted a sizeable share of Yadav

[56] Interview with Sharad Yadav, New Delhi, 10 Nov. 1997.

votes. After the anti-Mandal agitation started, Sharad Yadav was at the forefront of the counter-mobilisation in Delhi and elsewhere, till he launched his Mandal Rath Yatra in late 1992 and early 1993 in reaction to the Supreme Court's decision to exclude the elite of the OBCs from quotas. The 'creamy layer' controversy and the question whether caste had to be the criterion of the reservations, sheds much light on how the Janata Dal tried to protect Yadav interests.

The 'creamy layer' and the Yadavs. In September 1990 the Supreme Court stayed V.P. Singh's decision to implement the Mandal report in the petition *Indra Sawhney and others* v. *Union of India.* It pronounced its final verdict more than two years later, on 16 November, 1992: V.P. Singh's decision was upheld by the majority of the Court but the judges questioned the granting of reservations to all OBCs given the fact that some of them did not need any state help. In their order, they requested the Government of India to specify within four months 'the relevant and requisite socio-economic criteria to exclude socially advanced persons/sections [the creamy layer] from "Other Backward Classes" '.[57] The Expert Committee appointed by the Government in March 1993 under the Chairmanship of Ramanandan Prasad proposed to exclude all the progeny of the OBC elite (including the employees of public sector units) and of the OBC property-owners – which meant, for agricultural holdings, the son(s) and daughter(s) of a family which owned 65% of the statutory area.

The Janata Dal, with Laloo Prasad Yadav as President and Sharad Yadav as leader of the legislative group in the Lok Sabha then lobbied to exclude the middle peasantry from the 'creamy layer'. Eventually, the government bowed to their pressure and the latter restriction affected only OBC applicants of families owning 85% of their land ceiling allowance. The fact that the main bone of contention, for the Janata Dal, concerned the size of agricultural holdings testifies that it was primarily the spokesman of the middle caste peasants and above all of the Yadavs.

When the 27% reservation was eventually implemented at the Center after the Supreme Court decision of November 1992 and the Memorandum of 8 September 1993,[58] the upper castes ceased to

[57] 'Summary of issues, judgment and directions in Indra Sawhney v. Union of India', Appendix 1 in Prasad, *Reservational Justice*, op. cit., p. 312.

[58] This memorandum – with which the Mandal affair came to a close – explicitly recognised caste as the relevant unit for the reservation policy: 'The OBCs

resist it and resigned themselves to the rule of numbers. By then the economic liberalisation that was set in motion in 1991 provided them with a safety net: careers in the private sector had become more attractive and therefore they felt there was no need to fight for their traditional positions in the bureaucracy. Having won the battle over quotas, and with the upper castes relinquishing their confrontationist attitude, the lower castes no longer felt the need for solidarity as acutely as before. The very notion of OBCs started to lose its relevance and it seemed that this broad category was in fact often manipulated by a Yadav elite to promote its interests. Such élite manipulation was not uncommon in the past since the *kisan* identity promoted by Charan Singh was also perceived by many Jats as a means of mobilising a large social base, and Madhu Limaye, as noted above, deplored the use of the tactic during the SVD government in Bihar when B.P. Mandal cashed in on the low caste mobilisation to promote the Yadavs' interests through the Shoshit Dal. Lohia lamented even before this episode that 'Ever and ever again, the revolt of the down-graded castes has been misused to up-grade one or another caste . . . '.[59] Even then Lohia targetted the Yadavs as the main protagonists of such a strategy.[60]

The way Yadav leaders used the Janata Dal reservation policy to promote their caste interests is evident from the *modus operandi* of Mulayam Singh Yadav and Laloo Prasad Yadav after they became Chief Ministers of Uttar Pradesh and Bihar, respectively in November 1989 and March 1990. M.S. Yadav lost power in 1991 but governed the state again in 1993–5, whereas the latter won the 1995 state elections and then remained at the helm of Bihar after the March 2000 elections through his wife, Rabri Devi, who had taken over from him in 1997 because of the judicial procedure directed against him in the infamous 'fodder scam'.

---

for the purpose of the aforesaid reservation would comprise, in the first phase, the caste and communities which are common to both the lists in the report of the Mandal Commission and the State Governments' Lists' ('Office Memorandum no. 36012/22/93-Estt.', reprinted as Annex 1 of N. Verma and H.S. Verma, 'Criteria for Identifying the Creamy-Layer Among the OBCs in U.P. and Bihar', Paper presented to the panel, 'Marginalised groups and human rights', of the 22nd All India Sociological Conference, 16–19 Dec. 1995, Bhopal, p. 21).

[59] Lohia, 'Towards the destruction of castes and classes', op. cit., p. 90.

[60] Ibid., p. 103.

Mulayam Singh Yadav's return to Lohia politics? In Uttar Pradesh, Mulayam Singh Yadav epitomised the oscillation of Backward Caste leaders between Lohia's socialism and Charan Singh's politics and the final 'victory' of quota politics over *kisan* politics. He was born in 1939 in Etawah District, an early socialist stronghold.[61] Arjun Singh Badhoria, a veteran freedom fighter, was elected MP for this constituency in 1957 as an independent with socialist leanings. (Between 1957 and 1980, he won three times and lost three times as a socialist candidate in Etawah). Mulayam Singh Yadav was initiated into socialism through this local connections[62] and also because of the growing influence of Lohia, who came first to Etawah in 1954 to campaign against an increase in the irrigation levy.[63] In fact, he had launched this 'Nehar rate Andolan' in thirteen districts of Uttar Pradesh to protest against the hike in the irrigation fee introduced by the state government. Etawah was one such district and Mulayam Singh Yadav took part in the demonstration and courted arrest even though he was only fifteen at the time. Lohia had also come to his village for a '*jat todo*' (break caste) meeting.[64]

Mulayam came from a poor peasant family in a small village but was able to join K.K. College in Etawah in 1960, where he was highly influenced by *Jan*, the newspaper that Lohia then edited. This political commitment led him to contest the student union elections, of which he was elected president once. He passed his B.T. to become a teacher and gained an M.A. in political science at Agra University soon after. He was directly initiated into socialist politics by Natthu Singh, a local politician, who was impressed by Mulayam's talents as a wrestler! He was responsible for getting Mulayam Singh to contest the 1967 assembly elections when he became the youngest MLA in the Vidhan Sabha. After Lohia's death, he joined the socialist faction led by Raj Narain, which merged with the BKD to form the Bharatiya Lok Dal in 1974.

Mulayam Singh Yadav then combined the ideas of Lohia – whose writings he read assiduously when he was in jail for nineteenth

[61] *Uttar Pradesh Dvadesh Vidhan Sabha ke Sadasyon ka Jivan – Parichay, 1993*, Lucknow: Vidhan Sabha Sachivalay, 1994, p. 246.

[62] He had joined one of the schools setup by Bhadoria. Interview with Arjun Singh Bhadoria, New Delhi: 28 Oct. 1997.

[63] A.K. Dubey, *Mulayam Singh Yadav – Aaj ke netalAlochnatmak Adhyaynamala* (Hindi), New Delhi: Rajkamal Prakashan, 1997.

[64] Lal and Nair, *Caste vs Caste*, op. cit., p. 32.

months during the Emergency – and those of Charan Singh. In 1977, he was elected on a Janata Party ticket and became minister of co-operatives, animal husbandry and rural industries, in which capacity he developed a *kisan*-oriented policy: he distributed seeds and fertilisers to farmers – obviously those who owned some land[65] – and made loans cheaper and easier to obtain. At the same time, he also remained committed to quota politics since reservations for Scheduled Castes and Backward Castes were introduced in the co-operatives.[66]

Mulayam Singh Yadav lost the 1980 election but was made president of the Uttar Pradesh Lok Dal and then of the state Dalit Mazdoor Kisan Party that Charan Singh launched in 1984. His politics then combined elements of the socialist platform and the articles of faith of Charan Singh. He urged the government to implement the Mandal Commission recommendations, to increase reservations for the Scheduled Castes in the Lok Sabha, Vidhan Sabha and government services, as their numbers had substantially increased, and argued in a more Charan Singh-like perspective that 60% of government expenditure should be devoted to agriculture and that big factories should be replaced by cottage industries.[67] However, a more legitimate *kisan* leader, Ajit Singh, the son of Charan Singh, dislodged Mulyam Singh Yadav from the post of leader of the opposition in the UP assembly in February 1987.[68] The Lok Dal split into two, as we have seen already: the Lok Dal (A), 'A' for Ajit and the Lok Dal (B), 'B' for Bahuguna, a party whose real leader in UP was Mulayam Singh Yadav. In September 1987, Yadav launched a Kranti Yatra, 'Pilgrimage for Revolution', whose main themes combined *kisan* and quota politics: he asked for remunerative prices for farmers and the abolition of land auctions in cases of loan recovery, while at the same time demanding the implementation of the Mandal Commission report.[69] This campaign enabled him to visit most districts of Uttar Pradesh: he 'wanted to reach every nook and corner of Uttar Pradesh before the elections of 1989'.[70]

[65] Ram Singh and Anshuman Yadav, *Mulayam Singh: A Political Biography*, New Delhi: Konark, 1998, p. 47.

[66] Ibid, p. 49.

[67] Ibid., p. 65.

[68] Charan Singh was then ailing – he was to die in May 1987.

[69] Ibid., p. 72.

[70] Ibid., p. 87.

While Bahuguna refused to join the Janata Dal, Mulayam Singh Yadav committed his political party to it and joined its Central Parliamentary Board, like Ajit Singh. The victory of the JD in Uttar Pradesh led both leaders to contest the post of Chief Minister. Mulayam Singh Yadav was chosen by a majority of MLAs. His first public statement – after being sworn-in – was: 'Lohia's dream has come true. A *kisan*'s son has become the Chief Minister'.[71] By bracketing together Lohia and a reference to the *kisan* in the same breath, he suggested that he would pursue both *kisan* politics and quota politics at the same time. Indeed, his first decisions – besides replacing English by Hindi as an official language[72] – consisted in waiving agricultural loans up to Rs 10,000 and increasing sugar cane prices. Then, even before V.P. Singh's reservation policy was announced, he promulgated an ordinance providing OBCs with a 15% quota in the state administration.[73] Ian Duncan points out that even though he came from the Lok Dal, Charan Singh's party, Mulayam Singh Yadav decided 'to place a far greater emphasis on the collective identity of the backward classes than the Lok Dal had ever done'.[74] Indeed, he put pressure on the Janata Dal government to implement the Mandal report. Addressing a party convention in Etawah, he declared: 'Since the Janata Dal does not consist only of the socialists [*sic*], a struggle is needed to ensure the implementation of the Mandal Commision recommendations'.[75]

According to his biographers, Mulayam Singh Yadav was very upset by the political exploitation of the Mandal issue by V.P. Singh and disappointed by the way the latter focused only on reservations in the central administration, leaving aside educational institutions and promotions, although they fell within the remit of the recommendations.[76] However he supported V.P. Singh's decision and shifted towards quota politics in the context of the Mandal affair,

[71] Ibid., p. 93.

[72] As a true follower of Lohia, he always prefered to speak in Hindi – also because his command of English was far from perfect. (D.D. Dubey, *For a Secular Alternative*, Lucknow, Dr Ram Manohar Lohia Trust, no date, no page no.)

[73] Hasan, *Quest for Power*, op. cit., p. 149.

[74] I. Duncan, 'Agricultural innovation and political change in North India', *JPS*, 24(4), July 1997, p. 262.

[75] Cited in Singh and Yadav, *Mulayam Singh*, op. cit., p. 104.

[76] Ibid., p. 105.

whereas Ajit Singh became the main spokesman for *kisan* politics. In 1990, the Bharatiya Kisan Union, which had been orignally launched by Charan Singh and which primarily represented the affluent Jat farmers of western Uttar Pradesh, put forward a charter of demands that Mulayam Singh Yadav rejected allegedly because their implemenation would have been at the expense of the poor and landless labourers. The fifty six Janata Dal MLAs of the Ajit Singh faction threatened to resign from the assembly, in vain.

He further distanced himself from Charan Singh's *kisan* politics when he prevented the BKU from holding a demonstration (a *kisan panchayat*) in Lucknow in July 1990. In spite of this ban, the Jat-based organisation demonstrated to put pressure on Yadav's government on behalf of the farmers' interests. The state's response was very heavy-handed: 20,000 people were arrested, including Tikait, the BKU leader, and 2 people were killed. Yadav then mended his ways and went in December 1990 to Tikait's village along with Chandra Shekhar, the then Prime Minister, to announce that the farmers' unpaid electricity bills would be waived.[77] But the cleavage (and division of labour) between Mulayam Singh Yadav and Ajit Singh was clear. The former moved increasingly towards low caste politics and showed no interest in reconstituting the Jat-OBC alliance. He was hostile to the inclusion of Jats in the OBC list since it would dilute the quotas whose main beneficiaries were to be the Yadavs and deprive them of their newly established leadership of the lower castes.[78] Mulayam Singh Yadav returned ostensibly to the socialist tradition when he severed his links with the Janata Dal to form, at the Rammanohar Lohia Nagar of Lucknow, a new socialist party: the Samajwadi Janata Dal, the Socialist People's Party, which became the Samajwadi Party in November 1992.[79] The composition of the

[77] *Sunday Observer*, 16 Dec. 1990.

[78] A Jat politician, Satpal Malik, recalls that Yadav once said that the inclusion of the Jats among the OBCs 'could only be done on his dead body' (interview with Satpal Malik).

[79] In the inauguration speech on November 4 at Lucknow, Mulayam Singh Yadav evoked the names of Lohia, Jay Prakash Narayan and Acharya Narendra Deva to conclude: 'The disintegration of the socialist forces has been one of the major causes for the present state of affairs in the country. So long as the socialists were united, they used to have a positive influence both on the government and society. They not only used to oppose anti-people policies of the

party's National Executive showed that it was closely associated with the OBCs, who were far more numerous than the upper castes, and more especially with the Yadavs, who formed by far the largest group. The second largest group was made of Muslim leaders, the Muslim community being part of the social coalition Mulayam Singh Yadav had constituted. Similarly, out of the 90 presidents of district or city units of the SP in UP in August 2000, 35.6% were Yadavs and 25.6% were Muslims – other OBCs represented 19% of the total and the upper castes 15%.[80]

Soon after founding the SP, Mulayam Singh Yadav tried to make an alliance with the BSP. He was certainly anxious to benefit from the new strength of this Dalit-based party. The seat adjustment they eventually agreed upon in 1993, left 167 constituencies to the latter and 254 to the Samajwadi Party. This alliance won 176 seats in the 1993 elections and was able to form the government with Congress support. Mulayam Singh Yadav, who became Chief Minister once again, initially combined quota politics and *kisan* politics. As far as the latter was concerned, he met some of the demands of the BKU: the ban on free movement of wheat, paddy and coarse grains was lifted so that farmers – those who had a surplus to sell – could earn a decent remuneration for their produce, prices of sugar cane were again raised and the surcharge on electricity dues from private tube-wells was waived.

On the other hand, he relaunched the state's reservation policy. When he was Chief Minister in 1989–91, Mulayam Singh Yadav had issued an amending ordinance giving the OBCs of UP the same reservations – 27% – as the Mandal Commission Report had recommended. A stay order granted by the Allahabad High Court blocked the process and then the Supreme Court, in its 16 November 1992 judgement, asked the Centre and the states first to identify the 'creamy layer'. UP had been placed under President's rule after the demolition of the Babri Masjid on 6 December 1992. The governor, Motilal Vora was a Congressman from Madhya Pradesh. He resorted to obstructionism and appointed an Expert Committee in March

---

government but also came up with an alternative programme.' (Cited in R. Singh and A. Yadav, *Mulayam Singh*, op. cit., pp.131–2) These references were partly rhetorical but Mulayam Singh Yadav certainly aspired to rebuild a socialist alternative to sustain his political ambition.

[80] Interview with SP Office bearers in Lucknow in August 2000.

Table 10.17. CASTE AND COMMUNITY OF MEMBERS OF NATIONAL EXECUTIVE OF SAMAJWADI PARTY (as in 1995)

	1995
Upper castes	*30.6*
Brahmin	10.2
Rajput	3.4
Banya/Jain	6.8
Bhumihar	5.1
Kayasth	3.4
Khatri	1.7
Intermediate castes	*5.1*
Jat	3.4
Maratha	1.7
OBC	*42.4*
Banjara	3.4
Banya (from Bihar)	1.7
Darzi	1.7
Gadaria	1.7
Gujar	1.7
Kallar	1.7
Kurmi	1.7
Teli	1.7
Yadav	22
Others	5.1
Scheduled Castes	*5.1*
Christian	*3.4*
Muslim	*13.6*
Total	*N=59*

Source: Fieldwork.

1993 under the chairmanship of Justice (Retd.) Umesh Chandra.[81] The Committee submitted its report in May but then he waited till August to appoint the Committee charged with setting the percentage of reservations to be given to the OBCs. The Committee, under the chairmanship of Ramesh Chandra, recommended 27%

[81] In addition to Umesh Chandra, a retired judge and a Kayasth by caste, the committee comprised a university professor, B.K. Joshi (Brahmin), a sociologist, H.S. Verma (Kurmi) and an IAS cadre, Ramesh Chandra (Scheduled Castes) who was to preside over the committee in charge of fixing the reservation percentage.

reservation for the OBCs and the enhancement of the reservation percentage of the Scheduled Castes from 18% to 21%.[82] The SP-BSP coalition government was formed on 4 December 1993 and one of its first decision was to implement the 27% quota. Then the government had the *Uttar Pradesh Public Services (Reservation for Scheduled Castes, Scheduled Tribes and Other Backward Classes) Act* voted on 22 March 1994. This new law reserved 21% of public posts to the Scheduled Castes, 2% to the Scheduled Tribes and 27% to the OBCs. The 'creamy-layer' criterion that had been fixed by the Umesh Chandra committee suited Mulayam well since it was very generous with the small peasant-proprietors: the OBC farmers excluded from the quota were only those whose holdings were within the limits fixed under the UP Imposition of Ceiling on Landholdings Act (1960).[83]

Reservations were also introduced in the Panchayati Raj institutions along the same pattern as in the administration. While the 73rd Amendment to the Indian Constitution, in 1993, made reservation of seats for SCs (in proportion to their demographic weight) and for women (33%), mandatory at all levels of the Panchayati Raj system, in June 1994 the Mulayam Singh Yadav governement amended the *UP Panchayat Act, 1947* – in order to include these changes and add one more change, since it also granted a 27% quota for the OBCs.[84]

In addition to the administration and the local bodies, Mulayam Singh Yadav made provision for 27% reservation of OBCs in medical, engineering and management college. This decision was strongly resented in Uttarakhand where the OBCs comprised only 2% of the

[82] Verma and Verma, 'Criteria for identifying the creamy-layer', op. cit., p. 16.

[83] Ibid., p. 28. However, the Act – like the similar law passed in Bihar – was quashed by the Supreme Court in 1995 because the clauses regarding the 'creamy layer' did not comply with the spirit of its judgement in the Indra Sawhney Case. The Umesh Chandra committee excluded only the elite of the agriculturists since, in addition to the clause regarding land property, an income of Rs 1 million a year from sources other than agriculture, graduation of a spouse and family ownership of immovable property of at least Rs 2 million were among the key criteria – which meant that the affluent OBC (mainly Yadavs and Kurmis) would benefit from the quotas.

[84] G.K. Lieten and R. Srivastava, *Unequal Partners. Power Relations, Devolution and Development in Uttar Pradesh*, New Delhi: Sage, 1999, p. 250.

population.[85] Their agitation was judged illegitimate and politically motivated by Mulayam Singh Yadav who decided to crush it and launched a counter-mobilisation. He emphasised that he was fighting for the 95% who were deprived against the 5% who were priviledged.

In order to strengthen his image as a low caste leader, he transferred upper castes bureaucrats to non-essential posts. The number of Additional District Magistrates (Finance and Revenue) from the upper castes decreased from 43 (out of 63) to only 13 in six months. The Chief Secretary, a Brahmin, was replaced by a Kayasth.[86] These decisions – which were given maximum publicity – were partly made under pressure from the BSP but they were in tune with Mulayam Singh Yadav's strategy. In 1994 his government had also passed another reservation schema, the UP State Universities Reservation in Admission for Scheduled Castes, Scheduled Tribes and Other Backward Classes which provided a 21% quota for the Scheduled Castes, a 2% quota for the Scheduled Tribes and a 27% quota for the OBCs.

In 1995, the BSP withdrew its support from Mulayam Singh Yadav's government. Mulayam Singh Yadav had to resign and President's rule was instituted by the Governor Motilal Vora. But Yadav remained a strong advocate of quota politics. When Vora declared Uttarakhand as a backward region and thereby brought all its inhabitants – and not only the local OBCs – under the 27% quota, Mulayam Singh Yadav objected that such a move would deny them their due share in this area. He launched an *aarakshan bachao* (Save Reservations) campaign in January 1996. This was quota politics *par excellence*: even though the potential beneficiaries of the reservations were a handful of low caste people in Uttarakhand, by agitating over the issue, Mulayam Singh Yadav intended to mobilise his OBC 'vote bank' of large. However, while Mulayam Singh Yadav tried to federate all the OBCs behind him, he was keen above all to promote his caste fellows, the Yadavs.

The over-representation of Yadavs in the National Executive of

[85] On the Uttarakhand issue, see E. Mawdsley, 'Uttarakhand Agitation and Other Backward Classes', *EPW*, 27 Jan. 1996, pp. 205–10.

[86] I. Duncan, 'New political equations in North India – Mayawati, Mulayam and government instability in Uttar Pradesh', *Asian Survey*, 37, 10, (Oct. 1997), p. 992.

the Samajwadi Party was a clear indication of the way this caste identified itself with the party. Moreover, while in office Mulayam Singh Yadav, was well known for 'his tendency to distribute benefits of power largely to his own community'.[87] Out of 900 teachers appointed under his second government, 720 were Yadavs. In the police force, out of 3,151 newly selected candidates, 1,223 allegedly belonged to this caste.[88] Such a policy alienated the BSP, the SP's ally, but also the Kurmis, the second largest OBC caste of the state, which, incidentally, was well represented in the BSP. Sone Lal Patel, the Secretary General of this party presided over the Uttar Pradesh branch of the All India Kurmi Mahasabha. One year after the formation of Mulayam Singh Yadav's government he organised a Kurmi Rajnitik Chetna Maha rally (Great Meeting for the Political Awakening of the Kurmis) in Lucknow to protest against the Yadavisation of the State.

Even though the SP does have Kurmi leaders – such as Beni Prasad Verma – it has not been able to project itself as representing the second largest OBC caste of Uttar Pradesh and has remained identified with the Yadavs.[89] The Kurmis represented less than 2% of the National Executive of the Samajwadi Party in 1995. In 1993 only 8% of its MLAs were Kurmis (as against more than one-third Yadavs) and in 1996 they were less than 3% (as against one-fourth Yadavs).[90] In 1996 a pre-assembly election opinion poll showed that the OBCs were politically divided in Uttar Pradesh; while 75% of Yadavs remained strongly behind the SP, the Lodhis supported the BJP of Kalyan Singh, a Lodhi himself and the Kurmis divided their votes, chiefly between the BJP (37%) and the BSP (27%).[91] A *summa divisio* took shape within the OBCs with the

[87] N. Verma and H.S. Verma, 'The OBCs and sharing of power in the Panchayati Raj institutions in Uttar Pradesh', unpublished paper, p. 11. I am grateful to Jasmine Zerinini for providing me with a copy of this remarkable paper.

[88] *India Today*, 15 Oct. 1994, p. 37.

[89] The Vermas point out that he is 'an anathema to the Kurmis' (N. Verma and H.S. Verma, 'The OBCs and sharing of power in the Panchayati Raj institutions in Uttar Pradesh', unpubl. paper, p. 11).

[90] I am grateful to Jasmine Zérinini-Brotel for this piece of information.

[91] *India Today*, 31 Aug. 1996, p. 53, and A. Mishra, 'Uttar Pradesh – Politics in flux', *EPW*, 1 June 1996, p. 1300 and 'Uttar Pradesh – Kurmis and Koeris: emerging 'third' factor', ibid., 4 Jan. 1997, pp. 22–3.

(Most Backward Castes – MBCs) expressing a strong preference for the BJP and a more limited inclination in favour of the SP (25%) and the BSP (19%). These statistics suggest fairly conclusively that the OBCs do not form a 'political community'.

However, the performances of Mulayam Singh's party in the general elections in UP in the 1990s suggest that the SJP and then the SP have gradually broadened their base. From about 13% of the valid votes in 1991, it reached about 20% in 1996–8 and then 24% in 1999, only 3.6 percentage points less than the 'winner', the BJP.

The geographical spread of the SP has also become more evenly distributed over the course of time. While the SJP tended to have its strongholds in the lower Doab, it rose everywhere in the second half of the 1990s, except in Uttarakhand where the OBCs are very few in number.

In contrast, the social basis of the SP is much more unevenly distributed. Even though about one-fifth of non-Yadav OBCs voted for the party of Mulayam Singh Yadav in the 1996 and 1999 Lok Sabha elections, the Yadavs supported it on a much greater scale (between 72.7 and 75%) and more persistently than even the Muslims, the other traditional supporters of the SP (in 1999 Muslims tended to return to the Congress(I)) and their vote for Mulayam dropped from 77% in the 1996 Vidhan Sabha elections to 40%. In 1996 and 1999 his party could not attract more than one-tenth of the upper caste voters and one-tenth of the Scheduled Castes voters.[92]

Laloo Prasad and the transformation of Bihar into a Yadav Raj? As in Uttar Pradesh, the rise of the OBCs in Bihar is above all the rise of the Yadavs. They represented the largest caste group among the Bihar MPs after the Mandal affair, in 1991 (17.3% as against 7.7% for Rajputs and Bhumihars). In 1996 they accounted for twice the percentage of the second largest group, the Rajputs, 22.2% as against 11.1%. The other OBC castes, especially the Kurmis and the Koeris lagged behind. And while the representation of the Yadavs increased, that of the Koeris declined – they ended up with 2% of MPs in 1999 – and that of the Kurmis varied considerably. The composition of the Patna assembly bears out the same picture. While the Yadavs had

[92] CSDS Data unit, surveys used in K. Chandra and C. Parmar, 'Party strategies in the Uttar Pradesh Assembly elections, 1996', op. cit., p. 216; *India Today*, 31 Aug. 1996, p. 53 and *Frontline*, 19 Nov. 1999, p. 41.

Table 10.18. ELECTORAL PERFORMANCE OF M.S. YADAV'S PARTY IN UTTAR PRADESH (GENERAL ELECTIONS), 1991–9

	1991 (Samajwadi Janata Party)	*1996 (Samajwadi Party)*	*1998 (Samajwadi Party)*	*1999 (Samajwadi Party)*
% votes	13.1	20.8	20.9	24
Seats won	4	16	20	26

Sources: G.V.L. Narasimha Rao and K. Balakkrishnan, *Indian Elections: The Nineties*, op. cit., p. 51, and *Frontline*, 19 Nov. 1999, p. 41.

Table 10.19. VOTE SHARE OF THE SJP AND THE SP IN UTTAR PRADESH BY REGION, 1991–9 (%)

	1991 Assembly elections	*1996 Lok Sabha elections*	*1999 Lok Sabha elections*
Uttarakhand	3.7	8.1	5.6
Rohilkhand	12.2	25.5	23.7
Upper Doab/West UP	5.8	18.2	14
Awadh/Central UP	15.9	21.7	24.1
Lower Doab/Central East UP	20.2	20.9	28.3
Bundelkhand	8.8	17.3	25.6
Poorvanchal/East UP	11.6	19.9	28.6

Sources: *Frontline*, 3 Dec. 1993 p. 24, 15 Nov. 1996, p. 22 and 19 Nov. 1999, p. 41.

always been better represented than the other OBC castes in the Patna assembly, they continued to strengthen their position in the 1990s, whereas the Kurmis and the Koeris could not match this dynamic.

Laloo Prasad Yadav was its first beneficiary, as well as its architect. He was born in 1948 in a village of Gopalganj district. His father 'had barely a *bigha* of land'[93] but made it possible for him to follow veterinary studies up till university level. Like M.S. Yadav he began his career as a socialist student leader. In Patna University he was president of the student union between 1967 and 1969, when Karpoori Thakur was gaining prominence. Laloo Prasad Yadav, who regards Thakur as his mentor, was brought into the socialist fold at that

[93] S. Thakur, *The Making of Laloo Yadav*, New Delhi: HarperCollins, 2000, p. 25.

time. After working for two years at the Patna veterinary hospital as an assistant, he joined the JP movement in 1974. He went to jail during the Emergency and was elected MP in 1977 on a Janata Party ticket, but he returned to state politics soon after; he became leader of the opposition in the Vidhan Sabha of Bihar in January 1989 and Chief Minister in March 1990.

Laloo Prasad Yadav has deliberately introduced a new style of politics, highlighting the rustic qualities of the low castes of Bihar. For instance, he makes a point of speaking the Bhojpuri dialect or English with a strong Bhojpuri accent, to the horror of the upper classes. He was also adept at confronting them. One of his early slogans was 'Bhurabal Hatad', wipe out the Bhumihars, Rajputs, Brahmins and Lalas (Kayasths). A few months after he became Chief Minister, he utilised his control of the state media to describe the opposition to Mandal as the conspiracy of the upper castes.[94] The impact he made was all the more important as he took his message to the rural masses himself. (Indeed, Laloo is very good at visiting villages. It seems that he went to almost all of the villages of Bihar during his seven years in office.)

During the 1990 election campaign the JD had assured the voters that it was the only party prepared to reserve posts for the OBCs in the State administration and at the Center. Once voted to power, it increased the quota for OBCs from 20% to 27%, the law being officially voted in 1992. The 3% quota for the economically depressed, irrespective of caste, was abolished. In August 1993 the *Patna University and the Bihar University Amendment Bill* was passed, according to which, from then onwards there would be 50% reservations of seats for the OBCs in the senate and syndicate of these universities.[95]

Table 10.20. THE THREE MAIN OBC CASTES IN THE BIHAR ASSEMBLY, 1967–95 (%)

	1967	*1969*	*1985*	*1990*	*1995*
Yadav	11.63	14.78	14.59	19.5	27.2
Kurmi	4.08	4.08	5.27	5.57	4.6
Koeri	4.39	3.77	3.72	3.71	7.7

Source: Personal communication of Anand Kumar and, for 1995, *Muslim India*, op. cit.

[94] A. Kumar, *Laloo Prasad Yadav. Aaj ke neta/Alochnatmak adhy aynamala*, New Delhi: Rajkamal Prakashan, 1994 (no page number – Hindi).

[95] S.N. Chaudhary, *Power-Dependence Relations*, op. cit., p. 209.

Most of the vice-chancellors and directors of the educational institutions have been selected from among OBCs. In 1993 an IAS from the Scheduled Castes replaced a Brahmin as Chief Secretary and an OBC took over the charge of Director General of Police from another Brahmin.[96] Three years after Laloo Prasad Yadav took over, seventy upper caste officials had sought – and obtained – their transfer to the Center, allegedly because of the humiliation and ill treatment they suffered in Bihar. In addition to these 'voluntary' moves, the state government has transferred 12 out of 13 divisional commissioners and 250 of the 324 returning officers, in order to have lower caste people at the helm at the local level. Many OBC bureaucrats were transferred from the sidelines to the main department and the number of District Magistrates and Deputy Divisional Commissioners – two strategic positions – held by OBCs increased so that they became at least equivalent to those from the upper castes (see Table 10.21)

The government also gave jobs to a larger number of OBCs. In 1996, the University Service Commission of Bihar recruited 1,427 lecturers for the universities and its constituent colleges in the state. Protests were immediately lodged because most candidates were OBCs and, more precisely, Yadavs.[97] In 1993 the Bihar Vidhan Sabha passed the Panchayati Raj Bill which 'provides for reservation of seats in favour of Scheduled Castes, Scheduled Tribes and Backward Classes in proportion to their population'.[98] Interestingly this Bill was unanimously passed by both houses of the state legislature. However, the Bihar government was obliged to amend its reservation policy to exclude the 'creamy layer'. It appointed a committee which delivered a similar report as in Uttar Pradesh and which, therefore, had to be struck down by the Supreme Court because it was too favorable to the Yadav-dominated OBC elite.

The fact that Laloo Prasad Yadav's party was largely identified with his caste is evident from the social profile of the Janata Dal MLAs in the Bihar assembly in 1995. With more than 57% OBC MLAs, the Janata Dal may well claim to represent the lower castes. However, the Yadavs got the lion's share – 38% – and no other caste,

[96] Ibid., p. 241.

[97] Ibid., p. 262.

[98] 'The Bihar Panchayat Raj Act, 1992' in W. Ashrafi, *Laloo Prasad*, Delhi: Educational Publishing House, 1994, p. 108.

Table 10.21. COMPOSITION OF DMs AND DDCs BY CASTE IN BIHAR, 1995

	District magistrates	*Deputy divisional commissioners*
OBCs	26	30
Minorities	4	4
Forward castes	20	16
Total	*50*	*50*

Source: *India Today*, 28 Feb. 1995, pp. 100-7.

not even the Koeris – with 8.4% – could rival them. These figures suggest that the rise of the Janata Dal in Bihar may be the rise of the Yadavs. Such a conclusion flows even more naturally if one examines the caste composition of the governments headed by Laloo Prasad Yadav and his wife, Rabri Devi, between 1990 and 2000.

While the share of Yadavs in the 1990–5 government is not available, their over-representation in Rabri Devi's cabinet is quite remarkable and could only be resented by other OBCs, such as the Kurmis, who had only two ministers in a government of seventy-six people. The Kurmis also resented the bias of Laloo Prasad Yadav in favour of his caste fellows when he appointed Yadavs as heads of important boards such as the Bihar Public Service Commission, the Bihar Secondary Education Service Commission, the Bihar State Electricity Board and the Bihar Industrial Development Corporation.[99] Kurmi leaders felt sidelined and one of the most prominent among them, Nitish Kumar, left the Janata Dal in 1994 and set up the Samata Dal along with George Fernandes. This party forged an alliance with the BJP in the mid-1990s. As a result, the Janata Dal of Laloo Prasad Yadav became even more clearly than before a 'Yadav' party. During the 1995 state elections, the JD gave 28% of its tickets (72 out of 260) to members of this caste, while the Kurmis received only 5% of them (12 tickets).[100] Simultaneously, the Samta Dal fielded only 11 Yadav candidates, even less than the Congress Party.[101]

The caste polarisation of the OBCs in Bihar was most obvious during the 1999 general elections. The RJD – by far the most

[99] S. N. Chaudhary, *Power-Dependence Relations*, op.cit., p. 242.
[100] *The Times of India*, 1 Feb. 1995
[101] *The Hindustan Times*, 5 Feb. 1995.

Table 10.22. CASTE AND COMMUNITY OF THE MLAs IN THE 1995 BIHAR ASSEMBLY (*by party, %*)

	JD	*INC*	*BJP*	*CPI*	*Samata*	*Others*
Upper castes	*13.8*	*27.4*	*34.2*	*24*	*14.3*	*16.2*
Brahmin	1.8	3.4	9.8	4	14.3	3.6
Rajput	8.4	3.4	9.8			5.4
Banya/Jain						3.6
Bhumihar	3	17.2	2.4	20		
Kayasth		3.4	9.8			1.8
Khatri						1.8
Marwari	0.6		2.4			
Intermediate castes	*1.2*		*14.6*			*1.8*
Banya	1.2		14.6			1.8
Backward castes	*50.6*	*34.4*	*19.5*	*44*	*71.5*	*37.5*
Teli	1.2	3.4	2.4			
Yadav	38	17.2	4.9	40		14.3
Kirar						
Kurmi	2.4	6.9	4.9		42.9	7.1
Panwar						
Koeri	8.4		4.9	4	28.6	10.7
Munda		6.9				5.4
Nishad	0.6					
Sonar			2.4			
Most backward castes	*7.8*	*3.4*	*2.4*	*4*		*1.8*
Bhuiyan	0.6					
Gangota	1.2					
Gaud	0.6					
Kahar	0.6					
Dhanuk	0.6					
Kharbar				4		
Mehtar	0.6					
Nai	0.6					
Nonea	0.6					
Rajwanshi			2.4			
Rajwar	0.6					
Kewat	0.6	3.4				1.8
Mallah	1.2					
Scheduled Castes	*16.8*	*6.8*	*9.7*	*20*	*14.3*	*7.2*
Chamar	3	3.4	4.9	8		1.8
Dhobi	1.2		2.4			
Dome	0.6					1.8
Dusadh	10.2			8	14.3	1.8
Pasi	1.8	3.4		4		1.8
Ravidas			2.4			
Scheduled Tribes		*10.3*	*9.8*			*25.1*
Adivasi		3.4				3.6
Ho			4.9			1.8
Oraon		6.9	4.9			3.6
Santhal						16.1
Sikh	*0.6*					
Muslim	*7.8*	*17.2*		*4*		*7.1*
Unidentified	*1.2*		*9.8*	*4*		*3.6*
Total	*100*	*100*	*100*	*100*	*100*	*100*
	N=166	*N=29*	*N=41*	*N=25*	*N=7*	*N=56*

Source: Same as for table 10.9.

Table 10.23. CASTE AND COMMUNITY OF MEMBERS OF JANATA DAL AND RASHTRIYA JANATA DAL GOVERNMENTS IN BIHAR

	Laloo Prasad Yadav 1990–5	*Rabri Devi 1995–2000*
Upper castes	*26.7*	*17.1*
Brahmin	*n.a.*	2.63
Rajput	*n.a.*	11.84
Bhumihar	*n.a.*	2.63
Upper OBC	*35.2*	*51.31*
Yadav	*n.a.*	31.58
Kurmi	*n.a.*	2.63
Koeri	*n.a.*	11.84
Banya	*n.a.*	5.26
Lower OBC	*11.3*	*6.58*
SC/ST	*15.5*	*13.16*
Muslim	*11.3*	*11.84*
Total	*100 (N=71)*	*100 (N=76)*

Source: S.N. Chaudhary, *Power-Dependence Relations: Struggle for Hegemony in Rural Bihar*, New Delhi: Har-Anand, 1999, pp. 219 and 251.

Table 10.24. CASTE AND COMMUNITY OF RJD-CONGRESS(I) AND BJP-JD(U) VOTERS IN BIHAR, 1999 GENERAL ELECTION

	RJD-Con(I)	*BJP-JD(U)*
Rajput	8	92
Other upper castes	13	86
Kurmi-Koeri	19	79
Yadav	79	20
Lower OBC	27	55
Scheduled Castes	49	43
Muslim	79	19

Source: CSDS Data Unit, 'Sharp polarisation in Bihar', *Frontline*, 10 Dec. 1999, p. 36.

important component of the RJD-Congress(I) coalition –, retained the Muslim vote and a large section of Dalit voters in spite of Ram Vilas Paswan joining the JD(U) – a party born from the merger of the Samta Party and a fraction of the Janata Dal. The support that these three groups – the Yadavs, the Muslims and the Dalits – continued to extend to the RJD largely explains how it managed to resist its competitors during the assembly elections of March 2000.

The Yadavs thus benefited more than any other low caste group from the policies followed by Mulayam Singh and Laloo Prasad in UP and Bihar, two states where they form the largest component of the OBCs. The notion of the OBCs has obviously been exploited by them to their own caste's advantage. The Yadavs were bound to be among the first beneficiaries of the quotas because they are more numerous and relatively more educated than other OBCs among the urban population. But they were also favoured by the governments of Mulayam Singh and Laloo Prasad and other OBC castes unsurprisingly distanced themselves from these so-called 'OBC' leaders.

In fact, the very notion of the OBCs as 'a political community' needs to be questioned since the cleavages between major – rival – castes such as the Yadavs, the Kurmis and the Lodhis now finds expression in terms of party affiliation and voting patterns. Castes classified as OBCs might have coalesced in the early 1990s, because of the Mandal affair, but this trend was not sustained for long. It does not mean that the rise of the low castes can be taken lightly, however. They may not be united but individually each of these castes has acquired a new political consciousness which has led them to vote more or less *en bloc* and obliged the political parties to field candidates from their ranks instead of relying on old clientelistic and paternalist vertical linkages. The growing importance of the lower castes in the public sphere shows that they have gained a new influence. Madhu Limaye, even though he regretted the 'casteist' attitude of B.P. Mandal in 1967–8, drew similar conclusions from this episode:

If the [socialist] caste policy had not been there, the factional abuse would have taken some other form. But this does not prove that the general policy

Table 10.25. ELECTORAL PERFORMANCE OF RJD IN BIHAR, 1998–2000 (%)

	1998	*1999*[a]	*2000*
	(Lok Sabha)	(Lok Sabha)	(Assembly)
Seats won	17	11	124
% votes	26.6	28.3	27.99

[a] Figures for the RJD-Congress(I) alliance.

Sources: G.V.L. Narasimha Rao and K. Balakrishnan, *Indian Elections in the Nineties*, op. cit., p. 48; *Frontline*, 10 Dec. 1999, p. 37 and website of the Election Commission of India.

was wrong. Throughout the zig zag and tortuous course of this policy, the rising consciousness among the Scheduled Castes, Scheduled Tribes and OBCs had been a fact of life. It was still not what Lohia called a 'resurrection of India – the destruction of caste. . .' [. . .] Still it was a step forward of sorts towards equality.[102]

Indeed, the Yadav leaders have betrayed Lohia,[103] who wanted to eradicate caste, but they have used caste in a social transformation perspective anyway since they have reconstituted castes as interest groups and built caste coalitions – the OBCs, mainly – which had the capacity virtually to dislodge upper caste people from power. This is the main achievement of quota politics.

While in North India, political mobilization against the urban, upper-caste establishment traditionally followed two routes that we have called quota and *kisan* politics, in the 1990s the former strategy was adopted by the Janata Dal and generated low caste mobilisation whereas, Charan Singh's approach was followed outside the party-based political arena by the Bharatiya Kisan Union. The implementation of the Mandal Commission Report was responsible for the crystallisation of a new social coalition, the OBCs, which had never before come to fruition not even in the 1950s and 1960s in the wake of the Kalelkar Commission. It was an alliance that relied on the amalgamation of castes and, in a way, it marked a logical, new step after the formation of caste associations and caste federations. Paradoxically caste therefore provided the Indian masses with the tools of social change: a social unit that was able to create new horizontal solidarities, simply because it was the criterion for policies of positive discrimination, it proved to be an effective means of questioning vertical, clientelistic linkages. In the 1990s, this new OBC identity led the lower castes to coalesce in the street and to vote more or less together for candidates from their own milieu, in such a manner that the social profile of the Hindi belt MPs was significantly affected.

This silent revolution has probably ushered in the second age of

[102] M. Limaye, *Birth of Non-Congressism*, op. cit., pp. 163–4.

[103] Old upper caste Lohialities hardly retain any influence within the party. I attended a very significant debate in Lucknow between the President of the UP branch of the SP, Ram Saran Das (a Gujar) and an ex-MP, Brij Bushan Tiwari, a Brahmin. While the former admitted that the SP was dominated by the OBCs, the latter maintained, that it simply believed in preferential opportunities.

Indian democracy. But the process has not affected the whole of North India in the same way – Rajasthan is still largely untouched, for instance – and one wonders whether the OBCs really constitute a social and political category. This notion has been interiorised by the low castes in the context of the Mandal affair, when it epitomised an avenue of social mobility through quotas and when the castes classified as OBCs had to mobilise against the resistance of the upper castes. But it soon appeared that the OBCs were stratified, according to what Ambedkar called 'graded inequality', and that the less backward of these caste groups, the Yadavs especially, instrumentalised this category to promote their own interests. The policies of Mulayam Singh Yadav and Laloo Prasad Yadav, as well as the fragmentation of the so-called OBC vote, bear testimony to this lack of solidarity. However, if the Yadav-dominated political parties of North India do not cater to the needs of those now known as the 'lower OBCs' or the Most Backward Castes and the Dalits, the Bahujan Samaj Party is intended to do so.

11

THE RENEWAL OF DALIT POLITICS

THE B.S.P., PARTY OF THE BAHUJANS?

The OBCs were not the only group that benefited from the coming to power of the Janata Dal. The Scheduled Castes profited from it too, though less substantially. Dr Ambedkar's portrait was placed in the main hall of Parliament alongside other freedom movement leaders, and a law was passed so that the benefits extended to the Hindu and Sikh Scheduled Castes would also be made available to Dalits who had adopted Buddhism.[1] The Lok Sabha also passed the Constitution (68th Amendment) Bill which sought to set up a five-member statutory commission for the Scheduled Castes and Scheduled Tribes.[2] More importantly, the political context created by the Mandal affair gave more visibility to the claims of the Scheduled Castes while Dalit politics had receded into the background after the death of Ambedkar.

The Republican Party of India, as mentioned above, had developed pockets of influence beyond Maharashtra – especially in Uttar Pradesh and Punjab – in the 1960s but had declined in the early 1970s largely because of factionalism and the co-option of some of its leaders by the Congress. In the 1980s and till the mid-1990s, no RPI candidate could win a single seat. Ambedkar's grandson, Prakash, took over from his father, who died in 1978, and strove for to unite the different offshoots of the original RPI. In 1984 he founded the Bharatiya Republican Party but Ramdas Athavale, who had severed his link with the RPI (Ambedkar) just before the 1985 assembly elections, refused to merge with this new party. He then persuaded the BRP to support the Congress during the 1990 assembly elections, even though Prakash Ambedkar was opposed to such a policy. Athavale was rewarded by a victorious Congress: he was given a berth in

[1] The Rajya Sabha approved this measure unanimously on 8 May 1990, *Statesman* (Delhi), 9 Sept. 1990, p. 1.

[2] Ibid., 31 May 1990, p. 1.

government. In February 1996, most of these groups formed a collective leadership. Three months later, the eleventh general election allowed this loose grouping to form an alliance with the Janata Dal to establish a third force – an alternative to Congress and to the Hindu nationalists – but it did not win a single seat. In the 1998 general elections, the RPI allied with the Congress and the Samajwadi Party. This conglomerate achieved startling results since it won 37 seats, including four for the RPI and 34 for the Congress. Interestingly, the four RPI seats were won in non-reserved constituencies, a clear indication that the party benefited from the support of non-Dalit Congress voters.[3] This unity was short-lived. While Prakash Ambedkar remained associated with Congress, Athavale made an alliance with Sharad Pawar's Nationalist Congress Party and R.S. Gawai formed a third faction. As a result, the RPI hung on to only one seat during the 1999 elections. By contrast, the BSP was becoming increasingly successful in North India.

Its chief, Kanshi Ram, had first tried to organise the Dalits through union-like organisations but he gradually stressed purely political activities and especially the building of a party. Whether as a social worker or as a party leader, however, he emphasised the need to reach beyond the Scheduled Castes, an attempt that was partly successful in some areas of northern India, especially Uttar Pradesh.

Kanshi Ram and the Bahujan Samaj: from interest group to political force

Kanshi Ram was born in 1932 in a Scheduled Caste family in rural Punjab – his native village Khwaspur is situated in Ropar district.[4] His exact social background is subject to controversy because he prefers to keep his original community secret in order not to be associated with a particular group. He seems to belong to a Ramdasia *jati* – Chamars converted to Sikhism. Whatever his community is,

[3] Jogdand, 'RPI-Congress alliance: softer option', *EPW*, 9 May 1998, pp. 1071–2.

[4] Parliament of India, *Tenth Lok Sabha Who's Who*, Delhi: Lok Sabha Secretariat, 1992, p. 326. Mendelsohn and Vicziany give another date for Kanshi Ram's birth, 1934 (O. Mendelsohn and M. Vicziany, *The Untouchables. Subordination, Poverty and the State in Modern India*, Cambridge University Press, 1998, p. 219).

he underlines that his first social environment in Punjab was not as oppressive as the one Untouchables suffered elsewhere:

Because of the Sikh religion, also because most of the Chamars have adopted the Sikh religion,[5] there was somewhat upward mobility. The teaching of the [Sikh] gurus is more egalitarian.[6]

Like Ambedkar's and Jagivan Ram's, Kanshi Ram's family – who owned 4 or 5 acres of land – benefited from the British policy of giving jobs to Dalits in the army. His father was the only one of the family who did not leave for the front during the Second World War, because at least one man had to stay behind. His grandfather had been in the army and his uncle too. Kanshi Ram therefore emphasises that he was born 'among these people who gave their life to the motherland and who, over the last forty years, have always paid allegiance to the country'.[7] The army not only provided a good salary, it also encouraged the self-esteem among the soldier-Dalits. This social and family context, which one doesn't find often in the Hindi-belt explains why Kanshi Ram was unaware of what Untouchability was in his youth. Because he was the eldest child, and given his background, he was able to study until graduation, unlike his four sisters and two brothers.[8]

After getting his BSc at Ropar College, he left the Punjab to work as a government chemist from 1958 until 1965 in a laboratory at Kirkee (near Poona in Maharashtra). Kanshi Ram is therefore representative of the small elite of Scheduled Castes who benefited from reservation. In Poona, the miserable life of the Mahars came as a shock for Kanshi Ram.

I was first exposed to the miseries of the Mahars and Mangs [an even lower Dalit caste of basket and rope makers] and then I read *Annihilation of Caste*

[5] In fact, the proportion of Hindu Chamars is still very high in Punjab. In the 1931 Census, they were 62.1% of the total, as against 14.4% for Sikh Chamars.

[6] Interview with Kanshi Ram, New Delhi, 12 Nov. 1996.

[7] Cited in, *Kanshi Ram – Aaj ke neta/Alochnatmak adhyayanmala*, New Delhi: Rajkamal Prakashan, 1997 (Hindi).

[8] Two of his sisters got married to landless labourers in Punjab, a third one to a class IV civil servant and the fourth one to a soldier. His first brother is a welder at the thermal factory in Ropar and the second cultivates the 1.5 acre family farm. (*Sunday*, 13 Feb.1994, pp. 28–31)

and *What Gandhi and the Congress have done to the Untouchables* [two books by Ambedkar]. These are the two books which have influenced me most. Later I came to know about the Mahatma Jyotirao Phule.[9]

Once again a North Indian low caste leader was to benefit from the Maharashtrian experiment, all the more so as Kanshi Ram was largely initiated into 'Ambedkarism' by one of his colleagues, a Mahar Buddhist, D.K. Khaparde. Kanshi Ram turned more actively towards political action in the late 1960s. He resigned from his job and wrote a 24 page letter to his mother in which he resolved never to marry and never to return to his village: he wanted to sever all family links to devote all his energies to the cause of the downtrodden. He abjured all family functions such as wedding parties, birthdays, and funerals from 1971 onwards.

When he resigned his job, Kanshi Ram had already joined the RPI. But he was soon disappointed by the party's leaders who were bitterly divided into many factions and who were joining Congress one after the other. More important, Kanshi Ram was very critical of the RPI's tendency to work only among the Dalits, and even more especially among the Buddhist Mahars. For Kanshi Ram, the RPI, by focusing so much of its attention on the Dalits, was betraying Ambedkar. His reading of *Annihilation of Caste* had convinced him that any organisation based on one particular community would fail.[10] In suggesting an alternative strategy he drew inspiration not so much from Ambedkar as from Phule's theory of endowing the lower castes with an ethnic identity. He transposed the motif of the Aryan invader versus the oppressed *bahujan samaj* in the democratic context of India:

> The bahujan samaj accounts for 85% of the votes. It is a shame that the foreign Aryans constituting 15% are ruling over the 85% [. . .] The Aryans have exploited us. An Aryan ruler can never work for our betterment [. . .] When our ancestors from the bahujan samaj were ruling over his country, India was known world wide for its prosperity. The *bahujan samaj* can rule this country even today. . . .[11]

Kanshi Ram tried to use the theory of the Aryan invasion as an emotional argument for uniting the lower castes, as the Dravidian

[9] Interview with Kanshi Ram.

[10] One of the BSP's slogans says: '*Bâba terâ mission adhûrâ Kanshi Ram karenge pûrâ*' (Baba [Saheb Ambedkar] your unfinished work will be fulfilled by Kanshi Ram).

[11] Cited in *Kanshi Ram*, op. cit.

parties have done in the past. And he combined this view with the notion that the *bahujan samaj* was large enough to capture power. From the outset Kanshi Ram included the religious minorities in his definition of the *bahujan samaj* since, in his view they suffered from the same oppression by upper-caste Hindus. His ideology of the *bahujan samaj* first found expression in the union-like organisations that he set up in the 1970s.

On 14 October 1971, Kanshi Ram created 'The Scheduled Castes and Scheduled Tribes, Other Backward Classes and Minority Communities Employees Association'. At that time he considered that the most urgent need of the *bahujan samaj* was to organise its elite, which was, like him, the product of educational reservations and largely employed in the administration. Among the five vice-presidents who assisted Kanshi Ram, there was one Mahar, one Adivasi (Tribal), one Mali (gardener-OBC), one Muslim and one Christian. They were representatives of what Kanshi Ram considered to be the *bahujan samaj*, which he defined in opposition to the twice-born upper castes, the *savarna* whom he also called the 'Manuwadi', those who follow the *varna* system as codified by Manu's *Dharmashastra.*[12] Kanshi Ram's motto was '*jat todo, samaj jodo*' (break castes, unite the [bahujan] samaj).

The association became a federation in 1973 during a three-day conference in Delhi where 70% of the participants were from Poona.[13] Kanshi Ram left the town three years later and created the All India Backward (SC, ST, OBC) and Minority Communities Employees Federation (BAMCEF) whose aim was still to organise the elite of the *bahujan samaj*, mostly educated wage-earners benefiting from quotas. The BAMCEF made rapid headway – in 1978 about 150 districts were covered all over India – and reached critical mass because of the growing number of educated Scheduled Castes civil servants.[14] In Uttar Pradesh, the state where Kanshi Ram was to be

[12] Kanshi Ram talks of 'Manuwadi' versus 'Manavwadi', those who believe in men as human beings. His hostility to Manu led him to ask for the removal of the statue of Manu from the premises of Jaipur High Court (*The Hindu*, 5 Sept. 1998, p. 4).

[13] Interview with Chandra Kant 'Torat', Poona, 14 Sept. 2001. Tarat, a Mahar from Poona, was a close associate of Komshi Ram in the late 1960s-early 1970s.

[14] Educated Dalits are often voracious readers who, through books and periodicals, acquire a political consciousness at a rather young age. For instance,

the most successful, the Scheduled Castes literacy rate increased from 7.1% in 1961, to 10.2% in 1971, to 15% in 1981 and to 27% by 1991. In Uttar Pradesh among IAS cadres Scheduled Castes officers 'form the largest number next to the Brahmins and Kayasths'.[15] Yet these officers felt frustrated because they were denied 'important posts in the districts as well as the state capital'.[16]

Kanshi Ram travelled for years in North India and Maharashtra to convince the low caste officers to organise themselves within the BAMCEF.[17] He did not want to make the BAMCEF into a mere employees' union; instead he wanted it to become the organisation of the educated employees, the 'think bank', 'talent bank' and 'financial bank' of the *bahujan samaj*.[18] Gradually he built a network of activists.[19] In UP he not only attracted Ambedkarites but also socialists like Jag Mohan Singh Verma, a Kurmi lecturer at Lucknow Univer-

---

the weekly magazine *Sugathi* that was set up in the early 1980s in Karnataka is published in Kannada and deals with films, book reviews and 'Dalit affairs'. It has a circulation of 65,000. In the North also things are changing. S.S. Gautam, of the Dalit Sahitya [literature] Research Foundation, which was set up in 1994 to publish low-priced volumes of Dalit stories and poems, explains that at the Delhi book fair his institution sells books worth Rs 90,000 on just one stall: 'Our forefathers never even saw a book. Today Dalit officers even spend their Provident Fund in buying books. Our homes are mini-libraries and the pen is our sword.' (Cited in Sagarika Ghose, 'The Eklavya Complex', *Outlook*, 16 Nov. 1998, p. 67)

[15] R. Ramaseshan, 'Dalit politics in U.P.', *Seminar*, Jan. 1995, p. 73.

[16] Ibid.

[17] One of the Congress MPs from the Scheduled Tribes in Madhya Pradesh, Ajit Jogi, who joined the Indian Administrative Service before turning to politics, testifies that when Kanshi Ram called on him, as Collector in Sidhi district (Vindhya Pradesh), 'He looked very determined and clearly there was a messianic zeal in the work he was doing.' (Cited in *Sunday*, 7 July 1996, p. 16)

[18] Cited in *Kanshi Ram*, op. cit. BAMCEF members used to pay 6 to 12 rupees as a membership fee and to collect money for agitation campaigns was an important duty of the organisation's workers. In fact, there was a cashier in every BAMCEF office and he was changed by the district (or the block) organiser very often in order to minimise the risk of collusion and corruption.

[19] In Bilaspur, for instance, Dauram Ratnakar, who was to become the BSP chief in Madhya Pradesh, was approached while he was a student of BA, by T.R. Khunte, an engineer in NPTC who had come from Delhi on behalf of the BAMCEF. (Interview with D. Ratnakar, Bhopal, 2 Nov. 1997)

sity who was one of the architects of the BAMCEF in the state. In the 1980s the BAMCEF claimed to have 200,000 members, among whom were 500 Ph.Ds, 15,000 scientists, 3,000 MBBS graduates and 7,000 other graduate and postgraduate degree holders – most of them from Uttar Pradesh and Maharashtra.[20] The government became concerned about the organisation's progress because of the risk of politicising its Scheduled Castes employees. The cadres of the BAMCEF – Kanshi Ram estimated them to be about one thousand in the mid-1980s – were continuously transferred and harassed. This led Kanshi Ram, in 1985, to transform the BAMCEF into a shadow organisation:

> It has no office-bearers. There is no records of these thousands of office-bearers. Only *we* know the workers. They provide us brain power and money power. They can contribute. Most of the BSP offices are run by BAMCEF people.[21]

Kanshi Ram did not regret the way the BAMCEF receded into the background because in the 1980s he no longer regarded it as his priority to organise employees:

> I started with the idea of social transformation and economic emancipation. I still want my people to advance socially and economically. But I have realised that unless we are having political clout, we cannot advance much on those sides.[22]

Kanshi Ram was then in the footsteps of Ambedkar who also considered that capturing power had to be a priority.[23] The latter called power the 'master key' and the former translated it as '*guru killi*'.

Kanshi Ram founded his first political party, the Dalit Shoshit Samaj Sangharsh Samiti (DS-4: Committee for Fighting for the Dalit

[20] G. Omvedt, 'Kanshi Ram and the Bahujan Party' in K.L. Sharma (ed.) *Caste and Class in India*, Jaipur and New Delhi: Rawat, 1994, p. 163.

[21] Interview with Kanshi Ram. The vice-president of the BSP unit of Madhya Pradesh, IMP Verma defines today's BAMCEF as being made of those 'who can pay money, mind and time for their community'. (Interview with Indra Mani Prasad Verma, Bhopal, 10 Nov. 1997).

[22] Interview with Kanshi Ram.

[23] However, some BAMCEF people, including the president of the Jhalli organisation, disapproved of this shift to party politics and stayed behind (interview with Jag Mohan Singh Verma, Paris, 4 March 2001).

Community and the Oppressed) on 6 December 1981 – again on the anniversary date of Ambedkar's death. The terms used in the name of this organisation departed from the official euphemisms (Backward Classes, Scheduled Castes etc.); Dalit and Soshit are the words that politicised Scheduled Castes use more frequently to refer to themselves. However, Dalit here does not refer only to the Scheduled Castes, as is often the case, especially in Maharashtra. The English mouthpiece of the DS-4, as the movement came to be known, *The Oppressed Indian*, recurrently published editorials where the Shudras (OBCs) and Ati-shudras (Scheduled Castes) were bracketed together and even included Tribals. This *bahujan samaj* continued to be projected as descending from the pre-Aryans inhabitants of India.[24]

In addition to Shudras and Tribals, the DS4 also tried to attract Muslims, especially in Uttar Pradesh. Dr Mahsood Ahmed, a temporary lecturer at Aligarh Muslim University, became one of its full-time organisers in 1983[25] in order to serve this expansion scheme. However, the main target of the DS-4 was the rural Dalits, in contrast to the BAMCEF which was more oriented towards the urban Scheduled Castes elite. The DS-4 was also more aggressive in its agitation campaign, so much so that it made quick inroads in North Indian villages. From the mid-1980s onwards, the communist All India Workers Union 'singled out the DS-4 as the major "disruptive" or "divisive" force among agricultural labourers in UP and found it necessary to campaign actively against it'[26] on behalf of class-based politics against caste-based politics.

The BSP entered the electoral arena in 1982 and immediately targeted the Congress party as its main, historical enemy. Kanshi Ram even considered that his party had to contest elections because of the Congress attitude to the Scheduled Castes. On the eve of the 50th anniversary of the 1932 Poona Pact, which the Congress was about to celebrate with great pomp, Kanshi Ram published a booklet, *The Chamcha Age*, where he denounced this agreement as sealing the political fate of the Scheduled Castes. He argued that the system of

[24] 'Marching to awaken the Ambedkarite Masses', *The Oppressed Indian*, 5, 1 (April 1983), p. 16.

[25] Mendelsohn and Vicziany, *The Untouchables*, op. cit., pp. 224–5.

[26] J. Lerche, 'Politics of the poor: BSP and low caste rural workers in UP', Paper presented at the 15th European Conference on Modern South Asian Studies, Prague, 8–12 Sept. 1998, p. 4.

reserved seats that had been forced on Ambedkar – who favoured a system of separate electorates – had helped the high castes to dominate Congress and to co-opt Dalit candidates who were mere sycophants (*chamcha*) or yes-men (*ji huzuri*) since the Scheduled Castes did not form a majority in a single reserved constituency. Facing such a situation, the DS-4 had to act as a political party and contest elections. It was the only way out since 'A tool, an agent, a stooge or a *chamcha* is created to oppose the real, the genuine fighter'.[27] The DS-4 put forward forty-six candidates for the assembly elections of Haryana in 1982, without making much of an impact, but the party leaders launched several agitation campaigns to make it better known. Between 15 March and 17 April 1983 the DS-4 organised a 3,000 km cycle procession covering seven states in order to 'educate the oppressed and the exploited people that they need to build up their own organisation and independent movement'.[28] The following year, the DS-4 launched a similar but bigger movement since on that occasion processions of cyclists left from five peripheral provinces of India to converge upon Delhi. This 100 day-campaign included 7,000 meetings which were held all over India and was concluded in Delhi with a huge gathering out of which emerged the Bahujan Samaj Party.[29]

The BSP, which was officially founded on 14 April 1984, the anniversary of Ambedkar's birth, took over the mantle of the DS-4.[30] It did not imply much more than a change of name, but by re-christening his organisation in this way, Kanshi Ram consummated his shift from social work to party politics. The BSP has made rapid progress on the electoral front. During the 1984 general elections, it received more than one million votes, a number that was multiplied

[27] Kanshi Ram, *The Chamcha Age – An Era of the Stooges*, New Delhi, 1982, p. 90.

[28] 'Marching to awaken the Ambedkarites masses' *The Oppressed Indian*, op. cit.

[29] 'First phase of 100 Days Social Action concludes in Delhi', cited in B. Joshi (ed.), *Untouchable! Voice of the Dalit Liberation Movement*, New Delhi: Selectbook Service Syndicate, 1986. p. 115.

[30] Like BAMCEF the DS-4 has not been dissolved. BSP workers have told me that it was now the party's youth wing which planned the campaigns such as the one in favour of reservations. But no action has been held on behalf of the DS-4 for the last 15 years.

Table 11.1. THE BSP IN GENERAL ELECTIONS, 1989–99

	Candidates	*Winning candidates*	*Valid votes*
1989	246	3	2.07
1991	231	2	1.61
1996	117	11	3.64
1998	251	5	4.7
1999	N.A.	14	4.2

Sources: Election Commission of India, *Report on the ninth general elections to the House of the people in India*, 1989, New Delhi: Government of India Press, 1990, p. 7; Election Commission of India, *Report on the tenth general elections to the House of the people in India*, 1989, New Delhi, n.d., p. 9; Election Commission of India, *Statistical Report on General Elections, 1996 to the eleventh Lok Sabha*, vol. 1, New Delhi, 1996; G.V.L. Narasimha Rao and K. Balakrishnan, *Indian Elections. The Nineties*, Delhi: Har-Anand, 1999; and Y. Yadav and S.Kumar, 'Interpreting the mandate', *Frontline*, 5 Nov. 1999, pp. 120–6.

six fold in 1989 when it won 6,215,093 votes, or 2.07% of the recorded votes and obtained three seats at the Lok Sabha. In 1991, it only won two seats and 1.61% of the votes but five years later it gained eleven seats with 3.64% of the votes.

The growth of the BSP enabled the party to obtain from the Election Commission the status of a national party after the 1996 elections. This growth chiefly resulted from Kanshi Ram's long-term efforts to get the *bahujan samaj* organised. In the 1990s, thanks to the activists trained by the BAMCEF and the DS-4, the BSP had committees in all the districts of Uttar Pradesh. In Madhya Pradesh, in the mid-1990s it did not have a unit in only six districts (Panna, Vidisha, Betul, Jabalpur, Ujjain and Khandwa). However, the rise of the BSP has also much to do with the party's mobilisation techniques and policies while in office.

Towards a 'bahujan' front?

The main objective of the BSP remained the same as that of the DS-4, the formation of a 'bahujan' front which would be able to seize power. This discourse was symbolised by the metaphor of the ball-pen, repeated endlessly by Kanshi Ram on platforms or before the cameras: the top of the pen represents the upper castes who, though being only 15% of the population rule the country, while the pen itself represents the remaining 85% who have to become aware of their fate and of their numerical strength. This logic is omnipresent in the slogans, often extremely aggressive,[31] designed by the BSP for political as well as educational purposes:

> *Jiskî jitnî samkhya bharî uskî utnî bhagîgârî*
> The highest number has to be the best represented.
>
> *85 par 15 kâ râj nahîn chalegâ, nahîn chalegâ*
> 85% living under the rule of 15%, this will not last, this will not last.
>
> *Vot hamârâ, râj tumhârâ, nahin chalegâ, nahîn chalegâ*
> We have the votes, you have the power, this will not last, this will not last.
>
> *Tilak, tarâjû aur talvâr isko mâro joote char*
> The tilak [emblem of the sectarian affiliation of the Hindus which is applied to the forehead and symbolises the Brahmin], the balance [symbol of the merchant castes] and the sword [the symbol of the warrior castes], hit them with your shoes [symbol of the Chamars, the principal Scheduled Caste of North of India, who are leatherworkers].[32]

Thus Kanshi Ram tried to emerge as a spokesman for the *bahujan samaj* by advocating the interests of all its components including the OBCs against the upper castes.

Kanshi Ram and the OBCs. Even before the Mandal affair, when the debate (in the Lok Sabha and outside) on the Mandal Commission Report was gaining momentum, Kanshi Ram emphasised the claims of the OBCs. This is evident from one of his speeches during the election campaign for the Vidhan Sabha of Haryana in 1987:

> The other limb of the Bahujan Samaj [in addition to the Scheduled Castes] which we call OBC or Other Backward Classes, needs badly this party [the BSP]. Thirty-nine years after independence, these people have neither been recognised nor have they obtained any rights. Improvements have been introduced in the legislation for the Scheduled Castes and the Scheduled Tribes, but nothing similar has happened for these people. The truth is that the government of this country is not ready to recognise them. In accordance with section 340 of the Constitution, which was drafted by Dr. Ambedkar for the welfare of these people, the Kaka Kalelkar and Mandal Commissions

[31] Kanshi Ram also began many of his public speeches with an injunction to the upper castes who happened to be here to leave the meeting-place.

[32] Some of these slogans come from Kanshi Ram, *Bahujan Samâj ke lye âshâ kî kiran*, New Delhi: Bahujan Publications, 1992, p. 67.

were constituted, but the reports of both the commissions were thrown in the waste paper basket on the pretext that they had identified 3,743 castes which could not be called Other Backward Classes. Our central government is not ready to recognise any of these castes.[33]

He thus admitted that in some respects the conditions of the Scheduled Castes were better than those of the OBCs. He also concluded that the Scheduled Castes and the Scheduled Tribes had a larger presence in the bureaucracy than the OBCs because of reservations:

In this country, out of the 450 District Magistrates more than 125 are from SC/STs but those from the OBCs are very few. [. . .] The number of OBC is 50 to 52% but we don't see any of them as District Magistrate. The issue, which is special for us, is that reservation is not a question of our daily bread, reservation is not a question of our jobs, reservation is a matter of participation in the government and administration. We want participation in the government and administration of this country. There is democracy in this country. If 52% of the people cannot participate in the republic, then which is the system in which they can participate?[34]

Similarly, he noted in 1994 that of some 500 IAS officers in Uttar Pradesh, 137 were from the Scheduled Castes whereas there were only 7 OBCs (6 of them Yadavs).[35] Mendelsohn and Vicziany emphasise that 'Kanshi Ram has become increasingly critical of the institution of reservation in government employment' because it is 'a positive handicap for someone who wants to run on his own two feet' and a mark of a condescending Brahmanical attitude.[36] He developed this argument *vis-à-vis* the Scheduled Castes but not regarding the OBCs.[37] Kanshi Ram was very much in favour of reservations for this group, which he regarded as unprivileged. One of the BSP's slogans has been '*Mandal ayog lâgû karo, kursî khâli karo*' (Implement the

[33] Kanshi Ram, 'Bahujan Samaj Party aur Haryana Pradesh ke chunav' in Kanshi Ram, *Bahujan Samaj ke lye, âshâ kî kîran*, op. cit., p. 23.

[34] 'Azadi ke 44 sal bad bhi bahujan samaj (anusuchit jati, janjati, pichre varg va dharmic alpasankhyak) anyaya tyachar ka shikar', in ibid., p. 58.

[35] Mendelsohn and Vicziany, *The Untouchables*, op. cit., p. 224.

[36] Ibid., pp. 223–4.

[37] It is not true so far as women are concerned either. In 1998 Kanshi Ram said that his party sought 'reservation' for them: he wanted that, within the 30% women quota that was contemplated by the then government, 22.5% seats in Parliament and State assemblies be reserved for Scheduled Castes and Scheduled Tribes women, and 27% for OBC women. (*The Hindu*, 21 Dec. 1998)

Mandal Commission [Report] or vacate the seat [of power]). This is part of his strategy of constituting the *bahujan samaj* into a political force and therefore the BSP undoubtedly benefited from the atmosphere created by the 'Mandal affair' and tried to tap the OBC vote at the time of elections.

The BSP, not only a Dalit party? The case of Uttar Pradesh and Madhya Pradesh. While the BSP's vote has reached double digits in another state – Punjab – Uttar Pradesh is the only place where it has made real inroads in the last ten years, Madhya Pradesh being the only other state where the party remains above 5% of the valid votes.

In UP the electoral presence of the BSP began to be felt in 1984, as mentioned above, and then in by-elections. In 1985 Mayawati contested the Lok Sabha seat of Bijnor. She lost to Meira Kumar (the daughter of Jagjivan Ram) but got 65,000 votes. In 1987 she

Table 11.2. ELECTORAL PERFORMANCE OF BSP IN FIVE STATES OF NORTH INDIA IN GENERAL ELECTIONS, 1989–99
(% of valid votes; number of seats won in parentheses)

	Haryana	*Punjab*	*Uttar Pradesh*	*Madhya Pradesh*	*Jammu and Kashmir*
% of SC in 1991	19.75	28.31	21.05	14.5	*n.a.*
1989	1.62 (0)	8.62 (1)	9.93 (2)	4.28 (0)	4.06 (0)
1991	1.79 (0)	*No election*	8.70 (1)	3.54 (1)	No election
1996	6.6 (0)	9.35 (3)	20.61 (6)	8.18 (2)	6 (0)
1998	7.7 (1)	12.7 (0)	20.9 (4)	8.7 (0)	5 (0)
1999	1.7 (0)	3.8 (0)	22.1 (14)	5.2 (0)	4.8 (0)

Table 11.3. PERFORMANCE OF BSP IN ASSEMBLY ELECTIONS OF UTTAR PRADESH, 1989–96

	1989	*1991*	*1993*	*1996*
Seats	13	12	66	67
% of votes	9.4	9.3	11.1	27.8*

*Figure for the BSP-Congress alliance.

Table 11.4. BSP SHARE OF VOTE IN UTTAR PRADESH ELECTIONS BY REGION, 1991–9 (%)

	1991 Assembly elections	*1993 Assembly elections*	*1996 Lok Sabha elections*	*1999 Lok Sabha elections*
Uttarakhand	3.5	4.2	10.1	6.7
Rohilkhand	5.9	2.7	20.5	22.6
Upper Doab/West UP	3.5	5.7	18.5	23.8
Awadh/Central UP	8.8	5.6	18.8	22.8
Lower Doab/ Central East UP	10.2	9.9	22.8	22.8
Bundelkhand	20.3	26.1	25.8	28.9
Poorvanchal/East UP	13.5	21.9	20.2	23.6

Sources: *Frontline*, 3 Dec. 1993 p. 24, 15 Nov. 1996, p. 22 and 19 Nov. 1999, p. 41.

contested in Haridwar and again lost to the Congress candidate but came second ahead of Ram Vilas Paswan who lost his deposit. The following year Kanshi Ram lost in Allahabad – where he contested the Lok Sabha seat against V.P. Singh but nonetheless made an impact. In 1989 the BSP emerged as a force to reckoned with when it polled 9.9% during the ninth general elections – as against 7.4% for the BJP. In the 1990s it became the third political force behind the BJP and the Samajwadi Party – it even came second in 1996. In the late 1980s and early 1990s, the BSP's zones of strength were confined to Bundelkhand and East Uttar Pradesh but since the mid-1990s its influence has become more evenly distributed.

Its main success has been among rural, not urban, Dalits. The CSDS exit poll that was organised after the 1996 Lok Sabha elections showed that the party drew 62.7% of its votes from illiterate voters and that those engaged in white-collar jobs and business constituted only 1.6 and 2.6% of BSP voters respectively.[38] The CSDS opinion polls of 1996 and 1999[39] also show that the BSP electorate, though dominated by Dalit voters, is not confined to them.

Certainly, most supporters of the BSP come from the Scheduled

[38] Pushpendra, 'Dalit assertion through electoral politics', *EPW*, 4 Sept. 1999, pp. 2614 and 2616.

[39] The main results of these surveys have been published in *India Today*, 31 Aug. 1996, P. Kumar, 'Dalit and the BSP in Uttar Pradesh – Issues and Challenges', *EPW*, 3 April 1999, and *Frontline*, 19 Nov. 1999, p. 41.

Table 11.5. CASTE AND COMMUNITY OF BSP VOTERS IN UP, 1996–9 (%)

	1996 Vidhan Sabha elections	*1996 Lok Sabha elections*	*1999 Lok Sabha elections*
Upper castes			
Brahmin	–	–	2
Rajput	–	–	1
Banya	–	2.9	–
Other	–	2.9	5
Intermediate castes	–	*1.9*	–
OBC			
Yadav	4	4.3	4
Kurmi	27	–	–
Koeri	–	24.7	–
Pal/Gadariya		11.8	–
Other	Lower OBCs 19	Peasant 16.7	13
		Artisan 14.9	
		Other 20.6	
Scheduled Castes	*65*		
Chamar	–	73.8	74
Pasi		45.7	–
Other		60.6	39
Muslim	5	–	*5*
Muslim (low)		6.5	–
Muslim (high)	–	3.1	–
Other	–	*23.1*	–

Sources: CSDS data unit, *India Today*, 31 Aug. 1996, p. 53 ; P. Kumar, 'Dalit and the BSP in Uttar Pradesh', *EPW*, 3 April 1999, p. 822 and *Frontline*, 19 Nov. 1999, p. 41.

Castes, and more precisely from the Chamars who were already the mainstay of the RPI. In fact, the BSP faced the same difficulty as Ambedkar's political parties since the SCF and the RPI had not been able significantly to attract voters beyond the Mahars in Maharashtra and the Chamars in Uttar Pradesh. Does it mean that the *bahujan* ideology has failed completely? The BSP is not only a Chamar party, as is evident from the fact that more than 45% of the Pasis voted for its candidates in the 1996 Lok Sabha elections. It is not even only a Dalit party: in the same election 24.7% of Koeris voted for it and in the Assembly elections, 27% of Kurmis did likewise, according to the CSDS data unit.

In 1999, however, the BSP received only 13% of the non-Yadav OBC vote. At that time, the Kurmis had deserted the party[40] – largely because of the splits orchestrated in the mid-1990s by Kurmi leaders such as Raj Bahadur and Jung Bahadur and Sone Lal Patel who created the Aapna Dal. Sudha Pai argues that these splits resulted from inner tensions between Kanshi Ram and the OBC leaders of the BSP. According to Pai, in the mid-1990s, 'Kanshi Ram holds that lower backwards are not as politicised as the dalits and lack both a strong leadership and an understanding of the need to unite and fight the savarnas'.[41] As a result, the BSP allegedly developed a Dalit-oriented policy: 'In its post-bahujan phase, social justice has been defined not only as retributive but also *exclusive*, i.e., meant only for the dalits and not the entire bahujan community'.[42] The BSP changed its strategy once again in 1999 when 'the leadership decided to broaden the base of the party by giving tickets to carefully selected candidates belonging to the Muslim community, upper and backward castes, in the 1999 Lok Sabha elections thereby increasing its share of seats'.[43]

Pai's reading of the BSP's electoral strategy is not entirely convincing. In fact, the BSP has always tried to attract OBCs by giving them electoral tickets, including in what Pai calls the party's 'post-bahujan' phase. During the 1996 assembly elections, Scheduled Caste candidates were less than 29% of the total number of the party candidates in UP (see Table 11.6), whereas OBCs were more than 34% and Muslims 17.5% – and the same percentage came from the upper castes. Interestingly, the OBC candidates of the BSP were relatively more successful since there were 39% of OBCs among the party MLAs and the Scheduled Castes accounted for only 27%. In the 1999 Lok Sabha elections Kanshi Ram made this policy more systematic since he decided to nominate candidates in proportion to the caste and community composition of society. Out of 85 candidates, he fielded 17 Muslims (20%), 20 Scheduled Castes (23.5%), 38 OBC (45%) and 10 upper castes (12%) – five Brahmins and five Rajputs.[44]

[40] Till the mid-1990s, the BSP succeeded in attracting Kurmis from the region between Faizabad and Banda.

[41] S. Pai, 'The BSP in Uttar Pradesh', *Seminar*, no. 471, p. 40.

[42] Ibid., p. 42.

[43] S. Pai, 'BSP's new electoral strategy pays off', *EPW*, 30 Oct. 1999, p. 3100.

[44] *The Hindu*, 11 Aug. 1999, p. 9.

Table 11.6. CASTE AND COMMUNITY OF BSP OFFICE-BEARERS, ASSEMBLY CANDIDATES AND MLAs, UTTAR PRADESH, 1996–2000

	Office-bearers in BSP state executive			
	1996	*2000*	*1996 candidates*	*1996 MLAs*
Upper castes	*3.7*	*14.3*	*17.5*	*13.5*
Brahmin	10.3	10.7	4	4.5
Rajput	–	–	8.2	6
Banya	3.4	3.6	1.3	–
Khatri	–	–	1.6	–
Bhumihar	–	–	0.6	1.5
Kayasth	–	–	0.9	1.5
Other	–	–	0.9	–
Intermediate castes	–	–	*1.6*	*1.5*
Jat	–	–	1.6	1.5
OBC	*44.2*	*46.5*	*34.4*	*39.4*
Backward castes	*6.8*	*7.2*	*11.8*	*15.2*
Kurmi	3.4	3.6	6.3	12.2
Yadav	–	–	1.9	1.5
Lodhi	3.4	3.6	1.9	1.5
Most backward castes	*37.4*	*39.3*	*22.6*	*24.2*
Pal/Gadariya	3.4	3.6	1.9	6
Teli	–	–	0.3	–
Kachhi/Kushwaha	3.4	3.6	2.3	6
Gujar	3.4	3.6	0.9	–
Nai	3.4	3.6	–	–
Nishad	3.4	7.1	1.9	4.5
Baghela	–	–	0.6	1.5
Kumhar	3.4	3.6	0.3	1.5
Sunar	–	–	0.3	–
Chaurasia	–	–	0.3	–
Rajbhar	6.8	–	2.3	3.1
Shakya	–	–	1.6	1.5
Kashyap	–	–	0.6	–
Prajapati	–	–	1.3	–
Chaukan	–	–	0.9	–
Vora	–	–	0.3	–
Saithwar	–	–	0.9	–
Bair	–	–	0.3	–
Saini	3.4	7.1	1.6	–
Maurya	–	–	2.3	3
Others	6.8	7.1	1.3	–

(continued overleaf)

Scheduled Castes	*17.2*	*21.4*	*28.3*	*27.3*
Chamar/Jatav/Dhore	10.5	3.6	19.1	16.6
Kori	–	–	0.9	–
Pipil	–	–	0.3	–
Dhobi	–	–	0.6	1.5
Khatik	3.4	3.6	0.3	1.5
Pasi	3.4	3.6	4.2	7.6
Katheriya	–	–	0.3	–
Kuril	–	–	0.6	–
Chilpkar	–	–	0.3	–
Balmiki	–	–	0.9	–
Others	–	10.7	0.3	–
Muslim	*10.5*	*7.1*	*17.5*	*16.6*
Christian	–	–	*0.3*	–
Unidentified	*13.7*	*10.7*	–	*1.5*
Total	*100*	*100*	*100*	*100*
	N=29	N=28	N=303	N=66

Sources: Interviews at the BSPs office in Agra and Lucknow; *Bahujan Sangathak*, 11 Nov. 1996 and *National Mail*, 20 Sept. 1996.

Table 11.7. ELECTION RESULTS OF BSP IN MADHYA PRADESH IN 1996 LOK SABHA ELECTIONS BY REGION (%)

Vindhya Pradesh	*Chhattisgarh*	*Mahakoshal*	*Madhya Bharat*
19.6	7.4	2.9	1.2

Source: *Frontline*, 28 June 1996, p. 85.

The share of the OBCs is even more important among the state party office-bearers than among the BSP MLAs. Most of these lower caste leaders come from the Most Backward Castes, and not from the larger Backward Castes which often employ – and exploit – Dalits as labourers. Surprisingly, Dalit office-bearers are less than half as numerous as the OBCs. Interestingly, the President of Uttar Pradesh has been an OBC for years since Sone Lal Patel (a Kurmi) was replaced by Bhagwat Pal (a Gadariya-shepherd caste), who was himself replaced by Dayaram Pal, another Gadariya. Even though power lay in the hands of a Chamar, Mayawati, the table above shows that the BSP's image as a 'Dalit party' does not fully reflect the reality since the Scheduled Castes do not account for the majority of office-bearers and party candidates (or MLAs) in Uttar Pradesh. This picture, however, is more in tune with the social profile of its electoral basis.

The situation of the BSP is very similar in Madhya Pradesh, where the party developed pockets of influence in the districts of Vindhya Pradesh and Madhya Bharat bordering UP.

The figure for Madhya Bharat in Table 11.7 needs to be desegregated because in the northern part of this region, in Morena, Bhind and Gwalior districts, the BSP is at least as strong as in Vindhya Pradesh. These areas have been familiar with low caste politics for decades since they had been the strongholds of the Janata Dal and, before that, of the Socialists in the 1950s and 1960s.[45] Moreover, in 1993, the BSP snatched four MLA seats from the Janata Dal and one from the CPI, all of them in Rewa and Morena districts. In 1996, the party won two Lok Sabha seats as against one in 1991 and its nominees came second in four other constituencies, again located in districts bordering Uttar Pradesh and Chhattisgarh. While the party received only 8.18% of the valid votes in the state, in Vindhya Pradesh and in Gwalior region it polled about one-fifth of valid votes.

The social base of the BSP in Vindhya Pradesh offers a good example of the party's capacity to attract Dalits as well as OBCs. The first BSP MP in India, Bhim Singh Patel, was elected in this area, in Rewa, and he was an OBC (Kurmi). He won with 32.8% of the valid votes because he benefited from the support of his own caste fellows and from the Dalit vote.

Scheduled Castes and OBCs joined hands because of the local social context. Vindhya Pradesh has, indeed, many Brahmins –13.85% according to the 1931 census – who own land and are notorious for the atrocities that some of their number orchestrate against the lower castes. Caste conflicts are such that, as a reaction to the emergence of the BSP, local Brahmins sponsored a Savarna Samaj Party (Party of the Community of the Upper Castes) whose leader polled 13.43% of the valid votes in Rewa constituency in the 1996 general elections. In this context, in addition to the Kurmis, Kachhis also forcefully identified themselves with the Dalits and the Ambedkarite discourse, as is evident from the testimony of the BSP MP of Satna in1996-8:

[45] In 1997, the then Vice President of the Madhya Pradesh unit of the BSP, I.M.P. Verma pointed out that 'The OBC votes were automatically transferred from the socialists to the BSP when it emerged as a force in Rewa division' (interview with I.M.P. Verma).

I was born in that part of society which got since birth despise, insult, hatred and contempt. Humans have a birth right to live in dignity and honour but this Manuwadi social structure, which is the dominant structure in this society, took away from me this basic human right [. . .] We are grateful to the English that they came to India and opened the doors of literacy for all [. . .] [But] in today's world where we are educated and cultured, having our own notion of self-respect, the evil effects of the caste system continues to remind us of our position as social outcastes.[46]

A reader of Ambedkar before graduation in the mid-1980s, Kushwaha joined the BSP in 1989 and speaks as if he were a Dalit – Ambedkar might have said the same about the British. Kushwaha explains that he could defeat Arjun Singh, the Rajput 'feudal lord' in his stronghold of Satna because he received the votes of the Dalits and his own caste-fellows. Benefiting from the support of OBC castes such as the Kurmis and the Kacchis, the BSP is definitely more than a Dalit party in Vindhya Pradesh.

The BSP has tried to broaden its base beyond the Scheduled Castes in other sub-regions of Madhya Pradesh too. First, the party has nominated more and more OBC candidates, from 23.7% in 1993 to 50.5% in 1998. In 1998, the BSP's OBC candidates 'represented' twenty-seven different castes, among which the Kurmis were prominent with 12.4% of party candidates – the largest group. The decision to nominate more than half of the candidates from the OBCs was made not at the expense of the Scheduled Castes (whose percentage was stable at around 30%, with the Chamars and the Satnamis remaining the largest groups) but of Muslims and Scheduled Tribes. Acknowledging their strength in a state where they represent one-fourth of the population, the BSP had nominated almost 26% Tribal candidates in 1993 but reduced this percentage to 16% in 1998. In contrast to the situation prevailing in UP, the Madhya Pradesh unit of the BSP has not opened its ranks to the upper castes, either among party candidates or its office-bearers.

Second, the BSP has given various party posts to OBCs, who have often a BAMCEF background. While the president of the state unit, who was elected in 1997, Daulat Ratnakar, is a Satnami, the vice president, I.M.P. Verma is a Nai (barber).[47] And among the members of the 1997 state executive, OBCs represented 41.6%, as against 25%

[46] Interview with Sukhalal Kushwaha, Bhopal, 5 Nov. 1998.

[47] Interview with Ratnakar and Verma.

for the Scheduled Castes (see Table 11.9). At the local level almost half of the party district presidents are Dalits whereas OBCs – mostly Kurmis – represent about one-fourth of the total. Similarly, in contrast to the situation prevailing in UP, the BSP fielded many more Dalit than OBC candidates during the 1993 Assembly elections but not any more in 1998.

Contrary to Pai's interpretation of Kanshi Ram's strategy, our study of the BSP in Uttar Pradesh and Madhya Pradesh suggests that he has continuously tried to transform the party into the crucible of

Table 11.8. CASTE AND COMMUNITY OF BSP CANDIDATES IN 1993 AND 1998 ASSEMBLY ELECTIONS IN MADHYA PRADESH (%)

	1993	*1998*
Upper castes	*0.4*	*1.2*
Banya/Jain	0.4	0.6
Rajput		0.6
OBC	*23.7*	*50.5*
Aghariya		0.6
Bari		1.2
Bhoi		0.6
Chaurasia	0.4	
Dangi		1.2
Dhiwar		0.6
Dhobi		0.6
Gadariya	0.4	1.8
Gujar	0.7	5.3
Kachhi	3.2	4.7
Kallar		0.6
Kenwat		2.4
Kirar/Dhakad	0.7	3
Kolta		0.6
Kosta		0.6
Kumhar		0.6
Kurmi	5.7	12.4
Lodhi	0.4	1.8
Mali	0.4	1.8
Marar	0.4	0.6
Mina		0.6
Nai	0.7	0.6
Panwar		0.6

(continued)

	1993	*1998*
Rawat	0.4	0.6
Teli	3.9	5.3
Yadav	3.2	1.8
Others	3.2	
Scheduled Castes	*30.8*	*30.7*
Ahirwar	0.7	1.8
Bagri		0.6
Balai	0.7	2.9
Balmiki	0.7	1.2
Basor		0.6
Chamar	10.6	10.6
Khangar		0.6
Kori	0.4	1.2
Mahar	4.2	1.2
Rawat	0.4	
Satnami	7.8	8.2
Shakwar		0.6
Suryawansi		1.2
Others	5.3	
Scheduled Tribes	*25.8*	*16.1*
Barela		0.6
Bhilala		1.2
Gond	2.1	4.7
Kanwar		1.8
Kol	0.4	2.4
Kotwar		0.6
Muriya		0.6
Panika		1.2
Oraon		1.2
Others	23.3	1.8
Muslim	*8.5*	*1.8*
Sikh		*0.6*
Unidentified	*11.3*	–
Total	*100*	*100*
	N=283	*N=170*

Source: Fieldwork.

the *bahujan samaj*, by aggregating the Dalits, the OBCs and, to a lesser extent, the Tribals and the Muslims. However, his efforts to expand his party beyond the Dalits have not been entirely successful since the BSP receives only a small fraction of votes from the OBCs.

The way the BSP succeeded in consolidating its Dalit base remains to be elucidated. In Uttar Pradesh, this achievement can only be explained by the party acceding to power after 1993.

Using ladders to attain power. . . and consolidating the Dalit vote bank

Kanshi Ram, as mentioned above, looked at the conquest of power as his priority, hence his strategy of coalition-making. The grounds for his alliance with Mulayam Singh Yadav in 1993 were certainly laid by the Mandal affair. The mobilisation of the upper castes against the implementation of the Mandal Commission Report had triggered off a counter-mobilisation cutting across the caste cleavages. Not only had the OBCs discovered the need for more solidarity and more activism, but the Dalits developed the same feeling, especially when the very notion of reservations – including those for the Scheduled Castes – was questioned by some upper caste movements. The BSP was even more clearly a potential ally of the OBCs since Kanshi Ram acknowledged their need for quotas in the administration. The context created by the 'Mandal affair' was therefore conducive to the alliance between the Samajwadi Party and the BSP, although this alliance responded primarily to tactical considerations, as Kanshi Ram explicitly admitted: 'The reason why I concluded alliances with Mulayam Singh Yadav is that if we join our votes in U[ttar] P[radesh] we will be able to form the government'.[48]

In the 1993 Assembly Elections, the Samajwadi Party won 109 seats out of 425 and the BSP 67. Both parties were therefore able to form the government thanks to the Congress's support. Mulayam Singh Yadav became Chief Minister and the BSP obtained 11 ministerial portfolios in a government of 27. During the first month of

[48] Interview in *Sunday*, 16 May 1993, pp. 10–11. Once the elections were won he admitted the tactical character of the alliance: 'Up until now, neither Mulayam Singh nor me can stand alone in U[ttar] P[radesh]. That's why we are together' (interview in *Sunday*, 13 Feb. 1994, p. 26). Therefore, one cannot follow Sudha Pai when she writes that the BSP was converted 'from a social/cultural movement to an opportunistic party' in 1995 when it made an alliance with the BJP: the party had started making tactical alliances in 1993 and its move reflected more pragmatism than opportunism. (See S. Pai, 'Dalit Assertion in UP', *EPW*, op. cit., p. 2314)

Table 11.9. CASTE AND COMMUNITY OF BSP OFFICE-BEARERS IN MADHYA PRADESH, 1997 (*% in parentheses*)

	Presidents of district units	*Office-bearers in the BSP state executive*
Intermediate castes	*1 (2.5)*	
Maratha	1 (2.5)	
OBCs	*10 (25.5)*	*15 (41.6)*
Backward castes	*7 (18)*	*4 (11.1)*
Kurmi	5 (12.8)	
Yadav	1 (2.5)	
Lodhi	1 (2.5)	
Most backward castes	*3 (7.5)*	*11 (30.5)*
Teli	1 (2.5)	2 (5.5)
Kachhi/Kushwaha		3 (8.3)
Kirar		1 (2.7)
Gujar		2 (5.5)
Nai		1 (2.7)
Rawat		
Mali		
Marar		
Kallar		1 (2.7)
Gadariya		
Mallah		1 (2.7)
Other	2 (5.1)	
Scheduled Castes	*19 (48.5)*	*9 (25)*
Chamar	11 (28)	3 (8.3)
Satnami	1 (2.5)	4 (11.1)
Mahar	3 (7.7)	2 (5.5)
Khatik	1 (2.5)	
Other	3 (7.7)	
Scheduled Tribes	*6 (15.4)*	*6 (16.6)*
Muslim		*4 (11.1)*
Unidentified	*3 (7.7)*	*2 (5.5)*
Total	*39 (100)*	*36 (100)*

Source: Fieldwork.

this coalition, the BSP and the SP showed great solidarity. They stand firm against the BJP and some members of the Congress who protested vehemently against the implementation of Mandal Report quotas in Uttarakhand, a sub-region of Uttar Pradesh where OBCs represented only 2% of the population.

Relations between the two partners soon deteriorated. BSP was concerned about the 'Yadavisation' of the state, as mentioned above. Second, the Backward Castes, who were anxious to improve their social status and keep the Scheduled Castes in their place, reacted violently to their efforts to achieve social mobility. The OBCs and the Dalits' class interests are clearly antagonistic in some regions of Uttar Pradesh: while in East UP 'the OBCs and the Scheduled Castes labourers have a common enemy: the old elite'[49] made of upper caste landlords, elsewhere, the Scheduled Castes are often landless labourers or cultivators with a very small amount of land who work for OBC farmers. While conflicts about the wages of agricultural labourers and disputes over land ownership have always been acute, they became more frequent when both groups – the Dalit and the OBCs – became more assertive after the 1993 elections.

Indeed, these bones of contention partly explained the proliferation of 'atrocities'. The Commission of Scheduled Castes and Scheduled Tribes enumerated 1,067 cases of 'atrocities' in UP in its 1989–90 report; five years later, it listed 14,966 such cases in its report of 1995. This upsurge of atrocities in Uttar Pradesh was often caused by the upper castes, particularly Rajputs who were perturbed by the Dalits increasing political powers.[50] However, the OBCs – and especially the Yadavs – who had become more self-confident after the formation of Mulayam Singh Yadav's government, were also quick

Table 11.10. ATROCITIES AGAINST SCHEDULED CASTES

	1984	*1989-90*	*1995*
Uttar Pradesh	4,200	1,067	14,966
Madhya Pradesh	5,537	5,592	2,717
Rajasthan	1,648	1,501	5,204
Bihar	1,845	434	NA
Gujarat	582	710	NA
Tamil Nadu	689	334	NA
Maharashtra	570	426	NA

Sources: For 1984, V. Tatu, *Politics of Ethnic Nepotism*, New Delhi: Sterling Publishers United, 1991, p. 131; for 1989–90, *Lok Sabha Debates*, vol. 8, no. 2, 8 Aug. 1990, pp.622-30; and for 1995, H. Hanumanthappa, 'Dalits in India: A Status Report', *Dalit-International Newsletter*, vol. 2, no. 2 June 1997, p.9.

[49] J. Lerche, 'Agricultural Labourers, the State and Agrarian Transition in Uttar Pradesh', *EPW*, 28 March 1998, p. A-33.

[50] P. Swami, 'Conflicts in UP', *Frontline*, 11 March 1994, pp. 4–12.

to harass them.[51] Kanshi Ram protested vehemently and demanded that the Dalits should be protected more efficiently. Parallel to this move, the BSP leaders intensified their efforts to set up statues of Ambedkar in *mohallas* and villages. This idea, which was apparently suggested by Radhey Lal Boudh, a leader of the Dalit Panthers,[52] was intended to serve several purposes: to propagate the Ambedkarite iconography[53] and thereby to generate a kind of pan-Indian *bahujan* 'imagined community', and to assert the *bahujans'* control over land and polarise the upper and the lower castes, just as the building of new Hindu temples or Muslim shrines could be used to crystallise communal solidarities.

In March 1994, in Meerut, Dalits demonstrated against the removal of one such statue from a public park. The police dispersed them, killing two demonstrators. In Fatehullapur (Barabanki district) Yadavs protested against the installation of a bust of Ambedkar on a plot they had long occupied. Over a period of four months, about sixty incidents linked with the installation of statues led to 21 casualties among the Dalits.[54] The BSP insisted that Mulayam Singh Yadav should take all necessary measures. He may have tried his best, but without success. For Kanshi Ram the rising graph of atrocities was the main reason for the divorce between the BSP and the SP.[55]

However, the immediate reasons underlying this divorce were different. First, the 1995 Panchayat elections showed that Mulayam

[51] A. Mishra, 'Challenge to SP-BSP Government', *EPW*, 19 Feb. 1994, p. 409 and S. Chandra, 'Dalits versus the OBCs', *Sunday*, 27 Feb. 1994, pp. 10–13. In March 1994 *The Times of India* cited an intelligence report according to which 27 out of 54 cases of atrocities perpetrated against Untouchables were carried out by OBCs – half a dozen of them involved Yadavs. (*Times of India*, 2 March 1994)

[52] D. Mukerji, 'In the name of Ambedkar', *The Week*, 24 April 1994, p. 60.

[53] For decades the Ambedkarites have stylised 'Baba Saheb' by representing him as always wearing a suit, wearing round glasses and with carefully brushed hair. His portraits are quite often flanked by those of Mahatma Jyotirao Phule and Lord Buddha, so much so that a kind of pan-Dalit or even pan-Bahujan iconography has evolved.

[54] *India Today*, 10 April 1994, p. 56.

[55] 'BSP withdrew support in 1995 because Mulayam [Singh Yadav] tried to attract some of our people and because of atrocities against the Scheduled Castes, especially by the Yadavs. That was the main reason. I tried to warn him but he could not or did not want to do anything.' (Interview with Kanshi Ram)

Singh Yadav was about 'to capture the base of the power pyramid':[56] out of fifty districts where elections to the presidents of the district panchayats took place, thirty (that is 60% of the seats) were won by the Samajwadi Party, nine by the BJP, five by Congress and only one by the BSP. These results came as a shock to the SP's coalition partner. Second, Mulayam Singh Yadav was not slow to welcome BSP dissidents in his party, or probably even to entice them to defect.[57] For instance, he established a privileged relationship with the president of the BSP of Uttar Pradesh, Raj Bahadur. As a result, on 2 June 1995, the BSP withdrew its support for the government and its eleven ministers resigned. The following day Raj Bahadur and twelve other BSP MLAs joined the SP.

The BSP terminated its coalition with the SP to become actively involved in another, even more favourable, alliance, since on 3 June 1995 Mayawati became Chief Minister of the Uttar Pradesh government with the BJP's support. This alliance was even more tactical than that with the SP. It was primarily directed against Mulayam Singh Yadav whom the BSP and the BJP wanted to keep in check because of his increasing political influence – as evident from the Panchayat elections – which reflected the growing assertiveness of the OBCs, and especially of the Yadavs. The alliance of the BSP with the BJP epitomised the convergence between Dalit and upper castes leaders against the OBCs and above all against the Yadavs who now posed a threat as much to the Scheduled Castes, as they did to the elite landowners and civil servants, because of Mulayam Singh Yadav's reservation policy.[58]

The willingness of the BSP to come to terms with the BJP reflected the tendency of upper and lowest castes to make common cause against the increasing assertiveness of the middle castes – the Yadavs and the Kurmis – who threatened them both. Yet, to keep the Yadavs away from power was not the main reason for the BSP's association

[56] Verma and Verma, 'The OBCs and sharing of power in the Panchayati Raj institutions in Uttar Pradesh', op. cit., p. 1.

[57] A. Mishra, 'Limits of OBC-Dalit politics', *EPW*, 10 June 1995, p. 1356.

[58] This *rapprochement* of groups which were poles apart in the social structure was justified in those terms by Kanshi Ram: '. . . we can take the help of the BJP to advance our national agenda. We feel that the upper castes will be more amenable to social transformation than the intermediate castes.' (Interview with Kanshi Ram, *Frontline*, 28 June 1996, p. 35)

with the BJP: the alliance was especially valued because it enabled the BSP to remain in office. The end justified the means, and this approach was substantiated by Mayawati's first experiment in power.

Mayawati is a Chamar from Uttar Pradesh (her native village, Badalpur is located in Ghaziabad district). At the time of her birth in 1956 her father was employed in the telephone department (from which he retired as an MTNL supervisor). Mayawati was successful in her studies in Meerut (BA and B Ed) and in Delhi (LLB) where her family had settled when she was two years old. She became a school-teacher in 1977, and having experienced at first hand the typical discrimination that even educated Scheduled Castes routinely endured at that time – and still endure occasionally – she became an avid reader of Dr Ambedkar of whom her father was already a follower.[59] Her first brush with politics took place in 1977 when she vocally objected to the use of the word 'Harijan' in an 'Abolish Caste Conference' organised by the Janata Party. She was then approached by Dalit leaders for the first time. Three years later she was preparing for the IAS examination when she met Kanshi Ram[60] who persuaded her to enter politics. In 1984 she left her job to devote herself to the BSP. Apparently Kanshi Ram had been impressed by her oratory and indeed Mayawati made a name for herself through her deliberately aggressive and even provocative speeches.[61]

With Mayawati as Chief Minister, India's largest state for the first time was governed by a member of the Scheduled Castes, one who forcefully advocated the cause of the *bahujan samaj*.[62] For most Dalits she became a source of pride.[63] Mayawati's accession to Uttar

[59] Ku. Mayawati, *Bahujan Samaj aur uski Rajniti*, New Delhi, BSP, 2000, p. 96.

[60] The same year her family converted to Buddhism.

[61] For instance she declared that Gandhi was 'the biggest enemy of the Dalits. If Harijans means children of God, should it be considered that the Mahatma was the son of Satan?' (Cited in G. Singh, 'Power of Maya', op. cit.)

[62] Before Mayawati, there had been only three Dalit Chief Ministers – none of them a woman: D. Sanjiviah in Andhra Pradesh, Ram Sunder Das in Bihar and Jagannath Pahadiya in Rajasthan.

[63] However, some Dalits do not share this feeling because of rumors of her long term affair between her and Kanshi Ram. These rumors were reactivated by an article of *Dainik Jagran* in late 1995, in which it was said that, even though she had never married, she had a twelve year old daughter hidden in Delhi. Some of her caste fellows felt that such revelations made Dalits seen immoral (I am grateful to Owen Lynch for drawing my attention to this point).

Pradesh's top post thus played a major part in the consolidation of the BSP's vote banks.[64]

Such a consolidation also resulted from the special treatment Mayawati granted to the lower castes, of which the Dalits were the first beneficiaries. Mayawati started with a series of name changes: Agra University was re-named Dr Bhimrao Ambedkar University and the one in Kanpur, Chhatrapati Shahuji Maharaj University. New districts were carved out and renamed after Dr Bhimrao Ambedkar, Shahuji Maharaj and Mahamayana, the mother of Buddha. The Agra stadium was named Eklavya, etc. Dozens of Ambedkar statues were put up across the state. The acme of this symbolic conquest of public space was the Periyar Mela that the Mayawati government organised in Lucknow on 18 and 19 September 1995 in honour of E.V. Ramaswamy Naicker, or 'Periyar' – the wise-man as he came to be called in his old age. Periyar had been declared *persona non grata* in Uttar Pradesh after the translation in English of his book, *The Ramayana –A true reading*, where he portrayed Ram and Sita in a way considered blasphemous by many upper caste Hindus in the 'home state' of this divine couple (the book had been proscribed there in 1969). The Periyar Mela aimed at rehabilitating his name, at mobilising the Dalits and at provoking the upper castes, as did Kanshi Ram on this occasion by making derogatory remarks about Gandhi.

More importantly, the Scheduled Castes also benefited from concrete measures that were taken during the four and a half-months of Mayawati's first government. Mulayam Singh Yadav's Ambedkar Villages Scheme, which consisted in allotting special funds for socio-economic development under the IRDP (Integrated Rural Development Programme), for two years for villages with 50% Scheduled Castes population, was revised in order to include those with more than 30% (and even 22% in certain areas). Dalits in these villages were specially favoured by Mayawati since 'all the roads, handpumps, houses, etc., have been largely built in their *bastees* [neighbourhoods]'.[65] Grants were created for Dalit children to attend classes between level 1 and 8; those for Bhangi children were doubled. The Bhangis (or Valmikis), who tend to vote for the BJP, also

[64] Such a consolidation was part of a deliberate strategy: soon after the withdrawal of the BJP's support and the fall of her first government in October 1995, she declared in an interview: 'My biggest achievement has been consolidation of the Dalit vote bank.' (*The Pioneer*, 23 Oct. 1995, p. 9)

[65] S. Pai, 'Dalit assertion in UP', op. cit., p. 2314.

received special treatment as Mayawati announced a rehabilitation programme to free them from their traditional jobs as sweepers. Lastly, 20% of the posts of inspector of police (*thanedars*) were reserved to the Scheduled Castes.

As far as the OBCs were concerned, Mayawati announced that they would benefit from 27% of the state budget. Some new castes that had been neglected by the administration were included in the OBCs' list and the Nishads (boat-men also called Mallahs or Kewats) were allowed the privilege of renting plots alongside rivers.

Finally, Muslims were designated to receive the same grants as Scheduled Castes children and Mayawati implemented the recommendations of the second UP Backward Classes Commission which insisted, in its 1994 report that low caste Muslims should benefit from reservations in the state administration. Mulayam Singh Yadav had opposed the measure because it would have reduced the share of the Hindu OBCs. Mayawati granted the Muslims 8.44% of the 27% due to the OBCs. A comparable proportion – 8% – of police officers' posts was also reserved for the Muslims.[66]

In order to implement these measures Mayawati – who probably anticipated that she could not rely on the BJP's support for more than a few months – created a climate of fear in order to motivate her officials[67] and promoted her supporters in the bureaucracy to in replace of upper caste officers. The BSP government appointed its supporters in key administrative jobs: more than 1,500 transfers took place in Uttar Pradesh during the 136 days of Mayawati's government.[68]

[66] BSP, *Mukhya lakshay evan apil*, New Delhi: 1996. The Muslims also appreciated the way Mayawati government resisted the VHP's attempt at organising an important function at Mathura for Krishna's birthday in September 1995. On this site, that the VHP claimed to be Krishna's birthplace, stands a mosque and the VHP's intention was, as in Ayodhya, to mobilise Hindus in order to 'reconquer' this Muslim place. Mayawati allowed the VHP's function to take place provided that it was held more than 3 km away from the mosque.

[67] Mendelsohn and Vicziany, *The Untouchables*, op. cit., pp. 228–9.

[68] During his first term, M. S. Yadav transferred 419 members of the Indian Administrative Service and 228 members of the Indian Police Service between December 1989 and June 1991. His BJP successor Kalyan Singh transferred 460 IAS and 319 IPS personnel between June 1991 and December 1992. M.S. Yadav during his second term reversed the proportions with respectively 321 IAS and 493 IPS transferred between December 1993 and June 1995. After one month of exercise of power, Mayawati had already transferred 82 IAS and 96 IPS. (*India Today*, 31 July 1995)

This allowed her to post a Scheduled Caste District Magistrate at the helm of almost half of the districts,[69] a policy which alarmed the BJP as it helped the BSP to strengthen its local implantation. In December 1995 the local elections enabled the BSP to take control of one municipal corporation (out of the eleven of the biggest city councils), 9 middle-size municipalities and 22 small towns (as against respectively 1, 82 and 100 for the BJP and 1, 27 and 45 for the SP). The BJP withdrew its support on 18 October 1995 and the fall of the Mayawati government led New Delhi to declare President's Rule in Uttar Pradesh.

The BSP decided to stand alone, six months later, in the 1996 Lok Sabha elections. Yet the party doubled its share of valid votes in Uttar Pradesh, from 10% in the 1989, 1991 and 1993 elections to 20,6% (9,483,739 votes, fifty more than the SP). While Gail Omvedt considers that 'Short term gains from an opportunist alliance with the Bharatiya Janata Party yielded little in the end',[70] this electoral rise of the BSP can be attributed only to Mayawati's experiment in office. This episode has obviously enabled the party to broaden its base amongst the *bahujan samaj* by showing that a Dalit could occupy the seat of power (in itself a very powerful symbol) and exercise it to the profit of the downtrodden. The BSP was especially successful in consolidating the Scheduled Castes behind its candidates. As mentioned above, the CSDS survey conducted during the 1996 Assembly elections showed that 65% of the Dalit voters supported the BSP. The fact that the party was supported by two-thirds of the Scheduled Castes – who represent 21% of UP's population – was quite an achievement and could only be explained by the BSP's rise to power. While, for Omvedt, the '1998 elections [were] in some way a turning point because the Dalits then refused to be simply vote banks whose account [was] controlled by others; they [were] becoming voting blocks seeking to control their own destiny',[71] I would argue that the watershed was the Chief Ministership of Mayawati in 1995. Indeed, her popularity was such that she was the party's most effective crowd-puller during the election campaign.[72]

[69] *Frontline*, 1 Dec. 1995, p. 31.

[70] G. Omvedt, 'Dalit politics', *The Hindu*, 1 April 1998.

[71] Omvedt, 'Dalit politics', op. cit.

[72] A study of four villages in Meerut district showed that Mayawati was 'popular and acceptable to the jatav villagers because during her tenure as CM a number of welfare measures for Dalits were undertaken. [. . .] In the Ambedkar

The electoral dividends the BSP drew from the Mayawati government confirmed Kanshi Ram's feeling that any coalition was worth considering provided it allowed the BSP to come to power. The party was approached by several potential allies in view of the forthcoming Uttar Pradesh Assembly elections, to be held in September 1996, and eventually agreed to a seat adjustment with Congress. On 25 June P.V. Narasimha Rao, as Congress President, and Kanshi Ram announced the agreement at a highly symbolic press-conference: for the first time Congress played the role of a junior partner in Uttar Pradesh with a Dalit party. (It contested the elections in only one third of the constituencies compared to 300 for the BSP.) The BSP's decision to enter in such an alliance with the Congress was again purely pragmatic. As Chandra and Parmar argue, it was '(1) a short run strategy to catapult the party into a position to form a government in U.P. and (2) [. . .] a means to capture Congress' remaining dalit and backward vote in U.P. and in other states.'[73] The BSP repeated its score in the Lok Sabha elections (with about 20% of the votes, the alliance winning 27.8%) and obtained the same number of MLAs – 67 – as in 1993 (when it was associated with a stronger partner, the SP). No party won an overall majority and hence New Delhi once again imposed Presidents' Rule on the state.

The BSP leaders immediately announced that they would form a coalition with any political force willing and able to allocate the Chief Ministership to Mayawati. After six months of Presidents' Rule, the BJP accepted their conditions. This decision could be once again partly explained by the apprehension that Mulayam Singh Yadav generated in the BJP and the BSP.[74] According to the BJP-BSP agreement, Mayawati would be Chief Minister for six months,

---

villages [. . .] the land "pattas" which had been allotted to Dalits during the Emergency but not given, were actually distributed among them; "pucca" roads linking the villages to the main road, construction of houses, drinking water pumps and toilets in the SC sections of the villages; pensions for old persons; panchayat "ghars", installation of Ambedkar statues, etc., were some of the schemes implemented.' (S. Pai and J. Singh, 'Politicisation of Dalits and Most Backward Castes', *EPW*, 7 June 1997 , p. 1358)

[73] K. Chandra and C. Parmar, 'Party strategies in the Uttar Pradesh Assembly Elections', *EPW*, Feb. 1, 1997, p. 216.

[74] Being a Cabinet Minister in Dewe Gowda government, Yadav had indeed acquired a strong influence over the Governor of Uttar Pradesh, Romesh Bhandari.

followed by a BJP leader; thereafter they would function in rotation. As for the government, it would comprise 50% BJP and 50% BSP ministers. The BSP therefore came back to power thanks to a new reversal of alliances.[75]

Within the government the BSP and the BJP had respectively eight ministers and twelve ministers of state each, as Mayawati kept thirty-three departments from among twenty-four ministerial portfolios. During her six-month tenure, she transferred 1,350 civil and police officials.[76] Only two days after taking over she had announced that 250 constable-clerks would be soon recruited among the Scheduled Castes and Scheduled Tribes.[77] The Ambedkar Villages Scheme was comprehensively revived under the direct supervision of the Chief Minister. The 350 crores scheme covered 11,000 villages. In addition, 15,000 Ambedkar statues were installed throughout Uttar Pradesh, one of them, in Lucknow, at an estimated cost of Rs 250,000. Also in Lucknow, the 120 crores Ambedkar Udhyan (Park) was laid out on a massive scale.[78]

After six months in office, she left the post of Chief Minister to Kalyan Singh, the BJP OBC leader, but the BSP immediately criticised the government order he issued that the *SC/ST (Prevention of Atrocities) Act* should not be misused and withdrew its support. Mayawati, indeed, had implemented this Act in a more radical way than any of her predecessors.[79] A few weeks before Kanshi Ram had more or less explicitly announced his divorce with the BJP:

[75] Interview in *Frontline*, 18 April 1997, p. 15.

[76] *Times of India*, 18 Sept. 1997.

[77] Ibid., 23 March 1997.

[78] Mayawati had laid the foundation stone of this 28 acre park on 15 August 1995. The work stopped after she had lost power, but resumed in 1997 and the part was inaugurated before its completion in June that year. The entry plaque says that the Udhyan is dedi-cated to 'the sacred memory at the great hero of social change, Bharat Ratna Boddhisatva Baba Saheb Dr. Bhim Rao Ambedkar'.

[79] Lerche convincingly argues that 'jailing of anyone accused of such crimes while the case was investigated, and the award of Rs 6,000 to any victim of such crimes in order to enable them to fight the case in court, showed the seriousness of the pro-untouchable bias of the government.' (Lerche, 'Politics of the poor', op. cit., p. 7) While doing fieldwork in Jaunpur district after Kalyan Singh took over, Lerche discovered that 'the accused person is no longer put in jail while the case is being investigated, and the plaintiff no longer receives Rs 6,000 to fight the case in court' (ibid., p. 11).

My aim is that the BSP should move forward. At any given point, I'll enter into a tactical alliance with another party if I feel it will strengthen the BSP. And it is what I have done in the past. I did not enter into an alliance with the BJP because of any ideological common ground – in fact we are poles apart. [. . .] We entered into an understanding with the BJP last year to increase the base of the BSP and when we feel we are not benefiting any longer, we'll end it [...] I'm only looking for a suitable ladder.[80]

However, contrary to Kanshi Ram's expectations, the Kalyan Singh government did not fall because the BJP attracted enough defectors from the Congress and from the BSP to stay in power. The break-away group from the BSP comprised twelve MLAs who were all rewarded with ministerial berths in Kalyan Singh's cabinet.[81]

The BSP contested the 1998 Lok Sabha elections on its own in Uttar Pradesh and it polled almost the same number of votes as in 1996. However, it suffered a setback in Punjab where it had made an alliance with the Congress[82] and in Madhya Pradesh. Its seat adjustment with Laloo Prasad Yadav in Bihar did not really bear fruit either. In fact the 1998 elections revealed some of the weaknesses of the BSP's new electoral strategy. First, it had been so desperate to gain power that it did not refrain from co-opting politicians who were not as politically committed as people with a BAMCEF or DS-4 background. Kanshi Ram says that he was aware of the inherent risks in this approach.

The risk is there of diluting our identity, but for the sake of our growth we have to take that risk. We want a quicker growth and the empowerment of the oppressed. We do not give them [the new comers] any responsibility within the party apparatus, but only field them as our candidates. The organisers are from the DS-4, 95% of them. And we are also giving them tickets.[83]

[80] Cited in *The Times of India*, 21 Aug. 1997.

[81] The BSP petitioned the speaker, K.N. Tripathi since this breakaway group represented less than one third of the BSP legislative group and its members, therefore, should be disqualified. But Tripathi – who is a senior BJP leader – in his 148 page long report argued that the breakaway group, initially, had 26 members.

[82] This reverse, that was reconfirmed in the by-election of Adampur in late 1998, led the BSP state secretary-general, Avtar Singh Karimpuri, to revamp the party organisation. He announced that party offices would be set up in all the districts. (*The Hindu*, 1 Jan. 1999)

[83] Interview with Kanshi Ram.

However, veteran leaders the Dalit movement resented the fielding of newcomers during the elections, especially those from the upper castes, such as wealthy industrialists. During the 1998 elections, in Meerut district BSP activists resigned from the party to protest against the issuing of the ticket to one such former mayor, Arun Jain.

Second, the constant changes in alliances for the sake of power went hand in hand with a decline in party discipline: the BSP is especially prone to defections by its members as its leaders promoted a political culture based on the occupation of power. Over the last five years, the BSP has been repeatedly damaged by dissidence and defections which resulted also from its weak party structure. Nor is the organisation renowned for its democratic functioning: till 1997 the BSP had never held party elections, the office bearers being chosen by party grandees. In fact, Kanshi Ram adopted the same *modus operandi* as he had with the BAMCEF, in which every district organiser was personally appointed by him.[84] Similarly, to begin with, he appointed BSP presidents in the states and they selected the leaders of the district committees. In 1997 the chiefs of the State units were elected but they continued to select the members of the state executive committees and of the district bodies. More importantly, Kanshi Ram and Mayawati were quick to dispense with presidents of state units, as in May 1997, when the latter unceremoniously removed Bhagwat Pal from the party presidentship in Uttar Pradesh.[85] The concentration of power within the hands of Kanshi Ram and Mayawati alienated many second rank leaders. In 1998, the General Secretary of the Uttar Pradesh unit of the BSP, D.P. Bara, resigned because he felt humiliated by the so-called autocratic *modus operandi* of Mayawati. A few days later, partly as a reaction to what he regarded as an expulsion, an influential Kurmi leader, Ram Punjab Patel, a former MP, resigned from the National Executive of the party and then from the primary membership.[86] The most damaging split occurred in October 1996, however. As mentioned above, the party withdrew its support from Kalyan Singh's government after the latter had taken over from Mayawati in accordance with the initial arrangement, allegedly because of the order he had issued that the *SCs/STs (Prevention of Atrocities) Act* should not be misused. But Kalyan Singh

84 *Kanshi Ram*, op. cit.

85 *National Mail*, 24 May 1997.

86 *The Hindu*, 5 Sept. 1998 and 17 Sept. 1998.

was able to retain a majority in the assembly by gaining the support of breakaway sections of the Congress and the BSP. From the latter party, twelve MLAs were attracted by the promise of a ministerial portfolio in a 93 member ministry and therefore created the Jantantrik BSP, which supported Kalyan Singh.[87]

In Madhya Pradesh, to begin with, the steady progress that the BSP made till 1999 had led many congressmen to defect *to the BSP*. The most prestigious of them all was Arvind Netam, former Union Minister and Tribal leader from Chhattisgarh. Implicated in the Hawala affair, Netam had been requested not to contest in 1996 by the Congress, a party he left in 1997 to join the BSP on the occasion of Ambedkar Jayanti in April 1997. He was followed by Scheduled Caste Congress leaders such as Nathuram Ahirwar (a former minister) and Maya Salwar, an ex-MLA. In 1998 the BSP sustained its growth, largely because of a tacit agreement with the Congress against their joint priority target: the BJP.[88] Yet the party was unable to retain these new recruits who probably found that this growth was too slow: one year after joining the BSP, Netam returned to Congress. Kanshi Ram said that he did not want un-committed leaders anyway but, at the same time, he admitted during a public meeting at Raipur that he has 'not been able to create a leader in the midst of *adivasis* in Madhya Pradesh'.[89]

This is one of the reasons for the continuing weakness of the BSP in Chhattisgarh where the party relies mostly on the Satnamis' support. But even they did not support the BSP *en bloc* during the 1999 election campaign when the state party President, Ratnakar faced the candidature of a dissident, Ramakrishna Jangade, who cut into his vote. While indiscipline has always been a problem for the party in Madhya Pradesh,[90] things worsened after the 1999 elections.

[87] Five more BSP MLAs crossed the floor in March 1998 and were offered ministerial portfolios.

[88] Sukhlal Kushwaha pointed out: 'wherever the BSP is strong and can fight the BJP and the Congress we fight them both. But wherever by cutting into the Congress vote we help the BJP, we have stopped fighting it' (Interview with S. Kushwaha). This strategy suited the Congress Chief Minister perfectly since the BSP was especially effective in the strongholds of his main rivals within the Congress, Arjun Singh in Vindhya Pradesh and Madhav Rao Scindia in Gwalior area.

[89] *National Mail*, 7 Oct. 1998.

[90] For instance, in 1997, the BSP MP from Rewa, Buddhan Sen Patel joined Aapna Dal.

In 1999, the Congress and the BSP had no arrangement, probably because the former considered that it was strong enough after its success in the 1998 Assembly elections. This was one of the factors that explains the BSP's setback: the party's share of valid vote declined from 8.7 to 5.2%, and it was immediately hit by defections. Four of its eleven MLAs – all of them from the Gwalior area – formed a separate party in the Vidhan Sabha and joined the Congress Party a few weeks later.

Kanshi Ram became aware of the organisational weakness of the BSP after the 1998 elections and decided not to contest elections over the coming five years in order to concentrate on consolidating the party. His return to his initial focus probably had a positive impact on the party in Uttar Pradesh, a state where he toured extensively, but it has not been felt so far in the neighbouring states, including Madhya Pradesh.

The Scheduled Castes had long been politically marginalised and oppressed. Their leaders were unable to attract support from beyond their own milieu, did not fight as one and were prone to the co-option techniques of élite-dominated parties. The Ambedkar-inspired RPI was hindered in this way by factionalism and co-option by the Congress Party. Kanshi Ram's BSP is still affected by such problems but it may be able to complete Ambedkar's unfinished agenda.

Certainly, Kanshi Ram's thoughts are not as sophisticated as Ambedkar's.[91] He is not an intellectual and this is probably one of the reasons why he pays little attention, compared to Ambedkar, to educational issues. Some also reproached him for neglecting social reform whereas it was one of the areas of interest of Ambedkar.[92] Nor is Kanshi Ram interested in conversion to Buddhism, because, according to him, such a move would only make sense if all the Dalits converted en masse.[93] However, his approach to politics has much in common with that of Ambedkar. First, they both regard the capture of power as the main objective for emancipating the lower castes from elite domination – a prerequisite for social reform and

[91] Dr Ambedkar's widow emphasised that Kanshi Ram 'has no knowledge of his [Ambedkar's] principles and ideology' (interview to *Indian Express*, 18 Nov. 1997, p. 3).

[92] P. Kumar, 'Dalits and the BSP in Uttar Pradesh', op. cit., p. 822.

[93] Interview with Kanshi Ram.

redistributive justice. This priority implies the making of alliances that critics of Kanshi Ram describe as opportunistic but which reflects a pragmatic approach: he – like Ambedkar when he joined the Viceroy's Council – is flexible enough to collaborate with any ally in a position to give him access to power. This approach to politics is not revolutionary but legalistic. Kanshi Ram anyway regards communism (a revolutionary ideology) as irrelevant in the case of India, like Ambedkar. Thus both men opted for democratic elections rather than promoting violent change.

Both leaders also advocated the formation of a wide coalition of social groups with similar status. Ambedkar had oscillated between this position and the defence of the Dalits alone but ultimately opted for a broader front. Kanshi Ram took the same route by borrowing from Phule the notion of a *bahujan samaj* descending from the indigenous people of India. And, in contrast to Ambedkar, he succeeded in partially uniting the Scheduled Castes – around the Chamars – and in rallying around this core group some OBC castes and Muslims. The party's social basis remains narrow, however. It is no longer exclusively a Dalit party, but it is not a party of the low castes either since only a mere fraction of the OBCs have joined its ranks. It is still identified with the Chamars, just as the RPI tends to be 'a Mahar party' in Maharashtra.[94] Balmikis and Pasis instead vote for other parties, partly to distinguish themselves from the Chamars, whose hegemony they fear, – the former for the BJP, the latter for the party of Ram Vilas Paswan. Moreover the BSP recruits most of its supporters from the younger generations while their parents still vote for the Congress (as in Chhattisgarh, among the Satnamis, for instance).[95]

Over the last fifteen years the BSP has been almost constantly on an upward trend, a rise largely based on the groundwork of the BAMCEF and the DS-4, the organisational skill of Kanshi Ram, his efforts to reach groups beyond the Dalits and the dividends of Mayawati's governments. However, by the late 1990s, the BSP reached a plateau. It consolidated its base in Uttar Pradesh but was

[94] Mayawati, while confessing that she feared for her life declared in late 1998: 'If I am killed, members of the Chamar community would create a havoc.' (*The Hindu*, 12 Dec. 1998)

[95] One can argue that the BSP may therefore grow incrementally in the long run and, in the meantime, use its young partisans to win over their parents.

on the decline everywhere else. One of the main reasons for this setback probably lay in organisational difficulties, including factionalism: Kanshi Ram tends to concentrate power in his own hands, depriving his party of a strong structure and fomenting jealousy, with the notable exception of the UP unit which is dominated by Mayawati. The BSP is also affected by the reaction of upper-caste dominated political parties as evident from the co-option of some of its MLAs by the BJP in Uttar Pradesh and by the Congress in Madhya Pradesh. Besides co-opting MLAs of the BSP, these parties may also hijack part of its program. If so, the BSP will not be the only low caste party that may be affected – the Samajwadi Party may also be at the receiving end. But how far can the Congress and the BJP adjust to the rise of the lower castes?

Part V

THE UPPER CASTES' POLITICAL DOMINATION ON TRIAL

THE CONGRESS(I), THE BJP AND MANDAL

The way the Janata Dal and its offshoots – the SP and the RJD – on the one hand, and the BSP on the other hand consolidated their base respectively amongst the OBCs and the Dalits threatened the Congress and the BJP in North India. Till then, the former had owed most of its success to its catch-all party profile while the latter, and its earlier incarnation the Jana Sangh, not only had upper castes members at their helm but primarily represented the upper caste dominated urban middle class of North India – which could hardly compete with the OBCs and the Dalits in terms of numbers. Both parties had to adjust to the Mandal challenge. The BJP did so immediately by resorting to its Hindutva plank but soon realised that Hindu Nationalism could not subsume caste identities. The party, therefore accepted to mandalise itself, first by making alliances with low caste-based parties and then more directly by nominating more OBC electoral candidates. However, the upper castes continued to monopolise power within the party apparatus. Congress had to display some adaptability too but its discourse based on the idiom of consensus did not enable its leaders to tackle the issue properly everywhere. The party turned out to respond to Mandal in the most articulate manner in the stateof Madhya Pradesh.

12
THE CONGRESS(I) AND THE 'COALITION OF EXTREMES' REVISITED

Until the 1990s, the Congress(I) succeeded in attracting the votes of a wide range of social groups. It was a genuine 'catch-all party'. In 1967, for example, the vote in favour of the Congress varied hardly at all according to income level.[1] In North India, as mentioned above, it was more specifically based on a 'coalition of extremes',[2] to use the terms of Brass, since its principal support came from the Brahmins, the Scheduled Castes and the Muslims. The party thus blurred two cleavages, that opposing the high and the low castes, and that separating religious communities. The same technique turned out to be successful in other regions too. The all India opinion polls of the CSDS show that till the 1980s, the Congress party was able to attract between 35.8% and 50.5% of voters from any social group.

Table 12.1. EVOLUTION OF CONGRESS VOTE BY SOCIAL GROUP, 1967–98

	1967	*1971*	*1980*	*1996*	*1998*	*1999**
Upper castes	41.1	45.6	35.8	28.4	28.1	21
Dominant castes						31
OBC	38	39.4	42	21.7	22.5	35
Scheduled Castes	49.4	47.8	50.5	31.6	29.6	40
Scheduled Tribes	46.2	41.2	48.6	39.2	41.9	49

*These figures concern the Congress and its allies

Sources: Surveys by the CSDS data unit cited in S.K. Mitra and V.B. Singh, *Democracy and Social Change in India. A Cross-Sectional Analysis of the National Electorate*, New Delhi, Sage, 1999, pp. 134-5 and, for 1999, *Frontline*, 19 Nov. 1999, p. 32.

[1] D. Madsen, 'Solid Congress Support in 1967: a Statistical Inquiry', *Asian Survey*, 10 (11), Nov. 1970, p. 100.

[2] P. Brass, 'The Politicization of the Peasantry in a North Indian State – Part II', *JPS*, 8 (1), Oct. 1980, pp. 3–36.

In 1989, the Brahmins, the Scheduled Castes, the Scheduled Tribes and the Muslims were still over-represented within the Congress (I) electorate. According to an opinion poll survey carried out after the 1989 elections, where the Congress(I) won 39.5% of the valid votes, it received the support of 41% of the Brahmins who were interviewed, 44.2% of the SCs/STs and 45.8% of the Muslims.[3]

The end of a catch-all party

The implementation of the Mandal Commission Report generated a debate within the Congress(I). Low caste leaders of the party, such as Sitaram Kesri, a Banya from Bihar – where his caste is classified with the OBCs –, who was then Treasurer of the Congress, was favourably inclined towards it.[4] But the party chiefs preferred to maintain the traditional approach based on consensus. V.P. Singh's decision to implement the recommendations of the Mandal report was strongly criticised in the Lok Sabha by Rajiv Gandhi, the then Congress(I) President and leader of the opposition, on 6 September 1990. He considered that a 'national consensus' had to be evolved[5] and that caste-based reservations could only divide Indian society.[6] Alternatively, he suggested that the quotas should be based on economic criteria and that 'assistance should be given to the truly poor, to the landless, to the people falling in the poorest category'.[7] The Congress(I) tried to maintain its 'coalition of extremes' by indirectly promising quotas to the poor from the upper castes and new concessions to the Scheduled Castes and in doing so it continued to display the party's traditional indifference towards the OBCs, at the risk of further alienating this group.

The Congress(I) regained power, though without securing a clear-cut majority, after the May–June 1991 general elections. Soon after, on 25 September, Prime Minister Narasimha Rao issued an Office Memorandum amending that of V.P. Singh by reserving 10% of posts in government services to 'economically backward sections of

[3] *India Today*, 15 April 1991, p. 53.

[4] Yadav, *India's Unequal Citizens*, op. cit., p. 91.

[5] See the debate reproduced as Appendix 1 of Mustafa, *The Lonely Prophet*, op. cit., p. 206.

[6] On the following day, Rajiv Gandhi accused V.P. Singh of bringing 'the country to the edge of caste war' (*Indian Express*, 8 Sept. 1990).

[7] Ibid.

the people' who were not covered by the existing quotas – the poor from the upper castes were to benefit from this schema. The Congress(I) was still attempting to blur the cleavage between the upper castes and the lower castes and to recapture the former's allegiance. As mentioned above, this modification was ruled invalid by the Supreme Court in its November 1992 judgement when the judges emphasised that economic criteria could not be used in the definition of 'backwardness' under Articles 15 and 16 of the Constitution. The Congress(I) had to resign itself to the centrality of caste in the identification of the OBCs. It started to adjust to the rise of the latter, as was evident from the way the government negotiated the 'creamy layer' issue. The Supreme Court had asked them to exclude from the list of the OBCs eligible for quotas those who did not need any help from the state. The Prasad Committee appointed by Rao had considered that the progeny of the farmers owning irrigated land amounting to more than 65% of the statutory area were in such a situation. The Janata Dal, as mentioned above had protested that it was too strict a criterion. Now, the Welfare Minister, who was no other than Sitaram Kesri, displayed a very conciliatory attitude during an all party meeting that he organised and eventually the proportion of land was increased to 85% in August 1993. Subsequently he even invited the private sector to implement reservations for the OBCs.[8] During the 1996 election campaign the Congresss (I) even tried to project itself as the spokesman of the OBCs. Its manifesto argued that:

> Reservations for the Backward Classes was an idea of the Congress. Jawaharlal Nehru made this into a Constitutional Principle in 1952 [. . .]. In 1990, due to its ham-fisted and opportunistic approach, the Janata Dal Government triggered a virtual caste war in several parts of India.
>
> The election of a Congress Government in 1991 brought peace to a society that was threatened with disruption by caste strife.
>
> Quietly but firmly, Shri P.V. Narasimha Rao's Governement implemented the recommendations of the Mandal Commission.[9]

The Congress(I) was still trying to appear as a consensus party and, at the same time, to project itself as the defender of the OBCs. However, the party was unable to attract more than about one fifth

[8] See his interview in *Sunday*, 2 Oct. 1994, p. 30 and *The Times of India*, 4 July 1995.

[9] Indian National Congress (I), *Election Manifesto – General Election 1996*, New Delhi: AICC (I), 1996, pp. 11–12.

of the OBC vote in 1996 and 1998, and had to wait till 1999 to improve significantly its electoral impact on the OBCs (35%) and Dalits (40%). Yadav, Kumar and Heath convincingly argue that the Congress(I) was in a position to become the party of the underprivileged, while the BJP's 'social bloc' depended on upper caste, middle class voters. However, their two notes of caution need to be taken seriously. First, 'there is a residual quality to the Congress(I) vote' in the sense that the Congress(I) can only retain the support of those who are not attracted (or even targeted) by the BJP. Second, the creation of a counter-bloc of the underprivileged requires 'a painstaking building of social alliances and political coalitions, within or without the party'.[10] Now, the Congress does not seem fit to meet such a challenge in the Hindi belt.

For instance, it has nominated only a few non upper caste candidates in the Hindi belt during the 1999 elections – and its proportion of MPs from these background remains very limited.

Between 1989 and 1999, the percentages of upper caste and OBC MPs have remained about the same, the upper and intermediate castes representing about 50% of Congress MPs returned in the Hindi belt and OBC MPs about one tenth of the total. In contrast, the Scheduled Castes (except in 1999) and the Scheduled Tribes MPs are much larger in number, a strong indication that the old pattern of 'coalition of extremes' still prevails (see Table 12.2).

The upper-castes are also over represented among the Congress Working Committee and governing team of the All India Congress Committee. Till the late 1980s, the upper castes represented more than 50% of CWC members. Ten years later their percentage had substantially declined, so that much so they formed less than one third of the total; but the OBCs did not profit from this dramatic erosion. Its main beneficiaries were the Scheduled Castes, one more indication of the persisting 'coalition of extremes' pattern.

The Congress(I) remained especially reluctant to accept any kind of 'Mandalisation' in the two states where the OBCs were making the most significant impact in North India, Uttar Pradesh and Bihar. In the former, Jitendra Prasad took over from N.D. Tiwari as state party president in 1995. A Brahmin from Shahajahanpur, Prasad came from a landlord family as mentioned above. While he admitted

[10] Y. Yadav, S. Kumar and O. Heath, 'The BJP's new social bloc', *Frontline*, 19 Nov. 1999, p. 40.

Table 12.2. CASTE AND COMMUNITY OF CONGRESS MPs ELECTED IN THE HINDI BELT, 1989–99

	1989	*1991*	*1996*	*1998*	*1999*
Upper castes	*37.1*	*30*	*32.1*	*29*	*40*
Brahmin	17.14	11.67	18	8	20
Rajput	8.57	6.67	5.88	2.63	5.71
Bhumihar	2.86	3.33		2.63	5.71
Banya/Jain	5.71	3.33	5.88	8	5.71
Kayasth		3.33		2.63	
Khatri	2.86	1.67			
Sindhi				2.63	2.86
Tyagi					
Other			2.34	2.63	
Intermediate castes	*9*	*16.67*	*17.65*	*21.05*	*14.29*
Jat	3	15	17.65	13.16	8.57
Maratha	2.86	1.67		2.63	2.86
Bishnoi	2.86			5.26	2.86
OBC	*6*	*13.33*	*8.8*	*10.53*	*8.57*
Yadav		1.67		2.63	
Kurmi	6	5			2.86
Lodhi					
Kachhi					
Gujar		5	5.88	5.26	2.86
Koeri					
Mali					
Panwar		1.67	2.34		
Other				2.63	2.86
Scheduled Castes	*20*	*16.6*	*14.7*	*10.5*	*2.9*
Scheduled Tribes	*19.6*	*18.3*	*17.6*	*21*	*20*
Christian	*3*				*2.86*
Muslim	*6*	*5*	*5.88*	*5.26*	*5.71*
Sikh					
Unidentified			*2.94*	*2.63*	*5.71*
Total	*100* *N=35*	*100* *N=60*	*100* *N=34*	*100* *N=38*	*100* *N=35*

Source: Fieldwork.

that the Congress declined in UP because it could neither maintain its 'coalition of extremes' nor attract many OBCs, he refused to appeal to caste feelings in order to preserve the party's 'identity' based on consensus-making.[11] The Congress, which had never been very

[11] Interview with Jitendra Prasad, New Delhi, 17 Nov. 1996.

Table 12.3. CASTE AND COMMUNITY OF CONGRESS(I) WORKING COMMITTEE, 1981–98 (%)

	1981	*1987*	*1998*
Upper castes	*50.01*	*57.89*	*32.14*
Brahmin	40.91	31.58	14.29
Rajput		10.53	3.57
Bhumihar	4.55		
Kayasth			3.57
Khandait		5.26	
Khatri		5.26	3.57
Marar		5.26	3.57
Nayar			3.57
Other	4.55		
Intermediate castes	*4.55*		*10.71*
Maratha			7.14
Reddy	4.55		3.57
OBC	*13.65*	*15.78*	*10.71*
Yadav		5.26	
Banya	4.55	5.26	
Kshatriya (Gujarat)	4.55		7.14
Kurmi			
Other	4.55	5.26	3.57
Scheduled Castes	*4.55*		*17.86*
Scheduled Tribes			*3.57*
Muslim	*9.09*	*10.53*	*10.71*
Christian	*4.55*	*5.26*	*7.14*
Sikh	*4.55*	*5.26*	
Unidentified	*9.09*	*5.26*	*7.14*
Total	*100* *N=22*	*100* *N=19*	*100* *N=28*

Source: Fieldwork at the AICC office (New Delhi).

well implanted among the OBCs, gradually lost its Scheduled Caste voters, largely because of the competition of the BSP. J. Singh underlines that in the 1980s some of his respondents from among the rural poor in West UP already expressed their 'desire to support a better alternative if available', and the latter materialised soon after with the BSP.[12] This shift accelerated in the 1990s after the Mandal affair.

[12] J. Singh, *Capitalism and Dependence*, op. cit., p. 148.

According to the CSDS Data-Unit, during the 1996 Lok Sabha elections, only 8.2% of Scheduled Castes voters supported the Congress(I) and 8.6% of Yadavs and 6.9% of non-Yadav OBCs did likewise.[13] Even so, a few months later, two thirds of its 125 tickets were allotted to upper caste candidates in the Assembly elections, partly because of the Congress(I)'s short-lived alliance with the BSP: the former was supposed to attract upper caste voters and the latter Dalits; hence the Congress(I) targeted the upper castes.[14] However it not only failed to attract Scheduled Caste and OBC voters, but it also continued to lose ground among the upper castes: there were only 12% of Brahmins and 4% of Rajputs who voted for the erstwhile dominant party.[15] The Brahmins had already transferred their allegiance to the BJP (see below). Finally, the Muslims deserted the Congress(I) and shifted to the Samajwadi Party and, to a lesser extent, to the BSP, because they regarded Narasimha Rao as being responsible for the demolition of the Babri Masjid in 1992 and also because the party did not give many tickets to Muslim candidates. In Uttar Pradesh, for the assembly elections, it nominated only 10 Muslims (as against 53 on the BSP list and 43 on the SP list) and won only 9% of the Muslim vote.[16] The inability of Congress(I) to retain the vote of the lower castes was one of the reasons for its electoral decline. It won only 17.33% of valid votes in the 1991 state elections, 15.03% in the 1993 state elections, 8.3% in the 1996 state elections, 8.1% in the 1996 Parliamentary elections and an all time low 6% in the 1998 Parliamentary elections. It improved its position in 1999 with 14.8% of the valid votes but this resurgence was primarily due to the Muslim (40% of whom voted for the Congress), partly because a Muslim, Salman Khurshid, had replaced Prasad as PCC President.

Kurshid also tried to bring more OBCs and SCs into the party. In the 1999 Uttar Pradesh Congress Committee, five vice presidential positions were awarded to OBCs and five to Dalits (all Chamars, incidentally), while another five were Muslims, out of a total of twenty-five. Of 48 UPCC general secretaries, 9 were Dalits,

[13] K. Chandra and C. Parmar, 'Party Strategies in the Uttar Pradesh Assembly Elections, 1996', *EPW*, 1 Feb. 1997, p. 215.

[14] Ibid., p. 215.

[15] *India Today*, 31 Aug. 1996.

[16] *Muslim India*, no. 167 (Nov. 1996), p. 493.

7 OBCs, 4 Muslims, 2 Sikhs and 1 Jat. The Upper castes no longer represented a majority.[17] But they reestablished their supremacy, in the following PCC with 56% of the 32 members (including 31% Brahmin), whereas OBCs were only 9.5%, the SCs 15.5%, and the Muslims 9.5%. The situation was not very different at the local level: out of 74 Presidents of District Committees in August 2000, 36.5% were Brahmins, 24.5% were Rajputs and 5.5% were Banyas, whereas the OBCs were only 8% and the SCs 2.5%; Muslims were 12%.[18] As a result the party may meet much difficulties in attracting low caste voters in large numbers. While the party attracted 35% of OBC voters at an all India level, in UP only 2% of Yadavs and 20% of other OBCs voted for in 1999. Its performance was slightly better among the Dalits since it got 13% of the Jatavs but 39% of the other Scheduled Castes.[19]

In Bihar the party followed a similar trajectory as it slumped from 23.6% of valid votes in the 1991 elections to 13% in 1996 and 7.2% in 1998. The party remained in the hands of upper caste leaders whose conservative approach made them powerless to resist the rise of Laloo Prasad Yadav and the Samata Party. For the 1995 assembly elections, the Congress nominated 77 upper caste candidates out of 324 and fielded only 28 Yadavs (as against 72 on the Janata Dal list).[20] As a result, the Congress retained 30.9% of the upper caste vote but only 18.6% of the SC/ST vote, 7.6% of the Yadav vote and 15% of the vote from among other OBC castes.[21]

In 1998, the Congress(I) allied with the Rashtriya Janata Dal of Laloo Prasad Yadav, a coalition that revealed the growing awareness of congressmen that they could no longer stand alone. It was a case of indirect 'Mandalisation' in the sense that the Congress(I) preferred to make alliances with a low caste party than to promote OBCs and Dalits in its own party structure and among its election candidates.

[17] For more details, see Jaffrelot and Zérinini-Brotel, 'The rise of the low castes in Uttar Pradesh and Madhya Pradesh politics' in R. Jenkins (ed.) *Comparing Politics Across Indian States* (forthcoming).

[18] This is based on my fieldwork in Lucknow in August 2000. I am especially grateful to Ramesh Dixit for his help.

[19] *Frontline*, 19 Nov. 1999, p. 41.

[20] M. Jain, 'Backward Castes and Social Change in U.P. and Bihar' in M.N. Srinivas, (ed.), *Caste – Its Twentieth Century Avatar*, op. cit., pp. 148–9.

[21] *India Today*, 15 March 1995.

This strategy did not bear fruit since in the assembly elections of March 2000 the Congress(I) polled 10.83% of the votes and retained only 23 seats out of 324.

While the Congress(I) almost sank without trace in the 1990s in UP and Bihar, party leaders displayed more imaginative ways of maintaining themselves at the helm in Madhya Pradesh.

The Congress accommodating strategy in Madhya Pradesh: a new version of the 'Coalition of Extremes' pattern

In contrast to the situation prevailing in neighbouring Uttar Pradesh and Bihar, the OBCs of Madhya Pradesh have no tradition of political organisation and mobilisation, partly because the socialist movement was dominated by upper caste leaders as already mentioned above. The proponents of *kisan* politics were also very few, largely because of the absence of a strong middle caste milieu, like the Jats in Uttar Pradesh. There was thus room for manœuvre for Congress. The party tried at last to seize this opportunity in the 1980s. Arjun Singh, the Chief Minister in 1980–5, appointed in 1981 a Commission named after its chairman, Ramji Mahajan, a former state minister and himself a Mali (OBC), to establish a list of OBCs and to identify their needs in the state. The Mahajan Commission Report was submitted in late 1983, and it identified 80 OBC castes which represented 48.08% of the state's population (including 2.08% Muslims). The Commission's survey – an unprecedented endeavour in Madhya Pradesh – showed that in 1981–2, only 2.2% of OBCs attended school in classes 9 to 11 (that is, 56, 989 pupils out of 25.7 million OBC and lower caste children of school age). The report recommended that 35% of places be reserved for OBCs seeking admission to educational institutions either run or aided by the government.[22] Another recommendation was that the state should grant '35% reservation to the backward classes in all governmental, semi-governmental and public sector services', in selection, appointment and promotion as well.[23] The Arjun Singh government implemented two

[22] See Ramji Mahajan, *Madhya Pradesh Rajya Picchra Varg Ayog – Antim Prativedan – Bhag ek*, Bhopal: Dec. 1983, ch. 15 (Hindi).

[23] In addition, 'successful candidates of backward classes qualifying in the competitive exams on merit basis should not be included in the reserved quota' (ibid.).

other, minor, recommendations regarding quotas for OBCs in technical colleges and the granting of scholarships for higher studies but this decision was challenged before the High Court, which issued a stay order.[24] The Mahajan Commission Report thus lent itself to being exploited by the Congress(I) in the wake of the Mandal affair in the early 1990s.

Even though it was not of the same magnitude as in Uttar Pradesh and Bihar, an OBC mobilisation took place in Madhya Pradesh during the Mandal controversy. For instance, the Kurmis were increasingly mobilised in the early 1990s, especially during election campaigns. In November 1993, the Kurmis of Hoshangabad division held a large convention and lobbied for candidates from their caste to be given due weight in the allocation of tickets for the coming state elections.[25] In addition to forming individual caste associations, the OBCs organised themselves in order to further turn the policies of positive discrimination to their advantage. Some of them tried to unite the OBCs and the Dalits, like the Madhya Pradesh and Dalit Varg Sangh (The Madhya Pradesh Backward and Oppressed Classes Union) which aimed 'to awaken the feeling of love and unity amongst the people of the backward and the oppressed classes'.[26] Similarly, the Madhya Pradesh Picchre Varg Sangathan tried to gather together all the lower castes on the basis of a common work culture:

> All the people of the Scheduled Castes, Scheduled Tribes or Other Backward Classes, that is the oppressed [Dalits] who consider work as their only religion and who, with courage continue to do it are truly Karmavirs [heroes of work]. These people should use 'karmavir', that is 'KV' along with their names.[27]

However, the association paid more attention to the interests of the OBCs for whom it demanded reservations in the Lok Sabha, the Vidhan Sabhas and local bodies. Its programme was phrased in a Sanskritising perspective, its first objective being 'character building and self respect' through education.[28] These Sanskritisation leanings

[24] Interview with Ramji Mahajan, 19 Feb. 1994, Bhopal.

[25] *National Mail*, 19 Nov. 1993.

[26] *Sanvidhan*, Bhopal, Madhya Pradesh Picchra evan Dalit Varg Sangh, [n.d]. The founder of this association, in 1988, Jagannath Singh Yadav is not a Dalit but an OBC.

[27] *Karmavir Ekta*, Bhopal, MP Picchre Varg Sangathan [n.p.].

[28] Ibid.

were on a par with Congress patronage since OBC congressmen – such as Ramji Mahajan and Subhash Yadav (see below) – extended their blessings to the organisation. Others were more militant. For instance, the Madhya Pradesh Backward Classes Officers and Employees Association prepared a memorandum asking for reservations for the OBCs in land allotments, loans at subsidised interest rates, the filling of vacant posts, and the regularisation of daily rated employees of OBCs.[29]

Dalit associations mobilised in the same way in the wake of the OBCs. In October 1998 the Madhya Pradesh Balai Samaj organised a convention for the first time in Bhopal and asked Congress to nominate Balai candidates before the impending 1998 assembly elections.[30] The Valmikis did likewise. The MP Valmiki Samaj Election Committee pointed out that while 99% of the community supported Congress, not even one candidate from its ranks had ever been nominated by the party.[31] In addition to individual caste associations, the Dalits promoted Scheduled Castes associations and joined hands with Scheduled Tribes. For instance, the state unit of the All India Confederation of SC/ST Organisations held 'Save reservations' rallies and demanded reservations in the private sector as well as in the army and the filling of vacant reserved posts in government and semi-government offices in Madhya Pradesh.[32] Similarly, the MP Scheduled Castes, Scheduled Tribes Unemployed Graduate Engineers Association demanded the filling of vacant posts by graduate engineers in reserved categories and reservations in the private sector.[33]

In the context of post-Mandal politics, the Congress of Madhya Pradesh was therefore under pressures from the lower castes. The OBCs and the SCs tended to rally around the BSP in some areas but Congressmen were quick to exploit the new political mobilisation of the OBCs. In late 1991, the Sahu Samaj (Association of Telis) of Bhopal district held a convention where the Union Minister of State for Finance, S. Potolukhe, declared that he was in favour of complete implementation of the Mandal Commission Report.[34] In early 1992,

[29] *Madhya Pradesh Chronicle*, 26 Aug. 1998.
[30] *National Mail*, 12 Oct. 1998 and 22 Oct. 1998.
[31] Ibid., 22 Oct. 1998.
[32] *Madhya Pradesh Chronicle*, 26 April 1999.
[33] Ibid., 25 Feb. 1999.
[34] *National Mail*, 23 Dec. 1991.

the ninth annual conference of the Sahu Sangh of Raipur district was inaugurated by the Minister of State for Cooperation, Kriparam Sahu, who stressed 'the need for tightening the grip of the Sahu community on politics' and declared that the number of MPs and MLAs from the community should be increased.[35] The same year, a Congress MLA, Ramanand Singh, launched a Lodhi Sabha. It was a very timely decision because the then BJP Chief Minister, Sunder Lal Patwa was perceived as an enemy of this caste since he had clashed with Uma Bharti, the Khajuraho MP, a Lodhi who was a political rival.[36]

In 1992, a couple of weeks after the upholding by the Supreme Court of V.P. Singh's decision to implement the Mandal Commission Report, Ramji Mahajan challenged Sunderlal Patwa to discuss his report.[37] During the election campaign of 1993, Madhavrao Scindia and Arjun Singh demanded its implementation and the Congress(I) took full credit for implementing the Mandal recommendations. It was clearly stoking the political consciousness of the OBCs in order to attract their vote. In the same way the Congress(I) nominated a large number of OBCs: as many as 70 tickets – a record – were given to them. Scheduled Tribes and Scheduled Castes were given their due share, respectively 74 and 45 tickets: Brahmins received 57, Rajputs 39, Banyas 16 (if one includes the Jains in this category) and Kayasths (see Table 12.4).

The percentage of Congress candidates from the lower castes continued to increase in the 1990s. The Congress nominated about 35% upper caste and 20% OBC candidates in the 1998 assembly elections. (While the Brahmins lost ground, the Rajputs – who belonged to the same caste as the Chief Minister, Digvijay Singh – showed signs of resistance). Promoting low caste candidates was a sound strategy since the latter were elected more often than the former: OBC MLAs represented 24% of the total in 1993, whereas they formed only 18% of candidates; likewise the upper castes MLAs represented 35% of the total whereas the upper castes candidates formed 38% of the total. In 1998, the proportions between candidates and MLAs were almost the same.

The most striking aspect of Table 12.5 lies in the milestone that

[35] Ibid., 5 Jan. 1992.

[36] Interview with Tikamram Singh Naravya, 20 Oct. 1995, Bhopal.

[37] *Statesman* (Delhi), 1 Dec. 1992.

Table 12.4. CASTE AND COMMUNITY OF CONGRESS(I) CANDIDATES IN MADHYA PRADESH STATE ELECTIONS, 1993–8 (%)

	1993	*1998*
Upper castes	*38.1*	*35.7*
Brahmin	17.6	13.9
Rajput	12.6	14.6
Banya/Jain	6.3	4.4
Kayasth	1.3	1.6
Khatri	0.3	0.9
Sindhi		0.3
Intermediate castes	*0.6*	*1.2*
Maratha	0.3	0.3
Raghuvanshi	0.3	0.9
OBC	*17.8*	*20.4*
Bairagi	0.3	
Dangi		0.6
Darzi	0.3	0.3
Baghel	0.3	0.3
Gujar	1.3	2.5
Jaiswal	0.9	0.3
Kallar		0.3
Kirar	0.3	0.6
Kachhi		0.6
Kunbi		0.6
Kurmi	3.8	5.1
Lodhi	0.9	1.9
Mali	0.6	0.3
Pankha	0.3	
Panwar	0.6	
Rawat	0.3	
Teli	1.6	2.2
Yadav	1.9	3.2
Others	4.4	1.6
Scheduled Castes	*13.5*	*14.4*
Scheduled Tribes	*23.9*	*23.1*
Christian		*0.3*
Muslim	*1.9*	*1.9*
Sikh	*0.9*	*0.3*
Unidentified	*3.1*	*2.2*
Total	*100* *N=318*	*100* *N=316*

Source: Fieldwork.

Table 12.5. CASTE AND COMMUNITY OF CONGRESS(I) MLAs OF MADHYA PRADESH, 1980–98 (%)

	1980	*1985*	*1990*	*1993*	*1998*
Upper castes	*38.7*	*41.3*	*51*	*35*	*35.5*
Brahmin	17.3	17	24.6	13.3	12.8
Rajput	12.3	17	15.8	15.1	18
Banya/Jain	5.8	6.1	8.8	6	4.1
Kayasth	2.9	0.8		0.6	0.6
Khatri	0.4	0.4	1.8		
Intermediate castes	*1.2*	*1.6*		*1.8*	*10.6*
Maratha		0.4			0.6
Patidar	0.8				
Raghuvanshi	0.4	1.2		0.6	1.2
OBC	*14.2*	*15.2*	*14.2*	*23.4*	*19.2*
Bairagi	0.8				
Dangi					1.2
Baghel	0.4	0.4		0.6	
Gujar		0.4		2.4	1.7
Jaiswal	0.4	0.8	1.8		0.6
Kachhi		0.4			
Kirar		0.4		0.6	0.6
Kunbi					0.6
Kurmi	4.9	3.6	3.5	5.4	7.6
Lodhi	0.4	0.4		1.2	1.7
Mali	0.4	0.8	1.8	1.2	
Pankha	0.4	0.4		0.6	
Panwar	0.8	1.2	3.5	1.2	
Rawat				0.6	
Sondhia Rajput		0.4			
Tamoli	0.4				
Teli	0.8	0.8	1.8	2.4	1.7
Yadav	0.8	2.4		3	2.3
Others	3.7	2.8	1.8	4.2	1.2
Scheduled Castes	*13.6*	*13*	*3.5*	*8.4*	*11.6*
Scheduled Tribes	*26.7*	*26.3*	*29.8*	*30.1*	*27.9*
Christian	*0.4*				*0.6*
Muslim	*2.1*	*2*	*1.8*		*2.9*
Sikh	*0.4*	*0.4*		*1.2*	
Unidentified	*2.5*			*1.2*	*0.6*
Total	*100*	*100*	*100*	*100*	*100*
	N=243	*N=247*	*N=57*	*N=166*	*N=172*

Source: Fieldwork.

represented the early 1990s: Mandal was a turning-point for the Madhya Pradesh Congress, not in 1990 but immediately after. While the numbers of upper caste MLAs was above 50% in 1990, in 1993 and 1998 it fell to around 35%. The Brahmins were registered a decrease from 24.6% to 12.8%, whereas Rajput representation grew from 12% to 18% between 1980 and 1998. Simultaneously, the percentage of OBC MLAs rose from 14–15% to 19.23%. The largest group was the Kurmis who represented 7.6% of Congress(I) MLAs whereas they form 3.7% of the state's population according to the Mahajan Commission Report. Another interesting statistic concerns the Scheduled Tribes. They were the second largest group among Congress(I) MLAs after the upper castes, with 26%–30% of the MLAs, whereas only 23.4% of seats were reserved for them. In contrast to the Congress in Uttar Pradesh and Bihar, it seems that the Congress in Madhya Pradesh tried to adjust to the post-Mandal context.

This adaptability was one of the reasons for the party's electoral successes since it won a clear-cut majority of 174 seats with 40.8% of valid votes in 1993 (as against 33.5% in 1990) and 172 seats (40.6% of the votes in 1998). Immediately after the 1993 elections Arjun Singh initiated a debate within the party by suggesting that the Chief Minister should not come from the upper castes. This stand notwithstanding, a Rajput, Digvijay Singh, who presided over the state party unit, won the post. When in power he pursued policies that were accommodating to the lower castes and the Scheduled Tribes.

Digvijay Singh, who had become president of the Pradesh Congress Committee when he was 37 was elected Chief Minister at the young age – by Indian standards – of 46. He belonged to a new generation of Indian leaders like Chandrababu Naidu, the Chief Minister of Andhra Pradesh to whom he has been often compared in the media. Interestingly, Digvijay Singh expressed his uneasiness with this comparison saying, Naidu is 'more on the side of hi-tech whereas my focus has always been on social engineering'.[38]

While the 1993 election manifesto of the M.P. Congress promised that the backlog of SC/ST reserved posts (including those to be filled through promotion) would be cleared within one year if the party

[38] Cited in *India Today*, 21 Dec. 1998, p. 37.

were voted to power, it did not even mention the OBCs.[39] However, one of the first decisions of Digvijay Singh – who had already appointed Ramji Mahajan Minister in charge of Backward Classes Welfare – in December 1993 was to implement the 14% reservation for OBCs in government departments, public undertakings and local bodies that the Mahajan Commission Report had recommended.[40] This quota was extended to 27% in September 1995 through the *Madhya Pradesh Public Service Reservation for the Scheduled Castes, Scheduled Tribes and Other Backward Classes (Amendment) Act (1995)*, in which reservations for the STs and OBCs were increased from 18% and 14% to 23% and 27% in the two upper classes of the administration and from 20% and 14% to 23% and 27% in classes III and IV. It was difficult to go beyond 27% for the OBCs, since the total amount of reservations had already reached 69% in classes I and II (where 15% of the posts are reserved for the SCs) and 70% in classes III and IV (where 16% are reserved for the SCs) – 4% of the posts were reserved as a 'general quota' for the other underprivileged. The Act was passed unanimously by acclaim. During the Assembly debate BJP leaders from the OBCs and the SCs could only approve of this move, although they regretted that the 'general quota', implicitly intended to cater to the upper castes' needs, was so small.[41]

On the reservation question the main achievement of Digvijay Singh's term was evident from his decentralisation policy. Madhya Pradesh was the first state to introduce the new Panchayati Raj system by implementing the provisions of the 73rd and 74th constitutional amendments. Digvijay Singh admitted that this pioneering move was due to the fact that a severe resource crunch at the state level had made such a devolution of power necessary. But he seized the opportunity to extend reservations to the local bodies, at the village level (in the Gaon Panchayats), at the town and city level (in the municipal councils and corporations), at the *tehsil* level (in the Janapada Panchayats) and at the District level (in the Zila Panchayats). The

[39] Except for underlining that the need of the 'Muslim backward classes' should be catered to. (Madhya Pradesh Congress Committee, *Madhya Pradesh ki Dasavin Vidhan Sabha Chunav ka Ghochna-Pate*, Bhopal, 1993)

[40] Furthermore, his government relaxed by five years the upper age limit for the entry of the OBCs in government service. Madhya Pradesh Shasan, *Parivartan aur Vikas : Madhya Pradesh main Picchre Vargon ka Kalyan*, Bhopal, 1994, p. 13.

[41] *National Mail*, 20 Sept. 1995.

OBCs, the SCs and the STs benefited from quotas in these bodies, and the post of *sarpanch* (chief of the village *panchayats*), mayor, President of the Janapada Panchayats and President of the Zila Panchayats were also reserved for them in some places, according to the proportion of OBCs, SCs and STs in different sub-regions of Madhya Pradesh. In Tribal-dominated districts like Surguja, Mandla, Bastar and Jhabua, 100% of the posts of Sarpanchs and Janapada Presidents were reserved for Adivasis. The same rule applied in most *tehsils* of the 17 other districts. Elsewhere, the situation was more complex. For instance, in the 125 villages of Bilaspur district, where 12,125 *panchs* (members of *panchayats*) were to be elected in 1999, 20.5% of them were reserved for Scheduled Castes, 25.3% for Scheduled Tribes, 15.4% for OBCs and 33% for women.[42] In a city like Bhopal the wards were reserved for different categories including gender: out of the 66 wards, 17 were reserved for OBCs (including 5 OBC women), 8 to SCs (including 4 SC women), 2 to STs and 39 to the 'general category' (including 11 to women).[43]

In the run up to the *panchayat* polls upper caste petitioners challenged the 100% reservation at all levels of the Panchayati Raj three-tier system and the 75% reservation in some areas (mainly in Tribal districts) by arguing that the Supreme Court had spelt out that there should not be more than a 50% reservation in any one area.[44] However, in early 2000 local elections were held using the quotas established by the *MP Panchayati Raj Act, 1997*. In contrast, the election to the Mandi Samiti – the local market committees regulating trade in agricultural produce, in which the Digvijay Singh government had introduced a 60% reservation for OBCs, SCs and STs – were cancelled in 1999 because of a stay order. The introduction of such quotas in the Mandi Samiti was an important reform since they were often controlled by upper caste Banyas and/or rich farmers who influenced agricultural prices.

Besides the reservation policies of the Congress, the Digvijay Singh government initiated new education programmes which were

[42] Similarly, 39% of the 212 posts of Janapada Panchayat members were reserved to SCs, 26% to STs, 20% to OBCs and 32% to women. At the district level, the upper castes could retain most of their influence since out of the 16 posts of the Bilaspur district panchayat, 3 were reserved for the SCs, 3 for the STs, and 5 for women. (*Madhya Pradesh Chronicle*, 4 May 1999)

[43] *National Mail*, 23 Sept. 1999.

[44] Ibid., 8 May 1999.

implicitly framed in the interests of the lower castes and the Adivasi. In 1997, R. Gopalakrishnan, an energetic Chief Secretary who was known as the 'Vice Chief Minister' of Bhopal, launched an Education Guarantee Scheme (EGS) under the auspices of the Rajiv Gandhi Mission, whereby the state government was to provide a trained teacher if 25 people in a tribal area, or 40 in other areas, requested one and if there was no school within one km. If the community making the demand was in a position to suggest the name of a teacher from among its ranks, the teacher would be given twelve days intensive training. The government left the annual salary of the teacher with the village *panchayat* which would only have to provide the school building and supervise its smooth running.[45] This system was intended to circumvent the shortcomings of the formal government schools whose teachers were accountable not to the villagers but to a distant administration.[46] The main beneficiaries of this initiative were the lower castes and the Tribals who often lived in very remote places and were neglected by upper caste teachers. This initiative was so successful that by 1998 there were 19,289 schools, of which 10,325 were in tribal areas. Of the 707,393 registered pupils, 394,974 (56%) were Tribals.[47]

Special policies were also designed for the students from the Scheduled Castes and Scheduled Tribes. They were freed from the need to produce caste and income certificates every year and their scholarships were raised and linked to the price index. More importantly, a special recruitment drive was launched in April 1995 to fill the backlog of vacancies reserved for the SCs and STs – three years later some 30,000 vacancies had been filled.[48] In early 1999, when Digvijay Singh had just been appointed Chief Minister for a second, successive term, the Madhya Pradesh State Scheduled Caste Commission expressed satisfaction with the reservation of recruits from different Scheduled Castes in the State police force. The state police then had 35 Scheduled Castes IPS officers, 15 Scheduled Castes SPS officers and 79 Scheduled Castes Deputy Superintendents of Police.[49]

[45] *Madhya Pradesh Education Guarantee Scheme*, Bhopal: Rajiv Gandhi Shiksha Mission (no date), 22 pages.

[46] Interview with R. Gopalakrishnan, 2 Nov. 1999, Bhopal.

[47] *The Madhya Pradesh Human Development Report – 1998*, Bhopal: Government of Madhya Pradesh, 1998, pp. 21–2.

[48] *Madhya Pradesh Chronicle*, 13 May 1998.

[49] Ibid., 8 Jan.1999.

In 1995, the government formulated new rules under the *Scheduled Castes and Scheduled Tribes (Prevention of Atrocities) Act, 1989*: state and district level vigilance committees were constituted to prevent atrocities and monitor relief and rehabilitation of those affected by them; financial compensation was also increased in cases of murder, rape or dacoities.[50] Soon before the 1996 elections, 504 sensitive areas in 32 districts were selected for effective enforcement of the Act and 19 police stations were opened for this purpose.[51] In spite of these measures, the number of atrocities against the SCs and the STs continued to increase, from 6,064 in 1994 to 6,249 in 1995, 6,619 in 1996 and 7,747 in 1997. In 1998, the government therefore appointed 28 new Deputy Superintendents of Police at the district level and an Additional Director General of Police headed a separate wing meant to counter crimes against SCs and STs.[52] Naturally, this official claimed that the new set up was responsible for the slight decrease registered in 1998, with 7,514 atrocities.[53]

Digvijay Singh's first government also allowed Tribals to gather *tendu* leaves – used in the making of *bidis* – from sanctuaries and reserved forest areas. More importantly, soon before the 1998 election it ensured the forest dwellers their ownership rights to forest produce and increased the remuneration of *tendu* leaf pluckers by Rs 40 per bundle.[54] Finally, the state assembly passed a resolution in favour of the Sixth Schedule of the Constitution granting autonomy to Tribals in their districts, a reform the state government submitted to the Centre.[55]

These measures, which were populist, were also implemented by Digvijay Singh to defuse the demands of non-upper caste Congress leaders. They still asked for a Chief Minister from among their ranks, as promised by Arjun Singh after the 1993 elections. Scheduled Tribes leaders (such as Dilip Singh Bhuria and Ajit Jogi) were especially determined. Digvijay Singh tried to defuse these tensions by appointing non-upper caste office-bearers in the Congress party and as ministers in his government. Soon after he took over he appointed two deputy Chief Ministers, one from the Scheduled Tribes

[50] *National Mail*, 8 May 1995

[51] Ibid., 1 April 1996.

[52] Ibid., 19 June 1998.

[53] Ibid., 15 June 1999.

[54] Ibid., 15 May 1998.

[55] *Times of India*, 18 Apr. 1995 and 12 June 1995.

Table 12.6. CASTE AND COMMUNITY OF MEMBERS OF MADHYA PRADESH GOVERNMENT, 1980–99 (%)

	1980	*1985*	*1990*	*1993*	*1997*	*1998*	*1999*
Upper castes	*45.2*	*57.1*	*51.7*	*33.4*	*35.9*	*42.9*	*39.4*
Brahmin	19	33.3	19.4	11.1	11.3	8.6	7.9
Rajput	14.3	23.8	6.5	16.7	15.1	20	18.4
Banya/Jain	9.5		19.4	5.6	5.7	11.4	10.5
Khatri			3.2				
Kayasth	2.4		3.2		3.8	12.9	12.6
Intermediate castes				*2.8*			
Raghuvanshi	2.4					2.9	2.6
OBC	*19.1*	*14.4*	*22.5*	*19.5*	*28.4*	*14.3*	*15.7*
Jat			3.2				
Gujar					1.9		2.6
Jaiswal		4.8					
Kirar			3.2		1.9		
Kurmi	7.1	4.8	6.5	2.8	11.3	11.4	10.5
Lodhi			3.2		3.8	2.9	
Mali				2.8			
Pankha				2.8			
Panwar	4.8						
Teli			3.2	2.8	1.9		2.6
Yadav	2.4	4.8	3.2	8.3	5.7		
Others	4.8			2.8	1.9		
Scheduled Castes	*11.9*	*9.5*	*6.5*	*8.3*	*3.8*	*8.6*	*10.5*
Scheduled Tribes	*16.7*	*4.8*	*9.7*	*25*	*26.4*	*25.7*	*26.3*
Sikh	*2.4*	*4.8*		*2.8*	*1.9*		
Christian				*2.8*		*2.9*	*2.6*
Muslim	*2.4*	*4.8*	*3.2*	*2.8*	*1.9*	*2.9*	*2.6*
Unidentified		*4.8*	*6.5*		*1.9*		
Total	*100*	*100*	*100*	*100*	*100*	*100*	*100*
	N=42	*N=21*	*N=31*	*N=36*	*N=53*	*N=35*	*N=38*

Source: Fieldwork.

(Piyarelal Kanwar) and one from the OBCs (Subhash Yadav, a renowned leader of the cooperative movement who had contested five Lok Sabha elections – and won two, in 1980 and 1984 – and who had just contested for the first time, successfully, an Assembly election). Parasram Bharadwaj, a Scheduled Caste leader, was also appointed as PCC(I) chief in 1994. He was replaced by a Tribal woman, Urmila Singh in 1997. Then another Dalit, Radhakrishnan

Malaviya took over from her in 1999, as if the post of MPCC president was now unofficially reserved for SCs and STs.

The share of STs in the Digvijay Singh government increased substantially between 1993 and 1997 in successive reshuffles after Tribal leaders protested against upper caste domination and demanded the nomination of an Adivasi to the post of Chief Minister. Digvijay Singh responded by bringing in four more Tribal Ministers in his government. However, the SCs were also represented, among others by Doman Singh Nagpure, a leader of the RPI, a party with which Digvijay Singh formed an alliance before the 1998 elections. Nagpure replaced Ramji Mahajan as minister in charge of 'Backward Class Welfare'.

The table above confirms that 1993 was a turning point in Madhya Pradesh in the erosion of the upper castes' domination of political life: while they represented 45%–57% of the members of the government in 1980–90, in 1993, their percentage fell to about 33% and remained below 40% in the 1990s (except in 1998). Once again the Rajputs, 'resisted' more than the other upper castes, especially the Brahmins and the Banyas who have been solely well represented in the BJP government of S. Patwa in 1990–2: one more indication that the Congress tended to be associated with the Rajputs, while the BJP remained a 'Banya/Brahmin' party. In 1993–9, the main beneficiaries of the decline of the upper castes were not primarily the OBCs (who represent about one fifth of the ministers, with the Kurmis still much more numerous than any other low caste) or the Scheduled Castes (who remained largely under-represented), but the Scheduled Tribes, whose representation jumped to 25%–26%. This trend suggests once again that Digvijay Singh was eager to curb the influence of the upper castes but via a new version of the traditional 'coalition of extremes'. He offers an interesting variant of this pattern since the components of this vertical arrangements are not so much the Brahmins and the Scheduled Castes as used to be the case during the heyday of the 'Congress system', but the Rajputs and the Tribals.

In addition to diluting the domination of the state government by the upper castes, Digvijay Singh tried to promote non-elite groups within the machinery of the Congress party. The percentage of upper caste presidents of DCCs remained significant – almost 57% – as the decline of the Brahmins was compensated, once again, by the rise

Table 12.7. CASTE AND COMMUNITY OF CONGRESS(I) DISTRICT COMMITTEES PRESIDENTS IN MADHYA PRADESH (%)

	1994	*1996*	*1997*	*1999*
Upper castes	*61.5*	*53.8*	*50*	*56.7*
Brahmin	30.8	32.7	18.3	18.3
Rajput	13.5	9.6	15	18.3
Banya/Jain	17.3	11.5	13.3	15
Kayasth				1.7
Khatri			3.3	3.3
Intermediate castes	*5.8*	*5.8*	*3.3*	*3.3*
Maratha	5.8	5.8	3.3	1.7
Others				1.7
OBC	*17.1*	*15.2*	*26.7*	*23.6*
Bairagi				1.7
Dangi				1.7
Dhobi				1.7
Gosain				1.7
Gujar			3.3	3.3
Jaiswal				1.7
Kirar	3.8	1.9	1.7	
Kori				1.7
Kurmi	3.8	3.8	1.7	1.7
Panwar		1.9	3.3	1.7
Teli	1.9	1.9		
Yadav	3.8	1.9	1.7	1.7
Others	3.8	3.8	15	5
Scheduled Castes		*1.9*	*3.3*	*1.7*
Scheduled Tribes	*5.8*	*7.7*	*5*	*3.3*
Sikh				*1.7*
Muslim	*7.7*	*7.7*	*10*	*10*
Unidentified	*1.9*	*7.7*	*1.7*	
Total	*100* *N=52*	*100* *N=52*	*100* *N=60*	*100* *N=60*

Source: Fieldwork.

of the Rajputs. The trend favoured the OBCs since their share rose from 15%–17% in 1993–6 to 23%–26% in the late 1990s. In addition, the Congress of Madhya Pradesh was the first state unit of the party to reserve 53% of posts on the Pradesh Congress Committee as per the directive of the party high command in the wake of the

Pachmarhi resolution. As a first step, in March 1999, a meeting of the presidents of the District Congress Committees decided that 33% of the posts in the District Congress units should be reserved for women and 20% to SCs, STs and OBCs.[56] One month later, 13 new office-bearers were appointed to the Madhya Pradesh Congress Committee in conformity with the Congress constitution which now reserved 33% of party posts for women and 22% for SCs, STs and OBCs.[57]

In the Pradesh Congress Committee that was appointed in 1993, the president, Digvijay Singh, was a Rajput and the upper castes represented accounted for 55% its composition. Once again, the OBCs formed a small minority of 15.5% whereas the Scheduled Castes were almost as numerous with about 14%. Moreover, the three vice-presidents were, respectively, one Scheduled Caste member, one Scheduled Tribe member and one Muslim. The percentage of the upper castes decreased from 55.2% in 1993 to 45.6% in 1996, but this erosion did not benefit the OBCs who remained around 15%. By contrast, the share of the STs increased from 6.9 to 9.2%.

The OBCs remain clearly under-represented among Congress candidates to the Lok Sabha who are not selected only by local leaders – or not at all. In fact, Digvijay Singh complained that the nomination process began too late – compared to the BJP's practice – which implicitly refers to the headquarters' interference. Its hand in the selection of Lok Sabha candidates probably explains the over-representation of forward castes on the Congress list in Madhya Pradesh. Even though, in 1999, Digvijay Singh prevented V.C. Shukla from contesting[58] and Arjun Singh gave up electoral politics after two successive defeats, upper caste candidates were far more numerous than the OBCs, in stark contrast with the situation prevailing in the BJP. While the proportion of OBCs among BJP candidates reached 30% in 1999, it remained much less significant on the Congress(I) side. Simultaneously, the percentage of upper castes among Congress(I) candidates remained at 40% in 1999, whereas it was only 32.5% on the BJP side. This probably explains

[56] *Madhya Pradesh Chronicle*, 14 March 1999.

[57] Ibid., 7 April 1999.

[58] Digvijay Singh emphasised that 'caste equations' was one of the reasons why he had asked V.C. Shukla to withdraw in favour of a Teli candidate (interview with Digvijay Singh, *National Mail*, 4 Sept. 1999).

Table 12.8. CASTE AND COMMUNITY OF MEMBERS OF MADHYA PRADESH CONGRESS(I) COMMITTEE, 1993–6 (%)

	1993	*1996*
Upper castes	*55.17*	*45.57*
Brahmin	27.59	20.65
Rajput	12.07	11.41
Banya/Jain	10.34	8.7
Kayasth	3.45	1.09
Khatri	1.72	1.63
Other		1.09
Intermediate castes	*3.44*	*0.54*
Maratha	1.72	–
Patidar	1.72	0.54
OBC	*15.49*	*15.19*
Bairagi	1.72	0.54
Kirar	1.72	0.54
Kurmi	5.17	3.26
Mali	1.72	0.54
Pankha	1.72	–
Yadav	1.72	2.72
Other	1.72	7.59
Scheduled Castes	*13.79*	*8.7*
Scheduled Tribes	*6.90*	*9.24*
Muslim	*3.45*	*6.52*
Christian		*0.54*
Sikh		*1.09*
Unidentified	*1.72*	*13.59*
Total	*100*	*100*
	N=58	*N=184**

Source: Fieldwork in Bhopal.
* Including the 'special invitees'.

why Congress(I) could attract only 44% of peasant OBC voters and 48% of lower OBC voters, as against respectively 53% and 49% for the BJP.[59] On the other hand the Congress received about three quarters of the Tribal vote and 51% of the Dalit vote. It was also able to attract former BSP voters, a party which experienced electoral decline for the first time in 1998 as we saw in the previous chapter.

[59] These figures draw from the CSDS exit poll published in *Frontline*, 10 Dec. 1999, p. 42.

Table 12.9. CASTE AND COMMUNITY OF CONGRESS(I) AND BJP CANDIDATES TO LOK SABHA IN MADHYA PRADESH (%)

	BJP 1996	*BJP 1999*	*Congress(I) 1996*	*Congress(I) 1999*
Upper castes	*33.3*	*32.5*	*42.5*	*40*
Brahmin	12.8	15	17.5	20
Rajput	10.3	10	15	10
Banya/Jain	7.7	7.5	7.5	7.5
Kayasth	2.6		2.5	2.5
Intermediate castes				*2.5*
Maratha				2.5
OBC	*25.6*	*30*	*15*	*15*
Gujar		2.5		
Lodhi	5.1	5		2.5
Kirar	2.6		2.5	
Kurmi	7.7	10	7.5	
Panwar		2.5		
Teli	5.1	5	2.5	2.5
Yadav		2.5		
Others	5.1	2.5	2.5	10
Scheduled Castes	*15.4*	*15*	*10*	*15*
Scheduled Tribes	*23.1*	*22.5*	*27.5*	*22.5*
Muslim			*2.5*	*2.5*
Sikh	*2.6*			*2.5*
Unidentified			*2.5*	
Total	*100* *N=39*	*100* *N=40*	*100* *N=40*	*100* *N=40*

Source: Fieldwork in the BJP Office and in the PCC Office at Bhopal.

The Congress of Madhya Pradesh has been more inclined than most other state units in the Hindi belt to project a non elite image in response to Mandal. It was a strategy that did not rely only on rhetoric since Digvijay Singh actually implemented policies in this regard. This probably explains the electoral success of Congress in the 1998 assembly elections, when he was the only Chief Minister to overcome the anti-incumbency reflex that the India voter has developed since the 1980s.[60] Even though Digvijay Singh's strategy of 'social

[60] However, he benefited also from the unpopularity of the Vajpayee government at the Centre because of a sudden rise in inflation and of the state

engineering' was designed in order to adjust to the post-Mandal context, it is still biased in favour of the Scheduled Castes and, even more, of the Scheduled Tribes. Some OBC castes have undoubtedly benefited from his policy[61] but others protested against persistent upper caste domination, including the Kurmis,[62] who remain under-represented in the party apparatus and in the government in comparison to the Scheduled Tribes. In fact Congress(I), which remains dominated by the upper castes and especially Rajputs, prefers to promote Scheduled Tribes rather than OBCs. Whereas the latter may eventually challenge their power, the former, who represent an exceptionally high proportion of the population, are not in a position to compete with the upper castes. Digvijay Singh, while democratising the Congress(I) in Madhya Pradesh, has therefore initiated a new variant on the old pattern of the 'coalition of extremes'. The Rajputs tend to replace the Brahmins and the Scheduled Tribes the Scheduled Castes but the rationale of this arrangement may remain based on the logic of clientelism. Digvijay Singh candidly admitted that his strategy of promoting Tribal leaders has partly failed because none of them displayed statesman like qualities.[63] It means he has nothing to fear from any rival from the Scheduled Tribes[64] and may again activate the vertical linkages of the 'coalition of extremes' arrangement. This is certainly a good means of neutralising the OBCs, who remain under-represented in almost all loci of power.

Congress anti-corruption drive: seven ministers and 90 sitting MLAs were denied tickets. In the words of a very nuanced observer, 'The Congress was committed to taking action against party members accused of corruption and inefficiency.'(*EPW*, 5 Dec. 1998, p. 3093)

[61] The Gujar Samaj, a caste association, was grateful to the Chief Minister for appointing one of the caste member, Hukum Singh Karada to his government. (*Madhya Pradesh Chronicle*, 23 June 1998)

[62] The Kurmi Kshatriya Samaj, in a 600-strong convention in Bhopal expressed its anger at the political parties, including the Congress, for neglecting the caste it claimed to represent. (*National Mail*, 7 Sept. 1999)

[63] Interview with Digvijay Singh, Nov. 1997, Bhopal.

[64] This was even more evident after the formation of Chhattisgarh state in 2000 and the appointment of Ajit Jogi as its first Chief Minister.

13

THE HINDU NATIONALIST DIVISION OF LABOUR

SEWA BHARTI AND THE B.J.P. BETWEEN SANSKRITISATION AND 'SOCIAL ENGINEERING'

The Hindu nationalist movement has always had an upper-caste, even Brahminical character. This characteristic stems from the nature of Hindutva ideology which relies on a brahminical organic view of society where castes are seen as the harmonious components of society.[1] Since its creation in 1925, the Rashtriya Swayamsevak Sangh (Association of National Volunteers) tended to attract to its local branches (*shakhas*) Hindus who shared this ethos, either because they belong to the upper castes or because they wish to emulate them. The 'conversion' of the low castes to Hindutva therefore partly relies on the logic of Sanskritisation.

The announcement by V.P. Singh on 7 August 1990 that the recommendations of the Mandal Commission Report would be implemented was immediately attacked by the RSS. Reacting to the 'Rajah's caste-war', *Organiser* (the RSS's mouthpiece) criticised not only quota politics in favour of the OBCs, which it denounced as the pampering of vote-banks, but also from its traditional organicist angle, the policy of positive discrimination itself: 'The havoc the politics of reservation is playing with the social fabric is unimaginable. It provides a premium for mediocrity, encourages brain-drain and sharpens caste-divide.'[2] On the implicit assumption that it is virtually harmonious, the nation's 'social fabric' is regarded here as in need of preservation from state intervention.

[1] For details, see Jaffrelot, *The Hindu Nationalist Movement*, op. cit., ch. 1.

[2] *Organiser*, 26 Sept. 1990, p. 15.

Organiser came to embrace publicly the cause of the upper castes when one of its columnists wrote 'There is today an urgent need to build up moral and spiritual forces to counter any fall-out from an expected Shudra revolution.'[3] The RSS high command followed more or less the same line as its newspaper. The General Secretary of the RSS, H.V. Seshadri, reacted to the victory of the SP-BSP alliance in 1993 by arguing that: 'Social justice can be rendered to the weaker sections of society only when the entire society is imbued with the spirit of oneness and internal harmony.'[4] Rajendra Singh, the then chief of the RSS considered that 'There should be a gradual reduction in the job quotas,'[5] even for the Scheduled Castes. In response to the new caste-based politics, the RSS launched in January 1996 a new programme called *samarasya sangama*, 'confluence for harmony', which stated that RSS workers should each adopt a village in order to contribute to its development in order, in the words of Rajendra Singh, to promote 'social harmony between various sections of the society and social assimilation'.[6]

Among the front organisations of the RSS, one of the most recent creations, Sewa Bharti, Service of India, was charged with pursuing this agenda at the grassroots level in terms of social welfare, whereas the BJP implemented a more sophisticated strategy.

The welfarist strategy of Sewa Bharti

Social welfare work on behalf of Hindus has always been one of the mainstays of the RSS. Traditionally, it consisted in helping victims

[3] M.V. Kamath, 'Is Shudra revolution in the offing?', ibid., 1 May 1994, p. 6.

[4] *Organiser*, 19 Dec. 1993, p. 17. Seshadri had criticised the SP and the BSP in a similar way in a previous issue of *Organiser*: '. . . In any confrontation with the rest of the society, the weaker sections always stand to lose. It is only with the goodwill and cooperation of the entire society that they can get the necessary opportunities to raise themselves up. The very concept of social justice implies recognition of equality, dignity and opportunity in every sphere of national life by the entire society. And this is possible only when the society becomes imbued with the spirit of oneness and harmony among all sections just as a weak limb can get strengthened only when the entire bodily life-force is quite active and ensures that the entire body goes out to continuously nurture that limb. This is exactly how the Hindutva life-force works in the case of our society.' (Ibid., 5 Dec. 1993, p. 7)

[5] *Organiser*, 18 Dec. 1994, p. 20.

[6] *Organiser*, 14 Jan. 1996, p. 7.

of natural catastrophes or of 'Muslim aggression'.[7] This propensity to help coreligionists in order to foster Hindu solidarity acquired a new dimension when it became a technique for integrating and maintaining poor Hindus in the community. It became more systematic, even institutionalised, with the creation of Sewa Bharti in 1979. Sewa Bharti is not even an offshoot of the RSS: it is one of its departments. Its motto is 'social welfare is my duty' and its main official objectives are as follows:

> (1) to eradicate untouchability, (2) to imbue people with the spirit of service and unity, (3) to promote and perform literary, cultural, social and charitable activities among the poor and our underprivileged brothers who live in run-down districts and (4) to serve the economically needy and socially backward sectors by contributing to their physical, educational, social, moral and economic development without distinction of caste, language or region, so that they gain self-confidence and are integrated into society.[8]

Beyond these laudable aims, Sewa Bharti's ideological purpose is to divert the Dalits, who are naturally appreciative of charitable work, away from egalitarian ideologies and to assimilate them into a 'Hindu nation'. While these social groups were aspiring to emancipate themselves more effectively, neither the RSS nor its affiliates were in a position to make inroads among the Dalits. It was difficult for a movement dominated by the high castes to reach a segment of the population so different in terms of caste and social status. Sewa Bharti was intended to put up with these defects.

Sewa Bharti opened dispensaries, ran ambulance services providing virtually free medical assistance and put a strong emphasis on

[7] The RSS's first public action in, 1926, which was carefully selected by its founder, K.B. Hedgewar, consisted in providing essential supplies (especially drinking water) to the devout in the Nagpur region – the birthplace of the RSS – who were taking part in the festival of Dasara; the RSS also protected them from those priests known to cheat worshippers. Its network of disciplined activists lent itself well to this kind of activities. It later often intervened in the same way when natural or political disasters occurred. For instance, it set up a Hindu Sahayata Samiti (a Hindu mutual aid society) in 1947 to clothe and house in camps refugees fleeing West Pakistan. Similar efforts were deployed in the 1990s on behalf of the Pandits from Kashmir who were accommodated in camps at Jammu and Delhi. RSS volunteers have also made a name for themselves by aiding the victims of floods, earthquakes, plane crashes or train accidents.

[8] A tract entitled *Sewa Bharti*, New Delhi, n.d., Hindi.

education.[9] Vans with video equipment visited deprived neighbourhoods and slums to promote 'moral and cultural education'. Among the films shown were the *Ramayana* and the *Mahabharata*, epics which had enjoyed tremendous success when broadcast nationally on TV. More importantly, Sewa Bharti offered children a much sought-after free education through Sanskrit Kendra (Sanskrit learning centres) and Bal and Balika Samskar Kendras (*samskar* learning centres for boys and girls). *Samskar* refers to a rite of passage but also, more generally, to every positive influence that shapes the personality of the individual from childhood onwards.[10] 'To have good *samskars*' usually means having no vices (no smoking or consumption of alcohol, for example), having very polished manners, following a vegetarian diet, etc. – in short, imitating the Brahmins. This is a Sanskritization process. The RSS's uses of the term *samskar* reflects its aspiration to reform the national character in line with the Hindu high tradition.

Sewa Bharti against the BSP: the case of Agra. The ability of Sewa Bharti to propagate a conflict-free conception of society and its attempts at encouraging the Dalits to participate in Sanskritisation were clearly reflected in its activities in Agra. The city had been a priority area for Sewa Bharti because of the strength of the Dalit movement, and especially of the BSP. While Chamars are the largest caste of Uttar Pradesh with 12.7% of the population (as against 9.2% for the Brahmins) according to the 1931 census, they are even more numerous in Agra because the shoe-making industry – for which the city is well-known – attracts fellow caste-members from neighbouring villages. According to the 1991 census, the Scheduled Castes numbered 240,726, out of 948,063 – that is about one fourth of the population. It is generally accepted that two-thirds of the Scheduled Castes of Agra are Chamars (according to Owen Lynch the Jatavs represented one sixth of Agra's population in the 1960s).[11] If we go

[9] For details, see C. Jaffrelot, 'Hindu Nationalism and the Social Welfare Strategy' in A. Dieckhoff and N. Gutierrez (eds), *Modern roots – Studies of national identity*, Aldershot: Ashgate, 2001, pp. 196–216.

[10] L. Kapani, *La notion de Samskara*, Paris: Collège de France/de Boccard, 1992, p. 43.

[11] Owen Lynch, 'The politics of Untouchability: a case from Agra, India' in M. Singer and B. Cohn (eds), *Structure and Change in Indian Society*, Jaipur:

by Rosenthal statistics, the Scheduled Castes, with 18% of the population of Agra city, were second only to the Banyas (22%) and ahead of the other twice borns (Brahmins and Rajputs – 12%).[12]

Gradually shoe-making brought greater prosperity to the Jatavs, while the other Scheduled Castes, the Bhangis (sweepers, also called Valmikis) and the Khatiks (butchers), remained much poorer. Such economic development has generated a kind of Chamar middle class from the small layer of entrepreneurs within the caste as well as from the reservations.[13] But caste stigmas have remained. This contrast between some socio-economic mobility and a very low status, besides a steady increase in education, has fostered feelings of frustration and hence raised political consciousness. As mentioned above, the Chamars first claimed that they were Kshatriyas descending from the royal lineage of the Yadavs or Jatavs, the name they started to adopt in the early twentieth century. This move reflected the pervasiveness of the ethos of Sanskritisation, but the Jatavs moved away from it rather quickly. Their emancipation from the value system of the upper castes was largely due to the influence of Ambedkar who came twice to Agra – the last time, the year of his death, in 1956, to inaugurate a Buddhist temple which is still in use. The inroads his political parties, the Scheduled Caste Federation and the Republican Party of India, made in Agra in the 1946, 1952, 1957 and 1962 elections were largely due to Jatav voters.

This political tradition declined from the 1960s onwards because of the Congress' ability to co-opt Jatav leaders such as B.P. Maurya, as mentioned above. But this tradition has been vigourously reactivated by the Bahujan Samaj Party since the 1980s, so much so that the party won 32 seats in the municipal corporation (out of 80) in the 1995 elections, as against 35 for the BJP. The Congress was

---

Rawat, 1996 (1968), p. 214. According to the 1931 census, the Chamars represented one fifth of the Hindu population and the Scheduled Castes population, 28% of it.

[12] Donald B. Rosenthal, *The Limited Elites: Politics and Government in Two Indian Cities*, University of Chicago Press, 1970, p. 11.

[13] Nandu Ram points out that 'the economy of shoe-manufacturing which once linked them with the international market has borne two classes of *bare adami* (big men – factory owners, politicians and bureaucrats) and *karigars* (craftsmen and poor workers) among the Jatavs.' (N. Ram, *Beyond Ambedkar – Essays on Dalits in India*, Delhi: Har-Anand Publications, 1995, p. 247)

relegated to fourth position with only two seats (the Samajwadi Party held four). These figures suggest that there is no room left in Agra for a catch-all party: caste conflict is the order of the day and the Dalits and the upper castes are engaged in a proxy war through the BSP and the BJP.

Indeed, the BJP of Agra is probably more dominated by upper castes than in any other city of Uttar Pradesh because of the large local population of Banyas and Brahmins. Among the Banyas, diamond merchants contribute significantly to the funding of the Sangh Parivar. Ramesh Kanta Lavaniya, a Brahmin who was one of the founders of the Jana Sangh in Agra, explains that the party relied primarily on a team of five, of whom two were Banyas and two Brahmins.[14] In the 1990s the social composition of the BJP municipal corporators continued to reflect the upper caste profile of the party: out of 35 BJP members of the Municipal corporation, 22 were from the upper castes (including 10 Banyas and 7 Brahmins), 10 from the OBCs and 3 from the Scheduled Castes (including only one Jatav).[15]

The special context of caste conflicts in Agra[16] explains the importance that Sewa Bharti attached to its deployment in the city. While the organisation is active in 292 of the 780 towns and cities and in about 500 of the 3,900 officially registered slums of Uttar Pradesh,[17] it covers seventy of the 200 slums in Agra.[18] In 46 of these 70 slums, Bal and Balika Samskar Kendras have been established.[19] As in any of these schools, before teaching begins, the pupils recite the *Gayatri Mantra*, a ritual formula from the Rig Veda. That Sewa Bharti teaches such an upper caste ritual to Scheduled Castes is revealing of its relying on techniques of Sanskritization. Other of its activities

[14] Interview with R.K. Lavaniya, Agra, 8 Nov. 1997. Lavaniya became mayor of Agra in 1989.

[15] These figures come from interviews in the Municipal Corporation.

[16] For more details, see J. Zerinini-Brotel's fieldwork in C. Jaffrelot and J. Zérinini-Brotel, with J. Chaturvedi, 'The BJP and the rise of Dalits in Uttar Pradesh', forthcoming.

[17] Krishna Das, *Sewa Sadhna Aur Siddhi*, Agra, Sewa Bharti Uttar Pradesh, n.d., p. 18 (Hindi).

[18] 'Sewa Bharti Agra Mahanagar', *Sewa Sankalp*, n.d., p. 10.

[19] Sewa Bharti has also set up tutorial centers for students from needy families and electricity and electronics apprenticeship courses for youngsters who have dropped out of the school system. Girls are invited to attend dress-making centres with the goal of making their families 'economically self-sufficient'.

reflect the same objectives. For instance, Sewa Bharti encourages Scheduled Castes members to participate in Hindu festivals from which they used to be excluded or that they did not celebrate publicly like *Raksha Bhandan*, when sisters tie ribbons to the wrist of their brothers to remind them of their protective duties: Sewa Bharti women activists visit slums in this regard too. *Makar Sankranti*, a festival marking the day when the sun begins its northward ascent from the tropic of Capricorn – Makar Rekha – is also celebrated by Sewa Bharti. The festival is traditionally observed with alms-giving, not necessarily to beggars but to anyone less privileged than the alms-giver. In Agra, as elsewhere, Sewa Bharti has started mass feeding programmes for Dalits from 'Sewa Bastis' (the slums where the organisation is active) on *Makar Sankranti* day. They are usually given *khichri* because it symbolises the ultimate synthesis of rice and various kinds of *dals*: a model of social synthesis is offered to the Dalits to show them that they must aim to assimilate in Hindu society to form a *khichri* incapable of separation in all times to come.[20] Similarly, Sewa Bharti organises *Kanya Puja*, the worship of girls, in Dalit *bastis* whereas this ritual used to be reserved strictly for Brahmins. Its activists pay due respect to Dalit girls whose feet they wash. The *havan* is one of the rituals that Sewa Bharti performs even more systematically in Dalit *bastis*. Dalits are always associated with this Vedic ceremony, for which the organisation usually builds a *pith*, a good means of counteracting the construction of Ambedkar statues in the competition for the symbolic monopolisation of social space.

These activities are all part of the same attempt to contain the growing influence of the BSP by maintaining the Dalits in a logic of Sanskritisation.[21] The Sewa Bharti cadres are the staunchest advocates of this organicist brand of nationalism among the Sangh Parivar's activists. The chief of the Braj branch of Sewa Bharti,[22] Krishna Das, repeatedly uses metaphors of the body to justify the need to help

[20] Interview with Ashok Aggarwal, the RSS man in charge of the local branch of Sewa Bharti in Agra (Agra, 15 August 2000).

[21] One of its local cadres considers that 'the BSP is so strong because of caste feelings. This is not good for the country [. . .] The BSP is separating the Jatavs from the mainstream [of society].' (Interview with Inderjit Chauhan, Agra, 30 Oct. 1998)

[22] The RSS has divided Uttar Pradesh in four regions, one of them being Braj, with its headquarters in Agra.

the downtrodden: 'we don't call them either Dalit or Harijan; we believe that they were part of the Hindu society who has remained ignored for some reasons, like some part of the body is ignored or hailing. To serve it is natural *dharma.* If the thumb of the leg is hurt the hand rushes to it. No need to mistrust it. With this objective we have started our service work [*sewa karya*]'.[23] Metaphors of the body are never value free, as Schlanger has shown so well.[24] Here, they echo the Brahminical view of society, as it derives from the famous Rig Vedic myth of origin that describes how society is born from the sacrifice of the primeval man, when the Brahmin proceeded from his mouth, the Kshatriya from his arms, the Vaishya from his thighs and the Shudra from his feet. More or less unconsciously, the Sewa Bharti leaders regard the schema of the four *varnas* as an ideal arrangement. Correlatively they do not acknowledge the existence of Untouchables in Indian society. They never use words such as Harijans or Scheduled Castes. They prefer to say *abhavgrast*, 'the deprived', 'the downtrodden'. Thus, Sewa Bharti is less interested in emancipating the Dalits than in converting them to an active Sanskritisation by displaying compassion (*daya*), one of the key words of the organisation.

In Agra, this approach has been rather successful with the Bhangis. This caste – probably the lowest among the Scheduled Castes – manifested a propensity for Sanskritisation over many years. It was persuaded to do so by the Arya Samaj as early as the late nineteenth century and this is how its members adopted a new name, that of Valmiki, the Rishi who authored the Ramayana. The Valmikis have not benefited from the same socio-economic mobility as the Jatavs, whose overweening attitude they resent very much, especially because they have cornered most of the valuable reserved posts in the administration. The Valmikis might have remained more favourably inclined towards Sanskritisation because they were still very much dependent upon the upper castes. They obviously appreciate the work of Sewa Bharti and do not object to its paternalist attitude. For instance, they lend themselves to surprising intrusions such as the annual visit to their houses by Sewa Bharti cadres who inspect them and then classify the families according to the cleanliness of their

[23] Interview with Krishna Das, Agra, 29 Oct. 1998.

[24] See p. 19. Seshaoki's quote (on p. 464), is also very telling.

home and their compliance with religious orthodoxy (the visible display of the OM symbol is a plus point in this competition). Those who occupy the first five ranks are publicly rewarded.[25] However the Valmikis primarily support Sewa Bharti because it provides them with free schools and free medicine.

The way Sewa Bharti finances these institutions is interesting because it shows that upper caste people do mobilise to help Sewa Bharti to counter the mobilisation of the Dalits. In Agra, for example, its expenditure is Rs 466,400 a year, half of which is spent on schools whose cost cannot be covered by fees: the pupils pay 2 to 5 rupees a month whereas the teachers – when they are not housewives or retired people – earn 250 rupees a month. The money comes mainly from donations. During the first trimester of 1998, Sewa Bharti received Rs 138,868. Its monthly mouthpiece lists the donors and the amount they contribute,[26] which enables us to identify the social profile of these patrons. Banyas are overwhelmingly over-represented with 66 out of 101 donors, a figure to which one must add eight private companies probably owned by Banyas.[27] This social profile can be explained from two points of view. First, the Banyas have always patronised charitable institutions because of their relative wealth but also because they had to in order to maintain their status.[28] Second, since the colonial era Indian notables began to adopt the British pattern of charitable giving.[29] They now allocate their funds to philanthropic institutions. Sewa Bharti combines both dimensions, the religious and the social.

But how effective is the welfarist strategy of Sewa Bharti in helping to roll back the mobilisation of the lower castes? It may help in building a clientelistic network among some of the Scheduled Castes, but their claim for social equality will not be dissipated so easily. Sewa

[25] I attended one of these competitions in a Valmiki *basti* in November 1998 during the 'Sewa Bharti week' in Agra.

[26] *Sewa Sankalp*, April 1998, pp. 15-16.

[27] The same over-representation is in evidence in Aligarh (where half of the 20 donors are Banyas and in Bareilly (where 40 of the donors are Banyas, out of 63). (*Sewa Sankalp*, July 1998, p. 15)

[28] C. Bayly, 'Patrons and Politics in Northern India', *MAS*, 7(3), 1973, p. 83.

[29] D.E. Haynes, 'From Tribute to Philanthropy : the politics of gift in a Western Indian city', *Journal of Asian Studies*, 46(2), May 1987, pp. 339–60.

Barthi's Sanskritisation agenda seem to work with some castes, such as the Valmikis in Agra, but the Jatavs have no respect for Sewa Bharti whose attitude they regard as condescending. While the Valmikis tend to vote massively for the BJP, the Jatavs remain en bloc on the BSP's side. Unsurprisingly, many BJP leaders consider the welfarist strategy to be anachronistic and not robust enough to defuse the low castes' mobilisation. They look upon 'social engineering' as a more relevant method of broadening the party's social bases.

The BJP from Sanskritisation to graded 'social engineering'

The BJP reacted differently from the Congress to the Mandal affair and the rise of the low castes. The party also disapproved of caste-based quotas and made a strong plea in favour of economic criteria in the framing of affirmative action programmes.[30] But simultaneously Advani's Rath Yatra relaunched the Ayodhya agitation to reunite all the Hindus and make the OBCs regard themselves as Hindus first and foremost. While one of the objectives of the Rath Yatra was to defuse caste feelings, many upper caste people and non-OBC 'Shudras' became supporters of the BJP at that time. The rise of the low caste parties and that of the BJP ran parallel not only because the Mandal affair and the Mandir movement coincided but also because the BJP attracted new support as the only party which was against caste-based reservations. However, the BJP could not avoid addressing the Mandal issue, especially when the Mandir issue receded after the demolition of the Babri Masjid in 1992.

BJP leaders did not openly criticise V.P. Singh's decision regarding the implementation of the Mandal Commission Report because they were apprehensive of alienating OBC voters. Instead they fomented the students' anti-Mandal agitation behind the scene. However, when a Rajya Sabha member, J.K. Jain, began a fast against the implementation of the Mandal report, he was criticised by the BJP's high command and had to fall in line.[31] The upper caste character of Hindu nationalism had become a greater handicap for the BJP in the 1990s because of the growing political consciousness of the low castes, as the 1993 elections testified.

[30] This is evident from the BJP's bulletin, *About Us*, 7, 17 (3 Sept. 1990, pp. 6-7) and from interviews with some of its leaders. (See L.K. Advani's interview in *Hindustan Times* Sunday Supplement, 23 Sept. 1990, p. 2)

[31] For more details, see Jaffrelot, *The Hindu Nationalist Movement*, op. cit., p. 431.

These elections, in which the BJP lost both Uttar Pradesh and Madhya Pradesh, largely because of the OBC and Dalit voters, led party leaders to promote more low caste members in the party apparatus. In January 1994, Hukumdev Narain Yadav – an Ahir – was appointed as special invitee to the party's national executive and Uma Bharti – a Lodhi – became chief of the Bharatiya Janata Yuva Morcha (the youth wing of the BJP). The main advocate of the inclusion of more low caste members at all the levels of the party apparatus was K.N. Govindacharya, one of the BJP's General Secretaries. He called the policy 'social engineering'. It was a strategy that was opposed by some of his colleagues and RSS leaders who objected on principle to any artificial transformation of the so-called social equilibrium and who were loath to grant more importance to caste as a result of pressure from the 'Mandal affair'. Murli Manohar Joshi, a former president of the BJP, opposed the move and even implicitly questioned the wider notion of 'social engineering' by asking 'what social justice has been brought in the name of social engineering? Rural poverty has increased and most of the rural poor continue to be Dalits'.[32]

To some extent the BJP fell in line with its mother organisation, the RSS, during the all-party meeting on reservations that was held in 1995 under the auspices of the then Union Welfare Minister, Sitaram Kesri, as its representative, Atal Bihari Vajpayee, alone opposed the extension of reservations to promote Scheduled Castes and Scheduled Tribes and refused to agree to increase the 50% ceiling reservation for these two categories and the OBCs.[33] However, as the eleventh general elections approached, the BJP amended its earlier position on the reservation issue. Before the 1991 elections the BJP

[32] Interview in *Sunday*, 26 Jan. 1997, p. 13. M.M. Joshi was not alone in expressing reservations *vis-à-vis* Govindacharya's programme. Sunder Singh Bhandari, one of the BJP Vice-Presidents declared for instance: 'We will keep social equilibrium in mind. It is an expansion programme and there is no question of being lopsided.' (Cited in *Times of India*, 26 Dec. 1993)

[33] S. Kesri consulted the political parties before bringing before Parliament a constitutional amendment bill designed to nullify the 50% ceiling imposed by the Supreme Court on reservation and a bill seeking extension of reservations in promotions for the Scheduled Castes and Scheduled Tribes in government jobs beyond 1997. Addressing a convention of Scheduled Castes and Scheduled Tribes MLAs, ministers, mayors, deputy mayors, corporators and panchayat office-bearers in Bhopal, he denounced the BJP as the biggest enemy of the SCs, STs and OBCs on the basis of Vajpayee's stand (*National Mail*, Bhopal, 19 May 1995).

had expressed very general views: 'Reservation should [. . .] be made for other backward classes broadly on the basis of the Mandal Commission Report, with preference to be given to the poor amongst these very classes and [. . .] [a]s poverty is an important contributory factor for backwardness, reservation should also be provided for members of the other castes on the basis of their economy condition'.[34]

In 1996, it retained the social harmony discourse[35] but made precise promises to the OBCs:

1. Continuation of reservations for the Other Backward Classes till they are socially and educational [*sic*] integrated with the rest of society;
2. A uniform criteria [*sic*] for demarcating the 'creamy layer';
3. Flow of reservation benefits in an ascending order so that the most backward sections of the OBCs get them first;
4. Ten per cent reservation on the basis of economic criteria to all economically weaker sections of society, apart from the Scheduled Castes/ Scheduled Tribes and the Other Backward Classes.[36]

The BJP had admitted the inevitability of quotas for the OBCs but tried to combine the criterion of caste with socio-economic criteria. This compromise reflected the debate within the 'Sangh parivar' between the advocates of 'social engineering' in favour of the low castes and those who wanted to abstain from acknowledging caste conflicts and amending the virtually harmonious structure of society.

Another dimension of this compromise consisted in the BJP's strategy of indirect Mandalisation: the party did not promote low caste party men in large numbers, either as election candidates or office-bearers, but made alliances with parties which did have a base among the OBCs. The seat adjustment between the Samta Party and the BJP in Bihar was a case in point. In the 1995 state assembly elections, out of the 41 BJP winners, 4 were Brahmins, 4 were Rajputs, 1 was a Bhumihar, 4 were Kayasths and 6 Banyas. There were only

[34] Bharatiya Janata Party, *Towards Ram Rajya – Mid-Term Poll to Lok Sabha, May 1991: Our Commitments*, New Delhi: 1991, p. 27.

[35] The manifesto also said: 'The task is nothing short of rekindling the lamp of our eternal "*Dharma*", that *Sanatan* thought which our sages bequeathed to mankind – a social system based on compassion, cooperation, justice, freedom, equality and tolerance.' (Bharatiya Janata Party, *For a strong and prosperous India – Election manifesto 1996*, New Delhi: 1996, p. 5)

[36] Ibid., p. 62.

2 Kurmis, 2 Yadavs and 2 Koeris among the party MLAs. On the other hand the Samta Party, despite its bad performance, had 3 Kurmis, 2 Koeris and 1 Dusadh among its 7 MLAs (see Table 10.22, p. 382). While the BJP polled only 16% of the votes in 1991, largely because it remained identified with the upper castes and the tribal belt of the South, its alliance with the Samta Party enabled it to make inroads in northern and central districts thanks to their base among the Kurmis and the Koeris. In several constituencies, these low castes were allied to the forward castes (Brahmins, Rajputs, Bhumihars and Kayasths), which helped the BJP a great deal. The party won 18 seats (as against 5 in 1991). In Haryana, the BJP, whose influence has traditionally been confined to the urban dwellers, and especially the Punjabi refugees, eschewed an alliance with OBCs and opted instead for a party rooted in the countryside. Indeed, the Haryana Vikas Party launched by an ex-Congressman, Bansi Lal, has a strong base among the Jats. This alliance enabled the BJP to win 4 seats in a state where it had not won any in 1991. Bihar and Haryana were among the states where the party registered its best results in terms of valid votes respectively +5% and +11% of the valid votes, compared to the 1991 election: these were the states where it had made new alliances with regional parties commanding a complementary base among intermediate and low castes. The BJP admitted the need to become more rural and even to 'Mandalise' itself, albeit indirectly. This compromise may well be the outcome of the internal debate between advocates of 'social engineering' and of the *status quo*. In its 1998 election manifesto, the BJP depicted society as 'harmonious and conflict-free' but it did not repeat its preference for reservations based on economic criteria.[37]

After the 1998 elections, the BJP formed a coalition, the National Democratic Alliance, which enabled Vajpayee to become Prime Minister. This alliance was formalised before the 1999 elections, to such an extent that the party did not prepare its own election manifesto: there was only one manifesto for the whole NDA. As it was now the pivotal force of a larger coalition whose components were often less elitist than the BJP itself, the party toned down its stand on reservations. In the NDA's election manifesto one could read:

[37] Bharatiya Janata Party, *Election Manifesto – 1998*, New Delhi: BJP, 1998, p. 34 and p. 36.

If required, the Constitution will be amended to maintain the system of reservation [. . .]. We are committed to extending the SC/ST reservation for another 10 years. Reservation percentages above 50%, as followed by certain states, shall be sanctified through necessary legislation measures.[38]

Vajpayee himself, while campaigning in Rajasthan, declared that his government 'would implement the reservation policy in right earnest'.[39] Obviously, the BJP leaders had become more responsive to the OBCs' demands not only because of their lower caste partners but also in order to attract more OBC voters. To what extent has this strategy been successful?

The BJP and its predecessor, the Jana Sangh were popularly known as 'Banya/Brahmin' parties, and CSDS surveys bear out that they have always attracted many upper caste voters. The figures for the 1990s (in Table 13.1) deserve special comment. Those referring to the 1996 and 1998 elections concern the BJP and its allies. The first column for 1999 concerns the BJP's allies and the second the BJP alone. By comparing them both one sees that the BJP remained relatively less attractive than its allies to non upper caste voters.

Analysing the 1999 CSDS exit poll Yadav, Kumar and Heath

Table 13.1. CASTE AND COMMUNITY OF BJS AND BJP VOTERS, 1971–99 (%)

	1971	*1980*	*1996*[a]	*1998*[a]	*1999*[b]	*1999*
Upper castes	6.7	17.1	23.6	38.5	14	46
OBCs	3.5	10	23.6	34.6	23 (upper) 23 (lower)	21 (upper) 19 (lower)
Scheduled Castes	2.1	14.3	14.4	20.9	10	12
Scheduled Tribes	4.1	5.4	19	25.6	12	19

Sources: S.K. Mitra, V.B. Singh, *Democracy and Social Change in India*, op. cit., pp. 135–7 and, for 1999, *Frontline*, 19 Nov. 1999, p. 32.

[a] BJP and its allies.
[b] BJP allies.

[38] National Democratic Alliance, *For a Proud, Prosperous India – An Agenda. Election Manifesto, Lok Sabha Election, 1999*, New Delhi, printed and published at the Bharatiya Janata Party, for and on behalf of the National Democratic Alliance, 1999, p. 8.

[39] Cited in *The Hindu*, 25 Aug. 1999.

suggested that the 1999 election marked the emergence of the 'new BJP's social bloc',[40] that included the traditional upper caste supporters of the party but reached out beyond this elite. They point out that 'the BJP and its allies secure the support of 60% of upper caste Hindus and 52% of the dominant Hindu peasant castes (which are not classified as Other Backward Classes such as Jats, Marathas, Patidars, Reddys and Kammas)'.[41] The NDA, therefore, represents a cross-section of the Indian urban as well as rural elite, at least those experiencing some social mobility. This social profile can be identified through the criterion of caste, but class must also be factored in. Therefore Yadav, Kumar and Heath have built an index mixing caste-based and class-based criteria which reveals that 'the BJP [and its allies ?] draws as much as 69% of its votes from the 45% voters [representing the upper strata of Indian society according to these criteria]'.[42] While the BJP has always been an elite-oriented party, what is new is its capacity to reach beyond the upper caste urban elite, to incorporate rural elites from the lower castes.

However, this notion of the 'BJP's new social block' must be scrutinised from two points of view. First, the party does not attract so many voters from the dominant castes: the BJP and its allies receive 52% of their votes but the BJP alone, only 30%, less than the Congress(I) (31%). Second, the most important groups for measuring the social expansion of the BJP should not be the dominant castes, but the Dalits and the OBC. In 1999, the BJP only attracted 16% of Scheduled Caste voters, according to the CSDS exit poll, 21% of upper OBCs and 19% of lower OBCs – the BJP and its allies won one fifth of the OBC vote, as against 35% to the Congress and its allies. Thus the social bloc of the BJP remains dominated by elite groups. This specific feature is evident from the CSDS exit polls regarding states of the Hindi belt:[43] in Uttar Pradesh the BJP got 77% of the Brahmin vote and 74% of the Rajput vote, as against 11% of the Yadav vote and 29% of the votes from other OBC castes. In Rajasthan, it received between 62% and 98% of the upper castes' votes as against 12% of the Gujar vote (the Gujars being the largest OBC

[40] Yadav, Kumar and Heath, 'The BJP's new social bloc', op. cit.

[41] Ibid., p. 33.

[42] Ibid., p. 39.

[43] 'Election analysis – Emerging patterns', *Frontline*, 10 Dec. 1999, pp. 36-43.

caste). In Bihar, the BJP-JD(U) coalition won between 86% and 92% of the upper castes' votes and 79% of the Kurmis and Koeris, two important OBC castes. Unfortunately, the CSDS exit poll does not distinguish the BJP electorate from JD(U) voters. This is one of the reasons why it is useful to look at indicators other than opinion polls, such as the social profile of elected representatives, which generally reflect the social base of the party. The other reason is that we can use this indicator to analyse the *evolution* of the social profile of the BJP over the last ten years. We shall focus our attention on the Hindi-speaking area of North India, the stronghold of the BJP, where it won up to 74% of its seats in 1996.[44]

The last five elections have shown a steady erosion of the share of the upper caste vote among the BJP MPs of the Hindi belt, from 53.13%, in 1989 to 43% in 1998 and 37.96% in 1999. Those who benefit from this trend are not so much the OBCs but rather the dominant castes (mainly the Jats) or even the Dalit candidates who are often elected with the support of upper-caste BJP's voters. (The BJP leaders often emphasise the large number of reserved seats won by the party and use this as evidence of their large following among the Scheduled Castes and Scheduled Tribes. But the argument is a specious one since these seats are not won *with* their support but generally against them and with the support of upper caste voters.)

The rapid erosion of upper caste MPs confirms that the BJP leadership has admitted the need to nominate many more candidates from non-elite groups; but has the BJP initiated a transition from indirect to direct Mandalisation? These figures are deserving of careful analysis. First, the decline of upper caste MPs has not coincided with the diminishing attractiveness of the party *vis-à-vis* upper caste voters. Second, the efforts of the party to woo the OBCs are real but limited: the rise in the number of OBC MPs probably reflects the fact that more and more OBC candidates are being fielded by the party, but by and large the OBCs' share remains well below 20%. (Incidentally, this percentage is also that of the OBC voters supporting the BJP, according to the 1999 CSDS survey.) Third, while the party is steadily giving more tickets to OBCs from one election to another, it has not made room for them – or any other non-elite-group – in the party apparatus.

[44] For more details, see Jaffrelot, 'The BJP at the Centre. A central and centrist party?'op. cit.

Table 13.2. CASTE AND COMMUNITY OF BJP MPs RETURNED IN THE HINDI BELT, 1989–99 (%)

	1989	*1991*	*1996*	*1998*	*1999*
Upper castes	*53.13*	*52.49*	*46.28*	*43.8*	*37.96*
Brahmin	20.31	26.74	20.66	19.83	15.74
Bhumihar			1.65	1.65	2.78
Rajput	17.19	19.77	15.70	14.05	11.11
Banya/Jain	7.81	2.33	4.96	3.31	3.7
Kayasth	3.13	2.33	2.48	2.48	1.85
Khatri	3.13	1.16	0.83	1.65	2.78
Sindhi	1.56	1.16			
Other				0.8	
Intermediate castes	*1.56*	*4.65*	*4.96*	*6.61*	*7.41*
Jat		3.49	4.13	5.79	5.56
Maratha	1.56	1.16	0.83	0.83	0.93
Bishnoi					0.93
OBC	*15.62*	*15.1*	*17.4*	*19.8*	*16.67*
Yadav	1.56		1.65	1.65	3.7
Kurmi	6.25	9.30	6.61	9.92	6.48
Lodhi	3.13	2.33	3.31	2.48	1.85
Kachhi	1.56	1.16	0.83		
Gujar	1.56				
Koeri	1.56	1.16	0.83		
Other		1.16	4.15	5.79	4.64
Scheduled Castes	*17.2*	*18.6*	*21.5*	*18.8*	*19.4*
Scheduled Tribes	*7.8*	*5.8*	*7.4*	*6.73*	*8.34*
Muslim	*1.56*			*0.83*	*0.93*
Sikh	*1.56*	*1.16*	*0.83*	*0.83*	
Sadhu		*2.33*			*1.85*
Unidentified	*1.56*		*1.65*	*2.48*	*7.41*
Total	*100*	*100*	*100*	*100*	*100*
	N=64	*N=86*	*N=121*	*N=122*	*N=108*

Source: Fieldwork.

At the apex of its party structure, an indication of the elitist bias of the party is furnished by the over-representation of high caste cadres among the BJP National Executive Committee. While the 'Mandal effect' is evident from the fact that the percentage of OBC office-bearers increased in 1993 from 8 to 13% at the expense of the upper castes, who declined from 72 to 54%, this impact was rather short-lived: certainly the upper castes remained below 60%, but the

Table 13.3. CASTE AND COMMUNITY OF MEMBERS OF BJP NATIONAL EXECUTIVE, 1991–8 (%)

	1991	*1993*	*1995*	*1998*
Upper castes	*72.2*	*54*	*59.7*	*54.9*
Brahmin	26.2	24	27.9	21.7
Rajput	8.2	2.7	3.8	5.8
Banya/Jain	14.8	11.3	10.6	7.2
Bhumihar		0.7		1.4
Kayasth	6.6	3.3	5.8	5.8
Khatri	11.5	8	7.7	5.8
Marar		0.7		
Sindhi	3.3	1.3	1.9	2.9
Nayar	1.6	0.7	1	1.4
Others		1.3	1	2.9
Intermediate castes	*4.8*	*5.4*	*6.8*	*5.6*
Jat		0.7	1	1.4
Kamma		0.7	1	1.4
Lingayat	1.6	0.7		
Patidar	1.6	1.3	1.9	1.4
Reddy	1.6	2	2.9	1.4
OBC	*8*	*13.3*	*6.9*	*4.2*
Banjara		0.7	1	1.4
Jat		0.7		
Kachhi	1.6			
Kshatriya		0.7		
Kurmi			1	
Lodhi	1.6	1.3	1.9	1.4
Soni	1.6	1.3	1	
Yadav	1.6	1.3	1	
Others	1.6	7.3	1	1.4
Scheduled Castes	*4.9*	*4.7*	*4.8*	*4.3*
Scheduled Tribes	*1.6*	*2*	*1.9*	*5.8*
Christian		*0.7*	*1*	*1.4*
Jew		*0.7*	*1*	
Sikh			*1*	*1.4*
Muslim	*6.6*	*2*	*4.8*	*4.3*
Unidentified	*1.6*	*17.3*	*12.5*	*17.4*
Total	*100* *N=61*	*100* *N=150*	*100* *N=104*	*100* *N=69*

Table 13.4. CASTE AND COMMUNITY OF BJP MLAs IN MADHYA PRADESH, 1980–98 (%)

	1980	*1985*	*1990*	*1993*	*1998*
Upper castes	*39.3*	*40.7*	*36.8*	*42.3*	*35.9*
Brahmin	14.8	18.6	13.8	17.8	14.2
Rajput	4.9	8.5	8.9	10.2	7.5
Banya/Jain	13.1	11.9	11.6	11.9	11.7
Kayasth	3.3	1.7	1.3	0.8	0.8
Khatri	1.6		0.4	0.8	
Sindhi	1.6		0.4	0.8	1.7
Other			0.4		
Intermediate castes	*1.6*		*1.7*	*0.8*	*1.7*
Maratha	1.6		0.4	0.8	1.7
Raghuvanshi			1.3		
OBC	*19.4*	*27.2*	*19.2*	*16.6*	*21.7*
Bairagi		1.7	0.4		
Dangi		1.7	0.4	1.7	1.7
Gujar	1.6				
Jaiswal					
Jat	1.6		0.4	0.8	
Kalar			0.4		0.8
Kasar		1.7			
Khati		1.7	0.4	0.8	0.8
Kirar	1.6		1.8	0.8	0.8
Kurmi	3.3	5.1	4	3.4	4.2
Lodhi	1.6	3.4	0.9	0.8	2.5
Panwar	3.3	5.1	2.2	1.7	0.8
Rawat	1.6		0.4		
Sondhia Rajput			0.4	0.8	
Soni			0.4		
Tamoli			0.4		
Teli	1.6	3.4	1.8	2.5	1.7
Yadav	1.6	1.7	3.1	2.5	4.2
Others	1.6	1.7	1.8	0.8	4.2
Scheduled Castes	*21.3*	*13.6*	*15.9*	*21.9*	*18.3*
Scheduled Tribes	*16.4*	*16.9*	*24.4*	*15.3*	*19.2*
Muslim		*1.7*	*0.4*		
Sikh			*0.9*	*0.8*	*2.5*
Unidentified	*1.6*			*1.7*	*0.8*
Total	*100* *N=61*	*100* *N=59*	*100* *N=225*	*100* *N=118*	*100* *N=120*

Table 13.5. CASTE AND COMMUNITY OF THE BJP CANDIDATES TO VIDHAN SABHA OF MADHYA PRADESH, 1993–8 (%)

	1993	*1998*
Upper castes	*39.7*	*36.6*
Brahmin	15.8	14.4
Rajput	9.5	8.8
Banya/Jain	12	10.6
Kayasth	0.9	0.9
Khatri	0.6	0.6
Other	0.9	1.3
Intermediate castes	*0.3*	*1.5*
Maratha	0.3	0.9
Raghuvanshi		0.6
OBC	*19.3*	*20.8*
Dangi	0.6	0.9
Gujar		0.3
Jat	0.6	0.3
Kachhi		0.3
Kallar	0.3	1.3
Khati	0.3	0.3
Kirar	0.6	0.6
Kolahar	0.3	
Kunbi	0.6	
Kurmi	5.1	5.3
Lodhi	1.9	2.5
Mina		0.3
Panwar	0.9	0.3
Sondhia Rajput	0.3	0.3
Soni	0.3	
Tamoli		0.3
Teli	2.5	2.2
Yadav	1.9	2.5
Others	3.1	3.1
Scheduled Castes	*13.6*	*14.1*
Scheduled Tribes	*23.7*	*23.1*
Muslim	*0.3*	*0.3*
Sikh	*0.6*	*0.9*
Unidentified	*1.9*	*2.5*
Total	*100* *N=316*	*100* *N=320*

Table 13.6. CASTE AND COMMUNITY OF PRESIDENTS OF BJP DISTRICT UNITS IN MADHYA PRADESH, 1990–9 (%)

	1990	*1994*	*1999*
Upper castes	*63.4*	*67.9*	*58*
Brahmin	26.8	23.2	14
Rajput	7.3	19.6	14
Banya/Jain	19.5	19.6	21.1
Kayasth	2.4	5.4	1.8
Khatri	4.9		1.8
Other	2.4		5.3
Intermediate castes			*3.6*
Jat			1.8
Maratha			1.8
OBC	*22*	*19.6*	*26.4*
Gujar	4.9		
Kirar	2.4		
Kachhi			1.8
Kurmi		5.4	5.3
Panwar			
Teli	2.4	8.9	7
Yadav	2.4	1.8	3.5
Others	9.8	3.6	8.8
Scheduled Castes	*2.4*		*1.8*
Scheduled Tribes	*2.4*	*8.9*	*5.3*
Muslim			
Sikh		*1.8*	*3.5*
Unidentified	*9.8*	*1.8*	*1.8*
Total	*100* *N=41*	*100* *N=56*	*100* *N=57*

percentage of OBCs fell below 5% in 1998. However, to get a more complete picture of the social profile of the BJP in North India, one needs to complement this national overview by paying attention to the situation prevailing at the state level. We shall first consider the case of Madhya Pradesh, in order to make a comparison with the Congress(I), and then Uttar Pradesh, the state where the BJP proved to be the most OBC-oriented – at least till the late 1990s.

The BJP in Madhya Pradesh: is it still an upper caste party? The State BJP's social profile changed very little after the Mandal affair. While the Congress(I) MLAs who were returned in 1993 were less elite than in 1990, on the BJP side there were even more upper castes than ever before in the 1980s and 1990s. Moreover OBC MLAs had never been so few – in terms of percentage. There was a shift in 1998 when upper caste BJP MLAs fell to 36% and OBC MLAs rose to almost 22%. These figures are almost exactly the same as those we have for Congress. In 1998, the caste background of the BJP and Congress candidates and MLAs was identical. While the BJP has nominated a growing number of OBC election candidates in the wake of the Mandal affair to benefit from lower caste mobilisation, its party machinery remains dominated by upper caste people.

The composition of Patwa's government that was formed in March 1990 was a good indication of the persisting domination of the upper castes within the BJP in the early 1990s. As shown in Table 12.7, out of 31 members, 17 belonged to the upper castes, 7 to the OBCs, 3 to the Scheduled Tribes, 2 to the Scheduled Castes and there was one Muslim. In contrast, the government of Digvijay Singh, who succeeded Patwa as Chief Minister, while it awarded a smaller share to the OBCs, also reduced that of the upper castes and significantly increased that of the Scheduled Tribes.

According to the constitution of the BJP, out of 11 office-bearers in any unit, 2 must be SCs, 2 must be STs and 2 must be women. But in 1990, out of 41 presidents of BJP district units in Madhya Pradesh, 63.4% belonged to the upper castes and their share grew in 1994 to reach 67.9%. Among them, only 22% were OBCs in 1990, and the erosion of their representation left them with only 19.6% of such posts in 1994. The proportion of Tribals increased (from 2.4 to 8.9%) but that of the Scheduled Castes fell from a meagre 2.4% to zero. Thus, at the local level the BJP hierarchy was overwhelmingly dominated by upper caste members, even in 'Tribal districts'. In 1990–1994, except in Jhabua, in all the districts where Scheduled Tribes were in a majority, such as Bastar, Mandla and Surguja, the presidents of the BJP district units were Brahmins and Banyas. Things began to change in the late 1990s. In 1999, the percentage of upper caste presidents of the district units fell at 58% and that of the OBCs rose to 26.4%. However, this evolution did not affect the SCs/STs, nor did it seriously challenge the domination of the upper castes.

Table 13.7. CASTE AND COMMUNITY OF BJP STATE EXECUTIVE IN MADHYA PRADESH, 1991–2000 (%)

	1991	*1994*	*1995*	*1997*	*2000*
Upper castes	*65.1*	*56.9*	*66.6*	*61.7*	*59.6*
Brahmin	30.3	26.4	27.5	27.8	26.2
Rajput	10.1	10.7	14.5	13.9	9.5
Banya/Jain	15.6	11.6	20.3	11.1	17.9
Kayasth	6.1	6.6	4.3	4.2	2.4
Khatri	–	0.8	–	1.4	–
Other	3	0.8	–	2.8	3.6
Intermediate castes	*1*	*1.7*	*2.9*	*2.8*	*2.4*
Maratha	1	1.7	2.9	–	2.4
Raghuvanshi	–	–	–	2.8	–
OBC	*13*	*20.5*	*12.8*	*19.6*	*14.4*
Gujar	–	–	–	1.4	–
Kirar	–	0.8	1.4	–	1.2
Kachhi	1	0.8	–	–	–
Jat	1	0.8	1.4	–	1.2
Kurmi	–	2.5	2.9	4.2	4.8
Lodhi	2	4.1	1.4	4.2	2.4
Nai	–	0.8	–	–	–
Sondhia Rajput	1	0.8	–	–	–
Soni	–	0.8	–	1.4	–
Teli	2	3.3	1.4	1.4	2.4
Yadav	3	1.7	1.4	1.4	1.2
Other	3	4.1	2.9	5.6	1.2
Scheduled Castes	*4*	*5*	*4.3*	*1.4*	*4.8*
Scheduled Tribes	*8.1*	*8.3*	*2.9*	*13.9*	*9.5*
Christian	–	*1.7*	*1.4*	–	*1.2*
Muslim	*4*	*1.7*	*1.4*	*1.4*	*1.2*
Sikh	*1*	*0.8*	*1.4*	–	–
Unidentified	*4*	*3.3*	*5.8*	–	*7.1*
Total	*100* *N=99*	*100* *N=121*	*100* *N=69*	*100* *N=72*	*100* *N=84*

Similarly, the composition of the Madhya Pradesh BJP state executive committees elected in the 1990s shows that it remained dominated by upper caste leaders, who still occupied more than 61% of the seats in 1997 and 59.6% in 2000. The percentage of OBCs by contrast, oscillated between 13 and 20.5% in 1991–2000.

The over-representation of the upper castes among the BJP cadres results from the conjunction of two phenomena. First, the party apparatus comprises many former *pracharaks* who have been seconded by the RSS to the BJP for organisational tasks; and most RSS *pracharaks*, till recently, came from the upper castes, particularly from Brahmin *jatis*, often with a Maharashtrian background. Second, the traditional elitist profile continues because the party establishment has not undergone any significant renewal in the last few decades, which means that the traditional base of the Hindu nationalist movement among the Brahmins and the Banyas remains over-represented. Most of the state leaders are in their seventies.

As a result, the BJP could easily be portrayed as a 'Banya-Brahmin party'. Indeed, among the state executive committee Brahmins predominate; and if one adds the Jains, the Sindhis and the Banyas, the merchant communities outnumber the Rajputs who are far more numerous in the general population. The upper caste image of the BJP of Madhya Pradesh is still accentuated by the role some of its leaders play in upper-caste associations. Kailash Joshi, the former Chief Minister of the State in 1977–8 presides over the All India Baversa Bhraman Samaj. Kailash Sarang, who remained treasurer of the state BJP for years till the mid-1990s, is the president of the All India Kayastha Mahasabha. A former BJP MLA, Vijendra Singh Sisodiya –a Rajput – is President of the State unit of the All India Kshatriya Mahasabha. These BJP leaders are well known for their activities in these capacities since they chair functions of their associations in Bhopal or elsewhere at least once a year. The Congress' growing focus on non-elite groups (especially Tribals) and the rise of the Bahujan Samaj Party was to pose a threat to the BJP, however. The 1996 elections acted as a catalyst in this respect and it may explain why the state's BJP leaders began to accommodate many OBCs in the late 1990s. A second reason lies in the increasingly militant attitude of the party's low caste leaders.

The new militancy of the low caste leaders. For many years, the OBC leaders of the BJP did not project themselves as members of the Backward Castes. This was largely due to the Hindutva ideology: the RSS and its offshoots insist on the need to stress the Hindu sense of belonging to an organic community, the 'Hindu nation' [*rashtra*], rather than to particular castes. The RSS relied on the attractiveness of the Hindu 'high tradition' to members of the low castes, as shown by its use of the notion of *samskars.* And in fact many low caste *swayamsevaks* joined the movement as part of a desire for Sanskritisation:[45] their aim was to emulate high caste behaviour patterns and they remained wedded to this ethos rather than to manifesting pride in their lowly background. According to Uma Bharti, herself a Lodhi (OBC) from Vindhya Pradesh, the acceptance of such an outlook has given the low caste leaders of the BJP a 'Brahmin's mentality'. She even complains that the BJP low caste cadres 'have an upper caste mentality. They do not show their caste.'[46]

Such an attitude was especially prevalent in the case of Scheduled Castes. Satyanarayan Jatiya, who took part in both Vajpayee governments and who has been elected five times as the MP for Ujjain since 1980, joined the RSS as a youth and became heavily imbued with its ideology. He stressed that he had been determined to learn Sanskrit and that he belonged to associations of Sanskritists.[47] In 1977 he took the oath in the Vidhan Sabha in Sanskrit. He fully subscribes to the Hindu nationalist reinterpretation of the *varnas* by ideologues such as Upadhyaya and Golwalkar. During an interview conducted soon after the 'Mandal affair' he argued:

> '*Varna vyavastha* was the *vyavastha* in which there was no difference between men. It was the arrangement of the society in which some people will do this job and this group this job. But at a latter stage it became rigid. So this is the evil of the society that should be removed.'[48]

Jatiya explicitly appreciated the social complementarity of the *varna* system and did not show any interest in Dalit mobilisation.

BJP leaders from the OBCs also refrained from appearing as spokesmen for their social category. They are even reluctant to indicate their caste. Bherulal Patidar, a prominent minister in Patwa's government and the deputy-speaker of the Vidhan Sabha in 1993–98, did not easily acknowledge that he was a Kurmi.[49] Similarly Babulal Gaur, another prominent minister in the BJP government

45 This observation which was suggested by my field work in Madhya Pradesh probably applies to the whole Hindi belt. In their book, Andersen and Damle convincingly attribute the appeal of the RSS to the low castes of North India in part to the process of sanskritisation. (Andersen and Damle, *The Brotherhood in Saffron*, op. cit., p. 45 and p. 102)

46 Interview with Uma Bharti, New Delhi, 12 Feb. 1994.

47 He is secretary of the Sansadiya Sanskrit Parishad based in Delhi.

48 Interview with S. Jatiya, 3 Dec. 1990, Ujjain.

49 Interview with B. Patidar, 17 Feb. 1994, Bhopal.

between 1990 and 1992, expressed reservations about the introduction of quotas favouring OBCs when I interviewed him in late 1990. He then followed the official line of his party against caste-based reservations, declaring that 'Unconditional system is bad for our nation. We don't want to divide our society. We want to unite our society [. . .] If we divide our society, our nation will go to hell'.[50]

The Madhya Pradesh BJP certainly had a vocal OBC leader in Uma Bharti but she has never been fully accepted by the party chiefs in the state. She did not enter the '*Sangh parivar*' through the Rashtrasevika Samiti but was introduced into the Hindu nationalist movement by Vijaya Raje Scindia, via the Vishva Hindu Parishad. In addition, women have never played a prominent role within the overwhelmingly male-dominated party that is the BJP.[51]

The BJP nevertheless decided to deploy its OBC leaders more aggressively in reaction to the growing assertiveness of the lower castes on the political scene of Madhya Pradesh. The electoral performances of the BSP were an especially powerful catalyst. After the 1993 defeat, Vikram Verma, a Jat farmer, was appointed leader of the opposition in the Bhopal Assembly, where Bherulal Patidar, also a farmer, became Deputy Speaker and Babulal Gaur, well known for his trade union activities, Chief Whip. But power remained within the hands of senior leaders such as S. Patwa, a Jain, L.N. Pandey, a Brahman and K. Thakre, a Kayasth. The real changes began to occur after the 1996 elections.

The BJP was then so much concerned about the rise of the BSP that they appointed a Janadhar Badhao Samiti (Committee for broadening the base [of the party]) in order to suggest ways and means of resisting this new threat. Its first recommendation regarding the party affairs was to promote the low castes within the party apparatus. The authors candidly emphasised: 'Many upper castes members within the party do not like the idea of social equality. Our

[50] Interview with Babulal Gaur, 17 Nov. 1990, Bhopal.

[51] Anyway, she toned down her lower caste militancy in 1999 when she abandoned her traditional constituency, Khajuraho where she had become unpopular, to contest the Lok Sabha elections from Bhopal. In this city, the Kayasths were very numerous and influential since many of them are employed as civil servants in the state capital's administration. As a result, Uma Bharti tried to woo them by arguing that 'this election was not based on caste or religion.' Cited in 'Desperate Uma turns to Kayasthas for support', *National Mail*, 7 Sept. 1999

leaders from the high castes therefore should be influenced to welcome the feelings of equality'.[52] They also proposed that the party should 'demand proportional representation in Parliament and State legislatures' for the OBCs,[53] a completely new objective for the BJP.

The eight-member committee which authored the report was headed by Babulal Gaur, who increasingly projected himself as an OBC leader. In 1997 he advocated the need for reservations in favour of the OBCs while opening the annual convention of the BJP Picchre Varg Morcha (OBC Front), one of the party's wings. Three months latter he presided over the launch of an agitation by the Morcha for a '27% reservation'.

The militancy of Babulal Gaur on behalf of the non-upper caste groups stands in stark contrast to his earlier discourse. His transition from Sanskritisation to 'social engineering', a notion framed in a very positive light in his report, probably reflects personal ambitions: the party had promoted Gaur because it needed an OBC leader to respond to the rise of the BSP, but he might have realised that he could exploit this pivotal situation to play 'the OBC card' (another expression used in his report) for himself. He explicitly cashes in on the momentum created by the BSP to improve the representation of non-upper caste groups within the BJP apparatus:

In North India, all parties are dominated by Brahmans, Thakurs and Banyas. After fifty years of independence, we people could not get an equal share in politics. Therefore these people [who support the BSP] want to snatch the power from the upper castes. The Bahujan Samaj Party is not a party but a movement. It's a one man show and a one woman show. This party has no future but it promotes a good cause, it enhances the feelings of the people. Some of our party members do not give their share to the Dalits, the Tribals and the OBCs. They should meet these people and give them an equal share in all spheres of life. These people should be given proper respect on the *manch* [platform]. Our OBC leaders are brave, they fight in the field. They say 'our leaders are Vyaparis [merchants], where are we?' This is the loud thinking among the OBCs: they want their share. Though the RSS and the BJP do not believe in the caste system, due to circumstances and to the other parties, they'll have to think over these issues. L.N. Pandey [the State BJP president] and Patwa are bound to change over this problem if they want the party to go ahead. We have been given posts, Vikram Verma is leader of the

52 Bharatiya Janata Party, *Janadhar badhao samiti ka prativedan*, Bhopal: BJP, 1997, p. 5 (Hindi).

53 Ibid., p. 6.

opposition, Bherulal Patidar is deputy speaker, I am one of the party general secretaries myself, but this is only the first step.[54]

But in the late 1990s the state's BJP leaders decided to apportion responsibilities not to OBC leaders but to rather innocuous Scheduled Castes and Scheduled Tribes politicians. In November 1997, a Tribal, Nandkumar Sai was appointed President of the Madhya Pradesh BJP, replacing a Brahmin, L.N. Pandey – for the first time in its history, the chief of the Madhya Pradesh BJP was not from the upper castes. Like their Congress counterparts, the BJP leaders chose to co-opt a rather docile individual. Commenting upon his appointment, a BJP worker declared: 'His only qualification is that he is a tribal. [. . .] He does not even know most of his district presidents, so how can you expect him to know the party workers?'[55] Similarly, after the 1998 elections in which Vikram Verma lost his seat, the BJP replaced him as leader of the opposition by a Scheduled Caste MLA, G.S. Shejwar. Again, this decision was deliberately intended to woo the non-upper castes without taking the risk of promoting an OBC leader or a militant Dalit leader. As one of the – upper caste – party workers puts it: 'He is a qualified doctor but he has a fairly rustic personality. A relatively simple person with a very good sense of humour. Not expected to provide a dynamic leadership, but being a backward caste [*sic*] person, his election as leader of opposition has sent positive signals in terms of caste factors'.[56]

To sum up: the situation of the BJP in Madhya Pradesh suggests that the party's upper caste leaders have realised the need to adjust to the post-Mandal context but have not gone very far. They feel obliged to emulate the Congress to compete more efficiently with it and with the BSP. There are many indications of this new awareness, ranging from the increasing number of OBC electoral candidates it nominates – including for the Lok Sabha, as evident from Table 13.8 – to the promotion of non-upper caste leaders within the party apparatus. But as far as power inside the party is concerned, the upper caste leadership promotes innocuous Scheduled Tribes and Scheduled Castes cadres instead of ambitious OBC old timers. In Uttar

[54] Interview with Babulal Gaur, Bhopal, Nov. 4, 1997.
[55] Interview cited in *Sunday*, 31 Jan. 1999, p. 59.
[56] Interview at Bhopal on 28 Oct. 1999.

Table 13.8. CASTE AND COMMUNITY OF BJP CANDIDATES IN LOK SABHA ELECTIONS IN MADHYA PRADESH, 1984–99 (%)

	1984	*1989*	*1991*	*1996*	*1999*
Upper castes	*35.9*	*39.4*	*32.5*	*33.3*	*32.5*
Brahmin	17.9	12.1	15	12.8	15
Rajput	5.1	12.1	10	10.3	10
Banya/Jain	10.3	9.1	5	7.7	7.5
Kayasth	2.6	6.1	2.5	2.6	
Intermediate castes	*2.6*		*2.5*		
Raghuvanshi	2.6		2.5		
OBC	*12.8*	*12.2*	*22.5*	*25.6*	*30*
Gujar					2.5
Lodhi	2.6	6.1	5	5.1	5
Kirar				2.6	
Kurmi	5.1	6.1	7.5	7.7	10
Panwar			2.5		2.5
Teli			5	5.1	5
Yadav					2.5
Others	2.6			5.1	2.5
Scheduled Castes	*15.4*	*15.2*	*15*	*15.4*	*15*
Scheduled Tribes	*23.1*	*24.2*	*22.5*	*23.1*	*22.5*
Muslim	*2.6*		*2.5*		
Sikh		*3*	*2.5*	*2.6*	
Unidentified	*10.3*	*6*	*2.5*		
Total	*100* *N=39*	*100* *N=33*	*100* *N=40*	*100* *N=39*	*100* *N=40*

Source: Fieldwork.

Pradesh, the party leaders were not so cautious: they played the 'OBC card' more decisively and, in the end, it turned out to be incompatible with the upper caste character of the BJP.

The BJP in Uttar Pradesh: how far can an upper caste-dominated party play the 'OBC card'? In Uttar Pradesh, most of the indicators suggested that the BJP remained an upper caste party in the 1990s. As far as election candidates are concerned, the BJP nominated more than two times more Brahmins and Rajputs than OBC candidates in the 1991 and 1996 general elections – respectively 33 (22

Table 13.9. CASTE AND COMMUNITY OF CANDIDATES IN 1991 AND 1996 GENERAL ELECTIONS IN UTTAR PRADESH, BY PARTY

	Brahmins		*Rajputs*		*OBC*		*Muslims*		*Scheduled Castes*	
	1991	*1996*	*1991*	*1996*	*1991*	*1996*	*1991*	*1996*	*1991*	*1996*
BJP	19	22	20	13	15	15	0	0	18	20
		18	20							
Congress(I)	25	19	13	11	12	10	10	11	18	19
	11	18	19							
SP	2	10	7	10	21	18	14	17	16	18
BSP	2	0	5	0	30	13	23	12	22	37

Source: *India Today*, 15 May 1996, p. 32.

Brahmins and 13 Rajputs) and 39 (19 Brahmins and 20 Rajputs) against 15 OBCs on both occasions. The Congress(I) fielded more Brahmins in 1996, but less in 1991 and a smaller number of Rajputs.

Among the BJP MLAs, one notices a very limited increase in the OBCs and a slight decline of the upper castes between 1989 and 1996. The erosion of the upper castes is not linear: their percentage fell below 50% in 1993; but rose again above this 'magic figure' in 1996. The increase in the OBCs has been more steady – from about 18-19% in 1989-1991 to almost 22% in 1996 – but not so significant. Among the upper castes, the Rajputs – who came second behind the Brahmins in 1989 with 15.5% against 20.7% – represent the largest group since 1991 with 19-22%. Among the OBCs, the Kurmis have always ranked first – with more than 5% of the BJP MLAs – over the entire period.

The social profile of the BJP voters in Uttar Pradesh is even more elitist. The CSDS surveys showed that respectively 80% and 77% of Brahmins and 79% and 77% of Rajputs voted for the party in the 1996 assembly elections and the 1999 Lok Sabha elections. On the other hand the proportion of Scheduled Castes supporting the BJP was marginal, about 10%, and that of the OBCs uneven. While only 4% to 7% of Yadavs voted for the BJP, 37% of the Kurmis did so in the 1996 elections and 29% of non-Yadav OBCs in 1999 did likewise.

The BJP leadership realised that the upper caste character of their party was proving a liability while the lower castes were engaged in an unprecedented mobilisation process. In 1989, the Janata Dal had won the state elections with 29.7% of the vote and Mulayam Singh

Table 13.10. CASTE AND COMMUNITY OF BJP MLAs OF UTTAR PRADESH, 1984–96

	1989	*1991*	*1993*	*1996*
Upper castes	*56.9*	*51.12*	*46.6*	*50.54*
Brahmin	20.69	19.91	14.04	16.66
Rajput	15.52	19	19.1	22.41
Banya	12.07	7.24	8.98	6.89
Kayasth	5.17	2.26	1.68	1.72
Khatri	3.45	1.81	2.24	1.72
Bhumihar	–	0.45	–	0.57
Tyagi	–	0.45	0.56	0.57
Intermediate castes	–	*3.16*	*3.93*	*4.59*
Jat	–	3.16	3.93	4.59
OBC	*18.96*	*18.1*	*19.06*	*21.66*
Yadav	1.72	2.26	1.12	2.87
Kurmi	5.17	5.43	5.61	5.17
Lodhi	5.17	4.97	5.05	4.59
Gujar	–	0.9	1.68	1.15
Kewat	1.72	0.9	0.56	1.15
Mallah	–	–	–	–
Kachhi	–	–	–	2.29
Saini	–	2.26	2.24	–
Sainthwar	–	0.9	0.56	0.57
Gadariya	–	–	–	0.57
Jaiswal	–	–	0.56	–
Rajbhar	–	0.45	–	1.15
Other	5.17	–	1.68	1.15
Scheduled Castes	*22.41*	*25.8*	*19.07*	*21.82*
Chamar	5.17	4.52	5.05	4.02
Valmiki	–	0.45	0.56	–
Dhobi	3.45	4.07	0.56	2.87
Kori/Koli	6.89	3.16	3.37	3.45
Pasi	–	2.71	1.68	1.15
Khatik	–	1.35	1.12	1.72
Baiswar	1.72	0.45	0.56	–
Bahelia	–	0.45	0.56	–
Dharkar	–	0.45	–	–
Shilpkar	–	1.35	–	1.72
Gond	–	0.9	1.12	1.15
Dohare	–	0.45	0.56	0.57
Kureel	–	0.45	0.56	-
Other	5.17	4.97	3.37	5.17
Sikh	*1.72*	*0.45*	*0.56*	*1.15*
Unidentified	–	*1.35*	*10.67*	*1.15*
Total	*100* *N=58*	*100* *N=221*	*100* *N=178*	*100* *N=174*

Sources: Adapted from J. Zerinini-Brotel's fieldwork in C. Jaffrelot and J. Zérinini-Brotel, with J. Chaturvedi, 'The BJP and the rise of Dalits in Uttar Pradesh' in R. Jeffrey and J. Lerche (eds), *UP 2000*, Delhi, Manohar, 2002.

Table 13.11. CASTE AND COMMUNITY OF BJP VOTERS IN UTTAR PRADESH, 1996–9

	1996 Assembly election	*1999 Parliamentary election*[a]
Brahmin	80	77
Rajput	79	74
Jat	30	*n.a.*
Kurmi	37	29
		(non-Yadav OBC)
Yadav	7	11
Lower OBCs	43	*n.a.*
Scheduled Castes	11	(6 Jatavs)
		(13 other SCs)
Muslim	–	5

[a] The figures for the 1999 election concern the BJP and its allies.

Sources: CSDS opinion poll, as reported in *India Today*, 31 Aug. 1996, and *Frontline*, 19 Nov. 1999.

Yadav had become Chief Minister whereas the BJP only polled 11.6%. The BJP therefore played the 'OBC card' by projecting Kalyan Singh, a Lodhi who was deeply imbued with the Hindu nationalist ideology – he was a major figure in the Ayodhya movement – and a disciplined party worker.

Kalyan Singh, from Sanskritisation to OBC politics. Kalyan Singh was first elected MLA in 1967 on a Jana Sangh ticket in Atrauli (Aligarh district). The main reason for his electoral good fortune was his popularity among the Lodhis: he 'had built a following among his caste by many years of attention to their welfare'.[57] He continued to attract support from Lodhis and this explains why they were the second largest OBC group after the Kurmis among the BJP MLAs in the 1990s. Kalyan Singh was thus at the cross-roads of two traditions, caste politics and the Hindu nationalist emphasis on an organic view of society.

A teacher by training, he followed the path of Sanskritisation by learning Sanskrit. His biographer emphasises the fact that 'he uses so many literary words that it seems that he is delivering a speech even in informal talks'.[58] Apart from this Sanskritised ethos, which was

[57] R.I. Duncan, *Levels*, op. cit., p. 64.

[58] Arjun Kumar Tripathi, *Kalyan Singh*, Delhi: Rajkamal Prakashan, 1997 (Hindi).

markedly different from the behaviour of other OBC leaders such as Mulayam Singh Yadav or Laloo Prasad Yadav, Kalyan Singh subscribes to the RSS's social views. In a very perceptive portrait his biographer writes:

> Kalyan Singh is preaching the pro caste system ideas of Deen Dayal Upadhyaya [the RSS-trained ideologue of the Jana Sangh] at a period which has become a strong harbinger of Ram Manohar Lohia's anti-caste system ideas. [. . .] The problem of Kalyan Singh is that in spite of being well aware of these ideas of Lohia and agreeing with them from inside, he is unable to express them. Instead he has to adhere to Deen Dayal Upadhyaya's ideas like: 'People make divisions from castes. But caste is a part of our body and the body cannot be divided'. [. . .] But Kalyan Singh is in favour of enhancing backwards' share in power. He is also a symbol of elevation of castes and sanskritisation by emulation and adoption of high caste attributes. But alongside, his politics also involves keeping close contact with lower castes.[59]

Kalyan Singh stands mid-way between Sanskritisation and social revolt: he aspires to be co-opted by the upper castes whom he is emulating and at the same time he wants to dislodge them. This ambivalence is a result of the contradictory influences he has undergone since his youth: on the one hand he was brought up in an Arya Samajist milieu and took part in a RSS *shakha* since he was a child. On the other hand, he is a Lodhi and proud of his caste. He participated in the activities of the Lucknow-based Lodhi-Nishad-Bind Unity Front whose convenor is none other than Ganga Charan Rajput, a close associate of Kalyan Singh. He also contributes to the Awanti Bai Trust – to which he donated one million rupees in 1992 – which was set up to preserve the memory of Awanti Bai, the Lodhi queen of the Ramgarh principality of Mandla district in Madhya Pradesh who in 1857 fought the British and died as a 'martyr' on Dasara day. The attempt to Sanskritise oneself while simultaneously promoting pride in one's own caste is not contradictory: Kalyan Singh's father, Chaudhury Tej Pal Singh, had taken the *kshatriya* surname 'Singh' which the Lodhis had struggled to adopt but they were not only imitating the Rajputs, they were proud of being as strong and prestigious as them, as testified by Ganga Charan Rajput:

> This tribe [the Lodhi] may be culturally and socially backward but it is fearless and irrepressible. Especially those who belong to the mahalodhi

[59] Ibid.

sub-tribe are comparable to the Kshatriyas. These people are in general very generous but intolerant towards injustrice.[60]

Moreover, the myth of origin of the Lodhis presents them as Kshatriyas. According to this legend, Parashuram was clearing the earth of all the Kshatriyas in India when the Lodhi, who were born in Kazhakstan, hid themselves in a Shiva temple with the help of that god. As they were the only surviving Kshatriyas, they became kings. This is why, as the secretary of the Lodhi Mahasabha emphasised, the Lodhis want to be called Lodhi-Rajputs.[61]

Kalyan Singh was an ideal combination of staunch Hindu nationalism and non-militant low caste politics with whom the BJP could play the 'OBC card'. Indeed, he led the party to electoral victory in the 1991 state election when the party won only 31.5% of the vote but a majority of seats thanks to divisions among its rival. However, tensions between the OBC-oriented strategy of Kalyan Singh and that of the BJP, upper caste leaders increased after the SP-BSP alliance won the elections in 1993.

During the campaign for the Assembly elections in September 1996 Kalyan Singh wanted to give tickets to many more OBCs but the upper caste lobby and the RSS resisted his move. The BJP nominated OBC candidates in 190 of the 420 constituencies but this move 'alienated the upper caste support base of the party and adversely affected its fortunes.'[62] It won only 174 seats, whereas it had secured a majority in 236 of the assembly segments in the Lok Sabha elections. The upper caste BJP leadership argued that the relative alienation of upper-caste voters resulted from the distribution of 45% of the tickets to OBCs and also from the nomination of Kalyan Singh as the party candidate for the Chief Ministership. He blamed them and argued that the four organising secretaries of the party – key figures with RSS backgrounds who were all Brahmins, incidentally – had paid more attention to upper caste candidates during the election campaign. Shortly afterwards Govindacharya, one of the party general secretaries, was appointed convenor of a committee charged with examining the reasons for the party's setback. He concluded that 'BJP's penetration in the society is still incomplete'[63] and

[60] Cited in ibid.

[61] Interview with Tikamram Singh Naravya, Bhopal: 20 Oct. 1995.

[62] 'Uttar Pradesh – Calculations gone awry', *EPW*, Oct. 12-19, 1996, p. 2773.

[63] Cited in Arjun Kumar Tripathi, *Kalyan Singh*, op. cit.

militated for a strategy of 'social engineering', that is the promotion of non-elite groups within the party apparatus and the nomination of more OBC electoral candidates. This suggestion was immediately criticised by Bhanu Pratap Shukla, the editor of *Panchajanya* – the Hindi mouthpiece of the RSS based in UP – who advocated the relevance of the D. Upadhyaya's theory of 'society as an organic entity.'[64] Murli Manohar Joshi also reacted strongly on behalf of the Brahmin lobby of the UP BJP.

This lobby, comprising Brahma Dutt Dwivedi and Kalraj Mishra, was favourably inclined towards making a deal with the BSP in order to establish a formal 'coalition of extremes'. Kalyan Singh was hostile to this arrangement because it would have circumvented his group, the OBCs.[65] The negotiations started in late 1996, and were conducted in Delhi by all-India leaders – including Suraj Bhan, the Deputy Speaker of the Lok Sabha who headed the Scheduled Caste front of the BJP for many years. Mishra was kept informed but not Kalyan Singh. The latter's supporters instead campaigned against such an alliance. Ganga Charan Rajput was especially vocal. Eventually, the BJP-BSP coalition took shape. Kalyan Singh complied with the decisions of the party leaders but did not resign himself to this new balance of power.

In fact, the rift between Kalyan Singh and the upper caste lobby led by Kalraj Mishra was further accentuated by the former's 'coup'

[64] Ibid.

[65] Kalyan Singh never showed much interest in the Scheduled Castes. He protested the strict implementation of the Dalit Atrocities Act and joined hands with Mulayam Singh Yadav to denounce the 'victimisation' of OBCs at the hands of the BSP. The Scheduled Castes have been the first casualty of the rise of OBCs in the BJP's organisation. The only Scheduled Caste representatives in the 1999 BJP government in U.P. were one Kori, one Dhobi and one Bhangi. In 1998, Vajpayee government nominated a Chamar as governor, Suraj Bhan, who had been elected several times MP from Ambala (Haryana) on a BJP ticket. The induction of an active BJP politician and an outsider to U.P. was sought by the RSS to make up for the lack of any Chamar figure in the party state unit or in the government. This decision contradicted the constitutional tradition whereby one does not appoint as governor a man with an active political background. But obviously Suraj Bhan was expected to work as an ally of Kalyan Singh, not as a watchdog of the centre. Perceived by the BSP as a direct threat to their stronghold, Suraj Bhan has shown great dynamism in assessing the performance of schemes concerning Scheduled Castes, such as reservations or the virtually unused SC/ST MLAs Forum in the state assembly.

against the Mayawati government in October 1997,[66] which resulted in the breaking of an alliance that had been carefully put together by the upper caste lobby. As Chief Minister, Kalyan Singh further alienated his upper caste colleagues by appointing many OBCs in his government. There is a striking difference in the composition of the BJP Cabinet he headed in 1991 and that formed in 1999, again headed by him. Not only did the number of OBCs rise but they also cornered some real influence in U.P. whereas their allotment of power in 1991 was mostly a token measure.

In terms of the portfolios secured, in Kalyan Singh's first government while 89% of upper castes were awarded cabinet or state ministerial postings, only half of the OBCs had positions of the same rank. In contrast, in the 1999 BJP government most of the OBCs were of state cabinet rank. Kalyan Singh was promoting the formation of a lobby centred around his own power base, and he tried to prevent upper caste leaders from taking positions at their expense.

Besides promoting caste fellows in his government, Kalyan Singh projected himself as an OBC leader during the 1999 election campaign.[67] On 25 April 1999 he addressed a 'backward rally' where 'he urged the OBCs to ensure the election of backwards, no matter which party ticket they stood on'.[68] A few days later, 33 dissident MLAs sent their resignation to the BJP President, Kushabhau Thakre, to protest the continued incumbence of Kalyan Singh as Chief Minister. They were all from the upper castes, except one Yadav and one Scheduled Caste member.

The growing assertiveness of Kalyan Singh in turn fostered the

[66] Kalyan Singh succeeded in engineering enough defections in the Congress, the BSP and the Janata Dal to form a government of his own without needing BSP support.

[67] He had started to show such militancy even earlier, for instance in 1996 when he campaigned against the quotas for women in elective bodies. While the upper caste leadership of the BJP was favourably inclined towards the institution of such quotas, the OBCs of the BJP expressed their fear that such a move would reduce the share of the Backward Castes. Instead they proposed a quota for OBC women. To show his hostility to the Bill in its current form and seek the introduction of a separate quota for OBC women, Kalyan Singh is said to have strongly backed the attempts of a BJP MLA to organise members of the backward classes across party-lines.

[68] Smita Gupta, 'Any move on Kalyan Singh may change equations', *Times of India*, 8 May 1999, p. 9.

Table 13.12. CASTE AND COMMUNITY OF MEMBERS OF BJP GOVERNMENTS IN UP, 1991–9 (%)

	July 1991	*February 1999*
Upper castes	57.45	49.21
Intermediary castes	4.25	4.76
OBC	21.28	31.76
Scheduled Castes	8.51	7.94
Muslim	2.13	3.17
Sikh	2.13	–
Unidentified	4.25	3.17
Total	*100* *N=47*	*100* *N = 63*

Source: As for Table 13.10.

militancy of the upper caste lobby comprising K. Mishra (a Brahmin who belonged to his government), L. Tandon (a Khatri, also an important minister) and Rajnath Singh, a Rajput who became President of the state unit of the BJP. The important point here is that the party apparatus remained in the hands of upper caste leaders. In 2000, over 66% of the members of the state's executive committee were from the upper castes, mostly Brahmins (nearly 27%) and Rajputs (18%). Scheduled Castes accounted for 5%, while OBCs were more numerous with about 22% of the committee's members.[69] Out of 57 district presidents, 31.6% were Brahmins, 31.6% were Rajputs, 12.3% were Banyas, 5.3% were OBCs and 1.8% were SCs. Resentful of the way the OBCs were gaining power in the party, the upper caste leaders were apparently responsible for the denying of ticket to the outgoing Mathura MP, Sakshi Maharaj – a Lodhi close to Kalyan Singh. Sakshi Maharaj then left the BJP and went over to Mulayam Singh Yadav. Kalyan Singh did not canvass against him in this constituency or the adjacent districts. The upper caste lobby soon exploited this episode and the party's setback in the 1999 general elections, when it won only 29 seats (as against 57 in 1998), to have the Chief Minister removed.

Kalyan Singh was asked to resign by the party's high command in November 1999 to be replaced by a Banya Chief Minister, Ram Prakash Gupta. Kalyan Singh replied that he was the victim of a

[69] These figures are based on fieldwork in Lucknow in August 2000.

Brahminical plot whose architect was none other than Vajpayee.[70] The BJP Parliamentary board voted a suspension order immediately and then expelled Kalyan Singh for six years in December 1999. He then launched a new party intended to articulate the grievances of the OBCs. The BJP tried to promote a new OBC leader by appointing Om Prakash Singh, a Kurmi, as chief of the UP unit after 'promoting' Rajnath Singh as Union Minister. But a few months later, Mishra took over from him and Rajnath Singh came back to Lucknow to be appointed Chief Minister: the upper caste leaders had regained their former influence at the expense of the OBCs. This is evident from the caste composition of the UP government in 2001: while the upper castes were allotted 50% of the portfolios, the share of the OBCs fell to 21% and that of the SCs jumped to 12%.

The various elements of the 'Sangh parivar' responded to Mandal in two different ways. The RSS, true to its traditional view of society as an organic totality, refused to make any compromise with 'OBC politics'. For Hindu nationalists, caste politics could only divide the country. Though they did not spell out this argument openly, the RSS leaders were also apprehensive of the emancipatory potential of low caste movements: they more or less consciously referred to the *varna* system as an ideal because of its hierarchical arrangement. The strategy of Sewa Bharti was to promote social work among Dalits in order to defuse their militancy and even to maintain them in a framework of Sanskritisation. This technique was used in particular in places like Agra where the BSP was making inroads. Sewa Bharti's approach was successful among the most vulnerable and backward *jatis*, such as the Bhangis, but had little or no impact on the Jatavs who were more politicised and continued to support the BSP. The limitations of the welfarist tactic partly explained why the BJP adopted other methods.

The upper caste leaders who control the BJP did not all react in a similar fashion to Mandal. The most conservative continued to adhere to the approach of the RSS, a movement in which majority of them have been trained. Some of these leaders even displayed utter contempt for reservations. On the other hand, equally senior BJP

[70] C. Jaffrelot and J. Zérinini-Brotel, 'La montée des basses castes dans la politique nord-indienne', *Pouvoirs*, 90 (1999), p. 85.

leaders considered that the party could not ignore the growing political mobilisation of the lower castes and advocated 'social engineering', that is the promotion of OBC cadres in the party apparatus and among the election candidates. Both tendencies reached a form of compromise in the early 1990s through indirect Mandalisation, that is the making of alliances with parties representing the lower castes. However, the rise of the BSP, the SP and the RJD in the Hindi belt tilted the balance in favour of more 'social engineering'. In Madhya Pradesh, the BJP promoted OBC leaders like Babulal Gaur under pressures from the BSP and the party nominated more and more OBC electoral candidates. As far as the party apparatus was concerned, however, the upper caste leaders tried to induct innocuous Scheduled Tribes or Scheduled Castes figures in the posts of party President or leader of the opposition. In Uttar Pradesh, where the low castes' parties were more influential and the BJP even more identified with the upper castes, the party went one step further since it appointed an OBC leader, Kalyan Singh, as Chief Minister. A pure product of the RSS, he seemed to offer the ideal synthesis of an OBC leader with Hindu nationalist ideology. But he tended to assert himself as an OBC leader and to promote low caste party leaders at the expense of upper-castes ones, with the predictable result that he was dismissed.

In Madhya Pradesh and Uttar Pradesh, the BJP realised that it can not ignore the OBCs. It was even quicker than the Congres(I) in understanding that Mandal had transformed the political landscape of North India. However, the upper caste leaders' strategy of accommodating the lower castes without losing power turned out to be very difficult to implement. In the end, the party tended to imitate the Congress and construct a coalition of extremes, a strategy designed to circumvent the OBCs – either by promoting SCs/STs in the party apparatus or by making alliances with the BSP.

14
CONCLUSION

India has come a long way since the early days of its conservative democracy. The political system of the 1950s and 1960s was characterised by three inter-connected features that were the ideological legacy of Gandhi, with its emphasis on social unity in an organicist perspective, the domination of elites (the upper caste intelligentsia, the business community and landowners) which maintained the clientelistic arrangement of the 'Congress system' and a systematic attempt at weakening the organisational base of the lower castes, especially the Dalits, either by resisting their 'separatist' claim – like Gandhi in his confrontation with Ambedkar – or by co-opting their leaders. This system was democratic in the sense that there were frequent, competitive elections, that the press was free and the judiciary independent but its beneficiaries mainly came from the same upper caste groups. Even when the Congress lost power at the state level, the parties which succeeded it were dominated by the upper case elite. As a result, no large scale reform could ever be implemented. Land reform, for instance, did not address the need of the poor. Indira Gandhi allegedly intended to make the Congress a party for social transformation in the late 1960s and early 1970s but she failed, partly because she was more attracted by an authoritarian, populist style of polity, partly because she could not do without the Congress notables and their 'vote banks'. Certainly, she implemented some reforms during the Emergency when she no longer needed the 'vote banks' – since there were to be no elections – but the Congress was then confronted with a terrible dilemma: either it suspended democracy to implement social reforms or it maintained the pattern of conservative democracy.

India overcame this Hobson's choice thanks to social transformations from below which occurred in the realm of caste. Southern and Western India had already shown the way since in the late nineteenth and early twentieth century low caste groups had started to emancipate themselves from the hierarchical logic of Indian society. British orientalism had prepared the ground by presenting these castes as non-Aryan ethnic groups and in South India, for instance they evolved a specific Dravidian identity that helped them to develop some solidarity against the 'Aryan Brahmins'. But this move was also due to another aspect of British policy, the implementation of affirmative action programmes in the administration which were intended to empower Non-Brahmins. This new category was very keen to forge a social bloc as the best means of obtaining employment. These Non-Brahmins adopted Dravidianism, to the extent that the ethnicisation of caste and the quest for power were two faces of the same coin. In North India, the attempts at ethnicising caste were hindered by the pervasive ethos of Sanskritisation but the policies of positive discrimination had the same impact as in the South and the West several decades latter.

Among the political forces, the Socialists were especially quick to mobilise the lower castes on the reservation issue. Lohia's approach, in particular, was thus responsible for the early inroads made by the socialist parties he successively set up in Bihar and even Uttar Pradesh. His 'quota politics', however, was not the only ideology that was mobilising the low caste peasants in the 1960s and 1970s. Charan Singh was also canvassing for the protection of the interests of the 'kisans', a group which was largely identified with his own caste, the Jats, but among whom there were many low caste people. Charan Singh and the Socialists joined hands in the 1970s and their alliance culminated in the first Janata experiment in 1977–9. This episode was the first turning point in the rise of the lower castes in North India but it was short-lived and brought few benefits to the lower castes because the proponents of 'quota politics' were in a minority within the ruling coalition. The appointment of the Mandal Commission, however, suggested that 'quota politics' may well have a future in North India.

The second landmark in the low castes' rise to power was precisely due, in the late 1980s and early 1990s, to the electoral victory of the second Janata and the implementation of the Mandal Report. This move showed that 'quota politics' had taken over from 'kisan politics'. The Jats left the coalition whereas the lower castes mobilised in North India where they were still marginal to all the centres of power. They formed a front against the upper castes' vocal hostility to the new reservations. So the affirmative action programmes had at last prompted them to fight united as one group, the 'Other Backward Classes'. As a result, OBC leaders were returned in large numbers to Parliament and took power in Uttar Pradesh and Bihar. In the wake of this development, the Dalits deserted the Congress in favour of one force, the Bahujan Samaj Party which aggressively fought upper caste domination in North India. In 1997 the growing recognition of the Scheduled Castes in the Indian political system found expression in the election of K.R. Narayanan, a Dalit from Kerala, as President of the country.

India is therefore experimenting with a silent revolution. Power is being transferred, on the whole peacefully, from the upper caste elites to various subaltern groups. While riots did take place during the Mandal affair such transfers of power are generally accompanied by larger scale violence. The relative calm of the Indian experience is primarily due to the fact that the whole process is incremental: the upper castes are still in command, with OBCs forming a second line of leadership, a new generation in waiting. The educational and social backwardness of the lower castes is such that they will probably not be able to dislodge the elite for several decades. Second, the rise to power of the lower castes is very uneven. They have taken over in Bihar but remain in a subordinate position in Rajasthan, for instance.[1] Third, the conflict is not based on a clear cut political opposition since the upper caste-dominated parties have low caste members in their ranks and vice versa (even the BSP has upper caste office-bearers). Fourth, the upper castes are losing ground in the political sphere and in the administration but the liberalisation of the economy – which coincided with the implementation of the Mandal Commission Report – has opened new opportunities for the upper castes in the private sector, and hence they may no longer regret their traditional monopoly over the bureaucracy being challenged.

Fifth, and more importantly, the rise to power of the lower castes is not irreversible and linear. There is a trend, but they will have to overcome several handicaps in pursuing it. The lower castes suffer from a structural lack of unity. The divorce between the Samajwadi

[1] The classification of the Jats as OBCs in Rajasthan in 1999 has naturally changed the socio-political landscape.

Party and the Bahujan Samaj Party in 1995 showed that an alliance between the OBCs and the Dalits was very difficult to maintain, *inter alia*, because these two groups have conflicting class interests. Besides, the Scheduled Castes and the Other Backward Classes do not comprise discrete social categories. They are divided along caste lines according to the 'gradual inequality' principle that Ambedkar described even before Independence. Mahars will not join hands with Chambhars, Jatavs will looked down at Bhangis, Yadavs and Kurmis will remain locked in rivalries etc.

The rise to power of the lower castes is also hindered by the response of the upper castes to their new assertiveness and ambitions. Old strategies are still implemented successfully. The traditional Gandhian discourse on the organic unity of society is still articulated by the RSS in order to defuse Dalit militancy and the Congress has also resorted to its techniques of co-option and the 'coalition of extremes'. The BJP has followed suit to a certain extent but it has accommodated the OBCs in a more significant manner. The appointment of Kalyan Singh as the Chief Minister of the largest state of the Indian Union was a clear indication of this flexibility. But the experiment turned sour, and the ruling party may now be in two minds *vis-à-vis* 'social engineering', and prefer the coalition of extremes pattern, as suggested by the appointment of Bangaru Laxman (a Madiga – SC – from Andhra Pradesh) as party president in 2000 and by the decision of the National Executive, almost at the same time, not to create an 'OBC Morcha' parallel to the 'SC Morcha'.[2] Simultaneously the party has sought to thwart the rise of the lower castes by subverting their main avenue for upward mobility: 'quota politics'. In late 1999, Prime Minister Vajpayee included the Jats of Rajasthan in the list of OBCs, soon after, R.P. Gupta, the – upper caste – BJP Chief Minister of Uttar Pradesh granted the same concession to the Jats of his own state. These decisions are diluting the impact of the reservations from two points of view. First, they enabled a caste, the Jats, which is rather well-off and enjoys a fairly decent level of education to compete with lower castes in the framework of the reservation system and therefore to obtain jobs in the administration at the expense of the latter. Second, the addition of the Jats

[2] Laxman explained that the party wanted to organise those who were known as OBCs on the basis of their professions (Interview in Delhi, 24 Aug. 2000).

makes the 'OBCs' an even more heterogeneous category, so much so that it will prove even more difficult for low caste politicians to mobilise the 'OBCs' on issues such as the reservations.

The expansion of the social groups benefiting from quotas may well become the favoured tactic of the BJP in making 'quota politics' non-operational.[3] It may take an even larger dimension with the introduction of gender quotas in the elected assemblies: if 33% of seats are reserved for women, the upper castes may well be the first to benefit from of the reservations – a rather ironical conclusion which recalls that in Europe the conservatives were responsible for enlarging the franchise in order to exploit their influence over 'their' peasant voters. However, the peasants in question eventually emancipated themselves. In India too this tactical move may only slow down the democratisation process.

The state elections of Uttar Pradesh in 2002 reconfirmed this trend. The Samajwadi Party, with 143 seats out of 402, and the BSP, with 98 seats, bypassed the BJP (88 seats – 107 with its allies). Both parties represent about 48% of the valid votes (as against 24.5% for the BJP and its allies). Whether the new balance of power will result in a new equation so far as government politics is concerned remains to be seen.

[3] Another tactic emerged recently in UP where the Chief Minister, Rajnath Singh in August 2001 introduced a bill aiming at carving at a quota for the Most Backward Classes within the 27% that were reserved for the OBCs. Such a move was intended to attract the MBC voters.

SELECT BIBLIOGRAPHY

PRIMARY SOURCES

All Parties Conferences – 1928. Report of the Committee appointed by the Conference to Determine the Principles of the Constitution for India, Allahabad: General Secretary of the AICC, 1928.

Ambedkar, B.R., 'The Untouchables: Who Were They and Why They Became Untouchables?' in *Dr. Babasaheb Ambedkar: Writings and Speeches*, vol. 7, Bombay: Government of Maharashtra, 1990.

———, *What Congress and Gandhi Have Done to the Untouchables*, Bombay: Thacker, 1946.

———, *Writings and Speeches*, vol. 1, Bombay: Government of Maharashtra, 1979.

Birla, G.D., *In the Shadow of the Mahatma*, Bombay: Orient Longman, 1953.

Constituent Assembly Debates (hereafter *CAD*), New Delhi: Lok Sabha Secretariat, 1989.

Gandhi, M.K., *An Autobiography or the Story of my Experiments with Truth*, Ahmedabad: Navajivan, 1995.

———, *Indian Home Rule*, Madras: Ganesh, 1922.

———, *Socialism of My Conception*, Bombay: ?1957.

Das, Seth Govin, *Atma-Nirikshan* (autobiography), vol. 2, Delhi: Bharatiya Vishva Prakashan, 1958.

Implementation of Land Reforms: A Review by the Land Reforms Implementation Committee of the National Development Council, New Delhi: Planning Commission, 1966.

Memorandum Explaining Action Taken on the Report of the Second Backward Classes Commission, New Delhi: Government of India, Ministry of Home Affairs, 1982.

Montagu, E., and Lord Chelmsford, *Report on Indian Constitutional Reforms*, Calcutta : Superintendent of Government Printing, 1918.

Nehru, J., *A Bunch of Old Letters*, London: Asia Publishing House, 1960.

———, *An Autobiography*, New Delhi: Oxford University Press, 1987 [1936].

———, *India's Freedom*, London: Unwin Books, 1962.

Portrait of a President: Letters of Dr Rajendra Prasad written to Mrs Gyanvati Darbar, vol. II, Delhi: Vikas, 1976.

Prasad, Rajendra, *Autobiography*, Delhi: National Book Trust, 1994.

Pyarelal, *The Epic Fast*, Ahmedabad: Mohanlal Maganlal Bhatt, 1932.

Ram, Kanshi, *The Chamcha Age – An Era of the Stooges*, New Delhi, 1982.

Report of the Backward Classes Commission – Second Part, New Delhi: Government of India, 1980.

Report of the United Provinces Zamindari Abolition Committee, vol. 1, Allahabad: Government of the United Provinces, 1948.

Sampurnanand, S., *Memories and Reflections*, Bombay: Asia Publishing House, 1962.

Scindia, V., with M. Malgonkar, *Princess—The Autobiography of the Dowager Maharani of Gwalior*, New Delhi: Times Books International, 1988.

Singh, Charan, *Joint Farming X-rayed: The Problem and its Solution*, Bombay: Bharatiya Vidya Bhavan, 1959.

———, *India's Poverty and its Solution*, New York: Asia Publishing House, 1964.

Singh, C., *Land Reform in UP and the Kulaks*, Delhi: Vikas, 1986.

———, *Abolition of Zamindari—Two Alternatives*, Allahabad: Kitabistan, 1947.

SECONDARY SOURCES

Austin, G., *The Indian Constitution – Cornerstone of a Nation*, Bombay: Oxford University Press, 1972.

Bardhan, P., *The Political Economy of Development in India*, Oxford: Blackwell, 1984.

Bayly, C.A., *The Local Roots of Indian Politics – Allahabad 1880–1920*, Oxford: Clarendon Press, 1975.

Blunt, E.A.H., *The Caste System of Northern India*, Delhi: S. Chand, 1969 [1931].

Burger, A., *Opposition in a Dominant Party System*, Berkeley: University of California Press, 1969.

Dubey, A.K., *Mulayam Singh Yadav – Aaj ke netal/Alochnatmak Adhyaynamala*, New Delhi: Rajkamal Prakashan, 1997.

Frankel, F., *India's Political Economy, 1947–1977: The Gradual Revolution*, Princeton University Press, 1978.

——— and M.S.A. Rao (eds), *Dominance and State Power in Modern India: Decline of a Social Order*, vol. 1, Delhi: Oxford University Press, 1989.

Hooja, B., *A Life Dedicated – Biography of Govind Das*, New Delhi: Seth Govind Das Diamond Jubilee Celebrations Committee, 1956.

Jaffrelot, C., *The Hindu Nationalist Movement and Indian Politics, 1925 to the 1990s*, London: Hurst, 1996.

Jones, K., *The New Cambridge History of India* – III.1. *Socio-religious Movements in British India*, Cambridge University Press, 1989.

Jordens, J.T.F., *Swami Shraddhananda: His Life and Causes*, Delhi: Oxford University Press, 1981.

Joshi, B. (ed.), *Untouchable! Voice of the Dalit Liberation Movement*, New Delhi: Selectbooks Service Syndicate, 1986.

Kohli, A., *The State and Poverty in India: The Politics of Reform*, Cambridge University Press, 1987.

——— (ed.), *India's Democracy: An Analysis of Changing State–Society Relations*, Princeton University Press, 1990.

Kothari, R. (ed.), *Caste in Indian Politics*, New Delhi: Orient Longman, 1986.

Kumar, A., *Laloo Prasad Yadav. Aaj ke netal/Alochnatmak Adhyaynamala*, New Delhi: Rajkamal Prakashan, 1994.

Tripathi, Arjun Kumar, *Kalyan Singh*, Delhi: Rajkamal Prakashan, 1997.

Mahar, J.M. (ed.), *The Untouchables in Contemporary India*, Tucson: University of Arizona Press, 1972.

Mendelsohn, O. and M. Vicziany, *The Untouchables: Subordination, Poverty and the State in Modern India*, Cambridge University Press, 1998.

Masselos, J. (ed.), *Struggling and Ruling – The Indian National Congress, 1885–1985*, London: Oriental University Press.

Merillat, H.C.L., *Land and the Constitution of India*, New York: Columbia University Press, 1970.

Misra, B.B., *The Indian Middle Classes*, Delhi: Oxford University Press, 1961.

Mustapha, S., *The Lonely Prophet – V.P. Singh, a Political Biography*, New Delhi: New Age International 1995.

Neale, W.C., *Economic Change in Rural India: Land Tenure and Reform in Uttar Pradesh, 1800–1955*, New Haven: Yale University Press, 1962.

Pandey, G., *The Ascendancy of the Congress in Uttar Pradesh, 1926–1934*, Delhi: Oxford University Press, 1981.

Parekh, B., *Colonialism, Tradition and Reform—An Analysis of Gandhi's Political Discourse*, New Delhi: Sage, 1989.

Ram, Kanshi, *Aaj ke netal/Alochnatmak Adhyayanmala*, New Delhi: Rajkamal Prakashan, 1996.

Rawat, Gyanendra (ed.), *Chaudhury Charan Singh: Sukti aur Vichar*, New Delhi: Kisan Trust, 1995.

Reeves, P., *Landlords and Governments in Uttar Pradesh*, Delhi: Oxford University Press, 1991.

Seal, A., *The Emergence of Indian Nationalism. Competition and Collaboration in the Later Nineteenth Century*, Cambridge University Press, 1968.

Singh, Ram and Anshuman Yadav, *Mulayam Singh – A Political Biography*, New Delhi: Konark, 1998.

Sisson, R. and S. Wolpert (eds), *Congress and Indian Nationalism: The Pre-Independence Phase*, Delhi: Oxford University Press, 1986.

Srinivas, M.N., *Social Change in Modern India*, New Delhi: Orient Longman, 1995.

Thakur, J., *V.P. Singh – The Quest for Power*, New Delhi: Warbler Books, 1989.

Thorner, D., *The Agrarian Prospect in India*, Delhi University Press, 1956.

Varshney, A., *Democracy, Development and the Countryside – Urban, Rural Struggles in India*, Cambridge University Press, 1995.

Weiner, M., *Party Building in a New Nation – The Indian National Congress*, University of Chicago Press, 1967.

INDEX